POWER AND IDEAS

Volume II

POWER AND IDEAS

Milton Friedman and the Big U-Turn

by

William Frazer

In two volumes

Volume II
The U-Turn

Gulf/Atlantic Publishing Company

Copyright © 1988 by William J. Frazer

All rights reserved. No part of this book may be reproduced or transmitted in any form or by any means, electronic or mechanical, including photocopying, recording or by any information storage and retrieval system, without permission in writing from the Publisher.

Gulf/Atlantic Publishing Company
2920 N.W. 16th Avenue
Gainesville, FL 32605

Library of Congress Cataloging-in-Publication Data

Frazer, William Johnson, 1924-
  Power and ideas.

  Includes index.
  Contents: v. 1. The background.—v. 2. The U-turn.
  1. Friedman, Milton, 1912-   . 2. Chicago school of economics. 3. United States—Economic policy—1981-   . 4. Great Britain—Economic policy—1945-   . I. Title.
HB119.F84F73 1988   338.973   87-82665
ISBN 0-9619206-1-0 (v. 1)
ISBN 0-9619206-2-9 (v. 2)
ISBN 0-9619206-0-2 (set)

Printed in the United States of America by
Storter Printing Company

Typeset in California type style.

"If it were only the truth they were after, and not legends of greatness."

Rebecca Goldstein
from *The Mind-Body Problem*

"And ye shall know the truth, and the truth shall make you free."

JOHN 8:32

Contents

Volume II

Part IV. Political Economy (continued)

Chapter 11	Crises, Keynes, and Friedman	411
Chapter 12	The Philosophy and Economics of Freedom	457
Chapter 13	The Distribution and Permanency of Income	493

Part V. The Big U-Turn

Chapter 14	The British Connection	539
Chapter 15	The Thatcher Government	573
Chapter 16	The Reagan Presidency	631

Part VI. Epilogue

Chapter 17	Beyond Convention	701
Chapter 18	Economic Theory, Policy and Uses of Statistical Methods	735

Notes and References to Volume II   761

Appendixes to Part V

Appendix One: Analysis of a Tax Cut	802
Appendix Two: A Variant of the Laffer Curve	820

Index   833

In chapter 11 we return to the monetary revolution of the twentieth century. This revolution involved two main crises in economic thought—the first coming in Britain in the 1920s and 1930s and in the U.S. in the 1930s; and the second coming in the 1970s, and symbolized by the simultaneous occurrence of inflation and recession in the U.S. In the first crisis Keynes offered new direction—a revolution of thought in reaction to the crisis, as it were—and, in the second, Milton Friedman offered an antidote to Keynesian economics and new direction. There are, however, elements of thought which Keynes and Friedman shared in their respective revolutions, so we refer to both as a part of the monetary revolution of the twentieth century. The failure of Keynes to deal adequately with the first crisis anticipates the second.

As we reintroduce Keynes, we find the following: he gave too much weight to the rigidity of wages in Britain, albeit in a period of the rising power of trade unions; he gave a central role to monetary matters as a source of disturbances to the economy but he did so with a flawed treatment of interest rates and without freeing himself entirely from the old quantity theory of money; and he put too much confidence in the educated participants in government policy. Also, chapter 11 follows an outline of historical developments and introduces consumption function notions upon which discussion of income redistribution proceeds in chapters 12 and 13. The historical developments in chapter 11 range from the gold standard era through that for the labor and dollar standards and we discuss the prospect of what may be called a Friedman-rule standard.

In chapters 12 and 13, we discuss freedom and the redistribution of income through the tax and transfer powers of the state. Friedman is portrayed as seeing in the capitalist ethic the maximum amount of voluntary association. There, the tax and transfer powers of the state interfere least with the distribution of income. This lack of interference would leave income to be distributed according to the values of the various marginal products of labor and capital. Analysis along such lines leads to the flat-rate income tax. Nevertheless, redistribution is primarily involved with static notions that reflect household or agent utility as a function of income with the slope of the line for the utility function (say, marginal utility) declining as income increases. This early belief also parallels the analysis found in J. M. Keynes's simple consumption function. From the periods associated with J. S. Mill and the introduction of the amendment to the U.S. Constitution in 1913, the thinking has tended to be that fairness (or some sort of social justice) resides in a progressive income tax (often also said to be a tax based on "ability to pay").

As Friedman offered a new, more dynamic consumption analysis, he set the analysis of taxes as they relate to income on a different course, although this was not recognized when Friedman's consumption function work first appeared. This analysis, imposed on a Keynesian/income-expenditure plane, as introduced on page 83, puts the static consumption function schedule in motion and treats the Keynesian variables for income, saving, and consumption differently. All this brings further attention to what Klein called the great ratios of economics. Among these, as introduced on page 84, are the ratio of saving to income (S/Y) and velocity (Y/M). The former is brought forward later, along with attention to economic growth.

In Friedman's function, which is associated with the analysis of households's lifetime income, there is also social mobility—the poor are not permanently poor. (Indeed, we may think back to the "great migration" of Eastern European Jews and the New York environment of the late 1800s and early twentieth century as recounted in chaps. 1 and 5.) This social mobility appears to be absent in the static/Keynesian/consumption function context. Since, for sure, there may be a cultural as well as an economic problem with poverty and social mobility, the analysis for a free society that Friedman brought forward was accompanied by recognition that a society must support and inculcate social values such as concern the work ethic, charity, and social justice, if the society is to function well; and that a negative income tax could be called for as a means of alleviating adversity which Friedman treated as a temporary state for households in his consumption function analysis.

The thinking of freedom, taxes, and social mobility is discussed in part V, where we consider "The Big U-Turn" in reference to Thatcher and Reagan. There, we see notions about tax rates, a "safety net," a flat-rate income tax, economic growth, the "real" rate of interest, and reduction in the size of government in relation to the private sector. Unresolved questions are present about solutions to poverty, social mobility, the desirable extent of economic growth, and the historical roles of private charity. As social programs were attacked for waste, fraud, and corruption, Friedman raised a relevant question: Should people who want to do good do so with their own incomes and persuasive powers, or should essentially private values (say in a context of cultural heterogeneity and religious diversity) be imposed on the state so that those who want to do good appear to want to do so primarily with other peoples' incomes?

We call the redirection of historical and political events and thoughts encompassing Keynes's and Friedman's monetary revolution, their respective consumption function analyses and thinking about freedom, taxes and social mobility, and the historical and political events of the '20s and '80s, the U-Turn. This actual political turn around may be expressed metaphorically on what we call Hotelling's line (chap. 15), a continuum of ideological and political/economic positions running from the extreme socialist left to the extreme social economy right. The voters of a society are positioned about the line. They mingle about the line and politicians vie for their support.

There is a place on this line for economics as well as politics, for, naive absentmindedness aside, even "scientific economics" has latent ideological dimensions and cannot escape classification (as would also be consistent with *former* American Economic Review *editor George Borts's December '87 AEA-meetings paper "Ideology and the Content of Economic Journals"). The Marxist, socialist and collectivist economics on the left of the line includes historicism, the labor theory of value and the socialist ethic. Industrial policy and the "big models" (pp. 71-77), with their econometric, state planning dimension are also suggestive of the political left. They help make possible the use of force in control over the agents in order to get the real world to conform to the model. We may also envision so-called pure models, which proceed in static contexts from axioms implying the redistribution of income, and, further along the continuum, we encounter the conclusions of economists which offer a competitive equilibrium of prices and quantities.*

On the right of the line exists the economics where freedom is a main goal of the joint political and economic arrangements. "Institutional individualism," social mobility and voluntary association are elevated, "money" serves to facilitate the indirect satisfaction of wants and the maximum in voluntary association, and minimum government is sought in dealing with moral and economic matters (the use of persuasion aside), but the need to deal with damages to third parties and the environment is recognized. This monetarist economics is not without price-theoretic underpinnings, but we are not unmindful of two developments. For one, economics in the post-WW II years was set on a two track system in most teaching and professional treatments, where price theoretic economics was viewed as a distinct body. There we encounter neoclassical economics, which, exclusive of its anti-trust dimensions (pp. 304-321), can readily be viewed as apologetics for a capitalist society. Further, Friedman's monetarist non-neoclassical economics with its price theoretic statement of position may also be viewed as free society appologetics. For another, the role of money in twentieth century economics and the free society has taken some time to clarify.

Of course, voters, political figures, and economists may seek one position on the line when it comes to morals and the state and another when it comes to economics, and may, unwittingly or otherwise, claim political neutrality. In this we encounter paradoxes—the case of the Jew as a leftist who finds freedom in a market oriented society (pp. 166-172); the case of the moralists who want the state to impose morals but find freedom of advocacy in a society where power is dispersed; the case of military control where free markets may be allowed to function for a time exclusive of political freedom. In addition, there is a middle ground, which we encounter in volume II as being sought after by the parochial group we call the Keynesians. There is the question of the rise and ultimate failure of the middle over the decades spanning the 1930s through the '70s, with the result of greater polarization.

The recognition of Hotelling's line, different uses of statistical methods and analytical systems of economics (pp. 68-87; 453-456), does not preclude economists from being scholarly in the framing and defense of the best hypotheses.

Chapter 11
Crises, Keynes, and Friedman

The decades of the '20s and '30s mark a watershed. In these years, events coincided with changes in economic theory and the political implementation of ideas in the U.S. and the U.K. to set society on a course of development which culminated with the inflationary recession phenomenon, and the end of the Keynesian era (chap. 8), the labor government in the U.K. and the Carter presidency in the U.S. At this time, crises and a vacuum of power occurred which introduced a further watershed in history, accompanied by the Thatcher government in Britain and the Reagan presidency in the U.S.

The decades of this interwatershed period were an aberration in history in the sense that, with the Thatcher government in Britain and the Reagan presidency in the U.S., renewed emphasis was placed on pre-WW I ideas, policies and implementations stressing international trade, individualism, competition and flexible wages, and a relatively sound monetary medium. This emphasis was encouraged in the hundred years from approximately 1812 to WW I by a system with gold and the Bank of England as the centerpieces in international developments. In addition: the predominant ideas included a minimum role for an activist government in monetary policy matters; an economics of deficits to stabilize the economy, such as later came about, was unknown; and balanced budgets on the part of national governments were expected for the most part, national emergency aside.

To hint of a return to pre-WW I ways is not to say that history repeats itself in every respect for it does not. There are new ideas, practices and episodes. Indeed: Britain is no longer the lynchpin for the world; the predominant flow of economic thought is no longer from Britain to the U.S., as it was for the almost two centuries spanning from Adam Smith to J. M. Keynes; and the Bank of England no longer plays its historic role in combination with the gold standard and the avoidance of significant inflation. Nevertheless, there are some striking similarities between the century that preceded WW I and the early 1980s.

In part V, we discuss the rise of the role of money (defined as a stock, usually of deposit balances and currency) in the Thatcher/Reagan political arrangements. Importance is placed on open economies, international trade, and on individual initiatives, as opposed to dependence on government in crucial respects. Plus in later chapters on Thatcher and Reagan, we come to an emphasis on flexible wages as a means of facilitating full employment under conditions of international trade.

For now, we deal with the following: the economic ideas and practices spanning the 1930s through 1970s; special issues of the 1920s in Britain and the 1930s in Britain and the U.S. that have a bearing on development in the 1980s and on the '90s agenda; and Keynes, the Keynesians and Friedman.

Hicks's Drama

The Cambridge University professor and interpreter of Keynes, Sir John Hicks, wrote about the gold standard era and what we have called the aberration in history as a five act drama.[1] Hicks's acts are as follows: Act I, the automatic gold standard from 1812 to WW I; Act II, the attempted restoration of gold in the 1920s against the special backdrop of the rising strength of trade unions in Britain and rigid wages; Act III, the 1930s through WW II; Act IV, a return to a gold-flows mechanism with the International Monetary Fund and labor and dollar standards; and, Act V, no standard. We note the emergence of a monetary-rule standard, albeit one that does not necessarily require a formal, legislated rule, as suggestive of an Act VI and symbol of a return to an earlier era.

Though not as formal in its role as the old gold standard the Act VI standard would consist of the acceptance of Friedman's rule by influential thinkers, writers, and especially an informed segment of society in a major country of the world. The rule (pp. 548-549) is that the money stock grows at the same trend rate of growth as that for real output, but with allowance for secular trend shifts in the turnover of money balances. The acceptance of such thinking in the U.S. would for example, lead to the return of what we call below the dollar standard, which in its time substituted for the older gold standard and/or some variant such as the gold exchange standard. The gold exchange standard is a gold standard that is supplemented by some key currency. Under it gold bears a fixed relation to a country's currency (say the $ at $35.00 per oz) plus the currency becomes acceptable as a substitute for gold (i.e., the currency becomes a key currency). In earlier history, the definition of a key currency would require acceptance as a reserve currency by central banks other than that of the key-currency country, but under the envisioned Act VI this would be less important than the simple existence of a standard—most notably something that is acceptable as a unit of exchange with approximately fixed purchasing power.

Act I. Gold-Flows and the Quantity Theory

In essence we may envision as a standard something such as the British pound (£) which was a key to the gold standard of Hicks's Act I. Central to the standard and the role of the pound, however, was the performance of the Bank of England. The control of the Bank was arranged so that it avoided significant inflation for England and the surrounding territory with banks tied directly to London.[2]

In more general terms, the old gold standard had the property whereby important currencies were convertible into gold at a fixed price, and each of these was convertible into the others at a fixed rate of exchange (say, $/£ approximately constant). This property, however, is not so important as the gold-flows or specie-flows (or gold coin flows) mechanism it is a part of. The substance of this mechanism, which we associate with Adam Smith's friend David Hume, concerns several other concepts other than just gold at a fixed price, notably: economies are open to trade with one another; deficits on the trade account occur where imports exceed exports and these must be met with some other export, most obviously gold or monetary reserves or movements of capital; there is a form of price competition to sell traded goods and services, where a country's overall position is influenced by its price level in relation to the rest of the world (in other words, we may say, there is a "discipline" imposed via competition to keep prices and costs of production down, to achieve a gold-inflow position, and to influence the movements of gold, monetary reserves or capital); and the most important component of a price is usually the special price we call "wage cost."

Hicks's Five-Act Drama, Plus Act VI

Act I.

The gold standard,
1819-1914

Act II.

Attempted restoration of the gold standard, say 1924-33, following establishment of federal system in U.S. in 1913	The roots of the monetarist revolution of J.M. Keynes's famous *General Theory;* the issue enjoined by Winston Churchill and J. M. Keynes, the Great Crash, bank failures, etc.

	Act III.	
	The later 1930s and the years of the second world war—a search for a new standard	Continued depression; ownership of gold outlawed in U.S. under Emergency Banking Act of 1933; the International Monetary Funds as outgrowth of Bretton Woods meeting in 1944, and as basis for reconstituted gold-flows mechanism
	Act IV.	
The Keynesian era 1960-1980: Presidencies of J. F. Kennedy, Lyndon Johnson, Richard Nixon, and Jimmy Carter, for the most part; Keynes was not a Keynesian	The Early post-WW II years until 1971—a dollar standard	The dollar's fixed tie to gold; the breaking of the tie and devaluation by President Nixon in two steps in 1971 and 1973; removal of ban on ownership of gold by U.S. citizens in 1974
	Act V.	
	The early 1970s until the early 1980s—no standard	Decade with periods of price controls; ultimately double-digit inflation in U.S.
	Act VI.	
Monetarist revolution of this century; the Thatcher government and the Reagan Presidency	The monetary-rule standard(?)	The transition (the "hard slog"); deescalation of inflation; issues from Act II come forward

In Hume's thinking, there was a simple form of what we call the quantity theory of money. It may be symbolized as follows:

$$MV = PQ \text{ and } M = (Q/V)_{const.} P \qquad (1)$$

where M is the money stock, P is the average of prices or an index, Q is a country's measure of output in terms adjusted for inflation or deflation (i.e., Y/P where Y is total income or payment for output), and V (also = Y/M) is a measure of the turnover of money balances. Before J.M. Keynes's work in the 1920s and at Cambridge, there was the tendency to treat the Q/V factor as constant, and thus to think of changes in the left-hand side of equation (1) as impacting on P on the right-hand side. Friedman later reported, as we take up his *Monetary Trends* work with Anna Schwartz in chapter 14, that this is not a bad first approximation to reality, given what we came to in Keynesian terms.

The simple quantity theory has been greatly elaborated upon—including in Friedman's and Schwartz's (hereafter F/S's) *Monetary Trends*—and called the "new" quantity theory of money or, alternatively, monetarism.[3] In any case, the old theory fits into the gold-flows context without damaging the relevance of the concepts. It also becomes central to Act II of Hicks's drama, and to Keynes's reactions against the economics he received from the past and encountered at the hands of his peers.

Continuing with the mechanism, quite briefly but as elucidated in more detail elsewhere,[4] countries trade goods and services and compete for sales in domestic and foreign markets where attention is focused upon prices. There can be disturbing crises, but for the most part the trade of countries with the most competitive prices is favored. The matter may be viewed as if the respective countries have averages for their prices (or price indexes). As one country's relative position is favored [say, $-\Delta(P_{US}/P_{UK})$ for a favored U.S. position over a U.K. position] that country exports more and enjoys an inflow of monetary reserves. A balancing out of reserves occurs as the countries compete in terms of trade.

It is important that the competition regulates prices and disperses power that may otherwise reside in government bureaus. Under the arrangement, a country with efficient productivity (including as enhanced by new capital goods) is rewarded with rising income and reduced unemployment. No grand scheme of state or international planning and direct control is required. Exchange rates are for the most part fixed under the classical gold-flows mechanisms (say, $/£ = const. within fixed limits) and adjustments to trade imbalances are supposed to take place through price-level changes (e.g., P_{US} vs. P_{UK}) or product prices (and the special part of product prices called wages). Faced with unemployment, a country's position can be improved by enhancing productivity and having prices and wages adjust downward relative to those of other countries.

Another way to achieve adjustments in trade positions is to have exchange rate changes (e.g., Δ $/£). Where the rates are left to the forces of the markets for foreign exchange—rather than being fixed by governmental, exchange stabilization funds, and by agreements between countries—they are called floating exchange rates. Under these arrangements the relative price levels (say, P_{US}/P_{UK}) do not matter, as far as imbalances in trade and balance-of-payments accounting are concerned. The numbers in the accounting processes simply change to reflect exchange rate changes and balances in the international balances of payments. In any case, experience in the decade 1973-83, following the move by the U.S. and its trading partners toward floating rates in the early 1970s, has suggested that most national states do not like the consequences of fully floating rates. Weak-currency countries find themselves in effect bartering more goods for less and come to think of the market as being unjust to their cause.

Viewing a full float as the opposite extreme from a fixed-rate system, intermediate positions may be the "dirty float" (where some countries intervene in efforts to support or stabilize currencies) or the "dirty fixed-rate" (which allows for frequent devaluations and/or revaluations). Whatever the case, exclusive of full floating, some elements of economic efficiency and wage and price discipline (via relative prices, as under the gold-flows mechanism) enter from an international point of view.

Under the more rigid form of the old standard, gold was maintained as a fraction of the reserves and money supply it supports. Even so, for most of the 19th century the growth in the supply of gold kept up with the growth in the domestic economics and in the volume of international trade.[5] In the 1920s, the standards were more gold exchange standards where gold was supplemented by key currencies. These highly regarded currencies were freely convertible into gold, where they made stretching the reserves possible by serving as a substitute for gold and enlarging monetary reserves held by the central banks. The British pound played the role of a key currency in the 1920s, and, for a time in the post-WW II years (Hicks's Act IV), the U.S. dollar played the major role as a key currency.[6] Although American citizens could not own gold from 1934 to 1974, the U.S. government stood ready to exchange gold for dollars for official purposes with foreign central banks. As we will see, however, this could continue only so long as the U.S. had a very large stock, relatively speaking.

The old gold standard is thought to have worked pretty well from Waterloo to WW I,[7] and to have contributed to the long period of peace before WW I, with Britain and the City of London at its center. Hence, after the war (Hicks's Act II) many looked to the reestablishment of the gold standard with Britain at the center. In the meantime, however: labor unions had gained power in Britain (including through ties to the Labor party); Britain had liquidated much wealth in fighting the war; the political-economic issue of unemployment was in the forefront; its intellectuals renunciated old values, complacency prevailed in other respects, and the U.S. had come out of the war as the foremost industrial power.

In Act II, the rise of the Labor party as a major political party from 1922 to 1945, the unemployment issue, and the decline of Britain over that period predominate.[8] The issue of unemployment in an industrial society had been addressed by the socialists Karl Marx and Friedrich Engels,[9] who engaged in their lives' major effort in Britain. Against the backdrop of Britain in the 1920s, the issue attracted Keynes as he sought what some have viewed as a middle ground between the extremes of a socialist and an unfettered capitalist state. Keynes held an elitist political philosophy of sorts,[10] as we will see, and he held close to much that was dear to him in the British tradition of civility, but, as an intellectual of Britain's Bloomsbury generation, he was no slave to a "golden image," a "barbarous relic."[11]

A part of his reasoning was that we had already discovered the mystery of gold—its artificiality, the way it worked as a reserve in the vaults of banks, and the way it supported the creation of money and credit through bookkeeping entries. Having lost innocence, we could not go back to the gold standard rule as opposed to a managed currency and the related economic system.[12]

Act II. The Quantity Theory

In the early 1920s, Keynes (a highly creative monetary economist)[13] wrote about the quantity theory of money and reacted to the treatment of the constant Q/V in equation (1) above. In the Cambridge form found in Keynes's 1923 tract we may write,

$$M = k\,Py \qquad (2)$$

where we substitute y for Q in equation (1) and k, the Cambridge factor of proportionality, reflects velocity ($V = 1/k$). A difference between Keynes and his peers in this instance was Keynes's treatment of k (or velocity as it were) as a highly volatile variable. He in fact related it to the speculative demand for money, in particular speculation with respect to price level changes and hence the purchasing power of money.

Money was seen by Keynes as the most liquid of assets, the demand for which was subject to shifts. These shifts, moreover, affected the demand for current output of goods and services (whence began Keynes's attack on Say's law of markets, pages 58 and 195). There was, in other words, the beginning of an analysis of the interaction of monetary and real goods sectors that had been separated in the mainstream economies before Keynes where the Cambridge k (or the velocity of money) was constant. Attacking economists' separation of the sectors and the so-called long-run treatment of the separation, Keynes wrote:

> But this *long run* is a misleading guide to current affairs. In the *long run* we are all dead. Economists set themselves too easy; too useless a task if in tempestuous seas they can only tell us that when the storm is long past the ocean is flat again.[15]

Having become defiant toward the accepted quantity theory (velocity and 1/k constant), Keynes attempted to depart from it in his major work,

The General Theory. Even so, he was unable to completely abandon it, as we note below. Addressing the world of the 1930s and having become aware of the emergence of open market operations at the Federal Reserve Bank of New York, in his 1936 work he dealt with the speculative demand for money in relation to bond prices and interest rate changes. There were motives for holding money—for transactions purposes, as was traditional in economics (with 1/k constant), but also for precautionary and speculative purposes, which were not traditional. The new extensions of analysis concerned the uncertainty of the future, foreseen and unforeseen developments, and speculation concerned mainly bonds.

Keynes is brought into the monetary revolution in economics that Hicks and Lord Kaldor identified Friedman with,[16] for a variety of reasons: monetary analysis played a central role in Keynes's work and altered the study of real output and employment for both Keynes and Friedman; Keynes's expanded definition of money (uncertainty, speculation and so on) was accepted unaltered by Friedman; both Keynes and Friedman sought a monetary theory of the economy (in Friedman's case the statics of price theory and Keynesian economics as statement of position with monetary theory as a theory of motion), as opposed to the two tracks known as "micro" and "macro" economics following the late 1950s;[17] and both sought a more empirically oriented theory [what Hession called a "realitic" (sic) theory in contrast to analytic or pure theory in relation to the common interpretation of Marshall], and what Friedman identified in relation to Marshall as a search for a fruitful empirical hypothesis. Coming later to the main pillars of thought that grew out of Keynes's *General Theory* (most notably including the consumption function and the liquidity preference construction) Friedman made contributions by redirecting rather than abandoning the mechanical apparatus passed along via the Keynesians.

Friedman said that Keynes had the right idea in his approach and in the simplicity of statement, but he failed in other respects. Keynes was wrong in the exact form of his statement in the *General Theory* which implied behavior about velocity. He had not freed himself entirely from the quantity theory; there were hidden prospects (the velocity of money was implied in his liquidity preference construction). Moreover, positions Keynes took during Act II about wages, a closed economy, and the dependence on an informed civil service set the stage for what we have called the aberration in history—namely: the developments with roots in the 1920s that came to Britain's Westminster with the peak of labor government in 1945, and to Washington, D.C. with the Keynesian era; and the reversal of these developments at the time of the Thatcher government and the Reagan presidency (chaps. 15 and 16).

Act II (continued). Keynes, Churchill and Gold

In the 1920s the financial leaders of the world desired to return to the gold standard with the British pound and London at the financial center.[18] Even Keynes recognized its past success, and the reputation of respectability it acquired—"as densely respectable as ever encountered even in the realms of sex or religion."[19] A part of the effort toward having the standard achieve its function and the respectability upon which the function depended involved fixing the pound at its pre-war price for the dollar. When Winston Churchill was appointed Chancellor of the Exchequer, the resolution to return was a part of his first budget proposal in April of 1925. So it was that Britain returned to the gold standard in 1925 at the old parity of $4.87.

At the time, Churchill was more familiar with admirals and generals than London bankers and economists. Nevertheless, he became a focal point of the gold decision for years to come. This was perhaps abetted by J.M. Keynes and, in any case, Churchill became the topic of Keynes's essay written immediately after the return to gold.[20]

However, by the end of WW I, Britain had liquidated much of her wealth and had suffered enormous losses from the war. Following a mild economic expansion and a mild inflationary episode immediately after the war, the British economy was relatively stagnant, with unemployment continuing at high levels by pre-war standards. Further, the British labor party came on the scene and displaced Britain's old Liberal party as a major party in 1922. It increased its share of votes until, in 1945, it had its greatest sweep with 48.1 percent of the vote as Labor's Clement Attlee ousted Britain's wartime prime minister Winston Churchill. By American standards the trade unions were a strong part of the party backing even in the 1920s, and a socialist element was highly visible, as the rise of the Bolsheviks in Russia was debated.

The issues at the time were very similar to the monetarist issues during Margaret Thatcher's elections in Britain in 1979 and 1983 (chap. 15). A monetarist policy of bringing the growth of the money stock under control was advocated and defended by Thatcher. By the 1983 elections voters were faced with a stark ideological choice. On the one hand, Thatcher was campaigning to cut public spending and to curb trade union power, and, on the other, the candidate for the opposition Labor party advocated massive state intervention in the economy and close consultation with the unions.

Thatcher saw herself as attempting to change the character of the British people, as calling for a return to the "Victorian values" ("the virtues of thrift and self-reliance, hard work and a sense of duty"). Further, in her attempt to redirect the economy in her first term, unemployment reached a record high of 13.3 percent. On the wage issue, the American Keynesian James Tobin portrayed her thus:

> [She] threatens workers, managers, and plain citizens like an authoritarian school master disciplining an unruly class. You won't have your jobs, profits or prosperity until you stop inflating your wages and prices.[21]

Returning to the 20s and the gold issue of that time, Keynes argued that the return to gold "shackled" and "enslaved" the country. There was also the matter that the pound was over-priced in view of the assumption at the time of rigid wages and the state of the British economy in relation to the U.S. economy, as the latter began to boom in the 1920s. On the U.S. economy, Keynes said, "Wide fluctuations, which spell unemployment and misery for us, are swamped for them in the general upward movement."[22]

By 1925, Keynes had accepted the state of decline in Britain. Though he did not address the strong role of the trade unions as bad, he accepted the rigidity of wages and began to move toward the notion of a "managed" currency.[23] Indeed, in the period of the early 1920s he saw actual practice at the central banks as drifting toward what we now call a discretionary policy, as distinct from "the pre-war conceptions of the bank-rate, allowing the tides of gold to play what tricks they like with the internal price level."[24] He wrote about the return to the gold standard as "abandoning the attempt to moderate the disastrous influence of the credit-cycle on the stability of prices and employment."

In actuality, in the early 1920s Keynes envisioned the prospects of managing the creation of credit "to regulate the expansion and deflation of credit in the interests of business stability and the steadiness of prices."[25] He became interested in open market operations in the United States as the means of credit creation exclusive of any constraint on the part of gold flows. He made this comment about what he had learned:

> A regulated non-metallic standard has slipped in unnoticed. It exists. Whilst the economist dozed, the academic dream of a hundred years...has crept into the real world by means of the bad fairies...—the wicked Ministers of Finance.[26]

Keynes's approach had as its center two features. One was an interest rate orientation (the i-regime), as the control variable and link with credit expansion and capital expenditures. This is in opposition to what we call a money-aggregates regime (or M-regime) in the U.S. and the U.K. in the early 1980s. The second central feature in Keynes's approach was faith in government officials and civil servants to do the right thing.[27]

The first feature came to the forefront of the Keynesian-monetarist confrontation at Friedman's hands.[28] On the second feature, Friedman said the following on the occasion of the Keynes centenary:

> Keynes favored managed money and managed exchange rates [Keynes 1923, 177; 1932, 213]—that is, discretionary control by monetary authorities (the Bank of England in Britain, the Federal Reserve System in the United States) over the "supply of currency and credit with a view to maintaining, so far as possible, the stability of the internal price level"; and "over the supply of foreign exchange so as to avoid purely temporary fluctuations...in the relation between the internal and external price level". He was confident that the authorities had—or could have—sufficient knowledge to achieve these objectives and that, given the power, they would use it for that purpose.
>
> Discretion in the hands of public-spirited and competent civil servants fitted in well with Keynes's elitist political philosophy. But it must also be granted that, at the time he wrote, little or no experience existed to judge how such a method of regulating the supply of money would work in practice.[29]

In Friedman's orientation toward the U.S. and the U.K. in *Monetary Trends*, (chap. 14), we encounter, the following expression,

$$(P_{US}/P_{UK})/(\$/£) = 1.12 \tag{3}$$

where the left-hand member consists of a ratio of the U.S. and U.K. price levels (P_{US}/P_{UK}) over the market dollar-pound exchange rate ($\$/£$). The factor P_{US}/P_{UK} is the purchasing-power-parity concept of the exchange rate. The right-hand member of the expression, on the other hand, is a mean value expressed as a constant (1.12) to which the left-hand member returns, as shown in the accompanying illustration. The two members combined give expression and factual orientation to the law of one price, namely: allowing for transportation and location costs, a market basket of goods will come to sell for approximately the same price at different locations in the respective economies.

Friedman reported in connection with this mean-value constant that relative prices and exchange rates change, generating fluctuations about the number and a return to the number.[30] Efforts at control over balance of payments matters through exchange rates, along the lines followed by Britain from 1931 until 1979 (during much of what we have called an aberration in history), precluded the law of one price from working prop-

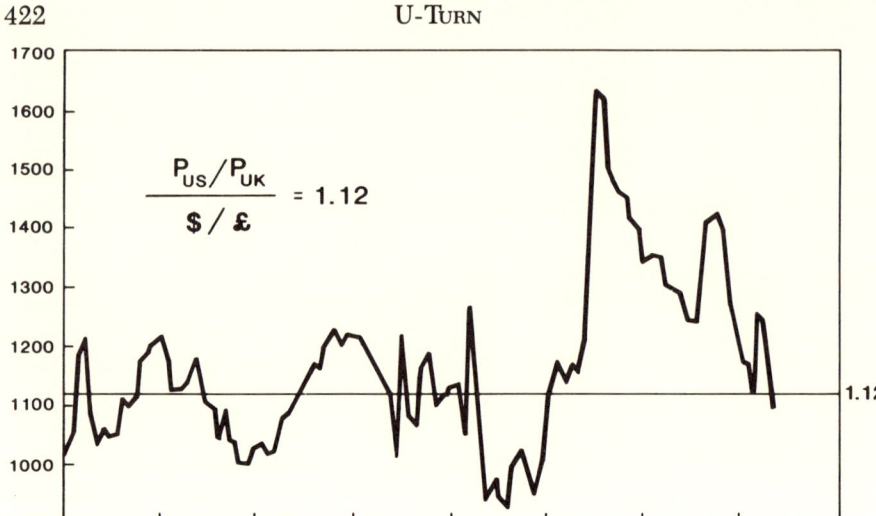

Source: Milton Friedman. "Prices of Money and Goods Across Frontiers." *World Economy* 2(February 1980): 497-511.

The Ratio of Purchasing Power Parity Exchange Rate (P_{US}/P_{UK}) to the Market Exchange Rate ($\$/£$), 1868-1978

erly. Adjustments are forced elsewhere, as in income and employment, and these interfere with the proper functioning of unified markets. But in the end we return to the constant 1.12.

Accepting the mean value of 1.12, a devaluation of the pound ($-\Delta \$/£$) calls for a decline in the ratio of U.S. to U.K. prices [$-\Delta (P_{US}/P_{UK})$]. In other words, in an open economy, where trade between partners is taking place, one economy cannot gain whatever permanent advantages are thought to lie in the discretionary devaluation of its currency, since these will be offset elsewhere.

Accepting the number 1.12, and, say, an over-valued pound, as was emphasized in reference to the dollar/pound exchange rate in the 1920s, we also see that either of two things must happen—U.S. prices must rise, or U.K. prices must decline. The booming economy in the U.S. in the late 1920s appeared to preclude inflation, where, even as discount rates were kept low in 1927-29, bank credit expanded most rapidly in the form of the extension of credit to the stock market.[31]

In Britain in the 1920s however, Churchill saw staying off gold as being a political as well as an economic matter. The return to it had been recommended by a standing committee of experts in 1918. Moreover, Prime Minister Stanley Baldwin (second ministry 1924-1929) who had appointed

Churchill as Chancellor declared: "All the workers of this country have got to take reductions in wages in order to help put industry on its feet." Hence the issue of flexible versus sticky prices.

Churchill was not inclined to see the matter of competitive British goods as a gold-standard problem but as an industry problem. Churchill emerged as being opposed to the strong unions, some of whose leaders were socialist advocates, but as being very charitably disposed toward the workers and welfare matters to help the less advantaged.[32]

An unfortunate incident arose shortly after the action of Britain to return to gold concerning the British coal miners, who were backed by the Trade Union Congress (or TUC). What followed was something like a Marx Brothers film of the time. It included a tragic general strike, with Churchill at the center of the government's opposition to an apparent threat from the union. Keynes was in the thick of things too.[33] He had accepted sticky wages as a premise from which to proceed and appeared also to favor protective tariffs, though on the latter he later reversed himself.

No doubt, partly because of Churchill's later prominence as a great wartime leader, there has been a tendency to find apologies for his actions, to see Keynes as having taken the proper position, to see Churchill as having been "baffled by twentieth century economics," and to point out that Churchill later "grasped the magnitude of his error in putting England back on the gold standard."[34] The facts of the matter are various, nevertheless, because Churchill was not wrong, unless he was prepared to accept a defeatist position for Britain. Britain needed a restoration of confidence, new capital (i.e., an increase in saving out of income), competitive wages and prices, and not simply concessions to charity that could not be carried through without improved economic performance and concessions to strong unions that would in time hamper the competitive prospects for the economy.

Keynes's *General Theory* (1936) came from these experiences of the 1920s and may have been right in its simplicity, "its concentration on a few key magnitudes, its potential fruitfulness." We may even have benefited from the apparatus that grew out of it over the long run. Even so, there have been those who were led to reject the theory because they "believe it has been contradicted by experience."[35] The theory and the more static apparatus that came from it failed to isolate the key factors in short-run economic change. The *General Theory*'s policy prescriptions placed confidence in enlightened leadership which has not been justified by the experiences since the 1920s.[36]

Act II (continued). British and U.S. Developments

The German reparations payments[37] and the return to gold with its associated U.S. policies as influenced by the fledgling Federal Reserve (established 1913) were the two crucial problems in the 1920s. They had major implications for the Great Depression and subsequent effects on social and economic thinking. From 1925 to 1929 in the U.S. wholesale prices fell by 8 percent, and agriculture was depressed. With attention to these variables and Britain's high priced pound there were efforts by the Federal Reserve System to ease credit and hence raise prices (ΔP_{US}) via maintaining low discount rates.[38] However, the New York stock market was experiencing the first of three great booms in its history, and the regulation of borrowing to purchase stocks was still in the future. The readily available bank credit found its way into stock purchases.

A peak in U.S. business conditions occurred in August 1929, and the period between August and October of 1929 was marked by uneasiness on the part of stock market participants. The Crash occurred on October 29 and was accompanied by building liquidity shifts in the U.S. that extended abroad (pp. 76-77). There was a fatal inconsistency in behavior and policy: for some time, some "agents" shifted their assets into cash and more liquid forms of wealth, even as banking developments occurred to destroy the liquidity being sought by the agents.

In addition, unemployment was increasing in Britain, where the British Labor party's ("right-wing," Kaldor would say) Ramsay MacDonald had formed a new government in August of 1931,[39] and where Churchill had been exiled to a political wilderness over issues concerning India.[40] Though MacDonald's Labor government had been reduced to impotence by the outcome of voting in May, Britain abandoned the gold standard on September 21, 1931. In a short time the pound lost over 28 percent of its value in gold and the dollar. Britain's action to abandon gold was preceded by runs to convert British pounds into gold.[41]

Between September 16 and October 28, substantial amounts of U.S. assets that were owned abroad were also converted into gold, all of which put pressure on the reserves of U.S. banks.[42] Combined with internal withdrawals of currency from U.S. banks, this reduced commercial bank reserves dramatically. From August 1931 to January 1932, the U.S. money stock fell at an annual rate of 31 percent.[43] Waves of U.S. bank failures came in 1931, 1932, and 1933, as the U.S. liquidity crises intensified.[44]

The details are numerous.[45] Open market purchases by the Federal Reserve did not compensate for the drains on bank reserves. A nationwide banking holiday was proclaimed on March 6, 1933 by President Roosevelt. It suspended gold redemptions and gold shipments abroad. Banking reforms of the 1930s followed and new international arrangements for the post-WW II reconstruction were put in place.[46] Mostly until the end of WW II, exchange controls, tariffs, and disrupted trade characterized international arrangements.

So, "Why Was Monetary Policy So Inept?" F/S asked. They noted that the actions called for to prevent U.S. monetary collapse did not require the knowledge of operations, monetary forces, and economic fluctuations that came later. Indeed, F/S pointed out, the pursuit of the policies outlined by the Federal Reserve System itself in the 1920s, or for that matter by London's Walter Bagehot in 1873,[47] would have "cut short" the catastrophic liquidity crisis "before it had gone too far, perhaps by the end of 1930."

In attempting to answer their big question, F/S saw shortcomings in the academic literature.[48] Even so, these do not explain "why an active, vigorous, self-confident policy in the 1920s was followed by a passive, defensive, hesitant policy from 1929 to 1933, least of all why the [Federal Reserve] System failed to meet an internal drain [the withdrawal of currency] in the way intended by its founder."[49] The explanation found here, on the other hand, lies in the death of Benjamin Strong in August of 1928, and in "the shift of power within the System [from New York to Washington] and the lack of understanding and experience of the individuals to whom the power shifted."[50] In the past, "in every banking crisis in our history," too much had depended on "the presence of one or more outstanding individuals willing to assume responsibility and leadership." The defect of the financial system was, then, "that it was susceptible to crises resolvable only with such leadership."

The Federal Reserve System's newly empowered Board in Washington and its later enlarged Federal Open Market Committee was no replacement for leadership. In a bureaucratic organization the tendency toward drift and indecision apparently reached full scope. The later, Keynesian era monetary policies were not much of an improvement.

Act III. The Post-1933 Years through WW II

Keynes's *General Theory* was a product of Hicks's Act II and Act III. Act II provided what Hicks called a labor standard for Act III. Keynes, Hicks might emphasize with some historical perspective, did three main things in the *General Theory*: (1) gave weight to the rigidity of wages in the 1920s in his objections to the gold standard with what he saw as an over-valued pound, and hence gave that rigidity a special role (as a standard that "expresses the value of money in terms of labor, just as the gold standard had expressed it in terms of gold"); (2) offered a monetary theory of a closed economy as distinct from an economy open to trade and the discipline of the old gold-flows mechanism; and (3) set full employment as the major economic goal.[51]

In advancing the familiar closed economy notion with respect to the *General Theory*, Hicks added that Keynes thought of it as being applicable to the world economy. Hicks argued:

> If the model was to be applied to a single economy, it could only have been to one where external trade was minimal, or to one (like Russia or the Germany of the date when he was writing) where it was tightly controlled. It is impossible to believe that such were the main applications that he had in mind. The only alternative is to suppose that it was meant to apply to the world economy.[52]

Whatever Keynes's intention, the idea of the closed economy was that domestic policies could be directed toward achieving full employment, given rigid wages and prices, without consideration of balance of payments problems which may call for wage and price adjustments, such as later appear as being painfully obvious to the Thatcher government and Reagan. In any case, extending the applicability of the theory to a world economy meant quite simply that major countries could proceed simultaneously to achieve full employment without the traditional costs of unemployed resources as a result of having to undergo economic adjustments to international matters.

Meanwhile on the domestic front in the 1930s in the U.S., Franklin Roosevelt's New Deal had come about in response to the economic problems of the early 1930s which were poorly understood and compounded by monetary contraction and bank failures, as induced by the 1913-founded Federal Reserve.[53] However, even the new president, taking office in March of 1933, offered no clear-cut ideas. Indeed: "Some of his advisors had specific plans, but his different advisers had different plans. Some wanted to print money, some to set floors under prices, some to inaugurate big spending programs."[54] Nevertheless, Roosevelt set about to elevate the public's mood, to inspire confidence, and to experiment. A result of the events was the acceptance of a new role for government, numerous statutes, and "programs and agencies that were not subject to annual reconsideration and that developed constituencies—bureaucracies and beneficiaries—that resisted counter-revolution."[55]

The Great Depression was a tragic event, where up to 25 percent of the labor force was unemployed at a time when the percentage would include a sizable portion of single-income families. The combination of the depression, Roosevelt as a personality, and Keynes as a worldly philosopher had great influence on thinking and policy, Herbert Stein said, "over the whole half century from 1930 to 1980."[56] It is not that Roosevelt himself or the policies of the 1930s were influenced by Keynes's *General Theory*, for that would require more time than many have allowed. The growing feelings about poverty, unemployment, the tax-transfer system, and income redistribution existed exclusive of Keynes.[57] Rather, the 1930s as an event may have done more to provide a market for Keynes's great book—which actually had its roots in Britain of the 1920s—than to influence it. The initial influence of Keynes's ideas was mainly at Harvard University, as introduced in chapter 7, where Professor Alvin Hansen ordered copies of the *General Theory* before its appearance at the book store. In time there was influence on the U.S. academic establishment more generally.[58]

Act IV. The Dollar Standard and the Labor Standard

Coming out of the 1930s and WW II, the U.S. and those who became its trading partners proceeded to establish new international institutions to help revitalize the workings of the old gold-flows mechanism.[59] This occurred on the international front, even as the U.S. proceeded on the domestic front to give attention to full employment goals. Ultimately the ideas and policies for achieving the domestic goals were Keynesian. In other words, we proceeded on ultimately inconsistent courses that could not be sustained. Internationally, the U.S. proceeded as if it were returning to the 1920s or even to Act I of Hicks's drama, where the country subjected itself to the effects of price level differentials in relation to the rest of the world. Domestically, however, the U.S. proceeded as if it were operating a closed economy, trading off a reduction in the unemployment rate for an inflation of the price level. This development could only function for a limited time, as we will see.

Among the centerpieces for economic policy that grew out of the devastations of the 1930s and WW II were the International Monetary Fund (IMF), on the one hand,[60] and the Employment Act of 1946 in the U.S., on the other.[61] The IMF provided member countries with temporary, helpful sources of liquidity to facilitate countries in making balance of payments adjustments. The temporary sources of funds were readily available and larger needs could be met for countries with fundamental problems in making deficit payments, if the countries agreed to undertake domestic programs to correct the payments problems giving rise to the deficits to begin with. Countries exchange rates were fixed, as under the old gold-flows mechanism, but devaluations were possible in the presence of some economic and political conditions. The corrective programs centered on the control over inflation and enhanced positions with respect to price competition, as symbolized by changes in the ratio P_{US}/P_{UK} under Act I of Hicks's drama.

In the U.S., the Employment Act of 1946 directed attention to the employment goal found in Keynesian economics. Even so, it was by no means strictly associated with the influence of Keynes's *General Theory*. Instead, the Employment Act was a part of the times in which Keynes had written and no doubt reflected the isolationist tendencies of the 1930s, as well as thinking about a closed economy (as far as the uses of monetary and fiscal policy are concerned) which we encounter in the development of Keynes's *General Theory*. The prevailing, potentially misleading thinking among economists in the U.S. was that wartime expenditure had achieved full employment in the U.S. The anticipated drop in these that would not be offset by domestic programs became a part of the basis for early post-WW II forecasts of recession.[62] The monetary thinking growing out of the 1930s, and the monetary control mechanism we associate with Keynes and Keynesian economics (the liquidity preference demand, an interest rate control orientation, and the liquidity trap, as taken up below under the Keynesian pillars), in effect diverted attention from a viable monetary policy role.

This thinking aside, an inadvertent monetary policy was followed. The Federal Reserve continued the rapid wartime expansion in the quantity of money, such that WW II inflation did not peak until August 1948. Recession followed in 1948-49, with the Korean War spanning the 1950-53 period. It provided another burst of inflation, Friedman said, "that reflected primarily an autonomous rise in velocity rather than prior excessive monetary growth."[63] Continuing, he said: "The outbreak of war only five years after the end of World War II and less than two years after the peak of the World War II inflation reawakened fears of inflation, which in turn produced a flight from money—that is, a sharp rise in velocity."

The Korean War helped produce the famous Treasury-Fed Accord of March 1951, from which we get much discussion about the independence of the Federal Reserve, as taken up in chapter 8.[64] Whatever, the Eisenhower years 1952-1960, with recessions in 1957-58 and 1960-61 set the stage for the presidential election of 1960, also as taken up in chapter 8.[65]

The election of 1960 and the mildness of the Eisenhower years set the stage for the Keynesian era which we identified earlier (pp. 231-240). As reported by Friedman, the Eisenhower years "laid the groundwork for a long expansion from 1961 to 1966." He said they were "the postwar 'high tide' of the Federal Reserve System comparable to the 1923-28 period."[66] After 1960, the rate of monetary growth doubled, rapid economic growth proceeded at first and then inflation started to gain ground.

In the early post-WW II period, these developments proceeded in the U.S. and Britain with relatively low rates of unemployment. For a time the U.S. advanced aid to the rest of the world and then in 1950 began to run deficits in its balance of payments with heavy losses of gold.[67] Even so, the dollar remained relatively strong and gold outflows continued in support of the dollar for a period of time which was only limited by the amount of the U.S. gold stock.

There were, of course, details to the transitions and episodes of the dollar-standard era as unemployment rates continued low.[68] However, the dollar standard era which ended in 1971, contained the seeds of its destruction in *General Theory* terms.[69] As Lord Kaldor said, everything in the *General Theory* was measured in terms of "wage units" which meant that "the rate of change in the price level was made to depend on the rate of increase in money wages relative to the rise in productivity." Continuing, he noted that fiscal and monetary policies could be "brought to bear to ensure the full utilization of resources," in keeping with the Keynesian era, but the Keynesian policies of moving toward a low rate of unemployment were useless for dealing with wage-induced inflation. Kaldor referred to the prospect of raising the unemployment rate in Britain from 1.5 to 2.5 percent, as a way of preventing excessive wage increases, and noted that this prospect won support for an elaborate scheme for a permanent incomes policy as early as 1950.

The point should be clear. By 1950 in Britain and 1960 in the U.S., the labor standard had broken down and the seeds for the destruction of the dollar standard were being sown. The standard could continue as long as the U.S. could export from its gold stock without dire consequences for the dollar. These came about in 1971.[70]

For a time wage agreements and expectations were slow to fully anticipate the inflation that was getting underway in the U.S. in the mid-1960s.[71] The events in the U.S. and the industrial successes in Germany and Japan set the stage for the dollar-mark-yen crisis and the U.S. actions to break the formal tie between the dollar and gold. Hence the end of Hicks's Act IV as it concerns the U.S.

Act V. No Standard

As seen by Hicks, the problem with the labor standard was that "many things affect the level of money wages, some economic, some 'social'." Real economic growth and moderate wage increases may combine to make the labor standard work for a time, but if monetary policy accommodates an upward push in wages in excess of productivity gains, the "social forces" gain in power. There are many of these, and Hicks mentioned the development of trade union power as one of them. It ceased to be exercised with moderation, as was evident in the U.S. by the end of the 1970s.[72]

Keynesian policies—such as we identify, including with the Nixon years in chapter 8—offered no firmness through which negotiations between the labor and management sides of industry might fruitfully proceed. Further, the Keynesian policies with roots in Keynes's work also carry the burden of being policies for closed economies. Closed economies were not what we came to operate in the post-WW II years nor did efforts toward floating exchange rates achieve any resemblance to closed economies. There were general reactions against inflation:

> It is true that even now there are regular Keynesians, if I may so call them, who believe that the money-wage level can safely be left to incomes policies and treaties with trade unions. But the evidence is that, while inflationary pressure may be temporarily checked by such devices, they offer no prospect of the longer-term stability, some degree of confidence in which has become a necessity for real recovery.[73]

Act VI. The Prospect

We encounter swings toward governments with monetarist leanings and reactions against Keynesian economics in the policy sphere first in the U.K. under Margaret Thatcher and then in the U.S., as later chapters indicate. In Britain the swing was dramatized by the results of 1983 elections, which came down to a choice on the voters' part along ideological lines with Margaret Thatcher's personality ("the resolute approach") and monetarist leanings as an issue. She was thought to have gained in support for her policies by her success in the handling of the Falkland's crisis in 1982 and by the failures of the policies of a socialist government across the English Channel in France. In any event, the 1983 elections showed Thatcher to be the strongest prime minister since the war-time Churchill, and offered her back-to-back terms, which in duration would be not equaled in British government affairs since the reign of Queen Victoria.

For now, we turn to the account of what happened. There was crisis, as Act V of Hicks's drama indicates, and, as comes up later, it facilitated the acceptance of an alternative way of viewing the world which we find at Friedman's hands.

The Keynesian Revolution

The period between the First World War and the Second, as outlined above, encompassed the best of times and the worst of times for the U.S. In the 1920s until 1929, production grew rapidly and, at the same time, the U.S. price level remained relatively stable,[74] partly in response to the enormous efficiency of production. In this era, there were further advance indications of the rise of the U.S. as a great power, as gold flowed into the country from abroad, and as the Bank of England turned to the Federal Reserve Bank of New York for assistance in returning the world to the gold standard.[75] With heavy dependence on trade from abroad, in this phase of the inter-war period, Britain overvalued its currency in relation to gold and/or failed in an industrial policy of flexible wage rates in response to payments deficits.

With whatever other complications were involved, two major events followed from the changing power alignment. The overtures of the Federal Reserve Bank of New York to provide leadership in support of the British problem and the competition between that bank and the Federal Reserve Board in Washington, led to an expansion of bank credit in the already rapidly expanding U.S. economy, with excessive amounts of the credit going toward trading on the margin in the stocks listed on the New York Stock Exchange. And, even as this occurred, the British economy experienced static conditions with high unemployment and no growth in real wages.

As the conditions and the extreme buoyancy in the U.S. fueled the stock market, with many innocent people entering the market, the unsustainable boom of the late 1920s and the continuous acceleration in stock market prices became dependent on the most subtle of changes in the economic outlook. As the subtle changes in outlook came about, the Great Crash of October 1929 also occurred. It was followed in turn by further contractions in commercial bank credit, business conditions generally, and waves of bank failures, as over-zealous Federal Reserve officials forced the repayment of credit that had been extended to the commercial banks through the discount windows of the Federal Reserve banks.

The contraction with its international overtones ultimately led to the abandonment of the gold standard, as it was known, and to a devaluation of the dollar in relation to gold in early 1933. There was also a breakdown in the efforts to achieve satisfactory reparation conditions for the German economy. This combination of breakdowns was accompanied by government breakdowns—first in Germany, then in Italy and Spain—and led to the rise of a liberal government in Britain and to the New Deal in the United States. (The communist revolution with its underpinnings of Marxist principles had already occurred in Russia in 1917.)

The consequences of these breakdowns were not solved in the 1930s by the forms of government that were known as democratic democracies. Germany was the first country to recover as it opted for state participation in private industry under the leadership of Adolf Hitler, as it abandoned the gold standard with the economic advice and assistance of Dr. Hjalmar

Schacht.[76] Adequate recovery from the 1930s for the U.S. economy only occurred, for whatever reasons, with WW II.

Against this background, Marxists saw the conditions of the 1930s as the inevitable consequence of the capitalist economy, as they noted on earlier occasions during recession. Marx himself, we recall from chapter 2, had posited the inherent instability of the market economy, with the tendency for the workers to be left unemployed in increasing numbers. The only ideologies offering appealing alternatives to the failures of capitalism with its related democratic institutions were socialism and fascism. All—the Soviet, the German, and the Italian models—depended on centralized control by government, although the ideals they were expected to attain differed somewhat.

It was in this setting that J.M. Keynes wrote his *General Theory*. He offered a solution to the unemployment problem of capitalism, and to that of his native Britain of the 1920s and '30s, without abandoning the principles of capitalist democracy.[77] Keynes's solution, however, is said with hindsight to have been temporary and ultimately to have led to a further weakening of the long-run conditions for its survival.[78] Samuel Brittan said, "It is this temporary success, but ultimate futility, of so-called 'Keynesian' spending boosts that is such a trap for a democracy."[79]

Essentially the solution associated with Keynes and the Keynesians focused on total spending, including by the government when it was not forthcoming in adequate amounts by the private sector, households and businesses. Government deficits were rationalized in the name of fiscal policy and as being in the interest of the economy. Facets of theory were altered to make the deficits politically acceptable. The main target for the policy on a short-term basis became the unemployment rate. This target was set irrespective of larger time frames and perspectives, irrespective of the inflation that may follow from setting the target rate.[80]

Government became active and responsive in these economic matters to an electorate that may not have understood the long-run consequences of the economic policies they were supporting. A term previously applied to such interaction between the elected politicians and the voters (pp. 213, 253) is "the political business cycle."

Brittan offered these reasons for the government's tendency to overstimulate demand and generate instability: "the benefits are short-run, while the costs are long-run; and the benefits are specific and easily attributable to the government, while the costs are general and less easily attributed to any single cause."[81] It would appear, with much later hindsight, that the public did in time, under the leadership of the Thatcher government and Ronald Reagan, key-in to the disadvantages of the "quick fix," as the short-run Keynesian measures came to be called by President Reagan and others.

Milton Friedman saw the sorts of instability indicated by the Great Depression and the interactions just described as being the consequences of government policies based on bad economic theory. This step in his work came with F/S's *Monetary History*, where they reconsidered monetary policy and policy-contributing causes of the Great Depression, as received under Act II. Another aspect of Friedman's work involved looking at larger time frames than had the Keynesians. He noted the destabilizing consequences of government policies that pursued target rates of unemployment irrespective of the stage of business conditions and without regard to the "natural rate of unemployment."[82]

The natural rate of unemployment turned out to be something the government had no control over through policies designed for the management of total demand, such as called for by Keynesian economics. It is in a sense a semi-permanent magnitude (or trend that may vary in the long run), but nevertheless it is the rate of unemployment that is consistent with a zero inflation rate. The government may through its non-demand-management policies control this rate. However, as stated, it does not do so through Keynesian demand management, and numerous changes—such as the extension of minimum wage laws to cover sectors with heavy teenage employment—actually raised the natural rate in the 1960s and 1970s. The Keynesian policy until late (too late) in the presidential administration of Jimmy Carter overlooked this latter prospect and pursued unemployment rate targets that ultimately compounded the twin problems of inflation and recession. The whole stance and theoretical underpinning led to divergencies in key economic variables that could not be maintained—at least not maintained without use of force on the part of the government over the behavioral units comprising the economy.

Said differently, in the era of fine "tuning" with respect to unemployment targets and Keynesian economics, the performance of the economy was pushed to the limits of its capabilities in the short run with destabilizing social, economic, and political consequences. In 1976-80, President Carter seemed more than most to personify the short-run risk taking associated with frequent shifts in policies, apparently with the view to improving his image in the news and TV polls.

As a reminder of the limits of Keynesian economics, Proposition 13 started in California in 1978, as a public initiative to limit spending by government. With the backing of Milton Friedman and others, its reverberations reached Washington, D.C. in that year with a message of warning about big government, big spending and big taxes. These reverberations carried through to a revolution in government policy under Reagan's presidency (chap. 16). The changes brought about signified what one columnist called "The Age of Limits."

The public and, in some measure, academic reaction we encounter to the Keynesian world is that the policies taxed "the survival capacity of our political institutions and social system."[83] Robert Skidelsky noted in 1977 that "such unity as Keynesian ideas may have given to the post-war economic system is unlikely to survive its present travails." With reference to a volume he edited, he noted further that the major assumptions of most of his contributors is "that our contemporary system of political economy is unstable."

Skidelsky stated why the terms "political economy" and "Keynesian" are appropriate with reference to the economic system he described. To begin with, he said, "Once government started to assume substantial responsibility for economic affairs, the old separation between politics and economics broke down."[84]

In the U.S. of Friedman's lifetime, the assumption of governmental responsibility began with the ad hoc measures of the New Deal and the Employment Act of 1946 (with accompanying statements about governmental responsibility to maximize employment, production, and purchasing power), as mentioned earlier, and the assumption extends throughout the Congressional Budget and Impoundment Act of 1974 and the Humphrey-Hawkins bill enacted at the end of the 95th Congress. The initial goal of the bill was to cut joblessness to 4 percent by 1983, but by the time the bill had passed, no new programs were mandated, and the targets were added for a reduced inflation, a balanced budget, a surplus in the balance of international trade, and higher price supports for farmers.

Previously, in the 1920s and through most of the nineteenth century, there was the usual belief that the extent of political interference in economic life would be decreasing for three reasons. First, it was thought that free trade would maximize everyone's position, and by the end of the century we had Pareto's criterion for the optimal performance of the economy, notably: it should not be possible to make some people better off without at the same time making others worse off. Second, the international gold standard was to serve as a disciplinary measure and regulate economic performance (especially efficiency in production and inflation rates) without the need for larger government. Third, certain political, institutional, and psychological conditions could be taken for granted. Most notably, there was "the hegemony of what Keynes was to call the 'educated Bourgeoisie'." They were to understand the economic laws and the environment necessary for their successful application.

Instead of these developments, government intrusion was legitimized by Keynesian economics and there was a change in the character of those attracted to government service. The three reasons for calling the system of economy prevailing over in the 1960s and 1970s in the U.S. and over most of the post-WW II years through the 1970s in Great Britain "Keynesian" are relatively straightforward. One is summarized by Skidelsky:

> Keynes alone provided an intellectually coherent justification for a certain type of governmental intervention, one which would save, not destroy, both capitalism and liberal democracy.... We have put his theory into operation and lived by it for the last thirty years. Before Keynes, most 'advanced' thinkers believed that some system of authoritarian planning, usually modelled on Russia, was the only answer to the problem.[85]

A second reason for the label "Keynesian" with reference to the economy is that "It draws attention to a crucial development which Marxists tend to deny." Notably: "the decline in the political power of private capital." Continuing, he noted, "This power has steadily receded in the face of the growth of working class organizations and the state. It was this change in the balance of social power that enabled Keynesian ideas to triumph in the first place."[86] There is the added suggestion that "big business" needed Keynes too, and J.K. Galbraith's *New Industrial State* supports the suggestion.[87]

A third reason for the label "Keynesian" with reference to the free-world sector of the post-WW II international economy is that it helped rationalize the role of deficits and the use of credit creating mechanisms, all with diminished attention to gold. On the international side, the dollar performed as a key currency (i.e., as a reserve for foreign central banks), at least until the early 1970s, and this depended on two things: initially on the U.S. having enough efficiency in production to support the Marshall Plan, and then on its being able to run deficits in the balance of international payments and thus export gold (mostly through supporting the dollar) and incur sizeable liabilities to foreign central banks.[88] Skidelsky said, "In a sense, America can be regarded as having played a Keynesian role on a (free) world scale." He said, "It is highly doubtful whether either the Americans themselves or the Europeans would have accepted prolonged American deficits without the understanding of their economic function which Keynes provided." And, continuing he said, "The World inflation to which they (the deficits) helped give rise," to be sure, was "part of the general problem of the Keynesian political economy."[89]

A main theme on the part of writers in the period of crisis in Keynesian economics was the disassociation of Keynes from the Keynesians, and the treatment of a distinct parochial American version of Keynes. In some measure this permits one to disassociate the master from his followers and thus to make the simple and sterile version more vulnerable to attack, for Keynes did indeed offer much redirection for an economics that was greatly in need of redirection. It just happens that certain things were lost in the translation, and some of this is Keynes's fault. It may have been his style of writing, the depth and complexity of the change he sought, and his attempt to offer redirection even while appealing to the orthodox whom he wished to influence. Keynes did, in any case, have great influence on the Keynesians and made their economics possible.

Skidelsky offered the following view about Keynes and the Keynesians:

> We cannot so easily separate Keynes from his consequences, from the style of thought and order of priorities to which his revolution gave rise. To say that had he lived he would have remained more flexible than his disciples is true but trivial. There was no more chance of his becoming "pre-Keynesian" again than there was of Copernicus once more becoming a flat-earther. One has to take Keynes with the Keynesians.[90]

There is room in the area of analysis for hair-splitting and for recognizing what we owe Keynes and even the Keynesians. Yet—when we consider policy and the influence Keynes had in the broad sweep of events—the Skidelsky view may not be far from what is possible. Certainly Keynes had influence on the Harvard professor, Alvin Hansen, and buoyed the intellectual spirits and zeal of the legion of Hansen students and Harvard Ph.D.s that entered the New Deal in the late 1930s and early 1940s.[91]

As discussed in the preface to volume one, in such revolutionary contexts the role of ideas is thought to weigh heavily. Indeed, Keynes himself dramatized their role in a last concluding note of the *General Theory*. His work legitimized for many intellectuals the system of political economy prevailing over most of the post-WW II years. In Skidelsky's interpretation, Keynes was related to the system that bears his name as Marx is related to Soviet Communism, and as Adam Smith is related to the classical liberalism that came to fruition in England in the early to late 19th century. Skidelsky said with reference to Keynes:

> Keynes provided an alternative model, an alternative theory of how the economy works and fails to work, with its in-built policy prescriptions. For the intelligentsia, inside and outside of the economic profession, it was essential to have such a theory. Mere inflationism would never have been accepted as a reputable alternative to centralized planning. The change in intellectual atmosphere from the 1930s to the 1950s and 1960s is striking. This was largely the work of Keynes.[92]

Most specifically, Keynesian economics dominated textbooks in a major portion of economics and in classroom discussions during the 1950s, '60s, and early 1970s and came to Washington, D.C. in the John F. Kennedy years. On the dominance of Keynesian economics at Keynes's own Cambridge University over the forty years following Keynes's *General Theory*, Peter Lilley commented at some length:

> For most of the last forty years the average student of economics in Britain or America has been shielded from any systematic critique of the Keynesian system. He is, of course, given an account—often little more than a caricature—of the obscurantist resistance put up by die-hard 'classical' economists to the original Keynesian revolution. Indeed, part of the appeal of the Keynesian system is that it presents itself as revolutionary and nonconformist whilst in fact being thoroughly established. Thus it satisfies the twin but conflicting desires of most young men—to rebel and to conform. But students have not, at least until recently, been taught about the genuinely nonconformist schools of thought which have continued to develop detailed criticisms of the Keynesian orthodoxy.
>
> This rather unacademic taboo certainly still operated at Cambridge a decade ago. I stumbled on its existence only because I happened to be too obtuse to grasp the sophisticated Keynesian justification for state control of the economy. My supervisor therefore reluctantly introduced me to some authors who would help me 'to express my outmoded prejudices in rigorous academic form'. But I was first required to swear not to tell anyone that I had been advised to read Friedman and his Chicago colleagues. Thus only under a veil of secrecy could one even discover the existence of an alternative to the Keynesian approach.[93]

The most specifically focused aspects of Keynesian economics came to Washington D.C. with Kennedy's astute political economist, Walter Heller, and in the underlying influence of MIT's Paul Samuelson, and ended with the Carter White House, as elaborated in chapter 8.

The Failure of the Revolution and New Direction

Just what went wrong with the Keynesian revolution? The answers offered below point toward changes in the government, the market for goods and services (including especially the labor market), and the inadequacies of the pillars of Keynesian economics.

The contributions of Milton Friedman both revealed the inadequacies of these pillars and, at the same time, offered new direction at the level of research and at the levels of national economic policy and politics. After a review of these pillars and Friedman's contributions as they concern the pillars, there are reviews of the political dimensions of the economic problem of full employment and short-term stabilization through governmental intervention, and of Friedman's approaches to coping with the political dimensions of the economic problem.

As to what went wrong, Skidelsky pointed to the government and to the market.[94] "Keynes," he said as Friedman had, "overestimated the possibility of rational economic management by democratic government." He saw the exercise of responsible intelligence as a preventative of inflation. As Brittan pointed out, Keynes took for granted that the political decisions "would ultimately be made by a small group of the educated bourgeoisie who were inspired by a disinterested concern for the public good."[95] Continuing, Brittan said, "He [Keynes] assumed that wrong decisions were taken out of intellectual error or, at worst, narrowness of vision, and that if correct ideas were promulgated with sufficient clarity and vigor they would certainly win the day."

In Keynes's world, the British civil service was made up of a relatively intellectual class, from Keynes's Cambridge and from Oxford mainly, and those elected to public office recognized and drew upon this.[96] Indeed, Keynes himself entered the prestigious civil service and his links with officials in government departments were important in the chain of events, although his undercurrent of rebellion led him to some anxieties about the service and to other achievements.[97] Further in Keynes's day, the electorate comprising the democratic base were more respectful of the government, and less organized than they later became. As Brittan further stated, "Both in personal and in public life he [Keynes] had an unquenchable faith in men's ability to work out directly the effect of each of their actions and behave in good faith."[98]

What went wrong with the government was multifold: a broadening of the political base, the emergence of labor organizations dedicated to self interest, the politization of economic decision, and the professionalization of politicians. In addition, in taking over the burdens of discretionary management of the economy in the short period, the system of government was overloaded. Too much was influenced by outside shocks to the economy and by the interaction of the short-term "self interests of politicians, officials and voters." The instability accompanied by this interaction, we have called "the political business cycle."

Skidelsky said, "Once economic life became a matter for continuous political decision, economic rationality (however defined) would be subordinate to political demands through the auction for votes of a competitive political system."[99] Friedman elaborated on this line of reasoning:

> The political crystal ball is even more clouded than the economic

crystal ball. There is no reliable way to predict whether particular economic-policy actions will be good politics. In many cases, it is equally difficult to predict their short-run economic effects.[100]

The gap between the costs of intelligent voting by voters and costs to politicians for staying in office may be another main area where things went wrong. For their part, the voters delegate decisions to politicians, partly because of the reduction in decision costs arising from delegating decisions.[101] The politicians for their part were once occasional representatives who served at costs to themselves, but who have since become more professionalized. Continuing on the professionalization of politicians, William Niskanen noted that it has been going on for some time and addressed several events of the 1960-75 period, while Friedman mentioned still other grounds.[102]

Thus, a final main area where things went wrong in the Keynesian world arises from the role the Keynesian system assigned to the marketplace. In his review, Skidelsky saw government drawn inevitably (and he thought irreversibly) into the sphere of the functioning of the economy at the firm and household levels and not simply into that of the economy as a whole.[103] In particular: Keynesian theory left off with the suggestion that the supply side of the economy would take care of itself if total spending could be adequately managed; the financial planning of large industrial corporations of the so-called market sector led to their avoiding the effects of interest rate changes on capital spending, at least in the ways envisioned by Keynesian economic theory; and an overzealous commitment to full employment led the government too frequently to "bail out" the two sides of collective bargaining decisions when they were in fact inflationary and in conflict with the price-stability goal.[104]

In time the continuation of this "policy of accommodation" had a twofold effect: it removed the discipline that market prices (and wages as a special price) could impose on the participants in the production process; and the role assumed by government led the participants to look to government rather than to themselves for solutions to the problems (say, e.g., declining productivity per worker and loss of markets to foreign competitors).

With this policy of accommodation, the Keynesian governments were drawn into the administration of wage and price guidelines of an involuntary or voluntary sort, as in the cases of the Nixon administration in 1971-72 and the Carter administration's policy in 1978-79.[105] This symptom of decline in the "disciplines of the market" had, Skidelsky said, "upset the original Keynesian balance between government and market forces."[106] Continuing he said, "at the same time the relative failure of democratic governments to plan successfully (for example, the repeated failures of wage-price policies) further weakened their credibility."

In response to what went wrong in the government and in the market, Milton Friedman offered some thoughts. He directed attention to the long run (to what we have called his more permanent time frames). He said of economic effects, "It is generally far less difficult to know whether they will promote the long-run health of the economy."[107] Continuing, Friedman said, "it is not chimerical to hope that our leaders might let long-run economic considerations determine their policies." Such "might be good politics."

The main pillars of Keynesian economics that led to its short-term successes and long-term failures concerned aggregate demand, the liquidity preference demand for money balances, and expenditures on capital goods by business firms. The two most original, and at the same time interrelated and basic, features of the first are the simple consumption function and the investment multiplier. This first pillar also called attention to covariance in output and the level of employment. It ultimately gave rise to the unemployment rate as a policy goal and to the "fine tuning" of the economy to achieve that rate, irrespective of the state of business conditions.

The simple consumption function depicted what Keynes called "the fundamental psychological law," but it also reflected a view of demand that did not require price adjustments (recall "sticky wages") to establish full unemployment. It posited a simple relation between expenditures on consumption and income which was to be supported by cross-section (timeless) data, but it had further out-reaching effects. Most notably in the hands of some it seemed to support the prospect that moderation in the unequally distributed income was desirable and that transferring income by governmental means from high to low income groups would increase total spending and hence alleviate unemployment, as appendixes to chapter 16 emphasize. (This is not the way Keynes himself may have used the simple relation, but it came ultimately to support some tax cuts and proposals, even as inflation pushed families into higher income tax brackets.)

The simple consumption function with its slope property, moreover, became the determinant of the expenditure multiplier. This feature suggested that deficit spending by the government (as in the absence of adequate spending by the private sector) would have an impact on total spending of some multiple amount. Thus, a stronger rationale was advanced than heretofore for deficit spending to increase production and reduce unemployment. In the hands of Keynesians, such as Walter Heller of the Kennedy White House, the matter became one of a high degree of "fine tuning" as it were, with respect to the achievement of low unemployment rates, to use so-called science for the betterment of mankind.

In viewing the multiplier effect of deficit financing and in selecting unemployment targets, the Keynesians committed two quite grievous errors. First, as matters developed, they did not allow for the "crowding out" effect of the deficit financing. There had emerged a view from the 1930s that the Federal Government had vast resources relative to other units of government. Its main ingredients depended on the tendency to think of spending (demand management, say) exclusive of the roles of bank credit (loans and investments), the stock of money balances, and financing. With money and credit matters minimized in their thinking, deficit spending decisions became easy for politicians to make in a world where two significant things could happen, namely: (1) where the sale of government bonds to finance the deficit could be supported by an excessively expansive Federal Reserve policy; and (2) where the inflationary result of the monetary expansion would push households into higher tax brackets (so-called "bracket creep") irrespective of action by the Congress to raise tax rates.

Only much later, in the first half of 1982, did there emerge a trinity of recognizable political/economic problems, notably: large anticipated Federal deficits; the likely crowding out of private financing in a world where the Federal Reserve no longer supported the government's financing; and the inflationary/high interest rate prospect whereby, somewhere along the line, the Federal Reserve would do as it had in the 1960s and '70s and support the government's financing.

Various subtle aspects of the analysis of deficit financing and crowding out concerned another part of Keynesian theory and the demand for money as will arise on later occasion in part V. Even so, these subtle aspects of theory—of the government's financing, inflation, and the like—were avoided by Keynesians and shunted aside by politicians in the presence of the prospect for temporary solutions to economic problems.

The First Pillar

As to the simple Keynesian consumption function and the way it shifted attention from price adjustments to income and expenditures at a point in time, analyses relying on it—as it may apply over time and as related to government efforts to redistribute income through tax and transfer payments—were called into question as a result of Friedman's *Theory of the Consumption Function* (1957). Subtleties of this contribution aside until later, it did a remarkable thing, and in the process it gave empirical foundation to a specific aspect of economic theory that was heretofore almost unheard of in economics. The remarkable thing was that Friedman's particular formulation reconciled the empirical evidence on the simple consumption function from the cross-section data and a long-run empirical finding that Simon Kuznets had brought out in one of his celebrated works,[108] plus the long-run orientation yielded the later definition of the natural rate of unemployment.

The Kuznets's finding concerned the constancy of consumption in relation to income over long periods of time:

> Estimates of savings in the United States made by Kuznets for the period since 1899 revealed no rise in the percentage of income saved during the past half-century despite a substantial rise in income. According to his estimates, the percentage of income saved was much the same over the whole of the period. The corresponding ratio of consumption expenditures to income—the constancy of which means that it can be regarded as both the average and the marginal propensity to consume—is decidedly higher than the marginal propensities that had been computed from either time series or budget data.... The average propensity to consume is roughly the same for widely separate dates, despite substantial differences in average real income.... Finally the savings ratio in the period after World War II was sharply lower than the ratio that would have been consistent with findings on the relation between income and savings in the inter-war period. This experience dramatically underlined the inadequacy of a consumption function relating consumption or saving solely to current income.[109]

In reviewing Friedman's work as having demolished a pillar of the Keynesian system, the Britisher Peter Lilley summarized the achievement:

> Friedman's achievement was to explain these two apparently contradictory findings and show them to be compatible with his own theory of rational consumer behavior. He realized that snapshot studies of savings patterns in one period concealed the fact that some people (authors, stockbrokers, farmers) have volatile incomes. In years, when their income is high they will appear among the rich and will, *if they are rational*, save a disproportionate amount for lean years. Those who are having a bad year will appear among the poor and will draw on past savings, so their current rate of savings will appear negative. Thus much of the apparent difference between the savings habits of rich and poor, which had seemed to confirm Keynes's mechanical consumption function, could be explained as a rational response to volatile incomes.

Friedman elaborated his findings into a consumption function which fitted the data quite well (by no means perfectly, but far better than Keynes's). This consumption function differs from Keynes's in that the specter of under-consumption in the long term as savings rise faster than investment appears decidedly less likely.[110]

The significance of the reconciliation of the budget and time-series data on the consumption function was compounded by the fact that the achievement was framed in a highly dynamic context. Indeed, perhaps more than any other single thing that has occurred in economic theory and analysis, this formulation and its empirical dimensions tended to move economic theory in a more viable and dynamic direction. The framing of the theory, furthermore, was such that it facilitated estimation and tests of the theory and came to permit a simultaneous treatment of short- and long-run changes, that could be handled without the abandonment of certain aspects of Keynesian mechanics.[111]

Friedman's formulation called attention to permanent (or quasi-permanent) phenomena as distinct from transitory phenomena, facilitated their incorporation as a part of economic theory, and hence facilitated analysis and treatment within the theory of both simultaneously. The attention to quasi-permanent magnitudes, moreover, facilitated subtle distinctions bearing on economic policy that may be directed toward transitory, quasi-permanent (or permanent), and/or episodic changes.

The Second Pillar

The second pillar of Keynesian theory which Friedman reacted to lay in the area of the demand for money, and consists of Keynes's liquidity preference analysis, which grew out of the interrelated ideas of a managed financial system, demand management, and "sticky wages." Once again Friedman's work had implications for economic theory and economic policy. In the demand for money literature, which grew rapidly in the presence of the modern computer, beginning in the early 1960s, Friedman was joined by many others who were engaged in research and writing but he managed to dominate the scene and keep others reacting to him.[112]

Nuances and technical details aside, Friedman's major contributions in the area of the demand for money stand out. *Monetary History* has already been cited and related to the consequences of monetary policy following the Great Crash, where Friedman and Schwartz drew attention to the money stock as a control variable. This attention to the money stock, as a monetary aggregate and control variable, became crucial in the confrontation with Keynesian economics and in empirical and theoretical study bearing on monetary policy. Initially at the policy level, the central bankers paid only "lip service" and made only small changes, but, then the money-aggregate analysis became crucial in monetary policy matters at the highest levels of government, as taken up in chapters 14, 15, and 16.

The Keynesian liquidity preference model gave special attention to the rate of interest as a control variable by the central bank, and fitted well with what we called an i-regime in chapter 8. The liquidity preference construction, nevertheless, contained an analysis of the velocity of money and hence the quantity theory of money from whence Keynes sought to escape. There was the idea that an increase (or decrease) in the money stock would give rise to changes in the reverse direction in the interest rate (a liquidity effect), and in corresponding banking and academic circles there was the view that an open market purchase of securities at the Federal Reserve's trading desk in New York would raise bond prices and lower interest rates. With such views as may be obtained from the theory, exclusive of support from empirical study, a decline in market interest rates was thought to signify "easy" money and an expansive monetary policy, with a rise depicting just the reverse. Thus, observing rising and declining interest rate changes in phase with expansions and contractions of a transitory nature, there was the view in some quarters that monetary policy was quite well timed and stabilizing, to the extent that interest rates were the appropriate policy measure.

In Keynes's formulation, raising or lowering the interest rate (i), was thought to change the value of real capital (as if it were a marketable bond), such that a lower rate raised values of additions to capital stock in excess of supply prices or costs for the stock and thus led to an expansion of capital spending (ΔI). In another instance, viewing the liquidity preference curve as a static curve, there was in the neighborhood of low interest rates a demand for a large stock of money. This was in fact such that the absolute value of the ratio of a percentage change in the money stock to the percentage change in the interest rate approached infinity [ignoring signs $(\Delta M/M)/(\Delta i/i) \to \infty$]. This trap idea was the basis for the closely related metaphor that one could not "push on a string." It meant that expansion of money and credit aggregates would have no effect on the interest rate, and that hence when interest rates were low as in the Great Depression there would be no use expanding the money and credit aggregates. On Friedman's analysis the linkage ($\Delta M \to -\Delta i \to \Delta I$), the trap, and all that was a faulty view of the world.

The liquidity trap notion, however, also was related to that of the interest inelasticity of the demand for real capital, namely: a given percent decline in the interest rate would call forth a smaller percent change in real capital expenditures. In relation to the trap, the expansion of the money supply so to speak may lower interest rates some but not enough to influence capital spending because, at the same time, the enlarged money stock was going to fill the liquidity needs of firms as well as households. Such analysis could be related to the stagnation thesis of the 1930s, namely: the economy had matured so that wants were satisfied with respect to consumption and opportunities for profitable investment were unlikely to come about in any way that would assure full employment.

The liquidity preference block was, at Keynes's hands, an analysis of the demand for money which he entered into in part as an escape from the simple quantity theory (recall M = kY, from the earlier equations). However, as Lord Kaldor said, "the way he presented this solution was a *modification* of the quantity theory of money, not its *abandonment*."[113]

Clearly there were mixed elements in Keynes's thinking. Those who relegated the importance of the money stock to the junkyard for historical relics as the Keynesian formulations ultimately lead some to do, preferred Keynes abandon the quantity aspect of money all together. Continuing in this line of monetary thinking, Kaldor cited Keynes from the preface to the *General Theory* with respect to "the difficulties of escaping from habitual modes of thought and expression, 'which ramify into every corner of our minds'." He then noted two equations that may be found in relation to liquidity preference.[114] One concerns the liquidity preference curve itself in the static Keynesian formulation, and the inverse variation between the money stock (M) and the rate of interest (r), given income (Y):

$$M = f(r, Y = \text{const.}).$$

The other concerned an asymptote to the liquidity preference curve (say, a Y = const.) and the money stock actually held as a proportion of income (M = kY). This second equation was written by Kaldor in the following terms:

$$Y = \text{const.} = M \, V(r) \qquad (4)$$

instead of Y = M V.

According to Kaldor, equation (4) implies, "that *all* the adjustments of monetary to real factors are through changes in the velocity of circulation [V]—since the quantity of money, M, is still shown as an independent variable, determined by the monetary authorities." Kaldor saw the prospect of this interpretation as having led Britain's Radcliffe Committee in its report in the late 1950s to rather extreme sounding statements that all monetary changes were absorbed by changes in velocity. In other words, if the money stock was increased, velocity would decline and income would remain unchanged (Y = const.) and if the money stock decreased, velocity would rise and income remain unchanged.

Friedman's interpretation of Keynes's *General Theory* was similar to Kaldor's.[115] Thinking of the static Keynesian curve for liquidity preference, velocity (Y/M) approaches zero in the liquidity trap and a very large value in the opposite range from the trap. Friedman concluded with the last of three propositions.

> The demand function for money has a particular empirical form ...that makes velocity [1/k] highly unstable much of the time, so that changes in the quantity of money would, in the main, simply produce changes in V in the opposite direction.[116]

Such thinking predominated in Britain as in the U.S. and supported the view that monetary policy was not very useful or powerful as a control procedure.

Now, Friedman reversed all of the Keynesian thinking on liquidity, where rather clearly money does not matter much in the performance of the economy. A first step in the reversal is in effect to deal with the metaphor about "pushing on a string" through George Morrison's dissertation.[117] The idea is in four parts: (1) under state-of-shock conditions, such as occurred in the 1930s, there is a greater demand for a store of liquid balances, including a stock of excess reserves at banks; (2) rather than contract bank reserves and thereby the money supply, as the Federal Reserve did in the early 1930s, in the 1937-38 recession, and in post-WW II recessions, the preference for liquidity should be satisfied via expansion of reserves; (3) the expansion of reserves would in turn lead banks to increase bank credit (bank loans and/or investments); and (4) the latter would lead to an increase in the money stock and hence spending on income via what Friedman will later symbolize as "helicopter money."[118]

Friedman's reformulation of the liquidity preference theory contains the main elements of his reformulation of the consumption function (the first pillar above). Most notably the theory is reoriented along dynamic, time-rate-of-change lines for the money stock and income, where there are special time frames (cycles and trends) and where the time series are viewed as composing transitory and permanent or quasi-permanent components (alternative labels for cycles and trends). Next, recognizing "helicopter money," the interesting question is what happens when the helicopter flies overhead and maintains a drop of adequately denominated twenty-dollar bills. The obvious answer is to increase spending (actual money stock greater than that desired for transactions and liquidity needs). There will be a rise in velocity (Y/M) as spending overshoots, and as a rise in the inflation rate imposes some penalty on the holding of cash balances. There are liquidity matters and one could add some uncertainty (σ) about the inflation rate forecast ($\dot{P}^e$). Hence we may write, e.g.,

$$M = k\,(\ldots;\, \dot{P}^e;\, \sigma)\, Y.$$

Friedman did the foregoing on the reformulation of liquidity preference, mainly in a 1968 publication, but then gave it a central role in *Monetary Trends*. As taken up in chapter 14, in the later work there are lags in the effect of accelerated money growth which yields first a liquidity effect, then an income effect with the overshooting of spending, and a long-run expectations effect (the nominal interest rate equals the sum of the real interest rate and the expected inflation rate). However, in the 1982 work F/S reported somewhat disappointedly, because of their theory with overshooting, that the structure underlying the formation of inflationary expectations shifted dramatically in the 1960s. This coincided with the beginning of the Keynesian era and the period just prior to the breakdown of the dollar standard of Hicks's Act IV.

The reported structural shift in the formation of inflationary expectations in the mid 1960s (and its reverse in the mid 1980s) is consistent with other findings about interest rates, expected inflation rates, and the uncertainty in the inflation rate forecast.[119] The mid 1960s shift led to what we have called in other contexts "New York's revenge."[120] The term suggests a combination of two developments: (1) that participants in the New York bond markets efficiently used information about the Federal Reserve's monetary policy, credibility, and forecasted deficits and all in forming views about future inflation and hence in setting interest rates; and (2) that policies and plans coming from Washington D.C. with inflationary implications in the period had adverse effects on the economy via a rise in interest rates (hence revenge for the Washington, D.C. orientation toward inflation).

In testing the early quantity theory, Friedman's own theory, and Keynesian theory, as outlined above, F/S dealt in *Monetary Trends* with three possibilities about the effects of an increase in the money stock (or accelerated growth) on velocity: (1) velocity may remain constant, (2) velocity may rise, say, as actual balances exceed those desired by "agents"; and (3) velocity may vary to offset any tendency for spending to accelerate as the money stock accelerates. The first effect is that associated with the American Irving Fisher of the pre-*General Theory* days. Fisher had taken over the assumption of Keynes's predecessor Alfred Marshall whereby prices adjust more rapidly than quantities (i.e., on short-run formal analysis $\Delta M \rightarrow \Delta P$, and V = const.). The second of the three effects is mainly Friedman's. The third is essentially the Radcliffe Report view. It is also Lord Kaldor's view about the effect of accelerated (and decelerated) money growth.[121]

The F/S work was offered as providing some support for the first possibility above, most support for the second, and no support for the third. However, there is much more which comes later. The present point is simply that Friedman's leadership began to have effect in Washington, D.C. in the late 1960s and to have some influence at the Federal Reserve in

1970, as taken up in chapter 8. There was more as the Federal Reserve officials yielded somewhat, and in 1975 House Concurrent Resolution 133 (later written into the Federal Reserve Act) formalized a new vision of the Federal Reserve's control perspective with respect to national economic policy and the money stock. Even so, there was more lip service than change, and in October of 1979, an announcement of a stronger view about the direct control over monetary growth vis-à-vis interest rates came out of the Federal Reserve. As taken up later (pp. 648-670), there was no turning point in policy as opposed to a technical matter concerning operations until the Reagan presidency.

The old ideas did not die easily. There was still some thrashing around in the news media, in the White House and the Congress, and at the Federal Reserve that occurred as late as the early months of the Reagan presidency.

The Third Pillar

The Keynesian theory of interest rates and monetary policy, is closely entwined with a third pillar of Keynes's and Keynesian theory, notably investment demand (or spending by industrial concerns in the capital goods sector). Keynes in effect treated the rate of interest as if it were a readily controlled variable (say, by the Federal Reserve through open market operations, and exclusive of any component for the expected inflation rate), and he set it opposite the rate of return on capital expenditures as a declining function of expenditures.[122] This latter relation (or schedule) was itself potentially volatile in response to volatility in the prospects for future returns from capital goods (producer goods and equipment) and thus inflationary prospects. In fact, these prospects were a main course of instability in the democratic/capitalist economy as Keynes saw it, but the main gist of the theory (with constant prospects) was that interest rates and capital expenditures would vary inversely (that capital spending could be controlled through control of the interest rate, all without inflationary expectations altering the interest rate).

The use of the investment demand pillar by Keynes and the later Keynesians focused upon the control over capital spending via the rate of interest (given expectations and some prevailing elasticity of investment demand). Keynes was especially at odds with Fisher's notion of the rate of interest (as a sum of the real interest and expected inflation rates), for to admit it was to render inoperative an important part of the theory.[123] Keynesians had the same investment demand view that Keynes had, but in fact the Fisher aspect of the interest rate was dropped from consideration until 1968. At that time it appeared in the paper by Friedman, in an empirical study by Yohe and Karnosky, and in a doctoral dissertation sponsored by Friedman.[124]

Other studies confirmed the presence of an inflation rate component in the rate of interest and several were to allow as well for uncertainty in the inflation rate forecast.[125] The importance of the prospects about the interest and inflation rates were highlighted by debate at a conference Friedman attended in Sheffield, England in 1971. At that time, Friedman took a stance on the side of the Fisher equation and Sir Roy Harrod, Keynes's biographer, assumed the position taken by Keynes thirty-five years earlier. He was adamant about admitting the view that some new-found expectation about "a certain rate of inflation" can affect the rate of interest.[126]

Perhaps it is needless to say that the studies about interest rates and money demand showed otherwise and, in addition and also in contrast to the Harrod view, uncertainty over the inflation rate forecast lowers the rate of interest rather than raises it as Harrod posited. In brief, what Friedman stated about the demand for money led to an extremely different theory and a more empirically rooted one than the Keynesian theory.

The Political Dimension

As we have seen, Keynes had an aristocratic view of government, of its being comprised of an educated elite with a concern for the public good. As so often was the case in his life, persuasion could make a difference and enlightened argument could bring about change to accommodate common goals. There may be differences among this elite, but they could be worked out through discussion and debate. It never occurred to him, as it did to the Austrian-American economist Joseph Schumpeter, Brittan suggested, "to see the political process as a market-place, governed by the self-interest of politicians, officials and voters."[127] Nor similarly would it have occurred to Keynes to view government and politicians as they were viewed by Milton Friedman, the Chicago school, and the Public-Choice off-shoot of the Chicago school. Thus, we have Schumpeter's and Brittan's view of democracy as a possible means of a better understanding of the political dimension of the economic problem of short-term stabilization through governmental intervention, and of Friedman's long-run view.

Joseph Schumpeter offered the view that all of the people in a highly populated country cannot participate in every political decision. There are limits to communication and to the inefficiency in the use of time by having all the people routinely involved. And, "In any case," as paraphrased by Brittan, "most people might well prefer a less convenient and burdensome system of organization." The electors themselves "are assumed to act according to their own self interest." As Brittan said, "This does not imply any view of their motives" because people as individuals and in small groups "can display great generosity." In contrast, however, in large groups "any individual who does not look after his own interests is likely to suffer in comparison with those who do." Consequently, "It seems realistic," to Brittan, "to assume that voters will, at least at the margin, vote according to their perceived interests."[128]

There is a basis for a theory of voter behavior that is partly built upon the economists' theory of the commercial marketplace. The individuals pursue their own goals in the expenditure of income, but their expenditures are limited by an income constraint and what they can borrow. The incomes are payments for contributions to production and the limits on borrowing depend on individual standings and controls over credit. As the "interest units" become large, as in the political marketplace, however, personal budget constraints and credit policies bearing on them can be influenced. "Electors," Brittan pointed out, "can rather more easily demand an increased slice of the cake without any agreement on the part of those who are supposed to have the thinner slices." He continued:

> The costs of the handouts, whether met through taxation or inflation, will not necessarily accrue to the groups who benefit from them. In each individual case, whether a subsidy is paid to council house dwellers, cheese eaters or car makers, there is a strong incentive for the interest group to press its demands as forcefully as possible without any real discipline on the sum total of interest-group demands.[129]

Traditionally, the ingrained "balanced-budget" principle and the properly functioning automatic gold standard placed limits on government spending and the creation of money respectively. However, results of the shocking consequences of the 1930s, the experiments of that period, and Keynesian thinking were the acceptance of a new role for government, numerous statutes, and "programs and agencies that were not subject to annual reconsideration and that developed constituencies—bureaucracies and beneficiaries."[130] Continuing on after the 1930s the economic-political system's bias towards deficits and then later inflation-causing growth in the money and credit aggregates, combined with the voter demands of an enlarged democratic base. The temptations to the politicians were too great, until the early years of the Thatcher government in Britain and the early months of the Reagan presidency in the U.S. Samuel Brittan stated the earlier temptation to the politician and the alternative confronting him:

> One... is to lose votes by failing to offer an interest group as much as other parties offer. The other is to join the competitive bidding and offer as much.[131]

Against such a possible occurrence of entering into this political bidding for votes in terms of special-interest politics, Schumpeter put forward the conditions for insulating representative democracy from the prospects that would tend to destroy it. The three conditions include (1) the limitation of the incursions of vote-seeking politicians, (2) the need for a well-trained and influential civil service, and (3) the exercise of political self-restraint and democratic self-control. In Keynes's world at least, the civil servants were the professionals at the center. They were aristocratic and well trained, mostly at Cambridge or Oxford, and they could limit the incursions of the politicians. The politicians were enlightened amateurs with means and independence, they "were professionals at dealing in votes," and they were dependent on the professionals. Since the latter were insulated from the voters, they could resist the pressures of the voters.

But democracy grew after Keynes's time, and the world changed in other respects. As Friedman said with reference to Keynes, the situation has differed from Keynes's time when "little or no experience existed to judge how...[discretion in the hands of political officials and a managed economics system] would work in practice. Continuing, he said:

> Since 1931 in Britain, since 1933 in America, both countries have had precisely the kind of managed systems that Keynes advocated and, since 1971, they have not even paid token obeisance to the "barbarous relic" [Keynes 1923, 172]. The results have been anything but the achievement of either stable prices or stable exchange rates. The era of managed money has also been an era of greater and more widespread instability in both prices and exchange rates than any earlier period, except only the immediate period after the first world war which stimulated Monetary Reform [Keynes 1923].[132]

Continuing along such lines, Brittan said, "Modern politicians and business chiefs lack the glamour of an aristocracy." He said, "With neither the trappings of tradition nor the heroic qualities of great war leaders or generals, they cannot excite the identification of hero worship which previously reconciled people to much greater differences of wealth and position than exist today."[133]

So how did Friedman handle all of this? As treated earlier, he was not born an aristocrat as Keynes was, and he functioned as a minority among economists in a much more restricted setting than did Keynes. Friedman's approach with its high degree of reliance on the individual and the market system may have been destined as a minority approach. Nevertheless, it gained ground in Chile in the second half of the 1970s, as we saw in the last chapter, and it came to London and to Washington, D.C.

Early on Friedman sought to handle the problems of a broadly based democracy through persuasion, education, a use of simple method, a marketing of ideology, and, in short, by fostering changes in political ideas. Individual freedom became "the prime objective of social arrangements," as the next chapter indicates. Friedman sought to promote individual freedom as an ideology, to have restraints imposed through rules in the short run. He spoke of reaching a broader consensus and he entertained the hope of long-run rationality on the part of the electorate.

In addressing the problem of special interest groups, as mentioned by Samuel Brittan above, Friedman noted "that the requests of each single interest group is small in relation to the aggregate of special interest and that each singularly is easy to give in to, especially where requests of the government seem worthy." In the aggregate, however, the small single interests become enormous, burdensome, and contrary to the vested interests of society. Hence, very early in his public sojourns, Friedman saw the need to treat special interests as a package, "to handle things together." "That's how," he said, "we keep Government out of the censorship business." Continuing he said "It's not a matter of taking one case at a time and deciding each case on its merits. If we did that we would have free speech for very few." Thus, we get a broader consensus to protect free speech which we think is to everyone's advantage.[134]

Setting aside Friedman's detailed suggestions about what can be done, the timing of actions by a strong leader was viewed as important for making changes. There needs to be a package of detailed programs in place to be implemented via presidential leadership during the first six to nine months of a new Congress, following a presidential election where the majority has expressed itself.

In going public Friedman himself showed no hesitancy in packaging things together and in attempting to communicate with a larger public about his monetary growth proposal, freedom, balancing the federal budget, and the flat-rate income tax, such as come up later. As he moved toward a larger audience, he also reduced the frequency of his contributions to Congressional Hearings. By 1968, he was responding to Congressional requests for participation in hearings and compendiums with letters rather than in person, and pursuing an arduous schedule on the lecture tour (including numerous appearances before business groups). Finally, he also extended his appearances to foreign countries.

One inside observer of Congressional hearings suggested that Friedman's reduced appearances at Congressional hearings was partly due to his frustration in effecting changes through those sources. Perhaps, too, there was the reflection that the influences on a broader public overall would not come through at those committee hearings.

The Overview

The period from WW I through the 1970s appears as an aberration in history. In large measure the ideas and actions of the Thatcher government and the Reagan presidency put society back on the pre-WW I track—monetary discipline, open economies, individualism, reduced national government, wage flexibility, incentives and personal initiatives. We ask: what happened initially, in the 1920s and 1930s to get society off the track? And we ask again: what happened to get society back on the track?

In the one instance, circumstances and Keynes played leading roles. The British and interrelated U.S. circumstances were essentially: the unsuccessful efforts to reestablish the pound at its pre-WW I price; the rise of trade unions which compounded matters with respect to downward flexibility in wages in response to inadequate demand for products; the attention directed to unemployment as a by-product of capitalism by Marx initially and then by Keynes as a compromise with socialism; and the Great Crash in the U.S., the failures of monetary policy, and the breakdown of the international gold standard. The developments were not well understood at the time but coincidental with them in part and in reaction in part, J.M. Keynes played a prominent role.

As an intellectual with Bloomsbury credentials, Keynes reacted against the gold standard and the failure of neoclassical economics to offer adequate analyses of money and the short run. Nevertheless, reflecting adequate aristocratic loyalty to the British tradition: he argued for a managed currency as a substitute for the automatic workings associated with gold; placed great confidence in the mostly Cambridge and Oxford trained civil servants; accepted inflexible, downward adjustments in wages as a fact; offered an essentially monetary analysis, although an excessively static and partially flawed one; and provided a rationale that gave respectability to deficit spending by government as a means of increasing production, reducing unemployment, and stabilizing business conditions.

The circumstances of the 1920s and 1930s in Britain, the 1930s in the U.S., and the influence of Keynes extended to the post-WW II years, largely via the Keynesians. The circumstances themselves had great effects on public reactions and political change, but especially Keynesian economics came to dominate at Whitehall and then in the 1960s and 1970s in Washington, D.C. This economics of Keynes and the Keynesians was for a closed economy, where foreign trade competition did not matter, certainly in relation to the domestic employment problems. However, as Britain and the U.S. proceeded along these lines, the U.S. was simultaneously providing leadership to reestablish a monetary-flows, trade system with the IMF at the center. There was support by the U.S. and a strong dollar for a time, as the U.S. used gold to maintain the dollar exchange rate. In time this failed, under Keynesian policies. There was an absence of monetary discipline on price levels and wage bargaining. There were changes in government and in those attracted to the civil service as well, as the democratic base broadened. Special interests and the self-interests of politicians received attention.

The failures of the Keynesian policies, the breakdown of the labor and dollar standards, the absence of monetary and hence budget discipline—all provided new circumstances. Under these Friedman played a leading role. Furthermore, in relation to economics, both Keynes and Friedman gave special attention to the definition and role of money in economics, to a "realitic" (sic) economics, and to economics as a theoretic policy-oriented subject.

Given the important role that money played in their respective views, and the sizable portions of definitions and concepts they shared—we see both Keynes and Friedman as playing leading roles in the monetary revolution of the twentieth century. Keynes, we say, reacted to a first crisis in economic conditions where social forces were taking over.

Friedman, on the other hand, was shaped by various but not entirely different lines of thought as he advanced economics and reacted to Keynesians and the circumstances of the latter part of the Keynesian era. The strands of his thinking are various: mathematical statistics, personalistic probability, cycles and trends—all as outlined in the uses-of-methods schema in chapter 3 (pp. 68-87); and his special reading of Marshall, his going back to Keynes's on the equation of exchange [namely, $M = k(\ )Y$], his reaction against the two-track micro and macro distinction, his retaining and giving motion to price-theoretic and Keynesian statics (including in relation to the indirect method and instrumentalism of chapter 4), and his dynamic treatment of monetary matters—all as linked in the current schema.

There we also show other strands of thinking which end with categories that have been introduced earlier and which arise later. These categories are conventionalism, the NCS, and post Keynesian economics.

In addition, in Friedman's scheme of things, we find interest in analysis with respect to the self-interests of politicians and special interest groups, and an economics of supply (price theory and the capitalist ethic) and demand (say, quantity theory of money). Reflecting a link between the monetary dynamics and the price theoretic statics, an increase (decrease) in the demand for money is a reduction (increase) in the velocity of money (Y/M), and the increase (decrease) in the demand for money coincides with leftward (rightward) shifts in the demand schedules in the various Marshallian, price-quantity planes. As with the Keynesian income-expenditure block, employment varies with output in the short run.

Deductive Analysis and Economic Thought

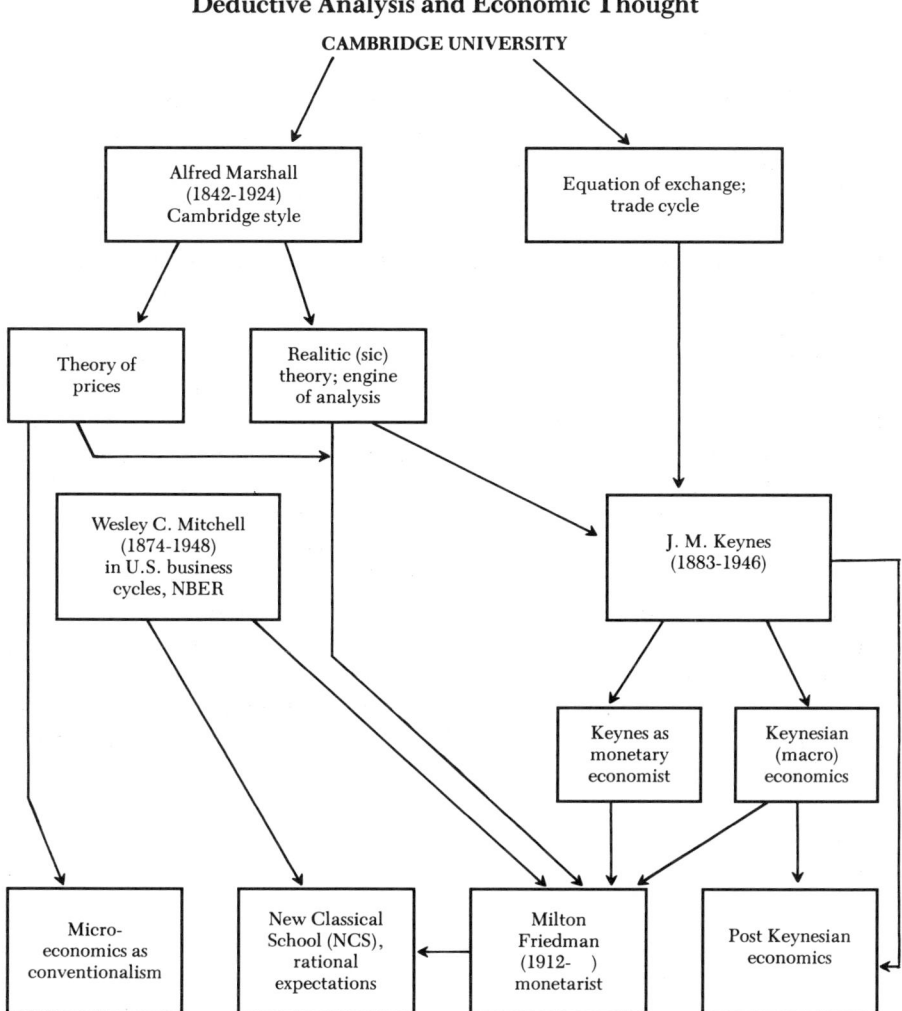

Under the circumstances of the crisis in Keynesian economics and concomitant economic conditions, Friedman's economics came to the forefront and offered both an antidote to Keynesian economics and new direction. It does this, as we have emphasized, without abandoning the mechanical apparatus advanced by Marshall and the Keynesians. In particular we encounter the following: consumption as a function of permanent income (incorporating the use of the Keynesian, income-expenditure block and Keynes's simple consumption function); and liquidity preference with overshooting (a dynamic variation of Keynes's liquidity preference model).

There is much more to Friedman's thought and orientation, as dealt with in other chapters. A present point, nevertheless, is: the particular shared interest in the definition and role of money, and the extended study offered by Friedman, constitute a monetary revolution in thinking within economics. Along this route we include Keynes and Friedman in the monetary revolution. The ideas there, with the attendant supply-side economics, ultimately come to Whitehall and Washington, D.C., as later chapters attest.

In essence, the shortcomings of Keynes's economics which Friedman remedied are as follows: its largely static quality (even as Keynes wrote brilliantly about change and expectations), its limited short-run time frame, the linkage mechanism (the i-regime vis-à-vis the M-regime, as it were), the fiscal policy defined as a government deficit exclusive of attention to the financing of the deficit, the implicit trust in government officials and civil servants, the closed economy concept, the absence of monetary discipline and the emphasis on inflexible wages, and limited attention to the supply or production side of the market (in particular its price-theoretic foundation). Remedying these defects and getting much accepted in the policy realm contribute toward getting society back on the pre-WW I track as it were—monetary discipline, individualism, international competition, economic incentives, freedom and the dispersion of power via reliance on markets.

Chapter 12
The Philosophy and Economics of Freedom

In the 17th century, economics was grounded in philosophy, particularly the deistic, natural order philosophy of John Locke.[1] In that context, one encounters the search for a socially harmonious natural order that continued until the middle of the 19th century. At that time, it became obvious to some, such as Karl Marx and Friedrich Engels (pp. 52-55), that society had not developed in accordance with the hoped-for harmony between "independent peasants and artisans who, serving each other, served themselves." Instead, Marx and Engels placed emphasis on apparent antagonistic encounters "between factory-owners and factory-hands, between the lucky heirs and the unlucky disinherited, between capital and labor which John Locke had fondly hoped to see forever united."[2]

Early Antecedents

At the same time as Marx's work in Britain, the free market concept had become so accepted that the groundwork was laid for a non-political, or neoclassical economics. Not to be mixed up with politically neutral, value-free economics, this economics abstracted from the polity so to speak and characterized mainstream thinking in economics for a time, as taken up below. Often characterized as "Robinson Crusoe" economics, it provided a basis for Frank Knight's reflection on and departure from the prospect of economics as an empirical science. At Knight's hands we encounter influences on Milton Friedman that support his special attention to economic freedom, and that connect with his departure from Knight over the matter of economics as an empirical science.

Faced with Marx's and Engels's "hard facts of reality," W. Stark said, "a new philosophy of economics was needed." The options confronting the predecessors of modern economic thought, Stark recorded, included taking up "the sordid task of capitalist apologetics," embracing the cause of socialist revolution, and shirking the issue. Opting for the latter, "it became fashionable to insist that political economy was not concerned with the happiness of human kind: that it is not a social philosophy, but a physical science."

Hence emerged the view of economics as a physical science—the view of an isolated, but free individual maximizing utility (or pleasure it was thought at the time) and minimizing pain, with antecedents that go back to a pleasure-pain calculus of Jeremy Bentham (p. 50).[3]

Herman Heinrich Gossen (1810-1858), a Prussian, writing in the middle of the nineteenth century, was among the earliest to take this physical science view of economics in lieu of the philosophical deism of the 18th century.[4] He and others began the trend that resulted in the definition of economics as a study of principles governing the allocation of scarce means among competing ends. This particularly narrow view is associated with an individualistic rationality of behavior, instrumental rationality, and an ability to adapt means to ends. The free operations of the laws of nature were thought to lead to the greatest possible well-being of each individual. Robinson Crusoe—political economist/journalist Daniel Defoe's shipwrecked adventurer and son of a middle-class English family—became the archetypical agent encountered in this limited economics.[5]

Though Gossen came to recognize the dependence of happiness on social cooperation, the starting point of his analysis was the socially "isolated individual." It was later said that "everyone is free as Crusoe is free."[6] Gossen's assumptions were said to "mirror the organization of production on Robinson Crusoe's island,"[7] and in the history of economic thought one encounters references by economists to "the simple situation confronting Robinson Crusoe," "the Crusoe method of illustration," "doctrinaire theorists of Robinson Crusoe stories," and to "the individual household economy (Robinson Crusoe economy)."

After considering principles of great importance for economics, Gossen asserted that the results tally "most exactly" with experience. For support of the proposition he drew on a German version of *Robinson Crusoe* "up to the point where he [Crusoe] finds his man Friday." Gossen felt the coincidence of the behavior and actions of Crusoe with the principles supported the proposition. (To use more contemporary language, the principles were to simulate the behavior).

In Gossen's work one encounters a declining pleasure (utility) and a parallel decline in value from the consumption of additional commodities, and an increasing displeasure (pain, or disutility) from additional effort (movement) in producing the commodities.[8] Initially, "movement—all movement—is in its first stages a pleasurable experience," but then pleasure decreases and displeasure increases. Value, like price for later economists, was determined by these marginal utilities, although a thing such as air may be of great use but of little value because it is available in such abundance.

The final result of Gossen's investigations have been expressed thus: "To achieve a maximum of enjoyment, man must divide his time and his energies between the pursuit of different gratifications in such a way that the value of the atom last created of any pleasure-giving object is equal to the magnitude of the pain which he would experience if he should create this atom in the last moment of his exertion."[9] Gossen's theory has been called a "theory of economic equilibrium" (the economic equilibrium of the *individual* and not that for society), and George Stigler translated the statement into the equality of the ratios for the marginal utilities of various commodities to their respective supply prices.[10]

In addition, one finds in Gossens's work a closeness to the egalitarian doctrine of the classical economists and the related tax and transfer-of-payments positions of the government. This doctrine has been stated by Stark:

> The last shilling of a rich man has less value—i.e., creates less happiness—than the last shilling of a poor man because the one has been able to descend much deeper on the scale of his desires, to ascend much higher in the satisfaction of his needs, than the other, and consequently that the transfer of it from the richer to the poorer would decidedly increase the aggregate well-being of both.[11]

The reasoning in this doctrine parallels that found in the declining marginal utility of income, in Cambridge's A. C. Pigou's *Economics of Welfare*,[12] and Keynes's statement of his simple consumption function (p. 83), as encountered in the next chapter. All are essentially static and without empirical foundation in any dynamic context, as they relate to income and wealth transfers of the type governments in the U.S. and Britain sought in the post-WW II years. And all were altered in treatment and conclusion by Milton Friedman's analysis of the permanent income consumption function (p. 83, chap. 16 and appendixes). Even so, the earlier, less dynamic doctrine, the assumptions, and the statements by Pigou and Keynes had profound effects on the minds of economists and through them on students of public finance and taxation and hence the world at large.

Positive and Normative Economics

Reacting to a view of economics as a physical science, along the lines introduced by Gossen, Frank Knight of the Chicago school did several things. He placed economics in the category of an assumer science, and he accepted the egalitarian view on the distribution of income, as did some of those upon whom he had direct influence.[13] Moreover, along with other major Chicago writers on the subject—namely Henry Simons and Friedrich von Hayek[14]—Knight especially influenced Milton Friedman in the philosophy of freedom and the quest for defensible principles of a "propaganda for economic freedom."[15] Friedman himself, moreover, extended the list of the Chicagoans that influenced him in this normative area.[16]

In this atmosphere Friedman was faced with sorting out conflicting strands of economic influence impacting on him very early in his career. As introduced earlier (pp. 111-112), these were classified as normative and positive economics. He drew on distinctions found in the work of Cambridge University's John Neville Keynes on the scope and method of economics, originally published in 1890.[17] Friedman thus cited the victorian father of John Maynard Keynes:

> John Neville Keynes distinguished among "a *positive science*...[,] a body of systematized knowledge concerning what is; a *normative* or *regulative science*...[,] a body of systematized knowledge discussing criteria of what ought to be...; an *art*...[,] a system of rules for the attainment of a given end"; comments that "confusion between them is common and has been the source of many mischievous errors"; and urges the importance of "recognizing a distinct positive science of political economy."[18]

Normative economics was also known in the parlance of Friedman's early years by the nondescript title "welfare economics" (pp. 152-153, 306, 311-314, 378 n51, 382 n42). Apart from early non-mathematical statements referring to social control and "welfare economics,"[19] with roots in the analysis of utility, welfare economics has largely been characterized entirely by theorems and proofs and/or deductions from assumptions rather than by empirical study. Hence, references appear to an "assumer" discipline, exclusive of any grounding in empirical study.[20]

As stated earlier (pp. 147-148), Friedman departed from Knight in his view of economics as an empirical science and in the normative area as well. There was one exception, but even that requires qualification. Friedman indeed departed from the egalitarian views of Knight and Simons, but extended the discussion of freedom found in their work.[21,22] Others coming under the Knightian influence carried on Knight's focus on complicated ethical and social detail through the "public choice" economics we mentioned in chapter 9 (pp. 297-301).[23]

Freedom, Economic Man, and Science

For Knight, the concept of freedom meant "freedom of the will" as opposed to "laissez faire" which simply means government non-interference in trade and individual choices and actions. In the broader freedom there must be choice, where "the practical political problem is said to center on the idea of freedom as voluntary agreement among responsible individuals." Continuing, John McKinney said, individual freedom is expressed in undetermined choice.[24] Each individual enters into transactions freely "in the sense that for any economic choice there are alternatives." Social freedom, on the other hand, takes the form of freedom of contract.

The notion in chapters 7 and 9 (pp. 194-196, 308-314) of the perfect market is an abstraction like that of the Crusoe individual, but it is conceptually necessary because it is the embodiment of complete freedom.[25] In the perfect market there are many individuals (or households) in the sense that no one has control. "There are no power relations," Knight said, "since everyone has a choice among a number of equally good alternatives." Further, McKinney said, "Each individual uses his own means to achieve his own ends," and the advantage of any association consists of one's ability to use other individuals as means, "under the principle of mutual free consent."[26]

Utilitarians, as mentioned in reference to early economists, argued the merits of free competition as a basis for maximization of satisfaction for the individuals. To the extent that actual markets approximated perfect markets, they tended "to provide the greatest possible aggregate of consumer welfare, under the given conditions of consumer taste and the distribution of income." In contrast to the utilitarians, libertarians like Knight view the freedom provided by the perfect market as an end in itself. "It is the embodiment of complete freedom."[27]

Knight recognized what he called "mechanical problems" in attaining the ideal. These concern the prospect of monopoly power, the possible need for legislation and action to deal with monopoly power, and the economic problem of the business cycle.[28] Plus there are externalities that may be defined as costs and/or possible benefits that accrue to the public generally rather than to the individual. Such costs to the public include dirty air and destruction of wilderness and the natural environment. Sometimes externalities are called "public goods," where there are benefits rather than costs, because there are goods such as clean air and wilderness that must be reckoned with collectively rather than through private competition.

Even in the most ideal market system, there remain conflicts of interest, and there must be discussion among groups in making and changing laws.[29] Since this group activity is a constraint on freedom, complete freedom requires the right to leave the group. However, the ability to give up citizenship in one modern state and join another is limited. The group is consequently political to the extent that one is not allowed to give up membership in it. The political then is inherently coercive. Even so, the moral quality of life is elevated to the extent that coercion is restricted.

Coercion includes persuasion by deception and "more importantly," McKinney said, "conditioning" as by advertising and political leadership.

The moral problem involves getting individuals to accept "all kinds of ends that serve the conditioner rather than the actor."[30]

Knight was aware of society and a complex of institutions, forces, and habits of thought that condition agents (the actors, the players, the behavioral units, etc.). The voluntary becomes elusive.[31] On the one hand, there is *radical moral individualism* and, on the other, there is *sociological determinism*. For Knight, this paradox of freedom and social conditioning is simply another aspect of man's pluralistic existence (say, as an individual and as a socialized person). McKinney reported that Knight's pluralism was the philosophical basis of his anti-scientism, but Friedman's retreat from "economic man" concepts and move toward empirical study allowed for both freedom and social conditioning with respect to culturally heterogeneous groups.

For Knight, the ethical side of man must be separated from the physical order. In addition, ethical values can exist in a state of contradiction. This comes out later in Milton Friedman's shifting the concept of freedom to encompass different cultural and religious entities at the expense of the agents being socially conditioned into some homogeneous set.

In Knight's anti-science view of economics, Robinson Crusoe is an economic man.[32] The use of the character Crusoe is analogous to that of the frictionless machine of theoretical mechanics. The Crusoe man doesn't exist but becomes the basis for discussion.

The economic man is exclusively concerned with the most efficient use of means for the realization of given ends (say instrumental rationality). We encounter this in the fairly common and restricted definition of economics (p. 458).[33]

For Knight, Crusoe's role as a model for problem-solving was beyond science. However, in the sense of abstraction, as from uncertainty and error, and in the sense of deduction exclusive of any empirical reality, it was a science. Writing in the British context, T. W. Hutchison simply referred to the fading away of the political concerns of Adam Smith, David Ricardo, and J. S. Mill in the 1860s and 1870s in Britain as the competitive market framework became so accepted. The rise of an abstraction from political and ethical considerations paralleled this "fading away." Of the emerging neoclassical economics, as it was called, Hutchison said, "Robinson Crusoe emerged as the personification of neo-classical, non-political economics." Continuing he said: "One may on a desert island have economic problems but no political problems. There is a kind of economy [a special form of abstraction, indeed, one may say] but no kind of polity…"[34]

So Crusoe is an "economic man," a "scientific man" in a limited sense, and an "individualistic individual." Moral and ethical problems are outside of this limited science (or non-science in a sense). In Knight's scheme, in fact, they centered about intelligent choice between ends and critical judgment, not instrumental rationality.[35]

The social values and the ends to be achieved in Knight's scheme are not merely a matter of preference. Indeed, valid values are to be achieved eventually by a consensus on the part of participants in a social process. Knight's notion of the consensus is more than just an agreement. It is analogous to the consensus among scientists in the natural science area.[36]

There is an acceptability of the values and the goals so to speak, and the method of arriving at the accepted values implies a commitment to a moral code. Knight noted that "without a sense of honor...among scientists...there could be no science." So Knight's political consensus in a democratic society is like that found in a community of scientists. "The pursuit of truth...is the ideal type of ethical association." Thus it is the ethic of science, truth seeking and honorable participants that provides the appropriate consensus.[37]

Here, Knight talked about what economists have labeled normative economics, which, since Knight's time and Friedman's 1953 essay, has taken various dimensions. The more formal early statements of "welfare economics"—viewed by T. W. Hutchison as "propounding of what were intended as *purely economic* criteria for policies on the basis of widely or universally acceptable value-judgements, without reference to political forces, while a quite Utopian degree of knowledge was assumed"—were written by Cambridge's A. C. Pigou and later Abba Lerner.[38] Related, but different sorts of analyses centering about public choice emerged at the hands of Buchanan via Knight, as introduced in chapter 9, and a further break with the past is found in Friedman's emphasis on the relevance of empirical study (positive economics) to normative economics (p. 112).[39]

In retrospect, we may find Knight's view very elitist. Like Galbraith, Knight may be seen as an intellectual seeking to impose his ethical views on others, although through persuasion and debate rather than through government (pp. 203-204).

McKinney recognized two reasons for F. Knight's anti-scientism as it related to economics (defined, we add, as the study of choice about the use of scarce resources to achieve competing ends).[40] McKinney noted that one is technical and the other ethical. On the technical side, the data of the social sciences are just different from that in the natural sciences. It consists of subjective meanings, opinions, attitudes, and social values rather than physical facts, and in addition in the narrow definition of economics (as stated above) there is no room for uncertainty because one has abstracted from it.

Knight's anti-science position is a consequence of his identification of economic science with instrumental rationality and the Crusoe economy. Crusoe, we may recall, was an isolated individual manipulating the objects of inert nature to his private advantage. Hence, questions arose in the larger context about every individual attempting to *manipulate* every other individual and/or about a dictator manipulating and controlling the society. The social problem, then, as viewed by Knight, became "one of *rational consensus*...not of control in the correct meaning of manipulation." Man could and has misused scientific knowledge for many purposes. So the philosophical problem of the extremely autonomous individual was reconciled by having man direct knowledge toward the ethic of science, and toward choosing better ends. The truth ethic of science (honor among scientists) was to rule out deception and manipulation by social technocrats. On the second matter, Roland McKean, a former student of Knight, quoted Knight thus: "The chief thing which the common-sense individual actually wants is not satisfaction for wants which he has, but more and *better* wants." Continuing he quotes further: "Life is not fundamentally a striving for ends, for satisfactions, but rather for bases for further striving."[41]

On the one hand, we have the perfect market and the society of Crusoes, and, on the other, the scientific community with its allegedly ideal ethical and moral standards. Knight apparently wished an extension of the principles of freedom found in the former to the activities of a larger social community as characterized by the scientific community. In social discussion there was to be a voluntary exchange and expression of ideas much like the free exchange in a competitive market. This larger society McKinney said, required "the design of appropriate institutions—linguistic, educational, cultural."[42]

Friedman departed from Knight's views in a number of respects in the moral and ethical realm. For one, he wanted science to depend on the method (including choice between conflicting hypotheses, and public debate in the case of the social sciences), rather than the men for the most part. Next, he resorted to rules rather than judgment by politically appointed officials in crucial areas of economic policy.[43] This distrust of the official in government to act in the interest of the public is generally seen in debate between Friedman and Franco Modigliani, and it is found in the literature on rational expectations.[44] Furthermore, Friedman's views on uncertainty departed from Knight's in that he both altered the views and treated uncertainty as a part of probability rather than simply abstracting from it as Knight did (and as Lucas-Sargent's new classical school did later, p. 71).

Individualism and Social Determination

Friedman, as we have noted, shifted weight away from Knight's sociological determinism, leading Gramm to address the issue of individualism "true" and individualism "false." Citing a 1945 lecture by Friedrich von Hayek, Gramm drew upon the title "Individualism: True and False" to deal with individualism in a social context as a "true" individualism as distinct from the treatment of the individual as a disassociated, independent atom. Gramm found the view of such early Chicago economists as Knight, Henry Simons, and Jacob Viner to be a true individualism, as captured above in Knight's view of the complexities of dealing with ethics and morals and the distinctions between instrumental rationality and critical judgment. He argued further that there is a "false" individualism associated with later Chicago economists.

The false individualism Gramm refered to is an individualism that is more limited to the concept of the perfect market and the naive view of Robinson Crusoe as a "ready-made" man, given to this world exclusive of any awareness of the social and cultural influences that shaped him. "For both groups," Gramm concluded, "the major means to the end of maximizing individual freedom is the institutional base of private markets and minimal government restraint of individual choice."[45] Continuing, he said:

> Freedom is equated with equality of opportunity which is, in turn, a function of a socially operational equality of economical and political power. The existence of equal rights (legal and social) is consonant with significant—but not extreme—inequality in distribution of income and wealth.

The predecessors of the early Chicago view represent a convergence of English and continental liberalism—a convergence of the liberalism of John Locke, Adam Smith, and Alfred Marshall, with that of Karl Menger and Friedrich von Wieser. The convergence is thought to be represented by the Cambridge spirit of economics (by "an intimate link between social philosophy and economic analysis"). The philosophical and ethical ground of individualism true (as shared by Knight, Simons, and Viner) has "equality of opportunity" (or steadily diminishing inequality) as the strategic base. In this view, democracy is a political norm "but emphasis on individual rights and the reality of great differences in individual interests and behavior necessitate restraint on the political tyranny of the majority." In addition, there was opposition among the early Chicagoans to the view that the scientific method of natural sciences was fully or directly applicable to social science.

Focusing on ideas rather than individuals, Gramm identified "false" individualism mainly with elements of method, and normative association. The first concerns the applicability of physical science-based methods to social sciences. And the second, in Gramm's view, concerned: (1) a displacement of an economics of ethics by an economics of efficiency; (2) a disassociation of economics from the process of social change, and (3) implicit support of authoritarian tendencies of advanced industrial capitalism.[46]

Without attempting to deal with Chicagoans generally, Friedman clearly offered a unique method of science for economics and not simply that of a physical science-based method (pp. 68-87 and chap. 4). In addition, Friedman placed freedom as the highest goal (over efficiency); stressed such matters as learning by the electorate in political and economic affairs; distinguished between force and persuasion and opposed the use of force; gave attention to the importance of social values; and supported an economics of markets which disperses power. This economics accommodates cultural heterogeneity and proselytizing activity by agents as they attempt to convert one another to various causes, hypotheses, and social views. (There is a later distinction made on page 723 between "institutional individualism" and the atomistic individualism of "conventionalism.")

Friedman's methods and his interest in freedom as encompassing heterogeneous agents in the market led to his both abstracting from complexities of culture change and social determinism and recognizing and accommodating them as important determinants of behavior. Pursuing thoughts along these lines led to Friedman's major popular work, *Capitalism and Freedom*, and beyond to empirical work and observations about economic development and the moral basis of capitalism.[47]

Capitalism and Freedom

The term "capital" has been associated with the financial means of getting title to the physical means of production and command over the services of land and labor. "Capitalism" has been associated with an economic system where this ownership comes about in the private sphere as with the private property of the capitalist, as distinct from public ownership. Aspects of what may be called free markets have entered this discussion, and the evolutionary historical nature of such a system received special attention from Karl Marx and other more recent writers.[48] Mostly, the system has been seen as developing, maturing and merging into some sort of controlled system, as under socialism (or "democratic socialism," to note that the political system of democracy can still be associated with public ownership and control).

The capitalistic/democratic system in the historical context, moreover, has been described as freedom ("laissez faire") and associated with an absence of government interference over periods ranging from the repeal of the Corn Laws to WW I in Britain and from the Civil War in the U.S. to the 1930s in the U.S. Often these historical notions of freedom and absence of government have been misconstrued to suggest that enterprisers should be free simply to do as they please. Such, however, is not the case of the free enterprise economy that is governed by competition and prohibited from imposing damaging effects on third parties.

Whatever the case for third parties, for now, the capitalist system discussed by Marx has attracted wide comment from numerous sources ranging from Marx's highly negative position, to Schumpeter's favorable but pessimistic position, to Friedman's enthusiastically supportive position.

Marx and his followers saw the system as necessarily evolving, a historical determinism because of internal laws, instability, and the system's (scientific laws, as they were pp. 332-333) alleged tendency to generate extreme inequality in wealth. Arthur Burns, former Federal Reserve Chairman and Friedman confidante (pp. 144-148 and chap. 8), summarized the Marxian perception:

> In his [Marx] vision, small business firms would gradually disappear as capitalism evolved. The concentration of production in a diminishing number of large enterprises would be accompanied by concentration of wealth in fewer and fewer hands. The middle class would thus be destroyed and the masses proletarized. Inadequate consumption would lead to recurring epidemics of overproduction, and depressions of increasing severity would follow.
>
> As the misery of the proletariat deepened, resistance to capitalist exploitation would intensify and become more militant. With such powerful tendencies at work, the capitalist order was bound to collapse; it was only a matter of time when the capitalists would be expropriated and all instruments of production socialized.
>
> Thus, according to Marx's theory, the failure of capitalism in its later stages to meet even elementary economic needs of the working masses would inevitably lead, although not without intense struggle, to the replacement of free enterprise by a socialistically planned regime.[49]

In more recent times, Joseph Schumpeter saw the capitalist system somewhat differently.[50] Again as summarized by Burns:

> In his view the capitalist spirit expresses itself characteristically through innovation—that is, developing new commodities, devising new technologies, harnessing new sources of supply, devising new market strategies, forming new types of organization. The competition of new products and customary procedures—that is the essence of the capitalist process. This competition of the new

against the old is what really matters in the business world; it has been continuing at a rapid pace, and it accounts for the vast improvement in living standards wherever capitalism has flourished.[51]

In continuing on Schumpeter, Burns offered a description of projected happenings that would reflect more widely held feelings at the time Schumpeter wrote in the early post-WW II days than in the more recent period of Thatcher and Reagan. Continuing on Schumpeter, Burns said:

> According to Schumpeter, capitalism would be destroyed by factors growing out of its own inner processes. As business corporations became larger, they would become bureaucratic and impersonal. The entrepreneurial function of innovating would be largely assumed by trained specialists. Increasing affluence would provide both the means and the will to expand social programs and thus lead to a growing role of government. The intellectual class created and nourished by capitalism would become increasingly hostile to its institutions. Animosity toward free enterprise would be exploited by government officials seeking additional power for themselves. The general public would fail to support free enterprise because the issues debated in the public arena are much too complex and often involve long-range considerations that go beyond popular concern. Even businessmen would become increasingly willing to accept the teachings of their detractors. In this social and political environment, capitalist enterprise would in time be undermined and finally replaced by socialism.

Whereas Schumpeter saw the capitalist system as evolving because in a democratic society the voters would recoil from the discipline it imposed on the agents and from the efficiency it imposed on production, Friedman himself held more positive views. Addressing the period of the least amount of governmental interference, Friedman said:

> The closest approach to free enterprise we have ever had in the United States was in the 19th century. Yet you and your children will hear over and over again in their schools and in their classes the myths that it was a terrible period when the robber barons were grinding the poor miserable people under their heels. That's a myth constructed out of whole cloth. The plain fact is that never in human history has there been a period when the ordinary man improved his condition and benefited his life as much as he did during that period of the 19th Century when we had the closest

approach to free enterprise that we have ever had. Most of us in this room, I venture to say, are beneficiaries of that period. I speak of myself. My parents came to this country in the 1890's. Like millions of others they came with empty hands. They were able to find a place in this country, to build a life for themselves and to provide a basis on which their children and their children's children could have a better life. There is no saga in history remotely comparable to the saga of the United States during that era, welcoming millions and millions of people from all over the world and enabling them to find a place for themselves and to improve their lives. And it was possible only because there was an essentially free society.[52]

Reacting to the Marxist view, Friedman questioned the inevitable, evolutionary nature of collectivism and directed attention to the burden imposed by freedom on the individual and to the complexity of sociological determinism.[53] He did all of this while addressing the matter of freedom for the individual, the family as a basic unit of society, ethnic and religious groups, and the conflict resulting from the reconciliation of individual differences in political matters.[54]

The complexity of determinism aside, Friedman stated quite simply the thing that amused him about the argument "You can't turn the clock back." Namely, he said, "The thing that always amuses me about that argument is that the people who make it and who accuse me or my colleagues of trying to turn the clock back to the 19th Century, are themselves busily at work trying to turn the clock back to the 17th Century."[55] Friedman continued:

> Adam Smith, two hundred years ago, in 1776, wrote *The Wealth of Nations*. It was an attack on the government controls of his time—on mercantilism, on tariffs, on restrictions, on governmental monopoly. But those are exactly the results which the present-day reformers are seeking to achieve.
>
> In any event, that's a foolish question. The real question is not whether you are turning the clock back or forward, but whether you are doing the right thing. Do you mean to say you should never learn from your mistakes?
>
> Some people argue that technological changes require big government and you can no longer talk in the terms of the 19th Century when the government only absorbed 3 percent of the national income. You have to have big government because of these technological changes. That's nonsense from beginning to end. Some technological changes no doubt require the government to engage

in activities different from those in which it engaged before. But other technological changes *reduce* the need for government. The improvements in communication and transportation have greatly reduced the possibility of local monopoly which requires government intervention to protect the consumers.

On this growth of government and the income redistribution matter which comes in the next chapter and on later occasions, Friedman said:

> Moreover, if you look at the record, the great growth of government has not been in the areas dictated by technological change. The great growth of government has been to take money from some people and give it to others. The only way technology has entered into that is by providing the computers which make it possible to do so.

There were, to be sure, ethical problems as to what the individual would do with his freedom if the state did not choose for him. And, in addition, freedom was a tolerable objective only for responsible individuals. "The free man," Friedman said, "will ask neither what his country can do for him nor what he can do for his country." He will ask:

> What can I and my compatriots do through government to help us discharge our individual responsibilities, to achieve our several goals and purposes, and above all, to protect our freedom? And he will accompany this question with another: How can we keep the government we create from becoming a Frankenstein that will destroy the very freedom we establish it to protect? Freedom is a rare and delicate plant. Our minds tell us, and history confirms, that the great threat to freedom is the concentration of power.[56]

Drawing on his Chicago background and Knight, and on the methodology of his *positive economics*, Milton Friedman offered new direction on the subject of freedom,[57] although in some measure his offerings seemed like a return to an earlier period of history. Leonard Silk wrote of "the Old-Time Religion," where Friedman often seemed to be searching the past for a valid orthodoxy.[58] As has been the case with the Chicago school, he spoke of his conservatism, to use the common term, as the true liberalism, "as the doctrine pertaining to a free man." On the term "liberalism," Friedman discoursed:

> Especially after 1930 in the United States, the term liberalism came to be associated with a very different emphasis, particularly

in economic policy. It came to be associated with a readiness to rely primarily on the state rather than on private voluntary arrangements to achieve objectives regarded as desirable. The catchwords became welfare and equality rather than freedom. The nineteenth century liberal regarded an extension of freedom as the most effective way to promote welfare and equality; the twentieth century liberal regards welfare and equality as either prerequisites of or alternatives to freedom. In the name of welfare and equality, the twentieth century liberal has come to favor a revival of the very policies of state intervention and paternalism against which classical liberalism fought.[59]

By the late 1970s, addressing the debate of welfare reform, Gordon Weil reported "that 182 federal benefit programs relating to income maintenance existed in 1977," and that they accounted for "69 percent of federal tax receipts for the year." Burns spoke along similar lines, and Friedman addressed a principle that animated people who wanted the power to be in government. "You see it everywhere," he said, you see it exemplified in a law "which was passed a few years ago which required the Treasury Department to report to the Congress a category called 'Tax Expenditures'."[60] Continuing:

Tax Expenditures are taxes which are not collected from you because of various deductions permitted by the law (such as interest or excess depreciation). The principle is that you are, after all, the property of the U.S. Government. You work for the U.S. Government, and the U.S. Government lets you keep a little of what you earn in order to be sure that they'll keep you working hard for them. But the rest of it is the property of the U.S. Government. And if the U.S. Government allows you to deduct something from your taxes, it's providing for the expenditure. It's not a right that you have to keep it. It's theirs!

The presumed right and power on the part of government denies freedom. Friedman saw this denial among intellectuals and businessmen. On the former he saw it as the government entered through the support of research as in the cases of the National Institute of Health and the National Science Foundation. He concluded:

I have often said about the only people who have any real freedom left are people who are in the fortunate position of myself—tenured professors at major private universities on the verge of retirement![61]

The businessmen, Friedman said, will still express general sentiments in favor of free enterprise and competition but rarely criticize particular measures taken by government. Both the professors and the businessmen, he said, want freedom for themselves but deny it to others. Reacting to pre-Reagan conditions, Friedman said of the businessmen's fears:

> I have heard very few get up and criticize particular measures taken by government. And I don't blame them. They would be fools to do it! Because any businessman who has the nerve to do that has to look over one shoulder and see what the I.R.S. is going to do to his books the next day. And he has to look over the other shoulder to see whether the Justice Department is going to launch an anti-trust suit. And then he has to find two or three more shoulders to see what the F.T.C. is going to do. You can take any other three letters of the alphabet and you have to ask what they are going to do to you. In fact, a businessman today does not have effective freedom of speech.[62]

The intellectuals and the business corporations, in their narrower perspectives, become the enemies of free enterprise:

> They are enemies for opposite reasons. Every one of my fellow intellectuals believes in freedom for himself. He wants free speech. He wants free research. I ask him, "Isn't this a terrible waste that a dozen people are studying the same problem? Oughtn't we to have a central planning committee to decide what research projects various individuals are to undertake?" He'll look at me as if I'm crazy, and he'll say, "What do you mean? Don't you understand about the value of academic freedom and freedom of research and duplication?" But when it comes to business he says, "Oh, that's wasteful competition. That's duplication over there! We must have a central planning board to make those things intelligent, sensible!"
>
> So every intellectual is in favor of freedom for himself and against freedom for anybody else. The businessman and the business enterprises are very different. Every businessman and every business enterprise is in favor of freedom for everybody else, but when it comes to himself, that's a different question. We have to have that tariff to protect us against competition from abroad. We have to have that special provision in the tax code. We have to have that subsidy. Businessmen are in favor of freedom for everybody else but not for themselves.
>
> There are many notable exceptions...

At about the same time as this speech, Jonathan Hughes wrote of the government's habit toward imposing market and non-market controls as a part of the control bureaucracy long after the controls had served their presumed purpose.[63] Hughes noted a tendency toward "regulated economic malfunctioning," and called for some change in the mix of social control and individual freedom.

In any case, Friedman did a number of things that were different from the early historical emphasis on capitalism, and from that of his forebears at Chicago. First, it was not the capital and the means of production that Friedman stressed in addressing capitalism. Rather it was the exchange economy with attention to choice in occupation and possible entry into business, in products, in values in the sense of ethical and religious values, and in voluntary cooperation.[64] Furthermore, Friedman addressed the matter of freedom in economic arrangements, voting, and constitutional matters. Thus, in doing so, Friedman directed attention away from the materialistic aspects of the economic system and clearly placed freedom as the highest goal, with attention to freedom in the market for ideas and in ideological debate.[65] Efficiency in production and the release of creative impulses from the dead hand of control were more of the nature of by-products, although they were not to be unimportant ones.

On the defense of freedom, Friedman said, "The believer in freedom has never counted noses." His statement pre-dated Barry Goldwater's, following his nomination for the 1964 Republican presidential candidate (N.Y.T., 7/17/64):

> I would remind you that extremism in defense of liberty is no vice.
> And let me remind you also that moderation in pursuit of justice is no virtue.

And, in fact, the publication of Friedman's *Capitalism and Freedom* was followed by his becoming Goldwater's unofficial advisor in the 1964 presidential campaign.[66] (We see this later in terms of antecedents to the Reagan presidency.)

In constitutional and in political matters, Friedman may be seen as getting broad agreement in a twofold way, which we later encounter as a strategy for achieving tax reforms during Reagan's second term. First, the strategy calls for selling ideas, and, second, the achievement comes via getting voters to give up what they see as their special interest. The possible resolution of the latter conflict is found in "bundling things together."[67] On "bundling things together," Friedman continued in 1973:

> That's how we keep Government out of the censorship business.
> It's not a matter of taking one case at a time and deciding each

case on its merits. If we did that, we would have free speech for very few. Someone would be able to get a law passed prohibiting free speech for Seventh-day Adventists. Or vegetarians. Or Black Panthers.

We talked earlier about reducing the tax rates and closing the loopholes. The right wing would be more than willing to give up the loopholes in return for lower rates; and the left wing would probably be more than willing to give up the high rates in return for closing the loopholes. So it looks as if there's a deal to be made. But you can't make a deal through the usual legislative channels, because neither side trusts the other—and both are right. The only way I can see to make such a deal is by a constitutional amendment that says, for example, Congress can impose an income tax as long as the only deductions are for strict occupational expenses and a personal exemption, and as long as the highest tax rate is no more than twice the lowest. Personally, I would prefer a flat rate, but to achieve consensus, it would be better to limit the degree of graduation. That would give both sides some assurance that the deal wouldn't come unstuck.

Friedman's approach to what may be called his normative economics was not to construct an elaborate formal system.[68] Rather, his approach was simple, as his scientific method was. Also, it has involved advocacy of the system he thought best for responsible individuals. There was no Marxian determinism and no alleging that scientific method decreed such a system. Rather there was simple advocacy, and there was a choice:

> I believe the choice is still open to us, that we can still decide, you and I and our fellow citizens, which of these two directions we want to go in—whether we want to return to the path that made this the great land of opportunity for millions of people, or whether instead we want to continue down the road toward a destruction of both liberty and prosperity.[69]

Knight, for his part, stressed the importance of selling the ideology if the system was to function properly,[70] and Friedman adopted this advocacy. In doing so, Friedman proceeded as one of the most masterful and optimistic peddlers of his time.[71] In this respect he contrasts noticeably with Adam Smith, whom Viner described as having been uninclined "to obtain acceptance and execution of his reforming ideas."[72] This skill in persuasion and an optimistic outlook about its effects characterized Friedman, as they did J.M. Keynes.

As early as 1962, at the end of *Capitalism and Freedom*, Friedman spoke of "The glimmerings of change that are already apparent in the intellectual climate" and in 1978 and 1979 he was still attuned to the straws in the wind, as he pushed for a constitutional amendment to limit taxes.[73] The earlier date preceded his support of Barry Goldwater and the setbacks of the J.F. Kennedy assassination in November 1963, the Vietnam distraction and Watergate.[74] The peddler was undaunted.

Keynes, as we noted in chapter 11, sought short-run control and appeal through intellect while Friedman was more directed in his political stances towards a dependence on the rationality of the voter in the long run and on Dicey's attention to long trends of opinion.[75] "The thing that is fascinating about Dicey," Friedman says, "is his emphasis on long trends of opinion."

Friedman visits Thomas Jefferson's Monticello during the 1979 production of the PBS series *Free to Choose*

The simplicity of Friedman's political/economic stance has a parallel in his empirical economics. Friedman himself recalled an often-recounted incident from his early days with the Division of Tax Research in the U.S. Treasury during WW II.[76] While testifying before a Senate Finance Committee, he was listing reasons advocating a policy or argument when Senator Tom Connolly interrupted with "Young man, one reason is good enough" (p. 22).

Social Process

In the simplicity of his approach, Friedman did not ignore the cultural and other forces that may influence and determine individual behavior. The market he addressed enabled economic activities to be coordinated in a general way, "impediments" to voluntary exchange aside.[77] These activities, Friedman stressed, were coordinated impersonally, "and without regard to the other activities of the participants [the values, religious beliefs, etc.]." The role of the market in enabling this coordination "is what's essential to the maintenance of political and social freedom."[78]

The entry of the cultural and related activities was facilitated by Friedman's retreat from the concept of economic man—a calculating pleasure-pain machine or a Robinson Crusoe on an island, as textbooks have addressed.[79] "Robinson Crusoe," Friedman said, "is subject to 'constraint'," he has limited "power," and he has only a limited number of alternatives, but there is no problem of freedom in the sense that is relevant to our discussion."[80]

For Friedman, the individual addresses complicated ethical matters about relationships and embraces values that are an important part of his freedom and choosing. The values, ethical and religious beliefs, are so important that Friedman's concept of culture is embracing of heterogeneity, of religious and ethnic differences.

Friedman addressed values and beliefs, as he did in reference to Chile and his early reactions to Galbraith. On the fundamental value he said:

> I do not believe that the fundamental value is to do good to others whether they want you to or not. The fundamental value is not to do good to others as *you* see their good. Neither is it to force them to do good.[81]

There is to be voluntary association plus persuasion. Continuing, Friedman spoke of the essential notion of a capitalist society as relying on voluntary cooperation and voluntary exchange:

> The essential character of a capitalist system is that it relies on voluntary exchange, on your agreeing with me that you will sell

something to me if I will pay you a certain amount for it. The essential notion is that both parties to the exchange must benefit. That was the great vision of Adam Smith in his *Wealth of Nations*: that individuals each separately pursuing their own self-interest could promote the social interest through exchange between people on the basis of mutual benefit.[82]

The exchange with voluntary cooperation is a part of the market's dispersing power and admitting freedom. Freedom—as in the case of the blacks or the Jews or any individual or minority, or dissenting individual or group—is best served by a market oriented society. It embraces cultural heterogeneity, and hence recognizes cultural, social, and individual differences.[83] The charge of false individualism does not apply, namely: Friedman was not talking about "the exaggerated individualism that disassociates the individual from society and the hyperrationalism that sees individual behavior governed by rational choice rather than jointly influenced by feelings and intellect." In contrast to this sort of individualism, Friedman said:

> On a scientific level it is true that what we are is affected a great deal by the society in which we live and grow up. Of course all of us are different than we would have been if we had grown up in a different society. So I'm not denying in the slightest the effect on all of us of the social institutions within which we operate, both on our values and on our opportunities. I am only saying that a set of social institutions that stresses individual responsibility, that treats the individual—given the kind of society in which he operates—as responsible for and to himself, will lead to a higher and more desirable moral climate than a set of institutions that stresses the lack of responsibility of the individual for what happens to him and relieves him of blame or credit for what he does to his fellow men.[84]

The terms "voluntary cooperation" and "persuasion" played key roles in Friedman's social thinking. His role for checks and balances minimized the use of force, even to the extent of minimizing force to achieve something he preferred on personal grounds.

The Exchange Economy

Voluntary cooperation of individuals arises in the market place as pictured by the model of an exchange economy, and this method of coordinating the economic activities, ultimately of millions, differs from the other fundamental method of coordination—namely, of *coercion*, "the technique of the army or the modern totalitarian state."[85] The model of an exchange economy starts with a collection of Crusoes, as it were, where "each household uses the resources it controls to produce goods and services that it exchanges for goods and services produced by other households, on terms mutually acceptable to the two parties to the bargain." There is the elementary proposition "that both parties to an economic transaction benefit from it," provided the transaction is bilaterally voluntary and the parties are informed.

As a division of labor occurs, and as money is added as a medium of exchange, the latter permits an indirect satisfaction of wants through exchange in a market (i.e., an exchange of a good other than money for money and then the use of money in the purchase of some good to ultimately satisfy a want). In the simpler market without money, "each household uses the resources it controls to produce goods and services that it exchanges for goods and services provided by other households on terms mutually acceptable to the two parties to the bargain." In the more complex market and in the monetary, market-oriented society, firms (business enterprises) arise as intermediaries between individuals and production and exchange may occur without the satisfaction of wants depending on the direct exchange of goods as in a barter context.

Since households have the alternatives of producing for themselves or for the market, they need not enter into exchange unless they benefit. "Hence, exchange will not take place unless both parties do benefit from it." Cooperation is achieved through the market. It is strictly individual and voluntary, provided: (a) that enterprise is private [that is privately owned], so that the ultimate contracting parties are individuals and (b) that individuals are effectively free to enter or not to enter any particular exchanges, so that every transaction is strictly voluntary.[86]

As the analysis of markets and market structures gets more complicated (chap. 9), specifying institution arrangements conducive to free markets gets more difficult. "The basic requisite," Friedman said, "is the maintenance of law and order to prevent physical coercion of one individual by another and to enforce contracts voluntarily entered into, thus giving substance to 'private'." In this context, "perhaps the most difficult problems arise from monopoly," and from "neighborhood effects," Friedman said, because monopoly "inhibits effective freedom by denying individuals alternatives to the particular exchange" and because there are difficulties in charging or compensating for the "neighborhood" effects (effects on third parties).

The Government and the Market

Several things happen as the analysis of markets gets more complicated: government enters as a forum for determining the "rules of the game" and as an umpire to "interpret and enforce the rules decided on," and the market serves "to reduce greatly the range of issues that must be decided through political means, and thereby to minimize the extent to which government need participate directly in the game." Said in the language of an earlier chapter, the market serves to reduce the burden on government. Further, the market widens the range of representation as to what to produce. "It is, in political terms," Friedman said, "a system of proportional representation." Each man can vote, as it were, through his purchases, to influence what gets produced. The result may be objects of art and ideas, as we note below. Quite significantly, however, "he [the individual] does not have to see what...the majority wants [as in a parliamentary majority voting context] and then, if he is in the minority, submit."

The concept of economic freedom is extended to encompass that of political freedom in that "political freedom means the absence of coercion of a man by his fellow men." Continuing, Friedman said:

> The fundamental threat to freedom is the power to coerce, be it in the hands of a monarch, a dictator, an oligarchy, or a momentary majority. The preservation of freedom requires the elimination of such concentration of power to the fullest possible extent and the dispersal and distribution of whatever power cannot be eliminated....By removing the organization of economic activity from the control of political authority, the market eliminates this source of coercive power. It enables economic strength to be a check to political power rather than a reinforcement.[87]

Monopoly is a problem in several respects. It may be the government, it may be technical monopoly in the market sector (exclusive of government), and it may concern "neighborhood effects." Technical monopoly is where the monopoly (the single producer) comes about as a result of the natural outcome of cost conditions or resource availability and of competitive market forces. In its presence there are three alternatives: private monopoly, public monopoly, or public regulation. Noting both sides of the private vs. public monopoly issue, Friedman said, "Having learned from both, I reluctantly conclude that, if tolerable, private monopoly may be the least of the evils." In a static, non-changing society Friedman would have little confidence in this solution, but in a rapidly changing society "the conditions making for the technical monopoly frequently change and

I suspect that both public regulation and public monopoly are likely to be less responsive to such changes in conditions, to be less readily capable of elimination, than private monopoly."[88]

This latter point about choosing between government as a single control unit and the monopolistic enterprise was an important point with Friedman in the political freedom context. Most notably, governmental power once entrenched is more difficult to decentralize than market power (exclusive of government). The preservation of freedom requires the elimination of such concentration of power to the fullest possible extent and the dispersal and distribution of whatever power cannot be eliminated—a system of checks and balances. Continuing, Friedman said:

> By removing the organization of economic activity from the control of political authority, the market eliminates this source of coercive power. It enables economic strength to be a check to political power rather than a reinforcement.[89]

A gray area, in addition to that of a technical monopoly, centers about "neighborhood effects" (effects on parties other than those immediately involved in the transaction). Examples of these effects would be the pollution of a stream by a private enterprise and the destruction of the wilderness and man's natural environment, although Friedman himself did not address the latter in his written works. In the case of pollution, the polluter is asking an innocent party in effect to exchange good water for bad. These individuals may be willing to accept the pollution at a price, "but it is not feasible for them, acting individually, to avoid the exchange or to enforce appropriate compensation." Hence, the government may have to step in where economics itself says very little about the public choice and where it is left to political voting.

Friedman, however, noted considerations that have been used to rationalize "almost every conceivable intervention." He saw this rationalization in many cases as "special pleading rather than a legitimate application of the concept of neighborhood effects." Continuing, he said, "Neighborhood effects cut both ways."[90] There are no hard and fast lines to delineate the role of government in the case of neighborhood effects. The use of government is difficult to circumscribe with respect to its use in accomplishing jointly "what it is difficult or impossible for us to accomplish separately through strictly voluntary exchange." There are advantages and disadvantages in any particular case, however, Friedman noted, "we shall always want to enter on the liability side of any proposed governmental intervention, its neighborhood effect in threatening freedom."

In the parliamentary sense of democracy, we vote to express opinions and values about the government we want and the limits that should be placed on it and on the undesirable effects of free enterprise. As an expedient, however, we accept in voting, majority rule in one form or another, and the size of the majority required depends on the seriousness of the issue involved.[91] On the one hand, "If the matter is of little moment and the minority has no strong feelings about being overruled, a bare plurality will suffice. On the other hand, if the minority feels strong about the issue involved, even a bare majority will not do." Continuing, Friedman noted, "Few of us would be willing to have issues of free speech, for example, decided by a bare majority." Thus, in such matters we make "minimal concessions to expediency," and one encounters a *self denying ordinance* where majority rule does not apply and something more like *essential consensus* (super or two-thirds majority) must be achieved in voting (i.e., in changing provisions in "constitutions or their equivalents prohibiting coercion of individuals"). These larger constitutional changes, as it were, "are themselves to be regarded as reached by free discussion and as reflecting essential unanimity about means."

In voting, "The number of separate groups that can in fact be represented is narrowly limited, enormously so by comparison with the proportional representation of the market." Thus, by viewing the market as an extension of voting we tend to reduce the burden on government and increase the number of individuals that can, in fact, be represented because the market is a form of proportional representation. In contrast, in voting, "the fact that the final outcome generally must be a law applicable to all groups, rather than separate legislative enactment for each 'party' represented, means that proportional representation in the political version, far from permitting unanimity without conformity, tends toward ineffectiveness and fragmentation." Continuing, Friedman said, "It [proportional representation in the political version] thereby operates to destroy any consensus on which unanimity with conformity can rest." A homely bit of political philosophy, which Friedman salted his remarks with on occasion, is: "while the free market yields 'unanimity without conformity,' government actions at best yield 'conformity without unanimity'."[92]

Proportional representation in the political version is impossible in some matters. Two individuals, for example, may not each separately get the amount of national defense they want. Even so, Friedman noted, they can "discuss, and argue, and vote." However, deciding they must conform to the majority view to protect the nation, they set aside "exclusive reliance on individual action through the market." In this context, we are employing political channels to reconcile differences.

Limiting the range of issues that must be decided by a majority rule increases the stability of society. "The strain is least," Friedman said, "if agreement for joint action need be reached only on a limited range of issues on which people in any event have common views."

Freedom

So freedom arises from an absence of coercion by monopoly powers, in one case, and from the ultimate limitation imposed by requiring an *essential consensus* on certain important matters such as the protection of free speech, in another. Between the limits of a bare majority and essential consensus in public political (collective, that is) decision making, there is potential unavoidable conflict.[93] On a matter like the amount of national defense, everyone cannot have the exact amount he/she wants. The amount to be agreed upon is indivisible, and having decided each individual must conform. The dissenting individual is coerced, but protection of the individual and the nation requires national defense to protect the individual and the nation from coercion.

In this attention to unavoidable conflict, Friedman is following Knight.[94] On Knight, McKinney noted that a 95 percent vote to impose a school tax on everyone in a community, leaves 5 percent subject to coercion. On the other hand, a rule of unanimity "provides an irrational bias in favor of the status quo." Continuing, McKinney said: "The rule of unanimity invites a tyranny of the minority. Plainly, the citizens of a free society must find a way to reconcile freedom with less than unanimous decisions."

So within the limits of a *bare majority* and *complete unanimity*, Friedman envisioned a special role for *persuasion* rather than for *force* (coercion) and a free market for ideas. Furthermore, restricting the range of decisions that must be made by a bare majority and leaving *divisible* matters to the market and morals to the individuals, all lead to release creative energies in arts and science and to responses by the business community to coordinate the number of divisible matters not left to collective (public) decision making.[95]

The freedom obtained by relegating certain matters to decision by a virtual consensus encompasses "the freedom of individuals to advocate and propagandize openly for a radical change in the structure of society—so long," Friedman said, "as the advocacy is restricted to persuasion and does not include force or other forms of coercion." The advocacy in, and as it touches upon, the political/economic/social spheres depends on (a) being able to earn a living (inheritances aside), (b) the role of a few wealthy individuals who have become persuaded (i.e., "a role of inequality of wealth in preserving political freedom…—the role of the patron"), and/or (c) success in gaining financial support for the ideas to be propagated. Continuing on the latter, Friedman said:

> Indeed, it is not even necessary to persuade people or financial institutions with available funds or the soundness of the idea to be

propagated. It is only necessary to persuade them that the propagation can be financially successful, "that the newspaper or magazine or book or other venture will be profitable. The competitive publisher, for example cannot afford to publish only writing with which he personally agrees; his touchstone must be the likelihood that the market will be large enough to yield a satisfactory return on investment.[96]

"In this way," Friedman said, "the market breaks the vicious circle and makes it possible to finance such ventures by small amounts from many people without first persuading them." Continuing he noted, "There are no such possibilities in the socialist society; there is only the all powerful state."[97]

Freedom in this advocacy of causes "does not require that such advocacy be without cost." For some who may think that advocacy should be costless (say, as subsidized by a state-financed election fund), Friedman noted, "On the contrary, no society could be stable if advocacy of radical change were costless, much less subsidized." He said, in fact:

> It is entirely appropriate that men make sacrifices to advocate causes in which they deeply believe. Indeed, it is important to preserve freedom only for people who are willing to practice self-denial, for otherwise freedom degenerates into license and irresponsibility. What is essential is that the cost of advocating unpopular causes be tolerable and not prohibitive.

On self-denial and advocacy Friedman continued:

> But we are not yet through. In a free market society, it is enough to have the funds. The suppliers of paper are as willing to sell it to the *Daily Worker* as to the *Wall Street Journal*. In a socialist society, it would not be enough to have the funds. The hypothetical supporter of capitalism would have to persuade a government factory making paper to sell to him, the government printing press to print his pamphlets, a government post office to distribute them among the people, a government agency to rent him a hall in which to talk, and so on. Perhaps there is some way in which one could overcome these difficulties and preserve freedom in a socialist society. One cannot say it is utterly impossible. What is clear, however, is that there are very real difficulties in establishing institutions that will effectively preserve the possibility of dissent. So far as I know, none of the people who have been in favor of socialism and also in favor of freedom have really faced up to this issue,

or made even a respectable start at developing the institutional arrangements that would permit freedom under socialism. By contrast, it is clear how a free market capitalist society fosters freedom.[98]

Friedman's free society, moreover, would use persuasion as the acceptable measure rather than coercive power (as may be imposed by a specific majority) to bring about changes in tastes and individual attitudes, and to deal with highly idealistic objectives such as equality and social justice.[99] As one general rule "any minority that counts on specific majority actions [rather than a general self-denying ordinance or constitutional change] to defend its interest [such as the avoidance of discrimination in employment because of color or race or religion] is short-sighted in the extreme." Friedman cited examples such as state actions to achieve fair employment (FEPC legislation) and right-to-work laws. One of his points was that if a bare majority can be used to support these matters, it can also conveniently be used to oppose one on other occasions. "Both", Friedman said, "interfered with the freedom of the employment contract..." Continuing, he added:

> Despite the identity of principle, there is almost 199 per cent divergence of views with respect to the two laws. Almost all who favor right to work oppose FEPC. As a liberal, I am opposed to both, as I am equally to laws outlawing the so-called "yellow-dog" contract (a contract making non-membership in a union a condition of employment).[100]

Freedom, Social Systems, and Ends and Means

In recognizing freedom as the highest goal and in envoking Goldwater ("I would remind you that extremism in defense of liberty is no vice") we touch upon a sensitive social issue about whether the ends (or goals) justifies the means. On it, Friedman noted that a common objection to totalitarian societies is that they regard the end as justifying the means. He said this objection is illogical when taken literally. "If the end does not justify the means," he asked, "what does?" He said:

> To deny that the end justifies the means is indirectly to assert that the end in question is not the ultimate end, that the ultimate end is itself the use of the proper means. Desirable or not, any end that can be attained only by the use of bad means must give way to the more basic end of the use of acceptable means. To the liberal, the

appropriate means are free discussion and voluntary cooperation, which implies that any form of coercion is inappropriate. The idea is unanimity among responsible individuals achieved on the basis of free and full discussion. This is another way of expressing the goal of freedom...[101]

Continuing on social systems in another context, Friedman said: "Capitalism, socialism, central planning are means not ends. In and of themselves, they are neither moral nor immoral, humane nor inhumane." The pragmatist, the empirical scientists, the emphasis on theory testing—were all revealed as Friedman continued:

> We have to look at what are the consequences of adopting one or another system of organization. From that point of view, the crucial thing is to look beneath the surface. Don't look at what the proponents of one system or another say are their intentions, but look at what the actual results are.
>
> ....
>
> Does the system—no matter what its proponents say—produce those results? Once you look at the results it is crystal clear that they do not. Where are social injustices greatest? Social injustices are clearly greatest where you have central control.

Friedman continued with rhetorical questions:

> Was it simply because Stalin took over from Lenin that communism went the way it did? Has capitalism succeeded despite the immoral values that pervade it? I believe that the answers to both questions are in the negative. The results would have occurred because each system has been true to the values it encourages, supports, and develops in the people who live under the system.[102]

"Capitalism," Friedman added, "is often reproached as being materialistic. It is often reproached as erecting money as a chief motive. Money is not a very noble motive, but it's cleaner than most. Look at the facts." Friedman continued:

> In a society in which people are free to do their own thing, in which people make voluntary deals, it's hard to do good. You've got to persuade people, and there's nothing in this world that is harder. But the important thing is that in that kind of society it's also hard to do harm.[103]

"Persuasion" and "coercion" play key roles. Friedman himself embraced persuasion for agents and leaders—say, with respect to social values, political policies, and so on—over force or use of power, which he saw as dispersed by the market. He saw the good working out, as it were, at least in the long run. On one occasion, we encounter him invoking Abraham Lincoln on deception:

> "You can fool all the people some of the time, but you can't fool all the people all of the time."[104]

For Knight, on the other hand, there was some overlap in meanings and related complexities. This overlap came about through his including "persuasion by deception and, more importantly conditioning," in his definition of coercion. Drawing on Knight, McKinney said, "Individuals can be conditioned by political dictators, fashion setters and evangelists to accept 'voluntarily' the most absurd beliefs and to act to achieve all kinds of ends that serve the conditioner rather than the actor."[105] By persuasion, Knight did not mean reasoned discussion and argument, the advancement of the best theory or policy, or moral value, "He meant sort of what would be called questionable bases for arguments, that is, sort of false arguments."[106]

Scientific and Public Debate: Friedman and Samuelson

With Friedman we encounter disagreements—conflicts over values, religions, hypotheses. Persuasion by individuals and groups is one way of reconciling these conflicts and disagreements, as are hypothesis testing and social debate. Later (chap. 18), we will encounter Friedman in reference to Leonard Savage, whom we introduced earlier (pp. 69, 156). Referring to Savage, he said, "the purpose of statistical analysis is to reduce differences of opinion among people about personal probabilities." He recalled Savage as saying we don't argue, yell or scream, and tear one another's hair. We "sit down and decide what data you would like to look at in order to resolve the difference of opinion." For Friedman debate over public policy simply extended this hypothesis testing. Along this line, in the economics and public policy sphere, we encounter Friedman and Samuelson in opposing positions over the axioms controversy, over Keynesian economics, and over capitalism and freedom.

In scientific and public debate on matters of economics and public policy, the Nobel laureate Paul Samuelson was Friedman's most enduring opponent. In methodological discussion we encounter them as adversaries in the axioms controversy. In economics and the public policy sphere we encounter them in the similarly opposing positions over Keynesian economics, and in public policy debates. In these, the closest Samuelson came to addressing the central issues of capitalism and freedom was in an interview for the Leonard Silk book, *The Economist*, and at a March 1980 program on the Texas A & M University campus (pp. 91-92). In those sources, his Keynesian learnings and two other related differences with Friedman stand out. These center about the mixed economy, the use of force, and the distribution of income.

Samuelson, Silk said (1976, 41), "is a philosopher of the mixed economy [the one in place in the 1960s and 1970s, other sources suggest], blending private and public sectors, market and political decisions, individual liberties and social responsibilities, personal and communal welfare."[107] Elsewhere Samuelson conceded, "the fact that the modern mixed economy is a *humane* economy lies at the root of the stagflation problem; unemployed resources no longer put the damper on price and wage raises that they used to under the cruelties of historic capitalism."[108] (Samuelson was no doubt referring to developments such as we took up under the labor and dollar standards of Hicks's acts IV and V.)

Furthermore, Samuelson was not against state coercion if worthy ethical norms required it, whereas the only norm Friedman took this position on is freedom (say the choice between the capitalist and socialist ethics respectively). From this position on Friedman's part followed the roles for persuasion, constitutional protections and the minimum use of force within the society. Thus, in contrast to Friedman, Samuelson is portrayed as establishing ethical norms where he set himself up as the arbitrator of right and wrong, but with hesitancy about imposing his norms on others. Examples of norms worthy enough to call for the use of force where persuasion fails are the overcoming of racial discrimination and the "killings by gas" of "suitable specified humans." Silk stated Samuelson's beliefs thus: "that life consists of minimizing multiple evils and maximizing multiple goals, by compromise when possible, while preserving as wide a role as possible for individual freedom—but not disdaining to use political means if they are necessary to achieve some social good."[109]

Finally, Samuelson was an egalitarian with respect to the distribution of income,[110] whereas Friedman accepted the distribution resulting from the interaction between freedom and payment according to the value of marginal product. For Samuelson, the issue of the distribution of income came down to matters of law and order versus class struggle, whether in the Mid-East, Argentina and Chile in South America, or Margaret Thatcher's government in Britain (also p. 773 n 74). As with Friedman, Samuelson said, "Order in society is as important to economic well being as is technology capital equipment, and labor skills." Then he quoted himself: "Class warfare is a receipt to undermine the well being and functioning of any capitalist system or for that matter any modern mixed economy. The breakdown of social consensus and preoccupation with the division of the social pie is often fatal to the growth of the pie."

Friedman, on the other hand, for reasons elaborated in the next chapter, opposed the use of the progressive income tax (i.e., a tax that rises more than in proportion to income) to redistribute income. Such use of the tax, of course, has followed from the implementation of static concepts such as found at the hands of Marshall, Pigou, and others, of the alleged declining marginal utility of income. In supporting a flat-rate tax but objecting to a spate of proposals on the legislative agenda in mid 1982,[111] Friedman noted that some of the proposals are not really for a flat-rate tax (say, equal tax rate on the tax liability), plus they retained deductions that led to "the outrageous kind of income tax from which we now suffer." Being careful to note that a flat-rate tax would not redistribute income "with more of the tax burden shifted from the rich to the poor and middle class," Friedman proceeded with a mixture of the rationale of getting voters through persuasion to give up what they see as their special interest and of the need for an "essential consensus." (This approach to resolving conflict, we may recall, is to be found in "bundling things together.")

Referring to bills with the label "flat rate" but exclusive of the substance, Friedman said:

> Such proposals seem extremely attractive. They offer a compromise between the so-called left and right. The left might accept a lower top rate as the price of gaining a broader base. The right might accept a broader base as the price for gaining a lower top rate.
>
> However, appearances are deceiving. Such a compromise is neither desirable nor feasible. Neither side would trust the other and both are right. If it were ever enacted, the left would go to work to raise the rates—and they would quickly be joined by persons on the right pleading fiscal necessity. The right would go to work to broaden the deductions—and they would quickly be joined by persons on the left pleading equity and social priorities. After all, that is how we got into our present fix. History would simply repeat itself.
>
> There is, I believe, only one way to make a bargain stick: by amending the Constitution to require that any income tax must be levied at a flat rate with no deductions from the tax base other than personal exemptions and expenses of earning the income.[112]

Continuing—in contrast to Friedman and referring to British Prime

Minister Margaret Thatcher and the first year of her five-year Parliamentary majority—Samuelson proceeded thus:

> By every test known to the political scientists, the temperature of the class struggle has heated up in Britain. That there should be macroeconomic consequences, I don't think is surprising. Strikes are proliferating. The inflation rate is re-accelerating—and this despite the pound exchange rate bolstered up by North Sea Oil. And there is some rise in unemployment. Now all this may be temporary—merely the necessary transition to a peaceful and prosperous market economy. Thatcher's admirers hope so, but historical experience suggests a certain scepticism and a reservation of judgement.

After further asides to his old teacher Joseph Schumpeter and to capitalism being economically stable but politically and socially unstable, Samuelson said,

> Now what I am stating is not a new idea. Karl Marx, of course, stressed the economic interpretation of history, but Macaulay, the historian (no Marxist he), warned that if the suffrage is made universal, the mob will come to act to try to equalize the distribution of income. And long before Marx—Madison, Hamilton, and John Adams had recognized that the privileges and prerequisite of private property would be imperiled by populist democracy. Schumpeter, in his heart of hearts, could draw but one conclusion from his analysis; he intended not to publish this conclusion, but I knew him well and I can bear testimony. He essentially arrived at the conclusion drawn by that so-called ideologue of fascism, Vilfredo Pareto: *undemocratic force will in the end have to be used to impose upon a society the capitalist mode of economic organization.*

In contrast to Samuelson's ideas on the class struggle and social instability, Friedman envisioned a social market economy (Samuelson's capitalism) with social mobility, as the next chapter emphasizes. The poor are not permanently poor. Even for the temporarily poor, a "safety net" of programs, to use a term that came out in the early months of the Reagan presidency in the U.S., is envisioned. The capitalist ethic and its related voluntary association must be widely understood and supported. To be sure, as attributed to Samuelson:

> To be healthy and stable,...a free society—one in which individuals are free to hold conflicting ideas and pursue ends of their own

choosing—must somehow arrive at shared ethical values. Shared values are those that most people believe to be in both the society's and their own interests. Those who violate such ethical principles usually recognize their deviance and experience guilt.[113]

An Overview

Democracy as we know it in the U.S. and Britain has an intimate link with Thomas Jefferson's efforts to draft a constitution for the U.S., in the one instance, and with Adam Smith's *Wealth of Nations*, in both instances. Smith's was among the early statements of economic freedom and Friedman's has been among the more recent on political freedom. As the economics and political systems emerged in the 19th century, capitalism appeared as a necessary condition for political freedom.

Smith and his more immediate followers saw the interrelationship between the political and the economic, but with the widespread acceptance of the competitive market in Britain following the middle of the 19th century, mainstream economists are credited with having given attention to the Robinson Crusoe economics that separated economics from the "polity." There was attention to an instrumental, problem solving approach that gave rise to the view of economics as "the study of the principles governing the allocation of scarce means among competing ends when the object is to maximize the attainment of the ends." In this view economics was separate, such that ethical considerations, uncertainty about economic outcomes, and stable monetary policies were taken for granted.

In time, Friedman's teacher Frank Knight took special views of the predominating economics, as had others on other occasions. Friedman was influenced by him, in part in the issues he addressed, and departed from him. He did this in such a way as to put the polity back into economics. He had the individual both influencing and being influenced by institutions. Juxtaposing Knight and Friedman further, we see that Knight viewed economics as an "assumer science," which is normative and "welfare-economics" oriented, and which led to the public-choice economics of James Buchanan's group; emphasized freedom and radical moral individualism which led Knight toward the study of ethical and social detail; looked at a political consensus analogous to the consensus found among scientists in a community of scientists which he saw as the ideal type of ethical association; favored the advocacy of economic principles and views, even while looking askance at the role of persuasion; viewed persuasion as a sort of social conditioning and false argument, and combined it with individualism to yield a view of the dual nature of man; and took on an anti-science view of economics (defined as the study of choice with respect to scarce resources to achieve competing ends).

In contrast, we see that Friedman deemphasized attention to detail, particularly with respect to the descriptive-truth component of axioms; adopted a variant of instrumentalism, as in chapter 4, as he moved economics along as an empirical policy-oriented science; accepted the method of the physical sciences, even as he recognized special problems in its application to the study of social/economic behavior; set freedom as the highest goal, which he saw as fostered by dispersing power; viewed the market as a means of dispersing power, along with the international gold-flows mechanism of the last chapter—and, at the same time, had the market coordinate culturally, ethnically diverse social entities into a harmonious whole; had the market system relieve the government of having to make politically destabilizing decisions about the distribution of income and related privileges; gave important roles to persuasion, advocacy, social debate, and the possibility of deception in the short run; saw hypothesis testing as a part of destructive criticism and extended it to ongoing social debate, as distinct from Knight's moral code and "ideal type of ethical association"; and adopted a long-run time frame, both in data analysis and political debate. There is, in the latter respect, Dicey's attention to long trends of opinion and Friedman's quoting Lincoln about the public not being deceived in the long run.

In the context of persuasion and political debate, Friedman showed considerable powers of persuasion in support of his reforming ideas. In this he was like Britain's J. M. Keynes.

Friedman's main political-economic tract is *Capitalism and Freedom*, although it is supplemented by numerous other writings.[114] The principles of *Capitalism and Freedom* center about the dispersion of power in government and in business and the protection of dissenting individuals. In dispersing power, the units are set as checks and balances in relation to one another. Freedom, we say, arises from an absence of coercion by monopoly, in one case, and from the ultimate limitation imposed by requiring an essential consensus on certain important matters such as the protection of free speech.

There should be a choice in employment and in the goods and services exchanged in the market. The scope of government is limited by leaving numerous decisions to the households and by allowing for the coordination of activities through the market.

The freedom thus obtained encompasses the freedom of individuals to advocate certain causes and changes in society through persuasion as opposed to coercion. Such advocacy, however, should not be without costs. This assures greater stability in the political/economic/social systems but provides for change also.

Morals and values are individual and social matters and effecting changes in them is best left to persuasion rather than force. Freedom is largely freedom to dissent, and freedom becomes the highest goal of a free society, as envisioned by Friedman. Short of a general self-denying ordinance, minority interests are best served by their not relying upon a special majority for the objectives of equality and social justice.

A system coordinated through the market place with attention to individual interest is an efficient economic system and releases creative impulses. However, an economic system itself is neither moral nor immoral, materialistic nor humane. The system is best judged by its results and the values it encourages. By these standards, history suggests that a moral climate flourishes where individuals are most responsible for their actions.[115] "In order for a society to be at once humane and to give opportunity for great human achievements it is necessary that the small minority of people who do not have materialistic objectives have the greatest degree of freedom." The market oriented society is the only society to have come close to achieving the greatest degree of freedom for the non-materialistic.

The market and social systems are not perfect, and we address them more in terms of abstractions.[116] "In the actual world we are always dealing with approximations, with more or less. In the actual world we always have impediments to voluntary exchange." These impediments concern technical monopoly, the need to address "neighborhood effects" (as on third parties not directly involved in the two sides of a transaction), and conflicts. Neighborhood effects, such as the destruction of the natural environment and wilderness by unfettered enterprise, can be a reason for expanding the activities of government. However, they may "cut both ways" and hence also be a reason for limiting the activities of government. Conflicts arise as we defend ethical and moral values, engage in persuasion (in lieu of force), and as we widen the range of issues that must be decided by a bare majority rule rather than the proportional representation provided by the market.

The foregoing are abstractions. To give concrete meaning to them Friedman considered a variety of particular problems including in one source, "the energy crisis," and including in other sources "the negative income tax," "the minimum wage," "housing," and "social security," and ranging in *Capitalism and Freedom* over "the control of money," "international financial and trade arrangements," "fiscal policy," "the role of education in government," "capitalism and discrimination," "monopoly and the social responsibility of business and labor," "occupational licensure," "the distribution of income," "social welfare measures," and "alleviation of poverty."[117] A major area receiving the attention of Keynesians, social engineers, Friedman, and others is that of the distribution of income with special attention to government efforts at its redistribution. Here Friedman departed from the Knight/Simon Chicago school, and from the Keynesians as the next chapter attests.

Chapter 13
The Distribution and Permanency of Income

There are major strands of thought in economics about the distribution of income with attention to government's involvement in its redistribution, mainly through tax and transfer payments. These strands appear in the British tradition of economics and also involve Karl Marx and American Keynesians, as Samuelson's positions in the last chapter indicate.

As we may recall from chapter 2 (pp. 52-55), Marx drew on Ricardo and espoused a labor theory of value. In Marx's hands it suggested that all the value of production was attributable in effect to a homogeneous mass of workers. Marx was very much aware, of course, that labor is unequal—that the bourgeois "tacitly recognizes unequal individual endowments and thus productive capacity as natural privileges." He said in fact, "One man is superior to another physically or mentally and so supplies more labor in the same time, or can labor for a longer time."[1] But for abstract purposes of his doctrine, labor was to be measurable *"only as workers* and nothing more is seen in them, everything else must be ignored."

Thus, after rejecting the principle underlying the bourgeois distribution of income, Marx proceeded to espouse what has been called the Ruskinian premise, after John Ruskin (1819-1900), English art critic and economist.[2] As quoted from Marx below, it is suggestive of the extent to which Ruskin inspired opposition to a laissez-faire philosophy. On the premise, one may paraphrase Ruskin's disciple, John A. Hobson, who said "that a quantity of goods attains maximum value when distributed according to the greatest need." Fain also found essentially this same notion in Ruskin's "Munera Pulveris."[3]

In the specific quotation attributed to him, Marx said: "From each according to his ability, to each according to his needs!"[4] Following the communist revolution, the state consequently was to perform the job of redistribution of income along Ruskinian lines.

Marshall's and Keynes's assumptions were not as extreme as those of Marx, but one posited the declining marginal utility of income and the other the declining marginal propensity to consume, with essentially the same result as that found in Ruskin, namely: that some total of social utility (or consumer spending, as the case may be) was enhanced by a more equal distribution of income.[5] In their respective static contexts, both notions lent themselves to the view—perhaps the common view in the history of the United States since Keynes wrote[6]—that society was better off, its agents happier, with moderation in the distribution, such as may be

493

brought about by government intervention. The primary idea underlying the redistribution efforts and embodied in the simple, static utility of income and consumption function curves was straight forward, namely: low income households had higher utility (consumption) from extra income than did higher income households. By taxing away the income from the high income household and transferring it through government transfer payments to the low income household, the total utility (consumption) would be greater than before the transfer. A secondary and most often unstated idea underlying advocacy (or approval) of the redistribution of income is that somehow the redistribution can take place without altering the amount of the product to be distributed.

On these Keynesian times, government services, and redistribution efforts, Friedman commented:

> Expenditures on the traditional services can and do generate discontent about waste and inefficiency, but they do not set group against group. Expenditures for social security, welfare, medicare, Medicaid and other transfer programs, as well as for the host of new regulatory agencies, also generate discontent about waste and inefficiency. But in addition they involve taking from some to give to others, or imposing some people's values on other people. In the process, they inevitably set group against group.
>
> Our government has been changing from a service state through which we jointly finance activities from which all or most of us benefit to a paternal state that increasingly decided for us what is good for us and increasingly redistributes income, taking from some and giving to others. Those who pay are understandably unhappy—but so are most of those who receive. They know that their cause is just and that they should get still more.[7]

The capitalist ethic always paralleled these views on equality in the distribution. In recent times, its formation has become more polished than as encountered in Marx's statement of it,[8] but essentially it has held that income should be distributed as payment for the value added to production by the addition of one's labor or capital to the production process. When initially confronted with this ethic and the opposing Ruskinian premise, Friedman vacillated in the selection of one or the other, on the grounds there was no scientific basis for choice. In time, he found the only basis for logical choice by setting some higher goal. It was freedom, with voluntary association among the social units playing a key role, as the last chapter attests.

With his early background in mathematical statistics and personal probability, moreover, Friedman abandoned the assumption of declining marginal utility of income, and found support for an alternative to the simple Keynesian consumption function. On these bases of logic and empirical research, often complemented with other results from data, decisive views about the distribution of income—indeed about government redistribution—followed. Milton Friedman addressed the matters with a consistency and breadth that has been unparalleled since Marx's time.[9] As his friend Leo Rosten quoted from Oscar Wilde's *Picture of Dorian Gray* with reference to him:

> I can stand brute force, but brute reason is quite unbearable. There is something unfair about its use. It is hitting below the intellect.

In addition, some of Friedman's critics might question "his judgment and ultimate political wisdom," but these qualities, of course, are not the same as truth and logic.

In any case, having set freedom as a goal by 1962, other cornerstones of Friedman's system of thinking came forward. Drawing on chapters 11 and 12, these were (1) his consumption function vis-à-vis the Keynesian function and (2) the perfect competition model where power is dispersed the most. The first gets us into dynamics and social mobility, as opposed to rigid income classes and the static utility and consumption function bases for progressive taxation and income redistribution via the government tax and income-transfer powers. In the dynamic function there is social mobility in that households are not permanently in a given income position over a long period of time. Some find themselves better off than others, the circumstances of the time play a role, and the poor/rich are not permanently poor/rich. In any case, there must be incentives and social underpinnings to support upward striving, and the incantation and support of the work ethic and other culture matters play their supportive roles in encouraging more social mobility.

As taken up in the last chapter with respect to morals and self-reliance, an economic system must be judged by its performance, by the values it encourages. An economic system is true to the values it encourages. Charitable instincts are important. A negative income tax is one means of setting a floor to personal income and reducing the harshness of adversity in an economic system that calls for a relatively high level of understanding about the system's rules and workings on the part of the "actors" and "players," and that places a burden of responsibility upon the individual.

The second important cornerstone—with the attention to freedom developed in the last chapter—brings attention to a personal income tax structure that was first given its particular underpinnings by Friedman in 1962, namely: "a flat-rate tax on income above an exemption with income defined very broadly and deductions allowed only for strictly defined expenses of earning income."[10] Over time Friedman kept the flat-rate tax under discussion. By the early 1980s we encounter variants of the original notion and related argument.[11] It comes forward in tax reform proposals, public statements by Ronald Reagan, and the Reagan-supported Tax Reform Act of 1986 (the most sweeping rewrite of the tax code since it was enacted in 1913).

The Saga

In the saga of the distribution of income, we start with David Ricardo, traverse a few lines in and out of the British tradition of capitalism, and then encounter Milton Friedman. Somewhat outside the system, but proceeding from Ricardo's partial labor theory of value, we encounter Karl Marx, as introduced in chapter 2. Returning to the main tradition, we encounter Alfred Marshall and then proceeding tendentiously again along the main accepted lines of thought, we brush once more with the Keynesians. The public issue about the distribution of income and freedom touches upon justice, entitlement to income, the paternal state, ethical considerations generally, unemployment, minimum wages, inheritance, the progressive income tax, the use of force, freedom, social mobility, free choice, and constitutional limitations.

Less immediately involved in the link between Ricardo and Marx is John Stuart Mill (pp. 50-52). Mill was the first major figure in economics to separate the theory about production from that of how the final product was to be distributed. The much later writer and Nobel laureate, Friedrich von Hayek, credited Mill in the British context of introducing the highly damaging concept of social justice to societal development.

In some measure, perhaps because of the breadth of Friedman's thinking and the timing of his ministration, there was some of Ricardo's approach in him. The abstract, bare-bone method is clearly present, but one hundred and fifty years more or less and the entry of the modern computer upon the scene separate their professional work and hence enhance the opportunities for empirical research. In addition, Friedman is more characterized by an optimistic outlook about prospects for social movement and opportunities in a voluntary exchange economy.

Ricardo, in fact, has been pictured as having viewed the workers, "undifferentiated units of economic energy," as being "condemned by their own weakness to a life at the margin of subsistence."[12] These workers got their bare subsistence, and Ricardo held no great prospects for their showing enough "self-restraint" and control to alter their lot. They are, further, accompanied in the society by capitalists and landlords, with only the latter's lot an easy one. The capitalist/entrepreneur organizes things and thus serves a function in the pursuit of profits, but competition erases undue profits which in turn hold wages down, while the landlords benefit from the organization and gain an income called "rent" from the ownership of the limited and most productive land in the presence of a growing population. For Ricardo, the landlords did little and thereby Ricardo was led to oppose the protective Corn Laws that favored the landlords and to stress the advantages of free trade and thus to permit the importation of lower priced grain to Britain.

The Corn Laws and trade aside, however, the value of the products of society for Ricardo, measured in more recent times by Gross National Product (GNP), embodied mostly labor and some capital, as revealed by the title "Ricardo and the 93 Per Cent Labor Theory of Value."[13] In time, Ricardo's work on labor's contribution to the value of products served Karl Marx and his strongly supportive and loyal collaborator Friedrich Engels.

In effect, the labor theory of value justified the overthrow of the capitalist, and the socialist premise associated with Ruskin dealt with the question of the distribution of income once capital was removed from the scene. The dictatorship of Marx's proletariat was to achieve this, pending a time when social behavior was so conditioned as to no longer require government.

In contrast to Marx in particular—but also along with a host of other economists in his time—Friedman saw a far more dynamic/evolutionary society, with less of the historical determinism associated earlier with Marx. The pursuit of profits and self interest was still present in Friedman's abstract system of thought, as was the desire to bequeath wealth.[14] In addition, however, self-sacrifice, creative initiatives, and charitable instincts were present.

These latter characteristics of behavior are strongest in a free society. The cornerstones to such a system are: a cultural heritage that leads people to seek out opportunities for self and social improvement; a theory of consumer behavior that embodies social mobility and dynamic analytic properties; a theory of evolving, nonrepetitive changes that serves to limit and otherwise mitigate the effects of private monopolies; adverse effects of business and production (as with those on the environment and from pollution) that must be dealt with politically by voting rather than market arrangements; a marginal productivity theory of labor and capital; a distinction between human and non-human capital that blurs the distinctions drawn by earlier writers between labor per se and real capital as an accumulation of prior gains from foregoing consumption; and roles for competition in ideas, for religion and other ethical and cultural aspects of society, and for persuasion. Nevertheless, the economic system is "true to the values it encourages, supports, and develops in the people who live under that system."[15]

The system, as viewed by Friedman, encourages moral behavior, places a burden on the individual and also in part shifts an emphasis to the responsibility of the individual for his behavior. As a floor to the harshness in the competitive system as historically envisioned by many, and as an improvement over many of the preponderance of welfare schemes associated with government, we find in Friedman's economic system opposition to minimum wages as a means of redistributing income and a substitution of the negative income tax for the host of welfare programs.[16] In some respects Friedman may be said to have placed too much emphasis on his own cultural heritage, even to the extent of arguing against the minimum wage laws that have often been viewed as a cornerstone for income redistribution schemes of the self appointed and politically appointed welfare reformers.

In addressing the unemployment and inflationary-induced aspects of minimum wages, some have drawn on the analytic and theoretic bases for wage and price guidelines.[17] These have most notably been those found in the economic reports of the president in the early 1960s. They held that wage increases on the average are noninflationary where they do not exceed the average growth in productivity (defined as output per worker). According to such guidelines, the increases in minimum wages are neutral in their effects on employment and inflation, where there are increases equivalent to the average trend rate of growth in real output per worker.

Friedman, however, viewed the presence of any minimum wage laws as opposing the interests of the poor and the unemployed, as did Ronald Reagan later. Friedman's analysis and his attention to his own background are of interest in the foregoing respect. First the analysis:

> *Playboy*: But you prefer the laissez-faire—free enterprise—approach.
>
> *Friedman*: Generally. Because I think the Government solution to a problem is usually as bad as the problem and very often makes the problem worse. Take, for example, the minimum wage, which has the effect of making the poor people at the bottom of the wage scale—those it was designed to help—worse off than before.
>
> *Playboy*: How so?
>
> *Friedman*: If you really want to get a feeling about the minimum wage, there's nothing more instructive than going to the Congressional documents to read the proposals to raise the minimum wage and see who testifies. You very seldom find poor people testifying in favor of the minimum wage. The people who do are those who receive or pay wages much higher than the minimum. Frequently Northern textile manufacturers. John F. Kennedy, when he was in Congress, said explicitly that he was testifying in

favor of a rise in the minimum wage because he wanted protection for the New England textile industry against competition from the so-called cheap labor of the South. But now look at it from the point of that cheap labor. If a high minimum wage makes unfeasible an otherwise feasible venture in the South, are people in the South benefited or harmed? Clearly harmed, because jobs otherwise available for them are no longer available. A minimum-wage law is, in reality, a law that makes it illegal for an employer to hire a person with limited skills.

Playboy: Isn't it, rather, a law that requires employers to pay a fair and livable wage?

Friedman: How is a person better off unemployed at a dollar sixty an hour than employed at a dollar fifty? No hours a week at a dollar sixty comes to nothing. Let's suppose there's a teenager whom you as an employer would be perfectly willing to hire for a dollar fifty an hour. But the law says, no it's illegal for you to hire him at a dollar fifty an hour. You must hire him at a dollar sixty. Now if you hire him at a dollar sixty, you're really engaging in an act of charity. You're paying a dollar fifty for his services and you're giving him a gift of ten cents. That's something few employers, quite naturally, are willing to do or can *afford* to do without being put out of business by less generous competitors. As a result, the effect of a minimum-wage law is to produce unemployment among people with low skills. And who are the people with low skills? In the main, they tend to be teenagers and blacks, and women who have no special skills or have been out of the labor force and are coming back. This is why there are abnormally high unemployment rates among these groups.[18]

With respect to his own background (pp. 18-21), Friedman restated the minimum wage position, as initially stated in *Capitalism and Freedom*.[19] The restatement concerning his background said:

My mother came to this country when she was 14 years old. She worked in a sweatshop as a seamstress, and it was only because there *was* such a sweatshop in which she could get a job that she was able to come to the U.S. But she didn't stay in the sweatshop and neither did most of the others. It was a way station for them, and a far better one than anything available to them in the old country. And she never thought it was anything else. I must say that I find it slightly revolting that people sneer at a system that's made it possible for them to sneer at it. If we'd had minimum-wage laws and all the other trappings of the welfare state in the

19th Century, half the readers of *Playboy* would either not exist at all or be citizens of Poland, Hungary or some other country. And there would be no *Playboy* for them to read.[20]

On his parents' background and the initiatives released by an essentially free society, Friedman further states the following:

> My parents came to this country in the 1890's. Like millions of others they came with empty hands. They were able to find a place in this country to build a life for themselves and to provide a basis on which their children and their children's children could have a better life.... And it was possible only because there was an essentially free society.[21]

The negative income tax provides a floor that in effect lessens the impact of poverty, which Friedman is inclined to think of as temporary because of the incentive to improve one's income position, given an appreciation of the values encouraged by the social market economy (or, say, that provided by the cultural background of immigrants of an earlier time). The matters come out early on in a dialogue between Daniel Schorr, CBS News Correspondent, and Friedman. At that time, the tax, as initially advanced by Friedman, was being offered as an improvement over prevailing welfare programs and an experiment just undertaken by the government was introduced.[22] Schorr described the tax as it would work in 1969:

> There are many different formulas, but here is one of the more conservative. Under the present tax set-up, for a man with a wife and two children, $3,000 a year is a kind of dividing line. If that's all he makes, his standard exemptions and deductions cancel out his earnings, and he pays no taxes. If he makes more than $3,000, he owes the government money. Under the Negative Income Tax, if a man made less than $3,000, that would be called negative income and the government would owe him money, a negative tax.
>
> A family with no income at all would get 50 percent of that $3,000 base, or $1,500. Anything they earned would reduce their guarantee, but only partially, as an incentive to work. A man making $1,000 a year would lose only half that amount, $500, from his guarantee. A man making $2,500 would lose $1,250. But by keeping 50 cents of every dollar he earns, a man would always be better off working than by living solely on his guarantee.

The dialogue otherwise proceeded as follows:

Distribution and Permanency of Income 501

Would you ask a family of four to live on $1,500?

Friedman: Well, in almost all states in the United States, this is well above the sum on which we are now asking a family of four to live. However, we're talking at the moment about a national system, like the national positive income tax. Just as New York State has a state income tax on top of the national income tax, so it would be highly appropriate for New York State to have a state negative income tax on top of the national negative income tax. And that would mean that this $1,500 would be the minimum amount that any family of four anywhere in the United States would be able to get, would be entitled to under the law.

The negative income tax Friedman was arguing for in the 1960s was to be an improvement over the then current welfare system.[23] Not everyone below the poverty level was expected to respond. The Schorr-Friedman dialogue proceeded:

Schorr: What is the greatest advantage of your negative income tax system as against the present welfare system?

Friedman: Under present welfare arrangements, in most states if a man goes out and works, he gets—he loses the whole of his additional earnings; here he has the incentive which is provided by getting half of those earnings. The other thing that I think is very important about this is that everybody's treated the same. We all of us file an income tax return. Some of us have a high income above the break-even point; we pay taxes. Some of us have a low income, as in the case of the man we were just talking about; we receive something. There isn't any demeaning distinction between two classes of people as there is under our present welfare system.

Schorr: You're making, it seems to me, certain assumptions, that if you could keep part of what you earn that you would have an incentive to go to work and get off negative income tax or any kind of public assistance. Are you sure this would work:

Friedman: It wouldn't work for everybody. There are always going to be some people who are going to—who are going to be satisfied to take $1,500 a year, let's say, for a family of four, and make no effort whatsoever and stay there. But I think a hundred years of American history is pretty strong evidence that it would work for most people. There is not in our history any experience of any large group of people, however poor they were, however indigent they were, who when they were given the opportunity to get jobs and to earn income with an incentive to do, didn't do so. So I don't think that that's a very real problem.

Continuing with reference to Friedman's overall economic system, cultural heterogeneity, competition for ideas, religious groups vie for their sets of values. The route of persuasion is open to the religious and other groups, and preaching a work ethic is not beyond those activities nor unrelated to the economist's theory of price.[24] Through competition in the areas of ethics and social values, persuasion is available to treat the otherwise permanence of poverty and thus lead the behavioral units of the economic system to a live-to-work (as opposed to work-to-live) behavior that is compatible with dynamic change. Further, in the presence of the negative income tax feature as a part of the tax, redistribution-of-income system, "There isn't any demeaning distinction between two classes of people as there is under our present [say 1969] welfare system."[25]

Two features of Friedman's approach to economics overall that bear on his addressing issues about the way the world ought to work (i.e., issues of normative economics) are: an economic system must be judged by the results it leads to, and there is no perfect economic (theoretical) system. On the factual/empirical side, a truly free economic system has never existed (by analogy to Euclidean geometry, a line without width and depth has never been seen); "In the actual world we always have impediments to voluntary exchange." Materialism is not an absolute quality of one economic system or another, so we must be guided by the qualities of one in relation to another (by the values one system encourages in relation to another) and by the results obtained from a comparison of alternative systems.[26] For Friedman these comparisons were to be made as a part of a factual/empirical economics.

For Karl Marx and Friedrich Engels, in contrast, the comparison of the existing capitalist system they described was with an ideal, a Utopian fantasy. An early work by Engels entitled "The Principles of Communism" contained a theme regarding the organization of the future communist economy ("the economic and technical assumptions on which the communist economy must rest") that was to follow the collapse of capitalism.[27] But, beyond this, and Engels proclaiming the task for economic science to uncover "the elements of the future new organization of production and exchange," Marx made no serious attempt to note what the future would be like. It was simply to be an economic and technological Utopia that would evolve given historical determinism and the socialization of the proletarians.[28] As Friedman frequently pointed out, there has been ever since, a tendency among academic, media, and other people to judge the communist/socialist system by its ideals rather than its performance.[29]

Essentially for Marx and Engels, as set forth mainly in the "Manifesto of the Communist Party,"[30] a sequence of events was attained: competition among the workers and overpopulation in industrial society drove the wages to a subsistence minimum; the livelihood was increasingly associ-

Distribution and Permanency of Income

ated with machinery and mass production such that commercial crisis led to mass unemployment, the combining of workers in Trades Unions, and hence the "industrial reserve army"; the army, made up of the proletariat, and guided by the intellectuals, was to overthrow the capitalist and bourgeoisie (exclusive of the intellectuals who went over to the proletarian's side); and the conquest of political power by the proletariat leads to a clean sweep of "the old conditions of production" and ultimately to the "abolition of its own supremacy as a class."[31] "In place of the old bourgeois society," Marx and Engels said, "we have an association, in which the free development of each is the condition for the free development of all."

In the foregoing sequence one encounters minimum wages—i.e., "that quantum of the means of subsistence, which is absolutely requisite to keep the laborer in bare existence as a laborer." There are also the "grave-diggers," created to bury the bourgeoisie,[32] and, as encountered later in Marx, "economic apologetics."[33] "The economic apologist," he said, "interprets this operation which 'fixes' capital and by that very act sets laborers 'free,' in exactly the opposite way, pretending that it sets free capital for the laborers." The Trades Unions try to work out some cooperation between the employed and the unemployed "in order to destroy or to weaken the ruinous effects of this natural law of capitalistic production on their class..." No sooner do they do so, however, than the capital and its "sycophant, political economy," cry out at the infringement of the 'eternal' and so to say 'sacred' law of supply and demand."[34]

One encounters early on in Marx the measures by which the proletariat is to "wrest" capital from the bourgeoisie. These consist of a list of ten means:

1. Abolition of property in land and application of all rents of land to public purposes.
2. A heavy progressive or graduated income tax.
3. Abolition of all rights of inheritance.
....
10. Free education for all children in public schools. Abolition of children's factory labor in its present form. Combination of education with industrial production, etc. etc.[35]

The Emergence of the Flat-Rate Tax View

As we have seen from earlier chapters, Friedman engaged himself almost entirely in the factual/empirical part of economics and in statistics from the 1933-34 school year at Columbia until well into the mid-1950s, when he started the first series of lectures on capitalism and freedom. There were, however, some distracting interludes, including an editorial experience at the National Bureau on the second volume of the Bureau's *Studies in Income and Wealth*, the 1941 to 1943 years in the Division of Tax Resources at the Treasury, and the early post-WW II experience on a book dealing with rent control. The review of these interludes reveals that Friedman had not yet formed the decisive views on the distribution of income aspect of normative economics that were to emerge. As his views did emerge after the 1946 book, they differed from the views of the earlier Chicago school, and Frank Knight in particular. With respect to the capitalist ethic, they placed Friedman rather clearly on the right of Hotelling's line (pp. 409-410), and remained a part of Friedman's normative economics.

In the editorial experience Friedman chided colleagues Copeland and Martin for introducing what he considered "ideologically biased analysis" (in other words, essentially ethical issues) into their work concerning in part the distribution of income.[36] Friedman asserted in his criticism of Copeland's and Martin's ethical predilections the following:

> Under a laissez faire economy individuals may be able to obtain the value product attributable to their activities; but this is fundamentally different from saying that such a system of distribution is ethically desirable. "To each according to his abilities" may be the rule; "from each according to his abilities, to each according to his needs" may nevertheless be the ethical objective.[37]

Next, at the Treasury from 1941 to 1943, Friedman was assigned to the early studies dealing with the withholding of income tax, a tax on spending, with aspects of forced saving as a means of controlling inflation, and with the withholding of income tax at the source.[38] Faced with the question of whether to raise the tax on income or instead to supplement the then existing income tax with a tax on spending," Friedman devised the spending tax (in later years viewed as a National Sales tax or value-added tax, VAT), supported it, and subsequently published an article analyzing it.[39] The devised tax was opposed within the Treasury by the Internal Revenue System (IRS) and later defeated in the Congress, Rose Friedman said, because under the influence of Harry White the tax had been presented "in the form of compulsory savings instead of a tax."[40] Continuing, she said, "The combination of two novel ideas served to make it unacceptable to the Congress and it was never enacted."

Also devised in this 1941-43 period was a U.S. plan (Germany and Britain already had such plans) for withholding the income tax at the source—"That is, the deduction by employers of an advance estimate of taxes due from the paycheck of employees." As R. Friedman further noted, "Prior to that time, taxes had been paid each year on the prior year's income." The introduction of withholding raised certain problems, and it was opposed by the IRS (the agency charged with collecting the tax). They insisted, R. Friedman said, "That it was not administratively feasible to collect taxes at the source, that the adjustments after the year was over would be too complicated to handle." She said, "It took months of discussion, of sending joint teams from the Division of Tax Research and the IRS out into the field to study payroll procedures, and of insistence from the Secretary of the Treasury to overcome the objections of the IRS."[41]

From the experience with the IRS as with later experiences with the Federal Reserve System (as Friedman observed, happens regularly), Friedman was impressed by the "law of bureaucratic inertia." That law he stated:

> Every large bureaucracy, government or private is certain that the way it conducts its affairs is the only way that they can be conducted.[42]

Continuing Friedman said:

> If today you were to ask a high Internal Revenue Service official whether income taxes could be collected without a withholding system, he would consign you to the loony bin. But in 1942, when we were devising our system, the IRS was the chief obstacle to its adoption. Its bureaucrats insisted that the way they were collecting the income tax was the only feasible way; that we were starry-eyed theorists to suppose that withholding at source was administratively feasible.

Rose Friedman herself expressed the view that withholding at the source is "a mistaken policy in peacetime." She said, "because it has eased the task of government in taking more and more purchasing power from individuals and transferring it to government." M. Friedman, moreover, noted: "My wife has still not forgiven me for participating in that project [withholding at the source]."[43]

Finally, in the rent-control episode (p. 152), Friedman and his colleague George Stigler from University of Minnesota at the time came out in favor of a free market solution to the housing shortage left in the wake of WW II:

1. In a free market, there is always some housing immediately available for rent—at all rent levels.
2. The bidding up of rents forces some people to economize on space. *Until there is sufficient new construction, this doubling up is the only solution.*

3. The high rents act as a strong stimulus to new construction.
4. No complex, expensive, and expansive machinery is necessary. The rationing is conducted quietly and impersonally through the price system.[44]

Having done this, Friedman and Stigler—as would have characterized their former teacher, Frank Knight—showed sensitivity to an egalitarian view about income equality that was to get them in controversy with and over the libertarian views of their "interest group" sponsorship.[45] On the income equality they wrote:

> The fact that, under free market conditions, better quarters go to those who have larger incomes or more wealth is, if anything, simply a reason for taking long-term measures to reduce the inequality of income and wealth. For those, like us, who would like even more equality than there is at present, not alone for housing but for all products, it is surely better to attack directly existing inequalities in income and wealth at their source than to ration each of the hundreds of commodities and services that compose our standard of living. It is the height of folly to permit individuals to receive unequal money incomes and then to take elaborate and costly measures to prevent them from using their incomes.[46]

The interest-group sponsor, Leonard E. Read, appended the following note to the passage:

> The authors fail to state whether the "long-term measures" which they would adopt go beyond elimination of special privilege, such as monopoly now protected by government. In any case, however, the significance of their argument at this point deserves special notice. It means that, even from the standpoint of those who put equality above justice and liberty, rent controls are "the height of folly."

So, as noted, the sponsor objected to the view about "long-term measures to reduce the inequality of income and wealth," and a vocal segment of the profession at large objected to the espousal of free market sentiments. The controversial aspect of this, as dealt with by Silk, could be overdrawn but, as he suggested, it apparently made Friedman more aware of the conflicts within himself—more aware of the positive economic dimensions going back to Wesley Mitchell, on the one hand, and the normative dimensions going back to Knight, on the other. Friedman indeed saw the two entwined and resolved the income distribution matter by favoring the results from voluntary cooperation in a relatively free, exchange market context with a flat rate income tax.[47]

On the positive aspect of controversy in the normative (the-way-the-world-ought-to-work) sphere, he stressed that economists and others disagree most about the means of achieving the economic goals than about the goals themselves. As arose in chapter 4, he saw this disagreement about means mainly as being disagreement over a choice between the alternative A and B means (p. 112). Drawing on Mitchell, he saw this as giving added importance to empirical study about the effects of policy A as opposed to B and so on. "I don't believe," he said, "the kind of people whom we're talking about—the kind of people in the American academic scene—differ fundamentally in the objectives they want to pursue"[48] (note, however, that Friedman differed with Galbraith on the grounds of social values, p. 203). Continuing, he added:

> They differ on how to pursue them, and differences in their predictions about what will happen if you do this and that...And so it is, I guess, it's always seemed to me more useful and more interesting to try and assemble evidence on how things are, what they are.

Ethics, Choice, Chance, and Taxation

Marx and Engels favored the use of the taxing powers of the state to redistribute income and, though less harsh in other respects on those seeking and possessing wealth, the tradition inherent in Marshall's assumption of the utility of income and in Keynesian economics has been along similar lines. In the respective cases, moreover, there was either class struggle with minimum wages at an absolute subsistence level or a relative permanence attached to one's income station in life. For Marx in particular, there was in addition, the 100 percent labor theory of value. This—along with Marx's early views of history, natural forces leading to subsistence minimum wage, inherent commercial crises, unemployment, and revolution—accompanied a list of means for wresting capital from the hourglass and hence for achieving a redistribution of income. Indeed, no matter what the form of production, it was reducible to labor directly or indirectly. Thus, Marx saw no room for profit and the ownership of capital.

The serious flaws in the foregoing socialist thinking, as Friedman pointed out indirectly, centered about the failure to recognize the role of time-preference in foregoing consumption, the tendency for income positions to be temporary in most cases, under free institutions with appropriate cultural underpinnings. The time preference was that for present over future consumption, as set forth in "appendix one" to chapter 16.[49] Economic "agents," the players, the behavioral units, as it were, required some form of inducement for foregoing present consumption in order to provide for future consumption (or, for setting aside the "seed corn" for the future planting, harvesting, and next round of consumption). There was, in other words, the need for some form of inducement (or force, in the case of the socialist, or mixed socialist-capitalist state) to encourage capital accumulation through saving (i.e., through foregoing present consumption).

Not anticipated, moreover, was the role of human capital, and the prospects that industry would not forever move toward the employment of an ever-increasing share of workers in mass production pursuits.[50] Indeed, the Marx/Engels model of the capitalist/industrial state was heavily influenced by Manchester, England where Engels worked first from 1842 to 1844 and then from 1849 to 1869. In the writing of *Das Kapital*, as in his other economic writings, Marx drew primarily from Engels's experience in the textile, industrial center of Manchester and from the general background of writing on the part of the classical British economists.[51] Though Marx and Engels presented what may be called "a dynamic theory of capitalist economic development," economists in general, as well as Marx and Engels, were long in coming to a view of the world that extended beyond a fixed period of their experiences and that, in contrast, incorporated evolutionary, episodic sorts of changes. Friedman's attention to a stable relation in the presence of episodic change, as taken up in the next chapter, may be the closest an economist has come to a view of the world that was not dependent on just the data for the decades of one's own life.

The awareness of human capital as a factor called attention to the skills, and qualities that improve humans from an income potential point of view. Increasing skills increases the value of humans in employment and coincides with their being technicians, professional managers, risk bearers and the like. Next—as a matter of secular, long-run trend—the technology of mass production soon became a factor of increasing productivity per worker, and the displacement of labor in mass production pursuits; and the shifts toward a technostructure in large industrial concerns and enlarged service sectors placed greater emphasis on the individual qualities of initiative, service, and innovative risk-bearing activity.

These shifts were reinforced by the energy crisis that emerged dramatically in 1973, and the need to redirect human values away from the more essentially materialistic, natural-resource depleting aspects of consumer behavior.[52] Said differently, the same sort of technology and the accompanying historical determinism that Marx saw as leading inevitably to the demise of capitalism and the socialization of the means of production held forth several quite alternative prospects, notably: an enlarged scope of choice to the individuals in their various pursuits; prospects for altering consumption habits, certainly in the more technologically sophisticated centers of the world; and growth prospects for the capital embodied in humans that would more readily support their coping with a free, social market system that placed greater burdens upon the individual and culturally diverse units functioning in a single society. Indeed, Friedman asserted, "This great achievement of capitalism has not been the accumulation of property, it has been the opportunities it has offered to men and women to extend and to develop and improve their capabilities."

Thus Friedman addressed very early the two conflicting ethical principles: the Ruskinian one and the capitalist one which harbored what was called "supply-side" economics in the early years of the Reagan presidency in the U.S. As early as 1938, Friedman chided colleagues at the National Bureau for bringing into scientific inquiry such predilections as the capitalist ethic. Later in his capitalism and freedom lectures he said:

> I find it difficult to justify accepting or rejecting it [the capitalist ethic], or to justify any alternative principle. I am led to the view that it cannot in and of itself be regarded as an ethical principle; that it must be regarded as an instrument or corollary of some other principle such as freedom.

And so, Friedman did in fact set freedom as the highest goal, and through this route and its tie with voluntary exchange, he accepted the social market principle that an individual should receive the whole of what he adds to the product. Unless the individual receives his payment for his efforts in producing products, "he will enter into exchange on the basis of what he can receive rather than what he can produce." Continuing, in 1962 Friedman said, "Payment according to the product is therefore necessary in order that resources be used most effectively, at least under a system depending on voluntary cooperation.⁵³"

A number of the features of Friedman's normative system follow from the goal of freedom and its tie with voluntary exchange. First, he said that the system is "unlikely to be tolerated unless it is also regarded as yielding distributive justice."

Social stability requires this and hence a core of value judgments that are "unthinkingly" accepted by the bulk of the members of the society. Friedman of course held that society accepts (should accept) the notion of payment according to product, as such a value judgment.

Having set this value judgment forth as a key institution, an "absolute," Friedman came to favor a flat-rate income tax (with allowable deductions for only "strictly defined expenses of earning income") over a graduated one, on two major grounds: the logical ground that it interferes less with the efficiency of the economic system, freedom, and voluntary association; and the fact that it would generate more revenue than the progressive tax he knew with its exemptions and loopholes.⁵⁴ The flat-rate tax as introduced at the 1962 date by Friedman became highly visible in congressional discussions in 1982.

A feature of Friedman's economic system that followed from his view of human capital, the goal of freedom with its tie to voluntary exchange, and from the role of the "absolute" value judgment involves the distinction often drawn between inequality resulting from differences in personal capabilities and from differences in inherited wealth (personal capabilities aside). Friedman found these sources of inequality difficult to distinguish on grounds of equity, and to tax inherited wealth in the latter form and not the former for redistribution of wealth purposes would besides partially lessen efficiency and partly alter the allocation of wealth as to the two forms.[55] The system of inheritance and of payment for contribution to production does indeed lead to inequality in income. However, there is far less inequality in income in the long run, and here we enter into the facts about Friedman's more formerly formulated permanent income hypothesis.[56]

In addressing the causes of inequality in income, the probability background in Friedman comes out, along with the matter of attempting redistribution after knowing the outcomes.[57] From the uncertainty point of view, entering into life itself is like entering into a lottery. Thus, addressing differences in attitudes of individuals toward risk very early led Friedman to drop the assumption in economics whereby the marginal utility of wealth to the individual was declining. Friedman saw a wider range of possibilities. Further, the impact of the graduated tax structure on inequality of income and wealth is for Friedman much less a tax on being wealthy than on becoming wealthy, as Ronald Reagan later emphasized.[58] So the progressive income tax thus impedes the accumulation of wealth but does nothing to reduce the wealth of the wealthy.

In addition, Friedman did not find a confiscatory inheritance tax a solution to inequality. On the contrary, expressing bewilderment, he made an analogy: "I have never been able to understand the worth of equality that would chop the tall trees down to the level of the low ones." He concluded, "The equality I should like to see brings the low ones up."[59] Later in chapter 15, along this line, we encounter Britain's Margaret Thatcher, then in a cabinet post for education, saying "I have sometimes thought that extreme advocates of equality would be happy if all the children were in bad schools as long as they were equally bad..."

On the matter of material inheritance, Friedman differed most with those who saw it as placing others in a disadvantageous position.[60] He did not dispute the inescapable facts of inequity in inheritance whether in the genes or in material form. He simply did not see a feasible basis of distinction and, as stated above, he even saw the graduated income tax as a tax on getting wealth rather than as a tax on wealth. It has the effect of freezing the wealthy in their positions. This becomes especially so when the selected representatives respond to special interests, as taken up below, and in doing so add deductions and loopholes to the progressive tax for the very wealthy, partly as a means of assuring a needed flow of new plants and equipment and growth in the productivity of workers.

Early in his writing Friedman saw the effect of the graduated tax as one of discouraging entry into highly taxed activity, into "activities with large risk and nonpecuniary disadvantages." Friedman also saw this latter effect of the graduated tax as the reason for so many "loopholes" in the tax law. He mentioned in particular "percentage depletion, exemption of interest on state and municipal bonds, especially favorable treatment of capital gains, expense accounts, other indirect ways of payment, conversion of ordinary income into capital gains." These "loopholes," he said, "are nothing more than devices that allow people with relatively high incomes to avoid high taxes."[61]

In effect, government presses one set of laws to improve a graduated income tax and a second set to undo the effects of the first, such that the net results are several: a maze of legal intanglements that the tax payer cannot understand; a diversion of income to support the avoidance of taxes, evasive maneuvers as it were, at a high cost by the well-to-do few; and the diversion of highly talented experts to the task of out-witting the government. In his early arguments, Friedman speculated about the Texas oil man H. L. Hunt spending $16,000,000 to avoid paying the government $20,000,000, and about other cases.[62] A decade later arguments such as the foregoing became common.[63]

Among the apparent facts on inequality of wealth in the United States as reviewed by John Britton are the following: (1) "Intergenerational transfers of wealth" in the form of gifts and bequests passed by parents to children as inheritance account for half or more of the net worth of wealthy men and for most of the net worth of equally wealthy women. (2) Great wealth is not mainly acquired as a lifetime accretion resulting from the productive career efforts of individuals as they earn, save, and reinvest. (3) Wealth is not actually acquired primarily through the productive efforts of individual holders of wealth.[64]

Marc Tool reviewed Britton's work as leading Britton to a "cautious advocacy" of the taxation of material inheritance. "*Unearned* income," he said, "may properly be taxed." Furthermore, Tool viewed Britton as having introduced evidence against what he called a "neo-classically based contention," namely: "That great wealth is mainly acquired as a lifetime accretion resulting from the productive career efforts of individuals as they earn, save, and invest." Such wealth, Tool noted, is often thought to be "equitable and just" because it is presumed to be accumulated as a reward for personal effort.[65] He mentioned "the equation of justice"—"justice is done when a balance is struck between effort and earnings." He also dealt with such truisms as, "Participants do not start even."

Referring to an earlier book by Britton, Tool said:

> Deference to competitive markets means opportunity for the advantaged to increase their advantages, to increase their wealth and income differential, to become the very rich, and to retain their wealth. Britton ably demonstrates that intergenerational transfers reinforce and extend inequality. He seems not to acknowledge that his deference to the earnings-as-productivity premise implicitly also reinforces and extends inequality.[66]

Proponents of a view such as Tool's seek progress in dismantling the so-called equation theory of justice, "which buttresses the neo-classical effort-earnings, market-linkage postulate..." On the other hand, proponents of views such as Friedman's sought to elevate the postulate (payment according to the value of the marginal product). The basic added distinction is to give more attention to social mobility rather than equality.

Friedman did the latter by giving more attention to voluntary association and to tax reform, namely: by removing the barrier to social mobility and revenue enhancement imposed by the progressive income tax structure with its inequities (such as different tax rates on those who spend and invest their incomes differently); by removing penalties with respect to leisure versus work (including special treatment of income for working and non-working spouses); and by removing loopholes, exemptions, and tax shelters. These latter features are indeed those with which U.S. citizens were most familiar in the 1960s, 1970s, and somewhat beyond.

The Lottery of Life and Social Mobility

In addressing the distribution of income Friedman's early background in probability comes out.[67] First, a redistribution of income after the event of a lottery, say, is equivalent to denying the outcome of the event to those who agree voluntarily to engage in it.[68] Considering a group of individuals who initially have equal endowments and enter a lottery with unequal prizes, Friedman noted, the result will be an unequal distribution of income, and most would agree. The time to think about the rules that govern the choice of a society by people who must live in it is before the event. One generation making rules for the next, may be a close prospect.

Continuing, Friedman maintained that individuals differ in their approaches to risk, attitudes toward leisure, taste for undesirable work, and hence choose occupations, investments, life styles, and the like according to such differences. "Actual inequality," Friedman said, "may be the result of arrangements designed to satisfy men's tastes." On a revealed preference note he said:

> If all potential movie actresses had a great dislike of uncertainty [the probability counterpart to risk], they would tend to develop "cooperatives" of movie actresses, the members of which agreed in advance to share income receipts more or less evenly, thereby in effect providing themselves insurance through the pooling of risk.[69]

Also, as previously mentioned, Friedman dropped the static assumption of a declining marginal utility of income,[70] for precisely the reason that it may not be warranted by the classes of the choices numerous individuals make, as just alluded to. Though there is no direct theoretical relation, this notion has an identical analytical counterpart in Keynesian economics in terms of the simple consumption function, as taken up earlier and in appendix one to chapter 16. Both notions, though static in formulation, tend to coincide with the ethical stances of numerous economists and politicians. The principals use the notions in rationalizing support for governmental actions to equalize the distribution of income, as through income taxes and governmental transfer programs.

Friedman recognized that—although much inequality in income and wealth is due to payment in accordance with product—initial inherited differences in endowment may account for a large part of the differences, both in human capabilities and property. This had led some to favor inheritance taxes to equalize initial endowments, as already reviewed.

For Friedman, however, the use of inheritance taxes just raised more ethical issues, for he soon found no greater ethical justification for confiscating the higher returns to the individuals who inherit property in its material form than from those who inherit human capacities. Besides, for him, confiscating the income from one source as distinct from the other will simply alter the allocation of the inheritance from one form to another. A wealthy person may pass on wealth in terms of sums of money to finance education and training as well as in terms of property, and, to repeat, Friedman found no basis for distinction on ethical grounds.

There are in Friedman's ethical, economic, social-market system a number of compensating features for those who abhor such an income distribution system as just outlined. Most notably, he did not find high income positions to be permanently held by the same individuals, the negative income tax is possible as a floor on poverty, and the extension and widening of educational opportunities may serve as a major factor for reducing inequality. In particular, in Friedman's consumption function work matters are dynamic (in contrast to the Keynesian function) and households may find themselves temporarily on a high or low side with respect to their budgets. In these categories, one may encounter some writers, actors, actresses, TV personalities, movie producers, professional athletes, football coaches, promoters of new ventures, small proprietors, corporate executives, casino gamblers, pornographers, wildcatters, and risk takers generally. In fact, even when Friedman contemplated the evils of public monopoly versus private, there were things going on to lessen the evils of the private monopolies and to make their status temporary. New products and enterprises are possible, and technologies in communication and transportation broaden and enlarge the geographical scope of markets.

No doubt Friedman's view as just outlined was a bit idealistic about social mobility and the fact that many get dispossessed in a highly viable market economy where disparate cultures coexist. Even so, at some sub rosa and other levels there is little of the protestant ethics, capitalist and judaic spirit which appear as motivating forces, and there may be as well initiatives, work ethics, and strongly held motives underlying the proper functioning of the system and getting rewarded. So, in Friedman's properly functioning system there are diverse groups, causes, and religious sects which proselytize and compete for men's minds, and hence there is plenty of work to be done among the dispossessed.

Taxation and Constitutional Amendments

So Friedman opposed the use of taxation in particular and the use of government generally to allocate and redistribute income as payment for the outcome of production.[71] He furthermore saw the question of government's role as being complicated by two interrelated developments: the unlegislated rise in taxes produced by inflation in the Keynesian era and in the presence of the progressive tax structure; and by a break in the nexus between the political cost to politicians of financing government spending by deficits as opposed to financing by taxes. Breaks with this past came about with what we characterize as "the Big U-Turn" with reference to ideological shifts along Hotelling's line. As taken up in chapter 16, Congress saw fit to index the income tax and Ronald Reagan's efforts in support of a balanced budget amendment preceded and coincided with the 1985, Gramm-Rudman, balanced budget bill.

The opposition to the performance of the redistribution functions by government was based on premises elucidated above. There we encountered the following: that the taxes used in the redistribution are after knowing the outcomes in the lottery of life; that the taxation interferes with voluntary association and the ethical principle of payment according to the value added in production; that redistribution dulls incentives to engage in income and production generating associations with others; and that the progressive taxes, as known in practice, have been taxes on becoming wealthy rather than on wealth. Moreover, in chapter 11 we encounter the prospect that government spending and the related redistribution consequences went beyond the reach of even a simple democratic majority of voters. This occurred in part because the cost of inflation induced tax revenues (even with given tax rates) and deficit financing appear in the long run while somehow the benefits of spending appear in the short run. In particular, Friedman saw the complication in terms of small, but strong and vocal interest groups, on the one hand, and the passiveness of the majority with respect to small measures that will benefit someone else, on the other. He said:

> The vested interests are not some big bad people sitting on money bags; the vested interests are you and me. Each of us is strongly in favor of small measures that will benefit us and each of us is not too strongly opposed to any one small measure that will benefit someone else. We are not going to vote anybody out of office because he imposes a $3 a year burden on us. Consequently, when each measure is considered separately, there is considerable pressure to pass it. The proposers have greater force than the opponents (who are often called "negative" or "obstructionists") and the total cost is never added up.[72]

Friedman concluded that there is "a fundamental defect in our political and constitutional structure." It is that "we have no means whereby the public at large ever gets to vote on the total budget of the government." Thus, tax limitation was aimed at correcting this particular defect.

Friedman's position, as just summarized, initially led him to address and support the limitation of taxes through constitutional amendment and ultimately to favor and actively engage himself in "a proposed amendment to the Constitution of the United States designed to limit government spending."[73] The idea in such an amendment was to give a matter such importance as to make minimal concessions to expedience, as in the case of voting by simple majority rule. This, said differently, is the "self-denying ordinance on certain kinds of issues..." Friedman saw the problem in implementing such matters as being twofold: selling the idea, and getting people to give up what they see as their special interest for the good of the whole and the respective interest as well.

In the case of income taxation in particular, Friedman envisioned the left wing giving up its support of progressive taxation in exchange for the right wing giving up its loopholes, and vice versa. And thus, he saw the diverse special interest yielding for the good of the whole and the special interest too. Along the constitutional limitation route, Friedman found himself supporting the 1978 tax limitation amendment to the California Constitution. He did so to the extent of going on television in California in support of the measure. Proposition 13, as matters turned out, was a first major reaction on the part of voters that was to take on national dimensions.

A later venture on Friedman's part was directed along with others through involvement in the National Tax Limitation Committee. Of the 34 states needed to ratify an amendment, such as drafted by that committee, 28 had done so by mid-March of 1979, and thereby provoked strong reaction from Congress at the fear of such constraint.[74] In early 1981, the U.S. Senator from New York reported with bewilderment that 30 states had passed resolutions calling for a national constitutional convention for the purpose of requiring a balanced budget[75] and Ronald Reagan continued to call for a balanced budget amendment in his 1985 State of the Union address.

The particular proposal that was drafted had a number of flexible features and Friedman believed it would achieve the twin goals of low unemployment and low inflation. Addressing at the same time the proposal and Congress's Humphrey-Hawkins bill passed in October 1978, Friedman said, "It [the acceptance of the proposal] would not be the first time that capitalist means were successful, and socialist means a failure, in achieving ends common to both those who favor capitalism and those who favor socialism."[76]

Reduction in the deficit, as may be encouraged by a balanced budget amendment was to have another desirable consequence. Namely, in the light of the political role the Federal Reserve came to play in supporting deficit financing by the Treasury in the 1960s and '70s, the reduction in the deficit would eliminate one excuse for excess growth in the money stock and hence the root cause of inflation to begin with. Addressing the monetary authority, Friedman concluded, "Inflation is made in Washington and can only be eliminated in Washington."

With what might appear as uncanny timing, the attention Friedman gave to the Federal Reserve and deficits on the public scene in early 1979 foretold the interrelated problems of high interest rates, high unemployment and forecast of Federal deficits in the U.S. in 1982 and in the United Kingdom a year earlier. In the U.S.—even in the presence of relatively stable and controlled money growth in 1982, on the Federal Reserve's part—interest rates held high, largely in anticipation of deficits and the prospect that the Federal Reserve would yield in their support of the Treasury's financing.

As Friedman saw economic performance, broadly reviewed in early 1979, inflation had the effect of raising taxes on income from all sources (including wages and profits), erratic inflation had generated uncertainty about the economic future and thereby had further discouraged capital spending, and inflation had been accompanied by additional regulation and spending by government.[77] Moreover, the higher taxes on income and profits, the low rates of capital spending, the uncertainty, and the regulations all contributed to higher unemployment rates viewed over the longer run period. Thus reducing the inflation would solve the latter economic problem. In this way, then Friedman saw the twin goals of low unemployment and inflation (as called for by the Humphrey-Hawkins bill) as being achieved by free market rather than by socialist means.

By 1982 Friedman had forcefully extended the prospect of a constitutional amendment to include one in support of his long-favored, flat-rate income tax. He, moreover, would not make exceptions to departures from the flat-rate tax, apart from the minimum floor set by the negative income tax (or its surrogate), personal exemptions and strictly defined expenses of earning the income. Noting the many so-called flat-rate-tax bills in the legislative hopper in 1982,[78] Friedman also noted some that seem attractive but that would in fact have rates "running from 14 percent to 28 percent—or a top rate double the bottom rate." These, he said, are attractive but "A far cry from a true flat rate."

The attractive appearances come from offering a compromise "between the so-called left and right." He said: "The left might accept a lower top rate as the price of gaining a broader base. The right might accept a broader base as the price for gaining a lower tax rate."

However, "special interests" are again a problem and Friedman, said that a compromise of the foregoing sort would not work, although it was present in the 1986 tax reform bill (chap. 16). Friedman said of the compromise in not going all the way with the flat rate concept:

> Neither side would trust the other and both are right. If it were ever enacted, the left would go to work to raise the rates—and they would quickly be joined by persons on the right pleading fiscal necessity. The right would go to work to broaden the deductions—and they would quickly be joined by persons on the left pleading equity and social priorities. After all, that is how we got into our present fix. History would simply repeat itself.[79]

Thus Friedman argued for the constitutional amendment route, as in the last chapter rather than the simple legislative routes. "Perhaps the time has come," he said, "to take the next step and outlaw the outrageous kind of income tax from which we now suffer."

"Freedom," as the last and present chapters have noted, is preserved by an economic system of markets and by constitutional means. As Friedman said earlier with reference to free speech, everyone's special interests must be banded together to keep government out of the censorship business.[80] "It's not a matter," he noted, "of taking one case at a time and deciding each case on its merits." Continuing, he said,

> If we did that, we would have free speech for very few. Someone would be able to get a law passed prohibiting free speech for Seventh-Day Adventists. Or vegetarians. Or Black Panthers.

So, as it is with free speech, it is with taxes, inflation and tax loopholes. Each group has its special interest—the one in a more progressive tax rate, the other in this loophole or that. Interest in the entire process is called for in the case of taxes as with free speech. The frailty of freedom, moreover, was further recognized by Friedman when he observed the need for checks and balances against the power of government as a means of preserving even constitutional protections.

The Negative Income Tax: An Income Floor for the Needy

In 1968, Milton Friedman surveyed the ways by which the United States had come to the grab-bag of programs to guarantee a minimum annual income.[81] He noted first that "poverty" is a relative concept (and hence also the relations between the family and other income receiving units as far as the distribution of income is concerned). Thus, in the perspective of this concept, "Economic progress and development have not and will not eliminate poverty." Even so, the facts about a rising standard of living for the "relatively disadvantaged," and the guarantee by one part of the population to another were viewed as credits to the economic system that generated the income and to the charitable instincts of the people respectively.

Against this background and from the vantage point of Friedman's normative economic views, Friedman's notions of the negative income tax and of gaining a consensus in political and economic matters came to bear. First, however, he found among the most satisfactory of the programs of the type under review "direct relief and aid to dependent children." Other programs "that have been justified on welfare grounds" would include at the time: "public housing, urban renewal, old age and unemployment insurance, job training, the host of assorted programs under the mislabeled 'war on poverty,' farm price supports," and so on at incredible length. "The welfare iceberg," Friedman said, "includes also measures that do not require direct government expenditures, except for enforcement."[82]

Continuing, Friedman said that "such legislation is always enacted in the name of helping the disadvantaged," but that its effect is to increase the number of indigent people." As an example he cited one of his favorite ones, minimum wages, even before a host of empirical studies confirmed predicted results. The example proceeded:

> The minimum wage...prices many unskilled workers out of the market and is the major explanation, in my judgment, for the tragically high unemployment rate among teenagers, especially Negro teenagers. These measures involve a confusion between *wage rate* and *family income*. Persons who are capable of earning only low wage-rates are for the most part youngsters or extra family members whose earnings supplement those of the main breadwinner. But even where the worker is the main breadwinner, it is surely better that he be free to earn what little he can than that he be unemployed, and better that if government funds are to be used to aid him, they be used to supplement his earnings, not to replace them.[83]

Addressing in 1968 the most satisfactory of the so-called welfare programs (direct relief and aid to dependent children) and looking at the flaws that offset the "great merits," Friedman said that they have ill effects: (1) adverse effects on incentives, because when a "person on relief earns a dollar, and obeys the law, his or her relief payment is reduced by a dollar," and because other costs are involved in working such as the wearing of better or different clothes; (2) loss of personal freedom and dignity for both the aid recipients and the welfare workers, because to gain assistance one must submit to a personal examination of circumstances and supervision by welfare workers in considerable detail (including the investigation of a mother's male visitors); and (3) in summary "weaken the self-reliance of the recipients, diminish their humanity, and make them wise in the stratagems for evading the spirit of the restrictions imposed on them." As Friedman pointed out, "Instead of bringing aid and counsel to the poor, the welfare workers become detectives and policemen; enemies to be outwitted."

Thus, in the light of the dehumanizing and costly aspects of the welfare programs as envisioned, "It would be far better to give the indigent money and let them spend it according to their values." Much of the way it is spent may not meet with approval but "at least some would grow in the course of making their own decisions and would develop habits of independence and self-reliance." Surely, Friedman said, "if social workers are hired on government funds they should devote their energies to helping the indigent, not spying on them."

So what this comes to is the negative income tax—the guarantee of a minimum annual income through the "use of the mechanism by which we collect the bulk of our taxes, namely, the personal income tax." On this, Friedman commented:

> At one time, citizens were required to contribute to the support of the commonwealth by payments in kind—forced collections of food or timber or forced labor on public projects. That is still the rule in many backward areas and is widely practiced in all totalitarian countries. Both freedom and efficiency were fostered by substituting taxes in money for taxes in kind.
>
> In our welfare programs, we are back in the earlier era, dispensing largess in kind, or trying to, and examining the detailed physical circumstances of the recipient. Here, too, the route to progress is to substitute payments in money for payments in kind and the single numerical means test of income for the ambiguous means tests we now use.
>
> I have termed this device for helping the poor a *negative income tax* in order to stress its identity in concept and operation with the present income tax. The essential idea is to extend the income tax by supplementing the income of the poor by a *fraction* of their unused income tax exemptions and deductions.[84]

Now, the wide interest in the negative income tax, from the time Friedman began to discuss it in the 1960s,[85] led to its having an influence on Richard Nixon (1968 GOP presidential candidate), on later tax and welfare program changes, and to the government's embarking on one of the most enormously costly research programs ever undertaken in the economic sphere by government. As the original negative tax concept emerged in the hands of Nixon and his then domestic policy advisor, Daniel Patrick Moynihan, however, it had few of its original virtues. Chapman stressed, that "it consolidated only a few of the federal income transfer programs and left the others alone." Continuing on the matter, Chapman mentioned the conservatives in 1968 and their 1980 counterparts as they anticipated the prospect of spendthrift presidential candidates:

> Some conservatives went along with it only out of loyalty and breathed big sighs or relief when it died. Their natural inclination to oppose anything smacking of a "guaranteed income" has naturally been reinforced by the public's skeptical mood. And their political instincts tell them that it will be good strategy and great fun to run in 1980 against a spendthrift president who wants to put millions more on the federal dole. Those Republicans from

farm states, of course, will have nothing to do with any attempts to prune or ax the food stamp program, which serves as a handsome subsidy to farmers.[86]

Before the results from the government's social experimentation study began to come out in 1978, President Carter proposed replacing the system he inherited with a system of direct cost outlay for families below a set income level (suggested as the then $6,200 poverty line which was $10,989 by 1985). The more money the families earned, the less assistance they were to receive.

The results from the costly government study, however, were devastating in two respects, as far as many were concerned who had hoped to reform welfare programs "with some form of national income maintenance or negative income tax program."[87] These two respects would not have been inconsistent with predictions from Friedman's normative views, at least about the progressive income tax,[88] but they were at odds with what many of the welfare reformers of 1968 and 1978 had hoped, according to Moynihan. The twofold results in question are: a cash outlay by the government in combination with a progressive tax feature leads to a substantial reduction in work effort as income increases, and the cash outlay as a substitute for existing programs leads to family breakup.

The research study began in New Jersey in late 1968, and further experiments were conducted in rural North Carolina and Iowa, in Gary, Indiana, in Seattle, Washington, and in Denver, Colorado. The latter two were the most comprehensive. There, 2,700 families were given direct cash assistance for three- or five-year periods, and an additional 2,000 families served as the control group by remaining on welfare or struggling along on their own. Among the first group, some were on welfare and others classified as "working poor." There were no job requirements and no strings attached other than researchers being able to study them.

In the experiment, male breadwinners receiving assistance and their wives worked an average of 6 and 17 percent fewer hours respectively, and women who headed households worked 12 percent less. In terms of the progressive feature for earned income, men worked 10.6 percent fewer hours when they lost 70 percent in benefits for every dollar earned, and they worked 6.2 percent fewer hours when the tax rate was 50 percent. Reflecting the possible absence of a work ethic and/or an expectation of upward social mobility, the disincentive for work was twice as high for blacks and Hispanics as for whites.

Over the two-year period of the Seattle-Denver guaranteed income experiment, family breakup increased 244 percent for whites, 169 percent for blacks, and 194 percent for Chicanos. Apparently these increases were due to the income guarantee applying separately to husbands and wives and thus having a "liberating" effect on women who may otherwise have remained in unpleasant marriages for financial reasons. The administrators of the experimental program, it may be noted, counted couples living together as married and therefore any separation the same as actual divorce.

On the timing of Senator Moynihan's subcommittee hearings[89] and the results of the government's study, Chapman elaborated.[90] He wrote as a proponent of the negative income tax and said, "These studies did not in any sense discredit the negative income tax."

Chapman, in closing, reflected on interest groups and the prospect of future welfare reform in a way that is remindful of Friedman's approach to the constitutional amendment on taxation. Namely, for the benefit of all, one must get the special interests to give up their favored position. The complication to be overcome centers about the twin tendencies: (1) for each of us to favor small measures that will benefit us, and (2) for each not to oppose too strongly "any one measure that will benefit someone else."[91] Somehow through persuasion and the like, the special interest must see the benefits to be gained through reform, through "bundling things together."[92] At the present, Chapman noted, "The existing welfare system provides so many benefits to such a broad range of interest groups—farmers, the construction industry, lawyers, doctors and, most important of all, bureaucrats—that it can never be dismantled." He said:

> No Congress will radically alter the welfare system until it is in the interest of some equally powerful interest group to do so. Right now, the only people who would benefit from a negative income tax are the poor.[93]

An Overview

Paul Samuelson has been referred to as a Keynesian and as an egalitarian with respect to income distribution and as a philosopher of the mixed economy. As he saw the distribution matter, it came down to one of law and order versus the class struggle. On this theme he invoked the memory of Schumpeter to the effect that *"undemocratic forces will have to be used to impose upon society the capitalist mode of organization."* In addition, there are technical bases in the Keynesian and related modes of thinking for taking up income distribution. These include the static constructions offered as the utility-of-income function and the consumption function.

In contrast, Friedman offered treatments of occupational choice, chance, and taxation and a dynamic consumption function. These coincide with his moving differently and combine with his setting freedom as the highest goal in choosing between the Ruskinian/socialist and capitalist ethics.

Instead of a class struggle and rigid income classes, Friedman observed and emphasized social mobility. Poverty is relevant, perhaps permanent in some cases and temporary in others but it needs to be dealt with. Friedman's means were as follows: persuasion to get the permanently poor and dispossessed into the system; the negative income tax (or a "safety net" as it were) to alleviate the hardships of low income and/or unemployment; and changes in the tax code to remove the progressive-tax penalty on getting rich rather than on being rich.

The innuendos of these positions for social change are variously stated. Two aspects of them from a legislative point of view are the pooling of special interests when trying to advance the general interest and the closely related emphasis on amendments to the constitution. Starting with ideas that progressive rates of income taxation enhance total social utility, in the case of static utility analysis, and total consumption, in the static consumption function analysis, we end with two developments: (1) a progressive income tax structure on the surface, and (2) numerous loopholes and shelters that not only in effect undo the progressive feature in practice for the very rich but hamper it from generating revenue. Under the progressive rate structure the shelters and loopholes come about partly as attempts to generate saving, capital spending, and income growth.

Plus, there are apparent disincentives involved also in the progressive structure. Arguments in support of this prospect, at a 1980 stage of thinking were partly just conjectural. They gain later recognition in review of the Tax Act of 1981, and some recognition as a result of the presently reviewed "social experimentation study" over the decade 1968 to 1978. That study indicated reduced work effort in the presence of a more progressive tax rate for income. It also dealt with cash outlays as a substitute for conventional welfare and a finding of further discouraging results. Most notably, family breakup occurred when cash outlays without the conventional restrictions were substituted for existing welfare programs.

Nevertheless, the Friedman arguments for the most part—the flat-rate tax, the pooling of special interests, the balanced budget amendment—gained White House attention, which we take up later. We encounter what Michael Evens called an "enduring truth of supply-side economics," in reference to Friedman's consumption function vis-à-vis the Keynesian function which provides argument for income redistribution. The static function suggests that higher income groups save a larger percentage of income more specifically, the marginal prosperity to save rises as household income rises, *ceteris paribus* (say, the cross-section or timeless data), plus there is the early Keynesian position that such a relation can be inferred over time. Hence there is the prospect many thought had arrived, namely a saturation of wants at higher income levels and over time for society as a whole. Next, the analysis and the information call for income redistribution to favor the higher-want/lower-income groups, with a possibly predictable outcome (notably: a lower personal saving to income ratio over time and slower income growth, as in "appendix one" to chapter 16). This comes about even as we may achieve higher spending on production and, hence, employment, for a time.

Friedman changed the initial interpretation of the Keynesian consumption function, as it were, after taking into account the Kuznets's finding reported in chapter 3 (p. 99)—i.e., the consistency of the saving-to-income ratio (s/y, and hence consumption-to-income, c/y) over a long period for which he observed data. Friedman saw the matter more to the effect that lower income households (high consumption-to-income, c/y, ratios) and high income households (low c/y ratios) at a given time are not permanently so. Some have temporarily low or high incomes. There is social mobility, as we elaborated (pp. 442-443, 489) plus a life-cycle pattern is suggested. Households at an early stage of formation may be high consumers and low savers, while at a later stage they become high savers and low consumers, all in relation to income.

The alteration of the tax analysis and the alteration of the budget-data/time-series analysis by Friedman are main pillars in argument for tax changes, which we take up later. In addition, Friedman's early position on the danger of big government, favored tax-cut arguments even where tax cuts potentially lead to high deficits. The high deficits we will see provide pressure for imposing cuts in spending by governments.

Part V
The Big U-Turn

The next two chapters extend the study to the politics of Britain under Margaret Thatcher. A third extends it to the Reagan presidency in the U.S. In reference to these chapters one should remember, as taken up in chapter 2, that Britain is the original home of that kind of market economy which has its roots in laissez-faire *capitalism and Adam Smith's* The Wealth of Nations. *Smith's book, we may recall (pp. 43-45), contained a masterful statement of how relatively atomistic units of household and business activity could function in a coordinated and harmonious way, while serving as well the interests of the public. Along with other ideas of its era, it engendered the seeds for a social system based on political and economic freedom.*

From Smith in the late 18th century to J.M. Keynes in the 1930s, British writers in economics influenced the course of British economic policy and history. Their ideas were influential abroad, particularly in the United States. Keynes's major work, The General Theory of Employment, Interest and Money, *however, was written against a backdrop of neoclassical economics, British socialist theory, and the apparent failure of the economic systems in Britain and in the U.S. The omission of monetary disturbances in the form of strengthened preferences to hold cash balances was emphasized by Keynes as a part of the inadequacy of neoclassical economics and of the failure of the economic system. In an effort to remedy the matter, Keynes gave special substance to the definition of money—to money's role in speculative activities and in dealing with an uncertain and often unforeseen future. However, there were also bases in Keynes's work, and especially in the work of U.S. Keynesians, for thinking that the British and American economies had matured to the extent that deficit spending by government was called for to assure full employment by Keynes's standards.*

Arguments were made in the 1930s that the economic system had matured, bringing about a satiation of wants on the part of households and an unwillingness of businessmen to engage in enterprise, on the one hand, and an excess of saving and inadequate capital spending, on the other. As arose in chapter 11, there were also notions about the simple Keynesian consumption function, the liquidity trap, and the closely related inelasticity of investment demand. The latter suggested, we may recall, that at low interest rates, little or no impact on capital spending could come from lowering rates further. Instead, expansion of the money stock went into the liquidity trap.

Such a story of saving to income and money stock to income ratios as we relate to Keynes was repeated many times in the post-WW II years as Britain and the U.S. embarked on economic policies based on egalitarian sentiments, socialist thinking, and Keynesian economics. However, the Keynesian theory—and the thinking of Keynes himself, as we noted in chapter 11—contained some major flaws, including as the theory applied under post-WW II conditions. Primary among these was the conclusion about rigid wages (or what Hicks called the labor standard, pp. 420-429); the advancement of an economic policy theory involving a closed economy even as the U.S. led part of the world moved toward economic recovery and a post WW II monetary system with the IMF and a variant of the old gold-flows mechanism at its center (pp. 427-429); and a faulty monetary-policy linkage scheme which centered about the money and bond model and the frail notion of open market purchases (sales) by the Federal Reserve which lowered (increased) interest rates and hence influenced capital spending (pp. 444-445). In the end, policies based on Keynesian theory led to problems of inflation, unemployment, and declining productivity.

The failure of Keynes's and Keynesian theory, in combination with monetarist thinking and theories of an earlier day, set the stage for the consideration of new ideas at the political level, and for Margaret Thatcher's Tory party victories in 1979, 1983 and 1987 (chap. 15). The leader in the development of the monetarist economics (with its attendant production, incentivist characteristics), as we have stated, was Milton Friedman. As early as 1970, Cambridge University's Lord (Nicholas) Kaldor wrote the following with reference to Friedman in Lloyds Bank Review:

> *This new doctrine is assiduously propagated from across the Atlantic by a growing band of enthusiasts, combining the fervor of early Christians with the suavity and selling power of a Madison Avenue executive. And it is very largely the product of one economist with exceptional powers of persuasion and propagation: Professor Milton Friedman of Chicago. The "new monetarism" is a "Friedman Revolution" more truly than Keynes was the sole fount of the "Keynesian Revolution." Keynes's* General Theory *was the culmination of a great deal of earlier work by large numbers of people: chiefly Wicksell and his followers, Myrdal and Lindahl in Sweden, Kalecki in Poland, not to speak of Keynes's colleagues in Cambridge and of many others.*

Against the backdrop of the historical flow of thinking in economics from Britain to the U.S., the fact that Friedman was an American suggests a reversal in the historically predominant flow of economic thought from Britain to the U.S. Failures in the British economy and Friedman's impact on worldly affairs is of interest for other, special reasons that will be apparent later. Included among these special reasons is Britain's historical regard for ideas in economics, its presence in the vanguard of capitalist development, the extreme shift toward a socialist society that occurred in Britain, and the role of the London press in communicating ideas at a relatively high level of sophistication for newspaper writing.

The next two chapters are about these matters—the extension of U.S.-based research to include study of the U.K., the impact of economic ideas on politics, the reversal in direction of the flow of economic thought from Britain to the U.S., and the arrival in London in the 1970s of significant blocks of Friedman's economic thinking. Chapters 15 and 16, in fact, are a brief history of political and economic matters, with some attention to the events that occurred when political leaders in the U.K. and the U.S. attempted to alter socialist/Keynesian trends along the lines of Friedman's economics.

The presence and central role of the economic, social and political ideas found in Friedman's work are clear in both Britain and the U.S., as we will see, but sorting out the links between the ideas, the officials, and the policies in the U.S. is made more complicated by the diverse groups under Reagan's political umbrella. Whereas we have essentially the same ideas in the U.K. under the single monetarist label, the label "supply-side economics" gained visibility in the U.S. and encompassed several different action groups that played highly visible roles in the U.S.

The political support Reagan gained from this diverse and not entirely consistent array of groups cannot be denied. Even so, Friedman's positions and ideas predominated among the positions we associate with Reagan, the Treasury Department, White House officials, and "the enduring truths of supply-side economics." These ideas were often clearer in the rhetoric of the strong communicative "symbolic" presidency than in his later policies. Friedman was quite able to live with the reasons for this. Most notably, he once said, "We know perfectly well that our sensible ideas are going to be mangled in the political process."

Aside from Friedman's intrusions into the developments in Britain, the role played there by Lord (Ralph) Harris's Institute of Economic Affairs must be emphasized as well as that of the academic economists. For its part, the IEA helped keep discussion of individualism alive in Britain over much of the post-WW II period, despite opposition from economists in the academic community. As sections of chapter 15 indicate, the British economists had, like many American economists (pp. 234-239), ideological positions different from Friedman's and a most superficial concept of his economics despite Friedman's impact at the highest levels of government in both countries.

The first chapter in part V deals at some length with Friedman's rather special work (with Anna Schwartz) on the U.S. and the U.K., published under the title Monetary Trends in the United States and the United Kingdom: Their Relation to Income, Prices and Interest Rates, 1867-1975. *The next chapter, chapter 15, will review again some relevant parts of Fried-*

man's more formal economics, with reference to original sources. A parallel treatment of the same topics, as they appeared in the London press (mainly The Times and The Sunday Times) over the second-half of the 1970s, is also examined. This treatment establishes that Friedman's more formal thinking was communicated relatively well to a private-sector audience in Britain and that it became a prominent element of political debate in the public arena.

Chapter 15 also relates Thatcher and her government to this background and to the reality of decelerating inflation, denationalization of industry, and transition from an inflation plagued socialist society with the attendant aspects of unemployment. Thatcher's suitability for the task confronting her and the British people arises on various occasions, as does the Falkland Islands crisis, Britain's 1983 and 1987 elections, and the resulting economic outlook.

As indicated, we are dealing with the impact of ideas about social and economic matters on British thought and politics during a time when a major effort was being made to redirect a socialist or Keynesian society, making it into a more individualistic, market-oriented society. Examining Milton Friedman's ideas as they have been presented in the London press, we find there a fairly complete statement of the problems in such a transition and of the ideas used to try to solve them.

As stated, the label applied in Britain to Thatcher's policies has been "monetarism," e.g., as encountered in Lord Kaldor's title The Scourge of Monetarism. As chapter 15 will reveal, however, attention was given to production and incentivist (or alternatively supply-side and tax) matters under the monetarist label. The points are, as variously emphasized earlier and later: that Friedman recombined the theories of production and distribution of income which were originally separated by John Stuart Mill; that the label "monetarism," as used in Britain, also encompassed policies and thoughts used in the U.S. at the time of Ronald Reagan's presidency under "supply-side economics" and "monetarism" labels; and that by treating the central bank's inadvertent impact on the money stock as a source of instability and, at the same time, offering to eliminate this source of instability, Friedman removed much of the basis for Keynes's earlier attack on classical economics symbolized by his attack on Say's law of markets (supply creates its own demand).

Under the economics symbolized by Say's law (pp. 58, 195, 417), no goods were brought to the market except to obtain income to spend (an indirect satisfaction of wants and also no overproduction). In the presence of inadequate demand, prices (including wages as a special price) adjusted downward to establish full employment output. For his part, Keynes saw a strengthened preference for money balances that reduced the demand for output, but instead of downward wage and price adjustments (sticky *wages, the labor standard pp. 417, 419-420, 429), a reduced aggregate demand for output was followed by more rapid adjustment in output and employment than in prices. Thus, for a time, the income obtained from employment (or production) did not create adequate demand to assure full employment.*

Following the period where Hicks reported the breakdown of the labor standard in the presence of monetary accommodation (Acts IV and V of chapter 11), the conclusions we came to are the following: prices and wages will not adjust properly to achieve the highest, non-inflationary full employment unless the economic climate is conductive to such adjustments (including a resolute position by government and less than an accommodative monetary policy); monetary policy (defined as time rates of change in the money and credit aggregates) had been a destabilizing force in the economy that could be eliminated; and in the presence of continued destabilizing policies, output in recession will still likely adjust more rapidly than prices. The roles of Thatcher and Reagan with respect to downward adjustments in wages and restraint in the wage bargains, nevertheless, provides ground for future research on wage flexibility under strong leadership and monetary discipline.

Some Shared Background

The backgrounds that Friedman, Thatcher, and Reagan share begin with the early 1960s, and the 1964 political campaign of Barry Goldwater (pp. 26-27). In the early 1960s, especially in connection with the 1964 campaign, Friedman and Ronald Reagan went public with their economic and closely related ideological views. In 1964, Milton Friedman became unofficial advisor to presidential candidate Barry Goldwater; Ronald Reagan, a Hollywood actor and former head of the Screen Actors Guild, took a step toward national political prominence in the U.S. by making a thirty-minute television presentation in behalf of Goldwater; and Margaret (Hilda Roberts) Thatcher became a "front bench" spokesperson for the opposition government in the British Parliament.

Friedman's 1964 role followed his going public with his political-economic tract entitled Capitalism and Freedom *(1962). Somewhat earlier, Goldwater had published a similar but shorter tract titled* The Conscience of a Conservative *(1960). Friedman said at the time his tract was published, "the believer in freedom has never counted noses." And Goldwater made freedom a central issue in his speech accepting the nomination of the Republican national convention: "I would remind you that extremism in defense of liberty is no vice. And let me remind you also that moderation in pursuit of justice is no virtue" (New York Times, July 17, 1964).*

Proceeding from what some saw as "a kind of safe middle ground," and discussing movement toward the upper and lower bounds on freedom (the "maximum of individual freedom consistent with law and order," and the minimum ["totalitarianism"]), Reagan said the following in the closing days of the 1964 presidential campaign: "Regardless of their humanitarian purpose, those who would sacrifice freedom for security have, whether they know it or not, chosen this downward path." Referring to a war with totalitarianism he said: "The guns are silent...but frontiers fall while those who should be warriors prefer neutrality." If we lose, he warned, "history will record with the greatest astonishment that those who had the most to lose did the least to prevent its happening."

Ronald Reagan's nationally televised talk on October 27, 1964 was thought to have impressed some, but at the time it did not get mentioned in the New York Times. *[Only later did it reappear in a book by Lee Edwards (1967, 235-246).] The Reagan speech combined an anecdotal style, "one liners," and an inspirational tone. The campaign was a triumph of ideology over politics, and Reagan's speech was soon seen as inspiration for the defeated supporters to hold on and fight another day. It is credited with keeping some workers in politics who twelve and sixteen years later would run Reagan-for-President headquarters. One such worker remembered the 1964 speech as the political equivalent of the George Gipper lines in the movie* Knute Rockne, All-American *in which Reagan had played the role of George Gipper. In the movie the mortally ill football star, "the Gipper," told Rockne the following: "Rock, some day when the team is up against it and the breaks are beating the boys, ask 'em to go in there with all they've got and win just one for the Gipper." Also, a week after the televised speech, Reagan was quoted as scoffing at non-Goldwater Republicans, saying: "We will have no more of those candidates who are pledged to the same socialist goals as our opposition."*

The rhetoric of this campaign was not forgotten by Margaret Thatcher in Britain. In a 1975 campaign speech to the Young Conservatives' (YC's) Conference, during efforts to achieve the leadership of the Tory party in Britain, she quoted the Goldwater lines about "backing the workers not the shirkers." Her speech drew two standing ovations; it was thought to have swayed a few waverers and to have made other people wince.

The 1964 campaign was not impressive in terms of the votes cast for Goldwater, but sixteen years later, with even more in the way of research, writing, and new ideas, the seeds of that campaign and much that Friedman set in motion in the same period came to fruition in the election of Reagan as president in 1980. Leaders were emerging who craved and celebrated new ideas at a time of economic crisis.

For Friedman in the U.S., the year 1980 was the sought-for destination of an unorthodox political odyssey that began in the early 1960s. The

Thatcher/Tory victories of 1979 in the U.K. presented a similar opportunity to reverse the trends of economic deterioration begun years before in the original home of the modern "social market economy," particularly those trends which had their beginnings in the 1920s and 1930s in the U.K. and the 1930s in the U.S.

Before Friedman went public in his reactions against the trends, he vacillated about a choice between the Ruskinian/Marxist ethic and the capitalist ethic, as reported on various occasions (pp. 151-152, chap. 13). He later argued against the leftist position that "capitalist freedom undermines capitalism both because freedom defines no moral basis for its results and because its successes are really dependent not on liberty but on bourgeois disciplines and restraints." Leftists have also assumed, since Marx's theory of historical determinism, that society is to evolve toward a communist state (pp. 332-333).

In 1978, Friedman wrote, in one case, about the moral/human basis of capitalism, and in the other about having a choice as to a socialist or "social market economy." He emphasized the need for freedom by "the small minority of people who do not have materialistic objectives." By 1980, Friedman's 1962 tract, Capitalism and Freedom, *was followed by* Free to Choose *and a ten-part television series (pp. 264-265).*

Accepting the principles offered in Capitalism and Freedom, *related elaborations, and in* Free to Choose, *one finds the market doing several things: (1) permitting the harmonious functioning of diverse, heterogeneous social, religious and ethnic groups; (2) harnessing an energy that can be expended on the crasser aspects of profits, but also on humanitarian, literary, and scientific work; and (3) dispersing power, partly by providing a means for making routine decisions about how, what, and for whom to produce goods and services without government being directly involved. A necessary support to a properly functioning market has been a satisfactorily functioning monetary system.*

These and Friedman's other ideas, as variously reviewed, come forward in the succeeding chapters. What essentially are those ideas that we find at the highest levels of government?

The Ideas and the Actions

The old ideas of freedom, individualism and monetary discipline were given new vigor at Friedman's hands, as were the new ones mentioned below. Here, we give attention to the interrelated nature of economic science and ideology and summarize the interrelated ideas, actions, and ideology.

1. The ideology with respect to the transition from the Keynesian era to more of what we may call a monetarist era (chap. 7). The role given to money in economic analysis, as we have indicated (chap. 11), carries with it some extra baggage—the view of an economy with money serving to facilitate an indirect satisfaction of wants as it enters into exchange in markets; and a reliance on markets with government providing an appropriate infrastructure (property rights and all, as in chap. 9) and stable monetary conditions to assure greater certainty and to facilitate trade. This monetary economy (in relation to barter and underground sectors of the economy) is a maximum under voluntary association on the part of agents in a market (as appendixes to chap. 16 indicate). Friedman saw this in association with a flat-rate income tax (chaps. 12 and 13). This feature is more obviously present in Reagan's rhetoric, positions, and tax-reform plans than in Thatcher's. However, Friedman and Thatcher, in the British context, stressed the incentivist aspect of reducing high marginal tax rates on income. In the U.S. supply-siders generally did this, but we find that Friedman, Thatcher, and Reagan had the following uppermost in mind with respect to tax cuts: (a) reducing the size of the government sector in relation to the private, and (b) setting freedom as the highest goal, as where Friedman chose between the capitalist and socialist ethics (chap. 12).

In Reagan's 1985, State-of-the-Union address the subject "freedom," as encountered in chapter 12, was mentioned no less than seven times. Examples:

> We said we would invigorate our economy by giving people greater freedom and incentives to take risks, and let them keep more of what they earned.
>
> promise of human freedom in a world at peace.
>
> And that word—freedom—is the key to the Second American Revolution we mean to bring about.

Later in February at a news conference, the President spoke of "a triumph of free people and their private institutions, not government."

2. The analysis of transition. The transition began with roles in government for monetary analysis, indexation, and taxes. First, inflation is a monetary phenomenon, and decelerating monetary growth causes a temporary retardation of economic growth as well as reduced inflation rates. There are no soft options, as Friedman's interrelated analysis suggests. Unemployment will be held above the "natural rate" for a time but the time and extent of the transition may be minimized (a) by facilitating downward adjustments in wage and other contracts (p. 223), and (b) by changing the tax structure along incentivist lines. Indeed, we have here what comes up in chapter 16 as the fundamental underpinning of supply-

side economics. A difference in the way the transition was debated in the U.K. and in the U.S. is present in the rhetoric of the "hard slog" versus "the economics of joy."

3. Checking the financing of deficits through monetary expansion. *We encounter here "the government budget constraint" (chaps. 8, p. 260, and 11). As money and credit growth are decelerated, inflation is brought under control, but the additional growth of credit that would support the purchase of the government's debt instruments which arise from deficits is lost (in the U.K., for example support for the public sector borrowing requirement was lost).*

4. Government deficits and the size of government. *Deficits become of secondary importance to the control of inflation if monetary growth is noninflationary. However: (a) there are the prospects of crowding out private financing and of having the monetary mechanism used to support credit expansion and facilitate the purchase of debt instruments by financial intermediaries generally; and (b), in the U.S., there is especially the argument associated with Friedman and Reagan that if you finance deficits by raising taxes you simply encourage government spending by giving government more revenue to spend. The emphasis on Friedman's and Reagan's part shifted back to the "freedom" and "noninflationary" analysis, and to their goal of constraining and reducing the growth of federal government.*

5. Deficits and the transition. *With deficits a major part of political debate in 1984-85 in the U.S., and with the indexation of the federal income tax to avoid "bracket creep" beginning in 1985 (chap. 16), an unusual event of special monetary significance happened internationally in the 1984-85 phase of the transition. First, the U.S. had run deficits most of the 1960s and 1970s, with energy payment and imports playing a main role in the 1970s even in the presence of a weak dollar (pp. 428-430). However, as the U.S. economy in 1984 turned out the best GNP performance since an 8.3 percent rise in 1951, and as the dollar reached record strength in the foreign exchange markets before intervention to reverse it in September 1985, there was an apparent paradox. The trade deficit hit a record level due to imports temporarily favored by the strong dollar, as may have been expected, but an unexpected inflow of capital funds from abroad came in to help finance U.S. debt even as interest rates declined in the U.S. The debt arose from record governmental deficits and from the private sector. And the inflow of capital funds came as a reflection of the soundness of the economy and its being a safe haven for funds. This perception of the dollar weakened, however, as U.S. budget deficits accumulated at record levels, even as the Reagan boom in the U.S. stock market continued at an extraordinary level, as the democratically controlled Congress persisted in increasing government funding of programs and as the President persisted in*

efforts to achieve budget cuts and contain the growth of government. As crisis came in response to the domestic and payments deficits, it took the form of a stock market crash comparable to that of October 1929 (pp. 421-425). This crisis, as we will see in chapter 16, led to some joint action by the President and Congress on the budget.

6. Friedman's rule standard (chap. 11). *The reason for the attractiveness of U.S. investments, consequently, was not the ordinary one cited in the press of high interest rates attracting foreign funds (actually an export of U.S. securities), plus much of the strength of the dollar turned on the control of inflation (a component of high interest rates). The reason for the attractiveness of U.S. investments was the stability of leadership in reducing inflation and hence maintaining the dollar, for a time, as a monetary standard, as it were—as a safe haven for funds relative to the rest of the world. As Reagan explained at a news conference with Thatcher on the occasion of a Thatcher visit in February of '85, markets help currencies whose governments help themselves. However, at the time of the 1987 market crash, he said that the market had overvalued the instruments traded on it.*

7. The interest rate analysis. *A piece of Friedman's work, which was central to Thatcher-Reagan positions and which appeared often in remarks by Thatcher, Reagan, and Reagan's support personnel, is the interest rate analysis (chap. 11). We have called it liquidity preference with overshooting. There, the nominal rate of interest is equated to the sum of a real rate and the expected inflation rate, plus there are additional results. Short of the use of force, the central bank cannot control the interest rate without controlling the expected inflation rate and uncertainty over its forecasted value; and—contrary to a legion of claims by economists about an ordinary stable relationship between the money stock demanded and the rate of interest variously defined—money-market rates of interest cannot be relied upon as a link for controlling money and credit aggregates.*

8. Constitutional amendment to balance the budget. *Friedman was the first economist to develop and publicize a proposition for a balanced budget amendment to the Constitution (p. 515). Due to institutional and constitutional differences this is more a matter for the U.S. than the U.K. The position was favored by President Reagan early on and placed in his 1985 and later State-of-the-Union addresses. He said, "I ask again that you pass, as 32 states have now called for, an amendment mandating the Federal government spend no more than it takes in." There was no doubt that there was the hope that a deficit crisis would foster this end.*

9. Free trade and the law of one price. *Free-trade principles have a long history (chaps. 2, 3, and 11) and were supported by Friedman, Thatcher, and Reagan. In addition, we encounter Friedman's treatment of the ratio from chapter 11, $(P_{US}/P_{UK})/(\$/\pounds)$, and its approximation with a constant*

number. In relation to the free-trade concept and the thought about the ratio, we find that Thatcher forsook incomes policies to control prices (the P_{UK} component of the ratio) and exchange controls to control exports (the $/£ component). She contended that British industry must be competitive internationally and that workers cannot have excessive wages and jobs both. Reagan for his part, announced in early March of '85, that voluntary import quotas on Japanese automobiles would be allowed to expire, and in October '87 he announced tentative agreement to eliminate all tariffs between U.S. and Canada. The first action was dramatic in the presence of a protectionist movement in the U.S., which took on some additional dimensions. Even so, the quota and tariff actions were consistent with Reagan's philosophy and agreements signed at preceding economic summit conferences.

10. The long-run view. *The long-run view ran throughout Friedman's distinction between transitory and permanent components of time series (pp. 82-83), his interest in Dicey's long swings in public opinion, and his analysis of such famous ratios as the income-velocity-of-money ratio (including liquidity preference analysis, as on pages 82-83, 443-448), the law-of-one-price ratio above, and the ratio of saving to income (in relation to his consumption function, initially introduced on pages 82-83 and 441-443). The latter became a part of the enduring truths of supply-side economics (chap. 16), but the long-run emphasis also extended to matters of monetary policy in both the U.K. and the U.S. where attention was directed to the "quick fix." The "quick fix" referred to short-run attempts to manipulate total spending through demand management. Thatcher said of it, "I will not stagger from expedient to expedient." And Reagan also took the long-run view.*

Apart from Friedman's ideas and the closely related actions of Thatcher and Reagan, there were other aspects of the developments beginning in 1979 that were distinctive with respect to Thatcher's and Reagan's efforts. First, as the economies lost the stimulus from sticking inflation on top of inflation, recession set in in both economies. This was more expected in Britain than in the U.S. because Friedman publicized the prospect in London, which was present in his analyses, as was the absence of any easy choices and because we had in the U.S. what Herbert Stein referred to as "the economics of joy," to suggest the supply-side views of Arthur Laffer and 1988 presidential hopeful, Congressman Jack Kemp.

Next, the control of monetary aggregates in any refined way was intermixed with other matters. In both the U.K. and the U.S. (chap. 15 and 16), there was a weak link between market interest rates and the money and credit aggregates for monetary control purposes. Also there were institutional features, where in the U.K. the authorities could not be certain about the composition of M3 (defined later), and where money control was tied directly to the public sector borrowing requirements (defined later). In the U.S. there were control problems brought about by the Depository Deregulation Act of 1980, NOW and super-NOW accounts, and lagged reserve requirements. In the latter case, the Federal Reserve had imposed difficulty for itself which was not corrected until Friedman analyzed and publicized the problem.

Moreover, as Thatcher moved in the U.K. special difficulties arose in getting cooperation from senior civil servants and in privatizing the nationalized industries. Revitalizing a private sector was complicated by the fact that half of industry was government owned and controlled. Reagan, for his part, showed great leadership but the passage of tax cuts, their minor impact on the U.S.'s personal saving-to-income ratio, and their effects lagged behind disinflation induced by monetary means in 1981 and 1982—all so as to further assure recession.

Finally, in both the U.K. and U.S., unusual leadership and determination were required to maintain support for the policies as unemployment increased during the transitions to less inflationary states.

The Personalities and the Times

Much has been written about Friedman—his underlying approach and ideas, his political odyssey, his intrusions into worldly affairs, his persistence in adhering to his vision. As we have seen and point to further in chapter 14, he offered an alternative to the Keynesian approach in monetary/macro economic matters when conditions in the U.K. and U.S. reached crisis states and social forces came to predominate over economic forces. The political-action people who came to share the vision of a return to a variant of individualism (later in chap. 17 called "institutional individualism"), moreover, were of a similar persevering mold. For Thatcher in the U.K. and Reagan in the U.S., voters had moved to share the positions of the leaders, all in contrast to the politics of a middle-ground consensus and public-opinion poles. When the Economist of London counseled Thatcher to move toward the middle ground where the votes were, Thatcher shifted the voters to the right, as we encounter later, and voters shifted to Reagan who had not changed ideologically from the Goldwater days when he and Friedman too were much maligned.

Furthermore, the candidates and the governments they later led shared their ideology and other experiences. The shared ideology, however, is more apparent in Thatcher's case—(1) because of "the economics of joy" in the U.S., a U.S. tradition of denying ideological entanglements, and what Robert Dallek called "the politics of symbolism"; and (2) because of the personality differences between the principal characters. Dallek saw sym-

bols as concerning perception, social values, and beliefs (chap. 16). He found much discussion proceeded in terms of symbols rather than in terms of details and political-issues papers.

Columnist George Will picked up on this latter theme in a March 1985 column. Will said:

> Reagan believes campaigns are to fill a reservoir of deference. (If the word "deference" grates on your democratic sensibilities, call it a reservoir of trust.) Reagan favors campaigns that set themes that bolster confidence in the theme-maker's character. His assumption is that the public's attention to politics is intermittent and its attention span is short. A constructive campaign convinces a majority that the candidate is a good fellow with a good idea of what he wants to do. These two perceptions by the public will translate into a lot of latitude for him when the game of governance begins.

An Anglophile of sorts, Will commented earlier in December of '84 on the personality differences between Thatcher and Reagan:

> One contrast between Thatcher and Reagan is especially striking. Many Americans do not consider Reagan formidable other than as a vote-getter, but almost all Americans like him. Most British voters respect Thatcher, but few feel any affection for her.
>
> Reagan's popularity gives him a cushion against political adversity. But Thatcher has a different advantage: "The enemy within." That is what she calls the "hard left" in and out of Parliament.

In December of 1984, Will predicted a third consecutive victory for Thatcher (the first prime minister since the 1832 reform bill to do so). Following Thatcher's third consecutive victory, in June of 1987, Will said Thatcher was the first prime minister whose name denoted a doctrine. "The essence of Thatcherism," he said on June 22, "is creation of an entrepreneurial, property-owning democracy."

Finally, both of the principal-action figures weathered difficult periods and had resounding victories. The difficult periods were in their first off-year elections, during recession, when the press and the polls asserted the failure of their policies, and the landslide victories followed in Thatcher's 1983 elections and Reagan's 1984 election. In June of 1987, as Thatcher won elections over the Labor party in Britain by 11.5 percentage points of the popular vote, Reagan faced a lame-duck ending as a two-term U.S. president. Iran-Contra difficulties and the failed nomination attempt of Robert Bork to the Supreme Court (p. 309) also complicated matters for the popular president.

Chapter 14
The British Connection

The series of studies envisioned in 1948, shortly after Milton Friedman took over the monetary portion of Wesley Mitchell's research at the NBER, ended with the work by Friedman and Anna Schwartz (hereafter F/S) which is known by the short title *Monetary Trends*. The other volumes, we may recall, were the *Monetary History* (1963) and *Monetary Statistics* (1970).[1] The majority of their research and writing spanned thirty years and took a few turns that were not entirely predicted at the outset. One of these was the extension of study in 1966 to include the United Kingdom.[2] Although F/S said that this extension delayed publication without commensurately resulting in new findings, the actual results of *Monetary Trends* do not bear them out. In fact, the added contributions, aside from the volume's attention to the "indirect approach," came from the extension of the research to include the U.K.

When *Monetary History* appeared in 1963, considerable controversy arose over two features of the research: the notion of a leading time rate of change in the money stock and the prospect of its instability being a main source of instability in business conditions (particularly with impact on income); and the notion that the Federal Reserve had exacerbated the bank failures and recession that followed the 1929 stock market crash in the U.S. (Act II, chap. 11). Following the publication of *Monetary History* some also claimed that F/S wrote as if they had an economic theory but that it was not spelled out. This feature of the review-period controversy was partly dealt with in the early 1970s.[3] It was updated and restated in *Monetary Trends*, along with new attention by F/S to their uses of statistical methods.

The testing of the theory and the uses of the statistical methods were entwined with the money-demand relation first denoted as equation (1) in chapter 3, pp. 79-80 [recall $M/P = f(y, w; \ldots ; u)$]. The main testing of hypotheses in *Monetary Trends* developed out of Friedman's return to the simple quantity theory of money and his confrontations with the Keynesians over the post-WW II years. These hypotheses concerned the simple quantity theory of money, the Keynesian theory of the velocity of money, and Friedman's theory as related to equations (1), (4), and the liquidity preference demand for money with overshooting, all in chapter 11.

Although the 1982 volume was entitled *Monetary Trends*, the analyses of data reported there provided another opportunity to discuss cycles (or transitory changes)[4] which had originally been the main feature of the *Monetary History*. With respect to both trends and cycles, and analyses of data concerning the interaction of the monetary and real goods sectors of the economy, *Monetary Trends* is best seen as a summation and extension of the major features of F/S's research as a whole.

By the time *Monetary Trends* came into review, most of the controversy over topics from the older *Monetary History* had subsided—a reflection of temporary acquiescence by some and the partial-to-wide acceptance of the major tenets of *Monetary History*. However, attention shifted to Friedman's uses of statistical methods.

In a review article, Charles A. E. Goodhart of the Bank of England said: "the *general* forms of data adjustment that they [F/S] used" are "more worrying." He also objected to the separation of trends from other components in the time series; cited Thomas Mayer and noted that "F-S are out of tune with current trends in econometrics"; noted that "modern econometricians may look askance at some of F-S's econometric methodology"; and said that F/S's statistical evidence was presented in a "somewhat *idiosyncratic manner*." In addition, Goodhart indicated in his review that F/S developed much of the data base themselves and that they sought out the best sources on the data base for the U.K. He then called attention to a study at the City University, London, the first volume of which appeared in 1985 with a parallel title to F/S's 1963 study.[5] Goodhart's guess at the 1982 date was "that such data revisions will not upset F-S's statistical results much."

Goodhart then expressed more concern about the "adjustments and manipulations imposed by F-S on their raw data before testing." Even so, he said, "Despite some reservations about these *particular* prior adjustments, I doubt if they seriously affected their results."[6]

As noted earlier, F/S themselves said that they proceed "indirectly"; that they examined variables a few at a time with reference to hypotheses generated by the theory; that their approach "yields insights that cannot be obtained from the more sweeping approach ["the prevailing fashion in econometric work"]; and that the more formal body of rational expectations literature (first shown in the schema on schools with respect to approaches, p. 70) "is not the open sesame to unraveling the riddle of dynamic change..."[7] Such divergence in the uses of methods, as reflected in Goodhart's and F/S's comments, had appeared in fragments of the literature with respect to structural equations methods, the Cowles Commission at the University of Chicago, and the "new classical school" approach to rational expectations (pp. 68-87). Nevertheless, sensational charges against F/S's uses of statistical methods were made in a study presented to the Bank of England's panel of academic consultants.

Details of these charges aside until chapter 18, important points for the present are: that *Monetary Trends* was received with considerable celebration for a technical work; that its research gave Friedman informed background for addressing British problems in London during the 1970s; and that the timing of the research also coincided with Friedman's influence on those who were later to be leaders in the Thatcher government. This influence in London was mainly via the economists of the City, Margaret Thatcher, and her associates (chap. 15). In effect, Friedman circumvented the intransigent academic economists and went directly to the higher echelons of those who would govern in Britain and the U.S. This contrasted with Keynes's influence in the U.S., where his main appeal and early influence through the *General Theory* was first upon academic economists and only indirectly upon government in later years.

Applause for *Monetary Trends* appeared in four early, lengthy, review articles. They emphasized the book's status as a classic,[8] its many new and important findings (including as a result of extending the research to cover Great Britain),[9] its views on the control of income by the money stock,[10] and the book's central role as a challenge to the Keynesians (even as Keynes's *General Theory* had challenged the classicists).[11]

As we will see in chapter 15, during the debate that surrounded monetarism in the early period of Thatcher's government, the academic economists opposed Thatcher as well as Friedman. Referring to "extreme dogmatism and lack of intellectual coherence" of the new wave of monetarism, Lord (Nicholas) Kaldor said, "the new creed made comparatively few converts among academic economists." This, he said, is "shown by the Manifesto signed by 364 University teachers in economics in March 1981—and the absence of any counter-manifesto in support of the Government's policies."[12]

As already indicated, we view Friedman's influence on policies and economics, albeit at the highest level of government in the U.K., as a reversal of almost two centuries of predominant flow of economic thought from Scotland and England to the U.S. This reversal phase will be taken up in the next chapter, following review of features of the indirect method, past themes and new contributions found in F/S's *Monetary Trends*, and especially, the sharing of U.K. and U.S. financial systems.

The Indirect Method

The "indirect method" was first discussed here on pages 77-84 with reference to the "primal equation," $M/P = f(y, w; \ldots ; u)$. As variously stated, F/S were not interested in estimating the demand for real-money balances (M/P) in terms of the right-hand side variables, nor were they interested in proceeding directly to a regression of real money balances on the other variables, as was the prevailing fashion among economists in the 1960s, 1970s and 1980s. Instead F/S were primarily interested in establishing the existence of a stable relationship by proceeding indirectly, studying the interaction of real and nominal magnitudes and the interaction of monetary changes with income, prices, and interest rates.

There is the view that the regression studies cannot be burdened by too much detail, as would come about from proceeding directly to introduce all the relevant variables. In the fashionable approach encountered in the U.S. and Britain and particularly at the U.K. Treasury in the early phases of Thatcher's government before she changed the practices of her civil servants, each relevant bit of detail was offered as if the effects of right-hand-side variables could be separated out and made a part of policy argument with the prospect of governmental control over the relevant detail and variables.

The alternative way of proceeding indirectly comes up both with respect to the mechanical apparatus found in economics (Marshallian demand curves, the Keynesian consumption function, and so on) and the use of statistical technique. This indirect method permeated Friedman's work. Its main interrelated parts center about the following: 1. Skepticism about what can be achieved along traditional lines with respect to the direct measurement of utility and the identification of static relations (say a Marshallian demand curve), and the notion of separating the effects of so-called independent variables by proceeding directly with multiple regression models. 2. The notion of the stable relationship [equation (1) p. 79], without the ordinary interpretation about causation and effects. 3. The separation of the variables in the theory and their time series counterparts into permanent and transitory (e.g., $Y = Y_P + Y_T$). Here, the permanent component (or quasi-permanent component, as the case may be) corresponds to the notion of secular trend, or trend in *Monetary Trends*. The transitory component becomes fluctuation about the trend (actually another way of separating out cyclical change). All of this is a part of combining both economic mechanics and statistics in the approach, as economic theory becomes more dynamic. 4. The treatment of the rate of change in the money stock as a leading rate in relation to business conditions generally, exclusive of the ordinary statistical approaches (distributed lag models, and regression equations with causation implied in right-hand side variables). Analysis of this lag between the peak (trough) rate of change in the money stock and the peak (trough) in business conditions becomes the causation issue (causation from $\Delta \dot{M}$ to $\Delta \dot{Y}$).[13]

As the above elements should indicate, at Friedman's hands the "indirect method" accommodated special time frames. It also facilitated the treatment of episodic change (say, a major shift in $\dot{M}$) in setting off other changes in such a fashion as to generate fluctuations about trend,[14] and the treatment of psychological time rather than the use of a single chronological time scale.[15] In psychological time the behavioral units forming expectations about the future may look back in time in other than some fixed time dimensions. Depending on the episode and their degree of certainty about the future, they may look far back in time at times and only at the less distant past at other times. This, moreover, becomes an integral part of the interacting uses of economic mechanics and statistical methods. Such treatment of variable lags in the formation of expectations contrasts with fixed lag time as obtained with distributed lag models, although again the apparatus of distributed lag models is present.

Quite briefly as further illustration, Friedman proceeded indirectly to deal with money demand rather than directly identifying the static construction (or an economic relation) ordinarily viewed in economics. There are the approximate determinants of the money stock, on the one hand, and the demand function for money balances, on the other.[16] The determinants of the latter two are not the same, because "A function calculated from such data could not be regarded as an estimate of a demand function—in the jargon of econometrics, the demand function would not be identified." From prior evidence, F/S took for granted that the nominal quantity of money available to be held is independent of the variables entering demand, and as a consequence, they treated the money supply (M_S) as "an exogenous variable entering into the determination of such endogenous variables as nominal income, prices, interest rates, and real income." In other words F/S treated M_S as a control variable.

The public can adjust to the stock M_S with relative ease by turning balances over faster or slower (actual M greater than desired and vice versa). Since this adjustment is a change in the velocity (or turnover) of money balances,[17] F/S studied variables affecting velocity a few at a time for the U.S. and the U.K. Their exploration dealt with "the hypothesis that the real quantity of money demanded can be regarded as a relatively stable function of a small number of variables." They said, "It [their exploration] isolated as the key variables entering into the demand function [1] the degree of financial sophistication, [2] real per capita income, [3] the return on nominal-value assets, [4] the return on physical assets, and [5] two episodic sets of events handled by dummy variables—postwar readjustment and an upward shift in demand [holding of more money balances] produced by economic depression and wars."[18]

Following the above, F/S estimated final equations for the U.S. and the U.K. for both levels and time rates of change. They found these results encouraging via what amounts to a fairly conventional analysis in the end, namely: the coefficients have the correct sign and most are different from zero by statistically significant amounts. F/S were pleased by their findings because there was consistency in their results for levels and for time rates of change, the separate coefficients for the U.S and the U.K. were close, and the extent to which they (F/S) accounted for "fluctuations" in the holdings of real money balances on the basis of six variables only [equation (1) p. 79].[19]

Both Mayer and Goodhart showed little awareness of Friedman's indirect uses of statistical methods and the traditional mechanical apparatus of economics. Mayer said early in his article, "To be useful and interesting it [a theory] must...deal with 'interesting' questions (a matter of 'scientific taste') and focus on those variables that are empirically important for these questions. It must be set up so that one can deal simply and directly with these particular variables." Along this line, Mayer appeared to have in mind, both in his review paper and his book on monetarism, movements along static curves and schedules in economics, and changes that come about from a comparison of static states.[20] All is at variance with Friedman.

Goodhart put the statistical aspect of Friedman's work thus:

> F-S are careful to show how they took each statistical step. Nevertheless, it may be difficult to untangle exactly what their results owe to such smoothing processes, which most other research workers are unlikely to want to copy.
> As Thomas Mayer has noted, in other respects also F-S are out of tune with current trends in econometrics. F-S argue (and I would agree) that "multiple correlations with many variables are almost impossible to interpret correctly unless they are backed by more intensive investigations of smaller sets of variables" (p. 215), and this latter is, indeed, what they give us.... Nevertheless, modern econometricians may well look askance at some of F-S' econometric methodology, though everyone should applaud the scrupulous care they show in handling their statistics.[21]

It did not occur to Goodhart that econometricians should learn from Friedman nor did it occur to him that Friedman had a coherent, whole, interrelated system of economic theory and data analysis (chap. 18). His success with data analysis and theory construction in the economics-core areas suggested they should.

Past Themes

Subordinate to the overriding theme of testing one theory against another found in F/S's *Monetary Trends*, additional old themes centered about the effects of changes in the money stock on inflationary expectations and interest rates ($\Delta \dot{M} \rightarrow \Delta(1/P)/(dP/dt)^* \rightarrow \Delta i$), and causation from money to income ($\Delta \dot{M} \rightarrow \Delta \dot{Y}$). Both of these themes concerned the business cycle as Friedman viewed it, and also extended beyond it for two principal reasons: (1) there was, as already noted, a shift in the structure underlying the formation of inflationary expectations beginning in the 1960s, such that changes once thought to occur in the long-run become more immediate in the case of interest rates and what we have called New York's revenge (p. 447), and (2) monetary changes have not been simply a cyclical phenomenon, as noted below in reference to long swings.

Friedman's earlier writings in the monetary area addressed the leading time-rate-of-change in the money stock with reference to peaks and troughs in business cycles. It was this work that set off the controversy over the topic of causation from money to income, which we took up earlier in chapter 11. When it came up again in *Monetary Trends* F/S principally concluded, "The process is two-way, not unidirectional, so there undoubtedly has also been a feedback from income to money, yet the element that gives consistency to the century as a whole is the influence from money to income."[22]

However, reverse causation as set on its course by James Tobin and taken up by Lord Kaldor and the post Keynesians was contrary to this. Tobin's argument was largely a priori, but Kaldor added a post Keynesian argument for the relevance of the institutional considerations. Giving attention to the Keynesian preference for detailed manipulations, fiscal and monetary policy and a multiplicity of policy instruments, Kaldor gave theoretic justification for deficit spending by government up to the point of Keynesian full employment. Since monetary policy was to be accommodative of deficit spending, the spending caused the money growth (i.e., clearly the spending went for income to the factors of production which caused the money growth).

The implications about the multiplicity of policy instruments and the spending was as follows: where the effects of each of the instruments of policy cannot be separated by the means of econometric model building, the position implies using government force to make the models work. In other words, the models which appear as simply technical valid argument, become guides for the use of power by government in the implementation of economic programs.

Along this line, as inflation arose, from the accommodative monetary policy—also in conjunction with power units (oligopolies and trade unions)—prices would need to be controlled. Hence, price controls and incomes policy.[23]

London's Tim Congdon discussed "power theories," monetary approaches to inflation along with pay and price controls designed to curb inflation. He put the ideological aspect of controls and the use of power in perspective:

> Keynes's wage-unit assumption culminates in centralized pay negotiations between the "peak organizations" of labor and capital on the one hand and the government on the other. Moreover, in the Keynesians' opinion, these negotiations not only help overcome inflation, but may also contribute to the attainment of "social justice". By permitting larger pay increases to the low-paid than the well-off an incomes policy can reduce inequality. This the Keynesians consider a desirable end, partly because equality is good in itself, but also partly because they feel that the prevailing distribution of income, being determined by power, has no worthwhile economic function.[24]

Friedman, by contrast, took opposite views—inflation as a monetary phenomenon and income distribution as payment according to the value of marginal product.

The Newer Contributions

In brief, the newer contributions found in *Monetary Trends* were: 1. A further alteration of the Phillips curve argument, namely: the inflation rate was said to be negatively correlated with the ratio of output to capacity output rather than positively related as called for by traditional Phillips curve argument (pp. 213-214). 2. An elasticity measure of approximately 1 for the first right-hand side variable in equation (1) from chapter 3 (p. 79). It may be denoted in terms of monetary trends and data adjusted for episodes as $d \ln m (t) \cong d \ln y (t)$. 3. The finding of a common demand function for money for the U.S. and the U.K. with parallel and nearly identical rates of change in the velocity of money. 4. The law of one price (namely, support for the purchasing power parity notion whereby the same basket of goods will sell for the same price whenever it is sold, transportation costs aside). As additionally studied, the ratio of the ratio of the two price levels (P_{US}/P_{UK}) to the exchange rate ($/£) has a mean of 1.12, which we reported and used in chapter 11, pp. 421-422. For the part of the 1868-1978 period before 1931 the ratio fluctuates narrowly about the mean. Afterward with government intervention there are greater departures but a return to the mean. Government intervention to control exchange rates as a part of domestic incomes and full-employment policies simply disrupts and forces changes elsewhere, all to the detriment of the domestic economies. 5. Shared turning points in business conditions for the U.S. and the U.K., and a shared financial system: A coincidence of turning points in business conditions and interrelations doom to failure efforts at controls in one sphere that may be circumvented in others. The coincidence of turning points and related findings run counter to the idea that cyclical fluctuations mostly originate in the U.S. and spread from the U.S. to the U.K. 6. Long swings in growth rates for money balances and nominal income: The influences of destabilizing changes in the money stock are not limited to short-run and cyclical changes alone as previous monetary research held, and that earlier studies of long swings in business conditions left out an important determinant of business conditions. What we have in the earlier studies in effect is *Hamlet* without the Prince of Denmark.

All of these newer findings are germane to Friedman's intrusion into the U.K. debate over social and economic matters that brought forth Margaret Thatcher. The two that immediately stand out, apart from the prospect that the study of one economy is related to that of the other, are: the parallel percentage changes in the growth of real money balances and in real income; and the support for the law of one price.

The inflation/output-to-capacity-output correlation. Distinguishing between the price level and the output components of nominal income ($Y = PQ$) and retaining the notion of money impacting on income ($\Delta \dot{M} \rightarrow \Delta \dot{Y}$), F/S reported, as stated, that the inflation rate was negatively correlated with the ratio of output to capacity output rather than positively correlated as called for by the Phillips curve argument,[25] which had become an appendage of Keynesian economics. This came about after a long period of variations in Friedman's approach to the Phillips curve argument (p. 214). In fact it is not so entirely new as to a priori argument, including as found on the part of Friedman.

The Phillips curve arrangement was that of an inverse relation between inflation and the unemployment rate (itself viewable as short-run, negative covariation with the output-to-capacity-output ratio). The initial argument captured for a period of history an inverse variation in inflation and unemployment. However, if in a period of monetary deceleration, output adjusted downward more rapidly than prices, the higher prices would relate to a lower ratio of output to capacity output. This further is approximately the notion found in the downward sloping Marshallian demand curve (i.e., price negatively related to output).

Criticism of the Phillips curve may be reduced to four main points: (1) the trade-off is temporary and results only so long as the inflation is not fully anticipated; (2) accelerated inflation becomes necessary to maintain its effects with all the disruptive consequences of high and accelerating inflation; (3) as noted with reference to F/S, changes occurred in the structure underlying inflationary expectations so that initial levels for the rate become fully anticipated; and (4) in the long run the Phillips curve was simply vertical, showing no trade off at all for inflation and unemployment. A new point was added, namely: the inflation rate and output-to-capacity-output ratio are negatively correlated and not positive as the Phillips curve calls for.

The elasticity measure (Hicks's Act VI?). As already noted, the newer contributions in F/S's book came after the extension of the study to include the U.K. This may seem most surprising in the cases of the first contribution listed. Even so, in that case F/S were led to examining more closely their earlier finding from *Monetary History* for an elasticity measure of 1.8, and saw the earlier and the new finding for the U.S. as being associated with an increase in financial sophistication in the form of a changed financial structure in the U.S. during the period 1880-1906.[26] Allowing for this became the main basis for the new estimate of approximately 1 (actually 1.15 for U.S. and 0.88 for U.K). Goodhart gave further attention to the new measure.[27]

The emphasis on this measure for elasticity—along with the emphasis on the stable relation as a whole [equation (1), p. 79] and Friedman's review of the history of managed money since the establishment of the Federal Reserve System in 1913—is supportive of Friedman's advocacy of a monetary rule instead of discretionary management. In chapter 11, we associated the possible acceptance of this rule with the possible addition of a Friedman-rule standard for Act VI of Hicks's drama (p. 430). The standard may come about through the influence of an informed segment of the public or through statutory means.

Friedman himself made a judgment about the feasibility of his rule vis-à-vis a return to the gold standard and other alternatives, as have others. In a U.S. Commission report on gold, the majority position favored consideration of Friedman's rule as opposed to a return to gold itself. It was laudatory of F/S's work and a testimonial to the political feasibility of Friedman's rule that Anna Schwartz was executive secretary to the Commission and that it recommended on an evenly divided vote the following:

> "Whereas the inflationary process is ultimately related to excessive growth in money and;
>
> "Whereas it is clear that inflation cannot persist over the long run in the absence of excessive monetary growth then: "The Commission recommends that the Congress by legislation establish a rule specifying that the growth of the nation's money sup-

ply be maintained at a steady rate which insures long-run price stability."[28]

This result is essentially due to the influence of the inflation of the 1960s and 1970s and that of Friedman more than of any other economist. The Commission concluded that "*restoring a gold standard does not appear to be a fruitful method for dealing with the continuing problem of inflation.*"[29]

With respect to Friedman's money-growth rule, there were various prospects: for a strong, simply-fixed growth version; for a version allowing for secular shifts in the income velocity of money; and for the targeting of different growth rates. Early on, a range from 5 to 2 percent money growth was proposed, with the 2 percent rule expected to bring about some mild secular decline in the price level. The 2 percent rule was presented as the optimal one for improvements in the functioning of the economy, but Friedman at times indicated that he would settle on the 5 percent rule as a desirable objective with the possibility of a greater prospect of acceptance.[30] However, upon reflecting on the U.S. economy at year-end 1982 and the forthcoming expansion of economic activity, Friedman advised further deceleration of monetary growth in stages "until monetary growth is around 2 percent. Then keep it there."[31]

Keynes, in potential contrast to Friedman, had opposed deflation more than inflation, "because it is worse," he said, "in an impoverished world, to provoke unemployment than to disappoint the *rentier*."[32] In Keynes's context, the 2 percent rule would be thought to provoke unemployment. Keynes's time frame for this change, in any case, was the short run (immediate and sharp reduction), whereas Friedman's was the long run (gradual reduction). His gradual reduction was thought to avoid cyclical shifts in money demand and to do so without impact on unemployment, particularly where accompanied by incentivist policies in other respects.

The law of one price. In contrast to Keynesian economics, the F/S study demonstrated that the open economy and the old specie-flows mechanism matter (chap. 11, pp. 412-417). Price adjustments in one country call forth price adjustments in the other. National boundaries may have political importance and economic significance for differing physical developments and other characteristics, but financial unification of the two countries is accomplished through the old specie-flow mechanism. We add the provision for the period beginning in the mid-1960s that expectations by agents concerning the workings and the globalization of information make financial flows and financial markets even more interrelated than in the period covered by *Monetary Trends*.

Under the old species-flow mechanism, prices between trading partners "must move in a way that will keep international payments in adjustment which, broadly speaking [in the F/S time period of a few years] means that prices must move in harmony." If prices do not move, "they will lead to exports or imports that will produce balance of payments deficits or surpluses, setting in motion the specie-flow mechanism." F/S continued, "The requirement for money and nominal income (or exchange rates) is that they adjust in such a way as to keep prices in the appropriate relation." In other words, F/S said, "divergent movements in money and income will occur precisely to keep prices in line."[33] As stated on page 421, the law of one price holds.

Friedman and F/S reported that the law of one price for the U.S. and U.K. is more applicable before 1931 than after,[34] at least for the period covered by *Monetary Trends*. After 1931, problems with the law of one price arose because the respective economies became more isolated from one another. Efforts were made to control exchange rates, including British devaluations of the pound. Devaluation effects were only temporary, in any case, so there was a return to the law of one price, which may be expressed by setting the ratio of two price levels in relation to the exchange rate equal to approximately one, i.e., $(P_{US}/P_{UK})/(\$/\pounds) = 1.12$.

This purchasing-power-parity/exchange-rate ratio before 1931 had a mean of 1.12, and there were narrow fluctuations about it. Afterward the fluctuation widened. Each sharp rise in the purchasing power parity exchange rate after 1933 corresponded to a British devaluation of the pound, followed by market forces setting in to correct for the devaluation. Early 1970 devaluations by the U.S. (p. 650) speeded up the adjustment process, resulting in a return to the 1.12 level.

Efforts of the kind made by the British from 1931 until 1979 precluded the law from working properly and contributed to isolated rather than unified markets. The cliche since 1931, Friedman noted, has been that we have become one world. But in reality the reverse is true. "The technological improvements, which might have been expected to unify the world, have been more than offset by governmental intervention, which has fragmented the world into separate, isolated markets."[35] The F/S study showed how detrimental domestic economic policies were to the achievement of unified markets.

The need for adjustments in price indexes and/or in exchange rates actually appears in two ways. The one just anticipated, where Friedman gave advice to Britain, and in the matter of a country simply not able to control all of such key variables as the price average, the level and stability of aggregate employment, the level and compensation of the balance of payments (which is to say exchange rates also, given that the price averages are controlled). The latter comes up as we consider the late Lord Kaldor's policy positions for Britain and related methods of data analysis.

The disagreement Friedman expressed with Keynes's 1923 work (pp. 449-451) was with Keynes's views on discretionary control by monetary authorities. This disagreement may be more strongly found in later positions taken by Britain's Lord Kaldor during Thatcher's first term of office.

So why did Keynes accept discretionary control and why did Friedman denounce it? Friedman's answer:

> He [Keynes] was confident that the authorities had—or could have—sufficient knowledge to achieve these objectives and that, given the power, they would use it for that purpose.
>
> Discretion in the hands of public-spirited and competent civil servants fitted in well with Keynes's elitist political philosophy. But it must also be granted that, at the time he wrote, little or no experience existed to judge how such a method of regulating the supply of money would work in practice.[36]

In his centenary piece on J. M. Keynes, Friedman discussed the conflict between the stability of exchange by referring to Keynes's 1923 work entitled *A Tract on Monetary Reform*. Friedman proceeded:

> Though Keynes was a great theorist, his interest in theory was not for its own sake but as a basis for designing policy. In Monetary Reform, his conclusions about "the evil consequences of instability in the standard of value" led him to examine "the theory of money and of the theoretical foundations for the practical suggestions of the concluding chapters".
>
> His most original contribution, in my opinion, was his emphasis on the conflict between stability of prices and stability of exchange: If . . . the external price level lies outside our control, we must submit either to our own internal price level or to our exchange being pulled about by external influences. If the external price level is unstable, we cannot keep both our own price level and our exchanges stable. And we are compelled to choose.

Continuing to express a preference for internal price stability over stability in exchange rates, Friedman also supported Keynes:

> I have long shared Keynes's view on this subject, simply expanding it to include the rejection of exchange control as a device for

disconnecting the internal from the external price level. And clearly, actual policy in the major countries of the world has moved slowly and at long last in the same direction—not, indeed, in the sense of achieving stable prices, but of accepting flexible exchange rates and, for the most part, rejecting exchange controls in order to preserve independence in domestic monetary policy.[37]

A Shared Financial System

Particularly because of what we have pointed to as "the indirect method" and "the newer contributions," *Monetary Trends* is relevant to the relationship between Friedman, the politicians in Britain during Thatcher's early years, and complex economic ideas for a variety of reasons. First, in relation to the work, economists who were more oriented toward the fashions of movements along static schedules and the direct use of multiple regression equations had obvious difficulty in dealing with it. In their approach, variables are simply added to improve so-called "explanatory power" and there is the illusion that the effect of each relevant bit of the policy details can be separated out from the rest of the detail (pp. 71-77). Second, in relation to *Monetary Trends* we find Friedman had inside information when he lectured and visited in Britain during the period prior to the political shift that we associate with Thatcher. Third, the portrayed, shared financial system found in *Monetary Trends* suggested special problems for any detailed regulation of one economy in an interrelated system. And, fourth, some important economic findings bearing on one economy in the interrelated system may be shared with the other.

As already introduced, Charles Goodhart was one of those as late as 1982 having difficulty with Friedman's uses of statistical methods. We find Goodhart said:

> This is an important valuable book, in which the statistical evidence on the interrelationships between money, prices, output and interest rates is assessed carefully and rigorously, though in a somewhat *idiosyncratic manner*.[38]

To be sure, economists had struggled before with what Friedman actually said from the beginning of his first pieces. But this struggle was compounded when both American and British economists began to pick up on Friedman's "idiosyncratic manner" in relation to the past fashion in econometrics and what we introduced earlier as atheoretical econometrics (pp. 68-71).

The failure to appreciate this difference even accounts for some of the further difficulties at the Bank of England when it attempted to use expert opinion and switch from a traditional approach toward monetary policy to the M-regime. The traditional approach centered about interest rates and the idea that the central bank set these in a fairly direct way. In econometric approaches there was the idea of a variable on one side of an equation (say, an interest rate, i) and variables on the other (including say a monetary stock, M) such that stable relations existed (say that M and i are related in a direct predictable way). Further the approaches made no distinction between cyclical and trend components in the data.

Thus, Goodhart also objected to the concentration on distinct trends and cyclical components of the time series. He preferred data analyses without the separation of the data components of the type F/S undertook. At this point, on the one hand, he lamented "F-S are out of tune with current trends in econometrics" and, on the other, he applauded the approach where "a few well chosen graphs...are frequently far more illuminating than those generalized multiple correlations relating the dependent variable to a whole raft of possible independent variables." At this point, Goodhart concluded that "modern econometricians" would look "askance at some of F-S's econometric methodology." Prevalence of this latter use of methods gave a false sense of central bank control at a point in time, rather than within the time frames and interrelationships Friedman emphasized.

Moreover, the econometric fashion gave a false sense of control to central banks and others who embraced the method in other ways, as will come up on other occasions. There, we will encounter the notion of a left-hand-side variable (say real income or production) and right-hand-side variables (say, the dollar/pound exchange rate, the interest rate, and the inflation rate) that are said to be independent variables. There is the common illusion that, in a free society, each of the right-hand-side variables can be separately controlled by government to achieve whatever growth of production and employment is desired. In other words, in specific contexts, there is the idea that the exchange rate, the interest rate, and price averages can be set at desired levels without further consideration about freedom, incentives, adjustments in a free society, and so on.

A major conclusion of the F/S study was that the U.S. and the U.K. have many shared characteristics. The U.S. and the U.K. share common financial systems; a basic stable, monetary relation found in the one country is present in the other; the velocities of money balances (i.e., the portions of income expressed in weeks of pay that the "economic actors," Friedman's term for participants in economic activity, wish to hold) are highly correlated for the two countries, as are a number of other variables; and the two countries have in common the same determinants of the money demand functions. A major result of these findings was that no conditions special to just one of the countries need to be brought into discussion, as far as these important empirical findings were concerned.[39]

Parallel movements in "velocities" (the V, also V = 1/k, from page 417) and their rates of change, and other analyses of the U.S. and the U.K. indicated similar chronologies with respect to turning points and business conditions.[40] But when one juxtaposes this evidence with low correlations between the time rates of change for real per capita income in the respective countries, F/S reported "that the factors affecting the movements in real income over periods longer than a cycle but shorter than a sizable fraction of a century, are largely independent in the two countries." These may be due to special institutional factors, ideological shifts, government's role in the economy. In this sphere, moral and ethical considerations gain in importance. Here, we later encounter Margaret Thatcher's advocacy of what she considered to be the "traditional British way of life," in reference to a more distant past, and effort on her part to put "Great" back in "Britain."

Not dealt with in the F/S study, but bearing on the conclusion of a shared financial system and monetary controls, are some mechanical aspects of central bank operations. These require further introduction.

The Monetary Control Mechanism

In addition to a shared financial system, the U.S. and the U.K. have similar central banking systems and means for controlling money and credit aggregates. In both instances, special problems in the control of money and credit control arose when the respective central banks changed from a Keynesian control arrangement, with attention to interest rates, to a control of money and credit aggregates. That system was the almost single handed accomplishment of one man.

In the U.S., the switch from one method to the other began at the policy-making level in January 1970 (chap. 8, pp. 237-240). However, the change occurred slowly for two reasons: (1) central bank officials were reluctant to fully adopt the money aggregates approach; and (2) the use of interest rates in attempts to control the monetary aggregates persisted until October 6, 1979 (pp. 261-263). From developments in 1975 came the practice of announcing a range periodically for one year in advance for selected aggregates.

In that decade the financial markets became particularly sensitive to reports on the money stock that indicated governments' lack of resolve to achieve announced intentions. This problem continued to worsen until the Reagan presidency in the U.S. (chap. 16).

Efforts at change from an i-regime to an M-regime in the U.S. also appeared in Britain beginning in 1976. In 1980, the Bank of England reported such a policy as their current objective, "defined in terms of a target rate of growth for the money supply (sterling M3)."

We observe that a range for the money aggregate was reported in the U.K. just as it was in the U.S. In 1980, we further find this statement of the Bank's resolve: "The Bank seeks to affect the operations in the money market, which in turn influence short-term interest rates, and in the gilt-edge market where the aim is to finance the Government's borrowing needs as far as possible outside the banking system."[41]

Milton Friedman warned of the Central Bank's resolve:

> When we shift from the strategy of monetary policy to the tactics, it is essential to distinguish lip-service from a change in policy. Central bankers throughout the world have rendered lip-service to the control of monetary aggregates by announcing monetary growth targets. However, few have altered their policies to match their professions of faith. Most have continued to try to ride several horses at once by simultaneously trying to control monetary aggregates, interest rates, and foreign exchange rates—in the process introducing excessive variability into all three. And few have altered their operating procedures to make them consistent with the professed goal of controlling monetary growth. Bureaucratic inertia has been stronger than the pressure to fit actions to words. The United States is a particularly egregious example, mitigated so far only very partially by the Federal Reserve System's October 6, 1979 pronouncement [chapter 8, p. 262].[42]

British spokesmen at the time continued to attest to the importance of credibility in the newly evolved arrangements of announcements, and the influence of these announcements on the formation of expectations.[43]

As of 1980 the main differences in the control arrangements for the U.S. and the U.K. central banks were as follows: (1) The Bank of England made loans (discounts and advances) directly to its private customers and in practice it did not refuse loans to a special group called "the discount market,"[44] whereas in the U.S. the initiative for expanding bank reserves lay with the central bank and took place mainly through open market operations; (2) the Bank of England accommodated requests for advances to the Treasury, whereas in the U.S. the so-called independent Federal Reserve did not in practice accommodate the government directly, but might have done so indirectly by supplying more reserves to commercial banking institutions than would have been called for by the growth in real production;[45] (3) the arrangements with private banks in the U.K. for meeting reserve requirements were far "looser" than that in the U.S. and continued to be so, even with changes announced in late August of 1981.[46] The main reserve asset in the U.S. was deposits held by private banks at the Federal Reserve, whereas up until the changes of late August 1981, in the U.K. banks held a variety of assets to meet reserve requirements.[47]

Beyond these differences, the control mechanism and the issues involved in a transition to Friedman's approach were not too different. The U.S. mechanism of Friedman's approach is one in which bank reserves are controlled primarily through open market purchases and sales of securities and secondarily through the use of loan and discount facilities. In Friedman's approach, the reserves of the private institutions are controlled, and these in turn control bank credit (loans and investments) and money aggregates.

Partly because of the approach of the central banks to interest rates, and the poorly understood link between interest rates and money stocks, the central banks have at times exhibited an inability to control. This lack of ability has been confused at times with an unwillingness to control, possibly for political reasons (pp. 259-261). In both the U.S. and the U.K., the tendency of the narrower and broader measures of the money supply to drift apart at times further complicated the control of the money aggregates, but there is no apparent reason why this matter could not be dealt with (p. 658).

A step in finding a more stable target at the control level, involves shifting the control emphasis primarily to the "money base."[48] In the U.S. this meant control of the total for the reserves of the private institutions and the public's holdings of currency, including paper notes and coins. Beyond this the multiplier links between the reserves and the money and credit aggregates may be worked out, including with allowances for episodic changes which may impact on one or the other of the aggregates.

Whatever the details of the controls, there were two striking problems in the U.K. control mechanism, neither of which should appear insoluble. One was the multiplicity of assets that served as reserves for the U.K. banks,[49] and the other, shared with the U.S., was the presumption that short-term interest rates could be used by the central bank to control the money supply in a fairly specific way.

Though perhaps a more desirable than expected change, Friedman said, replacing the multiple reserve system with a single asset, "liabilities of the Bank of England in the form of notes or deposits (i.e. base money)," would be desirable.[50] Further, in the Keynesian (or historical banking) control mode, attention was on the interest rate, as we state on various occasions. In the early post-WW II years, expectations surrounding inflation rates were presumed to be independent of monetary policy and of interest rates. The assumption determining Bank of England operations was that accelerated growth in bank reserves, bank credit, and the money stock would lower interest rates, and that in such an environment market rates would fall below the Bank Rate set by the Bank of England (the term "Bank Rate" was later changed to "the minimum lending rate," MLR, which is a minimum rate at which the Bank of England stands ready to lend at last resort to a discount house). Setting the bank rate below or above the market was thought of as a part of the control mechanism. This thinking was such that an expansion of credit reduced market rates and thwarted borrowing from the Bank of England by the special customers of the discount market.[51]

Friedman spoke of the Bank of England's difficulties in getting away from its preoccupation with interest rates as being based in the Bank's history and the economic circumstances in which it functioned.[52] As matters developed, presumptions on the Bank's part about the formation of expectations (or their absence) was just the reverse of the facts that became so vivid in the U.S., and, Friedman suggested, in the U.K. also. Hence, on the basis of this new evidence the use of interest rates to control the money base or the other money and credit aggregates was brought into question.

After reading the 1980 British document called the "Green Paper" on *Monetary Control*,[53] Friedman commented:

> I could hardly believe my eyes when I read, in the first paragraph of the summary chapter, "The principal means [of controlling the growth of the money supply] must be fiscal policy—both public expenditure and tax policy—and interest rates." Interpreted literally, this sentence is simply wrong. Only a Rip Van Winkle, who had not read any of the flood of literature during the past decade and more on the money supply process, could possibly have written that sentence. Direct control of the monetary base is an alternative to fiscal policy and interest rates as a means of controlling monetary growth. Of course, direct control of the monetary base will affect interest rates (though not in the way that is implied in chapter 4 of the Green paper), but that is a very different thing from controlling monetary growth through interest rates.[54]

Sir Gordon Richardson, the Governor of the Bank of England no less, had said: "The main strategic instruments for influencing the growth of money supply are interest rates and fiscal policy—tax rates and public expenditures."[55]

Friedman continued on the control of the money supply through interest rates:

> The attempt to control the money supply through interest rates reflects a long-standing confusion between money and credit. Most credit is not money, by any definition of money; much money is not credit (as is clearest with a commodity standard such as gold). Bank of England notes used to be described, and perhaps still are, as "promises to pay." They are clearly not that today. They are simply fiat, not in any meaningful sense a credit instrument. Interest rates are the price of credit not the price of money. The price of money is the quantity of goods and services that will "buy" a piece of money (the reciprocal of the price level). Manipulating interest rates may have a decided influence on the demand for credit—though even that is dubious because of the limited range of interest rates that the Bank can manipulate. But it has a highly erratic and undependable influence on the quantity of money demanded over the kind of short periods which are crucial for monetary control (periods of a few months up to a year or more). Why else has it been that central banks seeking to control monetary aggregates in this way have had so poor a record in achieving their monetary targets, while they have had an excellent record in achieving their specific interest rate targets? Trying to control the money supply through "fiscal policy . . . and interest rates" is trying to control the output of one item (money) through altering the demand for it by manipulating the incomes of its users (that is the role of fiscal policy) or the prices of substitutes for it (that is the role of interest rates). A precise analogy is like trying to control the output of motor cars by altering the incomes of potential purchasers and manipulating rail and air fares. In principle, possible in both cases, but in practice highly inefficient. Far easier to control the output of motor cars by controlling the availability of a basic raw material, say steel, to the manufacturers—a precise analogy to controlling the money supply by controlling the availability of base money to banks and others.[56]

Following the publication of the Green Paper on monetary control to which Friedman responded, the Bank of England reported consultations and discussions directed toward improving operating and control techniques "within the existing framework."[57] By August of 1981 the Bank had made further changes[58] in response to the call for more forceful control of the country's "monetary base" and less emphasis on interest rates (including the MLR) in the conduct of the country's monetary policy. Staff at the Federal Reserve's Chicago bank further described the context of the changes at the Bank of England.[59]

Economic Thought in Transition

As we have emphasized, the flow of Friedman's ideas to Britain represented a reversal in a long history of economic thought. However, as also introduced, this flow of thought was not without some opposition and lags in adjustment. The lags are apparent, first, in the Thatcher government's efforts at a transition from an i-regime in central banking to an M-regime, and, second, in the discussion of the effort at a new policy as found in the collection of papers, memoranda, and reports provided by the government in 1980.[60]

The conflict between the "prevailing fashion" and Friedman's indirect method is present in a comparison of the Government's 1980 papers on monetary control and the uses of statistical method found there. In Friedman's case, the Treasury and Civil Service Committee (TCSC's) "Questionnaire on Monetary Policy"[61] contained statements attributed to the Chancellor of the Exchequer and the Financial Secretary which reflected rather clearly the new direction of policy in terms of a target rate of growth for a monetary aggregate (M3), analysis of expectations, and priority given to reducing inflation and "strengthening the supply side of the economy." The same was true of the Treasury's memorandum.[62]

In contrast to the changes taking place at the political level, matters at the economic level were in shams. Immediately following the staff-prepared questionnaire was an "Appendix on Econometric Evidence," presented as an aid in "weighing the empirical evidence submitted by witnesses." The investigator then encounters questions about the "Model Structure" and "Equation Estimation and Testing." There was interest in the model's principal equations and "how these are determined in 'complete' models." With possibly some minor refinements, the implied approach reflected the state of interest in large-scale economic models of the late 1960s, such as we associated with Lawrence Klein (chap. 3, pp. 71-77).[63] Even so, TCSC's later *Report* pointed to the state of model construction and said, "There is no generally agreed process of testing to which models should be subjected, such as that sought by the Committee's questionnaire."[64] (A similar conflict over econometric modeling comes up in chapter 16, where President Reagan's budget director, David Stockman played a role in the public discussion.)

In any case, even the TCSC's review of models suggested that, in some form, further research along the lines of "prevailing fashion in econometric work" may be worth the cost. The *Report* spoke of the need for published work on a "sustained systematic process of inter-model comparison, tracking down the reasons for differences between models and the justification of them."[65] The whole emphasis was suggestive of what Friedman called a Walrasian approach, an interest in elegance and detail.

This approach further reflected an interest in detail and the prospect of separating out short- and other-term, detailed relations—say as between interest rates, exchange rates, and some money or credit aggregate—all such that, through some Central Bank manipulation, targets for inflation and unemployment rates could miraculously be achieved.[66] A major change that came about in the use of the common econometric technique of the mid-1960s in the U.S. involved shifting emphasis from claims about policy questions and causal linkages among variables to one of simply forecasting without regard to policy actions and causal linkages. A body of literature on the evaluation of forecasting models emerged, but we still encountered the judgmental input of forecasters as being of overriding importance to successful forecasts (p. 74). In other words, the econometric claims of the '60s came to a point of embarrassment as to objective, scientific content.

A portion of the fault with the prevailing econometric approach of the 1960s and '70s, and a major part of what separated Friedman from the others, lay in a difference in the methods pursued in thinking and in research, as well as in methodology. These differences affected the entire discussion of the way the world works, albeit almost entirely below the surface. Work associated with David Laidler may be used to illustrate this point, both because he wrote widely on the demand for money and because of his presence among those who submitted memoranda in response to the 1980 questionnaire from the Treasury and Civil Service Committee.[67] Interestingly, in view of these differences, Laidler had been a graduate student at the University of Chicago.

Laidler proceeded, as we may also, with reference to a stable demand relationship with money balances (real or nominal M) as a left-hand-side variable and some other variables as right-hand side variables (say, the rate of interest, i, and the expected inflation rate, $\dot{P}$, and other things, u) in an equation. For simplicity, $M/P = f(i, \dot{P}, u)$. For Laidler, economic theory determined which variables to experiment with in the right-hand member, and explanatory power in a strict computational sense determined which variables to retain. Those retained on the right-hand side are those accounting for most of the variation on the left-hand side. Coefficients to the variables are estimated and stability is important, since the idea is to predict the effect on the left-hand side from the change on the right—all relying upon the stability of the coefficient attached to the right-hand side variable. For the Central Bank the idea is to control the rate of interest and, therefore, some part of the left-hand side variable. This control would come about at a point in time, although the prospect of lags in the effect from one side to the other may be introduced.

Now, indeed, Laidler saw this as basic scientific method in economics and incorrectly as the method Friedman adopted also. He proceeded with the idea of a basic/stable relation analogous to Friedman's basic/stable relationship mentioned earlier,[68] and also proceed to view Friedman not in terms of his alternative approach but as if they share a common approach. The next step is to view the policy control matter as if they have a shared view of it.

In contrast to Laidler's use of the presumably stable relation, with assumptions of causation of policy (the interest rate) implied, for Friedman, the stable relationship simply became a centerpiece in further study about the demand for money or its velocity.[69] The main question he asked was—"How do changes in the nominal quantity of money (as a rate of change) work to alter income, prices and output separately, and interest rates?" To deal with this question, Friedman used economic theory (or alternatively the mechanical apparatuses found in economics) in an indirect way to generate fruitful empirical hypotheses. The mechanical device Friedman used in this context was that of the liquidity preference demand for money.[70] He added motion, which we will illustrate in chapter 18.

Whether Friedman's hypotheses are useful depends on far more evidence than the statement of the basic/stable relationship.[71] Where time series vary so much together, as they do, the task of finding a regression equation with high explanatory power in the computational sense is too easy. So, for policy purposes, a policy-maker or an economist should not just go out and manipulate right-hand side variables in a presumed-to-be stable relation and expect to control target variables. At least this should not be expected to happen in the context of the fashion of the 1960s and 1970s.

Friedman's formulations of hypotheses and his statistical analyses were more persuasive than those of other economic theorists in his day precisely because of his method, which we take up further in chapter 18. His approach made a difference in the way evidence is interpreted and in the subsequent making of policy recommendations. In the outline of Friedman's views, we see changes in the monetary aggregates (time rates of change) affecting the demand for money, expected inflation, and then interest rates in the order listed here, not the other way around, as in the case of Laidler. Hence, in contrast to Friedman, Laidler said the following in summarizing evidence:

> The importance of the rate of interest for the demand for money is now estimated beyond any reasonable doubt...
>
> Of the many studies that have been carried out, we are aware of only three that have failed to find a significant negative relationship between the rate of interest and the demand for money.
>
> The orders of magnitude of the interest elasticity estimates found by Laidler...for Great Britain over the period 1900-1965 seem to be similar to those implied by United States data and again show little variation between sub-periods.[72]

(Only much later did Laidler express awareness of the extreme differences between Friedman's and other approaches to data analyses. This was after he had seen the *Monetary Trends* volume and Charles Goodhart's review of it).[73]

With respect to the demand function, Laidler and other economists who shared his views revealed a tendency to overlook the distinction between money and credit and to consider the rate of interest as the policy indicator. Their opinion was that a high rate of interest reduces the demand for money (i.e., viewed incorrectly by them, it reduces spending).[74] A rejection of this incorrect view of policy was present in Lord Croham's reply to the 1980 questionnaire, where he said: "The essential feature of any monetary policy in current conditions will be a quantitative target for the money supply. In inflationary conditions nominal interest rate objectives would be either meaningless or dangerous."[75]

Croham's statement implied the inappropriateness of using the interest rate as a policy indicator with the idea of its impact on spending, as well as the complications in using it to aid the central bank in controlling the money supply. F/S and Friedman, as taken up earlier in chapter 11 (pp. 446-447), expected to find a liquidity effect, plus a form of loanable funds effect (i.e., a negative correlation between money growth and interest rates), an income effect and then a Fisher effect (i.e., positive correlation). They found, instead, that beginning in the mid-1960s the structure underlying the formation of expectations changed. This change altered their interpretation so that, for example, the Fisher effect swamps the liquidity effect. Even uncertainty in the inflation rate forecast could be added.[76]

Of the eight individuals responding to the TCSC's questionnaire (D. E. W. Laidler, M. Friedman, J. Williamson, R. Dornbusch, Lord Croham, F. H. Hahn, Lord Kaldor, A. P. Minford, and Sir Alec Cairncross), four made specific reference to Friedman's work in connection with U.K. Government's policies at the time (Hahn, Kaldor, Minford, and Cairncross). Along with Friedman, the analysis of expectations, and the basis for the new macroeconomic policy, however, Minford mentioned the "Rational Expectations approach to economic policy pioneered in the USA by Professor Robert Lucas of Chicago and Thomas Sargent of Minnesota, and propagated in policy discussions by the Federal Reserve Bank of Minneapolis [chap. 3, pp. 68-71]."[77] Though it draws heavily on Friedman, as indicated earlier, and is largely Chicago based, it is not Friedman's monetarism, nor the monetarism that impacted on central banks in the U.S., the U.K., and elsewhere.

In his response to the U.K. Treasury questionnaire, Lord Kaldor discussed what he viewed as monetarists' propositions generally, and mentioned only Friedman by name in reference to them.[78] In some instances, as in the case of Laidler, there was some obvious misunderstanding of Friedman's theory, evidence, or approach. Only partly correct, Lord Kaldor noted in reference to monetarist positions, "In the 'long run'...real output and its distribution are fully determined by such 'real' factors [as technical progress, the growth of the effective labor supply and the rate of capital formation that are determined by market forces independently of changes in the money supply]." "There is," he said, "no scope for any macropolicies with the objectives listed in Q1 [(a) the level and stability of aggregate employment, (b) the level and composition of the balance of international payments, (c) the rate of inflation, and (d) the rate of economic growth] except for the control of inflation which can be achieved (and only achieved) by control of the money supply."[79]

Though Kaldor was correct in this statement, as far as Friedman's theory had been concerned in the past, and though his contribution dealt with many issues,[80] we may mention three overlooked facets of Friedman's work. Overlooked were: (1) the analysis of fluctuations about trends which became important to an overall understanding of causes and effects; (2) the prospect that social and political instability generated in the short run may be irreparable; and (3), contrary to Friedman's own hopes about the neutrality of money in the long swings in business conditions, the F/S finding that monetary disturbances are a principal cause of long swings also.[81]

As F/S began to deal with trends, they noted as early as 1972 that lengthening the period of analysis used to compute rates of change eliminated short, erratic movements, but reduced "only moderately the amplitude of the fluctuations in money and nominal income, leaving long, relatively smooth swings..." They highlighted the matter further by studying swings of three, five, seven, and nine business-cycle phases in duration. They saw these as being the same species as long swings in economic activity studies by such American investigators as Arthur Burns, Simon Kuznets, and Moses Abramovitz. The long swings were reported to be present not only in money and nominal income, but also in real income, with smaller amplitude in the latter. Though varying in the degree of clarity in some instances, the swings were present in both the U.S. and the U.K. The investigation was not as thorough as F/S would like, so much was left "to investigators concerned more centrally with long swings."

The finding that money impacts on long swings gains in importance when we reflect on the prospect that the harmful effects of excessive money supply distort the traditional role of prices in coordinating diverse interests in the market economy. In this respect, both Friedman and the 1974 Nobel Laureate and long time observer of the British scene, Friedrich von Hayek, made observations. Hayek noted: "The harmful effects of an excessive supply of money consist not merely of changes of the average price level, but quite as much on the distortion of the whole structure of relative prices and the consequent misdirection of productive efforts which it causes."[82] Friedman said: "At all times the forces determining relative prices are at work. What inflation, and in particular erratic inflation, does is to introduce noise into the signals that are being transmitted; it therefore tends to introduce friction into the relative price adjustments."[83]

On the other hand, Cambridge University's Lord Kaldor proceeded somewhat differently. Raising other questions, Kaldor dealt with the Walrasian model of the economy underlying a monetarist view. Among the quite reasonable questions he asked was why inflation is important if the "behavior of the 'real' economy is neutral with respect to monetary disturbances"?

The response to this question is twofold. First, there were monetarist implications in early references to Friedman's "primal equation" to the effect that monetary disturbances were neutral in the long run (the secular trend in Friedman's case). Second, however, the empirical results in *Monetary Trends* were not entirely what F/S had hoped for in the already reported shift in the structure underlying the formation of inflationary expectations in the mid 1960s and what they expected about the long run.

In clarifying the position on the Marshallian/Walrasian systems of equations, Friedman said:

> There is no conflict between Walras and Marshall with respect to the relative price systems we have in equilibrium. Marshall would certainly accept Walras's description of what that general price system would look like; there is no fundamental difference in that respect. The difference between Marshall and Walras is not that Marshall would say relative prices are different than Walras or that Walras would say they are different from Mar-

shall, but that Marshall deals with a very different problem than what the structure of relative prices would be at full equilibrium. He deals with the problem of how to analyze disturbances in that full equilibrium by examining particular sectors through partial as opposed to general equilibrium analysis. He has an engine of analysis rather than a description of the end product of full adjustment.[84]

According to a rigid statement of Friedman's approach, in the long run (the secular trend, the permanent component) all anticipations are realized, while in the short run there are unrealized expectations (money illusions, "irrationality"). In the long run, the balance (the equilibrium) is "determined by the Walrasian equations of general equilibrium, which determine the real variables, plus the quantity theory, which, for given real variables, determines the price level." This is another way of saying that, in the long run, all excessive growth in the money stock affects the general price level rather than real magnitudes.

In the short run, there is an adjustment process, in which "the rate of adjustment in a variable is a function of the discrepancy between the measured and the anticipated values of that variable or its rate of change, as well as, perhaps, of other variables or their rates of change." Now, however, in view of the evidence F/S reported in 1982, and the potential for more, the time at which Walrasian equations, as addressed by Kaldor, come into play may lie in an even more distant long run.

Monetarist Impact (continued)

As earlier chapters attest, Keynesian economics in general came to U.S. universities in the 1940s and '50s, to Washington, D.C. in the 1960s, and to London and Westminister somewhat earlier than it did to Washington D.C. In both instances, the shift in the structure underlying the formation of inflationary expectations, as reported by F/S coincided with Keynesian economics' arrival in Washington and with faster growth in money and credit aggregates in the U.K. As the Nobel laureate von Hayek himself said, "There can be no doubt that it was in Keynes's name and on the basis of his theoretical work that the modern world has experienced the longest period of general inflation." Continuing, he said that it has no gain to pay for the inflation because of widespread and severe depression.[85]

At the center of Keynesian economics, of course, was what came to be referred to as "demand management," management of total spending through monetary and fiscal policy. The monetary part, however, was not effective for a combination of reasons: its theoretical argument was flawed, and the empirical evidence to support that argument never adequately materialized. In Britain, especially, we encounter in the 1950 "Radcliffe Report" (so-called after Lord Radcliffe, the chairman of the committee that authored the report), a very strong view on the ineffectiveness of monetary policy,[86] and we encounter there the Phillips curve as well.

As inflation increased, the Phillips curve—so named after A. W. Phillips of the London School of Economics (p. 219)—provided a supportive argument, namely: that the acceptance of a permanently higher inflation rate could be traded for a permanently lower unemployment rate. As analysis and research later indicated, this was not only a relatively static argument, it was also false. The stimulating effect on spending came from upward movement in the inflation rate and not, Friedman pointed out, from the level it reached at any particular time.[87] In the end, accelerating inflation reached socially disruptive limits—attention on the part of the "actors" shifted from production to speculative, precautionary, and defensive activities. What we had—even in its mild stages—was a "trade off" different from that suggested by A. W. Phillips. We were asked to accept permanently higher inflation even for a temporary reduction in unemployment. The welfare losses of the one versus the gains of the other are questionable.

Lord Kaldor was among the British economists who first began to deal with these matters. While offering an argument for the most part contrary to that of Friedman on the Phillips curve, Lord Kaldor commented: "Nobody, I think would advocate hyper-inflation as a cure for inflation." He wrote, "it is like advocating the spread of a highly contagious disease in order to acquire immunity from it." Yet, analyses of change and empirical studies indicated that Kaldor's statement signifies precisely what the Keynesian/Phillips curve approach came to.

We find in Kaldor's memorandum to the Treasury and Civil Service Committee in 1980 the sort of advocacy that Friedman opposed in Galbraith and in American Keynesians. First, Kaldor advocated freezing "*all* wages, salaries, dividends and rents and *all* prices of home made goods, for an indefinite period." He argued for a "*permanent* incomes policy," a policy of controlling all items that are frozen. In this detailed control approach, he advocated achieving multiple goals through government "economic management." Kaldor saw these goals as including "(a) the level and stability of aggregate employment, (b) the level and composition of the balance of payments, (c) the rate of inflation, and (d) the rate of economic growth." Having many goals, Kaldor encountered the old mathematical problem of having more goals than instruments of policy, so he recognized the need for a multiplicity of instruments ("ideally the same number as there are objectives").[88] The mathematical idea of having enough goals and enough instruments to assure logical relationships between the goals and the instruments, however, is not the same as having stable parameters between each target and each instrument as may be estimated from actual data, nor does the mathematical idea assure an independence of instruments in relation to one another, such that the instruments can be adequately manipulated.

Whatever the real-world complications for policy implementation, there is in the mathematical notion of an equal number of targets and instruments, the idea that with all these controls government has only to set the dials to achieve the result. In Friedman's view, this is exactly what government is ill equipped to do. This problem of government is what Friedman saw in the U.S., following the creation of the Federal Reserve in 1913. Beginning with an incomes policy and government as the West has known it, one ends with government officials threatening intervention to put down the revolutionaries who "in effect" opposed the wage and price guidelines.

Congdon emphasized earlier the sense in which a free society depends on the proper functioning of a monetary system. "As the critics understand," he said, "monetarism is not politically neutral." Moreover, the expressed hostility toward monetarism is "more a matter of ideology." Along such lines we encounter Lord Kaldor's booklet titled *The Scourge of Monetarism*.[89]

Monetary policy along Friedman's line of thinking—as rejected by Keynesians and the Walrasians Friedman mentioned—enters variously into analysis. In two respects the credit and monetary aggregates (bank reserves, base money, bank credit, various measures of the money stock) got out of control: (1) as monetary officials (the Federal Reserve in the U.S. and the Bank of England in the U.K.) chased higher and higher interest rates in an attempt to keep them low, and (2) as the central bank supported the government's debt financing by faster growth in money and credit aggregates than real production would call for. This faster growth in the credit (bank loans and investments) aggregate facilitated the purchase of the government's debt instruments by the credit-creating, financial institutions.

In the first case, we encounter a variation on the relation posited by Irving Fisher in 1896, notably: the rate of interest is approximately equal to a real rate plus the expected rate of inflation. In Friedman's hands, accelerating the growth of money and credit aggregates was expected to have the following effects, in the order listed: (1) a Keynesian liquidity effect (in combination with a so-called loanable funds effect for bank credit), which is to say a temporary decline in interest rates; (2) and an intermediate income effect whereby accelerated money growth impacts on spending and shifts the static money demand curve outward with some overshooting (all such that interest rates rise rather than decline); and (3) the inflationary expectations effect as posited by Fisher (such that inflation drives interest rates up, irrespective of the central bankers' intentions).[90] What F/S reported, as cited earlier, is that the structure underlying the formation of expectations shifted in both the U.S. and the U.K. in the 1960s. Possibly this was the wide public attention increasingly directed to government economic policy, the effect being a greater sensitivity in the formation of inflationary expectations. Thus we come to move almost immediately from information on central bank policies to the reformation of expectations.

In the second case of bank policy listed above, we encounter the government budget constraint.[91] The perception of this, however, was altered dramatically when the analysis shifts from that of a monetarist-markets oriented approach to a collectivist approach.

International capital flows aside, the government budget constraint (259-260) indicated that government deficits can only be financed (1) through the support of the central bank, and/or (2) by the sale of bonds to the public without central bank support. The first is monetary policy, and the second route is called "crowding out" (the crowding out of private financing and capital investment). In his empirical research, Milton Friedman pointed out that the root cause of inflation is monetary policy, not government deficits or other causes. We call this Friedman's law. For him, inflation "over any substantial period, is always and everywhere a monetary phenomenon, arising from a more rapid growth in the quantity of money than in output." Control over the growth of money and credit aggregates leads to the control of inflation.[92]

Government deficits have the effect of a silent partner. The main reasons for controlling them are to control the growth of government and to lessen the prospect that monetary policy will be directed toward supporting their financing. If government is given revenues from any source, its officials will spend them. Thus, if one can restrain the central bank's inflationary tendencies, exhibited, for example, in the 1960s and 1970s, one can control inflation and reduce (or slow) the growth of government.

As in the U.S. (pp. 246-264), the question of the independence of the central bank arose in Great Britain. Writing shortly after the transfer of ownership of the Bank of England to the Government in March 1946, the Lloyds Bank's economic advisor, quite reasonably asked whether the Bank's Governor or the Government would act more responsibly. The partial answer he provided was that "it would certainly be incorrect to regard the Governor as the Chancellor's factotum [handy man] and the Bank merely as the Threadneedle Street branch to the Treasury." The simple issue Dacey envisioned was indicated by a question: "Whose resignation would be the more embarrassing to the government of the day—that of the Chancellor or the Governor?"[93]

The answer at that early date would be presumably that the Governor's resignation would be more embarrassing. In 1981, however, the answer would be different. With the rise of Friedman's new quantity theory and inflation in the U.S. and the U.K., the reputations of central bankers suffered. In the U.S. in 1981, one might have asked the question thus: In a political confrontation, who would win out, an elected minister (a president) or an appointed official?

The issue of central bank independence changed considerably when the prevailing theory shifted from one of presumed control through interest rates to one of control through money and credit aggregates. As defined earlier (p. 259), the culprit in the shift is known as the government budget constraint. In the aggregates system, a truly independent central bank has the power and authority to nullify the fiscal policy (measured in terms of government deficits) of the legislative branch. A truly independent central bank, then, would be in a position to control inflation and take the responsibility for it. Government, on the other hand, is in that position if the bank is government owned and/or controlled. The analysis of the Central Bank's position does not change, although we do encounter further argument by Lord Kaldor.[94]

An Overview

There is a history of economic thought in Britain from beginnings in Scotland, through the Cambridge years of Marshall and Keynes, as chapters 2 and 11 attest. With early common ties between the U.S. and Britain, this thought exerted its influence. However, Britain began to undergo rather dramatic changes in the 1920s and '30s, with J. M. Keynes playing a prominent role. It extended to the U.S. via the Keynesians and to what we identify in chapter 8 as the Keynesian era. Coinciding with and counter to some of these developments in Keynesian thought, we encounter intellectual developments in the U.S. in the person of Milton Friedman.

Friedman's monetary research was a positive contribution and served as an antidote to Keynesian economics. It is partly summed up in *Monetary Trends*, the culmination of parts of Friedman's thirty-four years of research. In time, Friedman's work with its distinct attributes—the indirect method, special time frames, time rates of change, money aggregates, price theoretic foundations, testing of one hypothesis against another, public debate, policy orientation, choice between the capitalist and socialist ethics, the failure of government, long swings in public opinion—had impact at the highest levels of government, as we will see in chapters 15 and 16. The acceptance of Friedman's work was fostered by the conditions of economic crisis—rising inflation and unemployment, with accompanying additional aspects of social disruption—in the U.K. and the U.S.

The story of Friedman's economics, the developing crisis, and the failures of government are interesting in themselves. Related themes include Friedman's impact abroad, which was partly the result of the incorporation of the U.K. in F/S's *Monetary Trends*. Friedman went public in the U.S. with his political tract and support of Goldwater as early as the early-to-mid 1960s, and his influence spread to London in the 1970s, and to those who later became leaders in the Thatcher government. In particular, the work undertaken in *Monetary Trends* with its extension to include the U.K. gave Friedman special familiarity with conditions there well before the published appearance of his work. Such findings as a shared demand function for money, and interdependence as depicted by the specie-flows mechanism and the law of one price supported the conclusion that Britain's economic-policy efforts in their Keynesian/socialist era were exerted in exchange for very little.

The study of money, as the Keynesian/monetarist confrontation indicates, and as we have duly noted, is not politically neutral, nor is its omission from economic study generally neutral, as some seeking refinement in the disguise of political neutrality may hope. Britain's Tim Congdon pointed out, as J.M. Keynes did much earlier, that a free society depends on the proper functioning of the monetary system. The function of money in commodity markets as an indirect means of satisfying wants is non-neutral ideologically, and the standard and store of value functions are too. Whatever assets serve the functions of money, and free gold no less, are the most liquid of all assets. Such monetary assets serve as a hedge on the part of the economic agents against some foreseen, unforeseen, and uncertain political and economic developments.

As we began to see in chapter 3 and on pages 409-410—as arises in the U.K. in the next chapter, and in the U.S. in chapter 16—the choice of an approach to the analysis of data is not itself neutral, as judged by analysis and historical developments and/or the scaling of theoretic/econometric topics as to the collectivist/statist and voluntary-association/monetarist implications. The choice of the large structural equations models, with attention to much detail, and Keynesian attributes has not been politically neutral. There have been the following: judgmental factors; inherent positions about the role of government to control the details of the models (the interest rates, exchange rates, and price levels, to start with) by the force of government where necessary; and the view of growth in the money and credit aggregates in relation to government deficits. Friedman proceeded differently but with no less political neutrality.

As may be expected from a new body of thought where old ideas of freedom, free trade, noninflationary price levels, reduced government, dispersed power, individual initiative, and, later, Thatcher's Victorian virtues enter—the new doctrine propagated from across the Atlantic was not adopted readily in the U.K. without some strong opposition and misinterpretations. In the U.K., the strongest opposition came from Lord Kaldor, a British Keynesian, and teachers of economics as a group, on the one hand; and the first acceptance, as we will see, came on the part of the economists of the City of London and those who entered into the Thatcher government.

The transition from the i-regime to the M-regime included some misleading positions on Friedman's part and some misinterpretations of Friedman's economics, models, and uses of methods. There are two senses in which Friedman's theory, more rigidly viewed, may be said to have met with shortcomings as a result of the empirical findings in *Monetary Trends*. For one, the structure underlying the formation of inflationary expectations shifted in the mid 1960s (and, we add later, shifted again in the mid 1980s). For another, the Walrasian, long run, end product of a full adjustment in prices may not be attained. Monetary disturbances, as reported in *Monetary Trends*, are capable of having very long-swing effects.

The transitional problems, furthermore, extended to the operations levels as well. The central bankers resisted in practice but offered lip service in support of change. The resistance in practice was partly inertia and lack of familiarity with the new, but there were also problems with the control arrangements and mechanisms. In one instance, tradition and Keynesian thought supported the notion that the interest rate could be used as a control variable to put the money aggregate on target. This arose in the U.K., as we have seen, and it comes up in the U.S., as we will see in chapter 16. In another instance, the fraction of bank reserves actually controlled by the Bank of England was small relative to the total of acceptable reserves, and the acceptable reserves included diverse loosely categorized instruments.

In brief, there are the transitional problems which come through in the next chapter, and there are the pillars of government policy which we consider along with the Thatcher government in the next chapter. The pillars are: the quantity theory of money; the open economy and the closely related law of one price; "supply side" and "incentivist" economics; and the analysis of expectations, at least along non-NCS lines (pp. 68-71).

Chapter 15
The Thatcher Government

As she emerged politically in the natural home of capitalism, Margaret H. (Hilda) Thatcher moved against the popular, historical-deterministic view of social evolution, denied its validity,[1] and moved toward Friedman's monetarism and the economics of individualism. To be sure, Marx's ghost in London's Highgate cemetery must have turned in its grave at the thought of Tories denying his theory of history.[2] Recalling Britain's history of vigorous individualism, Thatcher decried its decline into a "pocket-money society," where the fruits of one's work "belong mainly to the state." Out of the total value of their marginal product some were handed back a fraction each week for personal use.

In 1975 to 1976, *The Times* (of London) covered at relatively high technical levels the essence of Friedman's ideas as they may be found in his presidential address to the American Economic Association, his paper on liquidity preference, his "Comments on the Critics," his Nobel lecture on inflation and the Phillips curve, *Monetary Trends*, a few *Newsweek* columns, a negative income tax paper, and the lectures he gave in London on the transition from a Keynesian/socialist world to a free market arrangement with stable prices.[3] Hence Friedman's work received wide exposure at the time when Thatcher was making her move to become a philosopher of the right and head of her party.

The first of the lectures Friedman gave in the 1974-75 period was entitled "Unemployment versus Inflation," and the second "From Galbraith to Economic Freedom." Both were published in Britain by Lord (Ralph) Harris's Institute of Economic Affairs (IEA),[4] as was the Nobel lecture.

Lord Harris's institute was founded in Britain in 1957, partly as a reaction against the collectivist trends of the time. Its purpose was to educate and to publicize ideas. It emphasized the study of markets and prices and displayed a broad interest in conservative (radical right) opinion. The IEA established early contact with Friedman and extended its interest to what has been described as the "counterrevolution in macro-economics."[5]

This counterrevolution developed as a reaction to the influence of J.M. Keynes's major work *The General Theory*, itself a reaction to an earlier set of economic problems. Keynesian economics, as the emerging parochial view of Keynes's work was called, swept first the campuses of the major universities in the U.S. and the U.K. and then the halls and corridors of government in the post-WW II years. At first, as variously recounted, Keynes's work was viewed as offering a moderate prescription for the problem of inadequate employment of resources and labor. But in its impact on worldly affairs, the flawed, parochial view called Keynesian economics resulted in more economic problems than it solved: big government, rising inflation and unemployment, declining productivity and a decline in personal saving in relation to income. The failure of Keynes's and Keynesian theory to explain these problems was, in turn, widely viewed as a crisis in economic theory, which we introduced in chapter 11.[6]

On the negative side, the counterrevolution was simply a reaction against Keynesian economics, its accompanying socialist trends and the idea of a rigid private sector calling for a government actively involved in the management of the economy. On the positive side, it presented Friedman's economics as an antidote but also as offering new directions in economic theory and policy. Keynesian economics offered short-run solutions with temporary effects that resulted in the accumulation of long-run problems, as reviewed on an earlier occasion (p. 432). Friedman's body of economics directed attention toward the long run and to the transition from a Keynesian situation to a relatively more stable policy and political state. In this state, an activist, accommodative monetary policy is played down, supply-side (incentivist) aspects of production are encouraged, and the stable policy allows the private sector to adjust to contemporaneous and anticipated conditions.

The Keynesian activist policy started as a middle ground between the extremes of the political left and right, but that, as we have seen in Acts IV and V of Hicks's drama (pp. 427-430), broke down. Social forces took over the economics. As Thatcher's role indicates, the political/economic choice became a choice between extremes.

As indicated, Friedman's new body of economics emphasizes individualism, voluntary association, and social mobility. Picking up on such ideas, the new guiding spirits of the Conservative party in Britain in the mid 1970s put individualism back on the political agenda. Ian Bradley mentioned in particular the creation of "the Centre for Policy Studies by Mrs. Thatcher and Sir Keith Joseph in September 1974," and the circulation of a "bibliography of freedom" two years later throughout the universities and colleges by Sir Keith.[7] By 1975, Sir Keith was being referred to as Thatcher's political mentor. Joseph later served in various cabinet posts under Thatcher's leadership and in October '87 he was made a peer for life of the House of Lords. On a look backward in April '88 he recalled a change in the mid '70s in his views about the individual in relation to the state. He, Lord Joseph, had been a part of the political/economic problem before that date and, noting the time for change was right, he anticipated being a part of the solution. As a loyal supporter of Thatcher early on he said with the hindsight of April '88 that he had anticipated radical new direction of the type that did indeed come about—the taming of inflation, reductions in the ceilings on marginal tax rates, the privitization of industry and accompanying infrastructure changes. However, whether the politician's bravado or reality, he saw the more immediate monetary changes as only a first stage and saw the second, long-haul changes as more difficult—those of changing education and culture.

Friedman and Thatcher

The introduction of Friedman's economics in London may be dated by his giving the First Wincott Memorial Lecture there in 1969. It was entitled "The Counterrevolution in Monetary Theory," but could just as accurately have been entitled "The Monetary Revolution," for that was in fact what was under way.

Friedman's Wincott lecture of 1969 was published within a year by Lord Harris's Institute. Soon after, parts of his economics were rapidly accepted by the "economists of the city" (i.e., the commercial and investment banking economists).[8] The reaction against Keynesian economics had begun to appear in London, partly because of the emerging failures of previous policies and partly because of the plausible, empirically oriented alternative Friedman offered. In its most visible form, this alternative was called monetarism, albeit a textbook version as opposed to a more comprehensive system (pp. 209-211, 229). There were numerous researchers and writers involved in the emerging doctrine, but no one else was so much a part of it as Milton Friedman.

The same year as the Memorial lecture, Friedman gave a lecture at Northwestern University, where Alan A. Walters was on leave from the London School of Economics (LSE). Walters had previously been interested in the study of money and, in fact, had published the first edition of his *Money in Boom and Slump* at Lord Harris's Institute the previous year. Walters later served as economic advisor to Sir Keith (later Lord) Joseph and still later he became an intermediary in bringing monetarist concepts to the attention of Joseph and Margaret Thatcher. In 1975, Walters joined the faculty at Johns Hopkins University and became Advisor to the World Bank, but he continued his ties with Sir Keith and Thatcher, meeting with them on occasion when they were in New York.

In January 1981, Walters became Economic Advisor to Prime Minister Thatcher. However, other straws in the wind were having influence on her, as well as her links via politics and advisors. Lord Harris's Institute was publishing pamphlets and speeches and Thatcher actively followed the general discussion. To cite an example, TCSC's (Treasury and Civil Service Committee) *Report* noted in 1981 the influence of "monetarists" and that "the most prominent among them, Professor Friedman, has taken an active and critical interest in the application of these ideas to the U.K."[9]

Following Friedman's London appearances in the mid 1970s, discussions of policies associated with his work were linked with Margaret

Thatcher, as we shall see. Referring to what Friedman called the quantity theory of money and "the politician in the street" called monetarism, *The Sunday Times* writer Ronald Butt wrote that Thatcher had already been converted when she took over Tory economic policy from Mr. Heath in 1975.[10] There were also further links between Friedman and Thatcher via Sir Keith Joseph's position. Joseph was referred to in 1975 "as godfather to the new leader."[11]

Additional to the British situation, for the purpose of understanding Thatcher's role, there is a relatively unified structure to their government. The executive and the legislative are unseparated; the prime minister is the leader of the majority party in the parliament.[12]

Thatcher's Background

Margaret Thatcher's interest in political meetings dated back to her running errands in a 1935 election for a local party organization. She ran for parliament for the first time as a conservative (or Tory) party candidate in February 1950. In 1951 at the age of 26, she again ran for parliament, five weeks before getting married. A good student, she received a B.S. degree from Oxford in 1947 and later an M.A. degree. At Oxford she studied chemistry, along with the other subjects.

After starting a career as a research chemist, Thatcher began studying law the same year she was married. Two years later, in August 1953, she gave birth to twins, and four months after that she took her bar finals to qualify as a lawyer. In the next few years she practiced law, specializing in taxation and patent law. During that time, she faced some setbacks with respect to conflicts over the advancement of her career, renewed her determination to run for election, and soon accepted an invitation to run in Finchley—a north-London, upper-middle-class constituency. In October 1959, she won her election and took a seat in the 630-member House of Commons.[13]

As far back as 1966, Margaret Thatcher performed as an opposition spokesperson on taxation. In that role, she criticized the labor government's budget, was lauded in the press for her performance, and promised reductions in taxes when the Tories returned to power. When they did in June 1970, Thatcher was appointed to the Cabinet post of Secretary of State for Education and Science. In that post she was accountable for primary through higher education and charged with overseeing teacher training, financial aid to universities and students, and nonmilitary research and development. She was also responsible for close liaison with the teacher's union and local education authorities.

By 1972, Thatcher was embroiled in the issue of whether quality "independent" schools could operate side by side with "egalitarian" comprehensive schools. Her position was that flexibility and "freedom of choice" should be maintained in the school system. *Time* magazine quoted her: "I have sometimes thought that some extreme advocates of equality would be happy if all the children were in bad schools as long as they were equally bad..." She believed that there should be "a place for selected schools of excellence."[14]

In the cabinet post for education Thatcher also drew criticism for the government's cutback of funds to higher education "and for her move to establish stricter governmental control over student unions with the aim of depoliticizing them."[15] While she was still in the education post, the London *Observer* (10/10/72) congratulated her for her ten-year education plan "on the ingenuity with which she had been able to maintain reasonable standards while keeping up the drive for expansion in education right across the board."

The elections of 1974 brought the Labor party back to power with Harold Wilson as Prime Minister. Under Edward Heath's leadership, the Tories fared poorly in 1974 and 1975 even as Thatcher's role expanded in the important areas of economics and finance. Her views were thought to be well to the right of those of Heath, who in October 1975 appointed her as one of two "Tory front bench spokespersons on Treasury matters and economic affairs." As a spokesperson, Thatcher expounded views that sounded very much like those of Milton Friedman as early as 1974. Biographical sketches and press comments soon linked her name and that of her political associate, Keith Joseph, with Friedman.[16]

At this time, Thatcher maintained "that Britain's economic plight could best be alleviated by sharp reductions in public expenditures, a balanced budget, and sound monetary policies, rather than by efforts to control prices or guarantee full employment." "The tart-tongued Mrs. Thatcher," one biographical sketch stated, headed the opposition in the October 1974 election campaign by challenging the Labor government's finance bill, relentlessly attacking Labor's plans to raise taxes on inherited wealth, and provoking controversy "by suggesting that families should hoard canned foods as a possible hedge against inflation."[17]

Indicating her campaign style and rhetoric of five years hence Thatcher explained her party's October 1974 defeat as being caused by the party's not appearing "to stand firmly for anything distinctive and positive." In December of that year, she began "a low-keyed" campaign for leadership of her party with Sir Keith Joseph as her most influential supporter.[18] Three months later, in February 1975, Thatcher won her party's leadership in a vote of Conservative members of Parliament. Her vote was 130 against 119 for Edward Heath. When appointing her "shadow cabinet," as was customary for the opposition party in Britain, Thatcher created a new post for policy and research, headed by Sir Keith.

Shortly after Thatcher took leadership of the party, *The Economist* of London speculated over whether she could capture the center of the British electorate at the expense of the Labor party. *The Economist* expressed the view that after a "decent interval" she would likely "head for the center where elections are won." It further expressed the view that Thatcher needed "centrist henchmen" on the grounds that "oppositions are judged by men more than measures."[19]

Seven months later Thatcher made her first major overseas tour to North America. In the U.S., *The Economist* reported that Thatcher "dealt robustly with the worn convention that British leaders of the opposition do not run down their country abroad." They quoted her as saying: "It is not part of my job to be a propagandist for a socialist society."[20]

Upon her return from the U.S. *The Economist* noted a "boost given by her American stomp." It called attention to her theme "that the small man (or woman), the individual who without advantage pulls his or herself up by hard work, has been despised by the new establishment, 'the progressive consensus'." *The Economist* noted that Mrs. Thatcher's speeches "may make her ousted predecessor, Mr. Edward Heath, look like a faint-hearted liberal."

Four years later to the month, *The Economist* referred to Thatcher as "Atilla the hen" and noted the trouble her ministers were having with her. It stemmed, *The Economist* reported, "from the fact that, for the first time since the war, the party is being led not from the left of its center but from the right."[21]

By mid 1977, Thatcher was pictured as having "cast herself as her Tory party's philosopher queen." *The Economist* reported her as voicing "a widespread and justified frustration with bureaucracy, with high taxation and controls." Continuing, it noted, "In her recent speeches outlining the philosophical and religious basis of her free-market views she may also be satisfying a growing wish for a more serious moral element in political discussion." A little later *The Economist* stated that "Mrs. Thatcher is sorely aware that her acquired philosophy is not shared by all her colleagues."[22]

Contrary to what Margaret Thatcher's early positions on issues may indicate, like Milton Friedman and Ronald Reagan in the United States, she was not of aristocratic background. Eloquent, courageous, with piercing blue eyes, slight build, immaculate appearance, carefully enunciated speech, Margaret Thatcher was born as the second of two sisters in a flat above the family's grocery store. The date was October 13, 1925. The place was Grantham, "a market town in Lincolnshire, some 100 miles north of London."[23]

Deterioration, Transition, and Thatcher's Watershed Elections

Richard Rose, a student of British party politics for over a quarter century, reviewed in the late 1970s the post-WW II politics of Britain and found that parties had made little difference. When in power, the Conservative party had made concessions to the Labor party, and vice versa, with little difference. Rose found that consensus government usually dominated, and the consensus did not change much.[24]

The University of Liverpool's A. P. Minford came to similar conclusions.[25] He wrote, "The overwhelming problem we face in the U.K. economy is that of breaking, once and for all, the inflation psychology. This psychology consists in the belief that whatever strong words may be uttered by politicians and whatever actions may be taken to curb monetary growth and public sector borrowing, these actions will be temporary merely and the words ultimately meaningless." Such belief, he wrote, "has been reinforced by the actions of *every* post-war government." However, he found the freedom of government action restricted by the fixed exchange rate system before 1971, which we considered with reference to the "closing of the gold window" in the U.S. in chapters 8 and 11 (pp. 231-233, 429). Continuing, Minford said in accordance with what we called Act V of Hicks's drama, "we have seen first a Tory government and then a Labor government initiate a program of restraint only to discard it after a year or two, respectively in 1972-3 and in 1978-9."

In contrast, Margaret Thatcher's 1979 election campaign, election victories, and personal conviction offered the twofold possibility of real change in British economic life. First, she had new ideas to give substance to her convictions, plus more statistical results than had been dreamt possible by standards of the early 1960s. These ideas and statistical results had their origin primarily in the theories of Milton Friedman. Second, the failure of Keynesian/socialist policies in Britain favored the success of a leader with new direction rather than with the ordinarily viewed consensus. In the election campaign at Cardiff, Thatcher said:

> I am a conviction politician. The Old Testament prophets did not say, "Brothers, I want a consensus." They said "This is my faith. This is what I passionately believe. If you believe it too, then come with me."

In early May, *The Economist* reported that the British people had voted for a change, saying they "were ready to take a gamble on Mrs. Thatcher's personality in order to gain the benefits of her policies." Continuing, *The*

Economist said, "Since many of these policies depart starkly from existing practice, the gamble is a bold one."[26] Thatcher's victory and that of her party was of such magnitude by British experience that it seemed to assure her of a full five year term in which to establish her program.

Friedman first began to address the problem of unwinding a government that had pursued socialist/Keynesian policies in the U.S. in 1974. The question as he saw it, was how to move from one economic system to another (pp. 191-192). He addressed this matter further in Chile, and then lectured on it in Britain in late August of 1976 at a church in Westminister, where his lecture was later published by Lord Harris's IEA.[27] British readers, moreover, were presented with Friedman's analysis of deterioration in the British economy as early as 1974, even before Margaret Thatcher took leadership of her party in 1975.

The 1974 paper, entitled "Inflation: Causes, Consequences, Cures," was also later published by Lord Harris's Institute. *The Times* presented a synopsis of it in January 1975, under the title "Price, Stability and the 'Natural' Level of Unemployment." *The Times* writer Tim Congdon saw the theory as a restatement of what had already been presented in "American academic journals in 1967 and 1968."[28] Friedman's 1976 paper on the transition from a deteriorating state to a new and more vibrant Britain was later entitled "From Galbraith to Economic Freedom," in reference to J. K. Galbraith, who symbolized, for Friedman, rule by a "meritocracy." As taken up in chapter 7, Friedman saw Galbraith as representing a paternalistic state, where the masses will invite Galbraith and his fellow intellectuals to take charge, after, Friedman said, "the masses are properly instructed [of Galbraith's superior values] by enough of his books."[29]

"Heaven forbid!" Friedman continued, that "people who know that they are *abler* than their fellows" should rule. He found the rule of an aristocracy by birth more appealing. Referring to a group of 19th-century "Tory Radicals," Friedman thought their endearing feature to be that they "recognized they were accidentally in the position of leadership." Though Friedman found the aristocrats the more appealing of the two groups, he objected to being ruled by either the "natural-born aristocracy or by a meritocracy."[30]

The lecture in Westminister on the last Thursday of August of '76, at which Thatcher's Sir Keith Joseph was present, was reported in *The Times* in some detail. Extracting from the lecture, the reporter likened economics to a "martial art." He described how to be a superstar in economics "it is necessary to arrive at a fixed view of the world," and then "learn to state it forcefully and cast unremitting scorn on those who disagree."[31]

The Analysis of Deterioration

For inflation in both the U.S. and the U.K., the analysis is the same. Minor qualifications aside, inflation started with too rapid a rate of growth of the money supply. Historically, this came from many sources: gold discoveries, financing of private credit expansion, financing of government deficits. The larger government deficits came about either by the absence of effective taxing power (as after WW I in Germany and other defeated countries) or by rapid rises in government spending to wage war or to expand peace-time programs.

In the 1960s and '70s in the U.S. and the U.K., government programs were largely financed by deficits, inadvertent or otherwise, with central bank support. In the U.K., Friedman found an increase in government spending in proportion to national income which was complicated by the fact that "the willingness of the people to pay taxes" did not "increase proportionately." Inflation was a tax, but the people did not recognize it as such.

The good effects of inflation came first, as faster growth in money and credit aggregates stimulated spending and thereby reduced unemployment. Quoted in *The Times*, Friedman referred to the government's "full employment policy," and then said:

> "Whenever the opportunity has presented itself, the government has engaged in extensive spending and has stimulated the creation of money as a means of trying to stimulate the economy.
>
> "This can work for a time. As long as the extra spending which results from the over-issue of money leads people to produce more, it can work. But you can only do that for a brief time, until people find out what's going on. When they find out what's going on, prices are marked up and this results in inflation. After the inflation has gotten bad enough, there has been pressure on the government to slow it down, and at that point you've had the stop stage."[32]

Friedman's theory on the "natural rate of unemployment" (i.e., the non-inflationary rate), and the tendency of government to set, for policy purposes, the "target" rate below it, was summarized in the British press in early 1975:

> If the Government is too ambitious—if it chooses to keep unemployment at extremely low levels, the eventual choice will be worse than it is today. The price that has to be paid for a given level of employment is a higher rate of price increase.[33]

Contrary to earlier Keynesian opinion and the ordinary Phillips curve relation (pp. 213-214), the stimulating effect from inflation resides in the acceleration of inflation and in the inflation being unanticipated. Continuing with Friedman on accelerated inflation, *The Times* writer paraphrased:

> The situation moreover is, as economists say, "unstable". If in the first period 3 per cent unemployment is accompanied by 5 per cent plus a little extra to make, say, 10 per cent, and in the third period, by 10 per cent plus a little extra to make 20 per cent, and so on, the system degenerates from "creeping inflation" to "stratoinflation" to "hyperinflation".
>
> The theory that this is how the economy behaves, while a profoundly depressing one, is also rather suggestive. There is at least a case for saying that this is precisely what has happened in Britain since the late 1960s.
>
> The argument hinges on the idea of a "natural level of unemployment". This is the level which keeps supply and demand in the labour market balanced, and makes it impossible for unions, management or anyone else to achieve pay increases in excess of increases in output.[34]

As inflation starts, its stimulating effects, Friedman emphasized, depend on its being unanticipated. When the public learns of its presence, bad effects set in:

> "When they [the people] find out what's going on, prices are marked up and this results in inflation. After the inflation has gotten bad enough, there has been pressure on the government to slow it down, and at that point you've had the stop stage.
>
> "In the earlier part of the postwar period, the stop stage was brought on by fears about the exchange rate, because a rise in prices in Britain makes British goods less competitive with the outside world. So when either because of domestic inflation or because of a balance of payments crisis, the government has felt impelled to step on the brake, this has slowed down the increase in the quantity of money, slowed down the increase in government spending, and the result has been to reduce output and employment, and only after an interval has it had an impact on inflation.
>
> "Now as people have caught on to this process, increases in the money supply have had less and less effect in stimulating output and more and more effect in producing inflation. And at this point you come to the final step in the process. In order to try to stop the

inflation without fundamental changes, governments have imposed price and wage controls and interfered with the ordinary structure of business. Once you've done that, you find that higher inflation is going to be associated with higher not lower unemployment."[35]

The "natural rate" itself is a variable rate, though not via the demand-management means envisioned in the Keynesian era. Among other means of raising the "natural rate of unemployment" is that of making unemployment attractive. *The Times* writer quoted Friedman thus:

"And in Britain and the United States we have made unemployment a very attractive situation. In my country, many a person can have as high an income in real terms by being unemployed as he can by being employed. The laws of economics work very well: if there is a demand for anything, the supply will tend to rise to meet the demand. If there is a demand for unemployed people, as evidenced by a willingness to pay reasonable payments for being unemployed, then the supply of unemployed people will rise to meet it. Of course, there are many people who endure great hardships by being unemployed, but the numerical statistics are very misleading."[36]

As advanced by advocates of direct government control of prices and wages and others with equally good intentions, the main policy prescription for lowering the natural rate has been to introduce price controls or an incomes policy. This action should hold down prices while stimulative government policies of a fiscal-monetary nature are employed, and the public's inflationary expectations may be lowered. *The Times* writer then presented Friedman's opinion on this incomes-policy/"natural rate" issue:

Defenders of such a policy would argue that, both through its favorable effects on expectations and through direct compliance with the rules it lays down, it improves the inflation-unemployment trade-off.

In the IEA discussion [Institute of Economic Affairs discussion of 1974] Professor Friedman showed himself extremely reluctant to acknowledge any real importance in these qualifications. They were merely the institutional forms which the inflationary problem assumed.

If the Government's unemployment target is below the natural rate, stability cannot be maintained. But, Professor Friedman says, anything might be the first symptom of instability.

> "It might on one occasion be the creation of a few trade unions. ...It might be a change in the terms of trade. It might be the loss of export industry.
>
> "There is a sense in which, you can say in each of these cases that 'the cause of the inflation was a strong trade union or a trade deficit.' But surely it is analytically cleaner to say, that the fundamental cause of the inflation in all these cases is the adoption of a destabilizing monetary policy, namely, of an attempt to use a monetary weapon to fix something which it cannot fix."[37]

The Times writer conceded to Friedman:

> "After years of counterinflation programs, industrial relations Acts, special cases, "norms" and "ceilings", it is hard not to feel that Professor Friedman is right."

For Friedman, the role of inflation as a tax compounded the issue/analysis of inflation and unemployment. As reported by David Sinclair, Friedman noted the ease with which government came to finance expenditures by creating inflation. "Inflation we find is a form of taxation which never has to be passed by Parliament." Friedman continued, "No Member of Parliament has ever stood up and said 'I vote to impose a 10 percent tax on the people in the form of higher prices'." Parliament, he said, has three means of taxing through inflation:

> "It does it in the first place because as prices rise people are shoved into higher income tax brackets, and without Parliament passing a Bill the income tax is automatically raised on everybody.
>
> "Inflation generates revenue in the second place because the higher prices make the funds which government has previously borrowed worth less. In effect, the British government, like the American government, has been running a 'bucketshop' operation—the biggest in history—in selling securities to the unsuspecting public. People have bought government securities and when it has come time to redeem them, what they got back would not buy as much as what they paid in the first place. And to add insult to injury, the so-called interest on the money was subject to tax. The effect of this has been that the government has been able to raise large sums by, essentially, duping the people into believing that they were getting something valuable when they were not.
>
> "The third source of revenue from inflation is the new money which is printed. When the British government prints a pound note and hands it over to somebody and gets some goods for it,

that's equivalent to imposing a tax. Indeed the right way to look at the pound notes in your pocket is that they are vouchers for the payment of tax to the government."[38]

Reversing Direction

The problem with the deterioration in U.S and Britain economic conditions was that, unless reversed, the socialist, Keynesian-induced downward trend would only continue. Once established, the trend would be one of constant deterioration until the public perceived crisis and called for a reversal. The limits of tolerance for declining conditions depend on the people, their history, and broader circumstances. In November 1976, Friedman was quoted in England as stating that Britain was "on the brink" of economic and political collapse.[39]

Britain had not gone as far as Chile had gone in the mid 1970s (chap. 10), but Friedman predicted that Britain had only a 50 percent chance of preserving democracy because of the economic problems.

Mr. Lever, Chancellor of the Duchy of Lancaster, reacting with perhaps native resentment to Friedman's observations, was reported in *The Times* as saying: "In the past 70 years Britain has built up a free and civilized society while adopting policies which Professor Friedman has said were destructive."[40]

The question arises about whether the transition from the Keynesian world should be via a sudden "shock" or by a gradual transition. Some among those who have analyzed the shock approach hold the view that rapid adjustment in inflationary expectations can achieve a new floor from which to proceed which is combined with the prospect that the electorate will not endure and support the political leadership responsible for the shock for any extended period of time.[41] Friedrich von Hayek, the 1974 Nobel laureate reacted critically to the idea of a gradual transition for the U.K. He was quoted in *The Times* of London as linking the policy of gradual transition to the "advice of Milton Friedman." After further comment on the price structure, von Hayek said:

> "You can cure inflation suddenly or gradually. Politically, it is impossible to do it gradually. To put it crudely, I would say that it is possible to cause 20 percent unemployment for six months if you can hold out a hope that things will be better after that. You cannot have 10 per cent unemployment for three years."[42]

Von Hayek and others identified in the TCSC's *Report* recommended the shock treatment. So also did Lord Kaldor. Von Hayek said: "If, as the

Government proclaims, the elimination of inflation is a precondition for the resumption of sound growth, why not get inflation over as quickly as possible, instead of spreading it out over a number of years."[43]

Minford, on the other hand, explained gradualism as did Friedman and related Friedman's discussion of it to indexation (pp. 191, 223).[44] He saw Friedman as favoring gradualism "precisely in order to moderate the severity of the recession involved..." Where supply side policies may work to improve production and employment, the policy is not one of just spreading out the misery over a longer period. However, Friedman's gradualism was meant to allow adjustments in contracts between agents, etc., where they were entered into under very different conditions. Indexation, as for example when contracts for interest and wages have been tied to the inflation/deflation rate, was defended by Friedman partly on just such grounds, because it facilitates downward adjustments. Such adjustments could of course, be seen as mitigating the loss of total output since the extent of the misery to be spread out was less.

The transition from inflation is painful in any case, but in Britain the specific transition in question was complicated by the role of nationalized industries. The Thatcher government "was elected in 1979 above all else," *The Economist* reported, "to roll back the frontiers of the public sector, to leave resources free for private-sector expansion."[45] Though interlaced with controlling inflation, public spending, and interest rates, the transition here required more time, if output, employment, and productivity were not to be more severely affected than would otherwise be the case. These matters come later, as a part of Thatcher's policy. The nationalization came about in the first place with socialist changes. The public-sector enterprises came to include a "disparate collection of unprofitable lame ducks, profitable monopolies, large public undertakings and small organizations swept into state hands by the odd brooms of political history."[46]

Friedman emphasized that, putting aside the compounding complication of denationalizing state-owned industries, to reverse direction calls for a difficult withdrawal from the unsustainable stimulus of inflation. In Britain he advocated a gradual four-to-five year transition. *The Times* quoted Friedman as saying, "when a man has become sick, there is no miracle cure that will restore him to health the following day."[47] Steps in the transition (the "hard slog" as the British press labeled it on one occasion) included the following:[48]

•*Decelerate the rate of monetary growth.* "The Government should make some gesture which would banish inflationary expectations quickly and decisively." Continuing with his Friedmanian argument, Congdon, writing in *The Times* said, "This is the way hyperinflations are eventually resolved, with the Government introducing a new currency and announcing draconian budgetary measures to make it credible." He continued: "No such outcome is necessary or inevitable in this country, but it may help to maintain a sense of perspective to remember that currency reforms like this have taken place in both France and West Germany since the war and they don't seem to be doing so badly now."

•*Cut government spending.* "In a country where government spending amounts to more than 60 per cent of national income, it is going to be very hard to use explicit taxes to extract that fraction while at the same time preserving incentives for people to produce, to work, to save."

•*Change taxes to limit the "flight of capital" in both human and physical terms from Britain.* "If you are faced with taxes on income and wealth of more than 100 per cent, if you are faced with a growing government grip on activity, then I can well understand that any sensible man with property is going to try to get it out of the country. "One way for businesses to get property out of the country is to run their British business at a loss in a way that bids up their foreign assets, and then of course when the losses get large enough and threaten unemployment, the government steps in and subsidizes the losses. So in effect what has been happening is that the British Government has been borrowing overseas funds to finance the outflow of capital."

•*Abolish every aspect of control over foreign exchange.*

•*Possibly substitute "voucher schemes, or negative income tax," for conventional welfare programs.*

•*"Restructure the whole tax system so that it removes the present disincentives to work and save."*

•*"Four or five years hard slog."* This comes as unemployment is held above the natural rate, "combined with the cost reducing effect of productivity increases..."

•*Impose monetary restraints and encourage private enterprise.* However, "While monetary restraint is a sufficient condition for controlling inflation, it is a necessary but not sufficient condition for improving Britain's productivity—the fundamental requirement for restoring Britain to full economic health. That requires measures on a broader front to restore and improve incentives, promote investment, and give a greater scope for private enterprise and initiative." Later Friedman stressed even more the magnitude of the U.K.'s problem. "Doubling the trend rate of output growth in a few years would be phenomenal, yet for the U.K., that would reduce inflation by only two or three percentage points." The burden of controlling inflation then would fall on the monetary policy, which, to be successful, Friedman described as follows:

> A successful policy of reducing inflation will have as an unavoidable side effect a temporary retardation in economic growth. However, continuation of the present levels of inflation, and even

more further acceleration of inflation would at best postpone the retardation at the expense of a more severe retardation later. Past mistakes in economic policy have left us with no soft options. Our only real alternatives are to accept a temporary economic slowdown now as part of a program for ending inflation or to experience a more severe slowdown somewhat later as a result of continued or accelerated inflation.[49]

For the administration and political leadership of a transition from the socialist/Keynesian world, the British were offered Margaret Thatcher. By 1978, she had aroused the British electorate for a "watershed" election. In doing so, she was able to rely on some awareness of economic problems by the British public partly because Friedman's views had been getting considerable press attention in London since the mid-1970s. In January 1978, London's *Sunday Times* referred favorably to Friedman as "The Ghost of Montague Norman" a former, distinguished Governor of the Bank of England in the 1920s who had advocated and practiced orthodox views of economics.[50] He was seen in his time as a man of finesse and high intellect.

So Thatcher got swept into power in May of 1979 with a sufficient majority and under conditions that seemed to assure sufficient time to implement gradually a set of policies based on Friedman's theories. Seargeant recalled in *The Sunday Times* an earlier image of Friedman held by the British economic establishment, who viewed him there as "little better than Satan and the imps." Now, he noted, opinion has swung to the opposite pole; Friedman was the "chief intellectual begettor of Thatcher's new economic policy." Referring to BBC's screening of Friedman's television series under the *Free-to-Choose* title, Seargeant described it as propounding revisionist views with the interest of bolstering government moral.[51]

Later in describing a one hour meeting of Mrs. Thatcher with Professor Friedman at 10 Downing Street in late February, Seargeant entitled his column in the *The Sunday Times*, "Et tu, Milton (or Paradise Lost at No 10)." He suggested Friedman's talk with Margaret Thatcher might have opened with the following dialogue:

> Prime Minister, it is a great privilege to meet the one leader in the western world who is pledged to reverse the socialist policies pursued by all governments here since World War II.
>
> Thank you so very much professor. Changing hearts and minds is a long process. But we are absolutely determined to restore sound money and incentives to work. Attitudes are changing and the mood of realism is spreading fast. Let me introduce Sir Geoffrey Howe, the Chancellor, Mr. Biffen, Mr. Lawson, and Sir Ian

Gilmour; he's still a Keynesian you know but such a nice man and so very good with our European friends.[52]

Thatcher was yet to list the five basic truths Britain would have to face on the road to recovery: 1. To exact an ever-rising standard of living without creating the wealth to pay for it through higher output per worker simply raises prices and costs jobs. 2. The blame for all the economic and industrial ills did not rest upon the shop floor (say, in relation to the shop's workers). Contrary to what was believed, the government was well aware of that. 3. The government could not create wealth. It could, though, create the climate in which wealth producers flourished. Getting inflation down was at the heart of the government's strategy. If it failed there, it failed on every front. 4. The country could not prosper in any circumstances unless firms produced goods or provided services that consumers wanted to buy. And the customer would only buy if he was attracted by design, quality, reliability, service before and after purchase, delivery, and overall reputation, as well as the price. 5. The British have what it takes when it comes to innate inventive genius. As Thatcher stated it, "That genius in the nation of Newton, Watt, Arkwright, Davy, Baird, Barnes-Wallis, Rutherford and Fleming is alive and well and working all around us."[53]

In addition, a major change in attitude was required, Thatcher stated:

> First, a new respect for the risk-takers, for the producers of wealth, for the tradesmen of this world, who for so long have been looked down on instead of up to as a source of our prosperity. And second, new determination to succeed as a nation, by translating the risks, enterprise and invention into the rewards of new markets.[54]

A change also in how the word "profit" is viewed was essential. Thatcher observed:

> [that some businessmen] had started to use the term 'surplus' to describe profit [compare, p. 54], as though profit is almost irrelevant to the functioning of business. Yet if we had to point to one single notion which is calculated to damage our industrial performance, to prevent us from competing effectively in the world and ultimately to undermine the basis of a free and diverse society, it is the idea that profit is some how wrong.

Thatcher and Her Government

The Thatcher government was elected on May 4, 1979. The win was a reaction to Keynesian/socialist policies and consensus politics, and verified a sympathetic response to Thatcher, new ideas, and the prospect of redirection. The main economic trends of post-WW II Britain had been rising inflation, rising unemployment, and declining growth in productivity (defined as growth in output per worker).

Following her campaigning and debates, Thatcher indicated that the government was elected to bring about control of inflation through monetarist means by reducing the size of the public sector through cuts in government spending, taxation and borrowing. Her new government was also to free resources for the private sector, free the private sector from incomes policy and revitalize the will to engage in private enterprise.

Thatcher's analysis also contained the assumption that consensus politics and socialist inroads had made British national character a part of the problem. Even as Britain's J. M. Keynes shunted economic theory along lines that came to prevail in U.S. and U.K. economies, he recognized, as Thatcher did, the dependence of economic prosperity "on a political and social atmosphere which is congenial to the average businessman."[55] Thatcher thought the national character was malleable; Milton Friedman said it could be changed through persuasion. High Thomas, a Thatcher spokesman, asserted that Thatcher's "fundamental purpose is moral." There was to be a "revival of individualism." Thatcher herself said: "To adopt our policies is to be realistic and optimistic about our people."

The central ideas behind Thatcher's rhetoric, as her earlier interest in Friedman would indicate, are found in monetarist economics, supply-side (or incentivist) economics, and analyses of expectations. Referring to Thatcher and her ideas and concepts as outlined above, *The Economist* pictured her at election time as "a Friedmanite believer, committed to a fundamental shift in the character not just of Britain's economy but of its society." *The Economist* found this prime minister intriguing. Anticipating a split in the Labor opposition in response to Thatcher, which indeed did come later, *The Economist* described her as potentially Britain's most powerful leader since the war.[56]

In the meantime, the timing of Thatcher's election and early efforts at changing policy brought recession to Britain slightly earlier than in the U.S., as covered in the next chapter. This timing plus the larger transition problems for the U.K. foretold the greater difficulties facing Britain and the long duration of what may be called loosely the 1979-82 British recession. In the U.K. the recession was, in effect, mingled with and reinforced by the special transition problems.

The British Condition

The British transition was compounded by Britain having started earlier and gone further with Keynesian/socialist policies than had the U.S.[57] Beginning in the early post-WW II years, the socialist trend increased greatly the public sector and resulted in the nationalization of many industries, including British Leyland, British Rails, British Shipbuilding, British Steel, the National Coal Board, and Rolls-Royce. These state acquisitions in turn meant a larger overseer role for the British Cabinet with respect to decisions about the financing and growth of the nationalized industries and negotiation of wages with the unions. Though no problem in itself, trade unions in Britain were related to the Labor party through membership on the party's committees,[58] and, until Thatcher determined otherwise, the Cabinet negotiated directly with the trade unions.

Given the practice that each nationalized industry group deals separately with the Cabinet on plans for financing and expansion, one encounters here a situation which in America came to be called the problem of special interests. Each interest group (or industry in the U.K. case) does its own lobbying, and each case for expansion may look good on its merit and relatively small in cost, but these special interests become a costly and persistent problem when taken in the aggregate. In the U.S. the packaging of separate proposals, as long advocated by Friedman, was the approach Ronald Reagan used to weaken special interest influences on various occasions, including in getting tax reforms measures.

Though a boon in most economic respects, Britain's development of its North Sea oil and gas reserves in the 1970s was a mixed blessing for the transition policies of the Thatcher government. For one thing, it reduced their dependence on foreign oil, thereby reduced oil imports. For another thing, this relatively favorable balance of payments impact contributed to the strengthening of the pound sterling along with the greater prospects for control of inflation.[59] In turn, the strengthening of sterling favored British purchases from abroad, thus causing a weakened demand for domestically produced goods. The weakened demand for goods, or its analogue, a more costly pound, meant in effect greater pressures for improved competition by British industries, as had been the case in the 1920s when the pound was said to be "over-valued." Ordinarily the pound exchange rate could have been manipulated to temporarily offset its strength, but Thatcher was committed to less intervention in such matters and to what we encounter in chapter 11 as an open economy. Both Friedman and Thatcher thought that facing international competition was important.

In addition, and as a part of less intervention generally, there was the problem of mobility of labor resources in response to energy price changes, tax changes, exchange rate changes, and, in general, efforts to revitalize private-sector activities. To solve this problem, British government, and particularly that of Thatcher, has encouraged "an unusually large-scale resource reallocation, an unusual amount of search and job-changing activity...." Such large-scale changes ordinarily would raise unemployment until adjustments in the labor markets were completed, but these unemployment-reducing adjustments were further delayed because of socialist government induced impediments to the geographical mobility of labor. As Michael Parkin explained in U.S. proceedings of a conference on the U.K.:

> The key impediment concerns the way in which the housing market and the unemployment compensation arrangements interact. The housing market is, to a large degree, organized by local government on a subsidized first-come, first-served basis. Those who already have subsidized public sector houses in areas where the demand for labor is declining may find it unprofitable to move to areas where demand is rising. The relevant calculation for them is a comparison of the cost of a subsidized public sector house with an income generated from the unemployment compensation funds and a market rent for housing with a market wage rate.
>
> Given the combination of subsidized local authority housing and fairly generous and long-term unemployment compensation benefits, it may be predicted that large numbers of workers, especially older ones, who find it in their best interest to take what amounts to an early retirement but what, from the point of view of the data, shows up as unemployment.
>
> The essence of the above is that the British economy has experienced unusually high unemployment and unusually low real output growth in the latter part of the 70s and the early part of the 80s as a consequence of the behavior of the world price of energy and as a consequence of steady persistent trends in the changing composition of public sector expenditures and revenues.[60]

A further complication for the British was that of having professional senior civil servants at policy levels rather than appointed officials. This meant, particularly for Thatcher, that the presumably supportive experts may not be prepared for the ideological changes the shift in government policy required.[61] Indeed, in Thatcher's case, her economic advisor Alan A. Walters had to be brought back to England in early 1981 because of the need for advice that was not available from the senior civil servants.[62]

From the earlier background of analysis and a wide range of "indirect evidence," the policies associated with accelerating inflation (re-inflation, Thatcher would call it) provide a stimulus only so long as inflation is accelerating. Even a leveling off of the inflation rate is a withdrawal of the stimulus, which then calls for downward adjustments in employment and in production or its rate of change. Deceleration of inflation reinforces even these declines in production and employment. In a complicated economy like that of Britain, the declines can be further compounded. For example, tax changes can shift the emphasis from consumption spending to saving and investment expenditures, with some lags in the effects of that shift. Also, any restrictions on nationalized industries and the public sector which have as a goal the release of resources to the private industrial sector also can cause lags in the effects of the shift.[63]

In Thatcher's first year the government, which in part was elected to free the private sector, did in fact preside over a rise in the public sector's share of gross domestic product. "Thatcher's failure to cut back government in the first year came about," *The Economist* reported, "because she took office at the start of a surge in public-sector pay, and her ministers...lived too long in the cloud-cuckoo belief that this need not affect their aims." The public sector pay boost meant a larger public sector borrowing requirement, and this, in turn led to a revision in the targets for monetary growth, since the public sector borrowing required more central bank support or crowd out private sector financing.[64] Continuing on this topic, *The Economist* reported:

> Before this surge [in public sector pay] was over, Mrs. Thatcher's chancellor, Sir Geoffrey Howe, had laid down a medium-term path for monetary growth and public borrowing whose first markers have been missed by a mile. Because the government was pushing up the pay of its public servants by over 20 per cent in a year in which all Britain was plunging into slump, it had no hope of cutting its public-sector deficit. So the whole slump landed on private enterprise, whom Mrs. Thatcher's government was elected to help. Because it was leading a pay surge at the same time as it was unwrapping monetary controls (on bank lending as well as on movements across the exchanges), it had no hope of meeting its monetary target.[65]

Obviously, a renewed effort at reform was needed. Thatcher found that difficulties in getting the Bank of England to control the aggregates and shift from a Keynesian to monetarist stance were indeed present, which was complicated by the government itself backing off from its initially announced target ranges for the control of the money supply (notably, in this case, the series known as the pound sterling M3). Initially, the Chancellor set a target range of 7-11 percent per annum for the growth of £M3 until the end of the 1979-80 financial year and announced declining target ranges that were to end with a 4-8 percent range in 1983-84. The importance of maintaining confidence in the targets on the part of economic agents was stressed, in part to assure the greatest impact on expectations with respect to the inflation rate.[66] As the 1979-80 year unfolded, however, the large public-sector pay boost, the politics of recession, and technical flaws in the control mechanism all contributed to a too rapid growth in sterling M3.[67]

A technical factor in the control of £M3 was the so-called "corset," which, previous to Thatcher's government, was a restriction on the banking sector's ability to issue liabilities included in the definition of £M3. This "corset" was said to have generated a fair amount of substitution between three-month bankers' acceptances, which were outside of the classification for £M3, for short-dated liabilities called CDs, which were inside the designation £M3. "The actual difference between three-month CDs and three-month acceptances," Michael Parkin said, "may be presumed to be so slight as to lead to the conjecture that they may be almost, but importantly not quite, perfect substitutes." With this prospect for a substitution of securities, the removal of the "corset," along with the dismantling of exchange controls at the outset of Thatcher's administration, caused a shift in the supply of a whole host of assets, including the substitution of the CDs inside the designation £M3 for the acceptances that were outside. Indeed, the size of the switch back into £M3 after the removal of the "corset" was estimated to be of the order of 4 percent and to have contributed to the growth of £M3 in the middle of 1980. The possible distortion in the measurement and control of money growth led Parkin, who had examined £M1 as a possibly better measure of money growth, to note that the switching "had little or no aggregate demand (and therefore price level) implications."[68]

Following the episode of excessive growth in sterling £M3 in 1980, Thatcher commissioned Jurg Niehans, a University of Bern professor, to investigate the Bank of England's control arrangements further. Niehans's study recommended that the control arrangements be altered. This change was made in August 1981. Niehans, however, also reported that sterling £M3 was a misleading measure. He compared the phenomenon of money appearing to grow fast even as credit seemed tight to a distorted mirror in a fun house. "You see yourself getting fatter and fatter," he said, "so you diet and diet, but in reality you're losing weight and dying of anorexia."

Friedman himself had speculated that the U.K. economy was behaving in 1980-81 as if it were subject to more monetary restraint than indicated. Reflecting on the matter later in early 1982, after the August '81 change in the control mechanism, he said "monetary policy has been considerably more restrictive than one would gather from the £M3 figures alone, and that restrictiveness does seem to have brought the rate of inflation down." Continuing, Friedman saw this as "a minor quibble" relative to other aspects of Thatcher's program, including the lack of success in shifting resources to the private sector. Commenting on the effects of the recession on the economy, he said:

> I would also not be surprised if the actual depth of the recession has been less than it appears to be, thanks to the growth of a strong underground economy. That phenomenon seems to have become a very important one not only in Britain but also in the Scandinavian countries, and perhaps in its most extreme form in Italy in which unquestionably the official statistics grossly understate the level of income and overstate the level of unemployment.[69]

In any case, complexities of the control of £M3 led to revisions of the Bank of England's control mechanism, as discussed in chapter 14 (pp. 554-558). The failure to stay within the upper bound of the 7-11 percent range in 1980 led to the conclusion in the TCSC's 1981 *Report* that there had been no true "monetarist experiment."[70] Friedman himself struck a somewhat optimistic note on the possible success of the strategy of limiting monetary growth, in replying to the U.K. Treasury and Civil Service Committee questionnaire in 1980, but it was certainly dependent on firm adherence to targets.

Friedman said:

> The best evidence is from the prior experience of the UK and other countries. As I read that experience...I conclude that (a) only a modest reduction in output and employment will be a side effect of reducing inflation to single figures by 1982, and (b) the effect on investment and the potential for future growth will be highly favorable.[71]

The TCSC's 1981 Report noted this quote, but the report also said that the government's monetarist strategy "was not soundly based." Continuing, the *Report* said that the government's strategy "was overambitious in the first year, and in setting specific targets for a four year period." It spoke of the detailed design of a strategy with "more detailed evidence than the Treasury has yet been prepared to give or the Committee to provide for itself."[72]

There were two difficulties with such conclusions: (1) the comparison suggested for judging the strategy was some ideal that does not exist rather than the alternative the U.K. society was facing in the 1979 election; and (2) the search for more detail was what Friedman would characterize as Walrasian. It presumed the answers lie in the further pursuit of a "prevailing fashion in econometric work," whereas what might be called for were new channels of thinking.

Drawing on the F/S draft manuscript of *Monetary Trends*, Friedman said in an earlier note that "a successful policy of reducing inflation will have as an unavoidable side effect a temporary retardation in economic growth." In addition, in the fuller blown F/S work, as briefly summarized in chapter 14, two other points stand out for purposes of evaluating Friedman's conclusion. First, the historical regularity of the relations between money growth and expenditures became distorted by the shift in the structure underlying the formation of inflationary expectations in the 1960s. These shifts in the relationship and in the structure were such that monetary effects could work more directly on spending effects, in the sense that (decelerated) growth in the money stock led to the prospect of higher (lower) inflation, with less of a lag in the effect. These effects of decelerated (accelerated) money growth were further complicated by the other results, with uncertainty over the inflation rate forecast serving as a factor.[73]

Second, movements in real income over periods longer than a cycle may be independent of the monetary effects and hence more dependent on special institutional factors, trade unions, ideological shifts, habits about work and saving, and so on. Such a possibility suggested for a country like the U.K., with its post-WW II socialist trends, its sizable public sector, and relatively small private sector exclusive of an enormous financial center like London, that more thought be given to the long-run development of a private, nonfinancial sector.

As to controlling monetary and credit aggregates, even in the U.S., it took a decade, a dramatic change in the chairmanship at the Federal Reserve in 1979, and the election of a new president in 1980, to bring about such a shift, as the next chapter attests. In Britain, large disturbances in the industrial sector as well could be expected in response to the ideological and organizational changes represented by the Thatcher elections. These disturbances would be caused partly through expectations and uncertainty about the dramatic changes to come. Further, in the British "hard slog," as distinct from that in the U.S., the temptation to the government to ease temporarily the adverse effects of some aspect of the transition was very strong, when the government has at hand the nationalized industries for use as a possible mitigating force against the effects of a deceleration in monetary aggregates.

Stated briefly, the simultaneous pursuit of all the goals that Thatcher set for her government was probably more than human effort could achieve in a five year span, or to be more accurate, a four year span, since conditions in 1982-83 were the ones to be taken to the electorate in 1984. As matters turned out, however, an early election was called for June 9, 1983, where under the British political system, a Prime Minister can call an election any time within the five-year parliamentary term. By a similar token where the Prime Minister's party loses a majority of the seats in Parliament, the opposition government may call for an election.

Achieving the transition hoped for and thus undoing cumulative effects of the earlier thirty-five year trend would be a remarkable accomplishment for Thatcher, one she was approaching by the 1987 elections. As matters turned out, the first term set the tone for change spanning elections in '83 and '87. After the initial victory, Thatcher's policies and orientations simply stayed on the course upon which they were set in the first term. Further, her tax and government expenditure cuts did not have the potential for crisis found in the later U.S. redirection. Consequently, we deal here primarily with the Big U-Turn of Thatcher's first term.

Alan Walters

Advisor Alan Walters, who entered into Thatcher's service in January 1981, was British by birth, background, and citizenship at the time of his appointment at age 54. He had graduated in 1951 from University College, Leicester (later the University of Leicester). From there he went to Nuffield College, Oxford, and then, in 1952, to the University of Birmingham as a lecturer in econometrics. His interest in econometrics continued at that University, where he was appointed Professor and Head of the Department of Econometrics and Social Statistics in 1961. Later in the period 1968 to 1976 he became Sir Ernest Cassel Professor of Economics at the LSE in the University of London. In the autumn of 1966 he began at the University of Virginia a series of visiting appointments at U.S. universities, and in 1968 he published a textbook in econometrics which stressed the use of technique as a means of improving one's insights into the workings of the real world.[74] Some other such works in economics, we may note, had stressed such technique as a means of socialist planning and some may even be charged with doing so for its own sake ("for its intellectual attraction," some may say).[75]

In the econometrics textbook and in a selection of readings he later edited, Walters dealt with issues and topics that have the characteristics of Friedman's work. Rather than present his own unique views, he reported and brought together a collection of readings from Friedman's work. Early in his econometric study, he directed attention to the methodological issue raised by Friedman in his famous 1953 essay in which he attacked the "conventionalist" (or "assumptionist") approach of passing truth forward rather than stressing the use of economic theory in making predictions. Later in his econometrics text Walters discussed: Friedman's consumption function work; the question of causation from money to income (or vice versa) as introduced by James Tobin in the U.S. and as reviewed in various sources; an early controversy set off by Friedman on the money multiplier versus the investment multiplier; Friedman's emphasis of testing one model against another rather than against some naive alternative; and money demand topics in general. Walter's collection of readings in money and banking was unusual both in its focus upon Friedman's work and in the advanced level of difficulty of the selections.[76]

Walters first encountered Milton Friedman in the 1969-70 school year at Northwestern University, when Friedman delivered a lecture on the demand for money.[77] In the late 1960s Walters also began accepting a number of consulting activities in such highly practical areas as transportation and trade. He was a consultant to governments such as Israel, Singapore, and Malaysia. In 1976-80, prior to his appointment in the Thatcher government, Walters was Professor of Economics at Johns Hopkins University and Economic Advisor to the World Bank. By that time, he had the broad international background that would be needed by an economic advisor at No 10 Downing Street as a result of the international significance of London and Britain's markedly international role.

Along with Harry Johnson (University of Chicago, the LSE, and, briefly, the Graduate Institute of International Studies, Geneva, Switzerland) before his death in 1978, Walters was among the early British to be influenced by Milton Friedman and his works and to help in bringing "monetarism" to Britain. Both Walters and Johnson, though loyal British, were what has been described as a part of the "brain-drain" from the U.K. in response to high marginal tax rates in that country. Indeed, partly because of the tax difficulty, at the time of Walters's appointment at Downing Street, private outside money and a salary of £50,000 per year (about $100,000 at the time) were required to bring Walters back to London. *The Sunday Times* writers described the appointment and its background as follows:

> As Mrs. Thatcher's lunch party ponders the best way out of the mire, the conversation will undoubtedly turn to discussion of her new hard-line monetarist advisor, Professor Alan Walters, whose £50,000 a year appointment sparked off a major Commons row on Thursday.
>
> When 54-year-old Walters moves into Downing Street on January 5, it will make the end of a nine-month battle to bring him to Mrs. Thatcher's side from his highly paid Washington posts as a university professor and advisor to the World Bank. Her resolve to hire Walters—even at almost twice the salary of her senior civil servants—was confirmed in August when she made a trip to Switzerland, the home of monetary rectitude.

Unnerved by a 5% explosion in the money supply during July, she requested meetings with Karl Brunner, professor of economics in Berne and Rochester, New York. Why was monetary growth not slowing down in Britain, she wanted to know? Brunner, backed up by Fritz Leutwiler, head of the Swiss National Bank, replied that monetary control was partly a matter of will and partly a matter of technique.

Were there any economists in Britain who could help her find the techniques, she asked. Brunner said that most good British economists were no longer in Britain. He was especially flattering about Walters, who had already come to Thatcher's notice through recommendations from Sir Keith Joseph. Brunner recalls that she was determined to have her own monetarist adviser, independent of the Treasury and the Bank of England. "She doesn't trust the information flow she is getting from the government bureaucracy," Brunner told a colleague later.

At her Chequers lunch, Mrs. Thatcher and her two confidants will be reviewing the chapter of accidents which have produced something dangerously close to a crises of confidence in their economic strategy and its presentation to her increasingly restless supporters in the country.

It is now clear to everyone, including Walters, that the Thatcher administration has "lost" the crucial first 18 months of its parliamentary life. Far from being able to build on solid achievement on the economic front, there is a sizeable rescue operation to be mounted.

Alan Walters may prove crucial in providing the academic and technical support for Margaret Thatcher's unshakable belief that her economic policies are correct. What lies behind the failures of this year and last? Are they fatal for the credibility of the medium term strategy which is the heart of her policy?[78]

Reflecting on "The New Monetarism" long before Walters's appointments, Lord Kaldor offered some discussion and included Johnson and Walters in the monetarist fold thus:

They certainly use time-series regressions as if they provided the same kind of "proofs" as controlled experiments in the natural sciences. And one hears new stories of conversions they have made almost every day, one old bastion of old-fashioned Keynesian orthodoxy being captured after another: first, the Federal Reserve Bank of St. Louis, then another Federal Reserve Bank, then the research staff of IMF, or at least the majority of them, have become "secret", if not open, Friedmanites. Even the "Fed" in Washington is said to be tottering, not to speak of the spread of the new doctrines in many universities in the United States. In this country, also, there are some distinguished and lively protagonists, like Professor Harry Johnson and Professor Walters. In comparison to America, though, they write in muted tones and make more modest claims, which makes it more difficult to discover just what it is they believe in, just where the new doctrine ceases to be a matter of semantics and becomes a revelation with operational significance.

Walters's writings during the early stages of the rise of "monetarism" reflected his coming more from an econometric than a monetary economics background.[79] Milton Friedman, himself, had an unusual statistical background and brought it into monetary study where, in the decades of the 1960s and '70s, widespread use of the modern computer aided the advance of Friedman's empirical orientation with its emphasis on the testing of alternative theories.

Reflecting on the late 1950s, when monetary research by Friedman and his followers first became strongly characterized by the use of empirical investigation, Walters contrasted their work to the Radcliffe report by noting "the absence [in the report] of any statistical quantitative analyses of monetary matters..." The contrast, Walters noted here was indicative of the absence of statistical work he found generally on monetary matters in the U.K. It led him and his econometric/statistical group at the University of Birmingham to begin such studies in the U.K. The fruits of these studies appeared a decade later in his book *Money in Boom and Slump* (1971), which, with his other studies, helped focus attention on Friedman and his work.[80]

In Britain, as in the U.S., there were other early dissenters to the practice of excluding the study of money and its income velocity from economic study. None, though, mounted an effective onslaught against the Keynesian system, as Friedman did. Evidence of Friedman's effectiveness can be found in Walter's writing and research—the distinction he made between permanent and transitory magnitudes, his use of time rates of change in stock and flow quantities, the emphasis he placed on the interaction between monetary and real goods sectors, his study of lag structures and their changes, his analyses of expectations, including in particular liquidity preference with overshooting, and his presentation of an alternative to the approaches found in large-scale, short-term forecasting models and in "the prevailing fashion in econometric work."

In Friedman's early liquidity preference work (pp. 83-84, 443-448), accelerated growth in the money stock impacted by first lowering interest rates, then by increasing them, even above their original level, as the stock of actual money balances exceeds that economic actors wish to hold and as the spending on goods and services "overshoots" (say, exceeds) the initial increase in the money stock. In the long run, the increased growth rate in the money stock became fully reflected in the interest rate as stated in Irving Fisher's 1896 equation (namely, the nominal rate of interest is equal to the real rate plus the expected inflation rate). In time—with the shift in the structure underlying the formation of inflationary expectations, this otherwise long-run Fisher effect came about in a period of less than one quarter. Through such a route, Friedman reversed the direction expected of interest rate changes in response to money stock changes. Walters tuned in to such new thinking.

As in the U.S., Walters noted that in the U.K. "certain doctrines of macroeconomics...manage to survive the most damning evidence that has been adduced to discredit them." Just as in the U.S. in the 1960s and 1970s, Walters noted that in the U.K. such doctrines were convincingly discredited by experience in the late 1960s and early 1970s when both unemployment and inflation rose perversely together to new highs. The latter references were to the inflationary recession phenomenon beginning in the 1969-70 recession and to the Phillips curve (p. 214), as it was ably attacked by Friedman in lectures in the U.S. and the U.K. and in his Nobel lecture.[81] For Friedman, in the long run there was only a higher inflation rate and no effect on unemployment. And once again, inflation was mainly a monetary phenomenon.

Reviewing the 1973-76 period in the U.K. and declining monetary growth versus an increase in government spending, Walters proceeded as follows:

> From the end of 1973 monetary growth declined sharply from an annual rate of approximately 25 per cent for the period September 1971-September 1973 to about 10 per cent. This fall in the growth rate of the money stock was associated, however, with highly expansionary public spending and budgets. Here, then, was an acid test—monetarists predicted a sharp slump, whereas Keynesians would look to expansion. The outcome was a virtually unequivocal win for monetarism. Indeed the slump of 1974-76 was sharp and prolonged. The monetarist prediction that the inflation rate of prices would begin to moderate some 2 years after the end of 1973 was also borne out as the inflation rate declined to 13 per cent (year to July 1976). The consequences of the prolonged monetary squeeze which began at the end of 1973 have not yet run their course, although even at this stage the provisional conclusions are

clear, and it seems impossible to deny that monetary contraction played a major role in causing the slump and the arrest of inflation.[82]

The directness and forcefulness of this statement prepares us for the description of himself Walters gave in his econometrics text:

Although I have often indicated the state of debate on several controversial topics, I have tried to avoid fence-sitting. One must make up one's mind.[83]

On the occasion of Walter's appointment as economic advisor to Thatcher, Herbert Stein noted in the *Wall Street Journal* his regard for Walters who he considered to be a man with well developed views, not unlike those of Thatcher herself, and possessing a strong will. He was described as being of the "monetarist" persuasion, and even economists in the main, accepted flow of economic thinking were said to describe his brand of monetarism as "inflexible" and "rigid."[84]

The Further Reality

In October 1980 *The Economist* described Mrs. Thatcher as a kind of Dr. Jekyll and Mrs. Hyde—"drinking in great draughts of paperwork each night, the world never knowing which character will emerge to stalk the corridors of power the next day." At one time she could sound and act like the Friedmanite believer of the May 1979 elections—"radical to the point of revolutionary, committed to a fundamental shift in the character not just of Britain's economy but of its society." At another time, she changed into the traditional Tory, "a hesitant though increasingly astute practitioner of the art of compromise, adept at the commons dispatch box, obedient to the party's middle-class roots and to the dictates of electoral success in a mixed economy, and above all a pragmatist."[85]

At the same time this double image of Britain's prime minister was emerging some eighteen months after she had come in power, vocal frustration began to be heard in the trade unions and in the opposition Labor party as business conditions worsened and doctorinal disputes heightened. Thatcher's efforts to move the Tories to the right, as well as her persistence in maintaining her policies and even appealing over the heads of members of Parliament and labor leaders to the British electorate contributed to the frustration. Following the annual conference of the Trades Union Congress in Brighton, which closed on September 5, *Business Week* reported:

The powerful British labor unions that played key roles in toppling the last two British governments are in greater disarray today than at any time since World War II. They are being shoved off the political stage by Prime Minister Margaret Thatcher's free-market, monetarist economic policies that ignore the unions' traditional role in negotiating directly with the government over labor issues. The Thatcher government's revulsion to intervene in the economy leaves the unions without their usual influence on industrial decisions. At the same time, they have lost support among some rank-and-file members and are racked by internal dissent on several issues. Thatcher's policies, along with a solid 43-seat majority in the House of Commons that ensures her Conservative party a full five-year term in office, are allowing the government to ignore the unions as has no other recent government. The disarmed unions, taken by surprise, have yet to find an adequate response. "Unions are seen by the present government as at best irrelevant and at worst dangerous," says Lionel "Len" Murray, who is the TUC's general secretary.

Traditionally, both the Labor and Conservative governments have needed cooperation from the unions to work out wage restraint policies. But so far, Thatcher's Conservatives have only jaw-boned against high pay settlements. They have steered clear of getting directly involved in collective bargaining and of instituting a formal incomes policy, choosing instead to dampen inflation by controlling the money supply. "That leaves no terms for discussion with the unions," says Stephen J. Wood, an industrial relations specialist at the London School of Economics. The TUC's Murray, meanwhile, says that the few discussions union leaders have had with government ministers have been worthless. "It is much more difficult to have a conversation with them [than with past governments]," he says.[86]

Four weeks after the trade union conference, the Labor party held its annual conference. At that conference, there appeared evidence of a possible split in the party. The conference voted to extend the franchise for selecting its leader beyond simply its elected members of parliament. The block votes of trade unions at the conference did not hold together as the old leadership had expected, and Tony Benn, a leader further to the left, emerged as the strong man to fight for a socialist economy. Five months later, twelve M.P.'s, who objected to the Labor party's sharp shift to the left, resigned from the British Labor party to form a new party know as the Social Democrats.[87]

Some political observers saw the emergence of the new Social Democratic party (SDP) as a possibly new centrist movement in British politics. This prospect was heightened by the possible coalition of this new party with the old British Liberal party that had been replaced in 1922 by the Labor party as one of the two principal political groupings in British politics. Some election results at the midterm of the Thatcher government suggested this same possibility. In a July '81 special election at Warrington, Social Democrat candidate Roy Jenkins, a former Chancellor of the Exchequer, polled 42 percent of the total vote against the winning Laborite with 48.4 percent and a Conservative party candidate with only 12.5 percent. At other by-year elections Liberal candidate William Pitt won a long-sought seat in Croydon North West, and the even more newsworthy Shirley Williams, the well known Education Minister of the last Labor government who too was among the founding leaders of the Social Democrats, won a SDP seat with 49.1 percent of the vote of the electorate of Crosby, which previously had sent conservatives to Parliament for three decades. Speculation arose that SDP posed a threat to Britain's two-party system which had functioned since WW II, with the prospect of the SPD supplanting the Labor party. This speculation was tempered by the realization that national elections in May of 1984 would provide more of a test for Social Democrats than isolated by elections.[88]

In the Fall of 1980 as Thatcher's positions were driving the trade unions to the left, the U.S. presidential election produced a land-slide victory for Ronald Reagan, who in his zeal to transform government had embraced the same ideas as Thatcher. As a result of Reagan's election, interest in the Thatcher experiment increased in the U.S. press, especially after the inauguration and during Thatcher's late February visit to the U.S. as the first head of a major state to visit the new president.[89] The attempt to establish a parallel between the two countries, however, was overdrawn in the press, in that it focused on immediate solutions to inflation and unemployment. This concern for immediate solutions was pushed at the expense of addressing money-stock control difficulties, of describing accurately the new attitude toward a solution to the long-run problems created by years of temporary solutions, and on emphasizing the difficulties of transition from Keynesian/socialist orientations.

Reacting to the presidential election, Alexander Cockburn of New York's *Village Voice* wrote in an editorial, "Great Britain is providing fairly instructive parallels for Americans now wondering what the future holds in store for them." He then called attention to Milton Friedman, "dear to the heart of many of Ronald Reagan's economic advisors and supporters." Thatcher also came to power, Cockburn emphasized, "espousing the Friedman doctrine—announcing strict control of the money supply, fearsome onslaughts on deficit spending in the public sector, and a chance for the previously chained titans of British industry to prove their mettle."[90]

Cockburn continued:

Since which announcements, the money supply has roared up, inflation is running at 20 per cent, interest rates at 16 per cent, and unemployment at three million. With removal of currency controls, British capital has sailed forth to take up residence in other quarters of the globe, while the strength of the pound has permitted foreign imports to rush in. For the first time it looks as though the British might carry a trading deficit on manufactured goods. So much for the workshop of the world, where the managers of idle plants rush to the bank to get overdrafts, ever more costly as the interest rates soar.

The *Voice* editorial dismissed Friedman in the following terms:

So much for the Friedmanite theory that inflation is caused by growth in the money supply, and that attempted diminution of the latter is the answer to life's problems. It's amazing that the British let Friedman into the country at all. The French are more sensible. Not so long ago Milton traveled to Paris and sought a meeting with the French Prime Minister, Raymond Barre. When his assistants told Barre that Friedman was on the line, he was reportedly horrified and announced that he could not possible take the political risk of being seen in the same room, let along the same photograph as Friedman.

The night of the US election former British conservative Prime Minister Edward Heath reeled into a BBC radio interview with Friedman at three in the morning. Heath was somewhat the worse for drink after long hours of punditry on commercial television earlier in the proceedings. Finding himself sharing the same airwaves as Friedman, he became incoherent with rage, and denounced Friedman as the man who had brought misery and ruin to millions. The interview broke up in disorder.

Meanwhile Thatcher says that after just one more bout of pain, life will improve. She may be around to witness the dawn break. The first duty of a politician is to survive, and the British conservative party is beginning to reckon that survival may be an easier job if Thatcher ceases at some suitably early point to be prime minister.

On November 18 (nine days after the 1980 U.S. presidential elections), a new session of the British parliament opened with a confirmation by Thatcher of her determination to maintain current policies. The outline of the legislature program for the session, London's *Financial Times* reported, "contained no surprises and promised a less hectic year than in the administration's first session."[91] At that time more than 70 bills reached the statute book, which marked Thatcher's first session one of the heaviest legislative sessions of the century.

In early February 1981, as the media prepared for Thatcher's visit to the U.S., *Time* magazine did its cover story on Thatcher with the headings "Embattled but Unbowed" and "As Britain reels from recession and political turmoil, Thatcher soldiers on."[92] The article began by picturing Thatcher in debate in the House of Commons:

> Even by the rowdy standards of the House of Commons "cheer and jeer" debate, Prime Minister Margaret Thatcher was in for a bruising confrontation as she rose from the government front bench last week to answer hostile opposition challenges about the country's unemployment, the worst since the 1930s. Days earlier, when she wore a black dress, Labor M. P. William Hamilton had pointed a taunting finger at her and inquired derisively, "Is she dressed in black because of the unemployment figures?" Now she was meticulously turned out in a tailored gray suit, a soft white bow at her neck, to face another onslaught. In her coolly accented voice, she delivered a forceful and familiar message: only sound money and competitive industry can bring down inflation and eventually create new jobs for Britain.
>
> From the Labor benches jumped M. P. Dennis Skinner, a militant leftist. Stabbing at the air, he roared, "Same old story!" Thatcher, coming alive, snapped back, "Of course, it's the same old story. Truth usually is the same old story!" Almost menacingly, Skinner leaned toward her and charged, "We'll get you out—either in this place or outside it." The threat of going outside Parliament to bring down a government brought gasps from many M.P.s, Thatcher did not flinch. "Rubbish," she replied. Then she added, "Indeed, he is the face of the true new Labor party—not of its democrats—but those who have moved further and further left, towards the East European type of economy." Again came a momentary hush, and then Tory M.P.s broke into cheers at the flash of their leader's steel knuckles.

From Thatcher's performance in parliament, the *Time* article switched to demands being made on the industrial front. Leaders of the Trade Union Congress and the Confederation of British Industry were demanding that Thatcher reflate the economy before "there'll be nothing left to revive." Demands for pay boosts were being rejected. A negotiator for some civil service workers furiously rejected a 6 percent pay boost offered by the

Thatcher government with the remark, "I told them to get stuffed." The prime minister stood fast.

When Thatcher appeared on television from No 10 Downing Street the next week, *Time* pictured Thatcher as scoffing at past governments that "have taken fright and cut and run." The prime minister said, "If I could only get this message over: I will not stagger from expedient to expedient."

The rhetoric portrayed a lot. The pragmatist in Thatcher, though, came out as well, for she did yield on a pay raise to avoid collision with Britain's coalminers. Britain's coal subsidies were reported as modest in comparison with those of Continental European countries. There was some evidence of disarray from the cumulative effect of raising the borrowing powers of state industries to pay bills. Nonetheless, as Thatcher departed for the U.S. *The Economist* said that Margaret Thatcher "knows how to use a parachute." Noting that she was admired "precisely by those who believed she was prepared to do or die," it reported the frankest of her cabinet as having "said that he had not come into politics for a kamikazi trip."[93] In the coming month, *The Economist* described Thatcher's apparent imperviousness to the critics.

Thatcher's impenetrable position was no "inelegant scrabbling for friends" on her part as she had noted in the U.S. case of Jimmy Carter. Referring no doubt to politicians who may be sacrificed at a time of reelection and the unavoidable unemployment as a part of the transition from the socialist/Keynesian world, *The Economist* pictured Thatcher as seeming to her supporters "intent only on the senseless self-sacrifice of Tennyson's Light Brigade heroes."[94] One may recall, however, that the heroes of the charge made by British cavalry in the Crimea in 1854 were honored in London and memorialized in Tennyson's poem "The Charge of the Light Brigade."[95]

. . . .
Boldly they rode and well,
Into the jaws of Death,
Into the mouth of Hell,
Rode the six hundred.

. . . .
Cannon to right of them,
Cannon to left of them,
Cannon behind them
Volley'd and thunder'd;
Storm'd at with shot and shell,
While horse and hero fell,
They that had fought so well
Came thro' the jaws of Death

> Back from the mouth of Hell,
> All that was left of them,
> Left of six hundred.
> When can their glory fade?
> O the wild charge they made!
> All the world wonder'd.
> Honor the charge they made!
> Honor the Light Brigade!
> Noble six hundred!

In the meanwhile, Thatcher arrived in the United States on Thursday February 23 to a flurry of martial music and stately dining elegance. Welcoming the Prime Minister with a flourish of heraldic trumpets at the White House, the President, the *New York Times* reported, echoed Thatcher's sentiments that economic solutions "lie within the people and not the state." Mrs. Thatcher responded, "We are both determined to sweep away the restrictions that hold back enterprise." Continuing, she said, "We both place our faith not so much in economic theory but in the resourcefulness and decency of ordinary people."[96]

As Thatcher's U.S. visit was ending, she decided to stay over for a guest appearance with correspondent Barbara Walters on the ABC-Television program "Issues and Answers."[97] After preliminary remarks about a shared philosophy, shared problems, and international matters, the interview focused on the respective economies. It began with taxes and public spending, moved to financing of deficits, then to the relationship between inflation and unemployment, and ended with a discussion of trends, inflation, hyperinflation, and the painfulness of the transition from an inflationary trend.

These topics parallel those appropriate to a discussion of Milton Friedman's economics. One of the early questions in the Walters interview involved a statement by Treasury Secretary Donald Regan, made at a Congressional meeting at the time of Thatcher's U.S. arrival. The question concerned Thatcher's failure to cut taxes enough. In response, she stated her desire to cut more but felt it conflicted with her inability to cut spending more.[98] Though she did not mention it, she had to consider her large public sector and state industries, so she took the risk of printing too much money [having the central bank support the spending], as a means of meeting expenditures. She said, "if you have higher expenditures than you wish, you must match it reasonably well by higher taxes than you wish." Thatcher continued:

> But never mind, don't let me underestimate our achievement. Public spending is very considerably down from the previously

Prime Minister Thatcher with President Reagan at the White House

planned totals. Direct taxation is very considerably down. One figure—direct taxation on earned income. The top earned was 83 percent when we came into power. The top rate's now down to 60 percent. On savings income, the top rate was 98 percent. We brought it down to 70 percent. We've a long way to go. But we've made quite a good start.

Next, the questioning shifted to the concern West Germany's Chancellor Helmut Schmidt had expressed over high interest rates in the United States which, he thought, held unemployment consequences for his own economy. Thatcher noted here that Schmidt and Germany had kept interest rates down with low inflation. Continuing along impeccable Friedman lines she said:

But you see, Helmut Schmidt has rightly taken a very strict view of monetary policy throughout his period of office, and he, in fact, has controlled money supply. He's got his inflation right down. If Germany has five percent inflation, they're worried, really worried. But they've done it by precisely the methods that President Reagan is going to try to carry out. And so the answer to our good friend Helmut Schmidt is that you cannot deny the United States the very policies which were so successful in Germany. And he'd be the first to accept that. Because if the United States has high inflation, and high interest rates, then you must take the right steps first to get the inflation down. And that's very important. It's important for the future stability of the world.

Host Barbara Walters followed with a question on inflation and unemployment, dealing with what was addressed earlier as some combination of the Phillips curve, wage adjustments, and an open economy. Thatcher's reply may be viewed as coming directly out of Friedman's Nobel and related lectures.

MS. WALTERS: Prime Minister, I would like to ask you about the relationship between inflation and unemployment. In *Time* magazine last week you said, and I quote, "I'm afraid that in the early stages bringing down inflation means that you have increasing unemployment. I don't know any other way of doing it." Is it therefore a fact that if we do try to bring down inflation we must be aware that we will increase unemployment.

MRS. THATCHER: In the early stages, yes. In politics life's a question of alternative policies. Two policies. Supposing we start off with inflation. You have it. We have it. At very high rates.

Rates that have gone up over the last decade to far higher rates than we would have thought possible. And you also have a certain amount of unemployment. Now you can do two things. You can reflate. That means sticking inflation on top of inflation, and what I would call "suitcase money." Germany had it after the first World War. When you get that you get unemployment on a colossal scale. Now what's the alternative policy? You've got inflation. You try to pursue policies that will get the inflation down. That means not having so much surplus money in the economy so that prices come down. Unless people condition their wage claims to the lesser amount of money, then there'll be some unemployment. What usually happens is that people still want to take out quite a lot for themselves, they leave less over for others, and it comes out in unemployment. But in the longer run, you'll not get a competitive industry, good secure jobs unless your costs are competitive with other people's. That means fighting inflation now, it means short run unemployment, but long term good jobs, good prosperity, good prospects.

MS. WALTERS: So if we have to look forward—Not look forward, but if we have to bear some unemployment, in your country does this mean even at the very high rate, almost ten percent of unemployment, that you feel it will go down? That this is what you would consider short term?

MRS. THATCHER: If I reverse my policies and said I'm now going to reflate at the level of inflation we have now, which is 12-13 percent, all I would be doing would be going to hyperinflation. It means that British industry is not competitive. How can it compete with inflation at five percent in Germany? We should lose our markets. We rely on exports for jobs. We'd lose our markets and we'd get much, much higher unemployment in the long run. So we have to go through short term painful periods in order to come through in the longer run. I know you don't like long answers, but can I point out one thing?

MS. WALTERS: Oh, of course, yes.

MRS. THATCHER: In the last twenty years, the level of inflation...has gone steadily upwards. We used to have levels of about three percent. Then we went right up to 20, 22 percent. Each parliament has gone upwards. In its wake, each unemployment level has gone upwards. I've got to break the cycle, get the inflation rate down, down, and get it to stay down. Then gradually the unemployment will come down and then we shall have a foundation for a much more prosperous society. We're a very inventive people. We're very ingenious people. We've got good supplies of oil, gas, and coal. And when we do that, we shall be a very, very formidable competitor, and we intend to be.

When Thatcher returned to Britain from the U.S., two additional matters of some considerable importance confronted her. The two were (1) the budget for the fiscal year beginning April 1, 1981, and (2) the matter of the state industries.

The budget for the year through March 1982 was presented to the parliament by the Chancellor of the Exchequer on March 10. It was an austerity budget, coming at the time of a 10 percent unemployment rate, the highest since the 1930s. Excise taxes were raised on alcohol, tobacco, petrol, and other items, and income taxes were raised "indirectly" (i.e., not by changing rates but by lowering the minimum for taxable income and by not increasing the allowances that index income taxes against inflation). On the budget side, there was a cutback in government spending overall, but a rise in defense outlays. To supplement the fiscal restraint, the budget adopted the prevailing 7-10 percent target for money growth (the so-called M-3) for the period until Mid-April 1981, and a reduction to a 6-10 percent range for 1981-82, and to 4-8 by 1983-84.

The measures thus announced were expected to result in a 2.5 percent decline in Britain's GDP (gross domestic product, or GNP less net foreign investment) for the budget year. After that, growth was expected to average about 1 percent a year for the next three.

Michael Foot, the Labor party opposition leader, called the budget, "A no-hope budget from a no-hope Chancellor." Some of Thatcher's fellow conservatives in parliament worried about the election that had to be held in 1984. Labor's spokesman for economic affairs in parliament, Peter Shore, said the government's program was "as socially unjust as it is economically unjustifiable." He continued, "It is a budget for the accelerated decline of industry and the economy. Unfortunately, it is a budget of failure." Margaret Thatcher, on the other hand, defended the budget as "the only hope for Britain." Displaying her confidence in ultimately changing Britain's economy, she said, "We have laid the basis for a genuine revival of the British economy." The budget is tough, "Yes. But a firm budget, by a Government confident that its strategy is right."[99]

Even with the budget in place, the state industries were still owned by the government for the foreseeable future, and their controlling boards had chairpersons and sponsoring departments who also were part of Thatcher's cabinet. The sponsoring departments included chiefly industry, energy and transport. The industry department was headed by Thatcher's long-time associate Sir Keith Joseph. The nationalized industry matters that had come before Thatcher's cabinet concerned public-sector borrowing targets of the treasury, temporary short-term financial bail-outs for troubled industries, and the setting of priorities for worthwhile public-sector projects. Each industrial board viewed its projects as worthwhile in a special way, each was defensive, and many of them, notably coal, steel, and BL (British Leyland), had excessive expenditures. The pressure put on government programs to use them as means of bolstering spending and employment and as engines of reflation was an additional problem. Thus, industrial boards, sponsoring departments, public pressures for reflation and other factors of this kind may appear on one side of the argument, as the boards and departments support more spending, and the treasury under Thatcher's Chancellor of the Exchequer Sir Geoffry Howe on the other as Thatcher's Exchequer argues for restraint in spending.[100]

All this industrial decision-making was layered on top of the ordinary problems and conflicts of a political body. The burden was excessive, and various governments tried various means to use it. Further movement toward the east European type of economy was at one extreme and, denationalization was at the other. One distorted prospect falling between the extremes was the creation of public-private hybrids as subsidiaries of nationalized industries. These proposed hybrids would gain the freedom to raise capital exclusive of the treasury borrowing requirement. In other words, borrowing by them would not count under the law as part of the public-sector borrowing targets. But it did count, in fact, particularly when a government guarantee for the financing was implied or demanded. Yielding to this pressure for guarantees would make the so-called private-sector borrowing by the hybrid arrangement nothing more than public borrowing.

Margaret Thatcher's conviction, as evidenced in her public remarks, was that the nationalized industries should be turned over to the private sector—"lock, stock and barrel." What she actually achieved for a time, however, was more complicated. So an apparently exasperated Margaret Thatcher asked "the Central Policy Review Staff (SPRS) under Mr. Robin Ibbs to investigate every aspect of the relations between Britain's nationalized industries and its government." These studies were undertaken by Mr. Ryrie at the Treasury.[101]

The Hard Slog, the 1983 Elections and Beyond

The shift toward a socialist society in Britain had its start in the 1920s, but appeared most visibly in 1945 with the great sweep of the Labor party (chap. 11). The roots underlying the shift lay in the 1920s and 1930s—in the economic problems that appeared in those decades and in the major work of J.M. Keynes that emerged from the interwar period. Going back a bit further, there are also the works of Marx and Engels, of John Stuart Mill, and the misgivings about Britain's success in the economic sphere on the part of the heirs to wealth such as John Ruskin and Sidney and Beatrice Webb.

From 1945 until Thatcher's May 1979 watershed election, the succession of Conservative and Labor governments made little difference to economic and social policy.[102] The ideas behind the policies were socialist and Keynesian, the first being distinguished from the latter primarily by the forcefulness of their advocacy for government ownership and control of industry and by a less muted advocacy of the equality of outcome in the distribution of income to households.

The competition for votes by the political parties follows an analysis offered by Harold Hotelling (pp. 409-410).[103] In that analysis with two parties and voters strung out along a line (say, as a continuum of political views from left to right), the competition for votes between the parties "does not lead to a clear drawing of issues, an adoption of two strongly contrasted positions between which the voter may choose." Continuing, Hotelling concluded thus: "Instead, each party [candidate] strives to make its platform [speeches in general election] as much like the other's as possible. Any radical departure would lose many voters, even though it might lead to stronger commendation of the party by some who would vote for it anyhow. Each candidate 'pussy-foots,' replies ambiguously to questions, refuses to take a definite stand in any controversy for fear of losing voters. Real differences, if they ever exist, fade gradually with time though the issue may be as important as ever."

And so it was in Britain, where economic policies were inflationary and accompanied by efforts to control prices, alter the distribution of income, and occasionally manipulate exchange rates. Nice things happened first, but the economic problems accumulated as the inflation rate rose, as saving on the part of the private sector declined relative to total income and as production per worker declined. Ultimately the unemployment statistics revealed a rise as jobs and capital went elsewhere in the world and underground.

The stage was set for the acceptance by the public of a combination of old and new ideas, and of strong leadership. The ideas were about in London and elsewhere, as we have seen, and Margaret Thatcher appeared from outside the establishment of traditional Tory politicians as a leader with the needed courage, conviction and perseverance. The electorate appeared ready to gamble on her personality "in order to gain the benefits of her policies."[104]

The unwinding of government and the necessary steps for implementing a transition from a socialist/Keynesian society were discussed in London by Milton Friedman as early as 1974.[105] As discussed by him and Thatcher, the following were to occur: reductions in inflation (and expectations with respect to it); resources were to be transferred from the public to the private sector; the willingness of the men and women of business to engage in enterprising ventures was to be revitalized; and the social perception of profits was to change. Friedman envisioned a rather ideal set of changes that could occur over a four-to-five year period, with minimum hardships.[106] Friedman knew, as did Thatcher, however, that the factors determining real economic growth were not primarily monetary but instead resided in the institutions of the country and the character of its people.

Thatcher, of course, was very much aware of the changes she was making in the character of Britain's economy and its society. In an interview with *Time* magazine's London Bureau Chief while awaiting balloting for the 1983 elections, Thatcher said, "I think our biggest single achievement is the whole change in attitude in this country." Thatcher's program had indeed been viewed as calling for a return to "Victorian values." She means by these, "the virtues of thrift and self-reliance, hard work and a sense of duty."[107]

Thatcher also took note of a remarkable feature of her first term. "It is quite a lot," she said, "for a politician to be able to take the long-term view, knowing that it is going to give you immense short-term trouble."

Theories, Victorian values and the long-run view aside, the ideal transition toward the social market economy was not the reality: 1. The techniques of control over money and credit aggregates were not well understood by university and Bank of England experts. As in the U.S., there was a lingering tendency to rely on a presumed link between money-market, interest rates and the growth of a selected monetary measure even where in fact the link was not so close. 2. Top level civil servants rather than appointed officials held important positions, but were unprepared ideologically and academically for the Gestalt shift from the prevailing economic orientations. Technical factors (e.g., the "corset") were impediments also. 3. Questions arose about the adequacy of sterling M3 as the indicator of monetary policy such that monetary policy appeared more restrictive than sterling M3 indicated. 4. Thatcher took office at the start of a surge in public sector pay. Under the British arrangement for public sectors borrowing, this meant that the Bank of England would finance the debt by overexpansion of bank reserves and the money and credit aggregates, at least as measured by sterling M3. 5. Controlling the public sector borrowing requirement was also complicated by the presence of representatives of the boards of state-owned industries and chairpersons of sponsoring departments as part of the Cabinet government. Special interest arguments surface, plus as monetary tightness occurs the temptation becomes greater to support deficit spending and expansion of the public industries. 6. The "privatization" of government owned industry called for a sizable, private financial sector, which had not flourished under Britain's post-WW II trends. Closely related to this, the British tax structure had to be changed and the power of British labor unions had to be weakened. Taxes in Britain had favored the export of Britain's financial (and hence ultimately real) capital to the rest of the world and damped the incentive to engage in business enterprise. The export of capital and the power of the British labor unions meant the export of jobs for British workers. 7. Production from Britain's North Sea oil and gas projects overcame Britain's dependence on foreign resources, at the same time it favored the British pound. However, a strengthened pound worked to the disadvantage of export industries and hence employment (pp. 412-417). 8. The removal of any stimulus to domestic spending via decelerated inflation, the strengthened pound, and efforts to control public sector borrowing and the size of the public sector, all meant recession and added unemployment for a time until a revitalized private sector could absorb some of the unemployed. 9. Even the mobility of labor from one geographical region to another encountered impediments that were put in place by prior governments. 10. The "expected" inflation had to be reduced as a component of interest rates, in relation to some envisioned norm for future interest rates and inflation. These developments were crucial to the enlargement of private-sector business actively and the expanded employment of labor resources.

Conventional Wisdom

So Margaret Thatcher was put in the challenging position of asking special sacrifices from the British people for an extended period of time. Thatcher had forsaken the "quick fix" and the temporary approach to permanent problems. The "quick fix" had come to symbolize aspects of money and credit growth, and government spending without regard to the long-run consequences. These were inflation, recession, and declining productivity, in the one instance, and a growing public sector borrowing requirement, in the other. Against all conventional economic and political wisdom Thatcher opted for the long run.

The conventional economic wisdom had been best portrayed by the development in the U.S. of a literature about the political business cycle.[108] In that literature we encounter the notion that voting on the election of a government or candidate for high political office is decisively influenced by the state of economic conditions at the time of voting, as indicated by such measures as unemployment, inflation, growth in real income, and the misery index (the sum of inflation and unemployment rates). The bad state of conditions meant a loss of voter support and improvements meant the reverse.

This view credits the voter with a short memory. When improvements do come, as one writer stated with reference to American voters, "Americans—at least, those whose phone numbers Mr. Gallop keeps in his Rolodex—are like November-to-March agnostics overcome with religious feeling on the first sunny day of spring."[109]

As the economic measure of unemployment went against Thatcher in the early phases of her first government, the London press reported on the rise of the newly formed Social Democratic party (SDP) as the likely centrist party that would capture power in Britain. There was the view that Thatcher would not make a second term with her harsh policies, and coincidental with them, Thatcher's standing in the opinion poles declined.

However, Thatcher was not addressing temporary phases of a traditional business cycle but more permanent changes, plus the size of the Tory majority in Parliament at the date of the May 1979 elections virtually assured her of a full five-year term, unless she chose to call an election earlier. Thus it came about that Thatcher acted against the conventional wisdom on the political front as she had on the economic front. To be sure, Thatcher was on the extreme right by post-WW II standards and she remained so in her 1979 campaign, with discussions of monetarism, the individual who offers hard work, the historical character of the British people, and rewarding the workers "not the shirkers." Even as she continued her campaign on the right, *The [London] Economist* advised that she would likely shift to the center "where elections are won."[110]

Thatcher, nevertheless, continued to move the Tories to the right eighteen months after coming to power. This persistence, worsening economic conditions, and Thatcher's appeal to Britain's electorate generally contributed to frustration within the opposition Labor party. Reacting to Thatcher and the futility of the middle, the opposition party shifted sharply to the left.

A few months later, a small number of the members of Parliament resigned from the Labor party to form the new Social Democrats. There was the prospect too of a possible coalition of the new party and the old British Liberal party that had been replaced by the Labor party in 1922.

In terms of Hotelling's line and the continuum of political views described earlier, Thatcher altered the alignment of England's voters. Her constituency shifted right with her, Labor had shifted left, and what was once thought of as the popular middle ground was shared by the coalition of Social Democrats and the Liberal party. The stage for Thatcher's 1983, landslide victory was set after two years in power, not by her moving to middle ground, but by her influencing the distribution of voters along Hotelling's line, and by some changes in political districting in Britain to reflect population shifts (an increase in house seats from 635 to 650).

What may have happened in the early election called by Thatcher for June 9, 1983, is more speculative than would have been the case had not two developments occurred: (1) One was the dramatic economic failures that had developed under the socialist government across the English Channel in France, under the leadership of President Francois Mitterrand, and (2) the other was an unforeseen episode that took place fourteen months earlier on April 2, 1982.

The French Experience

With his bent for testing one theory against another rather than against some ideal, Milton Friedman pointed to the role of Mitterrand's France in the British election. "France," he said, "was suffering the same ills when Mitterrand was elected president as Britain when Mrs. Thatcher became prime minister and the United States when Ronald Reagan became president—high and rising inflation, high unemployment and slow economic growths."[111] However, "Mitterrand's attack on those ills was precisely the reverse of Mrs. Thatcher's" and with the reverse consequences. On attacking the ills, Friedman said:

> On coming into office, Thatcher reduced taxes; Mitterrand increased them. Thatcher reduced controls over prices and wages; Mitterrand expanded them. Thatcher eliminated foreign-exchange controls; Mitterrand made them tighter. Thatcher moved to denationalize enterprises and reduce regulation; Mitterrand nationalized private banks and other enterprises and increased government intervention into the remaining private enterprise. Thatcher tried to hold down government spending, albeit with little success; Mitterrand went on a spending binge.

Continuing on the comparison of the British and French policies, Friedman remarked:

> Had the Mitterrand policies succeeded, even if for only a year or so, Thatcher's opposition in Britain would have been enormously strengthened. The Labor party would have had a real alternative to offer—one that was consistent with its ideological propensities and that had worked on the other side of the Channel. The cry that Thatcher's "monetarism" was a tragic failure could not have been dismissed as mere campaign rhetoric.
>
> Instead, the Mitterrand policy was a clear failure. Inflation remained high. Unemployment went up. The government's budget

deficit soared. So did the deficit in the balance of payments. The franc had to be devalued three times in the past two years, despite massive government borrowing in a vain attempt to prop the franc up.

So there was no credible alternative to Thatcher's policies, and none, Friedman said, to President Reagan's in the U.S. On the alternative, Friedman continued:

> Thatcher's opposition was left intellectually bankrupt. It had no credible alternative policy to offer. The claim that she was an irresponsible demagogue imposing unnecessary costs on the British people rang hollow. Her persistence in the main lines of her policy was perceived by the voters as a realistic recognition that there was no easy cure for ills that had accumulated during decades.

The Falkland's Episode

On April 2, 1982, Argentina invaded a small British island colony 8,000 miles from London. The Argentines apparently had come to think of Britain as a "decadent" country, and underestimated the reaction to the April-2 invasion that temporarily ended 149 years of colonial rule by London.

The invasion was in part a surprise because the British Foreign Office in London under Lord Carrington chose to ignore as being unbelievable reports coming from the British Embassy in Argentina. A few days after the invasion Carrington resigned, accepting responsibility for the "humiliating affront." He was replaced by Francis Pym who announced at the opening of Commons debate on the matter that "Britain does not appease dictators."

One Tory backbencher wondered whether "Margaret means what Francis Pym says." The crisis it seems had touched off old wounds in a national psyche that surfaced after four decades that witnessed the loss of an empire, the decay of an economy, and British adjustments to second-class status in the world.

Thatcher apparently did mean what Francis Pym said. Britain prepared for an invasion against numerically superior odds, at a distance 8,000 miles away. The Prime Minister quoted Victoria: "Failure—the possibility does not exist." The British fleet sailed out of Portsmouth to liberate the Falkland Islands, causing one writer to reflect on Rudyard Kipling's words, written when the British Empire was at its zenith:

> "If blood be the price of admiralty, Lord God, we ha' paid in full."

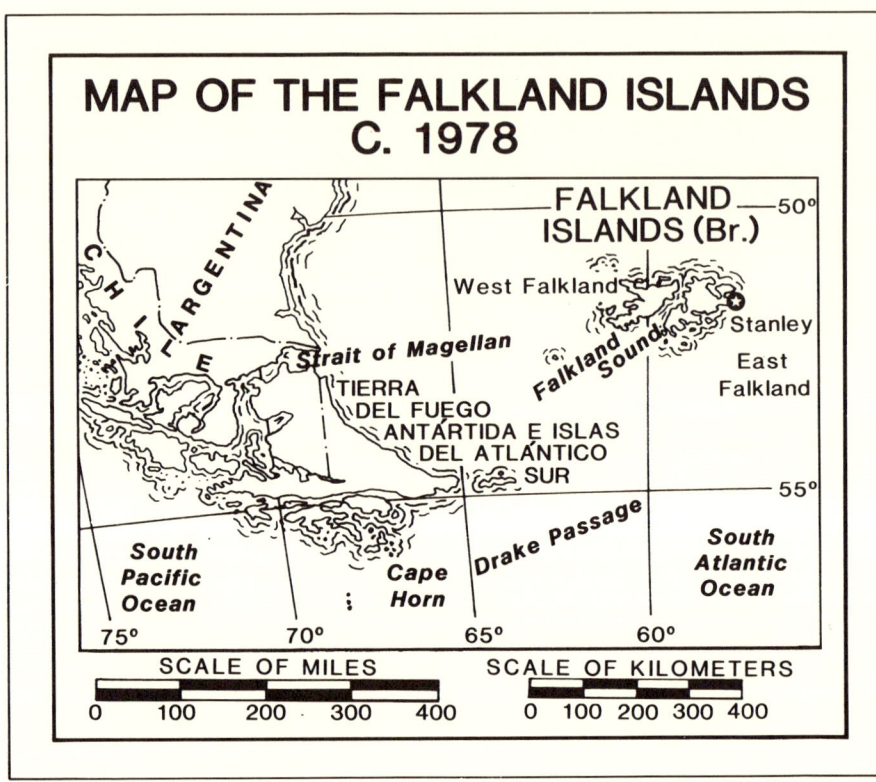

Falkland Islands, 250 miles east of Argentina's southern coast

Whatever the numbers, ten weeks after Argentina seized the South Atlantic archipelago, Thatcher won what many writers had viewed as the biggest gamble of her career. She had become more popular as Britain leaped from national humiliation to military victory. Thatcher told the House of Commons that Britain will hold the Falklands out of respect for the wishes of the local population which had opposed any link with Argentina. Of the 243 servicemen Britain reported killed, Thatcher said, "They died that many others live in freedom and justice."

In her handling of the episode, Thatcher portrayed the same character she had shown in dealing with the British economy, but there was an unusual twist. The success of the British under Thatcher's leadership in the

Falklands reinforced the confidence of the British people in themselves and in Thatcher. The reference "the 'Iron Lady' became an accolade, not an epithet."

The personality in the economic policy sphere is paradoxically portrayed in discussion by a Keynesian critic of Thatcher's policies in Britain and Ronald Reagan's in the U.S. James Tobin said, "[She] threatens workers, managers, and plain citizens like an authoritarian schoolmaster disciplining an unruly class. You won't have jobs, profits or prosperity until you stop inflating your wages and prices."

Continuing, James Tobin said:

> The Federal Reserve, it is true, has been following a Thatcher-like policy but in whispers...
>
> The Fed's muted threat is quite different from Her Majesty's first minister's standing up in Parliament and throughout her country to say that she doesn't care how much unemployment there is for how long, or what is the real rate of growth or decline; she will stick it through whatever the pain, however long it takes to eliminate inflation.[112]

The 1983 Elections

Thatcher's standing in the opinion poles, rising even before the Falkland's episode, rose further in response to the success there and then moderated somewhat. This, along with some local elections in early May suggesting a reduced Tory lead, caused some conservatives to push for a new-election while the strong standing still held. Thatcher herself noted an atmosphere of uncertainty over her incumbency, even as she played coy with respect to whether an early election would be held. The atmosphere of anticipation, Thatcher teased, reminded her about an old song "Maggie May." (The title referred to a ditty about a prostitute from Liverpool: "Some say Maggie may. Others say Maggie may not.")[113]

In any case, after a long session with aides at the prime minister's country estate known as Chequers, the decision was announced on May 9, for an election on June 9.[114] Holding a 36 seat majority in the House of Commons at the time of the announcement (down from 44 seats when Conservatives took office) polls suggested a substantial win and, indeed, her standing in the polls rose during the campaign period. There were moments, one reporter noted, when Thatcher "achieved the remarkable feat of appearing to be on the side of the people against the government, as if she and the government had nothing to do with each other."

The May 9 announcement, Mark Whitaker reported, set the stage for a fast, rough-and-tumble campaign that confronted British voters with a stark ideological choice.[115] Continuing he said:

> After four years at 10 Downing Street, Thatcher will ask for another term to carry on the Tory party's battle to cut public spending, curb trade-union power and maintain a strong nuclear defense. Michael Foot, the candidate for the opposition Labor party, will preach a very different gospel: massive state intervention in the economy, close consultation with the unions and unilateral nuclear disarmament. Squeezed on a small patch of middle ground will be the two-year-old coalition between Social Democratic defectors from Labor and the small Liberal party. The Liberal-SDP alliance will prescribe moderation in both domestic and foreign policy...

Main facts noted during the campaign were a rise in the jobless rate from 5.4 to 13.3 percent, and a decline in the inflation rate from 22 percent in early 1980 to a 15-year low of 4.6 percent. Putting together the unemployment and inflation rates, there was a decline in the misery index by approximately 8 percentage points, although there was no concession on Thatcher's part that unemployment would decline. The best hope for unemployment, as offered by Sir Geoffrey Howe in the last stage of the campaign, was that unemployment would stop rising before it reached the 4 million level. Mrs. Thatcher expressed the hope in a television interview on June 8 that the rise in unemployment could be reversed within two and a half years.

As reported in *The [London] Economist*, "Mrs. Margaret Thatcher campaigned mainly on her own personality ["the resolute approach" To-

United Kingdom Election Returns

Party	May 1979 seats	May 1979 % of vote#	June 1983 seats	June 1983 % of vote#	June 1987 seats	June 1987 % of vote#
Tory	339	43.90	396	42.40	375	42.30
Labor	268	36.90	209	27.60	22	30.83
Alliance	n.a.*	n.a.*	23	25.40	22	22.5
Other	28	19.20	22	4.60	24	4.32

#Popular vote
*SDP-Liberal alliance not yet formed

Source: British Information Services, New York

ries called it] and on her own record." The choice in the campaign was presented as being "between Mrs. Thatcher's brand of economic masochism—you've never had it so bad—and the 'fresh' approach which the Social Democratic and Liberal alliance says it offers Britain."[116]

Portraying a British electorate in a giddy state, *The Economist* presented its cover with the question, "Thatcher's Britain?" It called attention to 3 million unemployed ("They've never had it so bad"), to an anti-union stand ("Bash my union"), to national defense ("I love nukes"), and to monetarism and other things ("Hang'em, flog'em").

In terms of Hotelling's line and Britain's electoral system, electoral success could hardly be measured in terms of popular vote. Instead of two parties vying for votes in the middle, the majority parties since WW II shifted to the extremes and the SDP-Liberal alliance took the more intermediate position. Under Britain's electoral system the Prime Minister's standing in the government is determined by seats in Parliament's House of Commons. It is the elected body but the House of Lords itself may spend much time on initiating, debating, and giving detailed consideration to bills. A bill becomes a law only when it has been agreed to by the House of Commons (with some exceptions) and by the House of Lords. In addition to ceremonial functions, the House of Lords may help decide national policy through debate.

As of the June 1983 elections the 650 seats in the House of Commons were held by MPs who represent districts. Election victories in these are determined by a plurality (not necessarily a majority or more than half a total). On June 9, much of Britain's recent past converged, when Margaret Thatcher won a landslide victory,[117] just short of that for Clement Attlee in his 1945 sweep, but it was more remarkable in view of Hotelling's line and the presence of the SDP and the Liberal party in the analysis. No party leader since Lord Salisbury (the Tory successor to Benjamin Disraeli) had won by sufficient majorities to be assured of a second, full five-year term as prime minister.

As matters turned out, one-quarter of the unemployed and 29 percent of workers in trade unions voted for Conservatives.[118] The immediate aftermath of the election offered a few paradoxes.

Headlines reflected Thatcher's statement, "I am not an extreme person, and I won't be extreme now."[119] In a sense, she had been moderate in dismantling government ("privatizing" as it were), even though the simple idea of "privatizing" was extreme by post-WW II standards. She was reported as clearly committed to reducing inflation as a top priority, relying on the control of the money supply and cuts in public spending.

Shortly after this statement of moderation, a government priority to move further toward denationalization was pointed out,[120] and changes in Thatcher's Cabinet were announced. Somewhat later, Alan Walters left his

Prime Minister beams at supporters on Isle of Wright during 1983 campaign's final day

assignment at 10 Downing Street. Newly titled Sir Alan Walters, he returned to Johns Hopkins University and joined American Enterprise Institute as a resident scholar.

Although British Airways was moved from the trade department to transport, a part of the new trade and industry secretary's responsibility was to remit the introduction of private capital into British Steel, British Leyland, British Shipbuilders, Rolls-Royce and British Telecom (BT, the state owned telephone company). Even so, at the time of the 1983 election only the BT privatization looked practicable. The government was simply empowered to privatize BT by means to be decided later. Since BT was valued at £8 billion at the time, and was more than twice the size of Britain's largest industrial concern (the General Electric Company), even the idea of floating half of its stock was thought to be overwhelming to the London stock market.

British merchant banks were portrayed by the financial press as seeing good times again.[121] These, of course, were the financial institutions that traditionally raise private capital through the underwriting and sale of new security issues to the private sector. In the Golden Age of Britain, they were the hallmark of London as a financial center.

The new cabinet moves announced by Thatcher also accompanied plans to reduce the cabinet from 22 ministers to 21 by combining the previously separate trade and industry departments.[122] The major changes reflected economic policies, although Thatcher's office announced that overall the changes were "designed to reflect the range of opinions within the Conservative party."[123] Mr. Nigel Lawson, a convinced monetarist, was named to the Treasury post housed at No 11 Downing Street. He was said to be committed to the Thatcherite faith and "on the same wavelength as Alan [Walters, Downing Street adviser]." Lawson replaced Sir Geoffrey Howe, the staunch Thatcher ally and instrument of her economic policies from the first election in May 1979, and Howe in turn replaced the foreign secretary Mr. Francis Pym.

Recalling Thatcher's early days in Grantham, *Times*'s London staff reported that the new "Cabinet no longer contains a Tory blueblood."[124] Continuing they reported: Thatcher has taken the party out of the hands of the gentry and turned it over to people like herself who have worked their way up in the world and who sometimes see a sense of social responsibility as an unaffordable luxury. She has forged an alliance between skilled workers and the middle class; according to polls taken before the election, a majority of both groups planned to vote for her. Only unskilled workers were viewed as having remained safely in the Labor camp, and theirs was reported as a dwindling breed.

During 1984, for the first time, blue-collar workers were outnumbered by white-collar workers in the labor force. Meanwhile, surveys showed that voters were growing less and less likely to vote by class, simply along the lines of bowler hat vs. cloth cap. As if that were not advantage enough for Thatcher, Britain's population was seen as shifting from the big cities that had long been Labor strongholds to the Tory enclaves of suburbia. Parliamentary districts had already been redrawn for the 1983 election to reflect that migration, and the Tories clearly gained. Robert Waller, author of *The Almanac of British Policies*, wrote that "Social changes are taking place which make the Conservatives the party of the future and Labor the party of the past."

Following the 1983 Elections

Following Thatcher's 1983 elections, three matters stood out. First, she won a stunning victory in early March of 1985, whereas in 1981 she yielded on what appeared to be pragmatic political grounds to avoid collision with British coal miners (the bellweather of union strength since the days of "The Economic Consequences of Mr. Churchill" and the 1920s). In March 1985, the Marxist led, coal-miners union called off the longest and most violent walkout in British history. Following the 357-day-old strike, the miners were ordered by the union to return to work without an agreement or a promise to rehire fired workers.

Second, the plan to privatize British Telecom at the time of the 1983 elections came about. Following the earlier return of British Petroleum and British Leyland to private hands, the formerly state-owned communications giant, the world's fourth-largest telephone company, went public in early December 1984 in the biggest stock offering in history. The plan that was finally implemented called for the government keeping 49.8 percent of the total stock and selling 50.2 percent. Small investors were favored in the 39 percent of the stock reserved for the British public. Before trading began more than two million Britons had applied to buy 1.17 billion shares from the government at $1.55 each. When trading actually began on Monday, December 3, the price offered in London and New York was $2.08 a share.

Thatcher's task of moving from a Keynesian/socialist world was more complicated than that facing Reagan in the U.S. The U.K. had moved further along the socialist route and long-held views were more difficult to alter. The enormously robust recovery in 1983 and 1984 in the U.S. drove the dollar to record levels in the foreign exchange markets. The pound—valued at $4.82 in the 1920s, and traded in the neighborhood of $2.60 as late as 1972—declined from well above $1.60 in 1981 to as low as $1.07 at the time of a Thatcher visit in February 1985. The U.S. visit was the occasion for an address by Thatcher before a joint meeting of Congress—the first by a British prime minister since Churchill. Afterward, as the dollar turned down beginning in September of 1985 (p. 650) the pound came back to trading above the $1.60 neighborhood in '87 and was approaching $2.00 in April '88.

An Overview

Thatcher's party won elections in 1979 after decades of the socialist/Keynesian policies on the part of both leading parties in Britain. The long-run economic results of these policies were mounting, a new alternative had presented itself along Friedman/Thatcher lines, but, surprisingly for a dramatic change in political orientation on the part of the larger public, the British economy was not in recession. With the policy-actions Thatcher inherited, some policy changes were delayed for awhile. The inherited policies were a large pay boost for government workers and a large public sector borrowing requirement, which for a time would dominate monetary policy.

Even confronting the inherited present, Thatcher moved more on some than on other fronts: control of inflation through monetary means; reducing the size of the public sector through a cut in government spending, taxing, and borrowing; freeing resources for the private sector and revitalization of the will to engage in private enterprise. Further, on the international side, Thatcher moved toward freer trade, recognized the need for relative adjustments in wages, and recognized, as it were, the law of one price $[P_{US}/P_{UK}]/(\$/\pounds) = \text{const}]$. This plus the tie between interest rates and inflation meant that the government could no longer think of controlling employment through a trinity of changes in exchange rates, the price level, and the interest rate, as if the three were independent.

Recession soon followed monetary restraint in the U.K., as it later did in the U.S. The transitional difficulty was not unexpected, even under the ideal of getting quick response from the small private sector. There were difficulties with monetary policy not entirely unlike those that came in the U.S. The pursuit of the target range for £M3 resulted in even tighter money and credit conditions that appeared from the £M3 policy. In addition, on the operations side, the Bank of England had not broken free from its preoccupation with interest rates, so that it still regarded the latter as a useful means of achieving its targets, plus there was lack of clarity about what components of reserves the Bank of England actually controlled. On the academic side, the chief participants in the discussion of the ideas either fell short in the translation of Friedmanite positions or opposed them outright because of different political preferences. Lord Kaldor was the chief and most clarion of the spokesmen with a Keynesian point of view.

Other barriers to a quick recovery were a long history of impediments to labor mobility, the temporary unwillingness of workers to accept a relation between their wages and employment, the core of professional senior servants which reflected traditional orientation, and, as pointed to by some, the development of Britain's North Shore oil reserves. In actuality, the latter contributed to a stronger pound than would otherwise come about, but at the same time the higher-priced pound meant reduced foreign demand for British exports, exclusive of downward adjustments in nominal wages and product prices.

Thatcher with her "resolute/conviction" approach weathered the most difficult part of the "hard slog" and went on to win resounding victories for her party in 1983 and 1987 elections. In the 1983 elections, the party was thought to be favored by the failure of policies across the channel in Mitterrand's France and Thatcher's handling of the Falkland Islands crises. However, without these factors in the 1987 elections, she won again resoundingly, even without much mention of her achievements—the conquest of inflation through monetary means, the taming of the unions (and miners), the shift of public emphasis from the redistribution of income by government to economic growth, the increased attention to social mobility through the work effort and the spread of ownership, and attitudinal changes about the individual's control over his/her own destiny and the nation.

As the anglophile, U.S. columnist George Will extolled, Thatcher "wielded power in the name of ideas." She shifted voters to the right, away from the muddling at the middle of Hotelling's line. The ideas we encounter are: the monetarist/liquidity/interest-rate package; the counter argument to the short-run Phillips relation; the consumption-function/savings-to-income ratio analysis with attention to incentives and social mobility; the setting of freedom as the highest goal, payment according to the value of marginal product; the interdependence of what may otherwise be viewed as separate policy instruments (the interest rate, the inflation rate, the exchange rate); and the analysis of transition, say, "from Galbraith to Friedman." Most are admittedly against a backdrop of older British and Keynesian thinking.

As support for the claim about the primacy of Friedman's role and his contribution to dialogue by which the public interest is served, we take note of the following: the start in 1969 and '70 of well publicized lectures given by Friedman in London; the accounts of Friedman's ideas in the London press; the presence of the ideas and often the rhetoric in Thatcher's discussions; and accounts of ties between Friedman's ideas and Thatcher in the press, and between Alan Walters as a monetarist and his Downing-Street assignment. In brief, Walters started as an econometrician, encountered Friedman's monetary work, and replicated the latter to a large extent using British data. At first, his monetarist leanings were mild ones. Then later he becomes more ardent and an "in house" advisor at No 10 Downing Street from early 1981 through the 1983 elections.

As a preamble to a late-1983 assessment of the Thatcher government's policies and performance, Sir Alan Walters expressed the belief that the British were "on the road toward a free society shaped by individual liberty and moral responsibility." He expressed the further view that "Hitherto flexibility ["circumstances change: and so policies should be adapted *flexibly*"] in government had bread rigidity in the private sector; henceforth rigidity in government [the resolute leadership] would foster flexibility in the private sector." In this earlier stance by government, "Instead of commanding the nationalized industries, government's were largely commanded by them." Sir Alan took note of the graffiti; "Miners Rule, O.K.?"[125]

Walters's late 1983 assessment of the Thatcher government's record was, in brief, as follows:[126] 1. On financial control the performance of the Thatcher government should be scored at an eight or nine on a possible ten point scale. In 1982-1983 monetary aggregates were in range. Inflation had fallen from a peak of 23 percent in mid-1980 to 5 percent at the date of

Walters's lecture. 2. Reduction in spending and taxes was due only a modest five out of ten. The underlying and continuing cause of the relentless rise of public spending was "entitlement programs." The government did something but not much. A principle of "honest finance" was maintained. 3. A program of deregulation began auspiciously when Mrs. Thatcher abolished exchange controls in 1979. The elimination of wage and price controls quickly followed (with exceptions like certain minimum wage legislation). Walters gave Thatcher's government a high seven out of ten. 4. Denationalization proceeded too slowly, so a score of six out of ten. Even so, Walters saw auspicious signs for the selling off of the great nationalized concerns and for the sale of "publicly owned housing to the sitting tenants." 5. Recognizing Thatcher's long view, assessment of production and reduced unemployment at the 1983 date is complicated. Even so, there was a "remarkable, unexpected, and countercyclical increase in productivity" from 1981 onward. Managers were managing again and anecdotes of wonders abounded. But most remarkably, a newly found realism, was reported to have come about after 1980, namely: dramatically falling wage awards. Walters said, recognition of Thatcher's credibility (resoluteness) could in the future reduce joblessness. "The renaissance of Britain, which once seemed an impossible dream, now appears not only feasible but perhaps even likely."

Later in his 1986 book, *Britain's Economic Renaissance*, Walters reported some conclusions, such as:[127] 1. Productivity (per worker or per hour) had grown 30 percent over the 1980-85 period, even as the inflation rate declined. The performance was thought to be unprecedented (against Britain's normal performance and in relation to the great European competitors, West Germany and France) and to be due to the Thatcher factor ("the compendium of ambient macroeconomic stability and microeconomic reform"). 2. Unemployment persisted at high rates (above 12 percent) even well into the recovery, (a) because the wage cost of the jobless workers was too high and (b) because some unemployed workers were better off drawing benefits and supplementing them with income from the "black economy" than working. 3. Despite unemployment, real wages increased—undoubtedly because of trade unions and minimum-wage legislation. This rigidity of wages Walters saw as possibly due to the inflation rate falling more dramatically than expected. (He was skeptical of 3 million or more unemployed stretching into the future).

In Walters's summary of some provisional lessons to be learned from the Thatcher period 1979-83, we encounter the following: 1. Monetary policy is powerful in its effects by comparison with "the perversity of the effects of fiscal policy." 2. The shock of appreciation in the value of sterling, partly due to North Sea oil, did not appear as devastating in its effects as many thought. 3. The gains in productivity were partly due to "a certain macroeconomic stability" which provided the impetus for a favorable trend.

Chapter 16
The Reagan Presidency

By comparison with the British and Europeans there is a historic tendency among Americans to view politics as the exercise of middle-of-the-road pragmatism, to avoid entanglements with ideology, and to substitute bland euphemisms for ideological rhetoric. This is true even as we encounter Samuel Gompers as a rising leader of organized labor in the U.S.,[1] as we encounter the passage of the income-tax amendment to the U.S. Constitution, and as voters faced the elections of Franklin Roosevelt in 1932, 1936, and 1940. Neither Barry Goldwater, as a presidential candidate on the far right in 1964, nor George McGovern, as one on the extreme left in 1972, was able to attract more than a modest degree of popular support. And yet, following Jimmy Carter at the end of the Keynesian era, the public shifted resoundingly to Ronald Reagan in 1980.

Reagan offered a much more political and ideological agenda for reducing government and elevating the individual than Roosevelt had had in the 1930s for moving the country to the left.[2] To be sure, the second-term Reagan election was called "ideological" and on the occasion of Robert Bork's unsuccessful nomination to the Supreme Court (p. 309), the debate between the Republicans and Democrats on the Senate Judiciary Committee was entirely ideological—more along the lines of the debates over Thatcher's policies in Britain.

Indeed, during Goldwater's 1964 campaign, Reagan openly expressed contempt for the moderate, middle-of-the-road establishment, long before Milton Friedman's work had served as a serious challenge to the Keynesians.[3] A columnist later remembered Reagan in 1964 as being regarded in about the same light as the typical economist regarded Friedman—as being "anathematized as a dangerous, marginal, radical, troublemaking, sectarian ... *kook*." By 1980, nevertheless, economic conditions had worsened, the public had shifted, and a political agenda of researched positions was in place to be rapidly implemented during the six-month window of a first four-year term and, given the long haul, the first half of a second four-year term. The converging circumstances that made him especially effective in office were a crisis, strong centralized leadership for a considerable time by American standards, a political agenda containing numerous researched topics in economics, and a zest for action during the period when public support of the executive has the most leverage in getting changes through Congress (i.e., usually during the six-month window, before special interests can regroup with enough opposition to overrule the general interest).

Uppermost among those representing topics in economics were the Friedman monetarists, the so-called supply-siders variously viewed, and some public finance types. Apart from shared ideology, there were unshared positions, as we will see. Even so, there were plans to change monetary, tax, and fiscal policy matters, thereby stabilizing prices, providing incentives and ultimately restricting growth in the size of the Federal government in relation to peoples' lives. At the time this occurred, some pointed to the long series of single- and/or partial-term presidencies and to what appeared to be Carter's inability to govern.

The single-term office holders ran from John Kennedy through Carter, with Nixon as the only exception (and he had Watergate, p. 238). As discussion of lengthening the four-year presidential term spread, Carter linked the pessimism to "a national malaise," and others pointed to the "quick fix" and accelerating inflation. Even without a clear overall, shared view among the policy agenda groups, without agreement upon notions for implementation, and without adequate timing as to the monetary policy, tax and expenditure changes—the thinking about policy and the actions based on it in the early stages of the Reagan presidency were revolutionary over the longer haul of his two-term presidency. There was also the prospect of possible impact on the future political agenda.

The particular sort of leadership that came to Washington, D.C. should not be minimized. Some called it the "symbolic presidency" and wrote of the politics of symbolism; another referred in a similar vein to Reagan's incorrigible optimism. The symbolism had to do with perception, moral values, rhetoric, the long haul, and symbols as opposed to details surrounding each interest group and policy position with respect to reality, economics, production and resources, and the details about budget forecasts.[4] Robert Dallek, at the time an associate of the Southern California Psychoanalytic Institute, said of the first six-month window, "Reagan has achieved something of a political revolution" all without contributing much along substantive economic lines to the revolution.

Following such a distinction between "symbols" and "substance" facilitates a conclusion. Reagan was able to compromise on substantive issues partly because he held strongly to a set of social values or beliefs, and in not compromising on values Reagan was able to claim victory for his position most often (Dallek said, "symbolic victories"). This was because Reagan saw the values as uppermost rather than the "detailed" policies. In this way he advanced both his policy position and his political standing, served as a salesperson for ideas and values (i.e., right-wing ideology), and portrayed optimism. Like Thatcher, "the most consequential democratic leader of any nation" in the 1980s, Reagan "wielded power in the name of ideas," until faced with a Democratic congress in 1987, the revelation of the Iran/Contra fiasco in October 1986 to September 1987, and the lame-duck status imposed at the end of his two-term presidency. The fiasco concerned covert activities involving American hostages, U.S. arms shipments to Iran in connection with efforts to gain the release of the hostages, and the divergence of arms funds to support Nicaraguan Contras (freedom fighters) against the Marxist government of that country. As the leader of her party and with a parliamentary majority, Thatcher faced no such obstacles.

Reagan's "symbolism" stance meant that he could stay to do battle for the policies underlying his firmly held principles on another day when there was a greater chance of success. And his successes came in part from two sources—persuasion, which could in the meantime improve the chance of success, and mere problems such as budget deficits which became economic crises, such that action to deal with them became more acceptable to the public as the problems gained crisis proportions.

Palmer and Sawhill, editors of an Urban Institute Study, made some overall assessments: "The conservative cast of the Reagan administration's ideology and its proposals have caused some observers (including us) to label this redirection of domestic policy the Reagan revolution (or counter-revolution). What must be understood is that it has been revolutionary in purpose but evolutionary in practice."[5] Further, the importance of the President's rhetoric must not be underestimated, when the long-haul goal was to change the ideological basis of economic policy and hence the policy and possibly the future political/economic agenda. As early as 1962, Friedman gave attention to the need for a broad base of public acceptance of the ethical underpinnings of the economics if the system was to function properly. Continuing on ideology, Palmer and Sawhill said that Reagan saw government as the economic problem whereas other recent presidents, whether Republican or Democrat, "accepted the basic premise that if something went wrong, it was the government's responsibility to fix it."

Writing in anticipation of the 1984 election, a *New York Times* writer entitled his piece "The Ideological Election." He noted that Reagan had redefined "populism." Pointing out that "William Jennings Bryan and Franklin Roosevelt and George C. Wallace each mobilized millions of individuals against 'elite' institutions like Wall Street," Reeves saw Reagan as redefining popularism—as "selling the idea that 'big government' was now the real enemy."[6]

The organization that was so effective early on in getting Reagan's policies through Congress had several features: a centralization of executive decision making, "almost like a board of directors"; a series of "cabinet councils" that were intended to bind cabinet members closer to the President than to the agencies they headed; a centralization of executive decision making for the major economic and budget decisions in the office of the President and, more specifically, in a relatively small group of key advisors in the White House; appointments by Reagan to subcabinet positions on the basis of "an uncommon degree of ideological consistency" (even extending to "moving ideologically screened appointees" into career, federal-employee positions); direct dealing with key groups in Congress; and a radical centralization with respect to control over the federal budget in the Office of Management and Budget (OMB) as an institution, and in David Stockman, budget director, as an individual.[7] The key advisors early in the administration were presidential aids James Baker, Michael Deaver and Edwin Meese. Donald T. Regan at the Treasury became the administration's official economic spokesman and chairman of the cabinet-level Economic Policy Group. His success was recognized in the early days of the President's second term, when he was appointed Chief of Staff at the White House. There, he functioned less successfully, and resigned as political problems surfaced regarding what came to be known as the Iran/Contra affair.

Stockman in particular gave attention to the White House's Legislative Strategy Group which included Meese, Baker, Stockman and Regan, and White House staffers Martin Anderson, Richard Darman, and Craig Fuller. It was not on the organization charts, but in the early days it served as a policy discussion and coordination group with frequent meetings at Baker's table and on occasion in the Oval Office.

The OMB structural change with Stockman extended to the use of Congressional Budget Committees, which had grown out of the 1974 Congressional Budget Act (p. 242).[8] These Senate and House committees were given responsibility for formulating budget policy in terms of an overall fiscal policy (or shaping total spending and revenue measures into a deficit and economic impact policy). They became helpful to the administration in helping formulate an entire budget program and reform package.

The "triumvirate" of chief presidential aids for the most part "stayed the course" of the first administration, as did the controversial David Stockman. At the outset of the second administration, however, Donald Regan replaced the "triumvirate"; Baker and Meese of the "triumvirate" moved to the Treasury and Justice departments respectively; the seven cabinet councils of the first administrations were consolidated into cabinet-level agencies (the Economic Policy Council under Baker and the Domestic Policy Council under Meese); and Beryl Sprinkel, a main monetarist tie in the Treasury to Milton Friedman, was moved to the chairmanship of the Council of Economic Advisors (CEA). Following a period when the CEA had fallen from use by the executive, the Sprinkel move was a revitalization of the CEA to serve as Regan's personal policy shop. However, after the appointment in August 1987 of the economist and Ayn Rand philosopher, monetarist-leaning Alan Greenspan (pp. 257, 262), as chairman of the Federal Reserve, there was word of Sprinkel's leaving the White

House. Even so, he stayed on amidst the Iran-Contra scandal and the revelations of covert activities and was given Cabinet rank with his CEA assignment.

In radical contrast to Richard Nixon (p. 232), for Reagan and Thatcher, economics was high on the policy agenda, especially in connection with monetarist, supply-side tax, deficit, and incentivist policies. The fundamental underpinning of supply-side economics was the use of tax policy to stimulate supply-side activity at the same time monetary policy was used in opposition to tax policy. The monetary policy was to be aimed at controlling inflation and stabilizing the economy, via what we have called on various occasions the government budget constraint and Friedman's consumption function. The monetary, deficit, and tax matters are interrelated (appendixes to chap. 16). In this light, it is certainly surprising that so many books have been written about the Reagan presidency which give little or no attention to the interrelationships and developments with respect to monetary policy.[9]

There are three reasons for this inattention to interrelationships and monetary policy by generalist writers. First, the widely held myth that the Federal Reserve's Board is independent within the framework of government has made it easy to set aside discussion of monetary activity and study. Second, the study of money carries an enormous amount of complexity with it—especially in relation to analyses of real output, prices, employment, and interest rates—which most authors and analysts may prefer to avoid, especially when the Fed can serve as such a deep dark hole for obscuring many matters. Third, for specialists in the tax field, the study of taxes has been separated from the study of economics to a large extent. The real world, however, does not accommodate such neat and convenient categories for writers and analysts, nor do we resort to them.

Abstracting from the day-to-day details, the revolutionary pattern of changes which emerged is as follows: a disinflationary, if erratic, monetary policy with clear support from Reagan with the rhetoric and emphasis of what we may call a money aggregates (M-regime) orientation; an early cut in income tax liabilities of 5, 10, and 10 percent over a three year period, albeit poorly timed in relation to monetary policy and packaged with numerous "Christmas tree" ornaments as the political process worked its way through Congress; a hard-slog transition to a disinflationary state with worsening forecasts of federal deficits for reasons which arise later; a crisis (later symbolized by the stock market crash of October 1987 and dramatic declines in the dollar in foreign markets), with respect to emerging and anticipated domestic and balance of payments deficits; presidential refusal to raise income taxes and partly thereby set limits to the growth of federal government; the passage in 1985 of a balanced budget bill to force expenditure reductions in a Congress otherwise fraught with special interest group politics; and an ultimate move toward the flat-rate income tax, as the President pushed for tax reform over the cries of special interest groups.

A discerning reader will recognize that the concepts and proposals bearing on these changes are present in Friedman's economics, although there are partial overlaps with political matters called for by others. For example: the Jack Kemp group (designated LMWK below) and public finance supply siders favored the tax cuts but had strikingly few dealings with monetary policy except for some who advocated a return to gold; David Stockman championed the initial tax cuts, but only later showed more awareness of monetary policy than his initial LMWK ties suggested. He actually favored tax increases to balance the budget in contrast to Friedman and the President.

The Overall Ideas and the Cast

The label "supply-side economics" gains emphasis here in relation to Reagan's economic policies in two respects: first, a highly visible group of tax-cut proponents (designated LMWK below) used it in relation to a new emphasis on incentives to produce, increase saving, and renew growth in income and tax revenues; and, second, the label draws a distinction in relation to the approach to government in the Keynesian era (chap. 8). This approach has been called Keynesian demand management, plus it came up earlier in relation to J. K. Galbraith and price controls (chap. 7), large forecasting models (chap. 3), inflexible wages and the acts of Hicks's drama (chap. 11), the trusted aristocrats who were to run the economic system (chap. 11), theories and data analysis in the U.S. and the U.K. (chap. 14), and the Thatcher government (chap. 15).

As we point out, Friedman elaborated quite early on the requirements of monetary policy in the transition from inflation states such as he saw it in the U.S. and Britain (chaps. 8 and 15) and in Israel and Chile (chap. 10). In these contexts, indexation clauses in contracts were to enhance downward adjustments in wages and in other respects as money growth decelerated, and tax reductions and other measures were to enhance saving, production of goods, and reductions in the size of government, all as anticipated by analyses in chapter 13.

From Friedman's perspective the foregoing is a consistent whole package with three interrelated parts: monetary policy, freedom and voluntary association, and the consumption function. We find these in what gained public attention as Reagan's economic policies and positions. In the first we find that the monetary factor was the main destabilizing force in the past, at least since the founding of the Federal Reserve (chap. 11); stabilizing monetary growth in a partial sense removed the basis for Keynes's attack on classical economics as symbolized by Say's law of markets (pp. 58, 195, 417);[10] and the mitigation of money-supply shocks to the economic system and the achievement of a stable monetary environment for other economic activity brought the system of relative (separate market) prices into its own. In an ideal sense, we end with a system of Walrasian prices and markets (chaps. 14 and 15), except for Friedman there are equilibrium time paths (secular, growth trends) and not simply mathematical solutions to static models where levels (vis-à-vis time rates of change) are the focus of attention.

Next, just as Friedman's analysis of money and production are entwined, so also are the analyses of production and distribution. Setting the higher goal of freedom in choosing between the socialist and the capitalist ethic, Friedman found voluntary association in markets to be maximized when agents are free to receive in exchange in the market the value of the marginal products of their labor and capital. This association and the maximum suggest the flat-rate income tax or a comparably neutral arrangement of taxes with respect to the distribution of income. Moreover, freedom calls for the dispersion of power—as in market arrangements and as under the classical form of the gold standard (or some substitute, monetary-rule arrangement). Thus reduction in the size of government becomes another important goal. The government may provide infrastructure for the functioning of the monetary economy and markets and it may deal with damages caused to third parties (environmental damage and so on), but where federal deficits in spending may arise, cutting spending and reducing the size of government is preferable to raising taxes. At Friedman's hands we have a fresher view of the free-enterprise economy—the first since Keynes set thinking on a mixed [fiscal policy (income redistribution, power theories of prices), private sector] economy course and one quite distinct from Adam Smith's and the laissez faire view. It is more in tune with the prospects of the 21st century.

Closely allied with freedom and voluntary association is Friedman's permanent-income consumption function (chap. 13). Addressing the apparent disparity between budget (or cross-section data) in relation to the Keynesian consumption function and the long-run tendency toward a constant (or variable-constant) saving-to-income ratio, Friedman combined analyses into what may be called a life-time pattern of consumption and spending. Low income households may save less than high income households, and a household may start low, save and spend on the basis of long-run anticipations, and continue some spending even during unemployment. The approach is a more dynamic consumption function—the poor are not permanently so (and, normatively speaking, should not be). Some households and individuals may elect faster, more upwardly mobile status than others, plus there may be the need for temporary help in getting the dispossessed and less fortunate on the income and growth track.

There is in this consumption-function context the household choice between present and future income. Encouraging future income over present via means of the tax code increases saving, the saving-to-income ratio (or more specifically the personal saving-to-income ratio), the real rate of interest, economic growth, long-run consumption, and tax revenue to the government (appendixes one and two, chap. 16). We encounter, in fact, what Michael Evans has called an enduring truth of supply-side economics: the analysis of tax cuts, income, and revenue growth, which we associate with Friedman.[11] Here we encounter an alternative and more valid analysis of tax cuts than that we associate shortly with Arthur Laffer's original reflows argument. In this more valid approach questions arise about the means of replacing the revenue lost to the government by the cuts (about what we call the government budget constraint), and about whether the cuts are across the board (equal percentage cuts of tax liabilities) or whether they favor high or low income groups (exclusive of those classed as at the poverty level, a relative standard which shifts with growth in the GNP). Those tax cuts favoring high income we label "trickle down" theory and, retaining a symmetry in the analysis, those favoring low income we call "trickle up." As formally treated in the appendixes to the present chapter, "trickle down" theory yields a higher saving-to-income ratio, faster economic growth, and more tax revenue.

As indicated, Laffer's analysis had a strong reflows argument that exposed it to the label "the economics of joy." The reflows argument was unaccompanied by monetary analysis and dynamic perception, as David Stockman learned in his White House tenure. This was particularly so as to the power and timing of monetary effects vis-à-vis tax effects. In any case, the reflows argument offered the claim that tax cutting overall would revitalize spending, income growth, and tax revenue to the government—all such that the federal budget could be balanced and recession avoided during a time of decelerating inflation. In this analysis we encounter no distinction as to the receipt of benefits via higher- or low-income households.

As these points and counterpoints suggest, Ronald Reagan's political umbrella covered support from diverse groups of economic thinkers and doers. Six groups may be singled out—Friedman himself; the Arthur Laffer, Robert Mundell, Jude Wanniski, Jack Kemp (hereafter LMWK) group; David Stockman as a highly effective, idealistic ideologue and as the pointman on the budget; some public finance and tax specialists;[12] a bevy of traditional, pragmatic, conservative economists;[13] and the "Boll Weevils" and other congressional Democrats who were ideologically attuned to the President.[14] We confine ourselves to the ideas, actions, and/or positions of only the first three and then consider Reagan.

Friedman's Comprehensive Analysis

Friedman offered the most comprehensive and published analyses of all—a total monetary, tax, ideologically explicit system of thought, albeit sprinkled in books, articles, news columns, collections of essays, interviews in the print and televised media, technical papers, conference proceedings and interviews. His influence extends as follows: to Reagan directly, as where Reagan appeared as a prepublication reader of *Free to Choose*, to Reagan through Friedman's written work and through speech writers, as in the adoption of ideas, unique phrases, rhetoric, and positions; to Reagan through the monetarist in the Treasury and later the White House.

As mentioned earlier, Sprinkel was a strong tie to monetarism. He received M.B.A. and Ph.D. degrees from the University of Chicago, spent 28 years with the Harris Trust and Savings Bank of Chicago as chief economist, and authored a book with a "monetarist view" and introduction by Milton Friedman.[15] In the early and later parts of Reagan's administration, Sprinkel stayed mostly in the background, except in early television appearances.[16]

His 1984 move to the CEA was seen as strengthening the monetarist tie to the President. A *Newsweek* headline read "Don Regan's man at the CEA," and the *New York Times* reported that Regan was Sprinkel's "principal sponsor for the council post."[17] Even so, the President himself had been recognized early on as "A Friedmanite in the Oval Office,"[18] and Friedman's positions were clear on the part of the President, Regan, and Sprinkel. From the early 1982 date, President Reagan could be cited as saying, "Inflation is a monetary phenomenon" (note Friedman's law). Harking back to the Fed's chairman who followed Arthur Burns, *Fortune* magazine writer Ehrbar said of the President, "This man is not another Bill Miller."

In addition to the monetary analysis, the idea we associate with Friedman and Reagan is that of setting freedom as the highest goal. This we associate with individual initiative, reducing the size of government, social mobility (the progressive income tax as a tax on getting rich rather than being rich), the flat-rate-income tax, the role of deficits following tax cuts, and the legislative strategy for reducing high marginal rates on personal income. Friedman had developed most of these positions by 1962, but he elucidated them somewhat further. On the Kemp-Roth, tax-cut bill which comes up below, Friedman favored the tax cut but counciled against the reflows argument as early as 1978.[19] David Stockman, the key in-house ideologue on the budget during the crucial period of action on Kemp-Roth, only later regretted his early overzealous supply-side ties and his failure to recognize the frailty of the LMWK reflows argument early on.

Drawing on an earlier title, Friedman characterized the reflows argument as "a promise of a free lunch for everyone," as Stockman did later. Also, Friedman forecast deficits as a result of the enactment of the tax-cut measure, as David Stockman did later. Friedman saw the 1981 cut, nevertheless, as a good thing. For him, the deficits provided added pressure for reducing the size of government (i.e., restraining or cutting government expenditures as a percent of GNP).

The legislative strategy for moving toward the flat-rate tax (or some variant of it, such as the President's 1985 "tax-overhaul package") was set forth by Friedman quite early.[20] It appeals to the general interest over the special interest. You bundle things together. As we recall from pages 488 and 518, you get the higher income groups to give up loopholes in return for lower tax rates and you get the lower income groups to give up support for high rates on high income in return for closing the loopholes and increasing the initial amount of income for exemption.

This we see in Reagan's April 13, 1985 announcement (two days before the deadline for filing income tax returns), when he set a timetable for major overhaul of the nation's tax system with a package of ingredients—a sharp reduction in the ceiling on the marginal tax rate to 35 percent; significant increase in personal exemption, "which will be especially beneficial to lower-income families"; and broadening the tax base by eliminating "the tax shelters that make tax avoidance legal." Pointing to concerns for fairness and neutrality, the President also said, "we must not jeopardize economic growth." Overall, the President appealed in his message to the American people to help overcome expected opposition from "Washington's army of high-powered lobbyists." By May 1986 the Senate Finance Committee had bundled the special interests together and produced a tax package with a lower ceiling on the marginal rate than Reagan's Treasury had produced.

The LMWK Group, Reflows, and Gold

The LMWK group played a prominent role in the 1980 election and on into 1981, as numerous sources attest. It had a close tie to the Kemp-Roth bill[21]—supported by Friedman as attaching bad arguments for a good measure and supported by Reagan in the 1980 election, and later written into the 1981 Tax Reduction Act. Initially, the Kemp-Roth bill called for across the board cuts in the personal income tax over a 3-year period with 10 percent the first year, 10 the second, and 10 the third. As enacted later, the cuts were delayed and the first cut was lowered to 5 percent.

The LMWK group's beginning started with Laffer's recruitment to a teaching post at the University of Chicago, partly because of Mundell's presence there before moving to Columbia University. Shortly after locating at Chicago, Laffer moved to Washington, D.C. with Chicago's George Schultz, newly appointed director of Office of Management and the Budget and later Secretary of State under Reagan. As an economist at OMB, Laffer first met Wanniski, then serving as a columnist for *The National Observer*, in February 1971.

In the early 1970s and later, Mundell was a specialist in international trade. Even so, whether because he picked up on the ideas in the wind at Friedman's Chicago and/or because of his own less publicly visible views, Mundell defied "some received ideas of the profession, and the current policies of the Ford Administration," where at a May 1974 Washington meeting he urged "a tight-money policy to check inflation, combined with a large tax cut to stimulate the economy and thus to avert a recession." Laffer picked up on this, and soon Laffer and Mundell met to exchange views and pursue their interests. They continued as Wanniski's economics teachers at lunches and private gatherings. The latter in the meantime shifted to the editorial staff of the *Wall Street Journal*. His work there soon led to a popular book by Wanniski where Laffer and Mundell are treated as the world's leading economists.[22]

Michael Evans then picked up on this thrust of supply-side economics. He considered the myths and truths of supply-side economics, treated the Laffer curve, called its reflows argument a myth, and placed Friedman's substitute analysis of the saving-to-income ratio among enduring truths, but then got off track in the monetary analysis. There, he treated Robert Mundell ("considered by many the intellectual father of supply-side economics"), exclusive of Friedman's more valid role.[23]

Calling attention to the published views of Mundell in 1971, Evans said, "the optimal blend of government policies to fight recessions would be easy fiscal policies, by which he [Mundell] actually means tax cuts rather than increased spending, while keeping money supply growth tight." Evans called further attention to a December 1974 column by Jude Wanniski in which the latter espoused "the essence of the Mundell argument and quoting his views at length." Continuing along this line, Evans noted Robert L. Bartley's positions in November 1979. In effect, he agreed with Mundell's proposed tight money and big tax cuts. By this date, Bartley was editor of the *Wall Street Journal* and in 1981 Bruce Bartlett of that journal published his book, *Reaganomics*, with a forward by Congressman Jack Kemp. As a journalist, Bartlett noted his intellectual indebtedness to "Arthur Laffer, Jude Wanniski, Paul Craig Roberts, Norman Ture and Steve Entin."

However, the evidence is at odds with the role attributed to Mundell by the journalists and by Evans. A review of Mundell's textbook, *Monetary Theory* (1971), shows none of the elements of monetarist impact on Federal Reserve policy that began in 1970 and proceed in further steps in 1975, and on October 6, 1979 (pp. 220, 221, 262, 447-448). In the 1971 Mundell text we find an introduction of Irving Fisher's relation between interest rates and expected inflation,[24] but this and the other discussions in the text show none of the dynamic qualities, time frames, and empirical study that Friedman brought to the subject, to the Federal Reserve's attention, and at least indirectly, to White House and presidential statements. In addition, we find that Mundell advocated budget deficits as fiscal policy to stimulate spending on the demand side of the market for goods, whereas Friedman did not. He and the President preferred deficits to taxes as a means of maintaining pressure for expenditure cuts, and the LMWK group supported the return to the gold standard while Friedman and Reagan did not.[25]

Highly active supporters of the gold standard included Rep. Ron Paul and Lewis Lehreman, who later offered a minority report of the U.S. Gold Commission.[26] In fact, as we will see, a Gold Commission study was set in motion by the Congress even before the Reagan presidency. In its 1982 report, the only position with majority support called upon the Congress to give closer consideration to Friedman's monetary rule.[27]

David Stockman, "Trickle Down" Theory and the Forecasting Models

The extremely capable, ideological, highly motivated revolutionary of "free markets," David Stockman gained the President's attention after being selected as a practice-person for candidate Reagan to debate against after the 1980 convention. As an idealistic, principled person of Western-Michigan farm, Harvard Divinity School, and Congressional background, Stockman was the key person in dealing with Congress on budget cuts which were pushed by the President in 1981 and later, following the passage of the 1981 Tax Reduction Act. During his tenure first as a Congressional staffer and then a Congressman, Stockman had developed ties with Jack Kemp and the LMWK group. Soon he had in mind a "Grand Doctrine" that he would work tirelessly to implement at the White House. He identified with Kemp's larger group and with Kemp himself as a permanent friend, but he split strongly with the group once in the White House when faced with reflows problems, confronted more directly with the role of monetary policy, and confronted with the group's gold standard advocacy.

Though he took on tough assignments, Stockman stayed the course until August 1985. Early on he became involved in the higgling and haggling with the Congress and its individual members over expenditure cuts plus one issue that had been at the core of monetarist-Keynesian confrontation.

The first led Stockman to express frustration over the greed of special interest groups. And, as he began to see which programs were being cut the most, he labeled the theory behind the package of measures as just old "trickle down" theory. The second issue he brought attention to arose for Friedman as early as 1951, and received attention in chapter 3 where we took up the Tinbergen-Klein approach to the analysis of time-series data. Namely, we refer to the thinking behind the government's economic-forecasting models at the Congressional Budget Office, at the Treasury, and at OMB. These became a considerable source of the frustrations of OMB director David Stockman in the early part of the Reagan presidency, and of the Treasury and the President later.[28] In fact, nearing the end of the first year of the Reagan presidency, the magazine *The Atlantic* appeared with a cover story portraying the frustration of the administration's budget technician when given the responsibility for negotiating budget cuts and the closing of tax loopholes with the Congress. The story and its publication were unusual in that, sensing the historical importance of what he was undertaking, David Stockman breakfasted on a weekly basis with a journalist friend to whom he portrayed his thoughts and experiences in the major historical effort at reducing the size of government.

The matter started with the effort at tax cutting, when Stockman said, "None of us really understands what's going on with all these numbers." The question Stockman attempted to deal with was the supply-side one: "How is it possible to raise defense spending, cut income taxes, and balance the budget, all at the same time?"[29]

There was only minor attention to monetary policy and the prospect that it could have quick and powerful influence when supply-side changes (production, saving and incentives) would work more slowly.[30] Instead, the main responses to the question were: "That the growth of government would be displaced by the robust growth of the private sector," and that swift and dramatic action by the President could impact on expectations about the future to "reverse the gloomy assumptions in the disordered financial markets." Indeed, when the OMB computer forecasted budget deficits as the impact of Reagan's program on the federal budget, Stockman changed the OMB computer's model to include more "expectations" dimensions, and used the forecast for the deficits as a talking point for cutting expenditures.[31]

On the models and prospects, Stockman wondered about who knew about what was going on. As he became less optimistic, William Greider portrayed him as saying: "The 'random elements' of history—politics, the economy, the anarchical budget numbers—were out of control."[32] By December 1981, Stockman reacted against the Laffer-curve supply-side argument with its emphasis on what we have called reflows. Pointing to the monetary factors he said, "You don't stop inflation without some kind of dislocation. You don't stop the growth of the money supply in a three-trillion-dollar economy without some kind of dislocation..." Greider on Stockman said:

> Tight monetary control should continue, he [Stockman] believed, until inflationary fevers were sweated out of the economy. People would be hurt. Afterward, after the recession, perhaps the supply-side effects could begin—robust expansion, new investment, new jobs [as we report later]. The question was whether the country or its elected representatives would wait long enough.[33]

In brief, the respective groups of government not only had their own models which varied from one another as noted above, but they excluded prominent elements of monetarist and supply-side thinking which contained very strong emphasis on the state of expectations about inflation, innovative enterprise, and business conditions generally. At the extreme, and taken exclusive of its inconsistent parts, the world the monetarist, supply-side thinking was to bring about was itself supposed to go a long way toward making prophecy come true. The underlying reality was first that monetary disinflation was for a time more damping than tax cuts were stimulating and then there was the later concern of the financial markets over whether future deficits and tax reform would be forthcoming. The first led in late 1981 and in 1982 to decline in expected inflation, and hence in interest rates, and to a stock market boom; and the later 1985-86 developments on balancing the budget and tax reform led to further decline in interest rates and to the later phase of the Reagan stock market boom. An underlying idea on the market's part, in the latter case, was that the Federal Reserve would be less tempted to have to pursue inflationary policy to bail the government out of its financial problems.

In 1987, however, the actions and conditions favoring the stock market were reversed, as we discuss later. The democratically controlled Congress procrastinated on firm, sufficient spending reductions and the President held to his position in opposition to taxes. All this occurred at a time of growing deficits and growing anticipation that weakened political leadership on the right was such that it could not assure noninflationary financing and, hence, a strengthened balance of payments position. Matters soon turned, resulting in the second great crash in the history of the New York stock market. The stock drop reflected the twin domestic and balance of payments deficit problems. As analysis on pages 412-430 would lead us to expect, the prospects of inadequate adjustments in domestic U.S. prices were reflected in the declining value of the dollar in the foreign exchange markets (p. 650).

Returning to March of 1981, we see that Treasury Secretary Regan dealt with questions on the forecasting models which were similar to Stockman's. Dialogue with Robert MacNeil and Jim Lehrer proceeds:

> MacNEIL: Turning to some of your other forecasts: the administration's forecast that the inflation rate is going be down to 6.2 percent by 1983, and correspondingly in the previous years, are challenged by all the well-known private forecasters—Chase, and the others. Now, since you come from the private sector, and presumably relied on those private forecasters before, do your forecasts depend on getting the Reagan package through in its entirety, or do they leave room for some adjustment?
>
> Sec. REGAN: Well, first of all, Robin, let's discuss those forecasts and their baselines as compared to ours. They start from a Keynesian baseline with certain assumptions. As you know, most econometric models are about 50 percent assumptions and 50 percent mathematics. And it depends upon where you assumptions are. And then their models do not take into effect that there will be any reaction of human behavior depending upon what is done in the federal sector by the way of spending cuts, or by way of tax cuts. The net result is that they come out way apart from how we see it. Now, what we're saying is that there will be stimulative effects in production, in savings, in investment, as a result of our tax cuts. That's why we come down on the side that we do.
>
> MacNEIL: And they then say, "But there are no models to provide a kind of projected base for your element of hope there."
>
> Sec. REGAN: And then we say, "Look at their record." Out of the last eight quarters all of these forecasters that you've mentioned, in the private sector and CBO, have been wrong, not only in the size of their error, but in the direction. They can't even predict the direction that the economy is going. For example, in July of 1980 the CBO forecast that the economy—
>
> MacNEIL: That's the Congressional Budget Office.
>
> Sec. REGAN: Well, the Congressional Budget Office, if you wish. The Congressional Budget Office forecast that the quarter—the July, August, September quarter of 1980—would have a decline of five points—approximately five points—in gross national product. Do you know what happened in that quarter? It increased 2 percent. Now, when they can't even get things straight in the same quarter, why should we rely on them now?[34]

Continuing with the blame put on inappropriate forecasting models, we find that in March 1981 Regan reflected the position of the extreme supply siders in the Treasury such as Paul Craid Roberts and Norm Ture. Here, the Treasury's Secretary reaches for the reflows argument:

> LEHRER: Okay, the CBO—The Congressional Budget Office you and Robin were just talking about—also disputes your prediction about a balanced federal budget in 1984. You said in a speech up in Philadelphia yesterday that that's what is going to happen. The CBO says that that's not going to happen; there's going to be a $49-billion deficit in 1984. How can the two of you be so wrong? Or so different?
>
> Sec. REGAN: Well—
>
> LEHRER: I may have been right in my first question, but let's answer the [last] one first.
>
> Sec. REGAN: Well, I would say that one of us is right, and one of us is wrong. And I think I know which one of us is going to be right.
>
> LEHRER: Why are they wrong?
>
> Sec. REGAN: For the simple reason that they have started with the wrong assumptions, and then they proceed in the wrong direction with their Keynesian model. They do not take into effect any human behavior in their model. And we know that if you give people back some of their money, that is, we in the federal government do not take that money from them but allow a person to have his own money that he has earned, he's going to save; he's going to spend it; he's going to do as he pleases with it. We think that as a result of that, the total pie of the United States—the incentives to work—are there. More people are going to work, going to work longer, going to work harder, going to save more, invest more; and the new result will be greater GNP than the Congressional Budget Office is willing to admit.[35]

Whatever had come in 1981 and '82, by February 1985 the economy had gone through two years of real-output growth with declining inflation rates, as we report later. For now, we note *Newsweek*-staff reporting on a Reagan news conference and dissension among economists. Quoting the President: "Those projections, frankly, I pay no attention to them." Then continuing, *Newsweek* staff said, "Reagan has consistently pushed dramatic new policies that flatly contradict conventional economic wisdom."[36]

Reagan's Beginnings and Beyond

Most of the groups under Reagan's umbrella, though diverse, shared ideological perceptions with the President. This feature of Reagan's political economics was analyzed by Robert Dallek, cited earlier, in terms of Reagan's beginnings and beyond. In shedding light on them, Dallek pointed to Reagan's desire to speak out "for traditional American values of family, home, free enterprise, and rugged individualism,"[37] and, like others, cited Reagan's small-town beginnings. Dallek called attention to the 1920s, in relating Reagan to the objectives of Coolidge and Harding.[38] Referring to that period, Dallek mentioned pastoral harmony as part of Reagan's concern and noted Calvin Coolidge in the 1920s as "a new version of an old symbol"—"the rugged honesty of the New England hills, rural virtues, clean living, religious faith, public probity."[39]

In Reagan's background Dallek found some behavior "shaped by the traditional values he [Reagan] wishes to bring back for all Americans." "Without question," Dallek continued, "Reagan's life and career have been shaped by traditional ideas about freedom, hard work, and morality."[40]

Continuing from this background, there was along the way "the...consumer culture" which shaped and molded what Reagan thought and did. There were, indeed, the movies of the era—"the new ethos of entertainment and pleasure..."[41] The story moved on to the Goldwater presidential campaign in 1964.[42] A thesis is drawn out by Dallek, notably:[43] that of Reagan's dependence on others and his longings for independence. In constructing this thesis, Dallek discussed the dependence of Reagan's drunken father on others and the tendency in his mother to devote herself to rescuing many from their fates. In such a context, Reagan came to idealize self-reliance but at the same time showed a need to save others in his zeal for missionary work. Reagan's recollections of "heroic rescuers" and "needy victims" suggest matters of self-posession "at the core of Reagan's inner life" and "the driving force behind his evangelical commitment to individual freedom or personal self-control."

Though Dallek did not say so, it is not exceptional to recognize that individuals are bound in an interdependence on one another through family life, economic organizations, or culture (the "institutional individualism" of the next chapter vis-à-vis the atomistic individual). In addition, political tracts such as Friedman's 1962 work stress the freedom for heterogeneous and diverse cultural groups which is provided by the notions of democratic voting and the essential consensus (or 2/3rds majority) on certain important matters such as free speech, and the market oriented economy. The latter places great reliance on individual efforts and initiatives, and, moreover, major religious groups and associations that endured during what Richard Tawney described as the rise of capitalism, place some emphasis on helping others.[44]

In taking a look back, the coincidence of Reagan's rise with economic crisis and monetarist, supply-side ideas should not be overlooked, nor should his communicative skills be overlooked. On the latter, Dallek said:

> His conformity and personal charm...made him a formidable candidate for public office. Unlike Goldwater, he was a "soft sell" spokesman for the conservative ideology. Reagan, one political opponent observed, exploited "resentments and emotions not by being a loud and threatening figure but by making wisecracks or poking fun at his enemies."[45]

Again, though not stressed by Dallek, Reagan's triumph was not a return to old-fashion Republicanism or the welfare state of both parties at the end of the 1970s. On the contrary, there is much that is new which we align with Reagan's achievements as president.

The Turning Point in Monetary Policy: Recession and Analysis

Friedman's challenge to the Federal Reserve, the early moves toward the reporting of monetary policy along monetarist lines, the absence of the Federal Reserve's independence under the monetary-aggregates regime (M-regime) vis-à-vis the interest-rate-control regime (i-regime), the degenerative monetary policy in the closing years of the Carter administration, the dramatic October 6, 1979 announcement at the Fed, and the more immediately ensuing developments in monetary policy—were all introduced earlier in chapters 8 and 11. Additionally, we may recall the entire era from the end of the dollar-gold convertibility in 1971 through 1980, which we noted as the act of Hicks's drama in which there was no monetary standard (pp. 429-430). This followed Arthur Burns at the Fed for most of the 1970s, and included monetary policy under Carter-appointee William Miller (pp. 221, 261-263). It was even more accommodative of what some see as cost-push pressures under voluntary wage and price controls and of energy-price changes in 1979. It occurred as interest rates rose to record levels in October 1979, and as the dollar price of gold (principally a hedge against inflation and monetary policy in the U.S.)[46] soared, even as the U.S. Treasury sold gold and took other support actions.

Thus it was in July of 1979, under the developing crisis conditions, that Carter announced the appointment of Paul Volcker as chairman of the Fed's Board of Governors. At first some initially favorable reaction occurred. But then, as no concrete evidence of a change in monetary policy appeared, the financial markets reacted less favorably to Volcker's appointment.[47] This lack of confidence was reflected in rising interest rates

The Reagan Presidency   649

through early 1980, and declines in the value of the dollar in the free gold and foreign exchange markets. The latter was the occasion for the now famous October 6 announcement upon Volcker's return from a meeting with European central bankers. We observe some of the developments leading up to it and afterward in the accompanying art work for the value of the dollar measured against an index of 11 major currencies.

Questions that arise—as a result of the October 6 announcement, the strong monetarist component in the Reagan presidency, the rising value of the dollar that accompanied it through early 1985, and the transition to a more individualistic, less inflationary, monetary world—are:
1. Was a monetarist policy adopted as a result of the October 6 episode, as some have concluded?[48]
2. When in fact did a turn from an inflationary to a disinflationary policy occur in the period under review? Asked differently: Did a disinflationary policy come to Washington D.C. with Paul Volcker or with the politics ushered in by Reagan's election and what we have called monetarist/supply-side economics?
3. What was occurring in the monetary policy area in relation to what we call the W-recession with reference to the U.S. recessions of 1980 (bounded by a peak in business conditions in March and a trough in July) and 1981-82 (bounded by a peak in 1981:I and a trough in 1982:IV)?

In answering these question we do three things: (1) restate the policy recommendation we find in Friedman's economics; (2) review operational and institutional changes that occurred in the monetary area during the 1979-84 period; and (3) distinguish three parts of the 1979-84 period.

Friedman's Rule and Monetary Discipline

As we recall, Friedman's economics places emphasis on targeting monetary aggregates (preferably the more narrowly defined aggregate that enters most heavily but not entirely into monetary transactions), and steady growth in a specific aggregate. This gives rise to what we have called Friedman's rule (pp. 412, 548-549), it may be restated thus: "Money should be allowed to grow at a constant X percent per year, where X is determined to equal the secular rate of GNP growth after allowing for *secular* changes in the velocity of circulation of the money stock [italics added]."[49] Friedman's emphasis was on "achieving a steady and predictable rate of growth in whatever monetary aggregate is targeted." "Steadiness and predictability" do not necessarily mean constant, but Friedman favored a constant rate between 2 and 5 percent in the U.S.'s M1 aggregate (his earlier M2 aggregate). Taking the politics of monetary policy into ac-

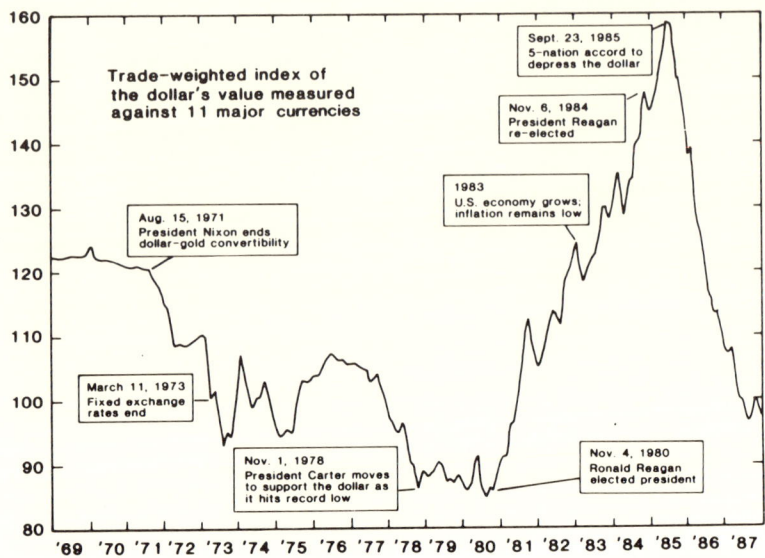

Trade-Weighted Index of the Dollar's Value Measured against 11 Major Currencies

count, he favored a simple mechanical rule rather than some ideal or more complicated rule. Whatever, Friedman saw monetarists as a whole as wanting to minimize the erratic and unpredictable element in monetary changes.[50]

Reacting to Friedman's preferred rule, Hadjimichalakis noted "rigid monetarism" and "flexible" or "pragmatic" monetarism.[51] He said, "flexible monetarism relies on predictions of velocity and recognizes prediction errors..." However, in the broadest outline and additional to Friedman's position, we simply want to recognize the presence or absence of monetary discipline for purposes of interpreting developments. The notion of the presence or absence of discipline here has two elements. The first concerns what we have called Friedman's law (namely: inflation is "always and everywhere a monetary phenomenon") and the notion of a price index (P = $w_1 p_1 + w_2 p_2 + \ldots + w_n p_n$ where P is the average of prices $p_1, p_2, \ldots, p_n$ and the w's are weights). Now by inflation we mean a rise in the price index (P) which implies a predominance of increases in the separate market prices. However, if the money stock (M) grows only with the real output (Q, pp. 417-418) (say adjusted for velocity changes or with velocity, V, constant), then the price average cannot rise (hence zero inflation). This means in effect monetary discipline in the sense that adjustments in the respective prices (and wages included) must take place, at least to reach noninflationary unemployment in wage and product markets.

Inflation then cannot be determined by labor unions pushing for excessive wage increases or by oil-price shocks such as in 1973 and 1979 in the U.S., although these may be accommodated by monetary policy along the lines associated earlier with Kaldor (pp. 97-98, 545). In the monetary discipline context, particular prices and wages may go up, but others must make compensating adjustments to achieve the zero inflation after some lag in adjustment.[52]

In the accommodative mode, on the other hand, the money stock grows faster than its noninflationary rate and assures the inflationary realization of excessive wage increases, oil-price shocks, and the like. Recalling discussion in chapters 11 and 15 where we deal with Lord Kaldor and the case of the central bank's purchasing the public sector borrowing requirement, we could say that the government's deficit spending caused inflation or validated oil-shocks and the like. Here there would be no monetary policy independent of fiscal policy. The executive leader, especially in the U.S. however, may predominate sufficiently over the monetary authority so as to assure that monetary policy and inflation are independent of federal deficits. As we develop the turn in monetary policy below, we observe that President Carter received approximately the monetary policy he wanted and that President Reagan did too, mechanical shortcomings and developments aside.

Much earlier (pages 248 and 260), we saw that Arthur Burns in effect compromised the independence of the Federal Reserve, because he did not see that Congress had intended it to be independent of Congressional wishes with respect to fiscal policy. President Nixon, we saw, was not much interested in domestic economic policy and left the field to others. Ronald Reagan, nevertheless put domestic economic policy at the top of his political plans.

As we will see, Reagan had monetarist learnings, and officials espousing the orientation rose in influence. The Reagan phenomenon, called variously monetarism and supply-side economics, had decisive influence over monetary policy. The influence may have involved what came to be called "Fed bashing" (verbal policy statements aimed in public at the Federal Reserve), and the results never attained the ideal of Friedman's monetarism. Even so, and even under Paul Volcker at the Fed, we have a different orientation in policy behavior after Ronald Reagan took office in January 1981. The former orientation reacted more to crisis with the "quick fix" and it was inflationary. Under Reagan, the effort to control inflation was persistent and we had no "quick fixes" with renewed inflation as before.

In a presidential address to the nation on October 13, 1982, with the economy still in deep recession, the President discussed the "quick fix." He said variously:

> Each time they applied the quick fixes, unemployment dipped for awhile, only to take off again. In that sense, you could say that we've been on a decade-long roller coaster ride.
>
> Unemployment would dip for a time, but the same quick fix that temporarily eased unemployment was sending inflation back through the ceiling.
>
> Inflation, and the high interest rates it leads to, are the real culprits. They create the economic climate that leads to unemployment.
>
> Like unemployment inflation has zigzagged over the last decade, but...the long-term trend has been upward. Again, as with unemployment, the old quick fix simply did not work.[53]

Such analysis of monetary aggregates and policy extends, moreover, to the previously introduced liquidity preference with overshooting (pp. 83-84, 444-448, 543-544). This centered upon the Fisher relationship (namely, the nominal interest rate equals the sum of the real rate of interest and the expected inflation rate), and the subsequently reviewed relation between money growth and income growth. From a minor variation of the Fisher relation, we can rearrange terms and get what appears in newspaper discussions as the real rate of interest (namely, the nominal interest rate less the current inflation rate).

The Fisher relation as considered by Friedman was originally treated as a long-run prospect, until Friedman encountered a shift in the structure underlying the formation of expectations in the U.K. and U.S. in the 1960s. After that date the financial markets were more sensitive in forming inflationary expectations in response to behavior of monetary aggregates, announcements concerning monetary aggregates, and inflationary prospects generally. Discussing the change in the market's processing of information in June of 1983, Friedman said, after a shorter lag in time, interest rates move in the same direction as monetary growth.[54] Since the 1960s, Friedman said, "inflation has had a very clear and very prompt impact on interest rates." For the period encompassing the Fed's October 1979 announcement, and the transition to the Reagan presidency, Friedman gave attention to short-run volatility in monetary growth, inflation rates, and the rate of interest on three-month Treasury bills in various sources.[55] The volatility of money growth and the closely related GNP above are pictured in the art work on the next page.

The Reagan Presidency 653

On the interest rate and the Fisher relation as advanced by Friedman, we see the President holding forth in a one-hour, CBS report in January 1982. He said:

> The Federal Reserve Board has missed its targets a few times in this last year, falling below its own planned increase in money supply and then catching up with a wild zoom that sets the funny—the money market off into a fear of inflation, and interest rates go up.
>
> He's [Paul Volcker] a good professional. I do feel that the board has missed its target both ways. In this past year for several months, as I said, you know, they have a bracket in which they're going to increase the money supply to a certain percentage, staying consistent with the economy.
>
> Now, that's what's known as a consistent, dependable monetary policy. And they got way below it and now they have suddenly zoomed. Well, that sends a message out to the financial markets. They see that great zoom, as they zoomed in late 1980 and interest rates went up. You'd think, well, with more money they would go down. No, they go up, because the money market looks and say, "Uh-oh, this could lead to inflation"—increase in the money supply.[56] [Note here the essence of what we have called "New York's revenge," pp. 447, 545.]

Now, a still further part of the liquidity-preference and money aggregates thesis is that changes in monetary growth impact on GNP in a direct

**M1 and GNP
One Quarter Later**

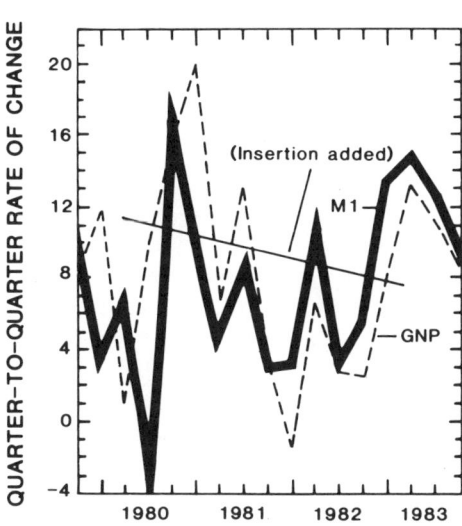

and powerful way. In fact, Friedman frequently reasserted the power of monetary policy when he increasingly stressed the importance of stabilizing monetary policy. Drawing on Friedman's presentations, additional pieces of art work were shown for the transition period. Readers of *Newsweek* were shown quarter-to-quarter rates of change for M1 and for GNP one quarter later.[57] In these pieces we note the close relation between the two measures; the volatility in the policy and the economic performance; the very high rates of monetary growth in the final part of Carter's administration; and the general downward drift in the monetary growth rate from its late 1980 peak through much of 1982.

Operational and Institutional Changes

Money was defined by J.M. Keynes (pp. 417-418) as (1) a medium of exchange, (2) a standard of value, and (3) a store of value. The first function has been related to the indirect satisfaction of wants—as in exchange in a market where money is accepted for use in some subsequent exchange—plus it has been related to what Keynes called the transactions motive. The second is mainly that of a unit of account (as in reckoning and making bookkeeping entries). And the third function, as formally introduced by Keynes in his 1936 work, concerned the holding of balances for speculative and precautionary purposes. In his famous work the following held: the speculation was in relation to bonds—a switching between money balances and bonds (but bonds quite broadly viewed, actually as only a generic category); and the precautionary purpose was in relation to a possibly uncertain, a possibly planned, and a possibly unforeseen future.

Although Keynes tried to free himself from the quantity theory of money in relating the foregoing definition and the liquidity preference demand for money in his 1936 work, he did not in fact do so (pp. 443-448). To be sure, we may bring forward from Keynes in the 1920s, $M = kY$, where the Cambridge k was the reciprocal of the income velocity of money $[k = 1/(Y/M)]$, and where k can readily be viewed as the number of months income held by behavioral units, and where the measure of balances held could be viewed as a function of the transactions, precautionary, and speculative demands for money. Friedman did not depart from this (p. 775 n69). In the hands of the Keynesians, nevertheless, there was not only effort to forget the quantity theory but to treat Keynes's category for bonds and actual holdings of debt-type instruments exclusive of other assets.

On the Keynesians part, this was such that when they introduced the demand for money balances in the static, liquidity-preference block, they had income velocity (Y/M) as a function of the interest rate (i). This was the switching from money to bonds (or simply money-market instruments) as interest rates rose. Writing the function $Y/M = f(i)$, it could readily be defined with a simple equation. And upon taking the logarithm of both sides and rearranging terms, we had another relation that expressed money balances as a function of income and interest rates (the first positively related to M, and the second negatively related). For a while as data were analyzed in the early stages of the modern computer, the correlation between velocity and interest rates appeared quite high and *incomplete* analyses of data indicated a stable relation between money, on the left-hand side, and income and interest rates, on the other side.[58] (We say, *incomplete* because the actual holdings of assets in relation to money-market interest rates or bond rates were not a part of the convention.)

Whatever, the idea of such a relationship became the basis for efforts at the Federal Reserve to attain a money supply with the aid of money-market rates of interest in the transition from an i-regime to an M-regime. The idea of the stable relation became widely accepted in Keynesian and macroeconomic circles, despite at least three significant developments: (1) examination of early statistical results taken as a whole did not support the Keynesian interpretation;[59] (2) income velocity and interest rates drifted apart dramatically in the 1960s and 1970s; and (3) the money relation Friedman offered as stable [equation (1) page 79 and chap. 14] was either overlooked, taken to resemble the Keynesian relation as to uses of statistical methods (pp. 68-84, and chap. 18), or misunderstood. [After all, he had obtained it using the indirect method (pp. 77-82 and chaps. 14 and 18). Further, using Friedman's method of adjusting the data for episodic change, which we take up in reference to the M1 money aggregate and deregulation in banking matters below and in chapter 18, we are able to reestablish through empirical research the former claim for a stable velocity-interest rate association over the post-WW II years (including for the inflation years of the '70s and the Reagan period).][60]

To be sure, what was taken by many at the time of the Fed's October 6 announcement as a change to a monetarist policy (pp. 262. 447), was actually only a change in the technique used for control over the money and credit aggregates by the Fed. The technique had been to use short-term market rates of interest as an intermediate link to the control of money and credit aggregates, partly because of central-bank tradition about interest rates and partly because money-stock data came with a few weeks lag, after the control date as it were, while interest rate information was available immediately to the New York manager of the federal open market account. The move on October 6, as noted earlier (pp. 262, 447), was hailed as a victory for Friedman, even as he expressed caution about the Fed's move. The caution appeared well justified, and in fact no turn in monetary policy as opposed to operative technique occurred. Monetary policy continued to be volatile, and the financial markets reflected no confidence that a change in policy had come about, as we recount shortly for the 1979-1980 part of the 1979-1984 period.

Now, not entirely unrelated, additional problems began to occur with respect to the deregulation of interest rates that commercial banks and thrift institutions pay on deposits; the development of new types of assets that are identified as a part of the narrowly defined money stock, M1; and the Fed's practice of lagged reserve requirements (LRR). These new accounts (which we view as episodic change affecting the raw, unadjusted data) which became troublesome are NOW accounts (negotiable order of withdrawal accounts), MMDAs (money market deposit accounts), and Super NOW accounts.[61] The first category of accounts were limited for a time to only an experimental basis, but were permitted nationwide, effective year-end 1980, under the Depository Institutions Deregulation Act of 1980. A 1982 act then provided for the new deposit account (the MMDAs) which could compete with money market mutual funds and did not place restriction on the type of depositor who may hold the new account. Further, the old NOWs became Super NOWs (essential old NOWs but without regulated interest rates). These became effective in January 1983, but were restricted to individuals, governmental units, and certain nonprofit institutions.

With the new accounts (the MMDAs and the Super NOWs) treated primarily as transactions balances and included in an M1 category, the new M1, as it were, became more like the broad measure Friedman and Schwartz used in the *Monetary History*. However, special problems of controlling the current M1 arose for what may be an obvious reason, notably: a rise in the interest rate may cause switching from M1 to money-market assets, but there is no longer the same inducement for switching out of (or into) the M1 category when an interest-yielding asset is included in the measure for M1. In any case, the institutional changes and growth in M1 beyond the original target range of 4.0 to 8.0 percent led the Fed at mid year to reset its goal for 1983, both by changing the base date and by setting the range at 5.0 to 9.0 percent. This, called "base drift," is shown in the art work for the M1 aggregate for 1983. Later for 1984, the growth range was set back at 4.0 to 8.0 percent, also as shown in accompanying art work, and still later a 4.0 to 7.0 range was set for 1985. However, in July of '85, the policy pattern shown in the art work for 1983 was repeated. In 1985, the Fed allowed the money aggregate to drift above its upper bound to an almost 12 percent rate. The prospect was that under the slow growth in the economy at mid 1985, an effort by the Fed to meet the original 4-to-7 percent range would bring on recession. Hence the officials validated the early '85 growth in M1 by shifting the base for percent change to mid year and by setting a new range of 3-to-8 percent.

M1 Target Ranges, 1983

M1 Target Range, 1984

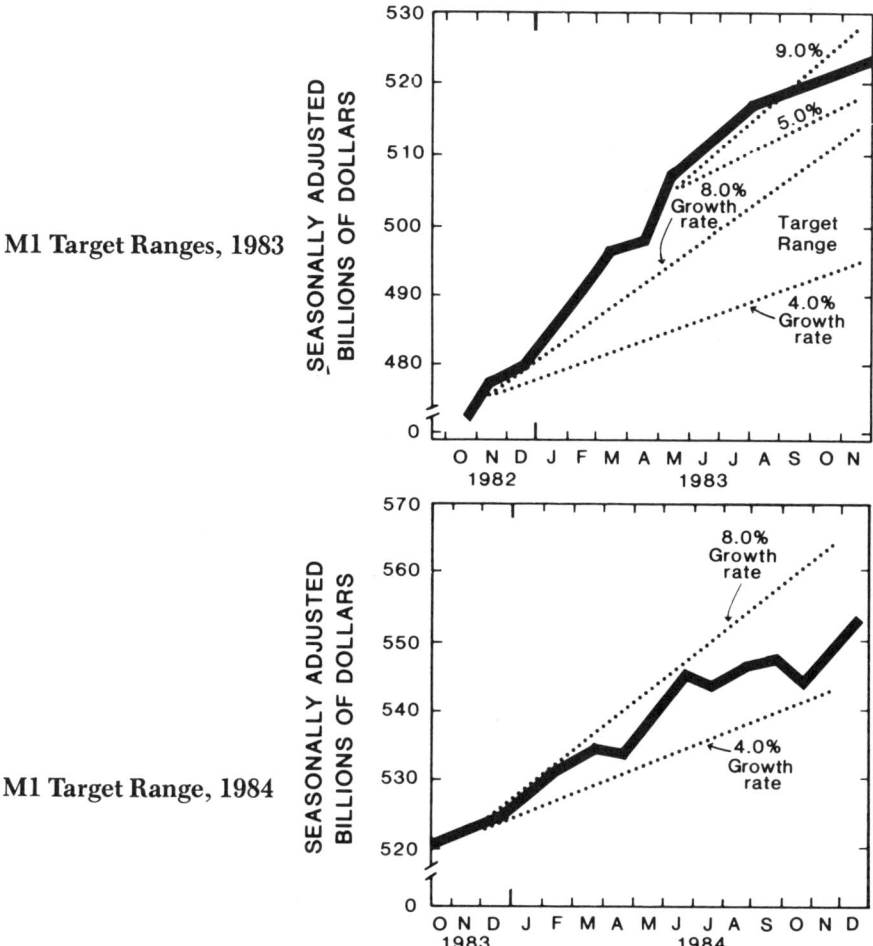

Source: Board of Governors of the Federal Reserve System

In brief, the Fed's approach to controlling money balances was on shaky ground in these 1980-84 transitional years. This could be because they relied upon interest rates (mostly the Federal funds rate, i.e., rate on trading in bank reserves), because of the inexperience with MMDAs and Super NOWs, or because of efforts to fine-tune control in a world where such effort brings less rather than greater success. To compound the control difficulty, the Federal Reserve had introduced the practice called lagged reserve requirements (LRR) in 1968. Under that practice, reserves required of banks were calculated on the basis of deposits held two weeks earlier. There was, as Hadjimichalakis reported, a good bit of opposition to this practice on the part of monetarists because it was shown to be a source of instability in the Federal Reserve's control of money balances.[62] This was especially so after the October 6, 1979 announcement when the Fed moved directly to controlling money and credit aggregates. As indicated, Friedman was among its first critics and soon pointed out in the *Wall Street Journal* and *Newsweek* that the LRR practice imparted some systematic instability in the narrowly defined money aggregate.[63] Following some of its own in-house study, the Board decided in June of 1982 to adopt contemporaneous reserve requirements (CRR) against transaction accounts for medium-sized and larger depository institutions. The new requirements became effective in February 1984.

In October 1982 in a changing regulatory environment, the Fed temporarily suspended its short-run objectives for M1 because of the large volume of all-savers certificates at that date. These certificates came about as a part of the add-ons to the 1981 Tax Reduction Act. Intended to benefit the small saver, the so-called all Savers bill permitted the purchase of tax-free deposits at commercial banks and savings and loan associations up to a maximum of $2,000 per tax payer during 1982. The certificates were not thought to generate much savings, nor to benefit savings institutions as also intended, but they did result in the transfer of funds from money-market funds or certificates at the same institutions.[64] The suspension of the M1 target concerning the certificates was then continued in anticipation of the MMDA and super NOW accounts, and diverse changes in the numerator and denominator of the velocity ratio (Y/M). Even so, the suspension of M1 as the target and the switch to other money aggregates (such as M2, or the Fed's money base) was not a change in policy so much as a recognition of episodic change impacting the data permanently or temporarily. Indeed, employing aspects of data construction known to Friedman years ago, the switch to another aggregate for current targeting was simply a recognition that episodically adjusted M1 can come about by using the pre-episode relation to construct a substitute segment for the M1 series.[65]

Though the targeting M1 was later resumed, the matter of control over M1, M2, or M3 still appears on highly subjective grounds because of uncertainty about the interplay between the money aggregates, the market rates of interest (i), and the velocity ratio (Y/M), as introduced on pages 443-446. A more stable economy and institutional arrangements may have lessened the operating problems with the control mechanism, but it did not provide a much firmer basis for Federal Reserve efforts at an active, discretionary, short-run monetary policy in the early to mid 1980s.

Moreover, the fact that contemporaneous reserve requirements are said to apply to transactions accounts [including "checking, negotiable order of withdrawal (NOW), automatic transfer, and share draft accounts"] in the Fed's regulations does not mean that M1 balances, which include these accounts, are not still held to satisfy the motives Keynes pointed to for the holding of money balances. Indeed, only a small fraction of currency (paper-note-and-coin or so-called "cash") holdings alone can be accounted for in terms of transactions alone.[66] There is little wonder that uncertainty in the economic outlook and speculations against purchasing power changes may still give rise to changes in the Cambridge k (M = kY) and hence to spending and the number of weeks income households hold in M1 balances.

The 1979-84 Period

The distinct parts of the 1979-84 period are: the Carter recession and "quick fix," 1979-80; the monetarist/supply-side recession, 1981-82; and recovery plus Friedman's forecast, 1983-84.

Carter recession and "quick fix." The first of the three parts encompasses the last of the Carter years, the first leg of what we have called the W-recession, and a renewed record growth in the money supply which was followed by a booming first quarter in 1981. As we have noted, some have said that a change in policy occurred in October 1979, but we see this instead only as a change in control technique, as foreign exchange and free-gold markets apparently did also. The dollar price of gold reached $875 per ounce on January 21, such that the early events of 1980 continued in crisis proportions.

In such a setting, in 1980 the Fed dramatically decelerated the growth of the money stock, as shown in the accompanying illustration, which

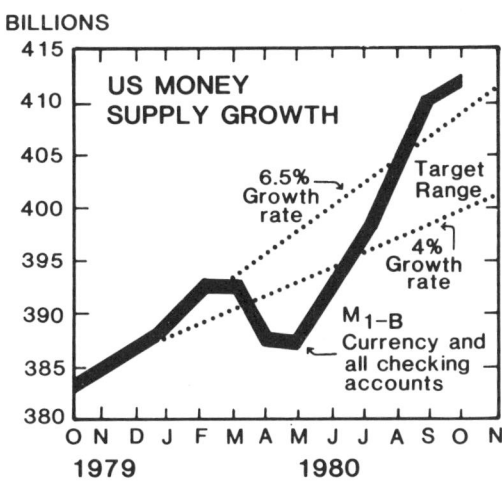

First Leg of the Fed
Dominated W-Recession

includes the first leg of the Fed dominated W-recession. This deceleration of money growth came about as the Fed imposed some selective controls over consumer credit as a result of an order from President Carter under the Credit Control Act of 1969. Then, as reported earlier (chap. 8), the money aggregate was dramatically accelerated as elections approached in November 1980. In his January 1982, State of the Union message, the President reported:

> In the last six months of 1980, as an example, the money supply increased at the fastest rate in postwar history—13 percent. Inflation remained in double digits and Government spending increased at an annual rate of 17 percent. Interest rates reached a staggering 21 percent. There were eight million unemployed.[67]

The monetarist/supply-side recession. The 1981-82 part of the 1979-84 period began with the new administration's criticism of past monetary policy and a call for more stable, declining growth in the money and credit aggregates. Monetary policy became highly restrictive, continued to be volatile, and continued to receive criticism from the executive branch of government and Friedman on all of these counts. Early on in the new administration, this dialogue between Beryl Sprinkel and Jim Lehrer occurred:

> Mr. SPRINKEL: ....Now, the Federal Reserve has stated for many years that they would reduce the rate of growth in the money supply, and they have not done so on average. It has accelerated. The reason it's particularly critical for the President's program is that if we continue to get rapid growth in money supply it will undo all of the other aspects of the program, and our program will be a shambles. For example, as we cut tax rate—trying to encourage incentives—if we have more and more inflation, we are all shoved into higher tax brackets, and it will nullify the effect. If we improve capital recovery provisions, and have added inflation, the capital goods will cost more and the recovery program will not work....
> LEHRER: In other words, you make no apologies for putting a lot of heat on the Fed?
> Mr. SPRINKEL: There are numerous discussion—ongoing discussions—between this administration and the Federal Reserve, as there has been in the past, the major difference as I view it is that in the past many administrations have pressured the Fed to pump in more money. We are doing the opposite....[68]

In January of 1982 attacks on the Fed continued as a result of instability in monetary policy. We encounter the following by-lines in the *Wall Street Journal:* "Reagan calls Fed's Money-Supply Figures 'the Wrong Signal' for markets to Heed," "Reserve Board Faces an Agonizing Choice, Amid White House Ire"; "Reagan Attacks Fed for Erratic Policies"; "The Steady Attack on the Federal Reserve Board"; "The Federal Reserve and Monetary Instability"; "The Attack on Monetary Targets."[69]

It was about these same dates that we note earlier (p. 653) the President discussing the Fisher relation as advanced by Friedman.[70] And, in early February, we encounter Beryl Sprinkel back on the MacNeil-Lehrer television show, where he is also addressing the Fisher effect and a surge in interest rates. The dialogue goes as follows:

> Sec. BERYL SPRINKEL: Jim, the most recent surge in interest rates in my judgement was due to an unanticipated and perhaps unplanned sharp increase in monetary growth. This has created uncertainty about our confidence that we'll get money supply under control, confidence that the Federal Reserve knows how to get it under control. This has been the most recent factor that resulted in a rise in rates.... Our hope is that we will actually achieve what the Federal Reserve and the administration both agree upon, namely a stable, moderate rate of growth in the money supply. That has not happened this past year.
>
> LEHRER: In other words, you think the Federal Reserve is responsible then?

The Dialogue continued.[71] By mid-year of 1982, Friedman also reported on the higher-than-expected, short-term interest rates. Referring to the art work which he presented in *Newsweek*, Friedman concluded:

> There is little doubt that the fluctuations in monetary growth account for the fluctuations in short-term interest rates. It is a more open question whether the abnormal volatility in monetary growth explains the abnormally high level of short-term interest rates. Yet I have been able to find no other explanation that is not clearly contradicted by the empirical evidence.
>
> The one mildly optimistic feature of the charts is that interest rates have been tending to become less volatile even though monetary growth has not. The market is apparently learning to live with the Fed's erratic performance, which also offers hope that the generally declining trend of short-term rates since the first half of 1981 may continue and even speed up.[72]

Looking backward a few months later and then one year later, Friedman also referred to the unusual drop in the velocity of money (Y/M) that occurred from the middle of 1981 to early 1983, as shown in the accompanying art work.[73]

He saw that drop as occurring in two stages, from the middle of 1981 to early 1982, and then from mid-1982 to mid-1983. The first stage, he associated with the sharp drop in inflation and an increase in uncertainty, where, in general, "an increase in uncertainty leads people to want to hold larger cash balances relative to their income." The second stage, which Friedman found more unusual (episodic, we may say), was associated with the extraordinarily rapid rise in the quantity of money ("money growth was about 12 to 13 percent higher than in the earlier 12-month period").

Friedman continued on the second decline thus:

> Historically, whenever monetary growth has increased sharply, the initial effect has been a decline in velocity because the initial effect is that the extra money goes into people's cash balances. For a time, they allow cash balances, which constitute a buffer stock, to grow and absorbed the extra money. But then after a lag, people step up their spending, and velocity tends to increase. So the

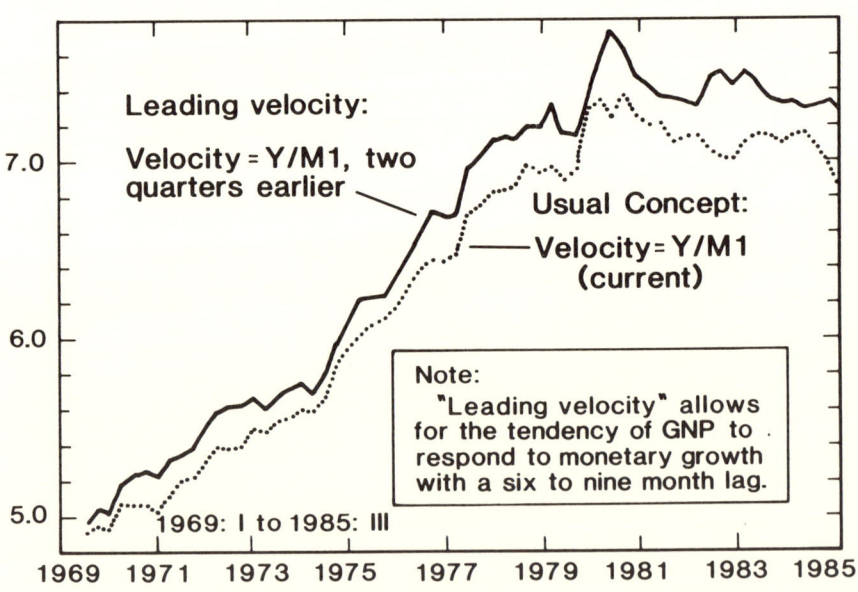

Velocity with current M1 and with M1 two quarters earlier

decline in velocity in the final two quarters of 1982 was one that, in the ordinary course of events, would have been reversed. However, it was not reversed. I believe the reason it was not reversed was the much-talked-about change in regulations, in particular, the introduction of Super NOWs (negotiable orders of withdrawal) in early 1983. The growth in Super NOWs was very sizable. And it reflected the existence of a component of the money supply which was paying very close attention to market interest rates.

As you know, historically, the kind of deposits that were included in M1 did not pay any explicit interest. They paid implicit interest in the form of services rendered, and other things, like being tied in with compensating balances and the like, but they did not pay explicit interest. Apparently, the introduction of explicit interest payments made deposits of that kind a more attractive asset, and thus lead people to seek to increase their holdings of M1. If that is the correct reason, that decline in velocity will prove a permanent decline, a once-and-for-all decline to a lower level, in response to the changed regulatory environment....

Now, what happened to that decline in velocity? How was it absorbed? There are two ways such a decline in velocity can be observed. One way is by a lower level of real income. Another is by a lower level of prices. I have tried to break the decline in velocity down into those two components. Speaking very roughly, I believe that about three or four percentage points was absorbed by a lower real GNP than otherwise would have prevailed and seven to eight percentage points was absorbed by a lower level of prices than otherwise would have prevailed. That is the major explanation why inflation came down so much more rapidly than was predicted from prior monetary growth.[74]

Now, with respect to the overall 1982-83 period, we conclude that the recession was led by monetary policy and, that though volatile, the policy offered the monetary discipline which ultimately reduced the inflation rate. This conclusion is associated with the art work for the quarter-to-quarter changes in M1 and GNP shown earlier. In addition, Hadjimichalakis offered the analysis and interpretation that the Fed intended disinflation but that the extent was more drastic than intended.[75] This was because the Fed over forecast changes in M1 which it associated with a growth of NOW accounts and high interest rates. Hadjimichalakis said, "Under the circumstances, the Fed chose to ignore the signals of low growth in M1, which foretold contraction, and concentrated, instead, on the signals emitted by M2 and M3 growth." He continued, "the Fed interpreted erroneously the above-target growth of these measures as too expansionist and, therefore, tightened monetary policy."

With all the volatility in policy, as reviewed, Friedman denied that we had a "monetarist policy" as opposed to a monetarist experiment or what we have cited as a monetary-discipline induced recession. Friedman said, "monetarist policy involves not only targeting monetary aggregates, but also—as a major and central element—achieving a steady and reducible rate of growth in whatever monetary aggregate is targeted. By this essential criterion the experiment was antimonetarist."[76]

Recovery, plus Friedman's forecast. The 1983 recovery, as we have seen above, was already being led by dramatic monetary acceleration in the second-half of 1982, and we had in place as well incentivist and capital recovery provisions that Beryl Sprinkel alluded to much earlier.[77] However, as tax cuts under the 1981 Tax Reduction Act took effect on the Treasury's revenues and as inadequately controlled expenditures by the government continued, the matter of deficit spending led some to say that we simply had a deficit spending, Keynesian recovery.[78] In fact, reporting such views, Dallek said the 1983 recovery "is a Keynesian, demand-side recovery driven by unprecedented deficits." Even Friedman said the close, visual relation in the art work for monetary growth and nominal GNP one quarter later was partly, in his opinion, an optical illusion. He said the illusion occurred, "because the fluctuations in money were so much wider." The reason he offered was that the fraction of noise in the wide fluctuation was smaller, "and so the relationship looks closer."[79]

There is the point, we add, that recovery occurred in Britain under an M-regime with monetary and tax policies similar to those in the U.S. but while still maintaining the principle of "honest finance," as noted in the last chapter. We may expect that causal analysis should require consistency in the explanation for the two countries.

Even so, the tax part of the fiscal measures may be distinguished from a deficit spending effect. Friedman said, "Those wider fluctuations in money had about the same relative influence on economic activity as the earlier fluctuations." Drawing the distinction between the tax and deficit effects, Friedman and others noted the expansion was not a consumer-led expansion. Friedman said, "Fiscal stimulus in the supply-side model comes in a different way."[80] And other analysts at the Fed of New York shed some light on the question: "what's behind the investment spending boom?"

To answer their question Sahling and Akhtar put together an analysis by searching for irregular sharp movements among the determinants of investment spending in two standard econometric models. (They designated them the FMP model and the BEA model.) Focusing on producers of durable equipment (PDE), they found that it accounted for almost all the unusual strength in business-fixed investment. They concluded:

> From 1982-IV to 1984-III the total expansion in real PDE equals almost $43 billion (1972 dollars). Over past cyclical upturns, the "normal or average recovery in real PDE amounted to about $15 billion. Our estimates suggest that the "extra" $28 billion comes from three principal factors:
> [1] the 1981-82 business tax cuts: $8 billion in direct effects; [2] the faster-than-average recovery in business output associated with personal tax cuts under ERTA [i.e. 1981 Tax Reduction Act]: $7 billion; and [3] the steeper-than-average fall in interest rates in late 1982: $6 billion.[81]

This last effect of course would reflect the monetary discipline and the resulting disinflation in the manner of the Fisher equation.

In a January 1985 interview, the President reported on the recovery:

> This is the first recovery in eight recessions, since World War II, that has been a real recovery. Unemployment has come down; at the same time inflation has come down; at the same time the interest rates have come down. Before we got here, we had double-digit inflation—that last three years, inflation is down to the four percent range. The prime rate was 21 percent. It's now 10.5 percent—and I think we're going to see it go lower. There are close to 108 million people working, more people employed than ever in the history of our country. These solid gains show that what we came into office to do has been accomplished—except that it takes time. We'll have to keep at it.[82]

Almost three weeks later, the President reported similarly in his February State of the Union message. There, he said:

> We did what we promised, and a great industrial giant is reborn. Tonight we can take pride in 25 straight months of economic growth, the strongest in 34 years; a three-year inflation average of 3.9 percent, the lowest in 17 years; and 7.3 million new jobs in two years, with more of our citizens working than ever before.[83]

An additional fact on 1984 is that GNP growth was 6.9 percent—the best for any year since an 8.3 percent rise in 1951, which included the onset of the Korean War.

Friedman underforecast the 1984 performance by both understating real economic growth and overstating the prospect for inflation. In this he was in the company of others who forecast the economy in its details, but he did so in terms of the subject matter of *Monetary Trends*. Although Friedman had shunned the world of short-term forecasting with big models (pp. 69-87), three factors drew him into short-term forecasting from his own monetary-studies base. The three are: (1) his position that the purpose of economic theory is to forecast the effects of policy on the economic goals; (2) his study of money and credit aggregates, prices, a stable relation [equation (1), page 79], and episodic changes; and (3) attacks on the Federal Reserve which included the outlook or forecast and what Friedman called the "backlook" or interpretation of what has happened. In his experiences on the "outlook" and the Fed he concluded, "I find it much easier to predict the consequences of what the Federal Reserve does than I do to predict what the Federal Reserve will do."[84] The contemporaneous or after the fact interpretation is what we engage in when we reconstruct, allow for episodes, and operate outside of a strictly computer-based forecast as it were. Friedman did not shun it entirely—and after all, the allowance for episodes as episodes was a part of his search for a stable relation [the equation (1)]—and, to be sure, the so-called forecasting or big-models was used with respect to it too. Such was the case with the Sahling-Akhtar study of the tax effects and the capital outlays which led the recovery from the 1981-82 recession.

In the 1984 case and on the basis of the 1979-82 patterns (see artwork for quarter-to-quarter rate of change in M1 and GNP one quarter later, p. 653), Friedman was led to underforecast the first-quarter GNP and to overforecast inflation. In late 1983, he had predicted a substantial slow down for the first quarter of 1984, as a result of the "close relationship between quarter-to-quarter changes in nominal GNP and money growth in the prior quarter."[85] The reason for the 1984:I prediction was the slowed M1 growth shown in the art work for the M1-targets Range.

Staying within his framework, Friedman saw a slowdown in nominal GNP. Thus he was wrong in the light of actual performance and he asked: "why was I wrong?" He then answered in two parts.[86] First, he said the Fed, "revised the figures to make them look better," and, second, "the actual outcome deviated unduly from the outcome predicted by monetary growth." Continuing, Friedman said:

> Given the revised figures, prior relations would have suggested that nominal GNP in the first quarter should have grown something like 5 to 6 percent. Actual growth was 13 percent. That 8-percent error happens to be just about two standard deviations. As

you all know, an error of two standard deviations happens about once in 20 times.

Back in the 1930s, I once heard a marvelous lecture by Ronald Aylmer Fisher, the great statistician (schema, p. 70), in which he said, "It's a funny thing—the one chance in a million happens just one time in a million. It only surprises you when it happens to you." That is an appropriate thing to say in Las Vegas. That is my interpretation. I have no explanation as to why that was such an aberration except that it was one chance in 20.

If it was simply a random aberration, you would expect it to come back in line. Lo and behold, so far as nominal GNP is concerned, it did come back in line. The second quarter's rate of nominal growth is exactly what would be expected from monetary growth in the first quarter. If you take the first and second quarters together, velocity grew at exactly a 3.5-percent-per-year annual rate, which is precisely a continuation of the earlier trend line. So the two quarters together are not an aberration, in terms of nominal GNP.[87]

On the underforecasting of inflation and the partitioning of nominal GNP into real growth and inflation, Friedman said:

Historically, we have a good deal of evidence on how nominal GNP tends to be partitioned between real growth and price inflation. And both the first and second quarters are out of line from that point of view. In both quarters, real growth is much stronger than would have been expected from earlier monetary growth. That is, of course, a good thing for the economy from a short-run point of view. However, it leaves a scientific puzzle about why real GNP growth has been so much stronger for these two quarters relative to inflation than would have been expected from earlier experience. Again, I have no satisfactory explanation. I conjecture that it may well be another aberration and that just as the aberration during the first quarter with respect to nominal GNP was corrected in the second quarter, the aberration with respect to real GNP may be corrected in the third or fourth quarter, or even maybe in revised second-quarter estimates.[88]

Following this comment at mid-year 1984, Friedman got back on track for growth in the second half of 1984, except for his inflation-rate forecast. For that he had the consumer price index rising at a cut-back rate of 6 or 7 percent for 1984 and in the neighborhood of 8 to 10 percent in 1985 when we "experience the delayed effect of earlier monetary growth."

Friedman missed his inflation-rate forecast for 1985. The reason we offer is that the Reagan phenomenon which permeated the media and discussion had a greater than anticipated effect on the damping of wages and costs, and the expectation of inflation, and hence a decline in velocity. The first meant that less monetary discipline was required to hold prices and wages in line and the second meant that more monetary discipline was being imposed on spending via declining velocity.

Quite possibly, in a state of considerable uncertainty, as in the period of high interest rates and expected inflation of 1981-82, the markets are likely to respond most immediately to the announcement effects of monetary policy (announcements of actual money growth and of plans for money growth but adjusted for confidence in execution). This is what we called "New York's revenge" (p. 447). On the other hand, with a change in the extent of uncertainty—say as occurred when it became clear Reagan would stay the course and as consideration of budget balancing and tax reform packages proceeded, the longer view takes on added importance. Here every little wiggle in the Fed's departure from target ranges becomes reduced in importance and may even work in a reverse fashion from the uncertainty mode. The longer run matter of whether the Fed will bail out the government and whether the tax of inflation will be reimposed become more important. The events of 1985 and 1986, as taken up later, favored a reduced inflationary and longer run outlook and hence a continued boom in the stock market of a magnitude first encountered in the 1920s (pp. 424-425). However, twin domestic and international deficits emerged as Stephen Marris warned against in his monograph, "Deficits and the Dollar" as a basis for potential crisis as control of the Congress shifted to the democrats in 1987. The domestic deficits, of course, were set on course by earlier entitlement programs, the 1981 tax cuts, and the closing of bracket creep as a source of tax revenue.

This sort of change in 1985 and '86 is quite possibly why Friedman's patterns of money growth began to predict less well. He had written of a change in structure underlying the formation of expectations in the mid-1960s that affected his historical patterns. And now, in the post-1981-82 recession mode, the structure was possibly changing again.

An Outline

We have traversed various routes—the policy recommendations we find in Friedman's economics, changes in executive-office personnel that coincide with monetarism, the operational and institutional changes occurring in the 1979-84 period, and the distinct 1979-80, 1981-82, and 1983-84 parts of the larger 1979-84 period. Having traversed these routes, we offer as an outline of the developments the answers to the three questions raised earlier (p. 649).

Most notably, no well defined, anti-inflation, monetarist discipline policy was adopted as a result of the October 6 announcement which came almost four months after Paul Volcker arrived as chairman of the Federal Reserve Board in 1979.[89] There was no distinguishable move toward monetary restraint (nor was such a move discernible in the behavior of the financial, foreign exchange, and free gold markets). What we find is renewed crisis as to inflationary expectations, rising interest rates and a declining dollar in the foreign exchange and free gold markets. This was met with credit controls which were intermingled with monetary policy, a rapid deceleration of monetary growth, an ensuing "quick fix," and hence the first leg of the W-recession. Inflation, interest rates, and monetary growth were higher in late 1980 and the first quarter of 1981 than previously. Next, a turn (or change in the direction of monetary policy) toward what we have called "monetary discipline" did not occur until after Reagan took office in 1981. The rhetoric that came from the Treasury and the White House at that time was essentially monetarist. Though the lines were spoken by Reagan, Regan, and Sprinkel, they were essentially what we find in Friedman's monetarism—"stabilize sharp swings in monetary growth," "inflation is a monetary phenomenon," and "the interest rate is the sum of the real rate and the expectation of inflation."

In 1981-82 we got a monetarist induced recession. Most ideally the tax part of the Reagan plan would have offset the loss of stimulus from decelerated monetary growth. Even so, the ideal did not come about (tax changes were put in place only slowly as earlier review indicates, and monetarists in any case expected some recession in the transition). At best, we find a recovery led by accelerated money growth and a partly tax-induced capital boom. Monetary and tax features of Reagan's plan were working. Recovery proceeded to approach performances not seen in over three decades, plus even as real output grew more than forecasters expected, the inflation rate declined more than expected.

As testimony indicated, Paul Volcker must have welcomed the Reagan developments. His rhetoric supported them, even if in the guise of the leader of a so-called independent Federal Reserve. However, the fact remains that the turn toward monetarist restraint with the underpinnings of Friedman's economics did not come to Washington, D.C. with Volcker rather than with Reagan. The Fed faced technical difficulties and imposed many on itself. Even as Friedman and others railed against the instability of LRR, the Fed was slow to change. Nevertheless they did change some in time. A point in retrospect may be made, notably: no Federal Reserve official since Benjamin Strong in the early days of the New York Fed (pp.

424-425) has had more influence on monetary policy than Milton Friedman. Essentially, he led the reorientation from the i-regime to the M-regime. At times his influence even extended to change in operating technique (e.g., that at the time of the October 6 announcement and the change from LRR to CRR).

The K-J and Kemp-Roth Tax Cuts

The Laffer curve as presented in its popular pre-1981 form was set on a plane with the tax rate (τ) on the vertical axis and tax revenue on a horizontal axis (T).[90] It did three things principally—depicted a long held view that tax revenue would be zero at two tax rates, zero and 100 percent; connected these two rates such as to show positive revenue at other rates, including one intermediate rate that yielded a maximum tax revenue (which was the public's preferred tax-rate position); and bounded an area under the curve but above the maximum-revenue tax rate which was associated with tax avoidance, barter, do-it-yourself, underground activity. The principal idea, as applied to the period of the 1980 elections and Reagan's 1981 tax cuts was that high tax rates had driven a sizable part of economic activity into these barter-underground areas. Hence a lowering of rates would release new activity into the more open, bookkeeping, monetary economy and generate more revenue. The focus of the lower rates was on expanding activity by some multiple amount (say, from reflows).

Laffer, Evans said, argued that the cuts "would stimulate the economy, reduce unemployment and raise productivity." Plus, Evans said, "The Laffer curve stated boldly that in addition the budget could be balanced by cutting taxes..."[91] The curve's principal analytical problems, as implied in technical appendixes to chapter 16, were as follows: the approach lumped all sorts of taxes and possible tax cuts into one category (whether encouraging saving or consumption in relation to income); it appeared to imply principally the progressive income tax but did not do so explicitly; and it treated an average tax rate (total tax revenue divided by total income say) rather than both marginal and average rates which we associate with the progressive income tax.

However, the more practical, empirically-suggestive results behind the Kemp-Roth bill were closely parallel to the reflows argument of the Laffer curve. They were derived from arguments about other broad-based tax cuts in the U.S. experience—the Mellon reductions in the 1920s and the Kennedy-Johnson (K-J) cuts from 1962 through 1965. Setting aside the earlier cuts as not too relevant and looking mainly at the ceiling on marginal tax rates, Evans proceeded with his analysis by noting differences before and after the K-J tax cut of 1964, when the top rate was reduced from 91 percent in 1963 to 77 percent in 1964 and then to 70 percent in 1965 and later years (still later reduced to 50 percent in 1981 and after that to 28). Taking data from *Statistics of Income*, Evans reported:

> After virtually no growth in income taxes for incomes over $100,000 for three years, taxes paid rose dramatically beginning in 1964 even though income was taxed at significantly lower rates. In the case of individuals earning over $1 million per year, taxes collected *actually doubled* in the two-year span during which the tax rates were being *lowered*. For income classes under $100,000, taxes either fell or rose less than the average growth in total personal income.[92]

Evans said these results led to the plank in the 1981 tax-cut bill which reduced the top marginal tax rate from 70 to 50 percent. The results themselves supported the dawning realization that the higher income groups "do not really pay marginal income tax rates of 70 percent any more than they did at 91 percent." This was coupled with the information "that heavy utilization of tax-free municipal bonds and other tax shelters was costing the Treasury a good deal more than the pound of flesh it was exacting from these high incomes..."

In comparing the K-J and Reagan tax cuts which started in 1981, Evans pointed to the similarities and the differences and in particular to the differences in circumstances under which the respective programs were put in place. In making the comparison he also emphasized in anticipation of his discussion of the myths of supply-side economics that overzealous supply siders overstated the similarity of the performance that could be expected from the K-J and Reagan cuts.

Evans found that the K-J cuts provided evidence favoring supply-side economics despite the underlying argument for them which appeared to follow Keynesian principles, as taken up in connection with Walter Heller (pp. 205-208 and chap. 8).[93] In fact, Evans said the K-J cuts were really more favorable to business. Corporate tax rates were lowered (a) by introduction of a 7 percent investment tax credit, (b) by a reduction in depreciation lives on new capital equipment by 30 percent to 40 percent, and (c) by "a cut in the top corporate tax rate from 52 percent to 48 percent." These changes, moreover, took place over a period from 1962 through 1965.[94] True, the personal income tax rates were reduced across the board by about 20 percent but not evenly so. Evans said:

> The reduction was actually flared slightly at both ends and squeezed in the middle; the lowest marginal rate fell from 20 percent to 14 percent and the highest rate from 91 percent to 70

percent, while the 50 percent marginal rate was cut only to 42 percent. This decline took place over a two-year period, with about two thirds of the reduction in rates occurring in 1964. The corporate income tax rate was also reduced from 52 percent to 48 percent in two steps.

On the comparison of the personal income tax and business tax cuts for the respective administrations, Evans continued:

> First, the [K-J] personal income tax cuts were only half as large relative to GNP as the Reagan tax cuts; the close equivalency implied by some ideological supply siders is fiction. Second, one third of the Kennedy-Johnson tax cut was received by corporations, as opposed to one fourth under the Reagan tax cut; indeed, when the 1982 rescindments are added back in, *only 10 percent* of the Reagan tax cut accrued to corporations.[95]

In calling attention to the circumstances underlying the K-J cuts vis-à-vis those of 1981, Evans noted with respect to earlier conditions the following: (1) First, the federal budget was virtually in balance at the outset, inflation was at 1.2 percent in 1963, and the latter assured low interest payments on the debt (virtually no inflation-rate premium in the rates); (2) second, the Federal Reserve could accelerate money growth and accommodate increased activity without major concern for inflation; (3) third, the K-J cut did not include any long-term provision such as a future indexation of the personal income tax schedule; (4) fourth, inflation increased only from 1.3 percent in 1964 to 2.9 percent in 1966; and, (5), "government spending increased only 1 percent in FY 1965, the year after the major portion of the Kennedy-Johnson tax cut was passed."[96]

The balancing of the federal budget that occurred in the two years following the 1964 K-J cut was attributed by Evans to the following:

1. A pause in government spending, followed by an increase which was partially offset by tax hikes.
2. Monetary policy which was able to encourage unhampered growth because of virtually no inflation. As soon as inflation rose and policy tightened, large budget deficits appeared.
3. An offsetting increase of $2 to $3 billion in other taxes.
4. An increase in the rate of inflation of 1 percent [percentage point] per year.[97]

Major differences alarming financial markets (and hence causing relatively higher interest rates, and other unfavorable conditions) in August

1981 and not in March 1964, were: (1) the economic environment, (2) the "Christmas tree ornaments" which were added to the Reagan proposal once action occurred in the Congress, and (3) indexation against possible inflation-induced tax increases in 1985 and later years.[98] To this, we may add spending by the Federal government, the specter of monetary policy in the light of the 1970s record and the fact that spending by the Federal government was accelerating in the 1981-84 period, including in relation to increases in the burden of personal income taxes. In fact, bracket creep and social security tax increases were main contributors to the income tax burden for the broad groups of households over the 1981-84 period. Along this line, other conclusions drawn from analyses of data were: typical households for upper, middle, and lower income groups faced higher tax rates in 1984 than in 1980; not surprisingly in the light of the 1980-84 rise in social security taxes, the tax burden fell disproportionately on low income households; and the effect of tax reductions in the 1981 tax act were not lower income tax revenues which contributed to deficits.[99]

Continuing with John Tatom's report, drawing on the analyses in the appendixes to this chapter, and considering the personal income tax burden alone, the 1981-84 tax changes probably discouraged consumption more than saving. Other features of the 1981 tax act, such as the IRA provision also supported saving over consumption.

Friedman's early discussion of arguments along the Laffer-curve lines and in support of the Kemp-Roth bill was prophetic.[100] He saw the arguments as bad but for a good cause. On the bad side, across-the-board cuts were unlikely to generate enough extra revenue via rising income to compensate for the reduction in revenue from lower tax rates. On the good side: reducing top-bracket rates for the personal income tax would reduce the spending by taxpayers that is directed toward avoiding tax payments; at lower rates upperbracket taxpayers may prefer to pay the tax and invest funds in the most profitable ventures; and the deficit that may arise from the tax cut would tend to inhibit spending by the government. Argument by Friedman about the deficit ran along the "government-budget-constraint lines, notably: there must be the hidden tax of inflation (say, from accommodative monetary policy) and/or a hidden tax of borrowing from the public (say, the crowding out of private financing and spending). On balance, the main desirability of a tax cut and resulting greater deficit is the pressure to cut government spending.

Friedman's 1978 discussion has implications for the support of the tax cuts and anticipated deficits in 1981, and for Reagan's approach to deficits, spending cuts, and tax reform in 1985 and 1986. Continuing with the 1981 tax cut episode, Evans said the myth about balancing the budget had two parts. First, he saw Reagan as believing he could actually get Congress to cut spending by the full amount of his original proposal, and, second (the "reflows" concept), there were to be higher revenues stemming from faster growth rates in income.[101]

On the possibility of cutting spending, Evans pointed to the big categories in the budget for FY 1982 which was $725 billion. Along lines later encountered in Stockman's book, Evans said:

> One does not have to be Ph.D. economist to realize that if the administration was serious about cutting spending, it had to attack the Big Three [retirement benefits and Medicare, defense expenditures, and interest on the public debt]. Even cutting all other programs in half would not satisfy the requirements of a balanced budget under the assumption of a 10 percent annual increase in real defense spending and no changes in retirement benefits, Medicare, or interest payments.[102]

The reflows concept, Evans said, "was based on misunderstanding of what happened following the Kennedy-Johnson tax cut."[103]

As outlined earlier, once the timing of the expenditure cuts was off and in fact not forthcoming to any relevant extent, a monetary-policy induced recession was well along. There were, as might be expected, lags in the effects of business tax cuts, and expectations about the future did not react as rapidly as ideal circumstances may have warranted. Soon the matter of anticipated deficits, the financing of these, the possible role of the Federal Reserve in supporting the deficits, and interest rates (with inflationary premia) were all real economic problems. Again, however, Friedman's position on the deficits anticipated the position adopted by the President. Referring to the anticipation of deficits that may follow from the 1981 tax-code changes, Friedman made the point: "The most effective—indeed, I would say the only way—to keep down government spending is to keep down government revenues."[104] While commending Phil Gramm—"the Texas Democratic congressman [later Republican U.S. Senator] who played a leading role in assuring passage of President Reagan's tax and spending cuts in the House of Representatives"—Friedman continued that the opposition and the broader group of Keynesian "big spenders" who opposed the cuts extending beyond 1981 as being "irresponsible" were really voting for future spending increases.

Reelection and Subsequent Developments

At mid-term congressional elections during Reagan's first term the economy was in deep recession. With the economy in this transitory state, numerous writers, journalists and Democrats chose the time to make pronouncements on the failures of Reagan's program. It was a time when, ruling out the "quick fix," all the President could do was to anticipate a more permanent state and expect his followers to "stay the course."

As it came to pass, 1983 was a year of unforecasted performance,[105] and the 1984 election year itself yielded economic growth unequaled in over three decades. Though not reported until after the event, Americans' income, after adjusting for taxes and inflation, rose at an average rate for the year of 6.8 percent (partly reflected in the accompanying GNP series). Thus it came to pass that the ranks of presidential opponents who lined up in 1982 thinned dramatically in 1984.

The President consistently led in public opinion polls, with only a temporary loss of points during the first of two debates between the candidates when the President was criticized for the complexity of his discussion.[106] Afterward, there was no contest and, with a strong lead, little inducement for the detailed discussion of decisive issues. An omen of later crises, the President simply ignored the deficit forecasts, noted a Treasury study directed toward tax reform, and pointed toward tax reform without any increase in rates for taxpayers as a group. (The tax plan, we note, was requested as early as December 1983, to be delivered after the 1984 election. Hence, during the campaign the complex job of overhauling the tax system was left to the Treasury's professionals.)

As anticipated, the President achieved a landslide victory in the November 1984 campaign—the biggest electoral total vote in the nation's history, a total of 525 electoral votes compared with 523 won by Franklin Roosevelt over Alf Landon in 1936, a 59 percent popular vote which carried every state in the Union except Minnesota and the District of Colum-

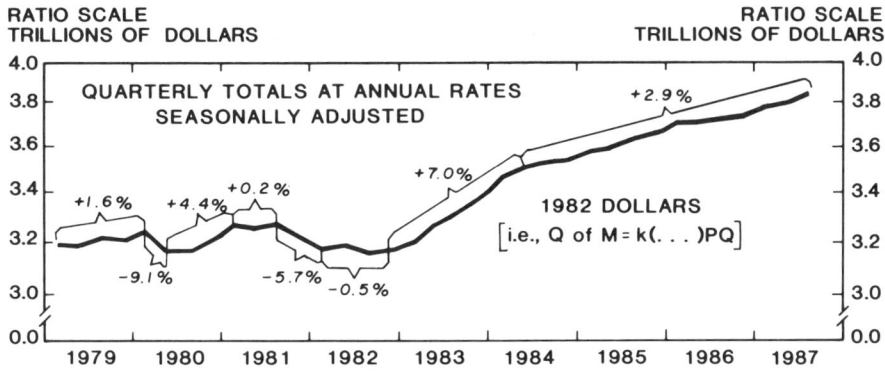

Gross National Product (constant dollars)

bia.[107] However, an issueless campaign and the margin of the President's victory themselves raised allegations: that the election was a personal triumph which failed to lift the party to major gains in Congress (a loss of two seats in the Senate, where a Republican majority was retained, and a gain of 14 seats in the House of Representatives where 26 seats had been lost at mid-term elections), and that the avoidance of hard-edge, issue oriented commercials failed to provide benefit for supporters running on the GOP ticket for Congress.[108] The President himself said the victory was an endorsement of his policies, and a campaign manager expressed the view that Reagan's strong showing in areas where Democratic incumbents won would still provide Reagan with support for his programs.

Steven Weisman of the *New York Times* reminded readers of the startling conservative vision of America which Reagan had outlined on the eve of Goldwater's 1964 defeat. He said, "Today Mr. Reagan savors a triumph even more lopsided than Mr. Goldwater's defeat." Continuing, he said: "It can safely be said that Mr. Reagan has not changed his views since his Goldwater speech."[109] Remindful of Robert Dallek's "The Politics of Symbolism," the view of Reagan was that he articulated a sweeping sense of direction through "his practice of speaking in the broadest of terms about values rather than issues..."

The 1984 election victory set the President on course for a major success on the tax reform front in 1986, although it fell short of its goal of a flat-rate tax with no loopholes. However, in the off-year elections of November 1986, his apparent personal popularity failed to provide him with a majority in the Congress, as the matter of growing federal deficits and controversy over tax and growth in the federal spending came to the forefront.

In this context, the President's (and also Friedman's) opposition to growth in the federal government and, hence, tax increases, set the stage for the later crisis effects of growth in the domestic deficits and trade account deficits in the balance of payments. In the context of chapter 11 (pp. 412-413), the trade deficits called for a decline in prices on the domestic front (say, $-\Delta P_{US}/P_{rest\ of\ world}$) and/or for a decline in the price of the dollar in terms of key foreign currencies (say, e.g., $-\Delta £/\$$). Having already put the U.S. economy through the ringer by lowering the inflation rate in 1981-1982 (actually, with little choice), it seemed from later Treasury department comments that the next choice was going to be to let the price of the dollar decline, hopefully bringing about the needed adjustments. As it later turned out, this means of adjustment required a much longer lag in time than expected, partly because it lacked the extra force from the announcement effects of monetary discipline (i.e., declining growth in M1 and related aggregates) and it targeted less specifically than a declining U.S. price level ($-\Delta P_{US}$) on those segments of the domestic markets where price adjustments were most needed.

The President's lame duck status combined in late 1986 with the unraveling of the Iran-Contra affair to weaken him and force the departure of Donald Regan as Chief of Staff. The early White House aides James Baker and Edwin Meese had moved to cabinet posts, and David Stockman and Michael Deaver had departed entirely (the idealistic Stockman to a New York investment house and Deaver to a Federal court conviction by a possibly illegally appointed prosecutor for perjury under congressional oath during questioning about his influence with the White House as a high paid lobbyist). In addition, the President lost on the Supreme Court appointment of Robert Bork (p. 316). The democratic majority in the Congress and pro-big government democratic hopefuls with a heritage of Keynesian leanings made political noises in anticipation of the 1988 presidential and congressional elections. (Regan, too, was to have his day in May '88. Seventeen months after his departure, with the help of what was reported as deep-background "media manipulation" and the President's wife Nancy Reagan, the former Chief of Staff went public with what had come to be called a "kiss-and-tell" book in the style of David Stockman's (p. 687). Titled *For the Record: From Wall Street to Washington*, the book depicted the first lady as a mystic relying on a later identified Vassar graduate astrologer in influencing the timing of the President's travel plans. *N.Y. Times* columnist William Safire said, "By throwing a hardball pitch, she [Mrs. Reagan] invited a hardball return.")

Even as Reagan moved in mid-1987 into his Iran-Contra scandal hampered, "lame duck" last year as president, he still found the opportunity to call for an "Economic Bill of Rights" at the Jefferson Memorial Independence Day celebration. The idea had first surfaced in Friedman's Reagan-endorsed, 1979 work, *Free to Choose*.

In referring to the President at the summer's end in 1987, there were those who recalled the protagonist of F. Scott Fitzgerald's *The Great Gatsby*. The book's narrator said of Gatsby's smile, "It was one of those rare smiles with a quality of reassurance in it that you may come across four or five times in life." Gatsby's house (an allusion to the White House) was juxtaposed against this quality. The house stood idle, the rooms were darkened, the sounds muted, and cocktail shakers dry. Some who had attended the parties hardly knew Gatsby (allusion to decline in Reagan's approval rating in *N.Y. Times*/CBS news polls). There were rumors about who he was—possibly the nephew of Kiser Wilhelm.

In the dark, lame duck, Gatsby-like period immediately following the October 19 market crash, as the budget remained unbalanced and the trade deficit continued, even at a reduced rate, Reagan held a press conference. There, ABC News White House correspondent, Sam Donaldson, asked the President what went wrong with supply-side economics to cause the crash. The President, correctly and consistently with the theme of chapter 8, "The Keynesian Era," engaged Donaldson in the following exchange:

> [Question] Sir, you feel very strongly about this, obviously. You've been one of the leading proponents of supply side economics. What went wrong?
>
> [Answer] What went wrong with what? Supply side economics?
>
> [Question] Why are we in the economic mess that we are in today?
>
> [Answer] Because for more than half a century, that was dominated entirely by the Congress of—both houses of the Congress by one party. They have followed, beginning with what they called the Keynesian Theory, deficit spending—openly deficit spending on the basis that they claimed was necessary to maintain prosperity—that you had to do it and it wasn't hurtful because we owed it to ourselves. And some of us said year after year that it would keep on to the point that it would just get out of control, and it has, just as we said it would. And they've got to give up that belief in that. I think I'd like to point out that [John] Maynard Keynes didn't even have a degree in economics.
>
> [Question] Was it the Democrats who did it?
>
> [Answer] What?
>
> [Question] Was it the Democrats who did it?
>
> [Answer] Well, you can look up and see who dominated both houses of the Congress for the last 50 years.[110]

Two further successes were to come for the President following the crash—a deficit reduction pact was made with the Congress following a brief interval in which the Gramm-Rudman bill kicked in, and, only tangential to the economic story, Reagan signed a historic arms reduction treaty, containing the first inspection provisions, with Soviet leader Mikhail Gorbachev. The talks also paved the way for a later summit with the Russians. Although the deficit reduction agreement extended for two years, it was only partially reassuring to the financial markets. No strong, positive resurgence, such as a renewal of the Reagan stock market boom, was expected until after the 1988 elections, and only then on the prospect of victory for a monetarist/Thatcher/Reagan clone.

Tax Reform/Simplification

Returning to the early, post-1984 elections, the tax plan called "Treasury

I" appeared in late November under the title "Report on Fundamental Tax Simplification and Reform."

As Leonard Silk of the *New York Times* commented in a December 2 column, there were not many directions for the plan to move since it was "to promote simplicity, equity and growth." Referring to the Greek myth about the Procrustian bed, he noted opponents of the President's fiscal strategy may see it as chopping off social programs when they don't fit the tax base. He then noted that Reagan was barring the way to new taxes and that a huge budget deficit exerted powerful pressure for cutting spending. He said, "A compromise will be hard to reach."

By the date of Reagan's February 6 State of the Union message to Congress, which carried the added title "A Second American Revolution," the issues Reagan put before Congress were well focused and drawn along the lines of the politics of symbolism. Except perhaps for Reagan's style, the rhetoric and ideas could just as well have been Milton Friedman's as Ronald Reagan's. First, the theme and goal of freedom, as in chapters 12 and 13, was foremost. Selected passages are as follows:

> Four years ago, we said we would invigorate our economy by giving people greater freedom and incentives to take risks, and letting them keep more of what they earned. We did what we promised, and a great industrial giant is reborn...
>
> ....
>
> It [the economy] doesn't need rest and supervision, it needs new challenge and greater freedom. And that word—freedom—is the key to the Second American Revolution we mean to bring about.
>
> ....
>
> Let us resolve that we will stop spreading dependency and start spreading opportunity, that we will stop spreading bondage and start spreading freedom.
>
> ....
>
> Every dollar the Federal Government does not take from us, every decision it does not make for us, will make our economy stronger, our lives more abundant, our future more free.
>
> ....
>
> We cannot play innocents abroad in a world that is not innocent. Nor can we be passive when freedom is under siege....

Second, referring to the Treasury plan for tax reform, the President outlined his variant of the flat-rate income tax which he now referred to as "tax simplification."[111] Stressing the principles behind the plan as guides for legislation, the President lobbied for the following points: reduction in tax rates along with the removal of "many tax preferences"; a top marginal tax rate of no more than 35 percent; reduction in corporate rates while maintaining incentives for capital formation; total exemption from the Federal income tax for "individuals living at or near the poverty line"; and a significant increase in the personal exemption "to restore fairness to families."

Third, there were to be cuts in government spending. Guidelines were: "overall Government program spending will be frozen at the current level"; "the social safety net for the elderly, needy, disabled and unemployed will be left intact"; "National security is Government's first responsibility"; "reduce or eliminate costly Government subsidies" such as the subsidy to Amtrak. Continuing along the spending line, the President requested "a two-year trial run of the line-item veto," and the passage of a balanced budget amendment ("an amendment mandating the Federal Government spend no more that it takes in").

Fourth, taking note of monetary policy, the President said he would seek "a steady policy that insures price stability without keeping interest rates artificially high or needlessly holding down growth." Though not the more rigid form of Friedman's rule, the position signified monetary policy and what we have called an M-regime. Further, in combination with earlier review of Arthur Burns's tenure at the Fed and the above analysis ("The Turning Point in Monetary Policy"), we no longer see the Federal Reserve as an independent policy-making agency (in this case, independent of the President).[112]

Finally, on the themes of reducing the size of government, cutting spending, balancing the budget, and variants of the flat-tax concept, we have a comparison of Friedman's ideas and the President's positions, with accent on those ideas and positions that they shared. However, a close parallel also extends to their negative stances as well. Additional to positions on the return to the gold standard, it extends to the widely discussed value-added tax (VAT) as a means of raising revenue for the Federal Government.[113] VAT was viewed as a way of achieving tax neutrality toward economic behavior and allocative efficiency, and as a tax on consumption spending rather than on saving and productive efforts. Nevertheless, Reagan held forth at a news conference in February of 1985 on this Friedman/Reagan position:

> But a value-added tax actually gives a government a chance to blindfold the people and grow in stature and size. First of all, you are kind of interfering with one of the principle sources of local government levels and state government in their use of the sales tax, since the Federal Government had so, you might say, confiscated the area of the income tax.
>
> But the other thing with that tax is, it's hidden in the price of the product and that tax can quietly be increased and all the peo-

ple know is that the price went up and they don't know whether the price went up because somebody got a raise or whether the company wanted to increase profits, or whether it was government. And I just am not enthused about it. I think I've said before, taxes should hurt in the sense that people should be able to see them and know what they're paying.[114]

By late May the President's own plan for tax reform, now called "Treasury II," was presented to the public and Congress.[115] As one expert said, we lost some major opportunities because "Treasury I" would have gotten the tax system out of people's business. "It would have relieved them of the need to bring tax considerations into business calculations to the degree that they now have to do."[116] Continuing Henry Aaron said, "the emphasis has been changed in the past few months from simplicity to more fairness..." As taken up in the press, Reagan was said to be setting a populist strategy. Possibly Reagan and his aids had seen political difficulties in the purer "Treasury I" plan. In any case, the winners under "Treasury II" were to be the lowest income groups and the losers were to be those "who make substantial itemized deductions, including individuals who invest heavily in tax shelters, live in high tax states or claim big deductions on loans they have taken to finance such items as second homes or cars."[117]

As these remarks imply, exemptions for self and spouse were to increase from $1,800 under 1986 law to $2,000, and there were to be no deductions for state and local taxes. In addition, there were to be only three tax brackets and the ceiling on the marginal rate was set at 35 percent. The guiding theme of the new proposal harked back to the State of the Union address. There was to be a "Second American Revolution," in the sense that the first revolution was also fueled by resentment to unfair taxation. There was more along these lines.[118]

The President did not deviate markedly from his positions nor from the "symbolic budget-cut and tax reform proposal." Nevertheless, in late July the Republican controlled Senate failed to break a filibuster by opponents of the line-item veto (58 voting to break and 40 opposing, with two short of 60 votes required), and legislative maneuvering and voting on the budget and tax-reform proposals were delayed by events that side-tracked the media dialogue on the budget and tax reform. The diversions were the hijacking of a TWA jet by terrorists in June and cancer surgery and convalescence for the President in July.

In his first news conference following abdominal surgery, the President resolved to mount a "Fall Offensive" in the domestic area.[119] Priorities included the constitutional amendment requiring a balanced budget, the line-item veto, and the plan to modify the income tax code. By December of 1985, the Congress passed what came to be called the Gramm-Rudman-

Hollins amendment (or alternatively the Gramm-Rudman balanced budget law). It muted the request for a constitutional amendment to require a balanced budget but nevertheless set Congress on a track to proceed in steps to achieve a balanced budget by 1991. Were the spending targets not achieved by the Congress, exclusive of certain exemptions, across-the-board cuts in spending were to be triggered. There were some court questions to be resolved about the trigger but in the meantime the Congress proceeded toward the bill's target.

On July 7, the Supreme Court ruled the automatic part of the budget cutting mechanism unconstitutional. The reason—the provision gave the automatic cutting power to the Controller General, who is subject to removal by Congress, and hence violated a separation of powers provision of the Constitution. Shortly after the court ruling, the "trigger" part of the bill was changed by giving the power to the budget director in OMB, but some uncertainty about Congress' resolve under Gramm-Rudman remained.

Five months after Gramm-Rudman, the Senate Finance Committee handed Reagan a tax improvement plan grounded in the work of New Jersey's Senator Bill Bradley and Chairman Bob Packwood of Oregon. It was even more sweeping than he had called for at the time of his "Second American Revolution" speech. The May 1986 plan reduced the top individual tax rate from 50 to 27 percent, and eliminated dozens of tax benefits to reduce the role that taxes play in the daily financial decisions of Americans. By mid-August, a "Reagan style bill" was out of the joint Senate/House Committee. It chopped tax rates to 15 percent for most tax payers and 28 percent for almost everyone else, closed many tax loopholes, removed about six million low-income households from the tax rolls, and added a 5 percent surcharge on income of $71,000 and above. Although one of the many outcomes was a strengthening of the marriage penalty on two-income households, the overall outcome was hailed as a "monument to Reaganism," which "Joins Populist Politics with Supply-Side Credo."

The Deficits and the Crash

Events and markets in economics and the time series that reflect them are highly interrelated. Among these encompassed by the 1981-1986 period were the budget and trade deficits as mentioned, and the strongest capital boom since the 1950s. All of this required financing—funds to pay for the government issued debt instruments, funds to pay for the imports on the trade account, and funds external to the corporations for new capital outlays. Further, all of this occurred at a time of declining inflation rates (a main goal of the Reagan presidency), and hence, interest rates (in view of the interest rate component for expected inflation).

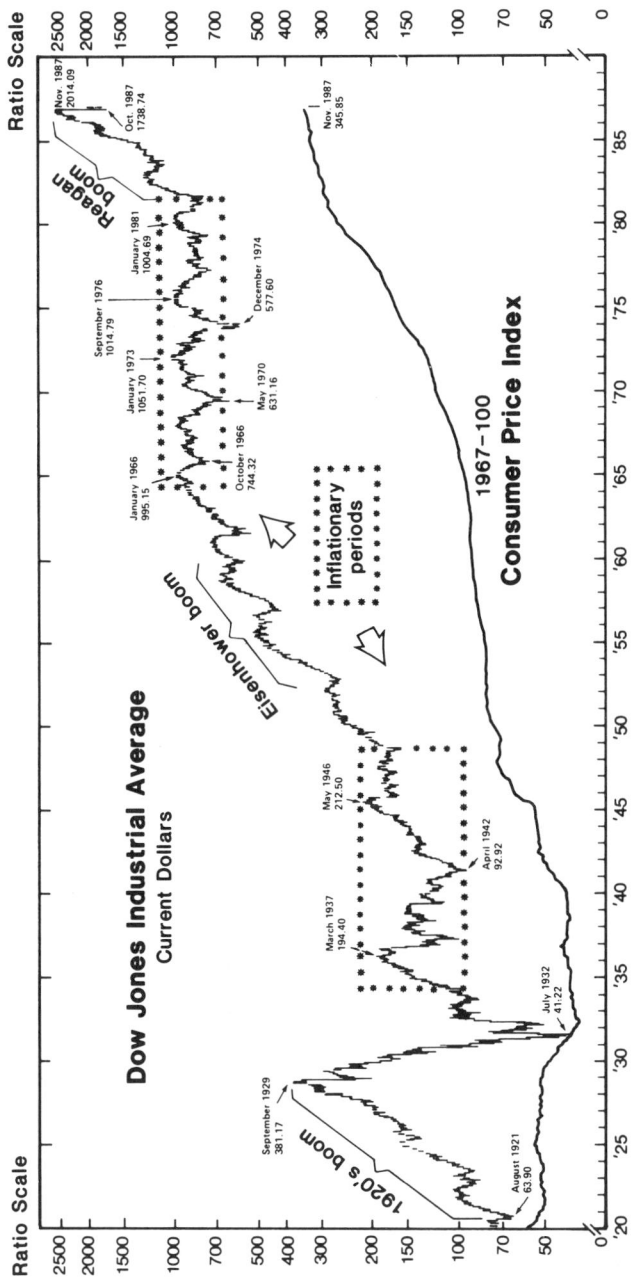

The Dow and the CPI from the 1920s through the Mid 1980s

A remarkable further feature of what would have ordinarily been a strain on financial markets for new funds was that foreign funds flowed into the U.S. in the form of direct investment, and the purchase of debt instruments and securities in general. This apparently could only occur in response to the success of the U.S. and the President in controlling inflation (a symbol of a strong economy) and providing strong measures and rhetoric along pro-enterprise lines. This appraisal of the times and conditions was confirmed by the performance of the New York stock market. As pictured by the accompanying series for the Dow Jones industrial average and the consumer price index, the market went through the third of its great booms in the period from August 1982 to August 1987. The other two are the Eisenhower boom and the market boom of the 1920s. All are associated with stable prices for the output of goods and services or a declining inflation rate, and all reflect a persuasive psychology associated with the times. To be sure, at these times and others, the growth in the stock market averages (such as the Dow) are poorly correlated, uncorrelated or negatively correlated with growth in sales and profits.

The euphoria of the stock market participants and the strong bond markets (coincident with declining interest rates) were related (as independent evidence) to the inflow of foreign funds (indeed, the U.S. was perceived for a time as a good opportunity exclusive of growth in profits and sales). Even the widely discussed spread between U.S. interest rates and foreign interest rates (the nominal interest rate differential, as reflected in the accompanying art work, page 685) revealed no clear pattern to account for the inflows of funds. The rate differential trended upward in the 1976-1981 period, and entering into the main period of capital inflows, it showed a sideways or declining trend [even when the dollar was appreciating in the foreign exchange markets (p. 650)].

The unusual combination of growing strain on the capital markets which was met with foreign funds at a time of large trade account deficits could not be sustained in the lame-duck period of deficits crises (pp. 677-678) in its dependence on Reagan's political leadership, policy advocacy and rhetoric. Although an early expected change was the peak and subsequent decline in the exchange value of the dollar (p. 650), the market had tied itself to Reagan whose time at the White House was running out. With the failure of the Congress to act persuasively on the domestic deficits and with the added prospect for the monetarization of the debt by the Federal Reserve under a different leader (p. 545), the levitation underlying the stock market vanished on Monday, October 19, 1987.

What went up on psychological grounds interacting with policy and leadership came down on the same combination. The market crashed—confronting inaction along monetarist, supply-side lines by Congress and the lame duck President. (Indeed, we have here a variant of what we

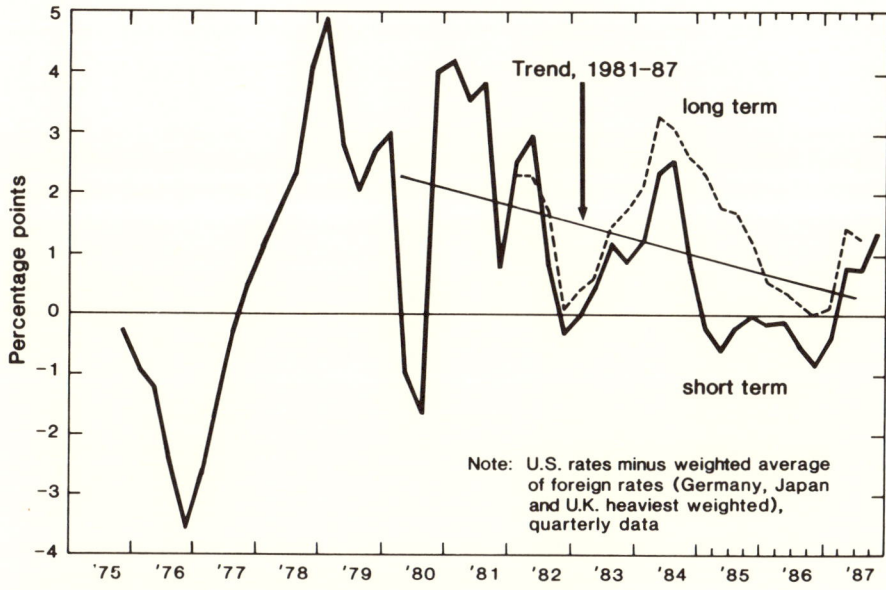

Nominal Interest Rate Differentials

called "New York's revenge," p. 447, where market rates of interest were adjusted as a countermeasure for Washington's inflationary policies.) There was a drop of 22.6 percent in the Dow on the black Monday, compared with a 24.5 percent drop (unaided by the elecronic computer) over the two day period of October 28 and 29, 1929. The October 19, 1987 market closed 1,000 points below its 2,722.42 peak on August 25, 1987. (Some contend the stock-market turn started in London, the day of a big storm there that disrupted communications and actions, and that the turn moved to New York before the market closed on Friday.)

Despite the comparable magnitude of both episodes on the crash dates the differences in the crash of 1929 (analyzed earlier pp. 424-425) and that of 1987 are significant: (1) The participants were more sensitive in the formation of expectations in 1987 than in 1929 (including those who failed to withdraw in the months and weeks before the 1987 crash). (2) The bank credit in the market in 1929 was a more significant source of funds (margined accounts as low as 10 percent compared to a legal 50 percent limit on the Fed regulated accounts). (3) The economy in 1929 had already reached a peak to business conditions whereas in 1987, GNP numbers were strong (reported at a robust 4.3 percent at the annual rate for the quarter ending in September). And, (4), in addition to the insurance for bank deposits, the

Federal Reserve was far more sophisticated in crisis management in 1987. This was in large part as a result of Friedman's and Schwartz's monetary works, the *Monetary History* in particular.

Friedman's monetary work and persuasion in general were the source for the shift from the i-regime to the M-regime in economic thinking and policy implementation, which we have widely recounted, and the *Monetary History* offered a new interpretation of the causes of the Great Depression (pp. 424-425). On Tuesday following the 1987 crash, Federal Reserve Chairman Greenspan met with the President, and the Federal Reserve moved through open market operations to provide liquidity to the nation's banks. They took similar steps on Wednesday after Greenspan announced they were ready to "serve as a source of liquidity." With a clear reference to the Federal Reserve's failures in the early 1930s, the chairman said that they would not repeat the mistakes of that period. Budget Director James C. Miller, apparently recalling the same Federal Reserve failures, said, "You need to apply the physicians code: first, do no harm."

Official reports after the '87 crash (the SEC's, the GAO's and a presidential panel's) gave attention to the role in accelerating decline of computer-based trading by large institutions, stock-options trading, and index-futures arbitrage. (There was a call for some limits and higher margin requirements for trading in options on credit.) But these reports (and the limits/margin prospect) do not account for the crash, its timing and the fact that the market did not rebound (computer-driven trading and all in reverse) in the immediately succeeding days.

Returning to the catalytic deficits (p. 534) and congressional inaction behind the market crash, we may still note the future agenda needed for the deficits problem. Certainly the dollar price of foreign currencies may fall further. However, for the political right, the future agenda would be a balanced budget that offers assurance of no more future growth in U.S. government debt and a large increase in the U.S.'s ratio of personal saving to income (i.e., foreign funds aside, the U.S.'s real rate of interest may be raised by tax and surely not monetary means). The political left (e.g., the post Keynesians) has an agenda too. It centers around more of a collectivist state (monetization of debt and so on). For its part the middle has little to offer—no solution, only a muddle.

An Overview

In his dejection about the failure(s) of the Reagan promise, David Stockman, idealist and pointman on Reagan's budgets from 1981 through August of 1985, wrote of the Revolution's abortive effort and said, "It defied the settled consensus of professional politicians and economists on its two central assumptions."[120] These he mentioned as being (1) that the ideologues believed themselves right and the politicians wrong "about what the American people wanted from government" and (2) that the inherited economy could be instantly healed. Indeed, in the first instance Stockman was incorrectly critical of the notion that strong central leadership can package tax and economic matters so as to have the general interest prevail over the ingrained special interest of groups. In the second, he saw only "the economics of joy" as being under the Reagan political umbrella, when in fact Friedman had publically warned for years about the power of monetary policy, advocated gradual deceleration of money growth and, even before the 1981 tax cuts, warned against the reflows argument of the LMWK group.

The anti-statist ideal of reducing federal spending as a percent of GNP was not achieved, but a lot was achieved. For one thing, the rhetoric and debate changed, and, not to be underestimated, the future agenda promised to be different. Indeed, the Gramm-Rudman bill and subsequent action by the Congress under it signified the greater difficulty inherent in the future acceleration of the growth of federal government, and the complexity of returning to the implementation of any Keynesian deficit-spending policy (all with the Federal Reserve accommodating the deficits). The experience with decreasing the ceiling on the marginal tax rate for personal income makes justification for reversing the action more difficult. Individualism, work effort, productivity and quality improvements were back.

For another major change, the President pursued Friedman/monetarist positions, and, as even David Stockman admitted, gave Paul Volcker at the Federal Reserve "the latitude to do what had to be done."[121] The monetary developments market the predominance of the change toward an M-regime over an i-regime, as we have widely discussed. In the larger perspective of economic ideas and their implementation, the Reagan presidency was a revolution in thought and action.

In brief, the major thrust of Friedman's ideas that were covered in part IV—and particularly in the crises/Keynes/Friedman chapter, the economics-of-freedom chapter, the income-distribution chapter—are found to be at the center of the policy thrusts of the Reagan presidency. *What essentially were these ideas?*

Answer: The analysis of the leading time rate of change in the money stock and liquidity preference with overshooting (including analysis linking interest rate to the expected inflation rate). These set about the basis for change from the i-regime to the M-regime and altered informed thought in the financial markets about money growth, inflation, and interest rates. There was also the setting of freedom as the highest goal (an ideological/symbolic goal) and Friedman's closely related arguments on reducing the size of government and moving toward the flat-rate income tax; his consumption function analysis which deals with social mobility (the tax on getting rich rather than being rich, etc.), income redistribution, and the saving-to-income ratio and what Evans called a "fundamental truth of supply-side economics." Special time frames were treated in relation to all of the foregoing.[122]

These ideas also bear on the transition from the Keynesian/elitist/inflationary world to the monetary/freedom world and center about the distinctions Friedman made as to transitory and permanent components in the time series, and the short and long run. Friedman extended the latter to a political dimension with attention to persuasion, the long swings in public opinion, the ability of the public to learn (long-run rationality with respect to inflation), the avoidance of the quick fix. These were all qualities found in the Reagan presidency—especially the uses of symbolism and persuasion, and the avoidance of the quick fix, even as pressures for such mounted during the 1981-82 recession.

Recognizing that there is no perfect translation from the economists workshop to the White House, Friedman said in 1975, "We know perfectly well that our sensible ideas are going to get mangled in the process..." What is amazing is that the correspondence between the ideas and the policies is so close. In the move from the i- to the M-regime, we do not encounter the implementation of Friedman's simply monetary rule exactly, but we do get major reorientation by the Federal Reserve, monetary discipline and a less inflationary world. Out of controversy during the transition from the i-regime to the M-regime, the political nature of the central bank is more clearly seen. Friedman himself switched from advocating his rule to advocating placing the Federal Reserve under the Treasury. This event was unlikely to happen. Nevertheless, with the experience gained from Thatcher's government and the U.S. presidency at a time of attention to monetary aggregates, we are less likely to delude ourselves that money aggregates are apart from politics and safe in the hands of appointed officials. The growth in money and credit aggregates will be more carefully monitored as a result of Friedman's efforts and Reagan's presidency.

Big deficits did emerge from the President's insistence on not raising income taxes, from the indexation of federal income tax with respect to inflation, from reduced inflation itself, and from the failure to cut spending as Friedman advised. Questions on the effect of deficits arise, as to whether they stimulate recovery (say, a Keynesian recovery in 1983) or whether there is the crowding out from the financing of the deficits. On the 1983-recovery matters we note two lines of argument: first, recovery occurred in Britain under policies similar to those in the U.S. but without the projection of large deficits. Second, drawing on the distinction between tax and deficit effects, the U.S. expansion was not shown to be consumer led. Federal Reserve Bank of NY economists pointed to a capital spending boom, as did others.

With the deficits of the mid 1980s we might under ordinary circumstances have expected the crowding out of private financing or excessively expansive monetary policy, in the manner according to the government budget constraint. However, a remarkable and unanticipated thing happened following the transition from the i-regime to the M-regime and during Ronald Reagan's presidency. Foreign funds flowed into the U.S. at unprecedented post-WW II rates. Initially this was predominately in the form of deposits and other assets at U.S. banks, but in 1984 and 1985 the predominant increases were in the purchase of stocks, bonds, and U.S. government securities. Common explanations were that the U.S. was becoming a debtor nation with maturity and without vigor and that high interest rates attracted the inflow of foreign funds.

The facts were just the reverse. U.S. interest rates were declining as inflation came under control (recall the nominal rate equals the real rate plus the expected inflation rate), and the soundness of the dollar domestically and vigor and soundness of the economy provided a haven for capital as the President and Friedman emphasized.[123] To be sure, in any case, in 1984 and 1985 there was a liquidity shift favoring the U.S. on a world scale. Hence there was a temporary respite from the restriction usually imposed on domestic economy matters by the government budget constraint.

The dollar remained strong in relation to the index of foreign currencies until September of 1985 (p. 650), when direct intervention to weaken it somewhat was announced by a 5-nation meeting called by the President. The move was taken to blunt protectionist moves in the Congress at a time when the strong dollar encouraged spending by U.S. nationals abroad,[124] and when some reversing of direction appeared to be in order. This would be because the U.K. was also following the policies of restraint, because some other countries were coming on line with more disciplinary policies, because spending by U.S. citizens on imports remained out of line with the U.S.'s gestures toward achieving a competitive position and possibly faster economic growth.

The international economic signal to the "agents" comprising the domestic U.S. economy was at this declining-dollar stage twofold: the need for further restraint in U.S. wage increases vis-à-vis the rest of the world, and/or faster economic growth in the U.S. (that is to say, a higher saving-to-income ratio) with wage increases lagging somewhat behind the productivity increases. These would be due to productivity-inducing capital accumulation (i.e., the S-Y ratio) and possibly work effort and improved organizational arrangements. In combination with adequately restrictive monetary policy, the greater growth, productivity and wage restraint would signify lower U.S. prices in relation to the rest of the world. Of course, any measures additional to price and quantity competitiveness to help U.S. firms penetrate selling in foreign markets would be of added benefit.

Next in the Reagan presidency we got tax reform of sorts—a lower ceiling on the marginal income tax rate, say from 70 to 50 to 28 percent; reduced tax shelters and loopholes; increased exemptions for lower income households; a reduced number of tax brackets; indexation of the federal income tax. The tax reform moved toward the ideal of the flat-rate tax and paid homage to the early idea of packaging the general interest and special interests, so as to get the latter to give up benefits for the former. The relevance of those ideas initially found in Friedman's efforts to the happenings of the Reagan presidency is amazing beyond ordinary belief.

And, finally, Friedman recognized, as did the President, that cutting taxes would lead to higher budget deficits if expenditures were not reduced. However, with restricting the size of government as a goal, the strategy involved forcing action on the part of Congress by allowing a crisis to catalyze it. The first major related event was the stock market crash of October 1987. Comparable in magnitude to the October 1929 crash (except for the major differences we outlined), the perceived market crisis led to congressional action, only slightly greater than that mandated by Gramm-Rudman, to balance the budget.

Other shared, related ideas included the constitutional ammendment requiring the federal budget to be balanced [with the usual prospect of making important rights protected by a "super majority" rather than just a simple majority (fifty percent plus one) voting]; a greater emphasis on the private sector; a linking of "economic freedoms" to "political freedoms" envisioned by Jefferson and the other founding fathers in the Declaration of Independence; and freer markets and greater world competitiveness in trade. Added to the ideas was a proposal called "truth in spending" which had the intent of tying specific tax-revenue costs to new programs begun by both the administration and the Congress.

Part VI
Epilogue

In The Background *we discuss the Jewish background and heritage of some prominent economists of Friedman's era; the sweep of over 200 years of British economics and conflicts within the pool of early Nobel economists. We highlight Friedman's efforts to combine his diverse educations at the early stage of the monetarist research, and his educational, teaching, and research experiences. We then focus on his "going public," his anticipatory ideas on the transition from the Keynesian, inflationary era, and the era itself. Discussion on the Chicago schools, Friedman's role there, antitrust economics and the law, and a counterrevolution in Latin America then end the volume.*

In volume II, The U-Turn, *we narrow the larger perspective to the period of the '20s through the '80s, focusing on the political economy topic of "freedom," the beginnings of Keynes's efforts at redirection in economic thought and policy, failures in the Keynesian era, and the monetarist revolution of Friedman, Thatcher and Reagan.*

The text could end with what we have called the "Big U-Turn," the implementation of Friedman's monetarist ideas by the Thatcher government and the Reagan presidency. But, as an extended finish, we take up, in chapter 17, the aspects of Friedman's personality which were necessary for his achievements, the "hidden-agenda" side of economics, and tensions within the wake of Friedman's onslaught. And, in chapter 18, we provide an extended treatment of the uses of statistical methods found in the controversies, analyses, and policy positions of the era.

Overlapping Themes

Below, we look at the themes of Power and Ideas, *paying special attention to those that may be found in the highly philosophical chapter 17 and the policy and statistical methods oriented chapter 18.*

Theme 1. *Friedman integrated and reoriented the parts of economics (like where he recombined the theories of production and distribution, the theories of money and real goods, and moved from* modus ponens *to* modus tollens*) that were separated during its development after Adam Smith. Along this route, he set freedom as the highest goal and backed away from economic man axioms and gave emphasis to unconditional predictions.*

In chapter 2, this theme is introduced through discussion of Jeremy Bentham's felicific calculus, which lay the groundwork for the "economic man" axioms in economics and anticipated the prominence in economics of calculus and particularly utility and profit maximization with constraints; Ricardo's separation of the theory of money from the theory of production and his setting up the labor theory of value for Marx; John Stuart Mill's economics, where he separated the theory of production from the theory of distribution (or demand side), and referred to economics as a "science" of "a body of deductive analysis resting on psychological premises..."

In chapter 12, we note that Friedman gave attention to voluntary association, choosing payment according to the value of the marginal product of one's labor and capital. This theme relates to the Keynesian consumption function, Friedman's dynamic consumption function, and the flat rate income tax, as it bears on Reagan's tax reform.

Theme 2. *Friedman saw the use of statistics as a means to resolve differences of opinion among economists. Through this route, he dealt with the meaning of the word "science" in "economic science" by introducing a method by which they could achieve agreement as to the superior hypothesis.*

The topics we encounter in developing this theme include the meaning of science as in "economic science" with reference to the Nobel prize; the emergence of econometrics and the big models of Tinbergen and Klein; Samuelson's neoclassical economics, Kuznets's GNP accounting, theorems and technique, the so-called "as if" methodology, Friedman's variant of instrumentalism, and Boland's logical defense of Friedman's view on the axioms.

In the decades of Friedman's monetarist research, much was learned about the free enterprise system and the way the world works. However, this knowledge was not of a difference-of-opinion-resolving type. Neither it, nor the statistics that revealed it did much to resolve the differences of opinion among the economists of the time.

There is more to these differences than theoretical and empirical matters indicate. Following Arjo Klamer's Conversations with Economists, economists tend to gather in separate groups, agreeing among their group, but disagreeing with others. "Neat and elegant" models abound, passionately defended but often without much relevance or empirical content. The voluminous analyses of data fails to bring economists of different persuasions together. In the case of Lawrence Klein and Milton Friedman (pp. 71-82), for example, we note that Friedman was quite explicit in his critical comments on a Klein inspired, structural equations model as early as 1951. But after over three decades and extensive analyses of data by such luminaries as Klein and Friedman, differences in approach and perceptions were unreconciled. Serious attention to the monetary variable, or the absence of it, reflects ideological interests, benign unawareness, or suspended disbelief.

Noticing such differences among economists, Klamer said that economists actually look beyond the strictly theoretical and empirical arguments to justify their positions and attempt to "appropriate history," as it were, to persuade others of the legitimacy of their views. This led him to consider what is discussed in chapter 17 as Lawrence Boland's "hidden agenda" (philosophical, non-explicit items underlying the visible agenda) for economic research, and to reintroduce the notion from pages 134-135 of epistemological arguments ("those that justify or legitimize the vision on how to formulate arguments").

Among old and new visions, in Klamer's interviews with economists, we encounter asides to Thomas Kuhn's notion of a revolution in science, a paradigm shift in economics, and "gestalt-switches." Although the NCS and its rational expectations (RE) were the focus of Klamer's Conversations with Economists, he noted that Lucas and Sargent elevated Friedman as a major figure and claimed that "they use the language of modern economics."

On what Boland called the "hidden agenda," Klamer said: "The confidence in empirical arguments...is overemphasized, and the suppression of normative or philosophical discourse only serves to hide philosophical elements in economic discourse." Along such a line, Klamer said that the epistemological arguments of economists give a more accurate presentation of what they actually do, and "that divergent visions, or beliefs, do play a large role in disagreements among economists." Introducing the persuasiveness of argument in favor of a particular vision, Klamer noted Lucas's and Sargent's appeal to rigor and precision as a foremost standard of scientific argument which may have an appeal and fascination for young economists, and the importance of the vision conveyed through the use of language with respect to the elucidation of economic concepts.

Personal and social factors which operate through the economist's judgments gain in importance as the economists support one vision or another of the world. The personal factor, he said, is manifested in the passion of economists ("the commitment with which economists adhere to a particular point of view"). Defining passion as an expressed commitment to a point of view, Klamer pointed to Robert Lucas and said, "His persuasiveness can be partly attributed to his ability to convey his passion." Similarly he referred to Tobin in his commitment to neo-Keynesian policies and "his disapproval of the new classical policy conclusions." On the personal side of the social process, Klamer noted Thomas Sargent's reference to "his experience in the Army as a reason for his suspicion of government intervention" (compare Armen Alchian pp. 301-305), and pointed out that Alan Blinder recognized the influence of his "middle class, Jewish background..."

On the operation of social factors within the world of economics, Klamer made additional observations. Purely individual judgments in economics do not account for much, apart from their being shared by a group. "In general, a judgment carries force when it is shared by a group of economists and is discussed in the context of a recognizable research *program."* Divisions in the world of economists can be quite sharp. They concern *"not only substantive ideas but the values and ways of arguing."* These divisions are controlled by a *"live-and-let-live attitude,"* which suppresses serious conflict by creating specialties and deferring to territories. Further, Klamer noted, *"One has to speak the technical language of economists to get their attention: empirical arguments, uncertain as they may be, are a necessity."*

All of these issues—the distinctiveness of Friedman's paradigm, and the personal and the social factors mentioned above—come up in chapter 17. Friedman, in contrast to the establishment economists of his time, exposed himself to criticism and cut broadly across the specialties. There was not a lot hidden in his research agenda. Early on, for a research orientation of wide scope, Friedman worked out the *"indirect approach."* He presented his highly controversial 1953 essay on a philosophy of science with respect to economics (chap. 4). Not much later, Friedman was quite explicit about the often suppressed ideological connection when he set *"freedom"* as the highest goal with reference to the choice between the socialist and the capitalist ethic (pp. 151-152).

There was confidence in the persuasiveness of Friedman's argument, to be sure—whether in devising a statistical procedure, or in proceeding with the publication of the 1953 essay against the advice of his friend Arthur Burns (p. 164). Indeed, from Friedman's statistical background, the war-related Statistical Research Group, and the late 1940s and early 1950s essays onward, there was a definite vision of what economics as a subject should be like. Further, Friedman not only accepted the language of economists and central parts of the mechanical apparatus of economics which was passed along by Marshall and the later Keynesians, he also showed expertise in devising statistical procedures, advancing Marshall's treatment of the demand curve, presenting a dynamic consumption function, and introducing liquidity preference with overshooting. To be sure, technique was important to Friedman's achievements, but it was never elevated to the primary role. He said, *"The test of a theory is its value in explaining facts, in predicting the consequences of changes in the economic environment. Abstractness, generality, mathematical elegance—these are all secondary..."*

Theme 3. *Friedman's system was "realitic"—favoring theoretic statements about the way the world works rather than technique and mathematical elegance.* There were different readings of Alfred Marshall, a principal figure of neoclassical economics (pp. 55-57), by such diverse economists as Galbraith and Friedman. Friedman's different reading of Marshall tied into the *"realitic"* theory some associate with Marshall and Keynes, and that we associate with Friedman.

Returning to the topics of chapter 2, Marshall translated Mill's economics into mathematics and set on its course the Cambridge method concerning static relations and what Friedman saw as an engine of analysis. Along this latter line, Marshall is said to have sought static relations that were to be combined with a "realitic" (sic) approach.

Marshall and his method resurface in chapter 11, where we see it at Keynes's hands. Hession, to whom we refer in chapter 11, touched on complaints by post-Marshallians about the obscurities in Marshall's work. As the obscurities were removed, the "realitic" flavor of the economics was lost. We see a parallel with Keynes, as the dynamic flavor of his work yielded to more static formulations.

It remained for Friedman to bring back the "realitic" and to extend it. Friedman treated Marshallian and static Keynesian statements of schedules in combination with an analysis of money. The first was a statement of position and the second the statement of motion not found in economics before Friedman. He said, in discussing aspects of his own work:

> But Keynes was no Walrasian seeking, like Patinkin, and to a lesser extent Tobin, a general and abstract system of all-embracing simultaneous equations. He was a Marshallian, an empirical scientist seeking a simple, fruitful hypothesis. And his was a new, bold, and imaginative hypothesis, whose virtue was precisely how much it could say about major problems on the basis of so little.

Theme 4. *Friedman gave his theoretic/empirical economics special time frames, distinguishing between the permanent and transitory components of the time series (also between trends and cycles in business conditions). These come forward in Friedman's monetary theory and empirical research where monetary disturbances play a main role in the cyclical instability and in other instances via shocks to the economic system; monetary disturbances are not the only class of episodes that must be allowed for in Friedman's analyses and his statement of a stable money demand relation, which came in chapter 3 (p. 79) and which reappears in chapter 14.*

Theme 5. *Friedman viewed equilibrium, an important topic in economics (pp. 81, 84, 91), as a time trend, distinct from a mathematical solution or even the idea of a balance in supply-demand constructs as common in economics. This is an empirically oriented extension of mathematical solutions to static equations.*

Friedman's equilibrium comes in the long run where the economic system is relatively free from monetary shocks and other episodic changes. In this instance, we arrive at a Walrasian equilibrium (the end to a long period of adjustments). Walras's system of equations, and unknowns comes into its own, when the economic system is freed of monetary and other episodic disturbances. In this secular, equilibrium state, the expectations of economic agents are rational. Even so, there is change in the sense of movement along growth paths for stock and flow variables. Moreover, in coming to equilibrium following disturbances, some sectors of the economy adjust more rapidly in the formation of expectations than others, plus the structure underlying the formation of inflationary expectations shifted in the U.S. and the U.K. in the mid 1960s (pp. 447-545). This was such that agents came to react more quickly to information bearing on inflationary expectations. Additionally, we point out in chapter 16 that the structure underlying the formation of inflationary expectations shifted again in the mid 1980s.

Theme 6. *Viewing Friedman in the perspective of the British tradition, his work was an antidote to Keynesian economics and was path breaking. It offered a reversal of the trend in Britain that was set on course in the 1920s and symbolized by the Labor party's 1945 election victory (pp. 419-425).*

Recalling the British connection (chap. 14), there was the change in the earlier trend in Britain under Thatcher's leadership. The role of monetarist thought was present in that leadership. Also, Thatcher rejected Marx's theory of the long-run failure of the market economy.

Paralleling the experience with Thatcher, there was a reversal in the U.S. of trends in government that were set on their course by the Great Depression and the shock of the Depression itself on society's outlook, in combination with Keynesian economics. Attention was given to the roles of Friedman's monetarist thinking and what may be called supply-side economics (chap. 16). The income tax, the tax and transfer powers of the government, and growth of the governmental and private sectors of the economy received attention.

Theme 7. *The failures of the Keynesian era were failures of the middle ground between the political left and right of Hotelling's line. In chapter 8, we encounter the failure of the middle, as the culmination of the Keynesian era. The unemployment crisis first faced by Keynes in the '20s was renewed in the '70s as a combination of inflation and unemployment. In chapter 11 we go back to the ideas on the monetary revolution of this century with attention to Keynes, Friedman, Hicks's five act drama, and the failure of the middle route between the Marxist's and market solutions to unemployment.*

Confronting the inflation/unemployment crisis as a symbol of the failure of the middle, we see the increased acceptance of monetarist and libertarian, right-wing ideas about freedom, markets, the individual, taxes, the distribution of income and social mobility which appeared on Thatcher's agenda and Reagan's.

Theme 8. *Friedman's Chicago school was a distinct school centered at the University of Chicago in roughly the third quarter of the twentieth century. Friedman's emphasis on the purpose of economics and the inadequacies of the theories of monopolistic and imperfect competition as positive economics extended his influence to areas beyond his immediate research and writing.*

Friedman's influences at Chicago were extended to an area that he did not himself participate in, namely antitrust law. Principal people involved in this extension were Stigler, Aaron Director, and, particularly, Robert Bork, through his writing on antitrust law. We see Bork's writings as another link between ideas and their impact.

A Sweeping Review

In Power and Ideas *we portray Friedman as larger than life, for the study of Friedman and his work reveals a distinct analytical system on his part, with results that were implemented politically. This study of Friedman's own breadth, consistency, scholarship, and public involvement has, in turn, made possible a glimpse of theoretic/empirical/political economics in a consistent way, not made possible by the study of economics as a well-defined scientific body with considerable analytical and philosophical depth. This glimpse, in other words, would not have been possible without an examination of Friedman's scholarship and his involvement. The glimpse reveals further that, as we approach the last decade of the twentieth century, we have several analytical systems in economics with distinct political and philosophical underpinnings, rather than the one true monolithic approach which had characterized macroeconomics textbooks. Ideology (as it bears on freedom, the disbursement of power, governmental and private power, and markets) and benign attempts at political neutrality enter in a significant way in the respective analytical systems and in the choice of a system by students and others.*

As we have said, two features of Friedman's background contributed to his success in cutting across the specialities, his diverse educations, and his empirical science orientation toward a world where data are generated without regard for traditional specialities of economists (price theory, monetary theory, public finance, business cycles, econometrics, economic history, economic policy, and so on). However, these features are not sufficient to account for Friedman's achievements as we have reviewed them. They required a special, not entirely academic personality—an "outsider" with some confidence, a belief in the task at hand, a touch of audacity, a willingness to expose beliefs to hostile criticism, and an ability to endure the criticism (possibly even when mitigated by belonging to groups such as his "Chicago school" and the Mitchell-Burns NBER).

In Friedman's holistic view, economic statics is a statement of position and monetary theory is a statement of motion, as we have said. This is distinct from the two-track "micro" and "macro" approach of the '60s and '70s. The statements of motion extend to the analysis of business cycles and the distinctions Friedman drew between cycles (transitory change) and trends (more permanent components) in time series data. As chapter 18 will indicate, episodic change and psychological time entered in Friedman's holistic view as well, both in relation to the treatment of expectations on the part of the economic agents and in relation to economic policy.

This text could end by viewing Friedman's impact and the changes signified by the Big U-Turn (Part V). For some readers the story may be finished there. However, we present the "Epilogue" to Power and Ideas *because a story about ideas and their impact has been told. We continue the story in order to bring further light to aspects of Friedman's personality which made it all possible, to conflicts in economics, to Friedman's economics as viewed in terms of the criteria of interest to science philosophers, and to uses of statistical methods in economics. We also examine the positions of econometric critics, who set standards for economic policy without revealing either the economic theory or the policies behind their approaches.*

In Friedman's orientation there are no facts without theory and no theory without facts; no policy without theory and no theory without policy. This is in contrast to much in economics, and to the theoretical econometrics which was initially noted in the schema on page 70. We may recall that the respective roles of economic theory and probability with its heavy philosophical emphasis were uppermost in obtaining the classification. The former gained its significance in Friedman's case as an instrument of prediction and as argument in support of a policy outcome. It further gained significance by its presence in the more traditional line of econometric thought and by its omission in Hendry's and Ericsson's "econometric approach."

Probability gained significance as a criteria for the classifications (p. 68) in terms of the distinctions between "actuarial probability" and "uncertainty," in the case of the NCS, and the more encompassing "personalistic probability," in the case of Friedman. This was compatible with Friedman's holistic view extending to prior knowledge of history, episodes, the data, the economics, and the policy.

Chapter 17
Beyond Convention

Convention is a conditioning and stabilizing force, governing, to a large degree, individual behavior and social and professional practices. It conserves and thus protects ideas, practices and beliefs rooted in earlier developments. The word "convention" refers to usages, standards, customs and practices, among other things. Convention is often in conflict and in friction with change, whether slow and unnoticed, or rapid, as in the case of some episodes and crises. Convention is often so accepted that it goes undiscussed, unspecified and taken for granted, as in the case of the "hidden agendas" of economic research.

Three separate views of social change and convention are present in the current discussion of economics. First, there is the concept of "historicism," where change is predetermined by the course of history (pp. 332-333). Next, at the other extreme, we have the atomistic individual of neoclassical economics, where human behavior is not influenced by the institutions surrounding it. The hidden agenda behind this view also holds that the reverse is true; the institutions are not affected by the individuals. The third view is found in the institutional individualism we associate with Friedman. There, the individual has some choice about the social and economic changes he or she makes. In turn, the individual is influenced by society. Thus, Friedman backed away from economic man concepts implying the atomistic individual, providing an unconventional alternative to the conventional economic man concepts.

A main focus of ideas, convention, and control through economic policy has been placed in the present work in three perspectives. First, we introduce the sweep of history ushered in by the events of 1776. It was the era of high capitalism following Smith's great work and the free trade arguments of Ricardo, influenced by the countervailing power of Marx's *Das Kapital*, Marx's and Engels's manifesto, and the orthodoxy of capitalism which followed with Marshall's efforts. In Marshall's era and in his work, so much could be and was taken for granted in the world (such, as the conventions of the gold standard, work effort, and a balanced budget on the part of government). Second, we look at the three score and more years ushered in by WW I, the loss of innocence about gold, Keynes's attack on the omission of the short run in neoclassical economics, the Great Depression, and the introduction by Keynes of a managed financial system—partly as a compromise between high capitalism and Bolshevism. Third, in an even more telescoped period, we present the failure of the middle ground of Keynesian economics (symbolized by high unemployment, inflation, and the breakdown of Keynes's labor standard), and the U-Turn (the countervailing ideas of Friedman's monetarism and freedom mainly, and the shift to the political right as symbolized by Thatcher's government and Reagan's presidency).

The complexity of convention and change in a field like economics may be compounded for a number of interrelated reasons—(1) because the study deals with society where social change takes place; (2) because social change as it relates to economics has an ideological dimension (e.g., as illustrated by the choice between the socialist and capitalist ethic, pp. 151-152, and/or the widely held Marxist/academic view of change called historicism); (3) because the conserving function of convention extends to the personalities of individuals and specialities they adopt; and (4) because the leadership in the wave of change and the lags in adapting to change may vary as to individuals, vested interests, cultural/religious-group activity, and ability to perceive and recognize change.

Indeed, the possible number of permutations and combinations of groups and individuals representing or promoting convention and change is quite large. Consequently, for our purposes we will limit the analysis to the following: the heterogeneous makeup of American society, the historical/cultural distinction of the Jew, the possible personal role of the individual with respect to change and groups, normative and revolutionary change, neoclassical economics as convention, and Friedman's entry into economics. In this last, he was an "outsider" (pp. 107, 145). As we have already stated, he and Keynes were the monetary revolutionaries of the 20th century in that they recognized monetary crises and offered new theories for dealing with them (chap. 11). Friedman moved counter to convention very much—both as an American with Jewish background and in offering a systematic, dynamic, analytic system of economics with implications for economic policy.

Friedman's was a high time for economics in the U.S. and for those in economics of Jewish and European background. In the first case, the breakdown of the gold standard, the Great Stock Market Crash of 1929, and the Great Depression combined as economic phenomena to raise ponderous questions about economics, society and the inherited economic system. These questions combined with the rise of the U.S. in the interwar and post-WW II years as a great power. In the second, the historical bent of the Jew toward both commercial and intellectual endeavors and a heightened social consciousness combined with developments in the early 1930s to direct Friedman and others toward the study of economics. More ordinary Americans of middle-class origin were less inclined toward the intellectual pursuit and economics, to be sure. In the America of an expanding economic frontier and abundant natural resources, the larger matters of the day seemed less relevant to the economics that was so much a British and European subject before the post-WW II years. For Britain, economics was part of the early developments along the Clyde River (pp. 41-45), the repeal of the corn laws (pp. 48-49), and, ultimately, the business of running a great empire with London as a financial center.

The '20s and the '30s were a time of change, reaction against convention, new ideas, and adaptation to change. Frisch, the early Nobel laureate (p. 71), spoke of the need for discovery of "regularities" to help society adapt, though Frisch hinted at socialist planning in their use. Others have simply noted social/political efforts at adaptation where an economic problem or crisis in the policy sphere occurs which calls for a change in argument underlying policy and in policy. There has been the question for positive economics of choosing among alternative theories about moving toward a goal society wishes to achieve (p.112, 153). To be sure, we have pointed to some quite broad alternatives about change, extending to Marx's historicism and to Thatcher's denial of it as she faced up to reversing the socialist trend in Britain.

When social change was first recognized by Plato, the Greek humanitarian, he observed the unhappiness of the Greeks and sought as the good state one where society would be held in place to conserve the ways of the past. Aristotle, on the other hand, opted for allowing change to take place and for an open society with its accompanying difficulties and rewards (pp. 335-336). In the 20th century, we have learned that convention, holding society in place, concerns many unspecified, undefined, unexamined, and otherwise taken for granted things, whether for society as a whole, or for a special area of study such as economics. There, individuals' adherence to convention holds the subject in place and imposes resistance to new ideas so that the initial area of study is not always in a state of flux. Here, convention prevents the subject from drifting into boundlessness, while slowing its professional acceptance of new ideas.

In times of change, counterargument, and their accompanying stresses, we often come to search out and examine the foundations that we have taken for granted. As a consequence of the phenomenon and its recognition, we have in economics what Lawrence Boland called "the hidden agenda"—the below-the-surface, usually unexamined and undefined rules. In economics, those who, like Boland, have dealt with this unexamined, undefined dimension have been called methodologists. As arose in our discussion of Tjalling Koopmans, the subject of methodology is unpopular in economics but it gains visibility when reexamination of the subject itself becomes important. From this reexamination, there is the hope that new understanding will come about. In the present case of the methodologists, Boland in particular, there has been attention to the methodology of neoclassical economies and to the criteria economics should meet to gain the status of acceptable science. We see Friedman's economics as meeting these criteria.

Along these routes of convention, friction, countervailing power, and the criteria for acceptable science, we reintroduce and extend five themes of *Power and Ideas*. They are: Jewish conventions at a time of rising U.S. prominence in economics; Friedman's style as a person and as an outsider with attention to orthodoxy and revolutionary change; normative and revolutionary change in science and in economics; neoclassical economics as conventionalism; and Lawrence Boland's criteria for economic science which we relate to Friedman's economics.

The 1930s and '40s: The Jewish Connection

As introduced in chapter 1, the major migration of Jews from Eastern Europe to the U.S. occurred in the decades just before and after 1900, and included Friedman's parents. It also included Friedman's friend Arthur Burns, and his associate from the NBER Simon Kuznets, as noted on various occasions. By 1980 six full Nobel prizes, including one each to Friedman and Kuznets (p. 99), had been awarded—all to Americans, and of the six recipients two others were of Jewish background.

In the broad perspective we seek, the Jewish historical inclination toward intellectual achievement combined in economics with the Jewish involvement with capitalism. The Jews thrived in its presence, opposed the systems' ideology for the most part, and viewed as antisemitic the prospect that they invented capitalism. By 1911, Werner Sombart's controversial book *The Jew and Modern Capitalism* had first appeared in Germany, and by 1919 a disturbing intellectual on the American scene had published "The Intellectual Preeminence of the Jews in Modern Europe."[1] All of this occurs near the end of a sizeable Jewish population movement to a relatively hospitable environment in the U.S. during one of the country's most open and unrestricted periods of development.

Werner Sombart's thesis was that the Jews invented capitalism. For this, however, they wanted no credit. Apart from dealing with a delicate topic for its day, the scientific criticism levied against the book suggested that Sombart had no knowledge of Jewish and religious philosophy before undertaking the work, that he did not know Hebrew and thus used secondary sources, and that the sources tending to invalidate the thesis of the book were inaccessible to Sombart.[2] Perhaps more in line with rabbinical authority and the thinking of the day were views expressed by Friederick Schweitzer.[3] He pointed out that a search through the Talmud (the written text containing the history, moral teachings and practices of Jews)[4] reveals a broad understanding of the rabbis in matters of currency, loans, banking practices, and trade, plus a keen mathematical sense, but that any such notions are more than offset by "warning in the Bible and Talmud against the acquisition of wealth for its own sake."[5]

Thorstein Veblen attributed Jewish intellectual achievements to the role of the Jew as an outsider—to the Jew in the alien gentile world. In that position, the Jewish intellectuals were made to realize the make believe character of both Jewish and gentile cultural foundations. They were thereby more able to appreciate the facts as they are. Thus, their peculiar intellectual position was due to their character as outsiders.[6] Following Marx's ideas, Paul Samuelson noted the guidance of the material conditions of making a living in shaping the "superstructure of ideology and analysis and choice of subject," and then proceeding along Veblenian lines. He noted, "The Jew, as a stranger, is sometimes alienated from the culture he is in, and therefore he's more critical."

We emphasize this cultural conditioning with respect to more than just religion. The two are not unrelated, but many, like Friedman, moved in a more secular world. Howard Sachar's observation is perhaps supportive. Calling attention to scientific discovery, Biblical criticism, Darwinism, nationalism, and Marxism, he noted they are all responsible "for widening the ever further gap between 'faith and reason'..." In the "age of materialism," he said, an antireligious point of view was proof of one's intellectuality.[7]

Whatever the explanation, the impact on economics of the Americans with roots in the Great Migration (pp. 14-21) and Jewish background was reinforced in the 1930s by the westward movement of many Austrian economists. However, the impact of these groups was, by no means, received harmoniously. The movement in the 1930s included John von Neumann, who began early work on game theory, and Oscar Morgenstern who, as director of an institute for economic research, employed Abraham Wald.[8] Von Neumann obtained a permanent position in the U.S. in 1931, but Morgenstern did not leave Austria until after the Nazis entered Vienna in March 1938 and dismissed him from the University and his Institute as "politically unbearable."[9] On Morgenstern's initiative before he departed from Vienna, and that of Ragnar Frisch, Alfred Cowles extended an invitation to Wald to become a member of the early Cowles Commission in Colorado Springs. Morgenstern himself later secured a position at Princeton with half of his salary paid by the Rockefeller Foundation for a three year period.

The Cowles Commission, which began at Colorado Springs and moved to Chicago in 1939, enters our story through two of its roles. First, it was a center with a mathematical and philosophical orientation which conflicted with Friedman (pp. 84-87). Second, it was the home of European and other economists who, with some exception, conflicted with Friedman. Although Abraham Wald entered the intellectual world of the U.S. through the Cowles Commission, his ties extended to the Hotelling/Wallis, war-related SRG (pp. 155-159). Wald accepted a position offered by Hotelling "on a grant from the Carnegie Foundation."[10] This Hotelling stream of thinking, as previously recounted, went with the assistance of Friedman, in a different direction from the more strictly European influences at the Cowles Commission.

Friedman and his cohorts with ties to Mitchell, the National Bureau and the SRG were in conflict in part with the later immigrant influence coming through the Cowles Commission. Recounting the story of general equilibrium analysis in economics, Roy Weintraub identified the Cowles Commission with mathematical economic theory in the U.S.[11] Particularly, a stream of thinking that came together under the Cowles Commission influence and was more strictly mathematical and econometric, along the lines of the early Tinbergen and Frisch influences. Jacob Marshak was made Research Director for the Cowles groups at Chicago in 1943, where he brought Tjalling Koopmans and Lawrence Klein in 1944, and, among later Nobel laureates, Kenneth Arrow and Herbert Simon in 1947. Koopmans originally came to the U.S. in 1940 via a research assignment at the League of Nations in Geneva from 1938 to 1940. He had received his doctorate from Leiden, the Netherlands, in 1936. Kenneth Arrow was more of a pivotal figure than the other Cowles participants in that he came to his interest in economics through Columbia University and Harold Hotelling's courses in mathematical economics and mathematical statistics, as Milton Friedman did in part.

As discussed by Weintraub, the equilibrium story "is one in which empirical work, ideas of facts and falsification, played no role at all."[12] He related it to mathematical economics, but a strange ideological dimension enters with the mathematics at Chicago and with Oscar Lange, who was appointed assistant professor in 1938, with the view to meeting certain departmental needs. Lange, an outspoken socialist, had for the time "considerable expertise in mathematical statistics and econometrics and was expected to supplement [Henry] Schultz in this area." The event, however, happened earlier than expected. Within six months of his arrival, "the death of Schultz in an automobile accident made Lange the senior mathematical economist-econometrician in the department."

Of personal charm and broad intellectual interest, Lange's views on departmental appointments have been described as "similar to those of Marschak, Tjalling Koopmans and other members of the Cowles Commission who more or less succeeded to his [Lange's] role in departmental affairs," following Lange's departure for Poland in 1945.

By 1944, an intense struggle in the economics department at Chicago was underway between Frank Knight and his former students on one side and the Cowles Commission and its adherents on the other. Hence, the late 1930s and war years influence of the Cowles Commission departed from Chicago in 1953, setting the stage for Friedman's dominance. However,

Friedman's dominance at Chicago was underway before 1953. The key was the appointments of Allen Wallis and Friedman in 1946, and the later return of Friedman's friend, George Stigler.

Personal Style

Comments by Melvin Reder and Allen Wallis of the war-related SRG point to an early buoyancy and confidence on Friedman's part. We see, indeed, a cheerful and confident individual who went public with his economics after engaging in technical work.[13] He was willing to simplify and expose his ideas "to criticism of all kinds."[14]

Simplicity was definitely a quality of Friedman's columns for *Newsweek* magazine, where for years his influence reached a wide public long after others of his era had departed the scene. One of Friedman's co-workers of many years said, as many had observed, "Milton has a kind of simplicity that can be understood by almost anyone..."[15]

In 1980 as presidential campaigning was getting under way in the U.S., Milton Friedman came out (along with Rose Friedman) with the most popular nonfiction book on economics in history, *Free to Choose*, which coincided with the popular television series by the same title (pp. 265, 588). The book itself was in the bookstores by Christmas of 1979, following a schedule that started at the beginning of that year. It was a phenomenal sales success, with early reviews appearing in London, New York, and elsewhere.[16] Following the first year of sales, *Publishers Weekly* reported that the nonfiction work had appeared on the best-sellers list for 47 weeks, more frequently than any other book.

As part of his appeal, Friedman dealt with some traditional values, and offered novelty even as he was critical of "peer review" and the government. He established ties to the past, to Adam Smith, Alfred Marshall, or J.M. Keynes, and set freedom as a major goal of social organization. He related freedom to the development of ideas as well, and extended discussion of it even to the practice of the "peer review" system in economics. Indeed, Friedman's major breaks with the past—as with his famous 1953 essay and on the later subjects of the consumption function, and liquidity preference with overshooting—appeared outside the "peer review" journals.

On the granting of research funds by the National Science Foundation (NSF) in the U.S., Friedman wrote in his *Newsweek* column:

> How can extra funds for research do harm? First by converting "grantsmanship" into as important an ingredient of professional success as original and penetrating contributions to the economic

literature. Second, by channeling economic research into directions favored by dispensers of NSF funds. For economics, that has meant highly mathematical research—certainly appropriate research, but not to the exclusion of other kinds. Third, the funding has stifled innovation. "Peer review" favors established scientists and directions of research. (Einstein was financed by government to develop the theory of relativity—through his earnings as a clerk in the Swiss patent office. How would his project have fared, if it could have been formulated at all, under "peer review"?)

It is noteworthy that no NSF funds, or their equivalent, financed the great economists of the past—from Adam Smith to John Maynard Keynes—or most of those of the present. Seventeen Western economists have been awarded the Nobel Prize in Economics since 1969. Fewer than a handful had government financing for the research for which they were honored. The innovative ideas that have stirred controversy in economics since NSF funding of economics began two decades ago owe little or nothing to NSF funding.[17]

Simplicity, open debate, and freedom in the marketplace for ideas aside, the hallmarks attributed to Friedman by professional associates are confidence and "brilliant intuition." Karl Brunner illustrated the latter quality by drawing a row of squares with the first being where we are and the last where we want to go. Brunner said most of us go square by square, whereas Milton does an end run around all the squares and lands in the final one.[18]

Such characterization comes from Friedman's use of a total system of social and analytical thought, which rarely comes out full blown, because of his penchant for simplicity. Indeed, some who have debated him have characterized him as being "unscrupulous."[19] This, we say, must come from Friedman's world view and practice of making simple points that draw opponents into argument which has great complexity. As debate progresses, related but somewhat removed points may come into the debate, much to the dismay of opponents. Sir Roy Harrod, J.M. Keynes's biographer, associated Friedman with Keynes and a kind of cleverness when he described a 1951 visit to Friedman's seminar on the Chicago campus (p. 25).

A journalist, writing in London's *Sunday Times* shortly after Friedman received the Nobel prize, noted a conflict between "the undoubted respectability of Friedman's academic work and his simplistic (sometimes almost simpleminded) statements as a guru that characterizes the Friedman phenomenon." Continuing, the *Sunday Times* writer said:

Milton Friedman actually looks like a guru should: small and in his mid-60's, still very neatly built; bald too. But he lacks a guru's gravitas. He is smiling and obliging, talking without patronizing the interviewer, who can rarely ask a question he has not heard before.[20]

On an earlier occasion, another British journalist discussed Friedman in a column headed "Economics viewed as martial art." The occasion was a gathering of economists and politicians at a church in Westminster in the early fall of 1976 to hear Friedman speak. The journalist noted that those present included Keith Joseph (who later served in Margaret Thatcher's cabinet). He said he did not know much about economics but that he did relish "superstars of the trade engaging without restraint in mutual denunciation." Continuing he said:

> To become an economic superstar it is necessary to arrive at a fixed view of the world, learn to state it forcefully and cast unremitting scorn on those who disagree. It also helps to gain a reputation for wit, which Friedman achieves cleverly by speaking with an almost permanent smile [see photo, p. 188], making you think he is making a joke even when a careful analysis of his words reveals nothing apparently funny.

The British journalist then recalled asking Friedman why "he and other star economists seem to spend so much time slandering each other, effectively turning their craft into a combative branch of show-business." He reported Friedman's answer in closing:

> "Nobody wants to hear economists talk about subjects on which they are agreeing", he explained. It was almost the only thing he said which was manifestly incontrovertible, the empirical proof of which is in the crowds he draws at demonstrations of verbal fisticuffs.[21]

Also, along these lines of style in debate, we encounter the Keynesian, James Tobin, assessing Friedman's appearance at Yale University for a talk called "Yale versus Chicago in Monetary Theory" before a house of 500 people. Tobin said:

> It was quite interesting. I didn't get much involved at all in public, but we had a small private session afterwards. The thing I remember most about the occasion was that there was a very earnest, well-meaning graduate student who stood up at the big

meeting and asked Friedman politely: "In your model, money is the basic concept, and yet, you haven't ever told us exactly what money is conceptually. Could you help us understand it now?" Friedman cut the guy down in the withering way he can do by telling him that he didn't understand scientific methods. He said Newton didn't have to tell what gravity was; he only had to tell what it does. The same applied to money. That illustrates Friedman's methodology of positive economics which I think has done great damage.[22]

Continuing on Friedman's vision, Tobin said, "But I believe that Friedman had a crusade that he was pushing all over the world, not just in the profession. He saw the big picture, and the big picture was right for him."

As these observations on Friedman, his style and the larger view of his work reveal, Friedman was a complicated subject who used brilliance and simplicity to achieve success in debate and public visibility in the name of his cause. Along the lines of an earlier comment made by A. Kemp (p. 178), this aspect of Friedman's work is revealed further in a bit of dialogue that appeared in an interview with the *Wall Street Journal* economics writer, Lindley H. Clark.

> *You're writing a book called "Milton Friedman: His Life and Our Times." How is that going?*
> I haven't finished it. I've got a lot of material written, but I'd hate to promise that I'll finish it. I found after I got into it that Mr. Friedman is a more complicated subject than I'd realized.
> *He's probably the single most famous economist in the country. What accounts for his fame?*
> He has a brilliant mind. He gets to the heart of a subject right away. He's certainly the most effective debater I've ever watched. No one who knows the kind of debater he is will willingly go up on the platform with him. The man is simply too brilliant.[23]

So brilliance and nontechnical features combined in Friedman to assure extraordinary success in economics in combination with unusual public visibility. We may measure this visibility using a sample of six economists selected by *NY Times* writer Leonard Silk,[24] and counting the length of space in inches taken up in the *New York Times*, over a period spanned by the awarding of the Nobel prize in economics from 1969 through 1982. The index shows Friedman, Samuelson, and Galbraith getting the most attention, with the attention to Friedman increasing with the passage of time. Overall, the attention devoted to either Friedman or Galbraith surpassed that of the others in every year but one. In that year Samuelson received the Nobel prize. Although Galbraith was a favorite of the *Times* as being newsworthy, Friedman overall met the standard Galbraith set and achieved the maximum visibility for any year.

Normal and Revolutionary Change

In the 1960 and '70s a philosopher of science named Thomas Kuhn gained attention by discussing the nature of scientific revolution. His influence extended beyond the confines of the philosophy of science to discussions about economics. Of special interest, in drawing on Kuhn, however, we encounter canons of theory choice during a period of rapid change, indeed "revolution," in a science.

Similar canons came up earlier as Friedman was singled out among the main figures in the British tradition in economics (chap. 2). In addition, authors in the area of the history of economic doctrine and methodology have moved to single out Friedman for having gone beyond conventional methodology in economics and for having moved it more along the lines of contemporary science.[25] To be sure, the attention to Friedman on the part of methodologists in itself meets one of the canons of revolutionary change.

Kuhn began his work on the nature of scientific revolution by defining "normal science" and discussing the nature of a paradigm. The meaning of the relatively vague concept of a "paradigm" was later extended by two new definitions for "exemplars" and "disciplinary matrices." "Normative science," Kuhn says, "means research firmly based upon one or more past scientific achievements, achievements that some particular scientific community acknowledges for a time as supplying the foundation for its further practice."[26] Elaborating on the subject, Bruce Caldwell said, normal science "is the hallmark of science, it allows progress because the legitimate areas and methods of investigation are clearly spelled out." Also, it requires the existence of a paradigm.[27]

By the concept "paradigm," Kuhn meant "some examples of actual scientific practice—examples which include law, theory, application and instrumentation together—[which] provide models from which spring particular coherent traditions of scientific research."[28] Along this line, Caldwell said, "The concepts of normal science and paradigm are intertwined." Continuing he said, "the archetype of mature scientific activity is normal science research taking place within the framework provided by a paradigm."[29] An example of the "normal science" activity in economics is provided below with reference to neoclassical economics, though as we discuss below one may not wish to consider neoclassical economics a science.

As characterizes Kuhn's view of normal science, in any case, we encounter research that is "mopping up activity." In a phrase, it is an attempt to force nature into the relatively inflexible box that the paradigm supplies." Caldwell said:

> Normal science does not seek to produce novelties; rather it is 'puzzle-solving' activity—the scientists proceed according to a well-specified set of rules; solutions are usually anticipated in advance; such activity tests the scientists' skill with the tools he employs; and a failure to reach a solution to a particular problem usually is taken more as a reflection of the scientist's competence than of the nature of the problem or methods used. In addition, it is through 'doing' normal science that a scientist learns the methodological, quasimetaphysical, theoretical, and instrumentational assumptions of his discipline; that is, those rules and values which are accepted within his own line of work. It is important to understand that little of that education is conscious; it occurs slowly, and over time, and is a result of scientific activity itself.[30]

"Exemplars," as related to the extended meaning of "paradigm," are "concrete, technical problem solutions which the students of a particular discipline encounter in getting their professional education." Also, as a part of the extended meaning, "disciplinary matrices" are "the symbolic generalizations, models, values, commitments, and exemplars shared by and which unite given scientific communities."[31]

Within normal science, departures from the regular arrangements, general rules, and usual methods may occur. These anomalies are basic to new discoveries. Nothing shattering to the paradigm occurs when they are of minor proposition and occurrence, and normal science proceeds. Even so, the anomalies may accumulate and emerge in a certain way so as to produce a crisis whereby, "much of the usual puzzle-solving activity breaks down."

The normal-science practitioners' initial reaction to anomalies is a defensive one. There is a resistance to change "which," Caldwell said, "serves a useful purpose in guaranteeing that 'scientists will not be lightly distracted and that the anomalies that lead to paradigm change will penetrate existing knowledge to the core'." As a crisis occurs, different attitudes emerge and research activity changes accordingly. In the crisis state there are competing articulations, expressions of discontent, a recourse to debate over fundamentals and to philosophy, and a willingness on the part of some to try anything.[32]

These developments set the stage for change, for "a 'gestalt-switch' in which a new paradigm emerges and a battle over its acceptability is joined."[33] It takes a new theory or approach to displace an older theory.

All of these developments are present in the Friedman Juggernaut. In particular, the crisis in Keynesian economics in the 1970s in the U.S. and Britain has been notably recounted and reviewed by various authors. The crisis was obvious from the predominant theory's inability to explain phenomena to which the theory had led to begin with. The phenomena included the coincidence of inflation, unemployment and ultimately declining productivity. In time, many recognized that "quick-fixes" for the unemployment problem on the part of monetary authorities and governments generally simply led to a compounding of the problems and recurring instability. The crisis, moreover, extended to the underlying philosophy about economics as a science, and to the uses of statistical methods and to econometrics, where reference is made to particular uses of statistical methods, multiple regression equations, and structural equations models of a fashionable sort.

An alternative to the Keynesian theory—and neoclassical economics—was provided, as variously outlined, by Milton Friedman. The new approach's fundamental, "gestalt-switch" is indicated by the presence of alternative provisions with respect to theory, uses of methods, philosophy of science, and the fact that methodological discussions emerged in leading journals.

Canons of Revolution

Canons of revolution call for a new paradigm that differs from the old, namely: (1) answers must be provided to anomalies that plagued the old paradigm; (2) there is often a new perception of which problems are relevant; and (3) methodological differences may emerge since a new paradigm dictates methods and standards of solution. The first of these canons was met when Friedman's theory served as an antidote to Keynesian economics (or, most notable, provided explanations and prescriptions for inflation, stagflation, and the economic instability associated with monetary policy in the Keynesian years before the Thatcher government in Britain and the Reagan presidency in the U.S.).

As to the second canon, the problem with the industrialized democracies became inflation, stagflation, and instability caused by government, where Keynesian economics addressed large-scaled unemployment and instability due to instability in capital spending, closely related volatility in expectations concerning the returns from capital expenditures, and inadequate demand for the full-employment output of goods and services. The problem of unemployment as witnessed in Britain in the 1920s and 1930s and in the U.S. in the 1930s, was addressed in greater generality, of course, by Karl Marx and Friedrich Engels.

Keynesian economics and its prescription, moreover, was thought of as a modest solution. A mixed government and business economy was to be a desirable compromise with the socialist prescription, plus it was accompanied by interest on the part of Keynesians to moderate the inequality in the distribution of income, and partly to favor consumption expenditures in relation to saving. Tax and government transfer payments were to be used in the latter endeavor. As inflation arose in the 1970s, the Keynesian prescription was most often incomes policies.

In contrast, Friedman's position was extremely different, as chapters 8, 11, 13, 15, and 16 should attest. Further, in reference to canons of a revolution, Friedman's approach brings with it alternative methods for data analysis, a shift of emphasis to new time frames during which the theory and mechanical apparatus comes into play, a breakdown of conventional ways of compartmentalizing economics and other related but new approaches. These features of Friedman's approach come out below, as we consider Lawrence Boland's treatment of neoclassical economics and recall Friedman's approaches to the analytical problems of aggregation and time in economics, and, in the next chapter, as we review and evaluate Friedman's uses of statistical methods.

The Hidden Agenda

To determine what neoclassical methodology and neoclassical economics are, Boland did more than simply look at what the economists said. Instead, he studied their works and he outlined attributes that a desirable theory should have. He took the idea of a research agenda, but he extended the agenda to include hidden items as well as the visible ones. The "hidden agenda" items were those taken for granted but that become relevant because they deal with the question of why the economists do what they do.[34] Along a related line, Arjo Klamer dealt with the arguments economists offer in defense of their positions and found that confidence in the ordinary uses of logic and empirical verification is overemphasized in determining the positions economists hold with respect to neoclassical, Keynesian, and monetarist economics. He spoke instead of the larger visions economists hold and found hidden philosophical elements or beliefs that were relevant.

The "hidden agenda," as seen by Boland, contained two related but separate methodological problems: (1) the problem of induction (also in relation to the problem of conventions), and (2) the pervasive explanatory problem of individualism (notably with respect to the psychology of individualism). The hidden philosophical elements as seen by Klamer concerned the following: the style of argument (whether model "neat and elegant"); personal factors (passion or feeling about whether right or wrong, experience in the military, middle-class Jewish background, recognition of specialties in reference to a live-and-let-live attitude); and social factors (values, whether judgment shared with a group, the need to speak the language of economists, the role for empirical arguments "uncertain as they may be"). Above all, Klamer came to the conclusion that the persuasiveness of the total package is important in whether an economist's vision is to carry the day.

The art of persuasion gains in importance in "the absence of uniform standards and clear-cut empirical tests." There is some overlap in the way Boland and Klamer proceeded. In particular we look at visions, the persuasiveness of arguments and what comes forward in the light of the methodological evaluations undertaken by Boland. To be sure, we find the following in the present and the next chapter: the neoclassical position, as outlined by Boland, is lacking in its uses of methods and relevance; Friedman's economics side-steps some unresolved problems in order to deal with policy questions in the present; Friedman treated time appropriately as indicated by Boland's criteria; and, above all, Friedman's economics is persuasive, in the U.K. and U.S. as we have seen (chaps. 15 and 16), and in its uses of economic theory and statistical methods (chap. 18).

Neoclassical Economics

Neoclassical economics was the main body of economics following Alfred Marshall's *Principles of Economics*. We encounter distinctive strands in Samuelson (pp. 91-92) and in the economics of Don Patinkin. These are dramatically in conflict with the way Friedman proceeded, although the post-Keynesian group of the mid-1980s falsely identifies Friedman with the latter.[35]

Subsequent discussion of neoclassical economics takes us back to Adam Smith's friend and contemporary David Hume, the early philosophical skeptic who noted among other things the absence of a logical justification for the common belief that much of empirical knowledge was based on inductive proofs.[36]

Hume, Boland noted, was the first to recognize the problem of induction, as Friedman did in later years.[37] It is, notable, that no finite quantity of true single statements could prove a general statement. One never has all of the facts, plus judgment about them cannot be made *a priori*. The acceptance of factual evidence by which to judge the relevance and selection of one theory as opposed to another becomes in the end an act of faith in the empirical/factual approach. For Friedman, this act of faith resided in using the best evidence available (including evidence often obtained only indirectly), in a process of ongoing criticism of accepted theories, and ultimately in a social debate over the selection of one economic theory over another. This comes about where for Friedman economics is primarily a subject oriented toward economic policy, and where we see him moving along the lines of what we called a "realitic" (sic) theory in chapter 11. Earlier we associated this view of theory with both Marshall and Keynes, and we disassociated it from the two-track system in economics which has been symbolized by the labels "micro" and "macro."

According to Boland, J.M. Keynes saw his work as an alternative to classical economics (in which he included neoclassical economics), as introduced in chapter 11. Even so, after Keynes, the main bodies of economics moved along two tracks—the so-called micro- and macro-economics. As treated by Boland and as the convention in economics, the neoclassical part came forward partly as micro-economics. This so-called micro-economics was for many equivalent to what Friedman called price theory. Its most basic parts, as variously reviewed, consists of (1) analysis and utility functions which lead to demand curves, (2) the theory of the firm with production functions and supply curves, and (3) interactions of supply and demand which take place in a market (pp. 194-195). Theories of the market structure, as one may recall, are those of perfect competition and monopoly. There is also that of "imperfect" or "monopolistic" competition (pp. 310-316) but Friedman claimed it "possesses none of the attributes to make it a truly useful general theory."

As has always been the case, neoclassical economics says things about the performance of the economy overall, despite the label "micro" which arose with the two-track system of the Keynesian era and which is associated with neoclassical economics by convention. And, indeed, beginning in the early 1970s we encounter what we have called Lucas-Sargent rational expectations and the new classical school (pp. 68-71) which some address under the title *Rational Expectations and the New Macroeconomics* and which John Muth introduced under the heading "Rational Expectations and the Theory of Price Movements" where he was dealing with price theory.[38] Along this line, moreover, we encounter the "macro" aspect of neoclassical economics, as described by Boland, particularly in the hands of the vanguard theorists.[39]

The neoclassical stream, as described by Boland, has two branches—(1) positive economics as conventionalism and (2) the analytical theory variant of conventionalism. This latter was extended by Boland to include what we have called Lucas's and Sargent's RE and NCS. Via discussion of the "problem of conventions" Boland returned to notions about the psychology of individualism. In addition, the positive and theoretical aspects of neoclassical economics are not entirely distinct, although on the extreme approaches of the "naive" empiricism and avant-guarde theorists they come out that way. Paul Samuelson's efforts toward setting out the operational significance of economic theory, as taken up in chapter 3 (p. 89), fall between the extremes.

Positive Economics as Conventionalism

Boland reported in his 1982 book on a review of journal articles concerning positive, neoclassical economics. The review revealed a standard format consisting of a section entitled "The Model," another entitled "Empirical Results," and a subsequent "Summary." Boland's attention to the empirical part then shifted to naive empiricism. What is clear about it is that Boland is talking about standard multiple regression equations where analysts proceed immediately to compute regressions "including all variables that can reasonably be regarded as relevant." This approach is along the lines referred to by Friedman and Schwartz in *Monetary Trends* as "the prevailing fashion in econometric work." F/S, in contrast, believed as reported earlier, "that multiple correlations with many variables are almost impossible to interpret correctly unless they are backed by more intensive investigations of smaller sets of variables."

The Analytical Variant

Lawrence Boland saw his analytical variant of conventionalism as following very much the format set forth by Tjalling Koopmans of the Cowles research group.[40] It is essentially, Boland noted, "the format of many mathematics textbooks of its day." The paraphernalia consists of, he noted, "'buzz-words': 'proposition', 'theorem', 'lemma', 'proof', 'corollary', 'hypothesis', 'condition', and 'definition'."

The theorems (propositions) most commonly take an "if..., then..." form where the "if" part is the hypothesis, and the "then" part is the statement to be proved. Among the theorists in question, there is a "universe of discourse" which incorporates all the givens that can be used in implementing a proof. This universe includes the acceptable premises, "established principles of algebra or set theory," plus "all major principles [of algebra or set theory]" since these are in the "public domain" by demonstration. The idea is to go from the "if" to the "then" part of the theorem by obeying the rules of logic. Other statements may be introduced and proof provided within the framework of discourse.

The literature of neoclassical theory grew beyond the main corpus of its foundations and mechanical structure through "new contributions." As provided in publications these are "new" proofs. "Anything novel or informative," Boland said, "will have to be provided in the 'universe of discourse'." Continuing, he said, "What we are saying here is simply that economic 'theory' today is nothing but exercises in puzzle-solving..."[41]

Now, the analytical/empirical problem which Boland raised is that of making reference to some "contingent" proposition as opposed to just yielding "tautologies." A "contingent" proposition will permit the statement to be "falsifiable" in some way. Here, we may find interesting explanations. Some classes of statements are conceivably false (e.g., "strictly existential" statements such as "There will be a revolution after 1984") but still can not be refuted.

The "tautology," on the other hand, "is any statement which is true by virtue of its logical form alone." It is true regardless of the interpretation of its terms. "If someone offers us an explanation which is true purely as a matter of logical form alone (i.e., all cases have been covered and thus all counter-examples are rendered inconceivable), we are not going to be very impressed, except perhaps with his or her cleverness."[42]

Boland soon came to further consideration of the "if..., then..." form of statement, and whether statements of the form are always admissible. He offered an argument for why they are not and "thus why the basis of analytical economic theory is not as secure as we are led to believe." He raised questions about the circularity of argument, and then argued that whenever the "if" part of the statement is false, the "if..., then..." statement cannot be considered true. Boland concluded "the ["if...then..."] statement is logically decisive only when it is false."[43]

In closing on the analytical variant of neoclassical economics, Boland saw its retention by some who adopt the view that there are no final inductive proofs. For them, the final rendering of truth can be put off. The problem of induction, as introduced earlier, is a primary item on their neoclassical "hidden" agenda. For them, only a valid logical argument with all the facts can even be considered acceptable. And, of course, all of the past, current, and future facts are never available.

Samuelson: The Methodology of Tautology Avoidance

In Boland's review of analytical economics, he inevitably encountered Paul Samuelson's celebrated Ph.D. thesis entitled *Foundations of Economic Analysis*, which we introduced in chapter 3 (pp. 89-91). Its prepublication subtitle was "The Operational Significance of Economic Theory."

In his thesis, Samuelson unquestionably illustrated that axioms about maximization by households and firms brought into economics from mathematics a main body of calculus. In effect, he showed that a good bit of economics is "nothing more than the analytics of maximization (or minimization)." Thus it would seem it would be no small accomplishment for economists, albeit no extraordinary feat to have rediscovered calculus.

Beyond the introduction of mathematics, however, Samuelson proceeded in two ways—one, with respect to his correspondence principle, and, two, with respect to the matter of "a hypothesis about empirical data which could conceivably be reputed if only under ideal conditions." Boland remarked, "Samuelson's methodological contribution was to recognize that in order to avoid tautologies we must be concerned with the correspondence of the analytical model of an equilibrium to a dynamic process."[44] At this point the empirical question became one of equilibrium—the correspondence between the economic model and equilibrium.

However, Boland saw this correspondence principle as being subject to being transformed into another analytical issue. He saw this as meaning "that Samuelson's method for avoiding tautologies—requiring testability through a correspondence principle—can, in effect, make the original model untestable and thus is self-defeating methodology."[45]

Aside from the differences in political values (pp. 91-93), the time-rate-of-change and monetary features of Friedman's work (pp. 84, 96-97, 446), and Friedman's uses of statistical methods (pp. 69-79), there may appear to be only a subtle difference between Samuelson's correspondence principle and Friedman's indirect method. But even here, the difference is considerable—Friedman backed away from *modus ponens* and used apparatus as an instrument of prediction about price levels, interest rates, and the cyclical and trend (equilibrium path) components of the time series. In doing this, Friedman did not reject the main parts of mechanical apparatus of neoclassical economics, Keynes, and the Keynesians, nor did he attempt to construct theories or assumptions which were grossly at odds with behavior as we know it for the sake of conclusions or mathematical elegance. The assumptions regarding behavior about agents' knowledge of actuarial probability distributions and long-run equilibrium in relation to static constructions would be wide of Friedman's notions about the search for a truthful hypothesis, positive economic theory, and the "as if" methodology (p. 131).

The Problem of Conventions

The mechanical apparatus of economics, as variously indicated, comes about from *a priori* reasoning along the lines of mathematics. Much of this, as also just stated, comes from the introduction of the extreme value (maximization) assumptions, which may not be fruitless or misleading in

Friedman's dynamic context where statics enter as statements of position. With the precursors to the extreme value assumptions come what we have called "economic man" notions about behavior, including in relation to a psychological view of individualism, dating back to John Stuart Mill and even further. In contrast to this deduction and reasoning from axioms, induction enters as we move from particulars (data observations) to general statements. The problem of induction enters here (pp. 115, 129, 377 n26, 378 n67), where we never have all the evidence, such that the verdict is never entirely in. As Friedman said, "Observable facts are necessarily finite in number; possible hypotheses, infinite." The outright solution to the problem requires an infinity of particulars that are not available. Accepting empirical results as an arbitrator of differences about theories is an act of faith in the facts as a way or reconciling differences. Plus there is the search for a stable relation as we move from the historical past to the period of forecasting proper [equation (1), p. 79, and as discussed, pp. 541-544].

"Conventions" on the part of the neoclassicists enter here, in that the neoclassicists use conventions about theory choice instead of facing directly the problem of induction. They substitute the problem of conventions for that of induction.

According to Boland's view, the neoclassicists' choice of a theory is to be based on conventional criteria or acceptable truth, i.e., on conventions concerning the "truth" of the "facts." The criteria offered by the conventionalists focus upon a choice of theory which maximizes some desired attributes.[46] Boland listed these and found two problems, namely: (1) the criteria relate to the goal of choosing the one "best" theory or model with attention to agreement, and (2) there are still remnants of inductionism in the sense that one must not engage in conjectures and speculations nor "jump to conclusions until the facts are examined."

As Boland said about agreement, "our profession's reliance on Conventionalism to deal with the Problem of Induction has always put a high value on agreement, that is, on having our views accepted by our Colleagues."[47] The conventionalist's emphasis on agreeableness is present in a combination of positions: that tentatively competing theories are simply different ways of looking at the same thing; that one theory must be chosen best but the choice can be postponed, since choosing will take a long time and since all the evidence is not in; and that jurisdictional boundaries receive professional recognition for purposes of specialization (e.g., so-called microeconomics, macroeconomics, market-structures or anti-trust economics, monetary economics, and so on), all such that inconsistent and alternative views go along side by side.[48]

In contrast to the attention to agreement that marks the conventionalists, Popper and Friedman are set apart by their conjectural and speculative stances. For them, the boundary between science and pseudo science is not carefully drawn (pp. 110-111).[49] This itself hints of a tolerance of others' views, as does other aspects of Friedman's position: his setting freedom as the highest goal in his analytical system, viewing the price system as coordinating a satisfactory functioning of heterogeneous social groups with divergent social values and interest, and calling attention to the protection of minorities and various dissenting views. However, there is conflict between scientists and social groups as well, where Friedman and Popper view social science as "an enterprise built upon systematic criticism" and social debate.

The Psychology of Individualism

Some form of individualism has long been recognized as associated with market forms of social organization as opposed to collectivists forms. Boland alluded to a more specific form of individualistic psychology, however, which puts the individual decision-maker at the center of the social universe.[50] He saw "methodological individualism" as being high on the hidden agenda of neoclassical economics. According to it, only individuals are decision-makers in any explanation of social phenomena. In contrast, Popper promoted another form of individualism in his book *The Open Society and its Enemies*. Boland called it "institutional individualism" while pointing out that it does not accept any individualism-holism dichotomy. This institutional individualism is also present in Friedman's approach and sets him apart once again from the conventionalist's view in neoclassical economics.

Methodological individualism has the problem of explaining individualism in a world where institutions exist. First, the institutions (customs, habits of thought, conventions, institutionalized values) must not be left unexplained, and they must be explained in individualist terms. Second, the institution "must be responsive to the choices of every individual." Along this line, the irreducible minimum might seem to be the given psychological state of the decision-makers, which in turn relates to the idea that psychological states are *exogenous* to the model. Again in contrast, however, Popper's institutional individualism does not require individuals to have only psychologically motivated aims. Individuals may be identified with problem-situations and furthermore institutions may be creations of decision-makers.[51]

Individualism and Equilibrium

Retaining the psychological view of individualism as found in neoclassical economics requires the attainment of equilibrium by adherence to the model of perfect competition. There is the added problem, however, with respect to the retention of the theory of imperfect or monopolistic competition as a part of neoclassical economics (pp. 306-316), since this theory deals with departures from the model of perfect competition.

With attention to assumptions, profit maximization in particular, neoclassical theory as held by conventionalists requires all individuals to be maximizers, which can be true only if all markets are in equilibrium. The key element to yielding both the social optimum and the equilibrium is the total reliance on individual decision-makers and the inability of one individual firm or consumer to affect the price (i.e., "competition must be perfect").

In this context, any imperfectly competitive equilibrium (where the firm has some control over price) presents a problem. "The imperfectly competitive world," Boland noted, "seems to be based on an arbitrary institutional assumption that restricts competition." And this would not be allowed by the commitment to the individualistic program.

There are a couple of ways theorists can deal with the problem of disequilibrium, but the main one Boland called attention to was the adoption of a view of the world "where everything is in long-run equilibrium," which we encounter with the NCS (pp. 68-71). Boland said avant-garde theorists seem to have come to an agreement "that a realistic short-run neoclassical theory must involve disequilibria that cannot be explained away, yet the requirement of individualism must be retained."[52] Boland described the solution, as seen by the theorists, as "depending primarily on expectational errors as the prime source of divergence from full equilibrium."

What we have called Lucas-Sargent RE and NCS offered apparently conflicting reasons for being, namely: some subtle aspects of monetary policy and inflationary expectations; and the resolution of problems about individuals and equilibrium. Boland recognized that the NCS position "opens up possibilities for the further use of the mathematical techniques."[53]

Early on, the NCS's attention focused upon the ineffectiveness of monetary policy where it was a repetitive or countercyclical policy that could be expected to continue in the future,[54] but the controversial position of the NCS became the equilibrium modeling rather than the policy proposition.[55] We encounter equilibrium everywhere.

The NCS has expectations errors, as Boland said, but, most crucially for our earlier and later discussion, the NCS introduced the distinction made years ago by Frank Knight between actuarial probability as risk and uncertainty as incomplete knowledge (pp. 68-71). Via this route, the NCS introduced errors, misconceptions and mistakes to explain deviations between actual and trend magnitudes. Klamer said, "So the combination of perfect information and stochastic variables explains the continuous discrepancies of actual and expected prices and, hence, deviations of real output from its natural level." In other words, the arbitrary confinement of probability to Knight's notion of risk facilitated the mathematical usage, but puts the NCS in a position on probability that Friedman and many others rejected as outmoded usage.

The NCS's approach, in any case, is not Friedman's more modest approach. With reference to "the recently popular theory of rational expectations" Friedman said (with Anna Schwartz):

> In applying this idea, it is common to proceed on two assumptions: (1) that participants in whatever market is considered have "correct" estimates of the probability distribution of outcomes (itself something that is difficult or impossible to define objectively), so that on the average anticipations are correct; and (2) that errors of forecast in successive time units are uncorrelated.[56]

Referring to a particular episode, F/S said, it "brings out sharply the difficulty of giving a precise meaning to the first assumption, and the ambiguity of 'time unit' for the second assumption. For that episode, the relevant time unit is about twenty years—so that averaging out may take a long time." F/S concluded:

> The formulation in the theory of rational expectations of the ancient idea that economic actors use available information intelligently in judging future possibilities is an important and valuable development. But it is not the open sesame to unraveling the riddle of dynamic change that some of its more enthusiastic proponents make it out to be.

Of the more formal NCS approach covered by Boland, he argued "that as a solution to the methodological problem of disequilibrium it is an illusion, as it is based on the acceptance of Inductivism."

Friedman's Monetary Economy

Conventionalists, as described by Boland, substitute choice criteria in the choice of a theory, all in the absence of an infinity of particulars; and the advocates of the so-called theories of monopolistic and imperfect competition incorrectly thought of the attention to the homogeneous-product axiom as leading to a more general economic theory (pp. 194-195, 310-313). Via this route, the advocates were led to incorrectly view simplicity on Friedman's part as a rejection of their attention to generality.[57] But Friedman's push for abstraction, simplicity, and empirical relevance is simply different from adding detail, either in terms of variables on the right-hand side of a regression equation, or in terms of the descriptive accuracy of the homogeneous-produce axiom.

For Friedman, the simplicity issue was centered about a Walrasian versus a Marshallian approach (pp. 117-119), where Friedman made a twofold distinction: (1) the common one whereby Walras is viewed as offering a statement of general equilibrium (say, equilibrium in all product markets) as opposed to Marshall's partial equilibrium; and (2) Friedman's own distinction wherein Marshall is said to also have his mathematical system of many (say, m-1) variables and many unknowns, and wherein Marshall searched for a fruitful empirical hypothesis while Walras added detail via an elaborate mathematical statement. This first distinction is a common one and accepted by conventionalists, and by Friedman, but Friedman departed from the emphasis on elegance and detailed facts, added the fruitful-hypothesis dimension, and went on to criticize the Walrasian approach. Friedman said:

> From a Walrasian approach, "abstractness, generality, and mathematical elegance have in some measures become ends in themselves, criteria by which to judge economic theory. Facts are to be described, not explained. Theory is to be tested by the accuracy of its 'assumptions' as photographic descriptions of reality, not by the correctness of the prediction that can be derived from it."[58]

Early on—in combining interest in economic theory with interest in facts—Friedman not only reacted against the theory of monopolistic competition and the econometric model approach to separating the effects of variables and constructing large models (adding detail) before isolating the key variables to the analysis, as we recall below, but he asked what a theory of the real world would look like. The early hints he provided as he set upon three decades of monetarist research are contained in Friedman's 1950 essay on Wesley Mitchell, the 1951 discussion of the Klein model (pp. 80-81), and the 1953 essay on methodology (chap. 4). The 1950 essay mentioned "the dynamic adjustment of the economic system as a whole," the process by which "a change in the supply of money affects prices" and so on, "different capacities for adaptation," "empirical regularities," "evolutionary science," "cumulative change," and a "satisfactory theory of economic change."

The 1951 discussion took note of the 1950 essay and even said that Mitchell's original judgments with respect to "orthodox relative price theory" were invalid. In the 1951 discussion there is lament about the way variables are added to regression equations and the notion that the theory for the economic system as a whole will combine theory as a statement of position and monetary theory as a statement of motion. The key to the difference with Mitchell the empiricist on the price theory was that Mitchell thought in terms of a direct approach to empirical relevance of supply and demand schedules and price theory generally, whereas Friedman thought in terms of his policy-oriented, indirect, monetary-theory-of-motion, approach.

The Theory and Data Analysis

For Friedman, the economic theory (or mechanical structure used to generate a hypothesis) and the analyses of data are not independent of one another. As we reflect on Friedman's background and his early instrumentalist learnings (chap. 4), quite clearly we see an instrumentalist influence on both his uses of the mechanical structure of received economics and statistical methods, which we will discuss further in the next chapter.

Economic theory represents an explanation of the way the world works, but for Friedman it was also an argument in favor of an empirical hypothesis. Proceeding along such lines in reconstructing Friedman's approach, Lawrence Boland took note of two basic forms of valid logical arguments—those for something and those against. "Arguments for something are formally in favor of the truth of a specific statement."

The arguments Boland described have two parts: "(1) the purported validity of logical relationships between all the given statements and the statement [say, hypothesis] in question, and (2) the purported truth status of *each* of the given statements."[59] In this context, but also as discussed previously, "Standard logic provides only the means of 'passing' along the truth of all the given statements to any statement which logically follows from them." This "is valid only for arguments from the truth of one's assumptions to the truth of one's conclusions."[60]

These latter lines of argument are unsound in various ways by the criteria of Friedman's positive economics. Accordingly, Friedman and Karl Popper shifted attention to the predictive aspect of economic theory. Friedman viewed the static mechanical apparatus, as it were, as the engine of analysis. Its purpose is to generate a prediction or successful conclusion. There will be competing theories, but these are to be dealt with by testing the predictions of one against the other as we have stated (pp. 80, 116, 539) and illustrated (pp. 437-452, 455, 544-545, 547).

Continuing with Boland's critiques and Friedman's economics, we find that not only did Friedman shift the attention to *modus tollens*, his work dealt with additional problems of economic theory as outlined by Boland as well. Looking primarily at those main bodies of economic theory that have been variously called neoclassical, micro- and macro-economics, Boland saw some rather archaic views about economics as a science and the closely related problems of economic theory. These included the following: (1) those surrounding aggregation; (2) the necessity of microfoundations for macroeconomics (or vice versa); and (3) those problems concerning the role of time in economic theory.[61]

Problems of Economic Theory: Aggregation and Time

The problem of aggregation is simply that of combining parts into a whole. It gains attention after the publication of J. M. Keynes's *General Theory* (1936). In broad outline, Boland thought that Keynes denied the adequacy of the macrofoundations of traditional theory and thereby argued that microeconomic theory is *false*![62] After Keynes, however, we come to two separate tracks for economic theory—the traditional, so-called microtheory and the Keynesian macrotheory. The two-part explanation for the separate tracks is (1) that some of Keynes's followers considered neoclassical theory to be false and (2) that conventionalism attempted to avoid a life-or-death struggle partly by compartmentalizing the discipline.[63] Some traditionalists offered discussion of the microfoundations of macrotheory, but Boland saw the reason for this to be the belief that "the strength of Keynes's critique of microtheory would be defused by the embarrassment of an inconsistency in Keynes's position."

As suggested below, Keynes's theory was thought to contain more core elements of a dynamic theory than did neoclassical theory. In any case, what Keynes offered with one hand he withdrew with the other, and a neoclassical approach to incorporating Keynes's theory seemed mostly to just put Keynes back into the classical mold of static schedules.[64] At this date of the approach a matter of aggregation came about but it came up in other ways also.

In the early Keynesian period a diagram representing total spending in relation to income was put in place (pp. 83, 141-143). There the concept of income was that of payment for output and national income accounts developing in the U.S. were to supply the income data (p. 99). (The concept was that of totaling the value of output but with the avoidance of double counting.) What we end with is a building block with an aggregate demand schedule (consumption plus investment) that is similar to the demand schedule depicted in the Marshallian, pre-*General Theory*, supply-demand cross, as far as the Cambridge style is concerned (p. 455). It is different in that the quantity demanded in a market is a function of price (ceteris paribus, including income) in the Marshallian tradition, and, in

Keynes's case, aggregate demand is a function of aggregate income but with sticky prices (or sticky wages, p. 420, a special price). We agree with Patinkin and Leith, who referred to this development with respect to aggregate demand as representing one of the great episodes in economics.[65] However, for the purpose of setting forth Friedman's economics, both the price theoretic function and Keynes's are statements of position. Additionally, as introduced earlier (p. 418), this treatment of position is at odds with the two-track, micro/macro system of economics.

The matter of combining the parts and the whole is accompanied by the use of indexes. There are those for prices and quantities, and others as well where Milton Friedman in particular was able to relate the price change as movement along a Marshallian demand schedule to the cost-of-living index.[66] This relation, moreover, was shown to have precise meaning in terms of the very fundamental Slutsky equation found in price-theoretic economics (called micro in the two-track system), and to relate to analysis with respect to money and inflation rates for the economy as a whole.

As suggested by the dating of the terms of a price index and by what we have said about the emergence of Keynesian mechanics, a problem about the treatment of time in the theory comes center stage. It is that of specifying how time enters with respect to changes. Since the changes that occur over time in economics have been troublesome for analysts attempting to develop a theory of the way the world works, early developments in economic theory in effect locked-up changes over time. Thus, what Friedman inherited from the past was static apparatus, including the Keynesian apparatus, and a theory of money which Friedman saw as providing the basis for a more satisfactory theory of motion. We moved Keynesian mechanics along dynamic lines and extended the empirically inseparable theory of money along dynamic lines.

Boland reviewed some efforts at introducing time without suggesting much hope for their success in moving economics along the lines of an empirical science. He came up with criteria for an appropriate treatment of time, namely:[67]

1. Time must enter in an essential way.
2. The individual's knowledge or learning in relation to behavior must have a role. Hence, expectations enter, and Boland wanted learning to be explained by the theory.
3. The role of money enters as having some importance in dynamic analysis. As Keynes said, "*The importance of money essentially flows from its being a link between the present and the future.*" A stock of money balances tides one over from one pay period to another and serves as a means of dealing with an uncertain and often unforeseen future.
4. The treatment of money enters in relation to the liquidity preference demand for money and Keynes's treatment of decision-making.

5. There should be some path fixed by a stable relation, or by stable constants as in physics, though Boland drawing on Sir John Hicks reflected pessimism about the prospect for such a constant in economics.

Contrary to Boland's sense of pessimism and additional to the criteria for the appropriate treatment of time, we add that Friedman's economics meets all of the criteria, in some strong measure if not fully. We stop short of the full measure because it is not difficult to think of complexities with respect to the criteria, and of unresolved problems. For example, in reference to criterion 2, there is episodic change, learning, and Bayesian elements in Friedman's economics, which we have already introduced, and which come up in the next chapter. But Friedman's work does not combine what some writers have looked for with respect to evolutionary change and learning, which is a theory that explains non-repetitive evolutionary change as if it were internal to the model. Also, in reference to criterion 5, we encounter what we may call Friedman's constants, but these are not viewable as flat-out numerical constants (pp. 75-76), as we see further in the next chapter. They simply may be obtained following Friedman's indirect approach, where we find allowances for episodic changes and adjustments to the time series.

Friedman's Theory

Dealing with matters of both aggregation and time, Friedman proceeded differently from others.

1. First, as already noted, index numbers are useful in moving from Marshallian markets to the economy overall. Friedman's treatment of these is readily extended internationally when we introduce the price index for a market basket of goods in one country relative to that in another and when we relate exchange rates for the respective countries $(P_{US}/P_{UK})/(\$/£) = 1.12$ as in chapter 11 (pp. 421-422).

2. Second, Friedman did not recognize the ordinary labels "micro" and "macro" economics and instead referred to price theory and monetary theory. On the false distinction in his time, Friedman noted that price theory also deals with the performance of the overall economy. In addition, Friedman's economics treats the price system as a part of the system of political and economic freedom.

3. Third, Friedman's notions about the role of axioms support his viewing essential parts of neoclassical and Keynesian economics as apparatus for generating fruitful hypotheses. We have the "engine of analysis" which Friedman would trace back to Marshall (p. 455).

4. Fourth, Friedman's treatment of time in the respective price and monetary areas facilitated his bringing the two areas together. As stated on

various occasions, price theory, and Keynesian mechanics are statements of position. Monetary theory is a statement of motion and hence the main source of dynamics in Friedman's economics.

The money and credit aggregates relate most directly to income growth and to inflation (deflation) rates. Money is part of the asset structure (or wealth) which generates a flow of returns (or income). That is the way Keynes viewed it, plus the functions of money and motives for holding money are retained by Friedman (pp. 417-418). Income may grow because of population growth, capital accumulation, and technological change, all as conditioned by underlying political and social institutions. Thinking of income per capita (and population constant) we still have income growth. This can be a trend line (or "permanent" or quasi-permanent magnitude). Expressed as a time path, the slope of the trend line is the rate at which the money stock (or the base money underlying it, more particularly) can grow without causing inflation.

This income growth underlies the money demand curve in the static liquidity preference block (pp. 83-84, 445-449), but in its presence and that of money growth everything is in motion along equilibrium time paths. The income growth (also "permanent income") determines consumptions, $C = k(...)Y_P$. The permanent magnitudes may but need not be identical with expected magnitudes. Expectations are present as the economic actors look back into the past and extrapolate to a future time horizon (T). This may be expressed mathematically, so that the expression contains a growth factor, a, that can be estimated separately. In any case, a complementary method of empirical treatment concerning permanent income is through adaptive expectations models. Substituting into $C = k(...)Y_P$, along this line, Keynes's simple consumption function (a cross section view of consumption by households essentially) may be isolated—only when Friedman's formulation is imposed on the Keynesian supply/demand block, everything is in motion (technical appendixes to chap. 16).

The foregoing process is essentially the same as with the liquidity preference block, which we recognized in chapter 11. In fact, the rule may be generalized: let all stock and flow quantities change at the same rate and the ratios (say income velocity, Y/M, saving to income, S/Y, sales to assets, etc.), rates and price level (rate of interest, rate of return, and so on) are constant.[68] Here we encounter the constants addressed in reference to Boland's criterion 5, but we envision rates of change as slopes to trend lines, and see the great ratios as constants only after allowances for episodes and adjustments to the time series, which we take up in the next chapter.

Now, Friedman dealt with the technical matter of identification, noted the supply of a quantity of money and money demand, and noted that supply is mainly exogenously determined. As Friedman and Schwartz noted, there will be some feedback from income to money, but the causation from money to income dominated in the period encompassed by *Monetary Trends*. What makes sense is that the money stock was historically determined by the gold flows mechanism or the central bank. As taken up on pages 97-98 and 545, Lord Kaldor offered an institutional arrangement that would reverse this F/S historical analysis of causation. Such an arrangement becomes central to the post-Keynesian economics of the mid 1980s.[69]

Supply-side, money shocks and cyclical patterns for the money stock have been the main sources of instability in income growth and unemployment in Friedman's approach. Keynes saw money as the ultimate variable too, but shocks impacting directly on the liquidity preference demand were the source of instability (including in relation to capital spending). Here we touch on the omission in neoclassical economics that Keynes railed about in his attack on J. B. Say's law of markets (p. 597), which he saw as symbolizing neoclassical economics. Keynes had the changes working through shifts in money demand, interest rates and employment, including as can be shown with a Marshallian cross analysis.[70] Friedman modified the cause of instability and showed it to be mainly money supply. In doing so, he *partly* neutralized the basis for Keynes's attack on Say's law (pp. 58, 195, 417).[71]

Following Friedman's rule of constant money growth (pp. 412, 649), a main source of instability in the U.S. and U.K. economies is removed. Whatever the case, the income growth accompanying the monetary rule operates to move demand schedules in the Marshallian crosses, as incomes change, and supply schedules, as technology and productivity change. These changes have a parallel to changes in the consumption function in the supply/demand, Keynesian cross (the later appendix, p. 828).

In Friedman's theory, behavior follows along the lines of Popper's "institutional individualism." Episodes and non-repetitive events in general are main sources of changes in equilibria (including in secular trends), though once changes are set in motion reverberations appear as processes that are internal to the economic system. In such a system, learning on the part of the economic actors is important, decision-making is sequential in that there are adjustments to episodic change, and the theoretical perception of behavior by the economists is influenced too, as Boland recognized. Early on, as recognized, Keynes's background and perceptions of behavior and the uncertainty of expectations led him to become a subjective probabilist, such as would be compatible with these perceptions. Friedman's thoughts moved along similar lines as he shifted early in his career from the classical notions of probability to the subjective probabilist notions where probability is the language of uncertainty (p. 70).

Friedman's early background with Harold Hotelling led him to focus upon the distinction between the permanent and the transitory components in time series. These enter into the economic theory, and also become a possible means of lessening some troublesome statistical aspects of the analysis of time series, as well as achieving agreement with the common policy orientations with respect to growth and stabilizing cycles. The permanent or growth part has been mentioned in relation to economic trends. The transitory component becomes another name for cyclical instability (chap. 14).

Quite simply, what we note above are very specific roles for time in the price and monetary theories, and in the roles of those theories in explaining economic changes. In the presence of all of this, at Friedman's hands, we even encounter psychological time in the formation of expectations. In psychological time, the time dimension is not always a fixed unit of time, and change is not always repetitive like the swinging of a pendulum in the case of clock time. Rather, depending on circumstances, the "agent" looks back in time to earlier events and changes, and may, on occasion, look far back in time, depending on the nature or trauma of the episode at hand. In chapter 16 (pp. 683-687), the look back at the crash of 1929, at the time of the crash of 1987 is an example of psychological time. It comes up in the next chapter.

Perhaps even more amazing, with respect to a theoretical system that treats volatility and so much prospect for disturbance, we still have at the center of Friedman's approach a stable relation [equation (1), p. 79, or the idea of one and that of separating repetitive and nonrepetitive change], and we have the closest thing to stable constants ever considered by economics,[72] namely: a real income elasticity of the demand for money in the U.S and the U.K. of approximately 1 ($d \ln m(t) \cong d \ln y(t)$); the closely related velocity ratio (Y/M); the law of one price, symbolized by $(P_{US}/P_{UK})/(\$/\pounds) = 1.12$; and the saving-to-income ratio (S/Y) as treated in the appendixes to chapter 16. Along similar empirical lines, we have Friedman's law: "Inflation over any substantial period is always and everywhere a monetary phenomenon arising from a more rapid growth in the quantity of money than in output."

An Overview

Friedman's career was partly the outcome of some bold moves: that of bringing Harold Hotelling, a mathematical statistician, into the economics department at Columbia University in the early 1930s; and that of inviting Milton Friedman to take over the monetary portion of Wesley Mitchell's grand design for economic research in 1948, at a time when Friedman's interests, and teaching and research backgrounds were not mainly oriented in the monetary area. Pieces undertaken shortly after Friedman began his monetary research reflect a special orientation, a coming together of diverse elements, that anticipates the monetary research. These pieces were about Wesley Mitchell, the economic theorist, and the relevance of economics to prediction and policy, plus a discussion of the emerging Klein-type models. The "indirect approach" that characterized Friedman's uses of mechanical apparatus and statistical methods was partly evident in his "Marshallian Demand Curve" paper of 1949.

In the work which followed the visions reported in 1950, Friedman was by circumstances, training, and personality an outsider. The circumstances included his Jewish background, and the training under Hotelling and Mitchell. He had a vision, as Tobin recognized, and his confidence in himself was extraordinary. He was not satisfied with "half a loaf" in life, as his friend Burns had counselled.

Being of Jewish background in economics after WW II, with ties to the Jewish migrations to the U.S. before World Wars I and II was a boon. The Jew there was no outsider, as he had been in much of history. However, in his emerging right-wing liberalism (Friedman would say, "classical liberalism") Friedman was also an outsider among Jewish intellectuals who, as a rule, had predominantly left-wing leanings. Also, as James Tobin said, with the hindsight of the early 1980s, "the time was to be right for him." Allen Wallis had written of his confidence in finding solutions to statistical problems.

Friedman's was an audacious mind. It had a Talmudic cast. We see that it followed things to a logical conclusion.

Friedman embraced much that was traditional (the static apparatus of inherited economics), that could have led him to "puzzle-solving" activities. He instead struck out boldly into empirical study ("no facts without theory, and no theory without facts"). He wrote brazenly about methodology, published much outside of peer review journals, and proceeded to demonstrate his thinking about methodology by example. Viewing economics as a policy oriented study, as had Keynes, Friedman was a part of a revolution in theory and policy.

Friedman's and Keynes's monetary revolutions were helped along by crises—the first crisis in neoclassical economics to which Keynes reacted, and the second crisis for which Friedman's work was partly an antidote. Above all, Friedman's was revolutionary science in the Kuhn sense. Following Lawrence Boland's analysis, Friedman departed from the methodology we associate with neoclassical economics. It was truth-of-axioms-in-descriptive-sense oriented, carried the baggage of "methodological individualism" (the atomistic individual, or narrow interpretation of Crusoe on an island before Friday arrived), and retained the problem of induction such as to postpone the final verdict on the theory until all the evidence was in.

Friedman, on the other hand, allowed for institutional individualism whereby individuals are both influenced by society, conventions, and circumstances, and in turn influence the society, conventions and circumstances; and sidestepped the unsolved problem of induction. Following him, we proceed as if we know what the truth is but we really do not know it. Rather there is a process of theories competing against theories, of destructive criticism, of ongoing social debate, and of reliance on one approach over another.

In the conventional approach there is (1) the methodology of tautological avoidance, (2) the problem of conventions, and (3) the problem with the psychology of individualism. All of these concern a preoccupation with equilibrium and special difficulties in moving neoclassical economics along the lines of an empirical science. The first recognizes a concern over the correspondence of the analytical model of an equilibrium to a dynamic process. The second substitutes conventions for dealing with theory choice instead of facing the problem of induction. The third comes from putting the individual decision maker at the center of the social universe, even where institutions must be explained in individualist terms.

In brief, Friedman went beyond convention—as to ideology among Jewish intellectuals; as to his Hotelling, SRG, NBER background in economics; as to personal style (confidence in himself, the illusion of a valid orthodoxy); as to what Popper and Boland called 'conventionalism'; as to instrumentalist learnings; and as a part of the monetary revolution. Friedman put in place an analytical system that meets the canons of revolutionary change and the independently derived Boland criteria for the appropriate treatment of aggregation and time.

Chapter 18
Economic Theory, Policy and Uses of Statistical Methods

Milton Friedman offered a distinct, philosophically based economics with antecedents in classical and Keynes's economics (schema p. 455). In bringing this about, he developed an approach to the analysis of empirical data in economics with its own methodological underpinnings and base in mathematical statistics (schema p. 70). Largely paralleling this development was that of econometrics in the form of the structural, simultaneous equations model with a reliance on the direct use of the multiple regression technique. The genesis and continuity of this approach have been celebrated by Jan Tinbergen's sharing of the first Nobel prize in economics and by Lawrence Klein's receiving the 1980 award (pp. 71-77).

Early on, Friedman's orientation was shown to be in conflict with this Tinbergen-Klein approach, which was the main fashionable econometrics of the 1960s and 1970s as portrayed in popular econometric texts and encountered in numerous studies.[1] The approach was heralded in the mid-to-late 1960s as offering considerable promise as a guide to monetary and fiscal policy, with attention to causation and policy linkages.[2]

With the passage of the decades of Friedman's and Klein's research, including in the presence of the "modern computer," Friedman's work was persuasive and had impact beyond the circles of Academia. At the same time, the emphasis on the large-scale model à la Klein shifted mainly to its role in forecasting as distinct from predicting the effects of policy actions with causation involved, as taken up in chapter 3 (pp. 71-84). Also, since the time of Friedman's early success in persuasion and the popularization of the direct use of multiple regression technique, there has been more questioning of the relevance of the econometric technique as presented, to wit a 1983 *AER* paper titled "Lets Take the Con Out of Econometrics."[3]

During the time from the 1950s to the early 1980s Friedman's particular uses of statistical methods themselves did not attract much attention. There was nevertheless considerable controversy over Friedman's closely related methodological work (chap. 4), and his dynamic-monetary orientation (chap. 11 and 14). These controversial matters that were only partly statistical we associate with the phrase "no facts without theory, and no theory without facts" (pp. 61, 153), and with the leading time rate of change in the money stock (pp. 96-98).

The controversy over the dynamic-monetary orientation began when Friedman examined turning points in the time rate of change in the money

---

This chapter draws from work undertaken with Kim R. Sawyer.

stock in relation to National-Bureau dated turning points in business conditions, and implicitly viewed business conditions as movements about growth paths (the trends of *Monetary Trends* and chap. 14, p. 542). The common interpretation that caused misunderstanding was that business conditions were more a matter of change in levels for stock and flow quantities than changes in growth rates.[4]

The second phase of controversy started with the introduction of the Granger-Sims test of causality,[5] and the third was advanced by Lord Kaldor. We presented him in chapter 14 as having income (or business conditions, as it were) determined by government spending (specifically the public sector borrowing requirement) with the central bank playing the passive role of simply supporting the spending (denoted Y, or GNP or GDP). There (pp. 97-98 and 545), the leading-time-rate-of-change issue got transformed from a statistical orientation to an institutional matter about the financing of deficits.

In the period of these controversies—and in relation to these conflicts, misunderstandings, the large simultaneous equations models and the multiple regression equations—there was a question about whether an economic variable is endogeneous (determined within the model) or exogeneous (determined outside of the model). In the structural models, the terms "exogeneous" and "endogeneous" had clear meaning, which we reintroduce shortly.[6]

As already noted also, Friedman's uses of statistical methods which were present all along were not the main focus of critics' attention from the early 1950s to the early 1980s. Instead, attention was directed toward the importance of the money stock as a variable (the Radcliffe report, the velocity of money, pp. 444-446, and the interest elasticity of the demand for money, and the luxury-goods hypothesis with respect to money demand p. 548). However, this was not so after the *Monetary Trends* volume, which we consider in chapter 14, was published. There we note Charles Goodhart's article on *Monetary Trends* and encounter him commenting (pp. 540, 544) on F/S's forms of data adjustment. He objected to the separation of trends and cycles, noted incongruity with econometrics, and said that F/S presented evidence in an idiosyncratic manner.[7]

Such divergence in the uses of methods as reflected in Goodhart's comments and Friedman's uses appeared in fragments of the literature with respect to structural equations methods, and the Cowles Commission at the University of Chicago (pp. 84-87). But in 1983 and '84 new charges surfaced against F/S in a study by David Hendry and Neil Ericsson (hereafter H/E) of Oxford University's Institute for Econometrics and Statistics and of Nuffield College. The H/E study was funded by the Social Science Research Council to challenge F/S's *Monetary Trends*. The resulting paper went through four stages early on: a presentation to the Bank of England's panel of academic economists in October 1983, a revision in December following comments from the panel, a presentation in July 1984, at an NBER conference, Sonesta Hotel, Cambridge, and a further revision under the imprint of the Board of Governors' *International Finance Discussion Papers*.[8]

In brief, Milton Friedman developed a distinct approach to theoretical/empirical economics, which extends to three interrelated parts of the subject: (1) the methodological underpinning, (2) the uses of mechanical apparatus, and (3) uses of statistical methods. The first was widely written about over an extended period, and later attention was given to Friedman's variant of instrumentalism and indirect ties to the pragmatic American philosopher John Dewey (pp. 133-135). The second part was related to the first in chapter 4, in reference to the use of the theoretic apparatus as an instrument for making predictions which serve economic policy.[9]

The discussion of the use of theoretical apparatus (pp. 82-84, 108, 114-115, 121-123) is extended in chapter 11 (pp. 441-448) and again in chapters 14 and 16 (pp. 544-545, 637-638, 649-652), where the liquidity preference and consumption function pillars of Keynes's, Keynesian, and Friedman's economics are discussed. The one bears mainly on monetary policy and the other mainly on tax and monetary policy. As should be clear, however, the apparatus and the policy are not independent of one another, nor in Friedman's case are they independent of his uses of statistical methods. It should not seem unnatural therefore that controversies over methodology, theoretical apparatus, and policy should somehow come to controversy which arose over the uses of statistical methods following the publication of *Monetary Trends*. Goodhart raised the initial issue, but H/E made the main case against Friedman and, they said, for econometrics.

This latter may seem to many mainly technical, but, we recall, Friedman was a public person and hence unprotected by the ordinary rules governing libelous charges, which H/E appeared to make. The H/E case first appeared in print in *The Guardian*, the left of center, highly intellectual British newspaper. We take it up there, recall the earlier section regarding the uses of statistical methods (pp. 68-84), and place Friedman's statistical work in the context of statistics and theoretic economics; evaluate F/S's statistical work, first on its own terms and then others; and evaluate *Monetary Trends* on H/E's terms. As on other occasions, the overall focus is upon Friedman, even though he undertook major monetary works with Anna Schwartz. This limited scope is because of the strong ties to numerous pieces concerning the monetary works in question which were authored independently by Friedman.

The Media

Once again, as it was in the professional literature, so it was in the media, as Friedman's statistical work was taken up in *The Guardian*.[10] A main headline read:

                Monetarism's guru 'distorts his evidence'

Another headline read:

                Why Milton's monetarism is bunk

Oxford Dons show why Friedman is 'devoid of empirical support'

The Guardian continued:

> The study will cause considerable embarrassment to the Government. One implication which has survived close inspection by the Bank's academic consultants, is that it is well-nigh impossible to set realistic targets for the money supply, and it could be dangerous to try.

> They [H/E] say he [Professor Friedman] reaches "conclusions devoid of empirical support" based on evidence of "dubious validity."

> Professor Hendry said yesterday that Professor Friedman resorts to "simply incredible" manipulations of official data and that "almost every assertion in the book is false." A Bank of England economist said that the study "blows Friedman out of the water."

> In an attempt to prove that inflation is "always and every where" due to too much money chasing too few goods, Professor Friedman manipulates official statics to reduce the supply between 1921 and 1955, and to increase prices after the second world war.

> But even then his theory just does not stand up according to Professor Hendry. It is essential for Professor Friedman to prove a stable link between money supply and total money spending, but the relationship varies so widely and unpredictably as to be random.

> A given level of money supply is thus able to finance widely different levels of total money spending and inflation, so that the money supply numbers themselves are a very poor indicator of the state of the economy. They could be unduly restrictive, despite an apparent overshooting of monetary targets.

> "David Hendry is the leading member of the younger generation of British econometricians," Mr. David Savage editor of the National Institute Economic Review said yesterday." Continuing, he said, "This devastating critique is a very efficient hatchet job."

Continuing in his back-page piece, Christopher Huhne said:

> It is a very long time since there have been any bomb-shells from Oxford University quite like the one which Professor David Hendry has just dropped on Professor Milton Friedman. The emperor of international monetarism, is roundly declared to have no clothes on.
>
> What is more, the critique of Friedman comes from a scrupulous econometrician who is widely respected throughout the profession, and who has in the past delivered shafts in equal measure at both the monetarist and Keynesian camps.
>
> He is at pains to point out that his work is "pro-econometrics" and pro-rigorous empiricism rather than "anti-monetarist," though anti-monetarist its results clearly are.
>
> In order to establish a more stable figure for velocity—the key number which ensures a stable link between money and prices—Friedman arbitrarily reduces the money stock by some 20 per cent for a period of no less than 34 years between 1921 and 1955—nearly a third of the entire span he studies. This is on the grounds that "war and depression" cause people to hold more money in their bedsocks.
>
> He also then boosts the price level in the period after the second world war to allow for price controls and rationing. In other words, Friedman argues that the price level must have been higher than official statistics showed, since the money supply grew more quickly than prices. He then uses the manipulated data to establish the link between money and prices. This is very circular, and very naughty.
>
> Professor Hendry's feat, however, is to take this severely massaged data and show that not even such distortions can save the empirical support for Friedman's theory. "One of the most amazing things about our study," says Hendry, "is that we have not been able to find any evidence that money supply creates either income growth or inflation." It seems, if anything, to be a passive respondent to the rest of the economy.
>
> Econometrics, though, is the science (art?) of putting into quantitative form the relationships (or lack of them) which we can see in a graph, so Hendry and Ericsson's work gives us a good idea of just how unpredictable—indeed, dangerous—the monetarist "relationships" are.
>
> Professor Hendry likens velocity to the walk home of a drunken

man: he's heading roughly in the right direction but one can never predict whether his next step will be backwards, forwards or sideways. It is a "random walk." What this means for policy-makers, and market watchers, is that a given money supply target could finance vastly different levels of transactions and inflation and in a wholly unpredictable manner.

Another important finding of Hendry and Ericsson's work is that the money supply is clearly not independent of events in the rest of the economy, yet the Friedmanite claim of independence ("exogeneity") is vital if he is to saddle governments and central banks with the responsibility for controlling it.

As reviewed by Christopher Huhne in *The Guardian*, H/E raised a lot of technical points. Friedman, they said, made adjustments to the data where they are shifted about by identifiable events, the numerator and denominator of the velocity ratio (Y/M) are linked by the shifting Cambridge k (Act II of chap. 11), M = k(...)Y; and the label "exogeneity" is vital to the role given to government responsible for the money supply.

What we see in the news media's remarks is not that monetarism's guru falsified the evidence, or that the emperor of international monetarism "is roundly declared to have no clothes on." Rather we see misunderstanding and a conflict of approaches uppermost. As we develop Friedman's position further, we see him as an "economic Bayesian" in his analysis of data (which is not the same thing as, say, an "econometric Bayesian" in the sense of Arnold Zellner and "Bayesian Analysis in Econometrics." Friedman brought the following into the analysis: familiarity with the data to be analyzed; knowledge of the experiment (world or universe) that generated the data; choice of the sample period; revisions of the data to reduce measurement errors; the use of an economic theory ("no facts without theory") to justify revision rather than just arbitrary statistical technique; and distinctions in the time series as to the permanent and transitory components which he found relevant to economics vis-à-vis the econometrics. Though not mentioned by Friedman, the independence/"exogeneity" matter from the last paragraph of the Huhne quotation is not necessarily something to be established by statistical testing (which may be shocking to conventionist econometricians). Rather it is a matter of whether the central bank is, apart from the presence or absence of correlation of the money measure with other time series, acting independently to some degree or whether it is accommodating other changes such as the shock of oil price hikes, excessive wage increases, and the government's deficits (which we have variously associated with Lord Kaldor, including in chap. 14, pp. 97-98, 545).

In contrast to this broad perspective, H/E were at pains to emphasize a purer econometrics, even exclusive of economic theory. As Christopher Huhne said of Hendry, "He is at pains to point out that his work is 'pro-econometric' rather than anti-monetarism..." What we find in effect is the old charge of "facts without theory" (pp. 53) only it is no longer applicable to the NBER of the Burns era, but rather to theoretical econometrics.

Friedman's Statistical Work in the Context of Statistics and Theoretic Economics

Friedman entered economics at Columbia University through mathematical statistics and acquired some very diverse backgrounds, as we have pointed out (pp. 146-151, 155-160). It was not, however, until 1948 that he set about the horrendous task of combining all of his early fields. He was aware of the common statistical problems of identification and the separation of effects in multiple regression equations (pp. 72, 78-79, 110), where time series are interrelated, and was aware of setting bounds on the "true" regression coefficient. The multiple regression and true-bounds matters were only later combined in the Leamer problem: As variables are added to the regression equation "it's extremely difficult to set limits on the regression coefficients..., and that beyond some point, you may be able to set no bounds...at all."[11]

Confronting practical economic problems, Friedman devised an approach with the uses of statistical methods and the interrelated "indirect" use of theoretic constructs from economics. F/S's *Monetary Trends* is the culmination of the more strictly monetary part of the foregoing.

Friedman's Uses of Statistical Methods

What are the most distinguishable features of Friedman's uses of statistical methods? *First*, there is the early distinction between permanent (the trend), and the transitory components (the cycles, which is not to say in econometric jargon "white noise" because there is order, rhyme and reason to the time series data exclusive of the trend and random variation), and the related time-rate-of-change feature for the trend component (pp. 79, 82-84, 146, 149, 210, 214-215, 443, 446, 542, and chap. 14). This component appears in *Monetary Trends* as "phase averaging" and as a "triplet." Time series data for distinct cyclical phases are averaged to get points between peaks (troughs) and troughs (peaks). Next, loglinear trend lines are fitted to the points for three phases at a time. The trend-line slopes yield time rates of change.

Second, as suggested earlier by the combination of statistical methods and theoretic constructs, there are to be no facts without theory and vice versa. Indeed, Friedman said: "It [the theory] may not be explicit, but there necessarily is implicit economic theory...You cannot have a set of statistical calculations without having an economic theory that describes [them]." Continuing Friedman said, "...I don't believe anybody makes policy on that [facts without economic theory]. They may try to make forecast on that."[12]

Third, the analysis of the expectations of economic agents is entwined with the transitory and trend components of the time series. In Friedman's formulation, trends depict equilibrium time paths and states where expectations by agents are fully realized. In the case of inflationary expectations, inflation is fully anticipated, and there is rationality, or an absence of "money illusion." In the shorter transitory part of change there is money illusion and irrationality in Friedman's scheme of things for over a hundred year period. Moreover, structure underlying the formation of inflationary expectations may change,[13] which we take up again below.

Fourth, along the later line, the distinction between chronological and psychological time and questions about episodes and adjustment to accelerated inflation enter.[14] Expanding upon this feature, F/S said, "In judging the future, participants look back for past evidence that they regard as the most relevant to the current situation."[15] That may involve looking at comparable stages of business condition, but on some occasion even that will not be relevant and agents reacting to episodes in the formation of expectations may look much further back to some comparable earlier episode, such as the experience following earlier years (e.g., the 1929 market crash at the time of the 1987 crash, pp. 683-686). Moreover, the agents comprising different sectors of the economy will react with differences in sensitivity. Uncertainty in forecasts enters too.

Fifth, Friedman and F/S used the simple method (p. 79 and chap. 14). This use of statistical methods consists of analyzing data for a few variables at a time, before proceeding to the more sweeping use of multiple regressions and correlations with all the variables that can reasonably be regarded as relevant. We encounter the idea of a "true" regression coefficient for two variables, and the extension of the idea by Edward Leamer to more than two variables.[16] Friedman said "that applying an upper and lower limit is really the most effective way to have some idea of knowing what I do know and what I don't know."[17]

Sixth, as stated, Friedman approached economics as a theoretic/policy-oriented/empirical subject. He focused on stabilizing the short cycle and questions of faster or slower economic growth. The first objective concerned the transitory component of time series data, the second the permanent or trend components. The separation of the two seems eminently plausible if the first component is ever to be identified and related to the measurement of turning points in business conditions. The averaging of phases in *Monetary Trends* is simply a step in the direction of analyzing a longer term, and trying to eliminate the shorter term movements associated with the business cycle. Friedman himself said he did *not* regard separating components in the time series as throwing away information. He called it, rather: "highlighting one class of information and trying to avoid its being diluted by a class of information relevant to a question we're not trying to answer."[18]

Seventh, Friedman did not think that we had enough information at the time of his work to build the "large scale" systems that came from the Klein approach (pp. 71-77), and he had a different sort of idea for the structure, which gave a lot of attention to episodes, as will come up again shortly. Starting with the question of identifying a demand curve, as raised by Elmer Working over a half-century ago,[19] Friedman saw more than one easy way of dealing with the notion of a structure and the interaction of different forces that may be affecting a particular relationship.

Eighth, Friedman's analysis of the demand for money proceeded along a very indirect route and concerned what we call a "primal equation."[20] This widely reviewed equation was denoted $M/P = f(y,w;...;u)$ on pages 79 and 541, where the left-hand member is real money balances. For Friedman and F/S, this later relation came from analyses of data which proceeded indirectly. In addition, the real money stock is not controlled by the monetary authorities, but by the agents (pp. 446-447, 543, 778 n69). The nominal stock is controlled by the monetary authorities, which is to say in effect that the inflation rate is controlled by the monetary authority.

This eighth attribute, we see, goes back to the seventh attribute in that a money shock can throw agents off of what we have called the primal demand curve. For example, for an accelerated growth, people for some time will hold larger real cash balances than they would have held if they had known what was going to happen. In that sense, they are temporarily off their basic demand curve. We deal with the shock and being off the demand curve, Friedman's said, in such a way as to get the movements of observation along the demand curve.

Ninth, Friedman's search was for a stable phenomenon, and not simply numerical constants. This comes up when Klein discusses "the great ratios of economics" (pp. 75-77). The more relevant ratios are the income velocity ratio (Y/M), the saving-to-income ratio dealt with in the appendixes to chapter 16, and the ratio of U.S. to U.K. price averages (P_{US}/P_{UK}) over the dollar pound exchange rate ($/£) which first appeared in chapter 11 (pp. 421-422). Now, Friedman said as Klein did that the velocity ratio is not a constant, but Friedman goes further.

Continuing on the ninth attribute, we may illustrate Friedman's use of episodes in relation to art work in chapter 11 (p. 422). It is somewhat in contrast to Klein's approach. Looking at the figure, Friedman brought in an episode to emphasize the departure from the 1.12 average during the 1931-1973 period. The period reveals an episode of exchange rate manipulation on the part of the U.K. with the measure $(P_{US}/P_{UK})/(\$/\pounds)$ returning to the average 1.12 when the return was speeded up by the U.S. move toward floating exchange rates in the early 1970s. Friedman got to the episode immediately as we do on page 658, and gave attention to the experiment that generated the data.

Tenth, Friedman accepted a Bayesian or personalistic probability view, as mentioned in relation to the schema on page 70. It holds implications for his economic views and uses of methods. First, from an analytical view, there was a lot of episodic impact (say, also, sampling from a changing universe) to be extracted from the data, during the search for a stable relation, i.e., $M/P = f(y,w;\ldots;u)$. Second, he did not use the elaborate statistical tests found in econometrics but instead tested one theory against another with reference to a consistency with the statistical results at hand, as well as prior evidence (say from different episodes, from time series, from cross-section matters, from anything). On the matter of testing one theory against another, Friedman was quite explicit. He held that "the purpose of statistical analysis is to reduce differences of opinion among people about *personal* probabilities (italics added)."[21] And, in close relation, Friedman said:

> The only definition of probability that is consistent is one which is linked to the experiment. It is what the individual would be willing to wager [on the predicted outcome], fundamentally. What he would regard as a 50/50 bet. There are no objective ways other than that of estimating probability.

The Economic Theory: Position and Motion

Friedman's distinctive approach entwines the unique uses of statical methods with a unique theoretic approach. Despite its uniqueness, it builds on aspects of works by Marshall, Keynes, and the Keynesians (see schema p. 455). The statics encountered there are statements of position, whereas Friedman added the money analysis as a statement of motion. We outline this further. (As an aside we suggest the future prospect of building a simultaneous equations system with features of Friedman's economics.)

As in Keynes's economics and the present liquidity preference construction (also, pp. 83-84, 443-448), money demand is considered in terms of income (Y, a flow variable) and the money stock (M, an asset). At a given time, there is the asymptote (aY) and the money demand relation, M = f (i, Y), with the interest rate which yields the liquidity preference curve at a given position in the construction shown (p. 745). Immediate differences with Keynes, however, are (1) the central dynamic property for all stock and flow variables, and (2) the closely related distinction between permanent and transitory components in all of the variables encompassed by the theoretic system. The central dynamic property is that of a time rate of change (commonly expressed in loglinear terms, e.q., d ln Y × 100 = percent change and as in the *first* feature of Friedman's uses of methods). It is illustrated in the second piece of art work (p. 747) with line C and income growth at 3 percent with which we start.

In this 3-percent, base position there is the motion shown in the liquidity preference construction by the movement in the asymptote (aY). Also, in the base position, the velocity ratio would be constant and the rate of interest would be constant (Y/M and i both constant). As we increase money growth from the 3 to the 5 percent rate, the permanent (i.e., trend) path shifts for the time rate of change for income in the second piece of art work (p. 747), and for the interest rate in the third piece. The change in money growth also sets off cyclical change (the transitory part) about the trend paths, in the second and third pieces. In addition, there is a long-run

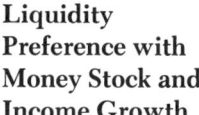

Liquidity Preference with Money Stock and Income Growth

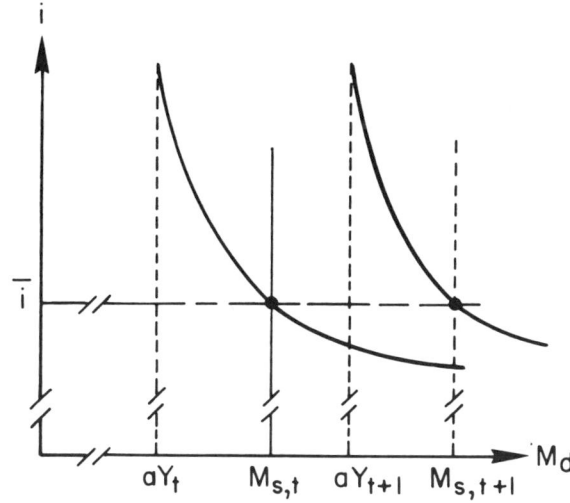

penalty on holding cash balances as the inflation rate and the interest rate rise by two percentage points (from path B to A and the rate from 4 to 6 percent).

All of this stock and flow analysis with levels for velocity and interest rates can be generalized to all of the basic statics of price theory and Keynesian mechanics (the supply-demand and Keynesian crosses, pp. 82-84, 194-195, 441-448, 637-639, 649-652). It is labored elsewhere and extended to Friedman's consumption function work,[22] including in the appendixes to chapter 16. As was the case with Keynes, nevertheless, significant developments come to the constructions from outside.

Keynes wrote of "autonomous" investment and attributed much to expectations except that in getting at policy prescriptions he impounded them in *ceteris paribus*. Friedman and F/S, on the other hand, introduced two (three) main features concerning expectations: first, the permanent (or "quasi-permanent") magnitudes are expected (the transitory unexpected) along the lines of the *third* feature of Friedman's uses of methods; second, there is psychological time, as in the fourth feature of F/S's uses of methods; and, third, the inflationary expectations feature with the expected inflation rate $[(1/P)/dP/dt)^*]$ is singled out for having the structure underlying its change in the mid-1960s (and we think again in the mid-1980s) as also taken up in the *fourth* feature of Friedman's uses of methods. So we have a lot of nonrepetitive (or "episodic") change going on (the psychological time and the episodes), even as Friedman searched for a stable relation.

The search was for a basis for predicting the effects of policy. The equation under the *eighth* feature of Friedman's uses of methods symbolizes the search. The left-hand member and the first term of the right-hand member are dealt with independently of the others. The former concern the income elasticity $d \ln (M/P)/d \ln(Y/P) \approx 1$ (also note the denominator and numerator of the ratio of Y to M), plus all the change is in relation to time series data which are adjusted for episodes.

Further, the four expected rates of return signified by the dots in the relation $M/P = f(y,w;\ldots;u)$ are all trends. They are dealt with in cycle and trend terms (as shown for the interest rate in the accompanying art work (p. 747), where the long-run Fisher equation (pp. 212, 234-235, 448-449), $[i = (i\text{-real}) + (1/P)/(dP/dt)^*]$, enters.

Continuing, the monetary part, as stated, provides the motion to the statics (even where accommodation enters, pp. 97-98, 545), as shown in the first two pieces of art work, where money impacts on income and where income has two parts (the price average, P, and output Q, including as on p. 414).[23] Hence, money impacts on the price average and output, where the price average comes from the terms of a price index. These have

Time Paths for Nominal Income with a Change in the Monetary Growth Rate from 3 to 5 percent

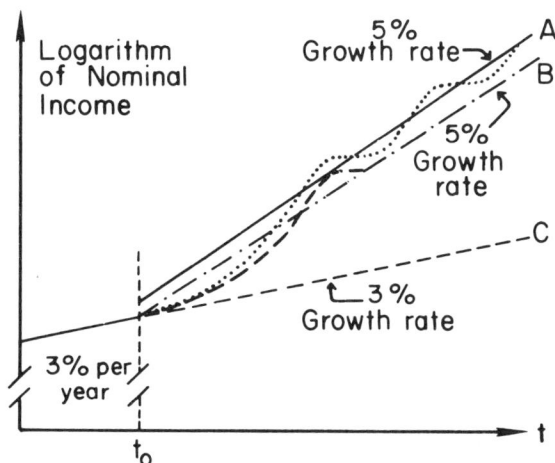

Secular Time Paths for the Nominal Interest Rate at 4 and 6 Percent

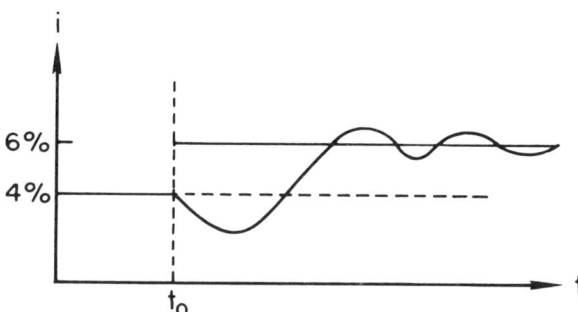

an exact counterpart to prices as depicted by a batch of Marshallian crosses (pp. 56, 210-211, 194-195).

There are two further points: (a) the difference between the slopes of the ordinary and compensated demand curves at a given time get related to the terms of a price index;[24] and we encounter in Friedman's work monetary change impacting on the prices firms face in the Marshallian markets.[25]

Traversing this route we end with a theoretic system that entails a lot of static analysis (the given time in the liquidity preference construction and the Marshallian crosses). All come together in the quantity expression,

$$M = Q/V\,P$$
or, the preferred Cambridge form (pp. 417, 446),
$$M = k(\ldots)\,P$$
where, for Friedman, money balances (M) may grow at the same rate as output (Q) and leave income velocity (Y/M) and the price level unchanged, and where we write k(...) to note that the Cambridge constant k (k = 1/V) shifts in response to changes in the demand for money. Here, we end with all of the motives and the psychology Keynes and Friedman associated with money balances, real capital, speculation (purchasing power risk and bonds) and uncertainty (another name for personal probability).

We need not labor the statements of position and motion further. They came about gradually, plus they entail a complex of time frames and expectations as well as exogenous (episodic) changes and psychological time. This theoretic system with episodic change has not yet been reduced to a structural equations model.

The Evaluation of F/S's (1982) Statistical Work

The evaluation of F/S's statistical work proceeds by viewing it in its own context and in the light of current econometric approaches introduced in chapter 3 (pp. 71-77). The most prominent of these is Klein's, which we showed in the schema on page 70.[26] Another, with the most direct challenge leveled at F/S, is that by H/E. In addition, H/E's attack started with a report at the Bank of England where Charles Goodhart shared ties.

Evaluation on F/S's Own Terms

When undertaken on their own terms, the evaluation of the statistical work in *Monetary Trends*, which brings to bear total statistical work covering over thirty years, is rather flattering to Friedman and F/S. In the first place, it had a major tie to the reference cycle work of Mitchell's NBER, with an added dimension. Notably, there were no facts without theory and no theory without facts (the *first* and *second* features of Friedman's uses of methods). In the second place, the economic-theoretic part was explicitly oriented toward monetary policy and pinned to the statistical part, as the previous section should indicate. The cycle, trend and episodic features of changes in the time series were exactly those with which monetary policy and Keynes's theory and Friedman's theory were concerned.

We need not traverse all the routes by which these changes came about since they are set forth in detail in earlier chapters. In essence, however, Friedman's work did three things: (1) it reoriented major blocks of monetary analysis from attention to the interest rate as the controlled variable (whether $\Delta M \rightarrow -\Delta i$, or whether i controlled directly by open market operations) to the money and credit aggregates; (2) it offered a persuasive body of statistical results giving support to the change in the analysis; (3) the theory and evidence gained attention in the political arena and brought about major policy reorientations at the Federal Reserve in the U.S. and at the Bank of England in the U.K. (chaps. 14, 15, and 16).

These interrelated accomplishments of Friedman's work were exactly what he saw as the goals of the statistical-theoretic effort. The major difference in accomplishments from other bodies of statistical-theoretic work is that they were rarely realized. Further, it is easy to single Friedman out in his role. When the experts of London were convened to discuss monetarist changes at the Bank of England, Friedman was the individual identified by the discussants, and when Lawrence Klein addressed monetarist matters in the U.S. they were all easily linked to Friedman.

Evaluation in the Light of Klein's Approaches

Friedman's distinctive uses of statistical methods are evident in the early 1950s. In his 1951 essay he directly confronted the emerging approach of the "big," structural equations models à la Klein and outlined his own approach. In 1953, he directed criticisms toward the methodology of the Cowles Commission at Chicago. As may be anticipated by his Cowles Commission orientation and Lawrence Klein's presence there, Klein moved along a different route (pp. 71-77). After writing a dissertation at M.I.T., Klein made contact with the uses of statistical methods through the Cowles Commission, where he moved in the econometric tradition that was set upon its course by Jan Tinbergen and Ragnar Frisch. Following changes in his dissertation, a revision appeared in 1966 which presented a simultaneous equations model that was both an updated Klein-Goldberger model and an extended version of the Keynesian system. The outline of a fuller-blown equation system with a Keynesian demand side, a Leontief supply side, and links to models for foreign countries appeared in 1983.

Klein's model started with a Keynesian orientation and did not fully lose it. Although a policy orientation is present, two developments came about over time: (1) the instability in parameters led to the addition of more and more detail, and (2) the emphasis shifted from serving as a guide to policy to forecasting primarily.

Friedman's approach to instability in the raw, time-series data is different from adding variables. Rather it is phase averaging, data adjustments, and cross-country comparisons. Friedman attempted to separate out many components of the time series in conjunction with a use of simple statistical methods, and specification analysis. As stated, this started early with Friedman when he entered economic research with an awareness we related to the Leamer problem. Indeed, this awareness reflected a use of prior information, through less explicit than in a formal Bayesian analysis. At this time, however—following all Friedman did with complex time frames, expectations, and episodic change—the work may be more nearly ready to proceed along the lines of structural equations models which Klein helped pioneer.

Phase averaging. Reflecting his experience at the NBER of the Mitchell/Burns/Friedman era, Friedman averaged observations across phases of reference cycles.[27] Within the phase, initial and terminal points were weighted one-half and intervening observations given a weight of unity. The phases themselves were also weighted.[28] This procedure constituted imposing a prior belief on the data, which was formed from NBER chronology. We note, moreover, that the revisions F/S employed in their reference points (for example 1966 and 1967 in the U.S. data and 1901, 1903, 1917 in the U.K. data), are predicted on other studies.[29]

The phase averaging helped F/S separate the phenomena they wished to investigate, but it is also technically regarded as filtering.[30] In the process, observations within a phase are grouped according to a triangular distribution. For the prior to be defensible, we require that the dependence of observations within a phase be greater than that between successive phases. This dependence may take the form of serial correlation, but also it may involve the higher moments or indeed more general forms of dependence.[31] A priori, we expect interdependance within phase to be greater than that between successive phases.

Data adjustments. F/S engaged in significant corrections of data at various stages of analysis. Essentially, Friedman's approach involved constructing instruments for variables where they are possibly measured with error. This represents prior belief extending to belief about an economic theory. Some of the major revisions centered about the series for net national product and corrections to allow for price controls.[32] In the first instance, we encounter two aspects of the income data. In one of these, Friedman accessed the quality of the series in part by its conformity with other series. Afterward he adjusted the data, as in *Monetary Trends*, to make it more conformable. In doing this, he enhanced the possibility of a stable money demand function, which we may see as necessary for progress in empirical economics when we reflect on the Leamer problem.[33]

The revisions above are a sample of numerous filters, both statistical and economic, used by F/S and summarized in tables 4.8 and 4.9 of *Monetary Trends*. With respect to these data adjustments, there are a number of salient issues, e.g., F/S drew heavily on the works of other authors, both statistical and economic, to make corrections.[34] Further, adjustments to the price series presupposed a conformity in the movements of prices, income and money.

These reservations aside, the emphasis Friedman placed on preliminary "data analysis" is appealing since it encourages a more detailed knowledge of the data, rather than simply a set of points conveying equal amounts of information.[35] This is in the spirit of traditional statistics, where we encounter John Tukey as its foremost proponent. Moreover, Friedman's preliminary examination of data was an attempt, partially involving theoretic economics, to deal with measurement errors.

The use of the term "measurement error" as it relates to controversy surrounding Friedman's uses of methods concerns a combination of sources of error with respect to time series (observations ordered over time, as pictured on pages 422, 676, 684, and 685). First, there is the error where the data do not measure what they propose to measure (e.g., the raw data provide a measure of, say, 6.5 percentage points when in fact, the error-free data would reveal 5.5 measured at a given time), and, second, there is what we now call "separation of effects" error. For Friedman, the first enters where a large change in the series is easier to deal with than a small change, principally because the error is a smaller part of the total change and the error-free part is more vivid.

The separation of effects error becomes especially complicated from a data analysis point of view when we introduce the compound prospects of business cycles and episodic change. There, indeed, we have a Friedman view of the cycle as largely exogenous or monetary-policy induced (pp. 98-99, 241),[36] and thus have episodes impacting on the time series, including where the cycle is not some smooth sine-curve phenomenon. Further, we are dealing with the well guarded distinction Friedman made between permanent (trend) and transitory (cyclical) components in the time series data.

The matter of episodic change arises where we have the following: an era of policy induced inflation (including monetary policy induced inflation to accommodate oil price shocks as in 1973 and 1979, inflationary wage and price changes as in the Carter years, and labor-union and/or monopoly induced wage and price increases, chaps. 8 and 15); a period of deregulation or administrative change (e.g., where new assets may arise to serve as what we call money balances (M1 or M2, pages 656-659); and a period of legislative procrastination which may induce uncertainty in the economic outlook (e.g., as in the case of U.S. inactions surrounding the Gramm-Rudman bill, the domestic budget and the balance of payments crises, pp. 654-659).

The potential for this separation-of-effects error starts to loom large where we encounter Friedman as, first, using simple methods and setting bounds on the true regression coefficient, and then as rejecting the prospect that a statistical equation with a batch of so-called "independent" variables on the right-hand side does in fact adequately separate the effects (p. 79). The question arose in his mind at a very early date in his statistical experiences as a student and under Harold Hotelling (pp. 69, 148), as a statistician with the SRG (pp. 155-159), and as he committed himself to monetary research in 1948-1953 (pp. 107-109, 180-182). It was thus that he proceeded along non-econometric lines to devise the separation of trend and cycle components and to deal with episodic change.

Friedman's handling of episodes and the use of simple methods was in effect a recognition of errors that could arise from the fashionable uses of statistical methods, and it offered an alternative to the use of dummy or exogeneous variables in a multiple regression framework to account for irregular observations. While Friedman's consideration of data was more thorough than for a typical econometric study, it incompletely assessed the robustness of the results to the selection of priors.

Estimation and specification analysis. Friedman's range of estimation methods was meager as attribute *five* of "Friedman's Uses of Statistical Methods" may suggest. Friedman almost exclusively used least squares (or simple regression) methods while ignoring questions of simultaneity, persistence in the errors, non-normality, exogeneity or a formal analysis of dynamics. Moreover, Friedman preferred to estimate simple behavioral models by simple methods, as we have indicated. This is a legacy perhaps of much of his earlier work and background, the expressed purpose of using methods with which he was familiar, and the limit of time placed on getting out the work. Viewing Friedman's work overall, there is no better example of Friedman's estimation and specification analysis than chapters 5 and 6 of *Monetary Trends*. The main characteristics found there are suggested by attributes *one*, *two*, *five*, and *nine* above, as found under "Friedman's Uses of Statistical Methods." They concern episodic change, dynamics, cross-country comparisons, reversal of the role of so-called dependent and independent variables, a focus upon doubtful variables, stability of a relationship, and specification tests.

Episodic change over a long period. The entire period 1867-1975 was examined by F/S, and special attention given to sub-periods and episodes. The use of episodes is an alternative to a more formal consideration of stability and structural change, as attribute *eight* may suggest.

The type of biases which motivated Friedman to consider phase averaging must also be present in the selection of episodes and the time period under study. Friedman did not consider this issue.

Dynamics. In dynamic analysis with trends, time rates of change, and all, Friedman apparently preferred the use of graphs to other standard methods.[37] For Friedman, graphical techniques were important because they lent credibility to his hypotheses without subjecting them to necessary exactitudes. Indeed, the maxim "a picture is worth a thousand words" probably explains the movement to graphical techniques in statistics.[38]

Another component of Friedman's dynamics is first differencing. Friedman used differencing to produce stationary time series and, while first differencing may not be optimal for a Box-Jenkins specialist,[39] it nonetheless was and should be adequate for assessing the interactions between money, income, prices and interest rates.

Cross-country comparisons. A major tenet of the F/S 1982 volume is the comparison of U.K. and U.S. data. The extra dimension added by considering two countries, gives support to the constancy of velocity, as noted below. The extension of analysis to other countries may be a part of future research.

Dependent and independent variables. Throughout chapter 6 of *Monetary Trends*, F/S considered regressions of money on income and income on money,[40] along the lines of attribute *five* under "Friedman's Uses of Statistical Methods." The apparent motivation for this reverse regression approach is presumably the close similarity between the money and income series and the measurement errors in both series.[41] In any case, from the reverse regressions, Friedman established upper and lower limits on income elasticities, which are theoretically justified.[42]

One may wish to extend the reverse regression techniques to the analysis of the interactions of other variables, such as money and prices, and money and interest rates. A point, however, is that money balances and income were most central to the relation found under attribute *eight*, namely $M/P = f(y,w;\ldots;u)$. This central role followed from the emphasis on the income elasticity of money demand ($d \ln m \cong d \ln y$) and on the velocity ratio (Y/M).

Focus on doubtful variables. Friedman was a strong proponent of simple regressions, preferring to examine variables one or two at a time. While this approach is advocated by some theorists,[43] it evokes strong criticisms from econometricians such as H/E.

The advantage of simple regressions is that the effect of measurement errors is readily established through the calculation of coefficient bounds from the reverse regressions. Additionally, problems of intercorrelation in the variables, as would ordinarily be the case with economic time series, are obviously reduced by considering simpler regressions. However, Friedman did not pursue the principle of simple regressions as far as possible. Simple regression methods are informative only if the parameter sensitivity is investigated, for example using methods of Leamer.[44]

Stability. A principal tenet of Friedman's economics is stability in the velocity of money as a phenomenon but not as a numerical constant. Friedman's conception of stability was markedly different from that of the classical econometrician who measures stability in terms of random variability of the coefficients. Rather, for Friedman, stability connoted several interpretations, including: the explanatory power and magnitude of coefficients should not vary greatly across episodes; and inferences on a given economic variate must be essentially the same for two different economies.

A seemingly latent aspect of Friedman's stability analysis is, as we noted in chapter 14, extension of research to the inter-country comparison. F/S found the coefficients in the money demand function for the U.S. and the U.K. to be close.[45] Indeed, they concluded that "only the coefficients of the income term from the level equation differ significantly between the two countries." The implication is that the same causal forces affect money demand in the two countries, underscoring a stable relationship for them. This concept of stability is arguably more realistic than the restrictive econometric definition of parameter constancy for two reasons: first, to expect constant coefficient relationships between variables as disparate as money, income and interest rates to be invariant over time is to impose an unnecessary degree of exactitude on the data;[46] and, second, to require money demand to have the same determinants in two different countries is a weak but surely necessary condition for stability. We note that the consideration of both U.S. and U.K. data lent credence to Friedman's contention that velocity is better explained as a numerical constant, such as found in the old quantity theory tradition, than as a "will o' the wisp," as encountered in the Keynesian and Radcliffe-Committee traditions (pp. 445, 447).

Finally, students of econometrics contemporary to H/E will almost surely dispute explanatory power, measured by $\bar{R}^2$, as a suitable criterion for stability. They will cite spurious correlations, particularly across time series, as evidence deeming explanatory power inappropriate as a measure of stability. Even so, by invoking an episodic study, Friedman went further than the use of explanatory power alone, and F/S examined the sensitivity of income elasticity to episodes.[47] Such an examination of stability, which partitioned the sample into economic episodes and compared the resulting coefficient, is more plausible than an artificial partition without economic premise—for example, that used by H/E[48].

Specification tests. A major aspect of Friedman's uses of statistical methods is the failure to completely test the model specification, which is an inherently controversial aspect of Friedman's simple method because "model specification" means adding all the relevant variables in a multiple regression equation and making statements in testable form. The use of simple method may have been defensible in some of Friedman's earlier work on the ground that the time called for to produce the major works with Schwartz was limited by the thirty year time span they required. Even so, looking to the future given the proliferation of specification tests in recent years, it is not acceptable. Friedman's assessment of model adequacy is simply in terms of goodness to fit (R^2), signs and significance of coefficients, and some investigation of parameter robustness. The only concession to the analysis of the residual or leftover variables takes the form of maximum residuals.[49]

That Friedman did not test for serial correlation in the velocity equation neutralizes the analysis somewhat, but not as seriously as implied by Goodhart and H/E. The presence of serial correlation does not bias the estimated coefficients. It does, nevertheless, bias test of those coefficients. The relevant question then, is whether the acceptance of hypotheses was distorted appreciably by such bias. We think not.

Evaluation in the Light of H/E's Approach

The comparison of Friedman's uses of statistical methods with H/E's econometric approach brings to mind the verse:
>Ships that pass in the
> night,... ,
>Only a signal shown and a
> distant voice in the darkness ...

On the one hand, Friedman's approach is policy oriented theory with data analysis. Policy and theory are explicit from beginning to end, plus the attention to cyclical and trend components of time series and the episodes that impact on them reflect the historical interests of the policy makers since the founding of the Federal Reserve System. On the other hand, H/E offered critical evaluation of F/S's *Monetary Trends* from a very fixed standard which they referred to as "modern econometric methods." Using these,[50] H/E analyzed data differently and rejected what they referred to as five of F/S's central empirical claims: "(1) the exogeneity of money; (2) their claims to the constancy and correct specification of their money-demand equation; (3) their interpretation of a dummy variable in that equation as capturing a 'shift in liquidity preference' for 1921-55; (4) their treatment of the interdependence of money, income, prices, and interest rates; (5) their use of phase-average data."

In rejecting F/S's claims, H/E went back to the annual "raw" data. They regarded the F/S adjustments to the data and the phase averaging as limiting the information in the data analyzed, whereas F/S regarded the matter as separating out the parts they wished to consider. By their standard, H/E claimed to achieve better results, which they did. A main question is whether the H/E results mean anything in terms of policy, since they offer no positive policy associations with their results. Rather, they said, they highlighted the "practical dangers of seeking to analyze complex stochastic [chance, probabilistic] processes while eschewing modern econometric methods."

Phase Averaging

The motive behind F/S's use of the phase average prior is to reduce cyclical variability. Although F/S argued that serial correlation may be reduced by such averaging,[51] H/E amply demonstrated that for the velocity series, serial correlation is by no means attenuated and high frequency variability is only marginally reduced. That serial correlation persists between members of a time series and leading or lagging members is due to the conjunction of expansion and contraction phases and also to the strength of two contractions in velocity.[52]

F/S also maintained that phase averaging diminishes the effect of measurement errors (or, we may say, it acted as a filter and thereby diminished the presence of extraneous information in the measurement). This, however, is conditional on the nature of the measurement error process. If this process were systematic as H/E contended, on the one hand, averaging is not helpful, but, on the other hand, the measurement error process may not be symmetrical, as Friedman contended (attribute *six* above, "Friedman's Uses of Statistical Methods").

A major question then is whether relevant information is lost by phase averaging.[53] H/E alluded to problems in using phase averaged data for Granger causality tests and for analysis of short-run dynamics. It is doubtful that these are serious problems, since Granger causality tests have rather low power and the short-run dynamics are ancillary to finding stable behavioral relationships. Indeed Friedman contended quite legitimately that phase averaging separates relevant information from information which may confound estimation of the parameters. In this sense, Friedman's use of phase averaged data is likely to be considerably more stable than for the original data, because positive serial correlation within a phase is at least partially removed, and because the effects of extreme expansions and contractions are dampened. To summarize, while phase averaging is not an appropriate filter for the entire set of observations, it can nonetheless be justified as a mechanism for reducing noise within expansion and contraction phases of the economy, and as a mechanism that may induce more regular patterns of serial correlation.

Velocity as a Random Walk

H/E used techniques to demonstrate that the velocity of circulation may be regarded as a random walk.[54] However, most importantly, the random walk hypothesis is refuted by the close concordance of velocity movements in the U.S. and the U.K. If velocity in each country is indeed a random walk ("a will o' the wisp") such parallel movements in velocity will surely

Simple Methods and Econometrics

From our present perspective, H/E's caustic criticism of Friedman's uses of statistical methods illustrates the wide divergence between Friedman's simple methods and a school of econometric thought based on specification analysis rather than substantive criticism. Briefly, H/E embraced the notion that for a model to be viable, it must survive a package of misspecification tests.[55] A preferred model was selected not from economic considerations, but rather as the result of an atheoretical screening process which massages the model to fit these misspecification test criteria. This approach has a number of disquieting characteristics, both statistical and philosophical. We cite only a few.

First, the small sample and confounding problems associated with excessive use of specification tests are probably less serious than the methodological questions raised. Foremost among these is the nature of specification testing itself. Tests for misspecification, such as the Durbin-Watson test or the Breusch-Pagan test for heteroscedasticity,[56] were designed to detect misspecification in a given model, not to select a preferred model nor to imply the direction of a better model.

There are typically a number of money demand functions acceptable to the gamut of specification tests H/E employed. Equally critical though, most of these tests will be economically implausible. H/E appear to have reversed orthodox econometric method in first finding a statistically acceptable model and subsequently discovering its economic rationale. Such an exercise is all too often obscure and arbitrary. It is no substitute for developing hypotheses and then subjecting them to empirical verification, as was the case with F/S.

As to specification tests generally, there are presumably an infinite number of alternatives against which we can test—e.g., an infinite number of types of heteroscedasticity. As the number of tests expands, it is possible that a previously acceptable model will be rendered unacceptable. Hence, just as Friedman's money demand function fails over the tests used by H/E, so the H/E model may fail if subjected to further and more refined testing.

Economic policy goes on and the research plays a role, but the conduct of policy cannot be postponed until the one true model appears (p. 133). We must be careful that the search for the true model does not preclude us from recognizing the best for a given time.

Overview

In reference to Friedman's view that the purpose of statistics is to reconcile differences of opinion, the outcome of controversy over his uses of methods is ironic. Over most of the post-World War II years, the main tracks in the developing uses of statistical methods as they related to empirical research in economics were (1) Friedman's, with its simple methods orientation, and monetary economics, personalistic probability, NBER ties, and (2) Klein's, with its structural equations orientation and Keynesian, Cowles Commission, and Frisch-Tinbergen ties.

The first was a search for a stable relation by proceeding indirectly and allowing for episodic change, psychological time, and permanent and transitory components of time series. The second proceeded more directly and the model size grew quite large as equations and variables were added to deal with matters of detail and unstable parameters. On Friedman's analogy, it was an attempt to build a foundation before constructing the house.

The second track also lost its early policy orientation, and came to be viewed by some as just an aid to forecasting and by others as a detailed system of analysis linking the domestic and foreign economies. Although statical results did little to reduce differences between Friedman and Klein, we see no reason why the structural equations methods cannot be extended to deal with the distinct Friedman approach including episodic change and all.

The broad differences in the uses of statistical methods continue with Friedman's and H/E's. They concern particularly the role of policy oriented, theoretic economics. On the one hand, Friedman's economics carried over to the role of economics in dealing with the goals of monetary policy; on the other hand, H/E reversed the approach by offering no economic rationale for the results they presented in their econometric tract and used in evaluating *Monetary Trends*. In the one instance we have facts and theory which give attention to policy and the historical interests of policy makers; in the other we only have data processed with technical econometrics. In future economic research it may be possible to discover the policy-economic rationale for results such as H/E's.

Judged by the pragmatic Friedman standard for theoretic, policy oriented economics, his uses of statistical methods were a smashing success. They made a difference at the policy-making level in both Washington, D.C. and London. The hallmark of Friedman's approach is reliance upon the following: a knowledge of policy, operations, history, and the experiment that generates the statistical data as it were; a closely related familiarity with the data being analyzed; prior information as it related to both theory and results from analyses of data; and a masterful use of relatively simple methods and variants of technique. Friedman's research in spanning four decades encompassed many variants of statistical technique. He was in part a personal probabilist, and a classical statistician but quite essentially a data analyst.

Friedman's data analysis as exemplified in *Monetary Trends* is neither in the tradition of the system theorist nor the atheoretical econometrician.[57] It is principally that of both an economist and historian.

The use of fundamental techniques and the knowledge of data are persuasive to a general readership. Friedman's uses of statistical methods are effective because they persuade and because nuances are overshadowed by the substantial evidence tending to support Friedman's position. Friedman's persuasive ability is linked to his variant of an instrumentalist, Dewey pragmatist philosophy. There, we encounter him asserting the stability of money demand and seeking to demonstrate the adequacy of his hypotheses in relation to it by generating unqualified predictions about the effects of policy. Friedman's uses of methods nonetheless were circumscribed with a strong emphasis on prior beliefs from economics and previous study.

Friedman's prior beliefs were from economic theory and past analysis of data, extending to studies conducted by others with respect to the economic theory. Traditional price theory and Keynesian mechanics are statements of position and monetary analysis adds the motion. Price indexes with terms tied to Marshallian markets combine with the elementary formulations found in the quantity theory of money. Money, price indexes, production indexes, income, and interest rates all enter.

As we have indicated, Friedman's work is a collage of contrasts. He was in one instance attentive to detail in his examination of data, yet in another he dismissed appropriate estimation methods. Econometricians can learn appreciably from his different statistical perspective, and from his uses of methods.

Along this foregoing line, there are some specific contrasts between aspects of Friedman's uses of methods and the contentions raised by H/E. Essentially, the difference between Friedman's money demand function and H/E's alternative is a matter of complexity. Friedman espoused simple, economic-theoretic hypotheses which were subjected to an empirical verification that did not demand an unnecessary level of exactitude. His model is readily interpretable and its ramifications readily implementable, consistent with his instrumentalist philosophy. He produced a tangible policy prescription.

In contrast to Friedman, H/E demanded a high level of refinement, which produced an especially complex model, and they said nothing about policy and the operations required for its execution. What H/E gained from refinement, they lost in interpretation and in applicability. The implication of this contrast for practitioners of econometrics is to appropriately balance the opposing themes of refinement and simplicity.

Looking to the future, we find that Friedman was perhaps too sparse in his specification analysis, while H/E were rather exacting. We challenge H/E and other atheoretical econometricians to specify the theory, policy, and operations that underlie the statistical achievements.

Notes and References
to Volume II

Notes, Chapter 11: Crises, Keynes and Friedman

Note: Citations in notes for chapters 1 through 18 refer to references which follow the notes for each chapter. For example, "Hicks (1983)" refers to Sir John Hicks's book which is listed under "References, Chapter 11" below.

1. Hicks (1983). 2. Santoni (1984). 3. The term "monetarism" has been widely used since 1968 to refer to the new quantity theory of money. Harry Johnson (1978, 126-127) discussed the term in the U.S. and British context and referred to Thomas Mayer as having given credit for its popularization to a 1968 article by Karl Brunner and a 1979 article by David Fand. 4. Frazer (1980, chap. 2). 5. Keynes (1923, 165; 1932, 201). 6. Frazer and Yohe (1966, sect. 23.3). 7. Keynes (1923, 165; 1932, 201); and Polanyi (1944, chap. 1). 8. de Cecco (1977, 18, 24). 9. Henderson (1976). 10. Hession (1984, 219, 221, 286, 362, 375). 11. The Bloomsbury group included Keynes, political scientist Leonard Woolf, novelist Virginia Woolf, biographer Lytton Strachey, critic-hedonists Clive Bell and Desmond MacCarthy, and three painters (Duncan Grant, Vanessa Bell, and Roger Fry). Charles Hession's book is an extended study of Keynes and his Bloomsbury connections.

Keynes for sure had a way with words. For this he owed much to his training in the classics at Eton and later at Cambridge, and to his association with the Bloomsbury group. Friedman too had skill with language, simplicity and all that, as we will see, but Friedman's use of language was different. As an undergraduate, he worked toward becoming an actuary. 12. Hession (1984, 87, 215, 207, 208, 247); and Keynes (1923, 170-171; 1932, 206-207, 218). 13. Hession (1984, 108, 162, 269-271, 288-289, 367, 378). 14. Hession (1984, 73, 81, 234, 237-238, 245, 261, 267, 301). 15. Keynes (1923, 80). 16. Hicks (1983); Kaldor (1982). 17. Hession (1984, 271, 290-291, 370). 18. Chandler (1958); Frazer and Yohe (1966, sect. 7.5); Manchester (1983, 782-814). 19. Keynes (1932, 183, 201). 20. Keynes (1925). 21. Tobin (1982, 338). 22. Keynes (1932, 233). 23. Hicks (1983, 17); and Keynes (1932, 119-212). 24. Keynes (1932, 208). 25. Keynes (1932, 207). 26. Keynes (1923, 173, 1932, 208-209). 27. Keynes (1923, 155, 164, 170; 1932, 196, 200, 206). 28. Frazer (1983b; 1983c; 1984). 29. Friedman (1983, 19). 30. Friedman (1980, 507-510). 31. Frazer and Yohe (1966, 146-151). 32. Manchester (1983, 782-814). 33. Manchester (1983, 787-799, 808-809). 34. Kaldor (1982, ix); and Manchester (1983, 808). 35. Friedman (1974, 134; 1983, 17). 36. Friedman (1983, 19). 37. Keynes (1920). 38. Frazer and Yohe (1966, sect. 7.5). 39. Stanley Baldwin, who appointed Churchill as exchequer, had his first ministry from May 1923 through January 1924, when he was briefly followed by MacDonald (January to November, 1924), before serving as prime minister from November 1924 to June 1929. Following Baldwin in June of 1929, MacDonald entered his second ministry, and started the third in August of 1931. He served as prime minister until June 1935, when Baldwin returned briefly. Baldwin was succeeded in May of 1937 by Neville Chamberlin, who was in turn succeeded in May 1940 by the wartime prime minister, Winston Churchill. Churchill was succeeded in turn by Labor's Clement Attlee in July 1945.

From Attlee to Margaret Thatcher's election in May of 1979, parties in Britain, whether Labor or Conservative, did not appear to make much difference in the country's economic policies. Thatcher's presence, however, is another story (chap. 15). 40. Manchester (1983, 833-855). 41. F/S (1963, 315). 42. F/S (1963, 316). 43. F/S (1963, 318). 44. F/S (1963, 308-311). 45. F/S (1963, chap. 7). 46. Frazer and Yohe (1966, 8, 21, 22, 23). 47. F/S (1963, 407-419); and Bagehot (1915). 48. F/S (1963, 411). 49. F/S (1963, 411). 50. F/S (1963, 414-419). 51. Hicks (1983, 18). 52. Hicks (1983, 17). 53. Friedman (1984, 24-25). 54. Stein (1984, 34). 55. Stein (1984, 312). 56. Stein (1984, 29). 57. Frazer (1984); Stein (1984, 53-57). 58. On the timing of the effect of the *General Theory*, see Hession (1984, 282, 369).

Stein (1984, 49) noted the prevalence of some of the "Keynesian" ideas evident in the New Deal before WW II. He said, "The most important of these was to maintain that the conditions which Keynes considered to exist at the bottom of the depression were general and permanent conditions of 'mature' economics like ours." Here, however, Stein must have had in mind Hansen's stagnation thesis (Scaperlanda 1977). On it, see also Hession (283-288, 298, 302, 375). 59. Frazer and Yohe (1966, chap. 22). 60. Frazer and Yohe (1966, chap. 22); Frazer (1980, chap. 2); Hession 1984 (257-259, 339). 61. Stein (1984, 76-77). 62. Stein (1984, 78-79).

63. Friedman (1984, 26). 64. Frazer and Yohe (1966, sect. 24.3); and Kane (1974). 65. Stein (1984, 65-87). 66. Friedman (1984, 26). 67. Frazer and Yohe (1966, chap. 21-24). 68. Frazer and Yohe (1966, chap. 21-24). 69. Kaldor (1982, 18). 70. Frazer (1980, chaps. 2 and 19). 71. Frazer (1980, chaps. 14, 17, and 18). 72. Frazer (1980, chap. 17). 73. Hicks (1983, 19). 74. F/S (1963, chap. 6). 75. Chandler (1958, 374-380, 423-470); and Frazer and Yohe (1966, 53-57). 76. Chandler (1958, 333-335); Shirer (1960, 112, 145-146, 189-190, 351-352, 918). 77. Fry (1969, 23-27); and Hicks (1974, 59-85). 78. Skidelsky (1977b, 33). 79. Brittan (1977). 80. Frazer (1973, 6-8; and 1977); and Friedman (1968a). 81. Brittan (1977, 46). 82. Frazer (1977; 1984); and Friedman (1968a). 83. Thirwall (1978, x). 84. Skidelsky (1977, vii-x). 85. Skidelsky (1977, viii). 86. Skidelsky (1977, ix). 87. In directing attention to planning for the future markets for products, Galbraith placed emphasis on the need for economic stability overall and in the product market. Said differently, there is a need for greater certainty about the economic future in order to call forth expenditures on capital goods. There was in Galbraith's writing the idea that government would be a source of stability for the economy instead of the instability that came to past. 88. Frazer and Yohe (1966, chaps. 21-23). 89. Skidelsky (1977, x). 90. Skidelsky (1977, 33). 91. Frazer (1980, chap. 4); Galbraith (1975); and Skidelsky (1978). 92. Skidelsky (1977, viii-ix). 93. Lilley (1977, 25). 94. Skidelsky (1977, 38). 95. Brittan (1977, 41-42). 96. Fry (1969, chaps. 1 and 2); and Harrod (1951, 3). 97. Harrod (1951, 13, 117-122). 98. Brittan (1977, 42). 99. Skidelsky (1977, 38). 100. Friedman (1978, 92). 101. D. Friedman and Selden (1975, 39); and Niskansen (1975, 30). 102. Friedman and Selden (1975, 49); and Niskansen (1975, 32-33). 103. Skidelsky (1977b, 39). 104. Frazer (1980, chaps. 8, 16, and 17). 105. Frazer (1973, 406-411; 1980, chap. 17). 106. Skidelsky (1977, 39-40). 107. Friedman (1978, 92). 108. Kuznets (1952). 109. Friedman (1957, 3-4). 110. Lilley (1977, 29). 111. Frazer and Boland (1983). 112. Frazer (1967; 1973). 113. Kaldor (1982, 21). 114. Kaldor (1982, 20-21). 115. Frazer (1983c). 116. Friedman (1974a, 15). 117. Frazer (1973, chap. 11); and Morrison (1966). 118. Frazer (1983c, sect. IV). 119. Bomberger and Frazer (1981); and Frazer (1980, chaps. 5 and 18). 120. Frazer (1984). 121. Camp (1962); and Kaldor (1982, xi, 2, 4-9). 122. Keynes (1936, chap. 11). 123. Frazer (1980, sect. 8.2); and Keynes (1936, 142). 124. Friedman (1968b); Gibson (1968); and Yohe and Karnosky (1969). 125. See note 123. 126. Harrod (1951; 1971, 62). 127. Brittan (1977, 41); and Schumpeter (1952). 128. Brittan (1977, 44-45). 129. Brittan (1977, 45). 130. Stein (1984, 312). 131. Brittan (1977, 45). 132. Friedman (1983, 19). 133. Brittan (1977, 48-49). 134. Playboy (1973, 65).

References, Chapter 11: Crises, Keynes and Friedman

Bagehot, Walter. 1915. *Lombard Street: A Description of the Money Market*, 14th edition. London: John Murray. The first edition appeared in April 1873.
Bomberger, William, and Frazer, William. 1981. "Interest Rates, Uncertainty and the Livingston Data." *Journal of Finance*, 36(June): 661-675.
Brittan, Samuel. 1977. "Can Democracy Manage an Economy?" In Robert Skidelsky, ed. *The End of the Keynesian Era*. New York: Holmes & Meier Publishers, Inc.
Camp, A.B. 1962. "Two Views of Money." *Lloyds Bank Review*, (July): 1-15.
Chandler, Lester V. 1958. *Benjamin Strong, Central Banker*. Washington, D.C.: The Brookings Institute.
Committee. 1959. [Radcliffe] *Report*, Committee on the Working of the Monetary System, Command Paper No. 827. London: Her Majesty's Stationary Office.
de Cecco, Marcello. 1977. "The Last of the Romans." In Robert Skidelsky, ed. *The End of the Keynesian Era*. New York: Holmes & Meier Publishers, Inc.
Frazer, William. 1967. *The Demand for Money*. Cleveland, Ohio: World Publishing Company.
_____. 1973. *Crisis in Economic Theory: A Study of Monetary Policy, Analysis, and Economic Goals*. Gainesville, Florida, University of Florida Press.
_____. 1976. "Review Article: Keynes and Feiwel's Intellectual History of Kalecki." *Southern Economic Journal*, 43(October): 1161-1169.
_____. 1977. "Income Distribution, Social Utility, and Unemployment." *Nebraska Journal of Economics and Business*, 16(Autumn): 37-60.

_____. 1978. "The Government Budget Constraint." *Public Finance Quarterly*, 6(July): 381-387.

_____. 1980. *Expectations, Forecasting and Control: A Provisional Textbook of Macroeconomics*, volumes I and II. Lanham, Md.: University Press of America.

_____. 1983a. *"Free to Choose*: A Review Article." *Wall Street Review of Books*, 11(No. 1): 14-22.

_____. 1983b. "Monetary Trends in the U.S. and the U.K." *Southern Economic Journal*, 49(January): 833-846.

_____. 1983c. "Lord Kaldor, Friedman and Pertinent Episodes." *Wall Street Review of Books*, 11(No. 4): 261-284.

_____. 1984. "Power, Ideas, and *Presidential Economics." Wall Street Review of Books*, 12(No. 3): 198-208.

_____, and Yohe, William P. 1966. *Analytics and Institutions of Money and Banking*. Princeton, N.J.: D. Van Nostrand Company, Inc.

_____, and Boland, Lawrence. 1983. "An Essay on the Foundations of Friedman's Methodology." *American Economic Review* 73(March): 129-144.

Friedman, Milton. 1957. *A Theory of the Consumption Function*. Princeton, N.J.: Princeton University Press, published for the National Bureau of Economic Research.

_____. 1961. "The Lags in Effect of Monetary Policy." *Journal of Political Economy*, 69(October): 447-466.

_____. 1968a. "The Role of Monetary Policy." *American Economic Review*, 58(March): 1-17.

_____. 1968b. "Factors Affecting the Level of Interest Rates." *A Savings and Residential Financing: 1968 Conference Proceedings*. Chicago, Ill.: United States Savings and Loan league.

_____. 1972a. *An Economist's Protest: Columns in Political Economy*. Glen Ridge, N.J.: Thomas Horton and Company.

_____. 1972b. "Monetary Policy." *Proceedings of the American Philosophical Society*, 116(June 1972): 196.

_____. 1974. "A Theoretical Framework for Monetary Analysis," and "Comments on the Critics." In Robert J. Gordon, ed., *Milton Friedman's Monetary Framework*. Chicago: University of Chicago Press.

_____. 1976. *Price Theory*. Chicago: Aldine Publishing Company.

_____. 1978. "The Politics of Economics." *Newsweek*, 92(October 16): 92.

_____. 1980. "Prices of Money and Goods Across Frontiers: The Pound and the Dollar Over a Century." *World Economic*, 2(February): 497-511.

_____. 1983. "The Keynes Centenary: A Monetarist Reflects." *The Economist*, 287(June 4): 17-19.

_____. 1984. "Monetary Policy for the 1980s." In John H. Moore, ed. *To Promote Prosperity: U.S. Domestic Policy in the Mid-1980s*. The Stanford University, Cal.: The Hoover Institution.

Fry, Geoffrey K. 1969. *Statesmen in Disguise: The Changing Role of the Administrative Class of the British Home Civil Service*. London: MacMillan and Co. Ltd.

Galbraith, John Kenneth. 1967. *The New Industrial State*. Boston: Houghton Mifflin Company.

_____. 1975. "How Keynes came to America." In Milo Keynes, ed. *Essays on John Maynard Keynes*. London: Cambridge University Press.

Gibson, William E. 1968. "Effects of Money on Interest Rates." *Staff Economic Studies*. No. 43, Board of Governors of the Federal Reserve System (January).

Harrod, Sir Roy F. 1951. *The Life of John Maynard Keynes*. New York: Harcourt, Brace and Company.

_____. "Discussion Paper." In G. Clayton, J.C. Gilbert, and R. Degewick, eds. *Monetary Theory and Monetary Policy in the 1970s*. Oxford: Oxford University Press.

Henderson, W.O. 1976. *The Life of Friedrich Engels*, vols. I and II. London: Frank Cass and Company Limited.

Hession, Charles H. 1984. *John Maynard Keynes*. New York: MacMillan Publishing Company.

Hicks, Sir John. 1974. *The Crisis in Keynesian Economics*. New York: Basic Books, Inc. Publishers.

———. 1983. "The Keynes Centenary: a Skeptical Follower: *The Economist*, 287(June 18): 17-19.

Johnson, Jarry G. 1978. "Comment on Mayer on Monetarism." In Thomas Mayer *et al.* *The Structure of Monetarism*. New York: W.W. Norton & Company.

Kaldor, Nicolas. 1982. *The Scourge of Monetarism*. Oxford: Oxford University Press.

Kane, Edward J. 1974. "The Repoliticization of the Fed." *Journal of Financial and Quantitative Analysis*, (November): 743-752.

Keynes, John Maynard. 1920. *The Economic Consequences of the Peace*. New York: Harcourt, Brace and Howe.

———. 1923. *A Tract on Monetary Reform*. London: MacMillan and Co., Limited.

———. 1925. "The Economic Consequence of Mr. Churchill." Reprinted in J.M. Keynes (1932, 244-270).

———. 1932. *Essays in Persuasion*. New York: Harcourt, Brace and Company.

———. 1936. *The General Theory of Employment, Interest, and Money*. New York: Harcourt, Brace and Company.

Kuznets, Simon. 1952. "Proportion of Capital Formation to National Product." *American Economic Review*, 42(May): 507-526.

Lilley, Peter. 1977. "Two Critics of Keynes: Friedman and Hayek." In Robert Skidelsky, ed. *The End of the Keynesian Era*. New York: Holmes & Meier Publishers, Inc.

Manchester, William. 1983. *Winston Spencer Churchill: Visions of Glory, 1874-1932*. Boston: Little, Brown and Company.

Morrison, George R. 1966. *Liquidity Preference of Commercial Banks*. Chicago, Ill.: University of Chicago Press.

Niskanen, William A. 1975. "The Pathology of Politics." In Richard T. Selden, ed. *Capitalism and Freedom: Problems and Prospects*. Charlottesville, Va.: University Press of Virginia.

Playboy. 1973. "Milton Friedman." *Playboy*, 20(1973): 51-74.

Santoni, G.L. 1984. "A Private Central Bank: Some Olde English Lessons." *Review*, 66(April): 12-22.

Scaperlanda, Anthony. 1977. "Hansen's Secular Stagnation Thesis Again." *Journal of Economic Issues*, 11(June): 223-243.

Schumpeter, Joseph A. 1952. *Capitalism, Socialism, and Democracy*. Fourth edition. London: George Allen & Anwin Ltd.

Selden, Richard T. ed. 1975. *Capitalism and Freedom: Problems and Prospects*. Charlottesville, Va.: University Press of Virginia.

Skidelsky, Robert. 1977. "The Political Meaning of the Keynesian Revolution." In Robert Skidelsky, ed. *The End of the Keynesian Era*. New York: Holmes & Meier Publishers, Inc.

———. 1978. "The American Response to Keynes." In A.P. Thirwall (1978).

Shirer, William L. 1960. *The Rise and Fall of the Third Reich*. New York: Simon and Schuster.

Stein, Herbert. 1984. *Presidential Economics*. New York: Simon and Schuster.

Thirwall, A.P. ed. *Keynes and Laissez-Faire*, New York: Holmes and Meier Publishers, Inc.

Tobin, James. 1982. "The Reagan Economic Plan: Supply-Side, Budget, and Inflation." In Richard H. Fink, ed. *Supply-Side Economics: A Critical Appraisal*. Frederick, Md.: University Publications of America, Inc.

Yohe, William P., and Karnosky, Denis S. 1969. "Interest Rates and Price Level Changes, 1952-69." *Review*, Federal Reserve Bank of St. Louis 51(December).

Notes, Chapter 12: The Philosophy and Economics of Freedom

1. Samuels (1977); Stark (1943). 2. Stark (1943, 149). 3. Mitchell (1950, 177-202). 4. Stigler (1965, 82-84); Stark (1943, 149-212); Walras (1952, 471-488). 5. Stephen (1917, 730-743). 6. Knight (1956, 263). 7. Walras (1952, 480). 8. Stark (1943, 149-159); Stigler (1965, 82-84). 9.

Stark (1943, 158). **10.** Stigler (1965, 83). **11.** Stark (1943, 156). **12.** Pigou (1920); and Hutchison (1981a, 65-66). **13.** Buchanan (1975, 52-77). **14.** Gramm (1976); Hayek (1944; 1978); Henderson (1977); Hirsch (1976); Knight (1956); Machlup (1976); Samuels (1977); and Simons (1948). **15.** McKinney (1976); and Samuels (1977, 490, 521). **16.** Friedman (1962, ii). Buchanan pointed out, however (1978), that Knight and his contemporaries "didn't use the words 'normative' and 'positive'." **17.** J. N. Keynes (1955). **18.** Friedman (1953, 3). **19.** Lerner (1944); and Pigou (1920). **20.** Hirsch (1976). **21.** Friedman (1962; 1978); and Selden (1975). **22.** Gramm (1965, 168). **23.** Buchanan (1962; 1975); and Niskanen (1975). **24.** McKinney (1976, 192). **25.** Knight (1956, 258). **26.** McKinney (1976, 192-193). **27.** Knight (1956, 258). **28.** McKinney (1976, 193). **29.** McKinney (1976, 195). **30.** McKinney (1976, 203). **31.** McKinney (1976, 203-204). **32.** McKinney (1976, 197). **33.** Stigler (1950, 12). **34.** Hutchison (1981a, 34). **35.** While there is a history of controversy about the "economic man," as if he operated in a vacuum from social and cultural matters, F. Knight's use of the Crusoe-type model does *not* deny the role of the social and cultural matters. Buchanan (1978) expressed the matter thus:

> "Rather,..., he [Knight] was using this [Crusoe-type model] as a model in which to get some handles on discussing some of the underlying forces in an interaction process, in which you sort of start with some acting, behaving, utility-maximizing person. Now Knight, of all people, fully recognized, as a matter of fact he, more than any established economist of that time, put great stress on the fact that the individual is a mixture of a whole lot of things and that the individual is not a simple unit that maximizes a utility function that does not change. In *The Ethics of Competition* [Knight 1935], for example, he stressed that the individual is always changing, he is subject to all these cultural, social influences. He put great stress on the fact that the individual also is part of a community. In all of these things—perhaps much more than modern economists and much more than Milton Friedman—Frank Knight fully acknowledged the sort of individualism that is really a construction of a lot of things....I suppose this in one sense is the reason that he and Clarence Ayers were great friends in spite of all their controversy. On one level they were in basic fundamental agreement. The disagreement was fundamentally that Knight was an analyst and Knight had to use these kinds of models because he wanted to get down to some fundamental analytics. And you start with the behaving individual. To Knight it made no sense to try to start with a social unit."

36. McKinney (1976, 198). **37.** Knight (1956, 132); and McKinney (1976, 198-199). **38.** Hutchison (1981a, 37); Lerner (1944); and Pigou (1920). **39.** Buchanan (1962); Frazer and Boland (1983). **40.** McKinney (1976, 199-201). **41.** McKean (1975, 92). **42.** McKinney (1975, 202). **43.** Frazer (1973, chaps. 16 and 17). **44.** Modigliani (with Friedman) (1977); and Frazer (1978). **45.** Gramm (1976, 167-189). **46.** Gramm (1976, 174-179). **47.** Friedman (1962; 1978a; 1978b; 1978c; 1978d; 1978e). **48.** Marx (1906, first edition, first published in 1867); Heilbroner (1953); and Schumpeter (1952; and 1954). **49.** Burns (1978). **50.** Schumpeter (1952). **51.** Burns (1978). **52.** Friedman (1977, 335). **53.** Friedman (1962, 12 and 33; 1978b, 3; 1978e, 11). **54.** Friedman (1962, 8, 12, 21, 23-25, 33, 108-118, 200; 1978a, 11; 1978e, 8). **55.** Friedman (1977, 335). **56.** Friedman (1962, 2). **57.** Novick (1974). **58.** Silk (1974, 47-93). **59.** Friedman (1962, 5). **60.** Burns (1978); Friedman (1977, 334); and Weil (1978). **61.** Friedman (1977, 334). **62.** Friedman (1977, 334). **63.** Hughes (1977). **64.** Friedman (1962, 3, 7-21, 26, 115-117). **65.** Friedman (1962, 2-35, 114). **66.** Davenport (1967, 148); and Friedman (1979). Davenport (1976, 149) reported that Friedman blamed Goldwater for his failure in the 1964 election on two counts: (1) for not giving his speech on civil rights much earlier, and (2) for not standing his ground on social security (including for not enlarging on the idea "that such security is best obtained by voluntary and private means"). **67.** Playboy (1973, 65). **68.** Friedman's position on welfare economics has been referred to on earlier occasions (chap. 8, note 51). We may quote him at greater length, however, where he responded to the question of why he never addressed "welfare economics." His answer starts by his recalling his view that empirical research would resolve differences of opinion, namely:

> "Well, I think fundamentally, for two reasons. The first and the more important was because of the belief that I have always had that most differences between

people derive from differences about positive economics and not normative economics. I don't believe that people differ fundamentally—i.e., the kind of people of whom we're talking about, the kind of people in the American academic scene, the people in the American political scene—I don't think they differ fundamentally in the objectives they want to pursue. But they differ on how to pursue them. And there are differences in their predictions about what will happen if you do this and that. Or else it's differences on their time perspective, whether they're talking about the long run or short run. And so it has—I guess—always seemed to me more useful and more interesting to try to assemble evidence on how things are, what they are.

Continuing Friedman recalled Mitchell's influence and ended by noting two theorems from welfare economics:

> I may say on this I do attribute a good deal of influence to Wesley Mitchell....For him there was no sense in talking about whether you're in favor of policy A or B unless you know what policy A or B are going to do. I have to know how something is going to work before I know whether I like it or not. And so fundamentally, it seems to me that—it's always seemed to me—that the problems of positive economics in that sense are very much more important than the problems of welfare economics in the sense of the formal analysis of the conditions of the welfare optimum zone. I think for example—I don't mean to run that kind of thing down—I think Ken Arrow's impossibility theorem [Sen 1985] is a very fundamental contribution. Coase's theorem in welfare economics had a very great influence. So I don't mean to be running it down, but it's not the thing I've ever been very much interested in."

The Coase theorem (1960), which came up earlier, is cited and discussed by Melvin Reder (1982, 22). As a result of the theorem, the following is said to be recognized, namely: damaging effects to third parties from production are produced jointly with positive output. The "consumers" of these negative outputs "must be compensated as the property rights of injuries and injured and the laws of liability determine." 69. Friedman (1978a, 9; and 1978e, 3). 70. Samuels (1976, 364-368). 71. Selden (1975, 21, 51, 112); and Stigler (1975, 321). 72. Viner (1952, 203). 73. Friedman (1962, 202); and Friedman (1978a; 1978f, chap. 2). 74. On these episodes and setbacks, Friedman (1969) commented:

> "I think we have to distinguish between the movement in the political sphere and the movement in the intellectual sphere. Now I am sure you are right about the political sphere. I don't have any doubt that if Kennedy had not been assassinated that in the 1964 election between Kennedy and Goldwater it would have been a wholly different story, and a much closer thing. So I don't disagree with you on the political sphere, but I think that so far as the attitude of the intellectuals was concerned, I don't believe the Kennedy assassination had much to do with that."

Continuing he said;

> "You know what set the intellectual thing back is at that time you had a movement among the young people of colleges away from the New Deal attitudes toward a freer, more individualistic style. I think what set that back was the Vietnam war. But particularly the draft.
> "Now in a way you might say that the draft would foster the approach away from government control, but the fact that it induced so many people to come on campuses, who had no business being on campuses to avoid the draft, and it gave them all a guilty feeling and drove all activism into protests against the war. And I think it just sort of killed an intellectual trend that was developing and beginning to gather force."

75. Dicey (1905); and Friedman and Selden (1975, 50-51). 76. R. Friedman (1976, 21-22); and Friedman (1979). M. Friedman's son David, commented on the simple method (1978):

You know Newton's laws of motion are extremely simple.... Ricardo in effect assumes that the capital-labor ratio is the same in all products. He knows it's not true. He says it's not true, but he's assuming it because he thinks that the errors that come from that false assumption are small, that he specifically argues they're small. This is the argument in Stigler's essay that Ricardo's is a 93 percent labor theory of value.

77. Friedman (1978b, 4; 1978e, 8). **78.** Friedman (1978a, 11; 1978e, 8). **79.** Heilbroner (1953, 28-29). **80.** Friedman (1962, 12-13). **81.** Friedman (1978b, 3; 1978e, 11). **82.** Friedman (1978b, 5; 1978e, 12). **83.** Friedman (1962, 8, 21, 108-118, 200); and Playboy (1973, 68). **84.** Friedman (1978b, 3; 1978e, 11). **85.** Friedman (1962, 13). **86.** Friedman (1962, 14). **87.** Friedman (1962, 15). **88.** Friedman (1962, 28-30), plus some of the dialogue in Friedman's *Playboy* interview is applicable (1973, 58). **89.** Friedman (1962, 15). **90.** Friedman (1962, 31-32). **91.** Friedman (1962, 24). **92.** Friedman (1962, 23). **93.** Friedman (1962, 23). **94.** McKinney (1976, 206, 208). **95.** Friedman (1978b, 45; 1978e, 12-13). **96.** Friedman (1962, 17). **97.** Friedman (1962, 18). **98.** Friedman (1962, 18-19). **99.** Friedman (1962, 114-115; 1978b, 2). **100.** Friedman (1962, 115). **101.** Friedman (1962, 22-23). **102.** Friedman (1978b, 3; 1978e, 10-11). **103.** Friedman (1978b, 4; 1978e, 12-13). **104.** Friedman (1976, 223). **105.** McKinney (1976, 203). **106.** Buchanan (1978). **107.** Silk (1976, 41). **108.** Samuelson (1979, 81). **109.** Silk (1976, 38). **110.** Silk (1976, 35-36). **111.** Friedman (1982). **112.** Friedman (1982). **113.** Silk (1975, 40). **114.** Frazer (1982). **115.** Friedman (1978b, 12). **116.** Friedman (1978b, 4; 1978e, 12). **117.** Brozen and Friedman (1966); Cohen and Friedman (1972); Friedman (1962, 37-195; 1966; 1968; 1978e).

References, Chapter 12:
The Philosophy and Economics of Freedom

Brozen, Yale, and Friedman, Milton. 1966. *The Minimum Wage Rate*. Washington, D.C.: The Free Society Association, Inc.
Buchanan, James M. 1975. In Richard T. Selden, ed. *Capitalism and Freedom*. Charlottesville, VA.: The University of Virginia Press.
_____. 1978. "Frank Knight, Chicago and Friedman." Taped Discussion (September).
Burns, Arthur. 1978. "The Future of the Free Enterprise System." Memphis, Tenn.: P.K. Seidman Foundation.
Coase, Ronald H. 1960. "The Problem of Social Cost." *Journal of Law and Economics* 3(October): 1-44.
Cohen, Webber J., and Friedman, Milton. 1972. *Social Security: Universal or Selective?* Washington, D.C.: American Enterprise Institute for Public Policy Research.
Davenport, John. 1967. "The Radical Economics of Milton Friedman." Fortune 75 (June): 131-132, 147-148, 150.
Dicey, A.V. 1905. *Law and Public Opinion in England*. London: Macmillan and Co., Ltd.
Frazer, William. 1973. *Crises in Economic Theory*. Gainesville, Fla.: University of Florida Press.
_____. 1978. "Evolutionary Economics, Rational Expectations and Monetary Policy." *Journal of Economic Issues* 12(June): 343-372.
_____. 1980. *Expectations, Forecasting, and Control: A Provisional Textbook of Macroeconomics*. Lanham, Md.: University Press of America.
_____. 1982. "*Free to Choose*: A Review Article." *Wall Street Review of Books* 11(Winter): 14-22.
_____, and Boland, Lawrence. 1983. "An Essay on the Foundations of Friedman's Methodology." *American Economic Review* 73(March): 129-144.
Friedman, David. 1978. "Taped Discussion." September 21.
Friedman, Milton. 1953. "The Methodology of Positive Economics." In *Essays in Positive Economics*. Chicago, Ill.: University of Chicago Press.
_____. 1962. *Capitalism and Freedom*. Chicago: University of Chicago Press.

_____, and Stigler, George J. 1966. "Roofs or Ceilings? The Current Housing Problem." *Popular Essays on Current Problems*.

_____. 1968. "The Case for the Negative Income Tax.: *Republican Papers*. New York: Frederick A. Praeger.

_____. 1976. *Price Theory*. Chicago: Aldine Publishing Company.

_____. 1977. "The Future of Capitalism: The Intellectual and the Businessman." *Vital Speeches* 43(March 15): 333-337.

_____. 1978a. "What is America." *Sohioan* 50 (February): 8-11.

_____. 1978b. "Is Capitalism Humane?" *Sohioan* 50(April): 2-4.

_____. 1978c. "Who Protects the Consumer?" *Sohioan* 50(June): 2-4.

_____. 1978d. "The Energy Crisis." *Sohioan* 50(August): 2-5.

_____. 1978e. *The Economics of Freedom*. Cleveland, Ohio: Standard Oil Company of New Jersey. Also lectures reported here have been videotaped and published by Harcourt, Brace Jovanovich, Inc.

_____. 1978f. *Tax Limitation, Inflation and the Role of Government*. Dallas, Texas: The Fisher Institute.

_____. 1979. "Taped Discussion." February 6.

_____. 1982. "How Flat is Flat?" *Newsweek* 100 (August 2): 52.

_____, and Samuelson, Paul A. 1978. "Answering the Big Questions." *Newsweek* 91(May 29): 80-81.

_____, and Samuelson, Paul A. 1980. *The Economic Responsibility of Government*. College Station, Texas: Center for Education and Research in Free Enterprise.

_____, and Friedman, Rose D. 1980. *Free to Choose*. New York: Harcourt, Brace Jovanovich, Inc.

Friedman, Rose D. 1976. "Milton Friedman: Husband and Colleague—(3) The Beginning of a Teaching Career." *Oriental Economist* (July): 18-23.

Gramm, Warren S. 1976. "Chicago Economics: From Individualism True to Individualism False." In Warren J. Samuels, ed. *The Chicago School of Political Economy*. East Lansing, Mich.: Association for Evolutionary Economics.

Goldwater, Barry. 1960. *The Conscience of a Conservative*. Shepherdsville, Kentucky: Victor Publishing Company, Inc.

_____. 1964. "Transcript of Goldwater's Speech Accepting Republican Presidential Nomination." *New York Times* 113(July 17): 10.

Hayek, Friedrich A. 1944. *The Road to Serfdom*. Chicago: University of Chicago Press.

_____. 1978. *New Studies in Philosophy, Politics, Economics and the History of Ideas*. Chicago: University of Chicago Press.

Heilbroner, Robert L. 1953. *The Worldly Philosophers*. New York: Simon and Schuster.

Hirsch, Eva, and Hirsch, Abraham. 1976. "The Heterodox Methodology of Two Chicago Economists." In Warren J. Samuels, ed. *The Chicago School of Political Economy*. East Lansing, Michigan: Association for Evolutionary Economics. 59-78.

Hughes, Jonathan R.T. 1977. *The Governmental Habit: Economic Controls from Colonial Times to the Present*. New York: Basic Books, Inc., Publishers.

Hutchison, T. W. 1981a. "The Market Economy and the Franchise." In *The Politics and Philosophy of Economics*. New York: New York University Press.

_____. 1981b. "The Philosophy and Politics of the Cambridge School." In *The Politics and Philosophy of Economics*. New York: New York University Press.

Keynes, John Neville. 1955. *The Scope and Method of Political Economy*. Fourth Edition. New York: Kelley and Millman, Inc.

Knight, Frank H. 1935. *The Ethics of Competition and Other Essays*. London: George Allen and Unwin Ltd.

_____. 1956. *On the History and Method of Economics*. Chicago: University of Chicago Press.

_____. 1960. *Intelligence and Democratic Action*. Cambridge, Mass.: Harvard University Press.

Lerner, Abba P. 1944. *The Economics of Control: Principles of Welfare Economics*. New York: Macmillan Company.

Machlup, Fritz, ed. (with foreword by Milton Friedman). 1976. *Essays on Hayek*. New York: New York University Press.

Marx, Karl. 1906. *Capital: A Critique of Political Economy*, Revised and amplified according to the fourth German edition by Earnest Untermann. New York: The Modern Library.

McKinney, John. 1976. "Frank H. Knight and Chicago Libertarianism." In Warren J. Samuels, ed. *The Chicago School of Political Economy*. East Lansing, Mich.: Association for Evolutionary Economics.

Mitchell, Wesley C. 1950. "Bentham's Felicific Calculus." In Wesley C. Mitchell, ed. *The Backward Art of Spending Money*. New York: Augustus M. Kelley, Inc.

Modigliani, Franco, with discussion by Milton Friedman. 1977. "The Monetarist Controversy: A Seminar Discussion." *Economic Review*. Supplement, Federal Reserve Bank of San Francisco (Spring): 5-26.

Niskanen, William A. 1975. "The Pathology of Politics." In Richard T. Selden, ed. *Capitalism and Freedom*. Charlottesville, VA.: University Press of Virginia.

Novick, Robert. 1974. *Anarchy, State, and Utopia*. New York: Basic Books, Inc., Publishers.

Pigou, A. C. 1920. *The Economics of Welfare*. London: Macmillan and Co., Limited.

Playboy. 1973. "Playboy Interview: Milton Friedman." *Playboy* 20(February): 51-74.

Reder, Melvin W. 1982. "Chicago Economics: Permanence and Change." *Journal of Economic Literature* 20(March): 1-38.

Samuels, Warren J. 1976a. "Chicago Doctrine as Exploration and Justification." In Warren J. Samuels, ed. *The Chicago School of Political Economy*. East Lansing, Mich.: Association for Evolutionary Economics.

_____, ed. 1976b. *The Chicago School of Political Economy*. East Lansing, Mich.: Association for Evolutionary Economics.

_____. 1977. "The Knight-Ayers Correspondence: The Grounds of Knowledge and Social Action." *Journal of Economic Issues* 11(September): 485-525.

Schumpeter, Joseph A. 1952. *Capitalism, Socialism, and Democracy*, Fourth edition. London: George Allen & Unwin, Ltd.

Seldon, Richard T., ed. 1975. *Capitalism and Freedom: Problems and Prospects*. Charlottesville, Va.: University Press of Virginia.

Sen, Amartya. 1985. "Review of Arrow's Social Choice and Justice." *Journal of Economic Literature* 23(December): 1764-1776.

Silk, Leonard. 1974. *The Economists*. New York: Basic Books, Inc. Publishers.

Simons, Henry C. 1948. *Economic Policy for a Free Society*. Chicago: University of Chicago Press.

Stark, W. 1943. *The Ideal Foundations of Economic Thought*. London: Routledge and Kegan Paul, Limited.

Stephen, Leslie, and Lee, Sidney. 1917. *The Dictionary of National Biography*. Volume V. London: Oxford University Press.

Stigler, George J. 1965. *Essays in the History of Economics*. Chicago: University of Chicago Press.

Viner, Jacob. 1952. "Viner on Bentham and Mill." In Henry William Speigel, ed. *The Development of Economic Thought*. New York: John Wiley & Sons, Inc.

Walras, Leon. 1952. "Walras on Gossen." Translated and abridged in Henry William Speigel, ed. *The Development of Modern Economic Thought*. New York: John Wiley and Sons, Inc.

Weil, Gordon L. *The Welfare Debate of 1978*. White Plains, N.Y.: Institute for Socioeconometric Studies.

Notes, Chapter 13: The Distribution and Permanency of Income

1. Marx (1875, 530). 2. Fain (1956); Ruskin (1862); and Stephen (1917). 3. Fain (1956, 95-96); Ruskin (1862, 178). The part of Ruskin's economic work in question originally appeared in *Fraser's* Magazine for June, September, and December 1862, and April 1863. It was not originally published as a book until 1872. 4. Marx (1875, 531). This work of Marx was actu-

ally not published until 1891 (Tucker 1978, 525). **5.** Frazer (1977, 39-48). **6.** Rivlin (1975). **7.** Friedman (1979a, 56) continued on government's changing role:

> "A simple calculation shows how drastic the shift has been. Not only has all of the increase in total government spending (Federal, state and local) gone into nondefense spending, but in addition, spending on national defense declined from 12 per cent of national income in 1957 to 11 per cent in 1967 and 6 per cent in 1977. As a result, nondefense spending rose from 20 per cent of national income in 1957 to 26 per cent in 1967 and 35 per cent in 1977—an increase of roughly a third in each decade. And this calculation seriously understates the size of the shift. Spending not only on defense but also on other traditional services has decreased as a share of total government spending."

8. Marx (1875, 530). **9.** On the subject of Friedman, inferences in statistical matters, and proofs as in mathematics, Leo Rosten drew a portrait thus:

> "Fenwick [Friedman] *likes* reasoning. He also likes people. So he listens carefully to anything you tell him, and promptly wants to know where and how you found out whatever it is you told him—and how you know it is so. Worse, he separates inferences from proof. Fenwick enjoys following every single little chug in your train of thought—indeed, he gets right on the train with you. And you have barely begun to move before Fenwick excitedly demonstrates that: (a) you have taken the wrong train; or (b) it doesn't stop where you want to go: or (c) the tracks don't lead from your premise to your preferred conclusion, or (d) that train will land you where you don't want to go and didn't even know you were going." (Rosten 1966, 14)

10. Friedman (1962, 174). But see qualifications in note 47. **11.** Some of these come in chapter 16. An extended position by Friedman in his 1980 book with Rose Friedman got into constitutional measures to assure freedom. **12.** Heilbroner (1953, 86-87). **13.** Stigler (1958). **14.** Playboy (1973, 60). **15.** Friedman (1978b). This notion of psychological conditioning by the socioeconomic system is found on other occasions in Friedman's work. For example, in addressing the disposition of high military officers to favor the "draft" over the "volunteer armed force," Friedman (1979c, 76) noted that the officers are sincere patriots with concern about national defense and then proceeded:

> "They have spent their lives in a system that is based on command. This is what they have been trained for. It is asking a good deal to expect them to understand, let alone be enthusiastic about, a wholly different approach in recruiting personnel."

In closing Friedman stated, "Our military will be far stronger if we recruit it by methods consistent with the basic values of a free society than if we resort to the methods of a totalitarian society." **16.** Continuing from note 9, Leo Rosten's passage on "Fenwick" (actually Friedman) and the minimum wage is revealing. An excerpt from it follows:

> Fenwick and a friend of mine from Washington were talking about the minimum wage, which Congress has voted to raise from $1.25 an hour to $1.40—and to $1.60 an hour in 1968. Fenwick stunned my friend by mournfully stating that these minimum-wage laws will create unemployment—and precisely among those unskilled workers (Negroes, teenagers, Puerto Ricans) whom the minimum-wage laws pretend to help.
> Fenwick said: "To begin with, the average wage earner today gets about twice $1.40 an hour. So the bill is not going to affect him—"
> "The bill helps the unskilled, the undereducated!" my friend sternly said.
> "An *admirable* intention," beamed Fenwick. "A large proportion of that group is unemployed—but if employers aren't hiring them at $1.25 an hour, will they hire them at $1.40 an hour?"
> I poured a stiff drink for my friend.

Fenwick went on: "Surely the unemployed will have less chance of getting a job under the new minimum-wage laws than they had under the old."

"What?" cried my friend. "Can you prove that?" "Yes," said Fenwick kindly. "Every time minimum wages have been raised, since 1945, the ratio of unemployed teenagers has risen. Every time you raise the minimum, you must push more unskilled, discriminated-against workers on to the unemployment rolls."

"What about the greedy employers," my friend demanded, "who cruelly exploit their workers by paying them barely enough to live on?!!"

"Oh, very, very few employers can hold on to workmen if they pay them less than the workers can get elsewhere." "It isn't what they can 'get,' it's what they're worth!" my friend thundered.

"Only God can decide how much a man is 'worth,'" sighed Fenwick. "We're talking about the best price a man can *get*—"

"Some men can't live on that! Or feed their children—"

"We certainly ought to remedy that!" said Fenwick. "Let's guarantee the poor a minimum income. That does far less damage than a minimum wage."

....

Rosten (1966, 14).

17. Frazer (1977). 18. Playboy (1973, 53-54). 19. Davenport (1976, 132); and Friedman (1962, 180-181; and 1973, 54). 20. Playboy (1973, 54). 21. Friedman (1977, 335). 22. Schoor and Friedman (1969); and Chapman (1978). 23. Davenport (1967, 150); Friedman (1962, 190-195; 1968); and Schnitzer (1968, 4-5). 24. Friedman (1976, 12-13). 25. Schoor and Friedman (1969). 26. Friedman (1978b). 27. Henderson (1976, 601). 28. Hutchison (1981, 9-11). 29. Friedman (1981). 30. Reprinted in Tucker (1978, 469-500). 31. The references to the sequence are respectively: Marx (1848, 485); Marx (1848, 480); Marx (1948, 400; 1906, 689-703); Marx (1848, 481); and Marx (1848, 484, 481). 32. Marx (1848, 483, 484). 33. Marx (1906, 701-703). 34. This apologetics role of economics and economists came up earlier. Leonard Silk's profile on Friedman (1976, 47-93) cast Friedman in the role of an apologist for the capitalist economy. 35. Marx (1848, 490). 36. Silk (1974, 56-57). 37. Friedman (1938, 129-130). 38. R. Friedman (1976b, 21). 39. Friedman (1943). 40. R. Friedman (1976b, 21). The Harry White in question is the Harry White who was somewhat of a Harvard Keynesian and somewhat of an American counterpart to Britain's J. M. Keynes during the World War II years (Harrod 1951, 507, 537-541, 557-560, 562-566, 569, 577-578, 581, 583, 590n., 629, 637). 41. R. Friedman (1976b, 21). 42. Friedman (1978c, 70). 43. R. Friedman (1976b, 21); and Friedman (1978c, 70). 44. Friedman and Stigler (1946, 9). 45. Silk (1974, 70-71). 46. Friedman and Stigler (1946, 10). 47. Friedman (1962, 174-176; 1979b; 1982). In the 1980-84, period of the Reagan presidency, the flat-rate tax received considerable attention, along with the production (or supply) side of the economy and not simply the receipt-of-income (or spending) side. (See references in chapter 16; Keleher 1982; and MacNeil/Lehrer 1982). In this period, Keleher et al. (1982) gave perspective to the flat-rate tax. They said: "In short, the low-rate, broad-based tax system finds its theoretical roots in the doctrines of the 19th Century classical writers. These economists emphasized all of the desirable features claimed for a flat rate scheme—equity, simplicity, and incentive" (Keleher 1982, 26). Friedman, however, as the present chapter indicates became the major modern economist to renew and extend its analytical foundations, to relate it analytically to freedom as a goal, to argue for it, and to mount criticism against the prevailing system with all its inequities, tax loopholes and shelters, and exemptions. 48. Friedman (1979b). However, see piece on Lawrence Klein and Friedman where their disagreements over three decades continued, even as they analyzed more data than probably any other economist (Frazer 1984), note references to Arjo Klamer in introduction to part VI, and note manifesto signed by academic economist who opposed Thatcher. 49.See also Frazer (1980, sect. 9.4). 50. Attention had been drawn to human capital by efforts of the 1979 co-recipient of the Nobel prize, Theodore Schultz, as taken up in chapter 7. His most important paper on the subject was presented as a presidential address to the American Economic Association (Schultz 1961, 1-17). The main figure to move toward the formalization of notions about human capital at the University of Chicago was Gary Becker, an early student under Friedman, though he later moved independently of Friedman.

Rose Friedman herself (1976a, 19-20) recalled Friedman's dissertation at Columbia University under the title *Income from Independent Professional Practice* (1945). Coauthored by Simon Kuznets, the dissertation was viewed by her as "a pioneer study in the field that subsequently developed under the label of 'human capital'." **51.** Henderson (1976, chaps. 4 and 6); and Hutchison (1981, 20). **52.** Frazer (1980, chaps. 2 and 16). **53.** Friedman (1962, 166). **54.** Friedman (1962, 174-176). **55.** Friedman (1962, 164). **56.** Friedman (1962, 168; 1957). **57.** Friedman (1962, 162-163); and Rawls (1971). **58.** Friedman (1962, 173). **59.** Playboy (1973, 60). **60.** Buchanan (1978); Britton (1978); and Tool (1979). **61.** Friedman (1962, 172); and Playboy (1973, 62). **62.** Playboy (1973, 62, 63). **63.** Kelcher (1982); and MacNeil/ Lehrer (1982). **64.** Britton (1978). **65.** Tool (1979, 259). **66.** Britton (1977); and Tool (1979, 260). **67.** Friedman (1953; and 1976, 76-84). **68.** Friedman (1962, 162). **69.** Friedman (1962, 163). **70.** Frazer (1980, appendix A to chap. 16). **71.** Selden (1975, 50). **72.** Friedman (1978a, 16). **73.** Friedman (1978a, 18); and Playboy (1973, 66). **74.** Frazer (1980, chap. 11). Friedman (1979a, 87); Goldman (1979); and Samuelson (1979, 79). Friedman's occasional Keynesian adversary, Paul Samuelson, opposed the notion of such a constitutional amendment. His argument was for maintaining flexibility in budget matters, but in its detailed reference to the 1930s conditions in the U.S., the supporting argument revealed an essentially Keynesian view of the 1930s. The argument follows:

> "Even from the standpoint of those anxious to contain and reverse the trend toward an expanding public sector, historical experience suggests that it is unwise to use the Constitution to fix upon the nation for all time some particular formula of macroeconomic policy.
> "Only recall 1930-32. Herbert Hoover tried disastrously to raise tax rates in the teeth of a worsening depression in order to balance the budget that inevitably had gone into deficit because of reduced tax collections. Had Roosevelt been forced by the Constitution to do the same, blood would have run in the streets."

Here Samuelson overlooks discussion of monetary policy as a solution to the crisis of the early 1930s and to the Fed's role in the liquidation of banks (pp. 424-425). Further, in his *Economics* with William Nordhaus (1985, 879)—referring to what would be essentially Thatcher's position on the wage rate (pp. 419-420)—he says: "Blood runs in the streets of nations trying to adjust to an overvalued currency by internal cost deflation [or, say, the downward adjustment in wage contracts (e.g., pp. 191, 223)]."

Samuelson concluded in 1979: "Government by law and not by men means flexible evolution through due process. It doesn't mean freezing into the Constitution each passing economic fad." (Samuelson 1979, 79)

75. Moynihan (1981). **76.** Friedman (1979c). **77.** Friedman (1979a). **78.** Friedman (1982, 52). **79.** Friedman (1982, 52). **80.** Playboy (1973, 66). **81.** Friedman (1968, 203-207). **82.** Friedman (1968, 206). **83.** Friedman (1968, 206-207). **84.** Friedman (1968, 209). **85.** Davenport (1967, 150); Friedman (1962, 190-195); Schnitzer (1968, 4-5). **86.** Chapman (1978). **87.** Moynihan (1978). **88.** Friedman (1962, 172-176; 1968, 214). **89.** Hearings (1979). **90.** Chapman (1978, 9). **91.** Friedman (1978c, 16). **92.** Friedman (1973, 66). **93.** Chapman (1978, 10).

References, Chapter 13:
The Distribution and Permanency of Income

Britton, John A. 1978. *Inheritance and Inequality of Wealth*. Washington, D.C.: Brookings Institution.
Buchanan, James M. 1975. "The Political Economy of Franchise in the Welfare State." In Richard T. Selden, ed. 1975.
—————. 1978. Taped Discussion, (September).
Chapman, Stephen. 1978. "Poor Laws," *New Republic* 179 (December 2): 6-10.
Davenport, John. 1967. "The Radical Economics of Milton Friedman." *Fortune* 75(June): 130-154.

Fain, John Tyrel. 1956. *Ruskin and the Economists*. Nashville, Tenn.: Vanderbilt University Press.
Frazer, William. 1977. "Income Distribution, Social Utility, and Unemployment." *Nebraska Journal of Economics and Business* 16(Autumn): 37-60.
_____. 1980. *Expectations, Forecasting and Control: A Provisional Textbook of Macroeconomics*, Lanham, Md.: University Press of America.
_____. 1984. "*The Economics of Supply and Demand* and Friedman." *Economic Notes* 13(no. 3): 47-71.
Friedman, Milton, ed. 1937, 1938 and 1939. *Studies in Income and Wealth*. Vols. 1-3 respectively. New York: National Bureau of Economic Research.
_____. 1943. "The Spending Tax as a Wartime Fiscal Measure." *American Economic Review* 33(March): 50-62.
_____. 1953. "Choice, Chance, and the Personal Distribution of Income." *Journal of Political Economy*, 61(August): 277-290.
_____. 1957. *A Theory of the Consumption Function*. Princeton, N.J.: Princeton University Press for the National Bureau of Economic Research.
_____. 1962. *Capitalism and Freedom*. Chicago: University of Chicago Press.
_____. 1968. "The Case for the Negative Income Tax." In Melvin R. Laird, Ed. *Republican Papers*. New York: Frederick A. Praeger.
_____. 1976. *Price Theory*. Chicago: Aldine Publishing Company. Chapter 2.
_____. 1977. "The Future of Capitalism." In *Vital Speeches* 43(March 15): 333-337. Reprinted as Chapter 1, in Milton Friedman, 1978, *Tax Limitation, Inflation and the Role of Government*. Dallas, Texas: The Fisher Institute.
_____. 1978a. *Tax Limitation, Inflation and the Role of Government*. Dallas, Texas: The Fisher Institute.
_____. 1978b. "Is Capitalism Humane?" *Sohioan* 50(April): 2-4.
_____. 1978c. "Inertia at the Fed." *Newsweek* 92.
_____. 1979a. "The Paternal State." *Newsweek* 93(January 22): 56.
_____. 1979b. "Taped Discussion." February 6.
_____. 1979c. "Implementing Humphrey Hawkins." *Newsweek* 93(March 5): 87.
_____. 1979d. "Jerry Brown's Kiss of Death." *Newsweek* 93(March 26): 87.
_____. 1979e. "Don't Draft GI Joe." *Newsweek* 93(April 16): 76.
_____. 1981. "A Biased Double Standard." *Newsweek* 97(January 12): 68.
_____. 1982. "How Flat is Flat?" *Newsweek* 100(August 2): 52.
_____, and Stigler, George J. 1946. *Roofs or Ceilings? The Current Housing Problem*. Irvington-on-Hudson, New York: Foundation for Economic Education, Inc.
_____, and Savage, L. J. 1948. "The Utility Analysis of Choice Involving Risk." *Journal of Political Economy* 56(August): 279-304.
Friedman, Rose D. 1976a. "Milton Friedman: Husband and Colleague—(2) The Beginning of a Career." *Oriental Economist* 44(June): 18-22.
_____. 1976b. "Milton Friedman: Husband and Colleague—(3) The Beginning of a Teaching Career." *Oriental Economist* 55(July): 18-23.
Goldman, Peter. 1979. "The Pop Politics of Jerry Brown." *Newsweek* 93(April 23): 24-29.
Harrod, R. F. 1951. *The Life of John Maynard Keynes*. New York: Harcourt, Brace and Company.
Hearings. 1979. *Welfare Research and Income Maintenance*, Senate Finance Committee's Subcommittee on Public Assistance. Washington, D.C.: U. S. Government Printing Office.
Henderson, W. O. 1976. *The Life of Friedrich Engels*, volumes I and II. London: Frank Cass and Company Limited.
Hutchison, T. W. 1981. "Friedrich Engels and Marxian Political Economy." In *The Politics and Philosophy of Economics*. New York: New York University Press.
Keleher, Robert E.; Cox, William N.; and Orzechowski, William P. 1982. "The Flat-Rate Income Tax: Boon or Boondoggle?" *Economic Review*, Federal Reserve Bank of Atlanta (September): 24-30.
MacNeil/Lehrer. 1982. "Simpler Taxes." Transcript: The MacNeil/Lehrer Report (July 12): 1-8.

Marx, Karl, and Engels, Friedrich. 1848. "Manifesto of the Communist Party." Reprinted in Robert C. Tucker, ed. 1978. *The Marx-Engels Reader*, second edition. New York: W. W. Norton & Company, Inc.
_____. 1875. "Critique of the Gotha Program." In Robert C. Tucker, ed. 1978. *The Marx-Engels Reader*, second edition. New York: W.W. Norton & Company, Inc.
_____. 1906. *Capital: A Critique of Political Economy*. New York: The Modern Library. Originally published in 1867, with first American edition in 1906.
Moynihan, Patrick. 1978. "Social Experimentation and Welfare Reform." Press Release from the Office of Senator Patrick Moynihan (November 15).
_____. 1981. "News Letter of the Presidents Budget Policy and Constitutional Conventions." (March).
Playboy. 1973. "Interview: Milton Friedman" *Playboy* 20 (February): 51-74.
Rivlin, Alace M. 1975. "Income Distribution—Can Economists Help?" *American Economic Review*, Proceedings 65(May): 1-15.
Rosten, Leo. 1966. "An Infuriating Man." 30, (November 15) 14-15.
Ruskin, John. 1862. "Munera Pulveris." In E.T. Cook, ed. 1905. *The Works of John Ruskin*, Volume XVII. London: George Allen.
Samuelson, Paul. 1979. "Too Much Democracy?" *Newsweek* 93(April 9): 79.
Schnitzer, Martin. 1968. Guaranteed Minimum Income Programs *Used by Governments of Selected Countries*. Paper No. 11, *Economic Policies and Practices*, Materials prepared for the Joint Economic Committee, Congress of the United States. Washington, D.C.: U.S. Government Printing Office.
Schorr, Daniel, and Friedman, Milton. 1969. "The Negative Income Tax and Social Experimentation." *60 Minutes*. CBS Television Network, vol. 1, no. 15 (April 22).
Schultz, Theodore. 1961. "Investment in Human Capital." *American Economic Review* 71(March): 1-17.
Selden, Richard T., ed. 1975. *Capitalism and Freedom: Problems and Prospects*. Charlottesville, Va.: University Press of Virginia.
Silk, Leonard. 1976. *The Economists*. New York: Basic Books, Inc. Publishers.
Stigler, George J. 1952. "The Ricardian Theory of Value and Distribution." *Journal of Political Economy* 60(June): 187-207.
_____. 1958. "Ricardo and the 93 Per Cent Labor Theory of Value." *American Economic Review* 68(June): 357-367.
Stephen, Leslie, and Lee, Sidney. 1917. *Dictionary of National Biography*, volume XXII. London: Oxford University Press.
Tool, Marc R. 1979. "Review of John A. Britton's *Inheritance and the Inequality of Wealth*." *Journal of Economic Issues* 13(March): 258-261.
Tucker, Robert C., ed. 1978. *The Marx-Engels Reader*, second edition. New York: W.W. Norton & Company, Inc.

Notes, Chapter 14: The British Connection

1. To this list a fourth volume by Philip Cagan (1965) may be added. Although the 1963, 1970, and 1982 volumes were co-authored by Anna J. Schwartz, the discussion is with reference to new directions offered by Milton Friedman. This is because the work is associated with Friedman's background and numerous pieces authored independently by Friedman (Frazer 1983a, 834). **2.** F/S (1982, xxviii). The U.K. (short for the United Kingdom of Great Britain and Northern Ireland) comprises the major part of the British Isles, a group of islands offshore from the European continent. Great Britain is the main island comprising England (by far the largest in population), Scotland and Wales. Ireland is a part of the British Isles, but the Irish Republic is not a part of the U.K. At times the terms "United Kingdom," "Great Britain," and "Britain," are used without their proper formal distinctions. **3.** Friedman (1974a; 1974b). **4.** Frazer (1983b). **5.** Goodhart (1982, 1541-1542, 1550); and Capie and Webber (1985). **6.** Goodhart (1982, 1541). **7.** F/S (1982, chap. 2, sect. 6.2, p. 629). **8.** Mayer (1982, 1538). **9.** Goodhart (1982, 1540-1541). **10.** Hall (1982, 1552). **11.** Frazer (1983a, 833).

12. Kaldor (1982, xi). **13.** Frazer (1973, 36-37, 49-53, 125-131). **14.** F/S (1982, 216-221, 569-573). **15.** F/S (1982, 568-569). **16.** F/S (1982, 32-36). **17.** F/S (1982, 205-206). **18.** F/S (1982, 342, 280-281). **19.** F/S (1982, 281-282). **20.** Mayer (1982, 1530; 1978, 6-8). **21.** Goodhart (1982, 1542). **22.** F/S (1982, 626). **23.** Interview (1982); Tobin (1972); Vinocur (1981); and Kaldor (1980, 87). **24.** Congdon (1978, 77-78). **25.** F/S (1982, 440-464). **26.** Goodhart (1982, 1544); F/S (1982, 148-149). **27.** Goodhart (1982, 1544). **28.** Staff (1982, 18). **29.** Staff (1982, 17). **30.** Friedman (1969, 48). **31.** Staff (1983, 66). **32.** Keynes (1923, 40). **33.** F/S (1982, sect. 7.2). **34.** Friedman (1980a, 507-510). **35.** Friedman (1980a, 510). **36.** Friedman (1983a, 19). **37.** Friedman (1983a, 19). **38.** Goodhart (1982, 1550). **39.** F/S (1982, sect. 5.4). **40.** F/S (1982, sects. 7.4 and 7.2). **41.** Commons (1980, 177-178). **42.** Friedman (1980b). **43.** Commons (1980, 18, 41, 131). **44.** Friedman (1980b, 58). **45.** The legal position, legislation, and principal statutes governing the Bank of England (including in relation to the U.K. Treasury) are noted in a memorandum by the Bank of England entitled "The Relationship between the Bank of England and the Treasury." See Commons (1980, 177-180). **46.** Staff (1981); and Wallace (1981). **47.** Command (1980, 17); Friedman (1980b, 58); and Staff (1981). **48.** Commons (1981a, xxxii-xxxiv). **49.** Commons (1981a, xxxii, and xxxv). **50.** Friedman (1980b, 58). **51.** Dacey (1951, 41-47). **52.** Friedman (1980b, 57). **53.** Command (1980). **54.** Friedman (1980b, 57). **55.** Commons (1980, 20). **56.** Friedman (1980b). **57.** Note (1980). **58.** Staff (1981). **59.** Staff (1981). **60.** Command (1980); Commons (1980). **61.** Commons (1980, 1-4). **62.** Commons (1980, 8-9). **63.** Chap. 7 of the present work; Frazer (1973, chap. 14; 1980, chap. 13 and appendix). **64.** Commons (1981a, xxxix-xc). **65.** Commons (1981a, xc). **66.** The criticism of the econometric method implied by the questionnaire would not apply to the Treasury's response to the questions about model performance (Commons 1980, 15-16). The response was clear about the overriding importance of judgment "about the plausibility of answers" provided by the model, and about different time frames. **67.** Laidler (1977; 1980). Laidler referred to the survey of evidence in his 1977 work as being reliable for addressing the issues before the British Government (Laidler 1980, 49). In fact, however, he mainly just addressed the question of a rapid vis-à-vis individual reduction in the inflation rate for Britain. **68.** Friedman (1956, 11); F/S (1982, chap. 2); and Laidler (1977, 72-74). **69.** There are numerous other technical problems that arise between Laidler and Friedman. Three are noted. One is that of the identification of a demand function (Laidler 1977, 114-117). Here again, Friedman proceeded very indirectly. Households and other "economic actors" can readily vary the quantity of real balances they hold by spending (or reducing its rate) and thereby altering nominal income and prices. The money stock, on the other hand, is a controlled variable fixed for the "economic actors" as a whole in various ways: by the gold standard, monetary authorities, institutions, financial sophistication of the society. In any case frequent and substantial changes are historically possible in the supply of money balances, and these can and do occur independently of any changes in demand.

Another problem arises in what Laidler viewed as the short-run evidence as opposed to the long-run, in referring to his 1977 book (Laidler 1980, 49). He noted the important distinctions, but the analysis of one and the other are not interacting as found in Friedman's work. Finally, in Laidler's interpretation and discussion of Friedman's basic/stable relation (Laidler 1977, 68-74, 103-104), he said, "Friedman's contribution to monetary theory is precisely to draw attention away from the motives that prompt the holding of money..." Yet, in contrast, we find all of the motives for holding money, as set forth by Keynes (1936, 170), present in Friedman's statement of the definition of money (F/S 1970, 107-110). Further, Friedman's treatment of the demand in anticipation of an increase in the expected inflation rate is no less than a speculative demand for money with respect to purchasing power risk. The expected rate of return on money in Friedman's basic/stable relation (F/S 1982, chap. 2) is primarily representative of speculation concerning the inflation rate. The functions of money set forth in its definition correspond to the motives found in Keynes (Frazer 1980, chap. 1, note 1). **70.** F/S (1982, sects. 2.3 and 6.2). **71.** Laidler (1980, 48-54). **72.** The three quotations are found respectively on pages 120-121, 127, 133 of Laidler (1977). **73.** Laidler (1982). **74.** This incorrect formulation is explicit in Laidler's treatment of the identification problem (Laidler 1977, 115). See also note 67 above. **75.** Croham (1980, 77). **76.** Frazer (1980, chaps. 5 and 18); and Frazer and Bomberger (1981). **77.** Minford (1980, 132). **78.** Kaldor (1980, 90-91). **79.** Kaldor (1980, 88). **80.** Kaldor (1980, 86-130). **81.** F/S (1982, chap. 11). **82.** Hayek (1981). **83.** Friedman (1983b). **84.** Friedman (1983b). **85.** F/S (1982, sect. 10.8); and Hayek (1983, 39). **86.** Committee (1959). **87.** Friedman (1977). **88.** Frazer and Yohe (1966, sect. 25.1); Kaldor (1980, 87, 99). **89.** Frazer (1983c); Kaldor (1982). **90.** F/S (1982, sects. 8.8 and 8.9). **91.** Frazer (1978). **92.** Friedman (1980b, 55). **93.** Dacey (1951, 36-37). **94.** Frazer (1983c). **95.** Sinclair (1976). **96.** Included here will be a treatment of uncertainty about the expectations or forecast values (Frazer 1980, sect. 5.3 and 18.4; Frazer 1982; and F/S 1982, chap. 10).

References, Chapter 14: The British Connection

Cagan, Phillip. 1965. *Determinants and Effects of Changes in the Stock of Money, 1875-1960*. New York: Columbia University Press for the National Bureau of Economic Research.
Capie, Forrest, and Webber, Alan. 1985. *A Monetary History of the United Kingdom, 1970-1982*, Vol. 1. London: George Allen & Unwin.
Clark, Lindley H. 1981. "The Monetarist." *Wall Street Journal* 198(October 7): 1 and 12.
Command. 1980. *Monetary Control*, Presented to Parliament by the Chancellor of the Exchequer by Command of Her Majesty (March). London: Her Majesty's Stationary Office.
Committee. 1959. [Radcliffe] *Report*, Committee on the Working of Monetary System, Command Paper No. 827. London: Her Majesty's Stationary Office.
Commons. 1980. *Treasury and Civil Service Committee: Memoranda on Monetary Policy*, ordered by The House of Commons (July 17). London: Her Majesty's Stationary Office.
_____. 1981a. *Treasury and Civil Service Committee: Monetary Policy*, Volume 1, Report. London: Her Majesty's Stationary Office.
_____. 1981b. *Treasury and Civil Service Committee: Monetary Policy*, Volume II, Minutes and Evidence. London: Her Majesty's Stationary Office.
Congdon, Tim. 1878. *Monetarism*. London: Centre for Policy Studies.
Croham, Douglas Albert Vivian Allen. 1980. "Memorandum to U.K. Treasury and Civil Service Committee." In Commons 1980, 74-78.
Dacey, W. Manning. 1951. *The British Banking Mechanism*. London: Hutchinson House.
Frazer, William (with William P. Yohe). 1966. *Introduction to the Analytics and Institutions of Money and Banking*. Princeton, N.J.: D. Van Nostrand Company, Inc.
_____. 1967. *The Demand for Money*. Cleveland, Ohio: World Publishing Company.
_____. 1973. *Crises in Economic Theory*. Gainesville, FL.: University Presses of Florida.
_____. 1978. "The Government Budget Constraint." *Public Finance Quarterly* 6(July): 381-387.
_____. 1980. *Expectations, Forecasting and Control: A Provisional Textbook of Macroeconomics*, Volumes I and II. Landham, Md.: University Press of America, Inc.
_____ (with William Bomberger). 1981. "Interest Rates, Uncertainty and the Livingston Data." *Journal of Finance* 36(June): 661-675.
_____. 1982. "The Velocity-Interest Rate Association: Inflation, Accelerated Inflation, and Uncertainty." *Economic Notes* (March): 144-156.
_____. 1983a. "Monetary Trends in the U.S. and the U.K." *Southern Economic Journal*, 49(January): 833-846.
_____. 1983b. *"Monetary Trends* and the Reviews." *Wall Street Review of Books* 11(No. 2): 105-123.
_____. 1983c. "Lord Kaldor, Friedman, and Pertinent Episodes." *Wall Street Review of Books* 11(No. 4): 261-284.
_____ (with Lawrence Boland). 1983d. "An Essay on the Methodological Foundations of Friedman's Economics." *American Economic Review* 73(March): 129-144.
Friedman, Milton. 1955. "Leon Walras and His Economic System." *American Economic Review* 45(December): 900-909.
_____. 1969. *The Optimum Quantity of Money and Other Essays*. Chicago: Aldine Publishing Company.
_____. 1974a. "Comments on the Critics." In Robert J. Gordan, ed. *Milton Friedman's Monetary Framework*. Chicago, Ill.: University of Chicago Press.

----------. 1974d. "A Theoretical Framework for Monetary Analysis." In Robert J. Gordon, ed., *Milton Friedman's Monetary Framework*. Chicago: University of Chicago Press.

----------. 1975. *Unemployment versus Inflation?* An Evaluation of the Phillips Curve. London: Institute of Economic Affairs.

----------. 1977. *Inflation and Unemployment*. Stockholm: The Nobel Foundation. The original spoken lecture is also reproduced verbatim as occasional Paper 51 by Lord Harris's Institute of Economic Affairs, with an introduction by Arthur Selden.

----------. 1980a. "Prices of Money and Goods Across Frontiers: The Pound and the Dollar Over a Century." *World Economy* 1(February): 497-511.

----------. 1980b. "Memorandum to U.K. Treasury and Civil Service Committee." In Commons 1980, 55-61.

----------. 1980c. "Monetarism: A reply to the critics." *The Times* (March 3): 19.

----------. 1982. Correspondence with respect to Frazer (1982b).

----------. 1983a. "The Keynes Centenary: A Monetarist Reflects." *The Economist* 287(June 4): 17-19.

----------. 1983b. "Correspondence on Walras's General Equilibrium" (July 22).

----------, and Schwartz, Anna Jacobson. 1982. *Monetary Trends in the United States and the United Kingdom: Their Relation to Income, Prices and Interest Rates, 1867-1975*. Chicago, Ill.: University of Chicago Press for the National Bureau of Economic Research.

Goodhart, Charles E. A. 1982. "Monetary Trends in the United States and the United Kingdom: A British Review." *Journal of Economic Literature* 20(December): 1540-1551.

Governor, Bank of England. 1980. "Memorandum to U.K. Treasury and Civil Service Committee." In Commons 1980, 17-36.

Hayek, F. A. 1981. "The Muddle of the Middle." Paper presented at a conference in Freiburg, Germany (February).

----------. 1983. "The Keynes Centenary: The Austrian Critique." *The Economist* 128(June 11): 39-41.

Hall, Robert E. 1982. "Monetary Trends in the United States and the United Kingdom: A Review from the Perspective of New Developments in Monetary Economics." *Journal of Economic Literature* 20(December): 1552-1556.

Kaldor, Nicholas. 1970. "The New Monetarism." *Lloyds Bank Review* 97(July): 1-17.

----------. 1980. "Memorandum to U.K. Treasury and Civil Service Committee." In Commons 1980, 86-140.

----------. 1982. *The Scourge of Monetarism*. New York: Oxford University Press.

Laidler, David E.W. 1977. *The Demand For Money—Theories and Evidence*, second edition. New York: Harper & Row, Publishers.

----------. 1980. "Memorandum to U.K. Treasury and Civil Service Committee." In Commons 1980, 48-59.

----------. 1982. "Friedman and Schwartz on Monetary Trends: A Review Article." *Journal of International Money and Finance* 1(December): 293-305.

Marx, Karl. 1891. "Critique of the Gotha Program." Reprinted in Robert C. Turker, ed. 1972. *The Marx-Engels Reader*, second edition. New York: W. W. Norton & Company, Inc.

Thomas, Mayer. 1978. *The Structure of Monetarism*. New York: W. W. Norton & Company.

----------. 1982. "Monetary Trends in the United States and the United Kingdom: A Review Article." *Journal of Economic Literature* 20(December): 1528-1539.

Minford, A. P. 1980. "Memorandum to U.K. Treasury and Civil Service Committee." In Commons 1980, 131-143.

Note. 1980. "Methods of monetary control." *Bank of England Quarterly Bulletin*. 20(December): 428-429.

Phillips, A. W. 1958. "The Relation Between Unemployment and the Rate of Change of Money Wage Rates in the United Kingdom, 1861-1957." *Economica* 25(November): 283-299.

Sinclair, David. 1976. "Inflation: 'The tax that never has to be passed by Parliament'." *The Times* (September 13): 3c.

Staff. 1981. "Changes in the British System of Monetary Control." *International Letter*, Federal Reserve Bank of Chicago (August 28): 1.

_____. 1982. *Report to the Congress of the Commission on the Role of Gold in the Domestic and International Monetary System*, vol. I (March).

_____. 1983. "How to Get the Country Moving Again: Advice from Six Nobel Prize Economists." *U.S. News & World Report* 94(January 3): 66-71.

Tobin, James. 1972. *The New Economics One Decade Order*. Princeton, N.J.: Princeton University Press.

Vinocur, John. 1981. "Tobin of Yale Wins Nobel in Economics." *New York Times* (October 14): 1, D. 22.

Wallace, Laura. 1981. "Patron on the Pound." *Wall Street Journal*. 198(December 17): 1, 23.

Walras, Leon. 1954. *Elements of Pure Economics*, English translation by W. Jaffé. London: First ed., Lousanne, 1874.

Notes, Chapter 15: The Thatcher Government

1. Guzzardi (1981, 38). 2. Some will recall that Karl Marx and his followers saw the economic system evolving, according to scientific laws, toward a socialist state. Their view of history has been called historical or sociological determinism (Friedman 1978c, 3). Indeed, this view has seemed at times to permeate teaching and thinking in the areas of history and social science. Karl Popper discussed these views under the label historicism, but noted that they are not peculiar to Marxism. "On the contrary," he said (1965, 338): "they are among the oldest doctrines in the world. In Marx's own time they were held...not only by Marx, who inherited them from Hegel, but by John Stuart Mill, who inherited them from Comte, and they were held in ancient times by Plato...They seem to be of oriental origin; indeed, the Jewish idea of the chosen people is a typical historicist idea—that history is a plot whose author is Jahwe, and that the plot can be partly unraveled by the prophets. These ideas express one of the oldest dreams of mankind—the dream of prophecy, the idea that we can know what the future has in store for us, and that we can profit from such knowledge by adjusting our policy to it."

Popper (1965, 339), like Friedman (1978c), found such views untenable. They do not imply that the task of the social sciences is historical prophecy. On the contrary, he drew the distinction between "scientific predictions" and "unconditional historical prophecies." The task of politics then is not simply to "lessen the birthpangs" of such prophecies. As Thatcher may have thought against this background of social thinking, "there is no need as yet to despair of reason." Continuing, Popper said (1965, 341), "Only those who do not distinguish between ordinary prediction and historical prophecy are likely to draw such desperate conclusions." 3. The *Times* references are Anonymous (1976), Congdon (1975), and Sinclair (1976). The other references are Friedman (1968a; 1968b; 1974; 1977; 1981; 1968c). 4. *The Sunday Times* economics editor Malcolm Crawford dated Friedman's first "open lecture" in London at 1970. The lecture was given "to a collection of civil servants, journalists and economists, on the futility of demand management." Continuing, he said, "Financial opinion connected with the City of London took to his ideas fairly quickly; in Whitehall and industry the response was more critical" (Crawford 1977, 62). The lecture in question (Friedman 1970) was also published by Lord Harris's Institute. 5. Collard (1981, 142-143); and Wood (1981). 6. Bell (1981); and Frazer (1973). 7. Bradley (1981, 187). 8. Friedman (1970); Walters (1978, 8-13). 9. Commons (1981a, xxxii). 10. Butt (1980, 16). 11. Staff (1975a, 14); Staff (1981m, 13-14). 12. Since the 17th century the supremacy of British government has resided in the Parliament. There are two houses—that of Lords and that of Commons—but since 1911 power has resided in the House of Commons, an elective body. It is supreme; judicial review of its actions is unknown. The constitution is unwritten but loosely understood through custom and tradition. There are numerous documents that provide guidelines (see Verney 1966, 16, 19, 20-21, 38-40, 42). The Prime Minister (PM) and her cabinet are the center of the government, with the PM being the leader of the party in power. Cabinet ministers are appointed, and they may be also members of the legislative body. The cabinet members may head departments but they remain collectively responsible for the government of the country. The power of Parliament is centralized in the Cabinet. Some say the political system is dominated by the Cabinet, others say by the Prime Minister. The PM, in any case, must keep the support of the Parliament, and the Cabinet requires its goodwill. Ultimately, leadership relies on public opinion in the U.K. just as in the U.S. 13. Murray (1978, 52-61). 14. Staff (1972, 48). 15. Moritz (1975, 406). 16. Anonymous (1978a; 1978b; 1981). 17. Moritz (1975, 406). 18. Moritz (1975, 407); and Staff (1975a, 11; 1975c, 14; 1979c, 15). 19. Staff (1975b, 12; 1975c, 11). 20. Staff (1975e, 11). 21. Staff (1979b, 16). 22. Staff (1977, 13; 1978, 17). 23. Moritz (1975, 405); Murray (1978, 13); Smith (1980, 23, 148). 24. Rose (1980, 142-161). 25. Minford (1980, 131). 26. Staff (1979b, 13). 27. Anonymous (1976); Friedman (1978a); and News (1976). 28. Congdon (1975, 17). 29. Friedman (1976, 62-66). 30. Friedman (1978, 65-66). 31. Anonymous (1976, 12a). 32. Sinclair (1976). 33. Congdon (1975). 34. Congdon (1975). 35. Sinclair (1976). 36. Sinclair (1976). 37. Congdon (1975). 38. Sinclair (1976). 39. Vogel (1976). 40. Felton (1976). 41. Frazer (1979). 42. Bradley (1980). 43. Commons (1981a, xxxiii-xxxiv); Kaldor (1980, 88). 44. Minford (1980, 132). 45. Staff (1981e, 11). 46. Staff (1981, b). 47. Felton (1976); Sinclair (1976). 48. These are found in Congdon (1975); Friedman (1980b); and Sinclair (1976). 49. Friedman (1980b, 56). 50. Anonymous (1978a). 51. Seargeant (1980b, 53). The 1980 book was widely reviewed in England, as was the television series (News 1980; Peele 1980; Roll 1980; Stephenson 1980). Roll's review opened thus:

> "Here we go again. Once more Milton Friedman goes into the breach, joined, as he was 18 years ago, by his wife to fight the "interventionist", "statist", "dirigist" hordes, to slay the dragon of bureaucracy, to reinstate freedom in her rightful place. Clearly advocacy of "the free market" has become a growth industry; and increasingly Friedman's writings, including this one, have become propagandist pamphlets, enjoying great popularity in their own country and in Britain (though not so much anywhere else). The present book is accompanied by all the razzmatazz of television series in the United States as well as here. Thus, in this field, and for the time being at least, Friedman's belief in giving the consumer what he wants—or at least what the media can make him feel he should want—seems to be working out all right." (Roll 1980, 12)

Writing from the Federal Republic of Germany, Von Hayek, provided the following short answer to the Roll review:

> "Sir, Sir Eric Roll makes fun of Milton Friedman (March 6) for having said that, the whole of Western civilization rests on the free market. Surely, if Professor Friedman has explicitly said what he clearly meant, namely that the whole of Western civilization rests on as much free market as government allowed, he would have been perfectly right.
> Yours faithfully,
> F. A. HAYEK,
> Urachstrasse 27,
> D-7800 Freiburg
> March 7."

52. Seargeant (1980b, 53). 53. Anonymous (1981, 19-20); and Hatfield (1980). 54. Anonymous (1981, 20). 55. Keynes (1936, 162). Keynes had said: "Only a little more than an expedition to the South Pole, is it [enterprise] based on exact calculations of benefits to come ["of a weighted average of quantitative benefits multiplied by quantitative probabilities"]." (Keynes 1936, 162) 56. Staff (1980a). 57. For the theoretical basis of modern British socialism, one is usually referred to Anthony Crosland's 1950 work "The Future of Socialism":

> "I no longer regard questions of growth and efficiency as being, on a long view, of primary importance to socialism. We stand, in Britain, on the threshold of mass abundance; and within a decade the average family will enjoy a standard of living which, whether or not it fully satisfies their aspirations, will certainly convince the reformer that he should turn his attention elsewhere....We should not now judge a Labour Government's performance primarily by its record in the economic field."

In November, 1970, Crosland told the Fabians that "Our record of economic growth has been lamentable." In "Socialism Now," written in 1974, he said, "Nobody disputes the central failure of Labour's economic policy. In 1970 unemployment was higher, inflation more rapid and economic growth slower than when the Conservatives left office in 1964."
"The Fabians" refers to Britain's Fabian Society founded in 1883, the year of J. M. Keynes's birth. Prominent among the Fabians were Sidney and Beatrice Webb (1859-1947, 1858-1943). On the "Fabian Society," see Robson (1972) and Clark (1981). **58.** Butt (1980) discussed the unions as being more of a problem in Britain than elsewhere. It has been suggested that the fundamental problem is the political tie-up between the unions and the Labour Party, which they control. When Labour is in, the unions try to run as much of the show as concerns them. And when the Conservatives rule, the unions put the pressure on the government and wait for Labour's return. The view has been that new union laws will not solve this. In the end, the government has to win the union rank-and-file away from the union leadership and from the Labour Party. **59.** Hafer (1981, 20); Seargeant (1981, 10-11). This strengthening of the pound was reviewed in the TCSC's 1981 *Report* (Commons 1981a, chap. 7 and xciii-xciv). **60.** Parkin (1981, 45). **61.** *The Times* writer Peter Hennessy (1980) reported in February 1980 on a two-and-a-half day seminar on "monetarism in practice" that was held in January at the Civil Service College in Sunningdale Park, Ascot. The principal speaker at the seminar was Mr. Terry Burns, "The new chief economic advisor to the Treasury and head of the Government Economic Service [GES]." The initiative for the seminar came from the Civil Service College itself.

Hennessy reported that the GES was "heavily suspect for its alleged Keynesianism by Conservative ministers on first taking office last year." The idea was that GES was beginning "to adapt to the new Whitehall orthodoxy of monetarism." According to Hennessy's report, "All members of GES at economic advisor and senior economic advisor levels who were interested in the subject were invited to attend." Over 30 were reported as accepting "from a wide range of departments..." One insider was reported as saying: "It was not a hatchet job or a sales job. No particular dogmatic view came out. It went down very well." Hennessy's report listed the names of the speakers at the seminar. However, the problem of expert opinion being outpaced by that at the political level did not appear to have been limited to civil servants. It also appeared among a wider range of economic experts as indicated by the memoranda reproduced by Her Majesty's Stationary Office (Commons 1980) and in a lecture given in August of 1981 by the University of Glasgow's Adam Smith Professor (see Wilson 1981, and Wilson as discussed by Frazer 1982). **62.** Walters (1981). **63.** Union power has been thought of as particularly disruptive of any denationalization, and the mechanics of the transfer from public to private ownership could be complicated. Milton Friedman's answer, though not that of Thatcher, was to denationalize outright. His position was twofold. First, if the government got the money supply right, both inflation and unemployment would eventually fall. The unions would then be without both the power and the motive to do damage. Since the responsibility is the government's, it is no use blaming unions for inflation. Second, since he appreciated the difficulty of finding buyers (and rightly did not favor selling off the best bits alone), he suggested parcelling it all up, and giving it away in shares to the people. (Butt 1980) **64.** Thomas Sargent (1981, 93) commented on the financing of public sector borrowing, the public-sector-pay episode, and some further effort by the Thatcher government thus:

> "Although it seems not to have been something that Keynes himself would have advocated, the widespread adoption of Keynesian ideas about fiscal policy after World War II has been accompanied by abandonment of the classical public budgeting and accounting procedures at the level of national governments (although not at the level of state and local governments in the United States). For example, in the United Kingdom the nationalized industries do not float their own debt. This arrangement is one that departs from or at least obscures the "earmarking" of revenues from particular projects to back a given bond issue. Moreover, the recent history of public finances in the United Kingdom displays little sensitivity to the capital account-current account distinction. For example,..., capital formation by the general government and nationalized industries has stagnated or actually fallen. Further,...while general government final consumption, current grants, and

subsidies have risen substantially in recent years and have continued to rise under Mrs. Thatcher, capital expenditures have not. Under both Mrs. Thatcher's government and the previous Labour government, belt-tightening has fallen largely on public sector investment items. According to the classic canons of public finance that we alluded to earlier, this structure of expenditure cuts is perverse from the viewpoint of anti-inflationary policy.

"The failure of Mrs. Thatcher's government to control public expenditures has been widely commented upon...Mrs. Thatcher has been criticized for a number of what are essentially tactical errors, for example, in her stance toward pay for public employees. Her early decision to stand by the Conservative Party's campaign pledge to honor the recommendations of the Clegg Commission, which the Labour government instituted to establish pay standards for civil servants comparable to those in the private sector, resulted in earnings increases for civil servants of 24 percent between 1979 III and 1980 III. Thatcher responded, albeit belatedly to that criticism, by eventually abolishing the Clegg Commission in the fall of 1980. Since that time, the government has announced the adoption of a 'cash limit system' which essentially creates a 'total wages fund' with which the government intends to confront a given public sector union or collection of unions. The idea is to force the unions to take into account a tradeoff between wage rates and the number of public sector employees. A problem is that such cash limits have been breached in the past and have already been breached by Thatcher in the coal miners' settlement."

Looking at the allocation of government expenditures for the 1975-80 period, Parkin (1981, 45) also noted that public sector investment declined as a percent of total expenditures. **65.** Staff (1980g, 11). **66.** Commons (1981a, xviii-xix). **67.** The range planned for money growth by the Bank of England and the actual growth during 1980 are shown in the accompanying artwork.

British Money Supply Growth

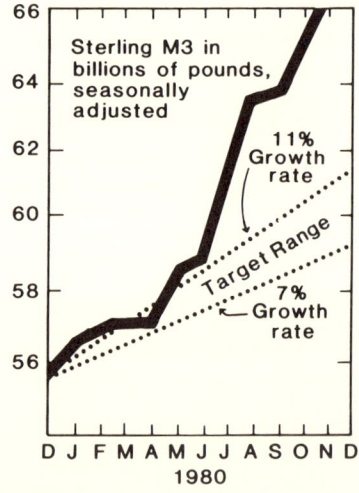

68. Commons (1981a, xxxi); and Parkin (1981, 44). **69.** Friedman (1982c). **70.** Commons (1981a, xxiii, xxxiii, xxxvi, xxxcvii, xcvii). **71.** Friedman (1980b, 61). **72.** Commons (1981a, xxxvi, xcvii). **73.** Frazer and Bomberger (1981). **74.** Walters (1970). **75.** Frisch (1970). **76.** Frazer (1973, 95-111, 126-129, and chap. 7); and Walters (1970, 177-189, 195, 245-275; 1973; 1979, 14-17). **77.** Friedman (1969). **78.** Bell and Stothard (1980, 19). **79.** There are two sorts of evidence. First, there is his service in a department of econometrics and social statistics, plus the econometrics textbook; and, second, there are statements in his work that one with background in monetary economics would not have made. Examples of the latter are: Walters's treating Irving Fisher's equation of exchange as a statement of the quantity theory of money (Walters 1971, 19); his treatment of "the quantity theory" rather than its different versions (Walters 1971, 16-17); his defining "the interest rate" as the "price of money" even as he discussed the "price of money" as the inverse of the price of goods (Walters 1971, 17-18). The interest rate in Friedman's work is the price of credit. The real rate is the rate at which goods today exchange for goods tomorrow (or one year hence), and, in some context it is the non-inflationary rate or the market rate less the expected inflation rate (Frazer 1980, sect. 9.4). **80.** Committee (1959); and Walters (1965; 1966a; 1966b; 1967; 1971, 20-21; 1973). **81.** Friedman (1976, chap. 12; and 1977); and Walters (1978, 8-9, 22-23). **82.** Walters (1978, 27). **83** Walters (1970, 10). **84.** Stein (1981, 28). **85.** Staff (1980a). **86.** News (1980). **87.** Borders (1981); Staff (1980b). **88.** Otten (1981b); Smith (1981); and Strasser (1981). **89.** Clines (1981); Johnson (1981); Nemy (1981); Otten (1981). **90.** Cockburn (1980). **91.** Owen (1980). **92.** Johnson (1981, 28-35). **93.** Staff (1981d). **94.** Staff (1981e). **95.** The poem, consisting of six stanzas, was first published in December of 1854. The charge is question was made on October 25, 1854. The Brigade had been sent to recapture guns lost to the Russians. (Marshall 1963, 135) **96.** Clines (1981). **97.** Walters (1981). **98.** Borders (1981b); Staff (1981a). **99.** Borders (1981c). **100.** Staff (1981h). The conflict described in this paragraph is illustrated by another from the June 20, 1981 issue of *The Economist*:

> "Britain's nationalized industries now threaten not only Mrs. Margaret Thatcher's economic strategy. They are undermining her control of her cabinet as well.
> Ministers at this week's well-trained cabinet meeting listened to her lectures on the need to cut their spending...[but some] of them are damned if they will cut while the coal industry is being allowed to crash through its borrowing limits. And nationalized industry chairmen have recruited... [some other] ministers into an unholy alliance against the beleaguered treasury, which is accused of perpetuating the slump by obstinately refusing state industries the freedom to invest." (Staff 1981i, 12)

101. Staff (1981h). **102.** Rose (1980). **103.** Hotelling (1929). **104.** Staff (1979b, 13). **105.** Congdon (1975); Friedman (1978a). **106.** Friedman (1980b); Sinclair (1976). **107.** Angelo (1983, 30, 36). **108.** Frazer (1980, sects. 10.3 and 18.5). **109.** Anonymous (1983, 29). **110.** Staff (1975b, 12). **111.** Friedman (1983, 51). **112.** Tobin (1982, 338-339). **113.** Whitaker (1983). **114.** Apple (1983a). **115.** Whitaker (1983, 30). **116.** Staff (1983a). **117.** Apple (1983b); Otten (1983); Staff (1983b). **118.** Feder (1983). **119.** Special (1983). **120.** Feder (1983); Staff (1983e). **121.** Staff (1983g). **122.** These departments were combined under Cecil Parkinson. He had risen from a humble background to become a prominent cabinet minister and a Thatcher confident. However, shortly after the new assignment as head of the combined departments, a secretary named Miss Sara Keays decided to reveal a love affair with Parkinson, who was married. Following the news that Miss Keays was pregnant, the unhappy Parkinson was obliged to resign. To the displeasure of some, Thatcher reappointed Parkinson an energy secretary following the 1987 elections.
The Economist's story on Cecil Parkinson and Miss Keays was also occasion for recalling some other titillating episodes in Britain's post-WW II politics. (See Staff 1983f). **123.** Staff (1983d; 1983e; 1983f). **124.** Kelly (1983, 33). **125.** Walters (1983, 2, 7). **126.** Walters (1983, 8-14). **127.** Walters (1986, 173-186).

References, Chapter 15: The Thatcher Government

Angelo, Bonnie. "Freedom is Working." *Time* 121(June 20): 30.
Apple, R. B. (Jr.). 1983a. "Election Called 11 Months Early by Mrs. Thatcher." *New York Times* 132(May 10): 1, 7.
──────. 1983b. "Conservatives Win: A Thatcher Sweep." *New York Times* 132(June 10): 1, 8.
Anonymous. 1976. "Economics viewed as a martial art." *The Times* (September 2):12a.

_____. 1978a. "The ghost of Montager Norman is in business." *The Sunday Times* (January 28):62.
_____. 1978b. "Economics viewed as martial art." *The Times* (September 2):12.
_____. 1981. "Margaret Thatcher, Prime Minister of Great Britain." *Sky: Delta Air Lines Inflight Magazine* 10 (March): 19-22.
_____. 1983. "The Talk of the Town." *The New Yorker* 59(June 6): 29-30.
Bacon, Kenneth H. 1983. "Reagan Wants Fed to Slow Money Growth but Urges It to Avoid Discount Rate Boost," *Wall Street Journal* 202(July 8): 3.
Bell, Daniel, and Kristol, Irving. 1981. *The Crisis in Economic Theory*. New York: Basic Books, Inc., Publishers.
Bell, John, and Stothard, Peter. 1980. "Monetarism: will she water it down—or Walters it up?" *The Sunday Times* (December 21): 19.
Borders, William. 1981a. "12 M.P.'s Quit British Labor Party, Plan to Form Centrist Group." *New York Times* 30(March 3):A1, A13.
_____. 1981b. "Britain Raises Taxes and Reasserts that Cutting Inflation is Key Goal." *New York Times* 130(March 11): A1, D18.
_____. 1981c. "Thatcher Budget is Denounced as 'Savage'." *New York Times* 130(March 12):A3.
Bradley, Ian. 1980. "The Hayek cure: bigger and better bankruptcies." *The Times* (November 21).
_____. 1981. "Intellectual Influences in Britain: Past and Present." In Arthur Selden, ed. (1981).
Butt, Ronald. 1980. "Friedman's blind shot." *The Sunday Times* (March 9):16.
Camp, A. B. 1962. "Two Views of Money." *Lloyds Bank Review* (July).
Clark, Colin. 1981. "The IEA and the Fabians: Comparison and Contrast." In Arthur Selden, ed. (1981).
Clines, Francis X. 1981. "Mrs. Thatcher Gives Support to Reagan as Trip to U.S. Opens." *New York Times* 130 (February 27):A1, A6.
Cockburn, Alexander. 1980. "Milton's Monument." *Village Voice* (November 12/18):36-37.
Collard, David. 1981. "Market Failure and Government Failure." In Arthur Selden, ed. (1981).
Command. 1980. *Monetary Control*, Presented to Parliament by the Chancellor of the Exchequer by Command of Her Majesty (March). London: Her Majesty's Stationary Office.
Committee. 1959. [Radcliffe] *Report*, Committee on the Working of Monetary System, Command Paper No. 827. London: Her Majesty's Stationary Office.
Commons. 1980. *Treasury and Civil Service Committee: Memoranda on Monetary Policy*, ordered by The House of Commons (July 17). London: Her Majesty's Stationary Office.
_____. 1981a. *Treasury and Civil Service Committee: Monetary Policy*, Volume 1, Report. London: Her Majesty's Stationary Office.
_____. 1981b. *Treasury and Civil Service Committee: Monetary Policy*, Volume II, Minutes and Evidence. London: Her Majesty's Stationary Office.
Congdon, Tim. 1975. "Price stability and the 'natural' level of unemployment." *The Times* (January 22):17.
_____. 1978. *Monetarism*. London: Centre for Policy Studies.
Crawford, Malcolm. 1977. "Inflation may rage on for decades Friedman now says." *The Sunday Times* (June 12):62.
Croham, Douglas Albert Vivian Allen. 1980. "Memorandum to U.K. Treasury and Civil Service Committee." In Commons 1980, 74-78.
Davenport, John. 1967. "The Radical Economics of Milton Friedman." *Fortune* 75(June):131-132, 147-18, 150.
Edwards, Lee. 1967. *Reagan: A Political Biography*. San Diego, Calif.: Viewpoint Books.
Elliott, John. 1980. "The Queen's Speech: Adopting policy to the needs of the public sector." *Financial Times* (November 21):10.
Felder, Barnaby J. 1983. "Mrs. Thatcher's Priorities." *New York Times* 132(June 11): 21, 28.
Felton, David. 1976. "Friedman hope of 'better chance' for Britain." *The Times* (November 10):19.

Frazer, William. 1967. *The Demand for Money*. Cleveland, Ohio: World Publishing Company.

———. 1980. *Expectations, Forecasting and Control: A Provisional Textbook of Macroeconomics*, Volumes I and II. Landham, Md.: University Press of America, Inc.

——— (with William Bomberger). 1981. "Interest Rates, Uncertainty and the Livingston Data." *Journal of Finance* 36(June): 661-675.

———. 1982. "Milton Friedman and Thatcher's Monetarist Experience." *Journal of Economic Issues* 16(June):525-533.

———. 1983a. "*Free to Choose:* A Review Article." Wall Street Review of Books 11(No. 1): 14-22.

———. 1983b. "Lord Kaldor, Friedman, and Pertinent Episodes." *Wall Street Review of Books* 11(No. 4): 261-284.

———, and Hess, Jane. 1979. "The Political Business Cycle: Adjustments through Persuasion Techniques." *Economics Notes* (August): 113-133.

Friedman, Milton. 1953b. "The Case for Flexible Exchange Rates." In *Essays in Positive Economics*. Chicago, Ill.: University of Chicago Press.

———. 1956. "The Quantity Theory of Money—A Restatement." In *Studies in the Quantity Theory of Money*. Chicago, Ill.: University of Chicago Press.

———. 1959. "The Demand for Money: Some Theoretical and Empirical Results." *Journal of Political Economy* 67(August): 327-351.

———. 1962. *Capitalism and Freedom*. Chicago, Ill.: University of Chicago Press.

———. 1968a. "The Role of Monetary Policy." *American Economic Review* 58(March): 1-17.

———. 1968b. "Factors Affecting the Level of the Interest Rate." *Conference on Savings and Residential Financing: 1968 Proceedings*. Chicago, Ill.: United States Savings and Loan League.

———. 1970. *The Counter-Revolution in Monetary Theory*, First Wincott Memorial Lecture. London: Institute of Economic Affairs.

———. 1973. "Public Spending and Inflation." Letters to the Editor. *The Times* (August 20): 15e.

———. 1975. *Unemployment versus Inflation?* An Evaluation of the Phillips Curve. London: Institute of Economic Affairs.

———. 1977a. "The Future of Capitalism." Vital *Speeches* 43(March 15): 333-377.

———. 1977b. *Inflation and Unemployment*. Stockholm: The Nobel Foundation. The original spoken lecture is also reproduced verbatim as occasional Paper 51 by Lord Harris's Institute of Economic Affairs, with an introduction by Arthur Selden.

———. 1978a. "From Galbraith to Economic Freedom." In Milton Friedman. *Tax Limitation, Inflation & the Role of Government*. Dallas, Tx: The Fisher Institute. Reprinted from Occasional Paper 49, Institute of Economic Affairs 1977.

———. 1978b. "What is America." *Sohioan* 50 (February): 8-11.

———. 1978c. "Is Capitalism Human?" *Sohioan* 50(April): 2-4.

———. 1980a. "Prices of Money and Goods Across Frontiers: The Pound and the Dollar Over a Century." *World Economy* (February): 497-511.

———. 1980b. "Memorandum to U.K. Treasury and Civil Service Committee." In Commons 1980, 55-61.

———. 1980c. "Monetarism: A reply to the critics." *The Times* (March 3): 19.

———. 1980d. "The Fed Fails—Again." *Newsweek* 96(December 1): 78.

———. 1981a. "Deficits and Inflation." *Newsweek* 97(February): 70.

———. 1981b. "A Biased Double Standard." *Newsweek* 99(January 12): 68.

———. 1982a. "Interest Rates and the Budget." *Newsweek* 99(June 28): 70.

———. 1982b. An Aborted Recovery?" *Newsweek* 99(August 23): 59.

———. 1982c. Correspondence with W. Frazer.

———. 1983. "Mitterrand Elects Thatcher." *Newsweek* 101(July 4): 51.

———, and Friedman, Rose. 1980. *Free to Choose*. New York: Harcourt Brace Jovanovich.

Gilbert. J. C. 1982. *Keynes's Impact on Monetary Economics*. London: Butterworth & Co (Publishers) Ltd.

Gilder, George. 1981. *Wealth and Poverty.* New York: Basic Books, Inc., Publishers.
Gilmour, Ian. 1977. *Inside Right: A Study of Conservatism.* London: Hutchinson & Co. (Publishers) Ltd.
Goldwater, Barry. 1960. *The Conscience of A Conservative.* Shepherdsville, Ky.: Victor Publishing Company, Inc.
Guzzardi, Walter, Jr. 1981. "Don't Sell the Great Thatcher Experiment Short." *Fortune* 103(May 18): 38-43.
Hayek, F. A. 1980. "Free market." *The Times* (March 18): 18h.
———. 1981. "The Muddle of the Middle." Paper presented at a conference in Freiburg, Germany (February).
———. 1983. "The Keynes Centenary: The Austrian Critique." *The Economist* 128(June 11): 39-41.
Hafer, R. W. 1981. "The Impact of Energy Prices and Money Growth on Five Industrial Countries." *Review*, Federal Reserve Bank of St. Louis 63(March 1981): 19-26.
Hatfield, Michael. 1980. "Mrs. Thatcher Refuses to Recall Commons Over Jobless." *The Times* (September 11): 1.
Henderson, W. O. 1976. *The Life of Friedrich Engels*, vols. I and II. London: Frank Cass and Company Limited.
Hennessy, Peter. 1980. "Treasury economic advisors adapt to new Whitehall orthodoxy." *The Times* (February 16): 15.
Herman, Tom. 1983. "Volcker Has 76.9% Support to Remain Fed Chief, in Poll of Investment Leaders." *Wall Street Journal* 201(June 8): 18.
Hotelling, Harold. 1929. "Stability and Competition." *Economic Journal* 39(Spring): 41-57. Reprinted in George J. Stigler and Kenneth E. Boulding, eds. *Readings in Price Theory.* Homewood, Ill.: Richard D. Irvin, Inc.
Hutchinson, T. W. 1981. *The Politics and Philosophy of Economics.* New York: New York University Press.
Johnson, Marguerite. 1981. "Embattled but Unbowed." *Time* 117(February 16): 28-32.
Joseph, Sir Keith. 1976. *Monetarism is Not Enough.* London: Center for Policy Studies.
Kaldor, Nickolas. 1980. "Memorandum to U.K. Treasury and Civil Service Committee." In Commons 1980, 86-140.
Kelly, James (reported by Bonnie Angelo, Mary Cronin, and Frank Medville). "Thatcher Triumphant." *Time* 121(June 20): 29-33, 36, 39, 41.
Keynes, J. M. 1923. *A Tract on Monetary Reform.* London: Macmillan and Co., Limited.
———. 1936. *The General Theory of Employment, Interest and Money.* New York: Harcourt, Brace and Company.
———. 1980. "Memorandum to U.K. Treasury and Civil Service Committee." In Commons 1980, 48-59.
Laidler, D. 1982. "Friedman and Schwartz on Monetary Trends: A Review Article." *Journal of International Money and Finance* 1(December): 293-305.
Marshall, George O. Jr. 1963. *A Tennyson Handbook.* New York: Twayne Publishers, Inc.
Marx, Karl, and Engels, Friedrich. 1848. *Communist Manifesto* London (February) Reprinted with editorial comment in Tucker, Robert C., ed. 1978. *The Marx-Engels Reader.* New York: W. W. Norton and Company.
Marx, Karl. 1891. "Critique of the Gotha Program." Reprinted in Robert C. Tucker, ed. 1972. *The Marx-Engels Reader*, second edition. New York: W. W. Norton & Company, Inc.
Minford, A. P. 1980. "Memorandum to U.K. Treasury and Civil Service Committee." In Commons 1980, 131-143.
Moritz, Charles, ed. 1975. "Margaret Thatcher." *Current Biography.* New York: H. W. Wilson Company.
Muller, Robert L. 1981. "Thatcher Taunted on Yielding to Miners." *Wall Street Journal.* 197(February 20).
Murray, Tricia. 1978. *Margaret Thatcher.* London: W. H. Allen & Company, Ltd.
Nemy, Enid. 1981. "Mrs. Thatcher at First Reagan State Dinner." *New York Times* 130(February 27): B6.
News. 1976. "Economists are schizophrenic, Friedman says." *Times Educational Supplement* (November 3): 20.

_____. 1980a. "Free market projections." *The Sunday Times* (February 19): 59.

_____. 1980b. "Thatcher's policies leave labor ruling." *Business Week* (September 22): 49.

Nordheimer, Jon. 1983. "Stern Doctor, Stern Remedy." *New York Times* 132(June 10): 1, 8.

Note. 1980. "Methods of monetary control." *Bank of England Quarterly Bulletin*. 20(December): 428-429.

Otten, Alan L. 1981a. "Tory Trend: Mrs. Thatcher Loses Support as Recession Drags on." *Wall Street Journal* 197(January 14): 1, 25.

_____. 1981b. "British Politics Altered by Rise of New Party and Tory Labor Ills." *Wall Street Journal* 198 (November 25): 1, 18.

_____. 1983. "Thatcher Wins by Large Margin." *Wall Street Journal* 201(June 10): 1.

Parkin, Michael. 1981. "Mrs. Thatcher's Management of the British Economy." In *Economic Policy in the United Kingdom: Proceedings of a Conference*. General Mills Foundation: University of Minnesota.

Patten, Chris. 1982. "Mrs. Thatcher and the British Economy." *Journal of the Institute of Socioeconomic Studies* 6(Winter): 34-43.

Peele, Gillian. 1980. "On the political battle lines." *Times Educational Supplement* (March 28): 28.

Popper, Karl. 1965. *Conjectures and Refutations*. New York: Harper and Row, Publishers.

Robson, William Alexander. 1972. "Fabian Society." *Encyclopedia Britannica*, vol. 9. Chicago, Encyclopedia Britannica, Inc.

Roll, Eric. 1980. "Gurus of the free Market." *The Times* (March 6): 12c.

Rose, Richard. 1980. "Do Parties Make a Difference?" Chatham, C.J.: Chatham House Publishers, Inc.

Sachar, Howard Morley. 1977. *The Course of Modern Jewish History*, revised edition. New York: Dell Publishing Company.

Sargent, Thomas J. 1981. "Stopping Moderate Inflations: The Methods of Poincare and Thatcher." In *Economic Policy in the United Kingdom: Proceedings of a Conference*. General Mills Foundation: University of Minnesota.

Seargeant, Graham. 1980a. "Not so much a program, more a way of life." *The Sunday Times* No. 8120 (February 10).

_____. 1980b. "Et tu, Milton (or Paradise Lost at No. 10). *The Sunday Times*. (March 2).

Selden, Arthur, ed. 1981. *The Emerging Consensus?* London: Institute of Economic Affairs.

Sinclair, David. 1976. "Inflation: 'The tax that never has to be passed by Parliament'." *The Times* (September 13): 3c.

Smith, Geoffrey. 1981. "Social Democrats: What's Next for Britain." *Journal of the Institute for Socioeconomic Studies* 6(Autumn): 1-12.

Smith, Hendrick, Adam Clymer, Leonard Silk, Robery Lindsey, and Richard Burt. 1980. In *Reagan the Man, the President*, New York: Macmillan Publishing Company, Inc.

Special. 1983. "Britain's Prime Minister Vows Not to Shift to Extremist Line." *New York Times* 132(June 11): 1, 4.

Staff. 1972. "The Milk Snatcher." *Time* (February): 48.

_____. 1975a. "The Reward for Courage." *The Economist* 254(February 8): 11-12.

_____. 1975b. "What Thatcher means for Labor." *The Economist* 254(February 15): 12-13.

_____. 1975c. "And for her own party." *The Economist* 254(February 15): 13-14.

_____. 1975d. "Maggie wins by a knockout in the second round." *The Economist* 254(February 15): 17.

_____. 1975e. "Liberty, inequality." *The Economist* 256 (September 27): 11-13.

_____. 1977. "Not quite Disraeli." *The Economist* 264(July 23): 13-14.

_____. 1978. "One Election till 1984." *The Economist* 266 (January 26): 17-18.

_____. 1979a. "Only one prime minister." *The Economist* 271(April 28): 13-17.

_____. 1979b. "Mistress of Downing Street." *The Economist* 271(May 5): 13-14.

_____. 1979c. "Doing it her way?" *The Economist* 272 (September 22): 13-16.

_____. 1980a. "Britain's two prime ministers." *The Economist* 277(October 4): 11-13.

_____. 1980b. "How Labor's left took power." *The Economist* 277(October 4): 55-56.

_____. 1980c. "In Thatcherland." *The Economist* 277(October 25): 13-16.

———. 1980d. "Not wet, just worried." *The Economist* 277(November 8): 20.
———. 1980e. "Which of her promises should Mrs. Thatcher break." *The Economist* 277(November 8): 57-58.
———. 1980f. "The cabinet does half it seems." *The Economist* 277(November 22): 75-76.
———. 1980g. "It's freezing." *The Economist* 277(November 29): 11-13.
———. 1980h. "No time for scapegoats." *The Economist* 277(December 6): 14-17.
———. 1980i. "The path to intervention marches through the free market." *The Economist* 277(December 13): 49-50.
———. 1981a. "And here's the rest of my budget..." *The Economist* 278(January 17): 51-52.
———. 1981b. "Where the rainbow ends." *The Economist* 278(January 31): 13-14.
———. 1981c. "All the prime minister's men." *The Economist* 278(February 14): 53-54.
———. 1981d. "Mrs. Thatcher bails out." *The Economist* 278(February 28): 17-18.
———. 1981e. "Charging the guns." *The Economist* 278 (March 21): 11-13.
———. 1981f. "Stuck in slump?" *The Economist* 279(April 4): 47-52.
———. 1981g. "Go take a break." *The Economist* 279(April 18): 13-14.
———. 1981h. "Publicize or privatise, don't ditherise." *The Economist* 279(June 13): 51-52.
———. 1981i. "Herbert's elephant roost." *The Economist* 279(June 20): 12-13.
———. 1981j. "1984 claims a seat at the cabinet table." *The Economist* 279(June 20): 61-62.
———. 1981k. "Make the railways run for their money." *The Economist* 279(June 20): 63.
———. 1981l. "Is slimmer fitter?" *The Economist* 280(July 4): 13-14.
———. 1981m. "Talking them out of their next pay raise." *The Economist* 280(July 4): 53-54.
———. 1981n. "Thatcher to shuffle." *The Economist* 280 (August 22): 13-15.
———. 1982. *Report to the Congress of the Commission on the Role of Gold in the Domestic and International Monetary System*, vol. I (March).
———. 1983a. "Thatcher's Britain?" *The Economist* 287(June 4): 11-12.
———. 1983b. "What is left for the left?" *The Economist* 287(June 18): 33-38.
———. 1983c. "Class is no guide." *The Economist* 287(June 18): 38, 41.
———. 1983d. "The rise of the money-men." *The Economist* 287(June 18): 41.
———. 1983e. "The accountants move in." *The Economist* 287(June 18): 44, 47.
———. 1983f. "Oh come on now!" *The Economist* 287(June 18): 14.
———. 1983g. "British merchant banks see good times again." *The Economist* 287(June 25): 83-84.
———. 1983h. "The rise of a populist." *The Economist* 29(October 22): 51-52, 54.
Stein, Herbert. 1981. "Britain and the Ordeal of Margaret Thatcher." *Wall Street Journal* (February 25): 28.
Stephenson, High. 1980. "The gospel according to St. Milton." *The Times* (February 26): 17d.
Strasser, Steven, and Clifton, Tony. 1981. "Britain's New Politics." *Newsweek* 98(December 7): 45, 47-48.
Thatcher, Margaret. 1981. "The Ideas of Free Society." Speech delivered at Georgetown University, February 7. Special collections Division, Georgetown University Library.
Tobin, James. 1982. "The Reagan Economic Plan: Supply-Side, Budget, and Inflation." In Richard H. Fink, ed. *Supply-Side Economics: A Critical Appraisal*. Frederick, Md.: University Publications of America, Inc.
Verney, Douglas V. 1966. *British Government and Politics: Life Without a Declaration of Independence*. New York: Harper & Row Publishers.
Vogel, Frank. 1976. "Friedman warning on 'U.K. road to disaster'." *The Times* (November 30): 1 and 25.
Wallace, Laura. 1981. "Patron on the Pound." *Wall Street Journal*. 198(December 17): 1, 23.
Walters, Alan A. 1965. "Professor Friedman on the Demand for Money." *Journal of Political Economy* 73(October): 545-551.
———. (with H. J. Kavanagh). 1966a. "Demand for Money in the U.K." *Bulletin of Oxford University Institute of Economics and Statistics* 28(July).

_____. 1966b. "Money Multipliers in the United Kingdom 1880-1962." *Oxford Economic Papers* (November).

_____. 1967. "The Demand for Money—The Dynamic Properties of the Multiplier." *Journal of Political Economy* 75(June).

_____. 1970. *An Introduction to Econometrics*, second edition. Macmillan First edition 1968.

_____. 1971. *Money in Boom and Slump: An Empirical Inquiry into British Experience since the 1880s*, third edition. London: Institute of Economic Affairs. First published in January 1969, with second edition in May 1970.

_____, ed. 1973. *Money and Banking: Selected Readings*. Baltimore, MD.: Penguin Books Inc.

_____. 1978. *Economists and the British Economy*, Eighth Wincott Memorial Lecture. London: Institute of Economic Affairs for the Wincott Foundation.

_____. 1983. *The British Renaissance*. Washington, D.C.: American Enterprise Institute.

_____. 1986. *Britain's Economic Renaissance*. New York: Oxford University Press.

Walters, Barbara. 1981. "Right Honorable Margaret Thatcher." (March 1). *ABC News Issues and Answers*: Washington, D.C.: Tyler Business Services, Inc.

Whitaker, Mark (with Tony Clifton and Ronald Henkoff). 1983. "Betting on a Landslide." *Newsweek* 101(May 23): 30, 31, 34.

Wilson, Thomas. 1981. "The Monetarist Controversy and the British Experiment." *Atlantic Economic Journal* (December).

Wood, John B. 1981. "How It all Began—Personal Recollections." In Arthur Selden, ed. (1981).

Notes, Chapter 16: The Reagan Presidency

1. Dulles (1949). 2. The evidence supporting this assertion is as follows: the general presence of the monetarist, supply-side ideas, their research base and links to Reagan, his speeches, appointed personnel, policy stances and legislative action, on one hand, and the absence of any comparable, researched agenda with ties to the actions, speeches, and deeds of Roosevelt. The events contributing to the Great Depression were poorly understood at the time by economists as well as others, and for some decades beyond. The analysis of the monetary role was not understood before Friedman's and Schwartz's *Monetary History*, and the explanations economists offered after Keynes's *General Theory* and on into the Keynesian era favored a movement toward big government (chaps. 8 and 11). The Keynesian explanations consisted primarily of the liquidity trap in relation to money, the closely related inelasticity of investment demand, and the declining marginal propensity to consume and hence the oversupply of goods. 3. The political changes brought about in Washington, D.C. with Reagan are best dated from this period of the early 1960s, when Friedman had done his *Capitalism and Freedom* lectures, when Goldwater had published his political tract, when Friedman had joined Goldwater as an unofficial advisor, and when Reagan had joined in to support Goldwater (Clymer 1980; Davenport 1976; Friedman 1962; Goldwater 1960; Greider 1981, 29; Tolchin 1984). 4. Dallek (1984, 64, 69, 94, 98); Frazer (1984c); Stockman (1986, chap. 12). 5. Palmer and Sawhill (1984, 23). 6. Reeves (1984). 7. Solomon and Abramson (1984, 42-43, 45, 59). 8. Frazer (1980, sec. 102.). 9. This list would include Bartlett (1981), Lekashman (1982), Palmer and Sawhill (1984). In Stone and Sawhill (1984b, chap. 2), on the other hand, monetary and fiscal policy will be related with the result that they see the 1981-82 recession very much a result of monetary discipline, as we do. However, even here treatment of topics like the government budget constraint, or tax effects on the real rate of interest (appendixes to chap. 16), or problems of monetary control and timing are avoided.

Evans's book (1983) provides more on monetary policy in relation to the tax policy than does others. However, even here monetary policy enters just as background, in undefined terms like "easy" or "tight" credit, in flawed discussion of Robert Mundell's role, which we take up in the present chapter. A passage cited to the effect that "the cyclical behavior of the post-war U.S. economy has been abetted by stimulative fiscal and monetary policy" (Evans

1983, 49) is almost the entire extent to which Evans suggests a monetary explanation of the cyclical behavior he utilizes so effectively in his analysis. He otherwise takes the cycles partly for granted and proceeds to make comparisons that support the predominance of monetary policy even as he deals with business-conditions effects or modifications in the tax code. For example, he finds major modifications that had the anticipated effects in expansion phases of business conditions (1983, 141-145) but failed in other instances in other phases and where inflation was a problem (1983, 145-149). "Indeed," he said (1983, 158), "while the tax advantage contained in the 1981 Tax Reform Act raised investment by $8 to $9 billion per year, the increase in interest rates lowered investment $25 billion." Continuing, he said, "on balance the net effect of the first two years of the Reagan program was to diminish capital spending in real terms by $17 billion." But in all this Evans failed to consider the interrelated and predominant monetary factors. **10.** The relevance of Say's law to supply-side economics has been widely recognized, including by Tyler Cowan (1982, 160-184), although both Cowan and Evans failed to see the significance of Friedman's monetary analysis as a part of supply-side economics and of renewed interest in Say's law. **11.** Evans (1983, 121-125). **12.** Some of the public finance group have ties to the public-choice economics which we associated with James Buchanan (chap. 9). It included Norman Ture, Undersecretary for tax policy in the early Reagan Administration. A number of others are listed in Charles Walker's and Mark Bloomfield's *New Directions in Federal Tax Policy for the 1980s* (1984). **13.** Principal ones in this group are Arthur Burns, Paul McCracken, and Herbert Stein who were players in the Nixon part of the Keynesian era (chap. 5). Others would include Charles Walker of the Treasury in the first Nixon administration, Murray Weidenbaum of Reagan's early Council of Economic Advisors (CEA) and Alan Greenspan, a former CEA chairman. Still others would include Martin Anderson, William E. Simon, and Walter Wriston. **14.** This group included W. Phil Gramm, formerly a professor at Texas A&M and leader of the Boll Weevils, Budget Committee chairman Jim Jones, and Means Committee chairman Dan Rostenkowski. **15.** Sprinkel (1971). **16.** MacNeil/Lehrer (1981; 1982).**17.** Kilborn (1985); Staff (1985b). **18.** Ehrbar (1981, 52). **19.** Friedman (1968). **20.** Friedman (1973). **21.** Budget Office (1978). **22.** Brooks (1982, 100-104); and Wanniski (1978). **23.** Evans (1983, 48-53, 200-205). **24.** Mundell (1971, chap. 2). **25.** Brooks (1982, 129, 143). **26.** Paul and Lehreman (1982). **27.** Staff (1982). **28.** Greider (1981, 39, 46, 54); Regan (1981); and Staff (1985a). **29.** Greider (1981, 29). **30.** Greider (1981, 29, 54). **31.** Greider (1981, 32). **32.** Greider (1981, 32). **33.** Greider (1981, 54). **34.** Regan (1981, 2). **35.** Regan (1981, 3). **36.** Staff (1985a, 60). **37.** Dallek (1984, 25). **38.** Dalamon and Abramson (1948, 41). **39.** Dallek (1984, 5-6). **40.** Dallek (1984, 7). **41.** Dallek (1984, 8-17). **42.** Dallek (1984, 7, 24-25, 30-33, 52). **43.** Dallek (1984, 13, 16, 17, 25). **44.** Tawney (1926). **45.** Dallek (1984, 32-35). **46.** Frazer (1980, sect. 191). **47.** The notion that a policy change was neither perceived nor believed before the election of a new administration is also supported by Blanchard (1984, 211) where he cites comments of market participants and analysts found in *Business Week*, for the period October 1979-June 1983. Friedman also makes the point about the credibility of the October 1979 announcement (1984a, 397). With respect to it, he said: "Such belief was not widely present...when the new policy was announced. And the wide gyrations in monetary growth rates in subsequent months rapidly disillusioned any naive agents who initially accepted the Fed's rhetoric as a guarantee of steady and predictable monetary growth." **48.** Benjamin Friedman (1984); Hadjimichalakis (1984, 38, 55); Hakkio and Higgins (1985); Sawhill and Stone (1984, 70, 79, 82, 104). **49.** Hoover (1984, 63). **50.** Friedman (1984a, 97; 1983, 4-5). **51.** Hadjimichalakis (1984, 22). **52.** This is the analytical case of recognizing the role of money. An example of its operations would be West Germany in the 1970s (Poehl 1984, 6-10). On the other hand, the more common interpretation of inflation imposes a special reading on the price index (or the price average as the left-hand-side of the equation may be read.) The special reading in effect attributes the cause of changes in the average to the components on the right-hand-side—oil prices, housing cost, food cost, etc. Indeed, no less an authority in econometrics than Lawrence Klein viewed the U.S. in the 1970s this way (Frazer 1984a.) Stone and Sawhill (1984b, chaps. 1 and 3) come very close to Klein's position only in their case on the analysis of decelerating inflation, 1980-83.

Though widely held views, the foregoing are simplistic in two respects: (1) they partly ignore the role of the money and credit aggregates, and (2) they ignore the reason why one country, such as West Germany with total dependence on foreign oil imports, may show less inflation than another during a period of oil-price shocks. Even so, the reasons behind the analysts' respective positions are probably more fundamental than we indicate and concern the social views held by the analysts themselves (Frazer 1984a). **53.** Reagan (1982b, 16). **54.** Friedman (1983, 3). **55.** Friedman (1980b; 1981a; 1981b; 1982a; 1982b; 1982c; 1982d; 1982e). **56.** Rather (1982, 3, 7). There were other instances where the President used the same analysis. One occurred in early July of 1983 (Bacon 1983), after short-term interest rates (the Federal funds rate and the 3-month Treasury bill rate) had showed upward movement in May, June, and July. The market speculation and the talk in the press was that the Fed would raise its discount rate(s), as it may to bring it in line with market rates. In the mid-1983 context, however, the president wanted rates to remain low, so he advised through White House spokesman Larry Speaks that the Fed should lower market rates by slowing the growth of money balances and hence reducing the fear of renewed inflation. **57.** Friedman (1984a; 1984b). **58.** Frazer (1967, chaps. 4-7). **59.** Gilbert (1985, 15, 19). **60.** Research undertaken at the University of Florida with David Hellier. **61.** Announcements (1982); Furlong (1983); Gilbert (1985); and Hadjimichalakis (1984, chaps. 4 and 5). **62.** Hadjimichalakis (1984, 80, 103-106). **63.** Friedman (1981a; 1981b). **64.** Gilbert (1981, 1a); and Evans (1983, 129). **65.** See Friedman (1962) and note 60 above. **66.** Avery et al. (1986). **67.** Reagan (1982b, 9). **68.** MacNeil/Lehrer (1981, 5). **69.** The respective sources are: Jaroslovsky (1982, 3); Bacon (1982a, 1); Bacon (1982b, 3); Bacon (1982c, 28); Friedman (1982a, 20); Roos (1982, 24). **70.** Rather (1982). **71.** MacNeil/Lehrer (1982, 2-3). **72.** Friedman (1982d, 70), and see note 55 too. **73.** Friedman (1983, 24; 1984b, 43). **74.** Friedman (1984b, 44). **75.** Hadjimichalakis (1984, 111-113). **76.** Friedman (1984a, 397). **77.** MacNeil/Lehrer (1981, 5). **78.** Dallek (1984, 120); and Friedman (1984a, 46). **79.** Friedman (1984b, 44). **80.** Friedman (1984b, 46). **81.** Sahling and Akhtar (1985, 27). **82.** Devroy (1985). **83.** Reagan (1985, 13). **84.** Friedman (1984b, 51). **85.** Friedman (1984b, 45). **86.** Friedman (1984b, 45-46). **87.** Friedman (1984a, 45). **88.** Friedman (1984b, 45-46). **89.** Volcker arrived from his post as president of the Federal Reserve Bank of New York, which meant that he had been serving on the Federal Open Market Committee. Hence, no time was needed for on-the-job-training. **90.** Wanniski (1978, 97-103). **91.** Evans (1983; 1984). **92.** Evans (1983, 199). **93.** Evans (1983, 17, 43). **94.** Evans (1983, 9, 45). **95.** Evans (1983, 40-41). **96.** Evans (1983, 39-40). **97.** Evans (1983, 43). **98.** Evans (1983, 43-44). **99.** Tatom (1984). **100.** Friedman (1978). **101.** Evans (1983, 85). **102.** Evans (1983, 87). **103.** Evans (1983, 85). **104.** Friedman (1981, 98). **105.** Greenwald (1984). **106.** Alpern (1984); and Raines (1984a). **107.** Raines (1984b). **108.** Rains (1984b); and Weisman (1984). **109.** Weisman (1984, 1). Invoking the time of two decades earlier, Goldwater himself appeared at the 1984 GOP convention in Dallas where he spoke his mind in his "inimitable, unvarnished style," a *New York Times* writer said (Tolchin 1984). His convention speech (Goldwater 1984) contained some of the famous (or infamous) old lines: "Extremism in defense of liberty is no vice." And, referring to Ronald Reagan, "And in your hearts, you know he's right!" **110.** Reagan (1987). **111.** Reagan (1984). The Treasury tax proposal has been described as a close cousin to other flat-tax proposals, most notably the Democratic Bradley-Gephardt "Fair Tax" plan and the Republican Kemp-Kasten "Fast Tax." For a comparison of proposals for fundamental tax reform, see Margo Thorning's piece (Walker and Bloomfield 1984, 393-416). **112.** We see instead Friedman's rationale for making the Federal Reserve a bureau in the Treasury under the secretary of the Treasury (Friedman 1982b; and Clark 1982). There is in this view recognition of formalizing the President's responsibility and letting voters know more clearly who is accountable. Other alternatives would include simply staying with Reagan's present course or implementing Friedman's rule as suggested by the Commission on the Role of Gold (Staff 1982, 17-18). On an evenly split vote the Commission recommended "that the Congress by legislation establish a rule specifying that the growth in the Nation's money supply be maintained at a steady rate which would insure long-run price stability." **113.** Friedman (1980); and Reagan (1985b). **114.** Reagan (1985b). **115.** Boyd (1985); Klott (1985); MacNeil/Lehrer (1985); White House (1985). **116.** MacNeil/Lehrer (1985, 4). **117.** Klott (1985). **118.** See references in note 113. **119.** Reagan (1985c). **120.** Stockman (1986, 395). **121.** Stockman (1986, 119). **122.** This list limits the ideas to the monetary, supply-side, deficit, and incentivist policies with which we deal in chapter 16. However, the list could be extended to the antitrust area we took up in chapter 9, where we noted that

Friedman had some influence. Extending the list to the area we may cite *U.S. News & World Report*'s issue on "Mergers" (7/22/85, pages 48-55). They note the fourth and largest wave of business mergers in this century and relate it to "a healthy economy, generous tax policies and virtual carte blanche from the Reagan administration." **123.** Kvasnicka (1985) and Rukeyser (1985). **124.** Kilborn (1985b) and Staff (1985c).

References, Chapter 16: The Reagan Presidency

Alpern, David M. 1984. "The Voters." *Newsweek* 104 (November 5):30.
Announcement. 1982. "Regulation D: Amendments." *Federal Reserve Bulletin* 68 (October): 625-626.
Avery, Robert B.; Elliehauser, Gregory E.; Kennickell, Arthur B.; and Spindt, Paul A. 1986. "The Use of Cash and Transactions Accounts by American Families." *Federal Reserve Bulletin* 72(February): 87-108.
Bacon, Kenneth H. 1982a. "Reserve Board Faces An Agonizing Choice." *Wall Street Journal* 199(January 22):1,18.
_____. 1982c. "The Steady Attack on the Federal Reserve Board." *Wall Street Journal* 199(January 29):20.
_____. 1983. "Reagan Wants Fed to Slow Money Growth But Urges It To Avoid Discount Rate Boost." *Wall Street Journal* 202(July 8):3.
Bartlett, Bruce. 1981. *Reaganomics: Supply Side Economics in Action*. Westport, Conn.: Arlington House Publishers.
Blanchard, Oliver J. 1984. "The Lucus Critique and the Volcker Deflation." *American Economic Review* 74(May): 211-215.
Boyd, Gerald M. 1985. "Reagan, Setting a Poyndist Strategy." *New York Times* 134(May 29): 11.
Brooks, John. 1982. "Annals of Finance: The Supply Side." *The New Yorker* (April 19):96-150.
Clark, Lindley H. (Jr.). 1982. "Make the Fed a Branch of the Treasury." *Wall Street Journal* 199(March 6):29.
Clymer, Adam. 1980. "A Star is Born." In *Reagan the Man, the President*. New York: MacMillan Publishing Co., Inc.
Cowen, Tyler. 1982. "Say's Law and Keynesian Economics." In Fink, ed. (1982).
Dallek, Robert. 1984. *Ronald Reagan: The Politics of Symbolism*. Cambridge, Mass.: Harvard University Press.
Davenport, John. 1967. "The Radical Economics of Milton Friedman." *Fortune* 75 (June): 131-132, 147-148, 150.
Devroy, Ann. 1985. "Reagan: I'm the Boss." *USA Today* (January 18):1, 4, 13.
Dulles, Foster Rhea. 1949. *Labor in America*. New York: Thomas Y. Crowell Company.
Ehrbar, A.F. 1981. "The Economy." *Fortune* (March 23): 47-52.
Evans, Michael K. 1983. *The Truth About Supply-Side Economics*. New York: Basic Books, Inc. Publishers.
Fink, Richard H. ed. 1982. *Supply-Side Economics: A Critical Appraisal*. Frederich, Md.: University Publications of America, Inc.
Frazer, William. 1967. *The Demand for Money*. Cleveland, OH: World Publishing Company.
_____. 1980. *Expectations, Forecasting and Control*, Vol. I and II. Lanham, MD.: University Press of America, Inc.
_____. 1982. "The Velocity-Interest Rate Association: Inflation, Accelerated Inflation and Uncertainty." *Economic Notes* 11(March): 114-115.
_____. 1983. "*Free to Choose*: A Review Article." *Wall Street Review of Books* 11(Winter): 14-22.
_____. 1984a. "*The Economics of Supply and Demand* and Friedman." *Economic Notes* 13(December): 47-71.
_____. 1984b. "*Supply-Side Economics* and Friedman." *Wall Street Review of Books* 12(Fall): 297-302.

———. 1984c. "*The Politics of Symbolism* and Friedman." *Wall Street Review of Books* 12(Fall): 292-296.
Friedman, Benjamin M. 1984. "Lessons from the 1979-82 Monetary Policy Experiment." *American Economic Review* 74(May): 382-387.
Friedman, Milton. 1962. "The Interpolation of Time Series by Related Series." Technical Paper 16, National Bureau of Economic Research.
———. 1973. "Interview." *Playboy* (February): 51-74.
———. 1975. "Tax Cuts and Recession." *Newsweek* (May 12): 83.
———. 1978. "The Kemp-Roth Free Lunch." *Newsweek* (August 7): 59.
———. 1980a. "Our New Hidden Taxes." *Newsweek* (April 14): 90.
———. 1980b. "The Fed Fails—Again." *Newsweek* 96(December 1): 78.
———. 1981a. "A Memorandum to the Fed." *Wall Street Journal* 197 (January 30): 20.
———. 1981b. "Monetary Instability." *Newsweek* 98(December 21): 71.
———. 1982a. "The Federal Reserve and Monetary Instability." *Wall Street Journal* 199(February 1): 20.
———. 1982b. "Monetary Policy: Theory and Practice." *Journal of Money, Credit and Banking* 14(February): 98-118.
———. 1982c. "The Yo-Yo Economy." *Newsweek* 99(February 15): 72.
———. 1982d. "Interest Rates and the Budget." *Newsweek* 99(June 28): 70.
———. 1982e. "An Aborted Recovery?" *Newsweek* 100(August 23): 59.
———. 1983a. "More Double Talk at the Fed." *Newsweek* 101(May 2): 72.
———. 1983b. "Monetarism in Rhetoric and in Practice." *Bank of Japan Monetary and Economic Studies*, Institute for Monetary and Economic Studies 1(October 1983): 1-14.
———. 1984a. "Lessons from the 1979-82 Monetary Policy Experiment." *American Economic Review* 74(May: 397-399.
———. 1984b. In Heller, H. Robert; Crockett, Andrew; Friedman, Milton; Niskansen, William A.; and Sinai, Allen. "Economic Outlook." *Contemporary Policy Issues* 3(Fall): 15-82.
Furlough, Frederick. 1983. "New Deposit Instruments." *Federal Reserve Bulletin* 69(May):319-326.
Gilbert, R. Alton. 1985. "Operating Procedures for Conducting Monetary Policy." *Review*, Federal Reserve Bank of St. Louis 67(February): 13-21.
Goldwater, Barry. 1960. *The Conscience of a Conservative*. Shepherdsville, KY: Victor Publishing Company, Inc.
———. 1984. "Text of Goldwater's Speech on National Defense." *New York Times* 133(August 23): 14.
Greenwald, John. 1984. "The Forecasters Flunk." *Time* 124(August 27): 42-44.
Greider, William. 1981. "The Education of David Stockman." *Atlantic Monthly* (December): 24-54.
Hadjimichalakis, Michael G. 1984. *The Federal Reserve, Money, and Interest Rates*. New York: Praeger Publishers.
Hakkio, Craig S., and Higgins, Bryon. 1985. "Costs and Benefits of Reducing Inflation." *Economic Review*, Federal Reserve Bank of Kansas City (January): 3-15.
Harvey, Jack L. 1986. "Foreign Direct Investment in the U.S. Rises." *International Letter*, Federal Reserve Bank of Chicago, no. 554, January.
Hoover, Kevin D. 1984. "Two Types of Monetarism." *Journal of Economic Literature* 22(March): 58-76.
Jaroslovsky, Rich. 1982. "Reagan Calls Fed's Money-Supply Figure 'The Wrong Signal' for Markets for Heed." *Wall Street Journal* 199(January 20): 3.
Kilborn, Peter T. 1985. "Economic Advisor with a Difference: Beryl Wayne Sprinkle." *New York Times* 134 (February 22): 29-30.
———. 1985b. "U.S. AS a Debtor Nation." *New York Times* 134(November 17): 1, 34.
Klott, Gary. 1985. "Reagan Asks Tax 'Revolution': $2,000 Exemption, 35% Top Rate, No Deduction of State Levies." *New York Times* 134(May 29): 1, 14.
Kvasnicka, Joseph G. 1985. "Bringing Down the Value of the Dollar." *International Letter* No. 552 (November).
Lekachman, Robert. 1982. *Reaganomics: Greed is Not Enough*. New York: Pantheon Books.

MacNeil-Lehrer. 1981. "Wall Street Jitters." Transcript, May 8.
———. 1982. "Why are Interest Rates Rising?" Transcript, February 5.
———. 1985. "Tax Reform..." Transcript, May 28.
Marris, Stephen. 1985. *Deficits and the Dollar: The World Economy at Risk*. Washington, D.C.: Institute for International Economics, December.
Mundell, Robert A. 1971. *Monetary Theory: Inflation, and Growth in the World Economy*. Pacific Palisades, Calif.: Goodyear Publishing Company, Inc.
Palmer, John., and Sawhill, Isabel V., eds. 1984. *The Reagan Record*. Cambridge, Mass.: Ballinger Publishing Company.
Paul, Ron, and Lehrman, Lewis. 1982. *The Case for Gold: A Minority Report of the U.S. Gold Commission*. Washington, D.C.: Cato Institute.
Poehl, Karl Otto. 1984. "Germany's Volcker." Transcript of Wall Street Week (June 8).
Raines, Howell. 1984a. "Chance of Revival seen for Mondale after TV Debate." *New York Times* 134(October 9): 1, 17.
———. 1984b. "Reagan Stresses Arms and the Economy." *New York Times* 134(November 8): 1, 10.
Rather, Dan. 1982. "A Conversation with the President." *CBS News Special Report* (January 27): 1-19.
Reagan, Ronald. 1982a. "State of the Union: An Era of American Renewal." *New York Times* 132(January 27): 8.
———. 1982b. "Economic Address." *New York Times* 132(October 14): 16.
———. 1985a. "State of the Union: Second American Revolution." *New York Times* 134 (February 7): 13.
———. 1985b. "Transcript of President's News Conference." *New York Times* 134 (February 22): 10.
———. 1985c. "Transcript of President's News Conference." *New York Times* 134(August 4): 10.
———. 1987. "Transcript of Reagan's News Conference." *New York Times* 137 (October 23): 6-7.
Reeves, Richard. 1984. "The Ideological Election." *New York Times Magazine* (February 19): 26-29, 80, 82, 92.
Regan, Donald. 1981. "Donald Regan Interview." *The MacNeil-Lehrer Report*, March 24.
Roos, Lawrence K. 1982. "The Attack on Monetary Policy." *Wall Street Journal* 199(February 3): 24.
Rukeyser, Louis. 1985. "The Return of Milton Friedman." Transcript of *Wall Street Week*, Owings Mills, Md.
Sahling, Leonard, and Akhtar, M.A. 1985. "What is behind the Capital Spending Boom?" Federal Reserve Bank of New York, *Quarter Review* 9(Winter): 19-27.
Solamon, Lester,M., and Abramson, Allan J. 1984. "Governance." In Palmer and Sawhill (1984, 31-68).
Sprinkel, Beryl Wayne. 1971. *Money and Markets: A Monetarist View*. Homewood, Ill.: Richard D. Irwin, Inc.
Staff. 1982. *Report to the Congress of the Commission on the Role of Gold in the Domestic and International Monetary Systems*, Vol. 1 (March).
Staff. 1985a. "What Good are Economists?" *Newsweek* 105(February 24): 60-63.
Staff. 1985b. "Don Regan's Man at the CEA." *Newsweek* 105(March 4): 46.
Staff. 1985c. "Will Moves to Curb the Dollar Really Work?" *U.S. News & World Report* 99(October 7): 28-30.
Stockman, David. 1986. *The Triumph of Politics*. New York: Harper and Row, Publishers.
Stone, Charles F., and Sawhill, Isabel V. 1984a. "The Economy: The Key to Success." I Palmer and Sawhill (1984, 69-105).
———, and ———. 1984b. *Economic Policy in the Reagan Years*. Washington, D.C.: The Urban Institute.
Tatom, John A. 1984. "The 1981 Personal Income Tax Cuts." Federal Reserve Bank of St. Louis *Review* 66(December): 5-17.
Tawney, Richard T. 1926. *Religion and the Rise of Capitalism*. New York: Harcourt, Brace and Company.

Tolchin, Martin. 1984. "Goldwater, Ignoring Laxalt Plea, Speaks His Mind at G.O.P. Parley." *New York Times* 133(August 23): 1, 15.
Treasury. 1984. "Report on Fundamental Tax Simplification and Reform." Washington, D.C.: U.S. Government Printing Office.
Walker, Charles E., and Bloomfield, Mark E., eds. 1984. *New Directions in Federal Tax Policy for the 1980s*, expanded. Cambridge, Mass.: Ballinger Publishing Company.
Wanniski, Jude. 1978. *The Way the World Works*. New York: Simon and Schuster.
Weintraub, Bernard, 1985. "Reagan Sketches Legislative Goals for Next 4 Years." *New York Times* 134(February 7): 1,14.
Weisman, Steven R. 1984. "The Politics of Popularity." *New York Times* 134(November 8): 1,11.
West, Robert Craig. 1982. "The Depository Institutions Deregulation Act of 1980: A Historical Perspective. *Economic Review*, Federal Reserve Bank of Kansas City (February): 3-13.
White House. 1985. "White House Summary of the Tax Package." *New York Times* 134(May 29): 15.

Notes, Chapter 17: Beyond Convention

1. Veblen (1919). 2. Sacher (1977, 39). 3. Schweitzer (1971, 168-169). 4. On the development of the Talmud, see Roth (1970, chapter 12). 5. Continuing:

"The Prophets, too, are full of devastating attacks on those who prefer riches to righteousness and wisdom; so, too, are the Proverbs. Intrinsic to Judaism is a far stronger sense of social justice than a capitalistic enterprise. This can be seen, e.g., in the long-standing tradition that called for wealth and land to be periodically and equally redivided during what was called the Jubilee Year. Moreover, the hero type in Judaism has always been the scholar, whereas the merchant is frequently regarded with contempt for his general ignorance." (Schweitzer 1971, 160)

6. In the writing about Jews, the emphasis is repeatedly on an intellectual orientation (Sachar 1977, 74, 139-147, 280, 316, 332, 346, 372, 394, 398, 406-407, 451-458): the rabbi is more of a scholar and a teacher than a priest (Roth 1970, 205); in the less secularized phases of Jewish education, the chief sustaining influence of the Jew was his religion plus the intense study of the Talmud imparted the discipline called for on the part of intellectual endeavor; Jewish housewives appear as being frequently engaged in business on a large scale in earlier periods "in some cases to leave their husbands more leisure for study" (Roth 1970, 204); "shrewd financiers became transmuted into acute scholars while their clients sat drinking in their castles" (Roth 1970, 205). 7. Sachar (1977, 406-407). 8. Von Neumann and Morgenstern (1964). 9. Weintraub (1983, 15-16). 10. Weintraub (1983, 19). 11. Weintraub (1983, 18-25). 12. Weintraub (1983, 18, 37). 13. Friedman's personality aside, Melvin Reder (1982, 32-33, 36) made a case for Friedman's success based on his role, taste, and aptitude as an ideologue. 14. On the exposure of a theory to criticism, see Popper (1962, 256-257). 15. Clark (1981, 1). 16. Frazer (1983). 17. Friedman (1981). 18. Clark (1981, 1). 19. Lerner (1978). 20. Fay (1976). 21. Anonymous (1976). 22. Klamer (1984, 105). 23. Staff (1987, 5) 24. Silk (1976, ix-xi). 25. Boland (1982); and Caldwell (1982). 26. Kuhn (1970, 10). 27. Caldwell (1982, 71). 28. Kuhn (1970, 10). 29. Caldwell (1982, 71). 30. Caldwell (1982, 71). 31. Caldwell (1982, 75). 32. Kuhn (1970, 90-91). 33. Caldwell (1982, 72). 34. Boland (1987, 6-9). 35. Patinkin (1956), and Frazer (1988). 36. Boland (1982, 13, 15, 24, 37, 149). 37. Boland (1982, 16-17). 38. Minford and Peel (1983); and Muth (1961). 39. Boland included in this group Robert Barro, Herschel Grossman, Robert Lucas, Robert Solow, and others. Articles by these authors were cited (Boland 1982, 197-204). 40. Koopmans (1957, 1-126). 41. Boland (1982, 132). 42. Boland (1982, 134). 43. Boland (1982, 137-139). 44. Boland (1982, 136). 45. Boland (1982, 136). 46. Boland (1982, 188). 47. Boland (1982, 188). 48. Boland (1982, 39, 89). 49. Popper (1962, 255-257). 50. Boland (1982, 28-30). 51. Boland (1982, 31-36). 52. Boland (1982, 63-

65). **53.** Klamer (1984, 230). **54.** Frazer (1980, chap. 17). **55.** Klamer (1984, 13-20). **56.** F/S (1982, 630). **57.** Boland (1982, 146). **58.** Friedman (1953, 91; 1974, 146). **59.** Boland (1979; 1982, 145). **60.** Boland (1982, chaps. 2 and 6). **61.** Boland (1982, 142-143). **62.** Boland (1982, 83-84). **63.** Boland (1982, 88-89). **64.** Patinkin (1956). **65.** Patinkin and Leith (1978). **66.** Frazer (1980, appendixes to chaps. 1 and 16). **67.** Boland (1982, 105-106). **68.** Frazer (1980, sect. 14.3). **69.** Frazer (1988). **70.** Frazer (1980, sect. 1.2). **71.** Keynes (1936, 18-20). **72.** Boland (1982, 107-109) notes and discusses the use of the methodology of physics in economics as calling for "the existence of stable constants." At the same time he questions their existence in economics.

References, Chapter 17: Beyond Convention

Anonymous. 1976. "Economics Viewed as Martial Art." *The Times* (London) (September 2): 12a.
Boland, Lawrence A. 1979. "A Critique of Friedman's Critics." *Journal of Economic Literature* 17(June): 502-522.
_____. 1982. *The Foundation of Economic Method*. London: George Allen & Unwin.
Caldwell, Bruce. 1982. *Beyond Positivism: Economic Methodology in the Twentieth Century*. London: George Allen & Unwin.
Clark, Lindley H. 1981. "The Monetarist." *Wall Street Journal* 198(October 7): 1 and 12.
Fay, Stephen. 1976. "The Friedman Phenomenon." *The Sunday Times* (December 12): 17.
Frazer, William. 1973. *Crisis in Economic Theory*. Gainesville, FL: University of Florida Press.
_____. 1980. *Expectations, Forecasting and Control*, vols. I & II. Lanham, MD: University Press of America.
_____. 1983. "*Free to Choose*: A Review Article." *Wall Street Review of Books* 11(March): 14-22.
_____. 1984. "*The Economics of Supply and Demand* and Friedman." *Economic Notes* 13(No. 3): 47-71.
_____. 1988. "The New Left" manuscript.
Friedman, Milton. 1940. "Review of J. Tinbergen, 'Business Cycles in the United States of America, 1919-1932'." *American Economic Review* 30(September): 657-660.
_____. 1955. "Leon Walras and His Economic System," *American Economic Review* 45(December): 900-909.
_____. 1972. "Capitalism and the Jews." Mont Pelerin Lecture.
_____. 1974. "Comments on the Critics." In Robert J. Gordon, ed., *Milton Friedman's Monetary Framework*. Chicago, Il: University of Chicago Press.
_____. 1981. "An Open Letter on Grants." *Newsweek* 97(May 18): 99.
_____. 1985. "Comment on Leland Yeager's Paper on the Keynesian Heritage." In *The Keynesian Heritage*, Center Symposia Series, C5-16. Graduate School of Management, University of Rochester.
_____, and Schwartz, Anna Jacobson. 1982. *Monetary Trends in the United States and the United Kingdom*. Chicago, Il: University of Chicago Press for the NBER.
Gilbert, J.C. 1982. *Keynes's Impact on Monetary Economics*. London: Butterworth & Co., Ltd.
Gordon, Robert J., ed. 1974. *Milton Friedman's Monetary Framework*. Chicago, Il: University of Chicago Press.
Hoselitz, Bert F. 1961. "Introduction to the American Edition." In Werner Sombart's *The Jews and Modern Capitalism*. Glencoe, IL. The Free Press. First published in 1939.
Hume, David. 1911. *A Treatise of Human Nature*, vols. I and II. London: J.M. Dent & Sons Ltd. First published in 1739.
Keynes, J.M. 1936. *General Theory of Employment, Interest and Money*. New York: Harcourt Brace and Company.
Klamer, Arjo. 1984. *Conversations with Economists*. Totowa, NJ: Rowan & Allenheld Publishers.

Koopmans, Tjalling Co. 1957. *The State of Economic Science*. New York: McGraw-Hill Book Company, Inc.
Kuhn, Thomas. 1970 *The Structure of Scientific Revolutions: International Encyclopedia of Unified Science*, vol. II, no. 2., 2nd enlarged edition, Chicago, IL: University of Chicago Press. The work first appeared in 1962.
Lerner, Abba P. 1978. "On Milton Friedman." Taped interview, September 15.
Meltzer, Allan H. 1982. "Discussion. In *Monetary Policy Issues in the 1980s*, A Symposium by the Federal Reserve Bank of Kansas City.
Minford, Patrick, and Peel, David. 1983. *Rational Expectations and the New Macroeconomics*. Oxford: Martin Robertson & Company Ltd.
Muth, John. 1961. "Rational Expectations and the Theory of Price Movements." *Econometrica* 29(July): 315-335.
Patinkin, Don. 1956. *Money, Interest, and Prices: An Integration of Monetary and Value Theory*. Evanston, IL: Row Peterson and Company.
_____, and Clark, Keith J. eds. *Keynes, Cambridge, and the General Theory*. Toronto: University of Toronto Press.
Popper, Karl R. 1962. *Conjectures and Refutations: The Growth of Scientific Knowledge*. New York: Basic Books.
_____. 1966. *The Open Society and Its Enemies*, fifth ed., vols. I and II. Princeton, NJ: Princeton University Press.
Reder, Melvin W. 1982. *Journal of Economic Literature* 20(March): 1-38.
Roth, Cecil. 1970. *A History of the Jew from Earliest Times through the Six Day War*, revised edition. New York: Schocken Books.
Sachar, Howard Morley, 1977. *The Course of Modern Jewish History*, updated and expanded edition. New York: Dell Publishing Co., Inc.
Schweitzer, Friederich M. 1971. *A History of the Jews since the First Century A.D*. New York: Macmillan Company.
Silk, Leonard. 1976. *The Economists*. New York: Basic Books, Inc. Publishers.
Staff. 1987. "Interview: Lindley H. Clark, Jr." *The Margin*. 3(November): 4-6.
Von Neumann, John, and Morgenstern, Oscar. 1964. *Theory of Games and Economic Behavior*, science edition. New York: John Wiley & Sons, Inc.
Veblen, Thorstein. 1919. "The Intellectual Preeminence of Jews in Modern Europe. *Political Science Quarterly* 34(March): 33-42.
Weintraub, E. Roy. 1983. "On the Existence of a Competitive Equilibrium: 1930-1954." *Journal of Economic Literature* 21(March): 1-39.

Notes, Chapter 18:
Economic Theory, Policy and the Uses of Statistical Methods

1. Cooley and LeRoy (1981); Johnson (1972); and Laidler (1977). 2. The early proliferation of large scale, simultaneous equations models with policy orientations is reviewed elsewhere (Frazer 1973, chap. 14). The naivete and promise of these models is best reflected in a presentation by Gary Fromm and in a paper by George Mitchell (1966; 1967). 3. Leamer (1983); and follow-up papers by McAleer (with Pagan, and Volker 1985); and by Leamer (1985). 4. Reviewed in Frazer (1973, 36-37 n11). 5. Frazer (1973, 128-129). 6. There is a literature on closely related reaction functions—functions which treat Federal Reserve policy as a left-hand-side variable which reacts to right-hand-side variables (Frazer 1973, 196). Plus there was a volume of literature on the Keynesian and money multiplier which largely ends with a definition of an antonomous variable which is similar to an exogenous variable (Frazer 1973, 95-133). 7. In addition to the reactions by Goodhart and Mayer, similar reactions are found on the part of David Laidler (1982) and Mario Tonveronachi (1983). 8. Hendry and Ericsson (1983; 1984). 9. The second part's detailed treatment as a theoretic system has been undertaken (Frazer 1988) 10. Huhne (1983a; 1983b). 11. Leamer (1985). 12. Frazer and Sawyer (1984, sect. vii). 13. F/S (1982, 569-573). 14. Stressing the general idea found in Maurice Allais's work (1966), Friedman translated the notion of psychological time. (Friedman 1968,

24) **15.** F/S (1982, 568-569). **16.** F/S (1982, 224-225); Leamer (1978 and 1985). **17.** Frazer and Sawyer (1984). **18.** Continuing on the sixth attribute and on the statistical problem of separating the components which in fact concern separate time frames for a relevant economic theory, Friedman said:.

> "The problem is that a set of data contains information about more than one question, and you want to eliminate information about questions you are not interested in. This is in order to concentrate on information about questions you are interested in....
>
> ....
>
> "Now if I had a perfect cycle, if I had a sine curve, or alternatively, if I had a perfect theory of the cycle, it might be possible to analyze the secular question using all the data but including in the multiple regression its equivalent variables that determine the cycle. But we don't have such a theory. We know certain things. We know that these cycles are irregular in amplitude, they are irregular in timing, we know that we don't have a satisfactory explanation. And given those limitations of our knowledge, we want to suppress the information about the cycle.
>
> "I wouldn't call it throwing away [information]. I would call it, rather...highlighting one class of information and trying to avoid its being diluted by a class of information relevant to a question we're not trying to answer." (Frazer and Sawyer 1984).

19. Working (1927). **20.** A primal equation is one which can be estimated separately from the other equations. It is predetermined; it is an equation which comes first and from which other relationships in the economy follow. **21.** Frazer and Sawyer (1984). Elaborating on this, Friedman said: "You have a personal probability about something now [e.g., Keynesian liquidity preference]. I have a personal probability about something now [e.g., Friedman's variant of liquidity preference]. It may be a very incoherent one, we may have little confidence in them, but we have them. They're very different. How do we decide the difference? ... Says Jimmy [Savage], you sit down and decide what data you would like to look at in order to resolve the difference of opinion." **22.** Frazer (1988). **23.** We are aware of the causation controversy (whether 00–00 with feedback or 00–00) which started in the early 1960s in response to Friedman's work (Frazer 1973, 36-38), was taken up by James Tobin and extended to the use of the Sims's test (Frazer 1973, 125-131), was reintroduced by F/S (1982, 626-627; Frazer 1983, 835), and received renewed attention in the mid-1980s at the hands of the post Keynesians. The latter is taken up in Frazer (1988). **24.** Frazer (1988, chap. 2); Friedman (1949). **25.** Friedman (1976, chap. 12). **26.** Poole and Kornblith (1983) were among those who addressed the controversy which followed from Friedman's and Meiselman's 1963 paper, which tested the predictability of a money multiplier (note 6 above). They felt this 1963 work set off debate about large versus small models (i.e., size of model as to numbers of variables and non-redundant equations) or alternatively the Fed-MIT-Penn model versus the St. Louis Fed's model (Frazer 1973, 304-310). That controversy was not Friedman's show, however. He did not participate in the controversy, plus the St. Louis Fed's model did not have the attributes of Friedman's uses of statistical methods. **27.** F/S (1982, 308). **28.** F/S (1982, 78). **29.** F/S (1982, 74-75, 308-309). **30.** Filtering concerns on the problem of determining the state of a system from noisy measurements. On filtering, see Jazwinski (1970) and see note 18 above. **31.** Eagle (1982). **32.** A full discussion of the data series is found in F/S (1982, 99-103, 105, 115-119). **33.** The survey by Judd and Scadding (1982) is an example of the fruitlessness of the search for a stable money demand function along traditional, non-Friedman lines. Judd and Scadding completely ignored Friedman's approach, while Hoover (1984) dealt entirely with Friedman as a leading monetarist. Moreover, J/S's review backed conclusions about parameter instability which Friedman confronted head on with his approach where he adjusted the series for episodic impacts. **34.** See studies of S. Necimura and D. K. Sheppard which are cited in Capie and Webber. **35.** The term "data analysis" is used in a narrow sense, akin to the work of Tukey (1977), where we emphasize knowledge of the data and the historical and economic situations that generated the data. This familiarity with the experiment that generates the data, as it were, should come before the estimation and testing takes place. **36.** Zarnowitz

(1985). **37.** Examples of his approach are charts 5.5, 5.6, and 5.7 of *Monetary Trends*. For a more detailed summary, readers are referred to Table III of H/E (1984). **38.** For examples, note Chernoff faces (1973) and Atkinson's graphical diagnostics (1981). **39.** Box and Jenkins (1970). **40.** See in particular charts 6.1, 6.2, and tables 6.9 and 6.10 of *Monetary Trends*. **41.** See F/S (1982, 171 and 224 respectively). **42.** F/S 1982, Table 6.4, and page 224, n 18. **43.** Notably Kalman (1980). **44.** Leamer (1977; 1983; 1985). **45.** F/S (1982, 208-215, 283). **46.** Compare note 33. **47.** F/S (1982, Table 6.7). **48.** H/E (1983, 11). **49.** F/S (1982, Table 6.1). **50.** H/E (1985, sections IV and V). **51.** F/S (1982, 78). **52.** F/S (1982, 86). **53.** H/E (1983, 6). **54.** H/E (1984, 9). **55.** In particular, tests with respect to auto correlation of prespecified order, heteroscedasticity of some form and non-normality. **56.** Breuch and Pagan (1979). **57.** Note, Kalman (1960) and Sims (1980) respectively. Friedman (1940; and 1937, 1950, and 1953 as cited in references to chap. 8); and Hollander and Douglas (1973).

References, Chapter 18:
Economic Theory, Policy and Uses of Statistical Methods

Allais, Maurice. 1966. "A Restatement of the Quantity Theory of Money," *American Economic Review* 56(December) 1123-1157.
Atkinson, A.C. 1981. "Two Graphical Displays for Outlying and Influential Observations." *Biometrika* 18(1981): 15-20.
Bera, A.K., and Jargue, C.M. 1982. "Model Specification Tests: a Simultaneous Approach." *Journal of Econometrics* 20(1982): 59-82.
Box, E.P. George, and Jenkins, Guilyn M. 1970. *Time Series Analysis, Forecasting and Control*, San Francisco, Calif: Holden-Day, 1975.
Breusch, T.S., and Pagan, A.R. 1979 "A Simple Test for Heteroscedasticity and Random Coefficient Variation." *Econometrica* 47(1979): 1287-1294.
Chernoff, H. 1973. "The Use of Faces to Represent Points in R-Dimensional Space Graphically." *Journal of the American Statistical Association* 68(1973): 361-368.
Cooley, Thomas F., and LeRoy, Stephen F. 1981. "Identification and Estimation of Money Demand." *American Economic Review* 71(December): 825-844.
Engle, Robert F. 1982. "Autoregressive Conditional Heteroscedasticity with Estimates of the Variance of the United Kingdom Inflation." *Econometrica* 50(1982): 987-1007.
Frazer, William. 1973. *Crises in Economic Theory*. Gainesville, Fl.: University of Florida Press.
_____. 1988. *Perspectives on Macroeconomics*, xeroxed.
_____, and Sawyer, Kim, eds. 1984. *Taped Discussion on Some Uses of Statistical Methods with Milton Friedman*, June 25, 1984, Las Vegas, Nevada.
Friedman, Milton. 1949. "The Marshallian Demand Curve." *Journal of Political Economy*. 57(December): 463-495.
_____. 1968. "Factors Affecting the Level of Interest Rates." In Donald P. Jacobs and Richard T. Pratt, eds., *Savings and Residential Financing: 1968 Conference Proceedings*. U.S. Savings and Loan League, 11-27.
_____. 1976. *Price Theory*. Hawthorne, N.Y.: Aldine Publishing Company.
_____, and Schwartz, Anna Jacobson. 1982. *Monetary Trends in the United States and the United Kingdom*. Chicago: University of Chicago Press.
Hendry, David F., and Ericsson, Neil R. 1983. *Assertion without Empirical Basis: An Econometric Appraisal of "Monetary Trends in...the United Kingdom: by Milton Friedman and Anna Schwartz*. A paper presented to the Bank of England's Panel of Academic Consultants in October 1983, and revised December 1983, in the light of comments made at the October 1983 meeting.
_____, and _____. 1984. *Assertion without Empirical Basis...*, paper presented at National Bureau of Economic Research Conference, Sonesta Hotel, Cambridge, July 12 and 13.
_____, and _____. 1985. *Assertion without Empirical Basis...*, International Finance Discussion Papers, no. 270, Board of Governors of the Federal Reserve System, revised December 1985.

Hoover, Kevin D. 1984. "Two Types of Monetarism." *Journal of Economic Literature* 22(March): 58-76.
Huhne, Christopher. 1983a. "Monetarism's guru 'distorts his evidence'." *The Guardian* (December 15): 1.
―――――. 1983b. "Why Milton's monetarism is bunk." *The Guardian* (December 15): 19.
Johnson, J. 1972. *Econometric Methods*, 2nd ed. New York: McGraw-Hill Book Company.
Jazwinski, Andrew H. 1970. *Stochastic Processes and Filtering Theory*. New York: Academic Press.
Judd, John P., and Scadding, John L. 1982. "The Search for a Stable Money Demand Function: A Survey of the Post-1973 Literature." *Journal of Economic Literature*, 20(September): 993-1023.
Kalman, Rudolph E. 1960. "A New Approach to Linear Filtering and Prediction Problems." *Trans. ASME, Ser. D: Journal of Basic Engineering* 82(March): 35-45.
Laidler, David. 1977. *The Demand for Money: Theories and Evidence*, 2nd ed. New York: Harper and Row.
Leamer, Edward E. 1978. *Specifican Searches: Ad-Hoc Inference with Non-Experimental Data*. New York: John Wiley & Sons.
―――――. 1983. "Let's Take the Con Out of Econometrics." *American Economic Review* 73(March): 31-43.
―――――. 1985. "Sensitivity Analysis Would Help." *American Economic Review* 75(June): 308-313.
McAleer, Michael; Pagan, Adrian R.; and Volcker, Paul A. 1985. "What Will Take the Con Out of Econometrics?" *American Economic Review* 75(June): 293-307.
Mitchell, George W. 1967. "Some Current Problems of Monetary Policy." *Southern Journal of Business* (July).
Nishimura, S. 1973. "The Growth of the Stock of Money in the U.K., 1870-1913." *Mimeograph, Hosei University*, Tokyo.
Pagan, A.R., and Hale, A.D. 1983. "Diagnostic Tests as Residual Analysis." *Working Paper no. 87*, Australian National University.
Poole, William, and Kornbluth, B. F. 1973. "The Friedman-Meiselman CMC Paper: New Evidence as an Old Controversy." *American Economic Review*, 86(December): 908-917.
Sargan, John D., and Bhargava, Alok. 1983. "Testing Residuals from Least Squares Regression for Being Generated by the Gaussian Random Walk." *Econometrica*, 51(January): 153-174.
Savage, Leonard. 1972. *The Foundations of Statistics*. New York: Dover Publications, Inc. Originally published in 1954.
Sheppard, David K. 1971. *The Growth and Role of U.K. Financial Institutions, 1880-1962*. London: Metheren.
Sims, Christopher A., ed. 1977. *New Methods of Business Cycle Research*. Minneapolis, Minn.: Federal Reserve Bank of Minneapolis.
―――――. 1980. "Macroeconomics and Reality." *Econometrica* 48(January): 1-49.
Tonveronachi, Mario. 1983. "Friedman and Schwartz on Monetary Trends in the U.S.A. and the U.K. from 1867 to 1975." *Quarterly Review*, Banca Nazionale del Lavoro (Rome). 36(June): 117-142.
Tukey, John W. 1977. *Exploratory Data Analysis*. Reading, Mass.: Addison-Wesley Publishing Co., Inc.
Vandade, Walter. 1983. *Applied Time Series and Box-Jenkins Models*. New York: Academic Press, Inc.
Working, Elmer J. 1927. "What Do Statistical 'Demand Curves' Show." *Quarterly Journal of Economics* 41(February): 212-235.
Zarnowitz, Voctor. 1985. "Recent Work on Business Cycles in Historical Perspective." *Journal of Economic Literature*. 23(June): 523-580.
Zellner, Arnold. 1986. "Bayesian Analysis in Econometrics." Paper for Conference on the Foundation of Statistical Inference, Breal, December 16-19, 1985 (reviewed May, 1986).

Appendixes to Chapter 16

Appendix One: Analysis of a Tax Cut

Analyses found in work on the consumption function, the mix of saving and consumption, and money and credit aggregates are drawn upon to generate three classes for the effects of tax cuts by the Federal government (designated "trickle-up," "trickle-down," and "neutral" cuts respectively) on income growth for the economy as a whole and on tax revenue to the government. The effects are shown to be dependent on monetary policy, such that the analysis of the effects of the tax cuts should not be treated separately from the monetary policy. Indeed, given a neutral cut (defined as no income-redistribution effect) and a smooth-growth, non-inflationary monetary policy, the positive effects of deficit-creating tax cuts on total spending are offset by negative effects from the crowding out of spending. Attention is also directed toward the following: tax cuts with reference to the size of the public sector in relation to the private sector with no change in tax revenues, "trickle-up" and "trickle-down" cuts that affect the real rate of interest (negatively in the first case and positively in the second), and cuts that appear unfavorable to household expenditures on the basis of static analysis but which may actually increase household expenditures.

Although this appendix is primarily technical and supportive of chapter 16, it makes points such as the following:

(1) An important standard by which to judge the tax structure (and tax cuts) is how it affects the division of income between consumption and saving and hence, as we show, the real rate of interest (defined later).

(2) Given appropriate monetary policy, a larger tax-induced aggregate saving rate calls forth a higher real rate of interest and higher growth rates in income and tax revenue.

(3) Households are generally better off and can consume more over a life-cycle even when income-tax policy may favor a reduction in consumption and an increase in saving at a given time.

The analysis that follows draws on separate bits of analyses that were prevalent in the late 1970s and early 1980s, during a time of unusual intellectual and social change. It is generally supportive of positions found in Milton Friedman's work, but the analysis presented was never put in its present form by Friedman. Rather, it pulls together points made by Friedman and others and combines them into a package.

The author wishes to express his appreciation to Eleanor Brown and Mark Rush for comments on earlier drafts of papers leading to the appendixes to chapter 16, and to Kim Sawyer for his helpful comments on the mathematics (presently omitted). The extreme value analyses contained in the appendixes were initially undertaken in an earlier unpublished paper with Charles Bennett.

I. Introduction

Approaching elections in 1980 in the United States and on into 1981, 1982 and 1983, there were widespread public discussions about tax cuts.[1] High visibility was given at the time to what has been called the Laffer curve (Bruce Bender 1984; James Buchanan 1982; Michael Evans 1983, 200-205; Jude Wanniski 1978, 97-103), to ending "bracket creep" (i.e., the movement of households into higher tax brackets as incomes were inflated), to the idea of a "safety net" for those who may be unemployed, to the tax revenue responsiveness of increase in income due to a tax cut, to the timing of a tax cut, to the sizes of underground economies in societies with different tax structures, and so on (Richard Porter and Amanda Boyer 1984). Within this set of ideas there were, to be sure, different positions, including on the part of such highly visible figures as Arthur Laffer and Milton Friedman. Friedman himself was supportive of tax-cut legislation in the early 1980s (Friedman 1980; 1981; 1982); he was a relatively visible figure at the time because of his television series "Free to Choose," and the publication of the best-selling, nonfiction book in economics (pp. 264-265, 782 n51), plus his *Newsweek* columns; and he was serving as an economic advisor to Ronald Reagan during the presidential campaign, in the transition to the Reagan White House, and afterwards as an outside advisor. He later deplored the excess claims given for the effects of a tax cut in some quarters, and he offered his own basis for supporting a cut.

This appendix deals quite simply with the theory behind a tax cut such as may be gleaned from Milton Friedman's views on the public versus the private sector, and from the consumption function and monetary works (Frazer 1983; and Friedman 1957). In the context of Friedman's analyses, a distinction may be drawn between: (1) tax cuts that simply transfer resources from the public to the private sector without altering the rate of income growth, (2) tax cuts that temporarily increase saving in relation to income and then contribute to faster growth in income and tax revenue, and (3) those cuts that temporarily decrease saving in relation to income and then decrease the growth in income and tax revenue. The first set of cuts may be called "neutral" tax cuts in terms of their impact on income growth and tax revenues. Even so, using terms that grew out of John Brooks's "Annals of Finance" (1982, 122-124, 141), the second set may be called "trickle-down" cuts, and the third set "trickle-up" cuts.[2] The formal statement of these effects is a main objective of the present appendix. Nevertheless, we may also note that the distinction drawn between the foregoing effects of a cut in taxes as percents of tax liabilities contrast dramatically with the results associated in the 1980-1981 tax-debate period with the Laffer curve (Bender 1984; Buchanan 1981; Michael Evans 1983, 108,

200-205, 261; Wanniski 1978, 97-103). Laffer lumped all tax cuts (reductions in tax liability) of an aggregative and overall nature in the same package with respect to the direction of their effect on tax revenue (Laffer 1981; Wanniski 1978, 97-103).

The monetary part of the analysis of tax cuts which we introduce is relevant for a variety of reasons: (1) the monetary approach as found in Friedman's work puts the tax-rate matters in a perspective that cannot be achieved by singling out tax-rate changes alone, since the effects of tax cuts are not independent of budgetary deficits and revenues, and the effects of deficits are not independent of the means of financing them, including in relation to monetary policy; and (2) the presence of the monetary analysis simplifies the theory by providing the means of assuring employment up to the "natural" (non-inflationary) rate, irrespective of the tax changes in question. The analytical means for treating the effects of deficits in the first instance concern the government budget constraint (Frazer 1978; and text pp. 260, 441).[3] It emphasizes that the sale of debt instruments to finance deficits must be (a) to the non-banking public for the most part or (b) to banking-type institutions and the public where monetary policy enters as a means of supporting (or not supporting) the financing via more (or unchanged) growth in the money and credit aggregates. Under (a) there is the crowding out of private financing (a substitution of government for private financing, as it were), and under (b) there is a monetary policy decision, inadvertent or otherwise, that accompanies the tax-cut decision.

Taken together, the reasons for introducing the monetary analysis are to reduce the reliance on the technique of artificially impounding important developments relating to tax-rate-changes in *ceteris paribus*. Instead, those interdependent changes that occur in fact are allowed to occur, although no elaborate equation is sought that depicts all of the presumed determinants of tax revenue. To be sure, at the state of econometrics when Friedman wrote of the "prevailing fashion in econometrics" and as elucidated in chapter 18, there is no demonstrable technique for proceeding to isolate for the real world the separate effects economists have commonly obtained using the technique of impounding troublesome changes in *ceteris paribus*.

As may surprise some, Friedman's analysis of a tax cut does several things: it develops almost entirely in terms of Keynesian mechanics; and it proceeds without explicit reference to production and the supply side, as may be found in supply-side analyses with attention to Arthur Laffer's early positions (Victor Canto et al. 1983). The use of Keynesian mechanics and the omission of attention to production itself are possible for three reasons: (1) Friedman did not reject Keynesian mechanics but rather directed them along dynamic lines in both the consumption function and liquidity preference cases; (2) a production side, so to speak, entered Friedman's work via his attention to the capitalist ethic and the flat-rate income tax (text, pp. 503-514); and (3) Friedman largely removed the basis for J.M. Keynes's attack (1936, pp. 18, 26, 363) on J.B. Say's law of markets (briefly, supply creates its own demand) by emphasizing monetary shocks to the economy that occur from the money-stock (supply) side of the economy. The capitalist ethic (payment according to the value of marginal product) and Friedman's attention to "freedom" and voluntary association connected the supply side to the demand side of the market for output. The basis for Keynes's attack on Say's law, finally, is partly undermined by the attention Friedman gave to monetary shocks on aggregate demand that arise from the money-supply side. (Keynes emphasized shocks impacting upon the demand side without reference to their coming from the money-supply side or errors in monetary policy as it were.) Most notably, monetary demands could prevent the achievement of full employment, but Friedman showed these to be induced mainly via destabilizing monetary policy.

The present appendix proceeds as follows: a further consideration of Friedman's consumption function (sect. II), the introduction of a parallel between Friedman's time paths and those of the Domar model (sect. III), a review of the real rate of interest, which we show may be influenced by tax policy (sect. IV), a review of the simple, Keynesian consumption function with attention to income redistribution (sect. V), and a summary (sect. VI). A number of the mathematical steps relied upon in the appendix were themselves originally set forth in a mathematical appendix. However, they are omitted on the ground that the steps are plausible in any case.[4]

II. Friedman's Time Paths

In Friedman's consumption function and monetary works we find analogous permanent (or time trend) measures for income and the money stock, plus the real income elasticity of the demand for money is unitary (Frazer 1983, 840). Growth in income depends on saving, the productivity of labor, technological change, and the non-monetary forces of the economy, once the monetary matters are functioning so as not to disrupt the workings of society (Frazer 1982).

A utility maximization notion enters Friedman's consumption function analysis, where we encounter households choosing between present and future consumption and hence between present consumption (C) and saving (S) out of income (Y) at a given time.[5] This choice and the utility-max mechanism gives rise to the concept of the real rate of interest (or return), namely the rate at which goods today exchange for goods a year hence as illustrated later (sect. IV). Further, the Keynesian variables (C, S, and Y) found in Friedman's approach also appear in the Domar model (1946), which yields growth paths for income that are equivalent to Friedman's permanent (or time trend) magnitudes, although Friedman actually analyzed data and offered a parallel analysis of expectations with respect to future income.

In these contexts, the maximization of utility in the choice between consumption and saving will determine the growth path for income. We may denote it,

$$Y_{max} = \bar{Y}_{max} e^{at} \qquad (1)$$

where a is the growth rate for income. Similarly we may write (via an excluded exercise),

$$T_{max} = \bar{T}_{max} e^{rt} \qquad (2)$$

where T is tax revenue, r is a growth rate in that revenue, and where T_{max} is some function of income, the tax rate (τ), and a portmanteau variable (u), i.e.,

$$T_{max} = f(Y, \tau, u).$$

(The notation $\bar{Y}_{max}$ and $\bar{T}_{max}$ is to suggest either or both of two possibilities: one, that the max arises from a choice between present and future consumption, as in section IV below, and, two, that the max may also be found to coincide with the extreme value for a static variant of the Laffer Curve which we present in a second technical appendix to chapter 16. Also, for the purpose of simplicity, the portmanteau variable which allows for forces of secondary importance does not reappear below.)

For the present purpose "the rate" symbolizes a package of rates. We are dealing with the Federal government's personal income tax, and we will be asking about the income-redistribution effects of tax rates on consumption and saving as formed in Evans (1983, chap. 6). Actually, we recognize the presence of both marginal and average rates on adjusted gross incomes, and that the marginal and average rates become the same at some rate as the ceiling on the marginal rate declines and approaches a flat-rate tax. This aspect of analysis is dealt with in an additional technical appendix ("A Variant of the Laffer Curve").

Growth curves as may be defined by equation (1) are shown in figure 1, plus each curve has its counterpart in terms of equation (2), where

$$T_{max} = \bar{T}_{max} e^{rt}, \ T = Y\tau, \text{ and } T_{max} = \bar{Y}_{max} \tau \text{ at any time (t)}.$$

Though not fitted to actual data in the present analysis, the curves in figure 1 have in Friedman's analytical system counterparts to expected income.

The expected income for some time horizon (T) is denoted,

$$Y_P(T) = \beta \int_{-\infty}^{T} e^{(\beta - a)(t-T)} Y(t) \, dt \qquad (3)$$

where β concerns a system of weights in which all the other variables and constants are as previously noted, and where the equation is simply a reduction from an omitted exercise. Also for consumption, Friedman wrote,

Appendix One: Analysis of a Tax Cut

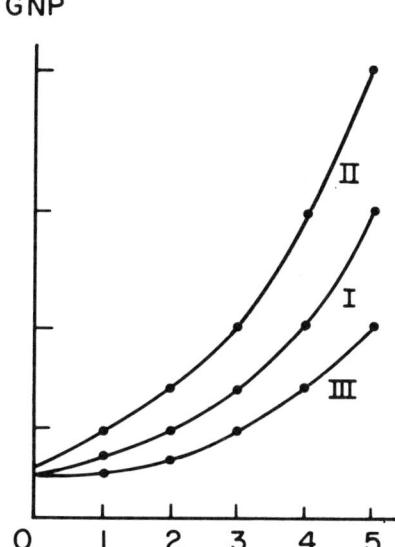

Figure 1. Growth Curves

$$C(T) = k(...)Y_p$$

Using this expression and substituting from equation (3),
$$C(T) = k\beta \int_{-\infty}^{T} e^{(\beta-a)(t-T)} Y(t)\, dt \qquad (4)$$
This result will be of use to us below, but with the weighting system associated with a mathematical analysis. Thus continuing with equation (3), substituting from equation (1) for Y(t) in equation (3), we have
$$Y_p(T) = \beta \int_{-\infty}^{T} \exp \beta(t-T)\, Y_{max} \exp at\, dt \qquad (5)$$
With operations performed on this (as in omitted analysis), the final results are:

$$\beta/(\beta + a) < 1$$
$$(\beta + a)T > 1$$

From this latter result, an increase in a increases permanent income and therefore consumption, as in equation (4), but with restrictions on β and T. For a time horizon of one year (T = 1) the effect of the current income on permanent income would be almost total (i.e., $\beta = 1$). As the time horizon becomes more distant (T = 1,2,3,...), the effect of current and lagged values for income would be reduced (i.e., β for current income would be smaller and declining with the length of the lag time), but it (β) should become smaller at a slower rate as the time horizon becomes more distant.

Thus, permanent income, $Y_p(T)$, and consumption are dependent upon the factor a. The larger the value of a, also the smaller the value of the (β-

a) in equation (3) and hence the larger the value of permanent income $Y_p(T)$. Since

$$C(T) = k\beta \int_{-\infty}^{T} e^{(\beta-a)(t-T)} Y(t)\, dt$$

consumption C(T) is maximized when the value of *a* is at the potential sustainable growth in income. In brief, as further analysis will indicate: *even those tax cuts that favor an increase in the rate of saving will increase consumption and, indeed, consumption may be made greater via this route than from policies that appear to favor consumption more directly.*

III. More Keynesian Mechanics

This section demonstrates the effect of an increase (decrease) in the saving component of national income on the growth rate in income (i.e., on the *a* factor of the last sections). It does so by way of tying up earlier discussion in terms of the Domar model (1946), which has as its solution a time trend. This model is used because of the consistency between its solution and Friedman's permanent income paths, as well as because of its consistency with standard Keynesian definitions and variables.

The Domar model consists of three equations and three variables:

$$S(t) = k\, Y(t) \qquad (1)$$
$$I(t) = g\, dY(t)/dt \qquad (2)$$
$$S(t) = I(t), k > 0, g > 0 \qquad (3)$$

where the flow variables S, I, and Y are defined as on earlier occasions. Equation (1) simply expresses saving as some proportion of income. Equation (2) and the conditions of a positive value for g (g = K(t)/Y(t) > 0) simply notes that businesses maintain capital (K) as a proportion of income.[6] Equation (3) is the condition for a solution in the static Keynesian model (Frazer 1980, chap. 7).

In reducing the model to a simple differential equation,

$$Y(t) = (g/k)(dY/dt) \qquad (4)$$

This equation says that income Y(t) is a constant multiple g/k of the change in the flow variable for income with respect to time. In the model's solution,[7]

$$Y = \overline{Y} e^{(k/g)t} \qquad (5)$$

The factor k/g in the exponent is the factor *a* from the last section. Thus an increase in the numerator, *k*, actually an increase in the saving rate, would yield faster growth in tax revenues, T = f(Y,τ). This would come about where monetary policy maintains full-employment, non-inflationary growth in income.

IV. The Real Rate of Interest: An Illustration

The real rate of interest reenters monetary analysis in the mid 1960s at

Friedman's hands, and as a part of *Monetary Trends* (chap. 14). In the mid 1960s he also drew on Knut Wicksell, when he used the term "natural" in relation to the natural rate of unemployment. Wicksell had meant by the term "natural" the non-inflationary rate, although he used it with reference to the rate of interest (Frazer 1977, 54-57). ("Natural," was not a reference to the "natural order" philosophy of John Locke and Adam Smith, as some thought.)

Shades of meaning abound. First, for Irving Fisher, whom Friedman drew upon in *Monetary Trends* and even earlier, the real rate was as we have already defined it (text pp. 212-213, 448-449, 545, 652, 653, 746),

$$i = i_{real} + (1/P)(dP/dt)^*$$

with i the nominal rate, i_{real} the real rate, and $(1/P)(dP/dt)^*$ the expected inflation rate. To this we may add as a weight in the last term the probability of the expected inflation rate $[Pb(\dot{P}^e)]$, and thus

$$i = i_{real} + Pb(\dot{P}^e)[(1/P)(dP/dt)^*]$$

Second, though not quite the same thing $[(1/P)(dP/dt)$ instead of $(1/P)(dP/dt)^*]$, Ronald Reagan and Walter Mondale discussed the real rate in their October 7, 1984 television debate as

$$i_{real} = i - (1/P)(dP/dt)$$

They noted a very high real rate on this calculation for their current period (Debate 1984, 16), and the president expressed the view that the market may be expecting a renewal of inflation. To this, we may add that as far as the market's requirements for a real rate go the high real rate could also be explained by additional generalized uncertainty about election time and future programs as well as the prospect that the tax cut in the 1981 Tax Reduction Act ultimately raised the real rate of interest or at least the personal saving out of income bearing on it (p. 814 below).

Third, for Wicksell the real rate (or non-inflationary rate) was more like a permanent magnitude for Friedman. It was the rate at which there would be no inflation (say, market rate equals the real rate). These Fisher and Wicksell rates, moreover, may be viewed as equivalent to a real rate defined as the rate at which goods today exchange for goods one year hence, and this latter may be treated further in terms of the analysis of utility maximization subject to constraint as found in Friedman's consumption function work (Frazer 1980, chap. 9 and appendix to chap. 9). Going this latter route, we relate the real rate to tax cuts that come up further below, that concern the rate of income growth ($a = k/g$, $k = S/Y$), and that concern the ratio of saving to income (S_o/Y_o).

In proceeding with the utility analysis of maximization subject to constraint, we only illustrate the real rate in terms of indifference curves and the constructions presented as figures 2, 3, 4, and 5. The quite elegant if classical mathematical underpinning need not detain us, as it is readily available elsewhere (Frazer 1980, appendixes to chap. 9 and 16) and not actually a part of the present results we obtain in the next two sections. In the art work, P is present income (with a specific value Y_0), F is future income $[Y_0(1 + r)]$ where r is the real rate of interest (i_{real} in other context), consumption and saving are among the Keynesian variables, also found in the Domar model (presently C_0, and $S_0 = Y_0 - C_0$), and $(1 + t)$ is the time preference for income expressed as a rate (also the slope at a point of the curve depicting a constant level of utility and the public's indifference between the choice of some portion of income today (C_0 as a portion of Y_0) and future income $[S_0 (1 + t)$ as portion of $Y_0 (1 + t)]$. Though it may sound foreboding and need not be a distraction in what follows, the indifference curves depict a constant level of the public's satisfaction so to speak, given income (say U_1, U_2, U_3 constant for different but increasing levels of income). Each curve in fact is the trace of a slice (U = const.) through a utility surface that rises and moves outward in a three-dimensional configuration, $U = f [C_0, S_0 (1 + t)]$. We say, "a trace of a slice" because each curve is a projection from the space on the floor of the three-dimensional space (the floor being the P-F plane as it were).

Figure 2 shows the income-constraint line relating present to future income. The line's intersection on the P-axis is the possible income today (Y_0) with no income one year hence, and the line's intersection with the F-axis is the income one year hence $[(Y_0 (1 + r)]$ with no present consumption. Point A is shown in the figure with coordinates C_0, and $(1 + r) (Y_0 - C_0)$, the choice between income today and one year hence is unlikely to be at the extreme possibilities. The slope of the budget line is the limit of the rise-over-the-run or incremental ratio,

$$\text{Limit}_{\Delta P \to 0} \Delta P(1+r)/\Delta P = 1 + r$$

Figure 2. Budget Constraint Encompassing Two Distinct Time Periods

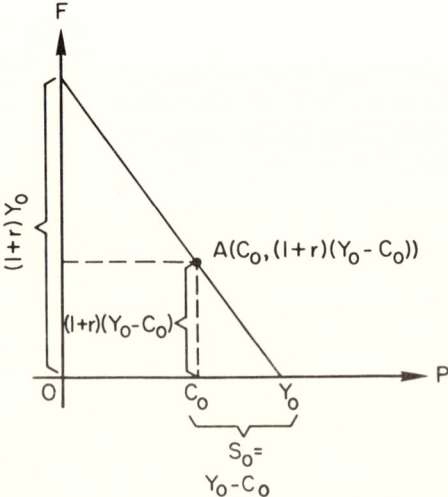

Appendix One: Analysis of a Tax Cut   811

Figure 3. Indifference Curves for Two Discrete Time Periods

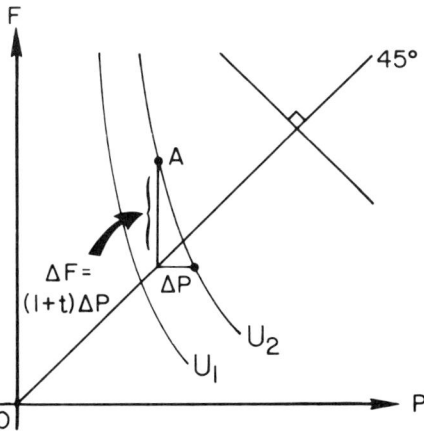

Figure 3 shows the slope of an indifference curve, also defined as the limit of the incremental ratio,

$$\text{Limit}_{\Delta P \to 0} \Delta P (1 + t)/\Delta P = 1 + t$$

and figure 4 denotes a point of tangency between the budget line and the curve for the highest level of utility obtainable at that budget. At this extreme point the slopes of the budget line and the indifference curves are equal $(1 + r) = (1 + t)$. This equality of slopes yields an equality of rates ($r = t$) and the rates r and t at this condition are the real rate of interest.

Now, in reference to figure 5, we introduce the prospect of a tax-package change that favors future income over present income. Such a package has no effect on the potential present income of Y_0 but it does raise the future potential from $(1 + r) Y_0$ to $(1 + r + \Delta r) Y_0$ which may be obtained a year hence. Said differently, we increase the slope of the budget line from $(1 + r)$ to $(1 + r + \Delta r)$ or we increase the real rate of interest. However, we are interested mainly in the current substitution of present for future consumption and not developments one year hence. To isolate this substi-

Figure 4. Maximum Utility from Consumption and Saving

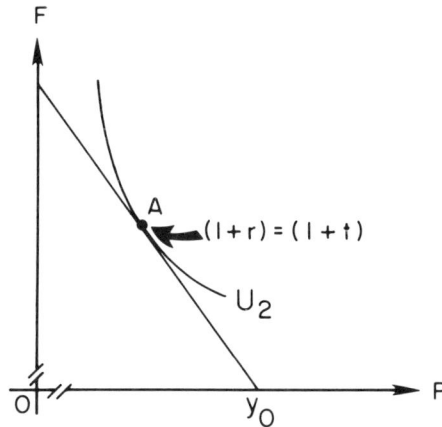

Figure 5. Substitution Effect

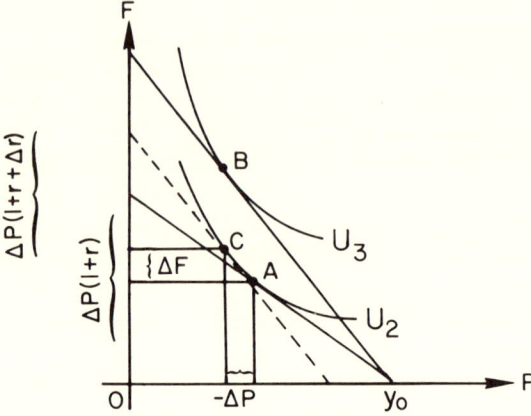

tution effect, we want to eliminate the income effect due to the higher real rate of interest. To do this we shift the budget line with the new greater (but negative) slope back toward the origin of the P-F plane, but keep the budget line being shifted in a parallel position to the line with the new slope. Such a line is the dotted line in figure 5 with tangency to the old utility curve (U_2 in the construction) at point C. At point C we have a greater (but negative) slope than at point A where we started ($1 + r + \Delta r$ or $1 + t + \Delta t$). In other words, we show an increase in the real rate of interest which followed from a policy change that favored future income over present income via an increase in savings. This change is one the Federal Reserve is unlikely to have any influence over. We say it below (p. 817) and may recall also that the Federal Reserve controls only the nominal stock of money, not the real stock (p. 745).

Trickle-Up, Trickle-Down, and Neutral Tax Cuts: Income Redistribution

As previous analysis has shown, an increase in saving (S) [also, a decrease in consumption (C)] in relation to full-employment income provides a faster growth in income (Y). With either a flat rate or progressive income tax, faster growth in income means faster growth in tax revenue (T) to the government, given $T = f(Y, \tau)$. Thus, combining these two notions, and changing the mix of saving and consumption or leaving it unchanged [i.e., $-\Delta(S/C)$, $+\Delta(S/C)$, and $(S/C) = \text{const.}$] yields three possible classes for the effects of tax-rate changes.[8]

These classes for the effects of tax-rate changes we will associate with "trickle-up," "trickle-down," and neutral tax cuts, for reasons that emerge below. There: (1) "trickle-up" cuts refer to the demand management, Keynesian, consumption function cuts (namely, cuts tending toward income redistribution that favor consumption over saving out of income, as may be recognized below in terms of analysis surrounding the simple consumption function); (2) "trickle-down" cuts give the weight of attention to increasing saving, capital expenditures, and enlarged incentives for work and production, and; (3) neutral tax cuts occur where the relative positions of the "agents," the households and the firm, are left unchanged. An across-the-board tax cut of a given percentage of tax liability of households illustrates this neutral cut. Further, as subsequent discussion should indicate, the present analysis of tax cuts proceeds from whatever tax and government-transfer-payment (tax/income redistribution) system exists at the time.[9]

In the post-World War II years, widely held views of consumer behavior have given support to policies that have attempted to moderate the inequality of income. These views center about Keynes's simple consumption function, c = f(y), and the independently stated social utility function, u = f(y), where c is consumption, y is income, and u is utility (all for households). Both simple functions may be viewed as essentially static statements as may apply to cross-section or budget-studies data, and both are presented below in figures 6 and 7 respectively. Indeed, the latter simple utility function is sometimes referred to as the Lerner justification for income distribution (Abba Lerner, 1944, chap. 3). The simple consumption function states that as income increases consumption increases too (i.e., that consumption is a normal good). The statement is also one of Keynes's first psychological law. The second law states that as income increases, then consumption as a proportion of income declines, that is, the income elasticity of consumption is less than unit, i.e., elasticity = $(dc/c)/(dy/y) < 1$ (Keynes 1936, pp. 29, 30, 75), and we posit a declining slope to the function in figure 6 as income increases.

Figure 6. The Simple Consumption Function

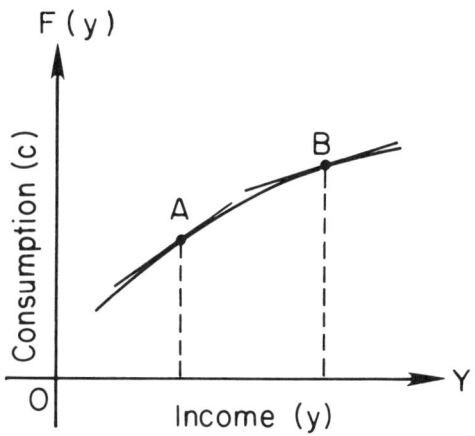

Keynes's first and second "laws" were accepted generally two decades after the *General Theory* (1936), but the second law has since come into question where the static curve is viewed as a time relation and where time-series and budget studies of the function revealed inconsistency in the time oriented and the cross-section relations. Friedman in fact has stated that the income elasticity of consumption is close to unity although there are some expressions to the effect that low income recipients are more likely to spend income (1957, 41, 126). In other words, Keynesian tax cuts increase the ratio of consumption to income (c/y) and stimulate present spending in relation to income.[10] This thinking is still present, but reversed with the argument that higher income recipients are more likely to save.

The social utility of income function, u = f(y), also received static interpretations along lines similar to the consumption function (Frazer 1977, and Phillips 1975). However, both functions were developed independent of one another and there is no theoretical connection between the assumption of diminishing marginal utility of income and diminishing marginal propensity to consume. Yet, as shown below, the utility function is drawn exactly the same way as the consumption function (Moggridge 1973, 70-85). The income elasticity with respect to utility, $(du/u)/(dy/y) < 1$, indicates the reasonably plausible principle that an additional dollar of income is worth less to a rich man that to a poor man because the marginal utility of income is decreasing. Therefore, the story goes, if income is redistributed from higher income bracket households to lower income bracket households, then total social utility (U) is enhanced. This reasoning has been tacit in plans that favor small tax payers with a larger percentage cut in tax liability, as well as has been the reasoning behind the consumption function.

Just as the prospect of declining marginal propensity to consume over time has come into question as a result of Friedman's permanent income hypothesis, the prospect of diminishing marginal utility of income over time may be reevaluated in light of Friedman's work on consumption as well as that on the utility of income (pp. 156-157). In other words, indirect theoretical and empirical support from Friedman's permanent income work may lead to a rejection of the assertion of diminishing marginal utility of income. Indeed, it is interesting to note that others speculate that if one utility function had diminishing marginal utility of income, another one equally consistent with consumer behavior could have increasing marginal utility of income.[11] The important point is that ratios of marginal utilities, not marginal utilities themselves, determine indifference curves and behavior.

The rationale surrounding the simple relations in figures 6 and 7 becomes the basis for changing selected constants and therefore the predictions about income growth, tax revenues, saving (investment), saving-to-

Figure 7. The Utility of Income Function

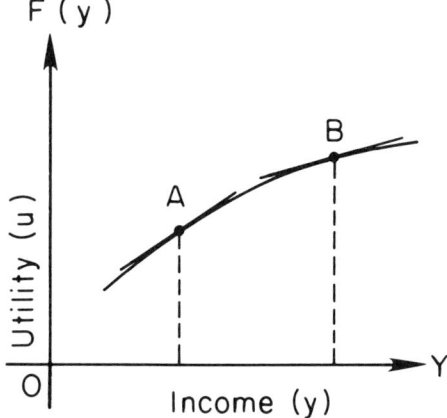

income ratios, and so on—all such as would follow from Friedman's treatment of consumption as a function of permanent income, and all such as may be summarized with reference to Keynesian mechanics, as treated earlier.

Recalling Friedman's permanent income statement in the form of equation (3) above (where Y_p is a growth path, and a is the growth rate in income), a rise in growth rate (a) increases income and thus tax revenues, $T = f(Y, \tau)$. The rise in the growth rate is depicted by an upward rotation of the permanent income line from line I to line II in figure 1. A decline in the growth rate (a) lowers the line from line I say to III. In the result from the Domar model, also presented earlier, $Y = \overline{Y} \exp (k/g) t$ (where k is the proportion of income going to saving and k/g is the income growth rate). Increasing k has the effect of rotating upward the growth path, plus the increase in k may result from an increase in the real rate of interest, as illustrated in section IV. Thus, on traditional argument with respect of figure 6, income redistribution via tax rate changes (say, a less progressive income tax structure) that favors high income recipients (point B over point A) increases saving, income growth, and tax revenues (T), $T = f(Y, \tau)$.

Moreover, the tax rate changes increase overall the rate at which goods today exchange for goods one year hence, as illustrated in figure 5. This would be as found in the choice, utility-max mechanism that arises in sections II and IV. Said somewhat differently, tax cuts that increase the real rate of interest will also increase saving, and rotate upward the paths for income and tax-revenue growth.

Continuing, income redistribution via tax changes that favor decreases in saving, income growth, and tax revenue at a given time have the reverse effects from those of the last paragraph. The real rate of interest is reduced by the changes, and the growth paths for income and tax revenue are rotated downward.

The third class of tax cuts, described as neutral tax cuts (across the board cuts in tax liabilities), provides for no change in tax revenue. In their presence, income still remains on growth path I in figure 1. This class of tax cuts, however, calls for further rationale. There are two parts to the reasoning, starting with no change in monetary policy (i.e., the monetary reserves, or base money, grow at a constant rate). First, the tax cuts with equal cuts in government spending simply transfer activity from the government to the private sector. The monetary policy (constant money growth) determines the path I for income growth in figure 1, as activity is transferred from the government to the private sector. Second, the tax cuts with deficits to be financed at a given time (i.e., with "crowding out" of private financing and spending, as introduced in section I) call forth offsetting results. The positive effects of the tax cuts on spending in this case are offset by the negative effects from crowding out of spending. (However, the result in this third class of tax cuts is strictly formal and implies that resources allocated to the government and private sectors respectively are equally productive. For Friedman, resources in the private sector were viewed as being more productive.)

VI. Summary

An analysis has been established on the basis of dynamic properties that facilitates a shift in attention to predictions of income growth rates and tax revenues, all on the basis of changes in saving out of income and hence those tax features that may influence saving one way or another. There is some simplification involved, perhaps over simplification. Even so special attention needs to be given to elements of taxation that influence saving out of income vis-à-vis consumption and that influence the real rate of interest.

A basic ingredient of the dynamic approach has been that of changing saving in relation to income, and hence changing the real rate of interest as in section IV. A decrease in saving as may be induced via tax means decreases the real rate of interest and at the same time decreases the saving to income ratio and thus the rate of growth in income and tax revenue. An increase in saving reverses these latter changes. An unchanged growth path for saving has neutral effects on income growth and tax revenues to the government.

Moreover, these respective classes of changes increase, decrease, and leave unchanged the real rate of interest such as that associated with Friedman's consumption function, the indifference curve analysis, and the work of Irving Fisher.

In brief, we have considered three classes of tax cuts, all with different effects on income and tax revenue, and all against a backdrop of monetary policy. The tax changes favoring a more egalitarian distribution of income have been called "trickle-up" cuts; those favoring a more unequal distribution have been called "trickle-down" cuts; and those that do not alter the relative income position of the economic "agents" have been called neutral. In the context of dynamic analysis, moreover, even those tax cuts that favor an increase in the rate of saving will increase consumption. This is indicated by the discussion surrounding the last equation in section II.

In addition, singling out these foregoing classes of tax cuts and tax-revenue changes points out an inconsistency in the tax-cut analysis that was associated with the Laffer curve of the 1980-81 era. There a tax cut—whether trickle-up, trickle-down or neutral in its effect—was to increase tax revenue beyond what it would have been in the absence of a tax cut.

Along the route we proceeded, we start to encounter by historical standards a peculiar prospect, namely: that the real rate of interest is more a result of non-monetary factors (say, the tax structure and the rate at which goods today exchange for goods one year hence) than monetary factors once monetary policy is directed toward stabilizing business conditions and the inflation rate. Before Keynes's liquidity preference demand for money balances there was the popular loanable funds theory of interest with the rate of interest being determined by the supply and demand for funds which could be influenced by the flow of bank credit (Frazer 1980, vol. I, 78, 450). Even so, tax matters were not as readily introduced as when we confront the real rate in relation to income today versus income one year hence (figure 5) and even in Keynes liquidity preference analysis, where we encountered the nominal rate of interest, it remained for Friedman to introduce the new quantity theory of money and the causal linkage running from accelerated money growth, to income and to the nominal interest rate ($\Delta \dot{M} \rightarrow \Delta \dot{Y} \rightarrow \Delta i$), where the nominal rate was the sum of the real rate of interest and the expected inflation rate.

Notes to Appendix One

1. See for example Paul Blustein (1981), John Brooks (1982), James Buchanan and Dwight Lee (1982), A. Ehrbar (1981), Michael Evans (1983), Paul Evans (1983), Milton Friedman (1980, 1981, 1982), George Gilder (1981), William Greider (1981), Arthur Laffer (1981), Douglas Shaller (1983), and Jude Wanniski (1978). 2. Brooks actually used the terms "trickle-down theory" and "trickle-up theory." The first is thought to derive from William Jennings Bryan's famous "Cross of Gold" speech in 1896. The democrats are said to have used the expression in 1932 to "deride Hoover's statement that his program was aimed at restoring prosperity to corporations and banks and that this would invigorate the economy." On the other hand, the opposite of trickle-down is "based on the premise that benefits to the poor will trickle up to the rich." This could be a fiscal policy action working through Keynes's investment multiplier, where a tax cut favored consumption and hence a more equal distribution of income. The analysis is developed later in the text.

This emphasis on the redistribution effects of tax-rate changes was one of the sources of mental anguish for David Stockman, Reagan's O.M.B. director, with reference to tax legislation in 1981. See Greider (1981, 46-47). **3.** The constraint attributes inflation to monetary causes alone rather than to fiscal policy (defined as a deficit), but, at the same time, it takes for granted the existence of a monetary policy. It is quite possible, as in the work of Lord Kaldor (1982), to construct monetary arrangements that entirely support fiscal policy and that exclude any role for monetary policy other than that of supporting fiscal policy and providing loan (or rediscount) facilities for other banking-type institutions. **4.** The Friedman analysis presented below, with reference to a tax cut, is in fact found to underlie less formal discussion in Michael Evan's book (1983, chap. 6). He drew the present distinction between Friedman's permanent income consumption function and the simple Keynesian consumption function, and gave attention to income redistribution arguments concerning tax cuts with reference to so-called "supply-side" economics. See also note 5. **5.** The work draws on Irving Fisher and other sources, as cited by Friedman (1957, 7). It is also discussed in Frazer (1980, sect. 9.4, and appendix to chap. 9). Though Evan's discussion, as introduced in note 4, lacked the formal treatment and results found in the present paper, he also gave special attention to the rate of return (or Fisher's real rate, say i) which follows from the utility maximization notion just introduced. Indeed, it is the rate found in Friedman's function below, where we may write $C = k(i,...)Y_P$. **6.** The growth feature upon which we proceed is that associated with technological change (growth in output per worker) and not growth in the labor force *per se*. For the stock and flow quantities—$K(t)$, $Y(t)$, $S(t)$, $I(t)$, and money, $M(t)$—policy shifts in the money growth rate or in the tax structure increase the growth rates for $Y(t)$, $S(t)$, $I(t)$ and so on, first and only after a time in $K(t)$ since it is the stock of capital accumulated over many years. Increasing $k[= S(t)/Y(t)]$ does not increase $g [= K(t)/Y(t)]$ because in the transition $Y(t)$ increases faster than $K(t)$ and because in the very long run, with $Y(t)$ and $K(t)$ going at the same rate, $g [= K(t)/Y(t)]$ does not increase. **7.** There are several methods of solution. For reference to them and the steps in the present solution see Frazer and Yohe (1966, 323). **8.** In a fourth class, tax changes may be undertaken mainly on the grounds of achieving equity and justice in taxation (Friedman 1962, chap. 10). **9.** This ignores the questions of tax reform that may be pursued on the grounds of equity and justice in taxation, or as a means of enhancing freedom and voluntary association in a monetary/market oriented society. Such may imply payments according to the value of marginal product of the labor and capital expended. **10.** Keynes himself, however, thought any short-run effect on income redistribution on spending to be unlikely and he favored such action only as a last resort, that is, if there were no productive investment left. See Moggridge (1973, 152, 159). **11.** The proof of this proposition is found in Becker (1971, 53).

References to Appendix One

Becker, Gary S. 1971. *Economic Theory*. New York: Alfred A. Knopf, Inc.
Bender, Bruce. 1984. "An Analysis of the Laffer Curve." *Economic Inquiry* 22(July): 414-420.
Blustein, Paul. 1981. "New Economics." *Wall Street Journal* 198(October 8): 1 and 16.
Brooks, John. 1982. "Annals of Finance: The Supply Side." *The New Yorker* (April 19): 96-150.
Buchanan, James M., and Lee, Dwight R. 1982. "Politics, Time, and the Laffer Curve," *Journal of Political Economy* 90(August): 816-819.
Canto, Victor A.; Joines, Douglas H.; and Laffer, Arthur, eds. 1983. *Foundations of Supply-Side Economics*. New York: Academic Press.
Debate. 1984. "Transcript of Louisville Debate Between Reagan and Mondale." *New York Times* 134(October 9): 14-16.
Domar, E.D. 1946. "Capital Expansion, Rate of Growth, and Employment." *Econometrica* (April): 137-147.
Ehrbar, A. F. 1981. "A Tax Strategy to Renew the Economy." *Fortune* 103(March): 92-96.
Evans, Michael K. 1983. *The Truth About Supply-Side Economics*. New York: Basic Books, Inc., Publishers.
Evans, Paul. 1983. "What Does a Tax Cut Do?" In Victor A. Canto, Douglas H. Joines, and Arthur Laffer, eds. *Foundations of Supply-Side Economics*. New York: Academic Press.

Frazer, William. 1977. "Income Distribution, Social Utility, and Unemployment." *Nebraska Journal of Economics and Business* 16(Autumn): 37-60.
_____. 1978. "The Government Budget Constraint." *Public Finance Quarterly* 6(July): 381-387.
_____. 1980. *Expectations, Forecasting, and Control*, volumes I and II. Lanham, M.D.: University Press of America.
_____. 1982. "Milton Friedman and Thatcher's Monetarist Experience." *Journal of Economic Issues* 16(June): 525-533.
_____. 1983. "Monetary Trends in the U.S. and the U.K." *Southern Economic Journal* 49(January): 833-846.
_____, and Yohe, William. 1966. *Introduction to the Analytics and Institutions of Money and Banking*. Princeton, N. J.: D. Van Nostrand Company, Inc.
_____, and Boland, Lawrence A. 1983. "An Essay on the Foundations of Friedman's Methodology." *American Economic Review* 73(March): 129-144.
Friedman, Milton. 1957. *A Theory of the Consumption Function*. Princeton, N. J.: Princeton University Press for the National Bureau of Economics Research.
_____. 1962. *Capitalism and Freedom*. Chicago, Ill.: University of Chicago Press.
_____. 1968. "The Case for the Negative Income Tax." In Melvin R. Laird, ed. *Republican Papers*. New York: Frederick A. Praeger.
_____. 1980. "A Simple Tax Reform." *Newsweek* (August 18): 68.
_____. 1981. "Which Budget Deficit?" *Newsweek* (November 2): 88.
_____. 1982. "Painless Revenue," *Newsweek* (April 5): 63.
_____, and Schwartz, Anna J. 1982. *Monetary Trends*. Chapter 14 of text.
Gilder, George. 1981. *Wealth and Poverty*. New York: Basic Books, Inc., Publishers.
Greider, William. 1981. "The Education of David Stockman." *Atlantic Monthly* 248(December): 24-54.
Kaldor, Nicholas. 1982. *The Scourge of Monetarism*. Oxford: Oxford University Press.
Keynes, John Maynard. 1936. *The General Theory of Employment, Interest, and Money*. New York: Harcourt, Brace, and Company.
Laffer, Arthur. 1981. "Supply-Side Economics." MacNeil-Lehrer Report, transcript (February 19): 1-9.
Lerner, Abba P. 1944. *The Economics of Control: Principles of Welfare Economics*. New York: The Macmillian Company.
Moggridge, Donald, ed. 1973. *The Collected Writings of John Maynard Keynes*, volume xiv. London: Macmillian for the Royal Economic Society.
Porter, Richard D, and Bayer, Amanda S. 1984. "A Monetary Perspective on Underground Economic Activity in the United States." *Federal Reserve Bulletin* 70(March): 177-190.
Phillips, Samuel T. 1975. "Rawls' Economic Position." *Public Finance Quarterly*, 3(January): 70-85.
Shaller, Douglas R. 1983. "The Tax-Cut-But-Revenue-Will-Not-Decline Hypothesis and the Classical Macromodel." *Southern Economic Journal* 49 (April): 1147-1154.
Wanniski, Jude. 1978. *The Way the World Works*. New York: Simon and Schuster.

Appendix Two: A Variant of the Laffer Curve

As chapter 16 indicates, groups with diverse theories about the economy and economic policy were included under Ronald Reagan's political umbrella when we discussed the Reagan presidency. Among those to write on such matters was Michael Evans. He discussed the diverse theories and thoughts, presented data analyses, and classified the diverse economic theories and thoughts in terms of the myths and enduring truths of supply-side economics. Moreover, we encounter him in his analyses of data as proceeding somewhat indirectly along lines associated with Milton Friedman. This is partly surprising because Evans started his career in economics under the guidance of the Nobel laureate and Keynesian Lawrence Klein (pp. 70-77 and Evans 1969). That is to say, in the case of the Laffer's analysis (Evans 1983, chap. 9), he analyzed revenue effects following tax cuts of the past, relied on separate studies of illegal tax avoidance, and used such independent evidence as may be obtained from market surveys, IRS estimates and government studies of income maintenance schemes. This contrasts with his trying to estimate an elasticity for a point on the Laffer curve.

Among the myths Evans treated are the excessive claims of the Laffer curve, which we introduced with references in appendix one ("Analysis of a Tax Cut," sect. I). As chapter 16 indicates, Laffer lumped all tax cuts into one class and had additional revenues following from income growth (or what Evans calls the concept of "reflows"). Laffer, Evans said (1983, 198), argued that the cuts "would stimulate the economy, reduce unemployment and raise productivity." Plus, Evans said, "The Laffer curve stated boldly that in addition the budget could be balanced by cutting taxes..."

However, among the truths Evans treated in his book, The Truth About Supply-Side Economics *(1983, Part II), are some principal ones we deal with. These concern (1) the flat-rate income tax, (2) elements of analysis with respect to "the discredited Laffer curve," (3) the real rate of interest, saving, and the distribution of income (appendix one, sect. IV). The first and the third of these categories are most strongly entwined with Friedman's efforts among the post-World War II generations of economists.*

I. Introduction

This appendix deals with principal areas of concern: the flat-rate income tax (sect. II), elements of the Laffer analysis (sect. III), the consumption function and income redistribution (sect. IV), and income distribution and monetary effects (sect. V). The appendix is technical in that it offers a reconstructed, new variant of the original Laffer curve, ties the new reconstructed curve to the formal analysis found in the first technical appendix, and, in doing the foregoing, also achieves agreement with the truth elements advanced by Michael Evans in relation to Friedman's work.

II. The Progressive Tax and the Flat Rate

The progressive income tax has its origins in the work of the British economist John Stuart Mill (pp. 50-52). It gained special support from the notion that additional dollars of income to a high income household yield less additional utility to that household than to a lower income household, and gained impetus in the U.S. in 1913 with the ratification of the sixteenth amendment to the constitution. Mill's contribution was to separate the analysis of production (the supply side) from the analysis of the distribution of income. Friedman for his part, however, was the leading figure in espousing a holistic view that put the two sides back together and added the analysis of money. Along this line, there is no explicit, separate attention to production and the supply side, as found in other supply-side approaches with attention to much detail and often traditional techniques that presume the separation of effects, *ceteris paribus* (Canto et al. 1983). Rather Friedman did the following: (1) partly removed the basis for Keynes's original attack on Say's law (1936, 18, 26, 363); and (2) advanced arguments in favor of a stable-growth, monetary policy (pp. 549, 649). This policy was to assure aggregate demand at full employment, even while tax changes might be introduced that influence the size of the government sector in relation to GNP, the real rate of interest, and the growth of income and tax revenues, as reviewed below. Indeed, reintegrating the supply and demand sides does several things—it reasserts payment according to the value of the marginal product of one's labor and capital, reasserts the notion of freedom as encompassing voluntary association in a market, and sets freedom as the highest goal (chaps. 12 and 13).

The latter calls for a flat-rate income tax because it interferes least with voluntary association in a market economy. Beyond that, however, Friedman argued that a flat-rate tax would yield more revenue to the government than the existing progressive tax with its tax shelters and loopholes (deductions for charitable contributions, interest payments, real estate taxes, special treatment of capital gains, oil depletion allowances, and all the rest except strictly occupational expenses).

In essence, with respect to the progressive tax, we think of adjusted gross income (AGI) with marginal rates (rates on additional income) and average rates (tax paid as percent of AGI). Viewing tax as a rate on a vertical axis and AGI on a horizontal axis, both marginal and average rate curves

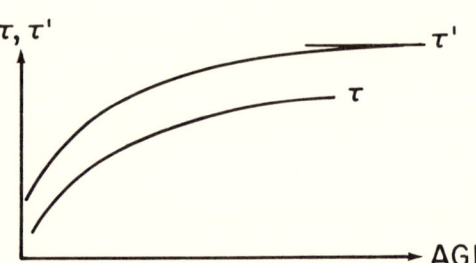

Figure 1a. Marginal and Average Tax Rates on AGI

may be drawn, as shown in figure 1. The marginal rate first pulls the average up more rapidly and then more slowly until at very high incomes a ceiling on the marginal rate (whether at 100, 90 or 50 percent, and so on) becomes the limit to the average rate. As the limit on the marginal rate is lowered to some flat-rate tax, the marginal and average rates become the same at that flat rate.

As the ceiling on the marginal rate is lowered under the K-J and Reagan cuts (chap. 16) the average rate simply approaches its ceiling more rapidly (i.e., at lower levels of income). Then, with loopholes and tax avoidance available to the higher income households, the higher income households may even be taxed at lower effective rates than lower income households. Moreover, in this tax system as it stood following the Tax Reduction Act of 1981 and the closely related Tax Equity and Fiscal Responsibility Act of 1982 (which closed some but left most loopholes intact)—there was the prospect of less tax revenue in relation to GNP in the future than in the past, as reviewed by Evans (1983, 266) for three reasons: (1) the removal of bracket creep as a source of revenue; (2) the addition of loopholes by the 1981 measure; and (3) the movement of more households into 40 and 50 percent brackets as a result of the past inflation means continued growth in legal tax avoidance and the underground economy.

Against such a background Evans (1983, 198-205) supported Friedman's earlier argument that lowering marginal rates will actually increase tax revenue to the government. Under his estimates, the marginal rate could be lowered to 25 percent without loss of revenue. Below the 25 percent

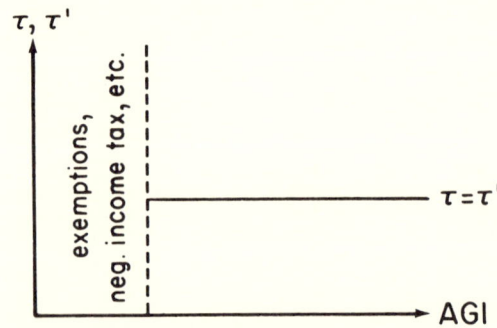

Figure 1b. The Flat-Rate Tax

rate, there are losses in revenue unless coupled with fewer deductions. With fewer deductions, Evans saw a rate as low as 15 to 20 percent as an excellent idea (less tax on work effort and incentive), if combined with a major broad-based value-added or consumption tax (more of a tax on spending than work effort, and so on).

The difficulty in going to the flat-rate tax with reduced deductions was for Evans (1983, 268)—as it was with Friedman—special interests groups. However, Evans said (1983, 268), even keeping basic deductions ("for mortgage interest, charitable contributions, catastrophic medical and state and local taxes") "and including a $2,500 personal exemption would only raise the necessary tax rate to 17 percent." Continuing, "In other words, even with all these deductions a 17 percent tax would raise as much revenue as does tax rates and rules in the personal income tax code at the 1983 date, even without taking into account any of the multifold benefits of such a tax."

In effect, what we have above are tax-rate conditions that maximize revenue, with reference to marginal and average tax-rate schedules in relation to households' adjusted gross incomes. The conditions thus far are taken up without the consideration of changes in saving to income ratios, and income growth rates such as come up below with respect to Friedman's treatment of consumption as a function of permanent income and the aggregative economy. There are some of what may be called dynamic elements in Evans's estimates due to increased work effort and reduced activity in the underground economy, but these would soon work themselves out under a flat-rate scheme. Even so, the analysis thus far takes us to a rate where curves for marginal and average tax rates in relation to AGI are identical (figure 1b). This will be a necessary condition for an extreme point on the variant of the Laffer curve which follows below, where we may think of the income tax system overall, GNP, and the average tax rate.

III. Elements of the Laffer Analysis

The present variant of the Laffer curve contains some of its original features, but with exceptions. The retained features are threefold: the long recognized relation between tax rates (τ) on a vertical axis and tax revenue (T) on a horizontal axis where at both zero and 100 percent tax rates the government gets no revenue (Kelcher and Orzechowski 1980; Kelcher 1982); the shape of the curve in the T,τ plane may change according to the public's willingness to be taxed and perception of the government's use of revenues (Wanniski 1978, 99); and the value of the tax rate (τ) that occurs at extreme value for the curve ($dT/d\tau = 0$) also specifies a separation of the area bound by the τ-axis and the curve connecting the zero and 100 percent tax rates. The upper part of the area symbolizes economic activity in the tax avoidance, barter, do-it-yourself economies, and parts of the underground economies (i.e., following Evans 1983, 204-213, some incomes from illegal sources, such as drugs, prostitution and gambling, will never be reported at any positive levels of taxation). The lower part of the area depicts the open, record-keeping economy where commonly accepted mixes of currency and transferrable balances abound as money facilitates exchange in the indirect satisfaction of wants on the part of economic agents. This latter we call the monetary economy. In the analysis, as tax rates decline to the level where the ceiling on marginal and average income rates are equal (i.e., $\tau' = \tau$), the economic activity in the tax-avoidance and so on economy vanishes to the extent possible (note, some incomes will never be reported).

The exceptions to the Laffer curve's early presentation include the following: the present orientation is toward the personal income tax entirely; its orientation is that of a static curve, such as a supply or demand curve in economics; the tax rate (τ) is an average rate (i.e., tax revenue over income, or $T/Y_{const.} \times 100 = \tau$) but one where the ceiling (floor) on marginal tax rates is above (below) the average rate as the ceiling (floor) on the marginal rate approaches the average rate from above (below) in the neighborhood of some revenue maximizing flat rate (i.e., until a flat-rate tax is attained that maximizes revenue); the average rate itself may vary between 100 percent and zero and, in any case, the average and marginal rates are the same at three points ($\tau = 0$, $dT/d\tau = 0$, and $\tau = 100$); and the extended analysis below distinguishes the effects of different classes of tax cuts rather than combining all in one category as Laffer did (1981, 1-9).

The variant of the Laffer curve, with the features indicated above, is shown in figure 2. As already suggested the extreme value for the modified Laffer curve may vary as to its position in the T,τ plane with public attitudes and perceptions in the way that taste may vary in the Marshallian demand curve. At the point of taxation where the government maximizes tax revenue, however, the necessary condition about marginal and average tax rates (i.e., $\tau' = \tau$) coincides with the tax rate that does in fact maximize tax revenue (i.e., the rate that occurs when $dT/d\tau = 0$). Both necessary and sufficient conditions are satisfied. These occur, where in Evans's terms (1983, 200), the Treasury sets the "personal income tax rate no higher than the level that maximizes total revenue."[1]

In brief, the analysis about the coincidence of marginal and average-tax-rate curves combines with the prospect of changes in the shape of the modified Laffer curve and the assumption about the government setting rates to maximize revenue. We have revenue maximization (T_{max}) given income ($Y_{const.}$). Income below will be given a growth feature [and hence T_{max} also, $T = f(\tau,Y,u)$ where u is a portmanteau variable] and Friedman's

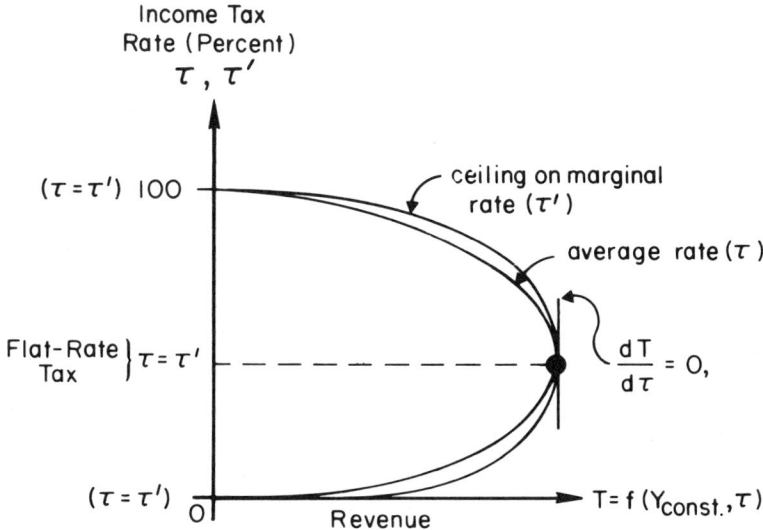

Figure 2. A Variant (static part) of the Laffer Curve

analyses of real rates of return, and consumption as a function of income (appendix one, sect. II) will be added below to the foregoing. However, the portmanteau variable will not be mentioned further.

IV. The Consumption Function and Income Redistribution

Evans recalled (1983, 120) a fundamental, linchpin hypothesis of the Keynesian system, notably "that the saving rate increased as income rose." The hypothesis in fact was embodied in Keynes's simple function depicting consumption as a function of income (text, pp. 83, 441-443), C = f(Y) as depicted in figure 6 of technical appendix one. In terms of household budget data, the thought was that consumption increased as income increased but at a declining rate. Though essentially a static or short-run relation, the simple function was nevertheless accompanied by the argument that over time consumption as a percent of income would decline and that the personal saving rate would rise [-$\Delta(C/Y)$ and $\Delta(S/Y)$]. Where private investment did not fill the spending gap, government spending was to step in. Further, where income redistribution effects were at issue, there was the further argument that tax-cut and government transfer payments that favored low income households would generate more spending and hence employment.

A contradiction was later posed to the foregoing by the finding "that the personal saving rate [S/Y] tended to remain constant over long periods of time" (Evans 1983, 120; text, p. 99). As Evans said (1983, 121), "A more comprehensive theory was needed, one which took into account the difference between short-run and long-run patterns of consumer behavior." Continuing, he said, "It fell to Milton Friedman to develop this definitive theory of consumer behavior..."

In the theory Evans referred to we encounter the difference between permanent and transitory components of time series. The first are trends and depict as well long-term expectations, as also found in Friedman's monetary analysis (chaps. 11 and 14). In the consumption function case, the permanent component of a household's income determined its consumption [say overall, $C = k(i,...)Y_P$] rather than the transitory or more temporary changes. The point, as developed in various sources (Evans 1983, chap. 6; and technical appendix one), need not be labored. As just denoted, the trend and the saving and consumption ratios (S/Y, and hence C/Y at a given time) could change as the factor $k(i,...)$ suggests, where in the present instance we stress the real rate of interest (i) as a variable that could alter the trends.

The interest-rate part of the theory Friedman drew largely from Irving Fisher's time preference for income. Most notably Friedman used indifference curve analysis with an income constraint as emerged in the early 1930s to depict the household choice between present consumption (c_O) and future consumption [$s_O(1+i)$] (first technical appendix, sect. IV). In this choice (say between, c_O, and saving, s_O) household utilities are maximized. In addition, the rate of exchange of goods today for goods tomorrow which reflects the time preference for income is the real rate of interest.

The stage was set by the simple Keynesian function to argue about the spending impact of tax cuts and government transfer payments, and it is enlarged by Friedman's more dynamic analysis as elucidated in the first appendix. Friedman's analysis is growth (or trend) oriented, plus it contained the rate for exchanging goods today for goods one year hence, and both the former and the latter have implications for income redistribution matters that are different from the implications of the simple Keynesian consumption function alone.

Evans touched upon the income redistribution part of the Keynesian analysis in the debate over the Reagan tax proposal of 1981, but he did not elaborate to the extent we do presently and in the first technical appendix. Evans noted (1983, 122) that "the share of GNP distributed between consumption and investment depends on the rate of return on saving [the i in the $k(i,...)$]."[2] In addition he noted, as would be the case in the foregoing framework, that tax cuts which favor saving increase this rate of return on saving. Continuing, with Evans's exposition, he said the following:

> It [Friedman's theory] also can be used as an argument against giving the poor more income through tax cuts and transfer payments in order to boost consumption. For if virtually everyone has the same saving rate, then consumption will not be increased by tilting the income distribution scale toward lower income groups. (Evans 1983, 123)

The implication of Friedman's theory for the analysis of tax cuts is in fact much stronger than Evans realized. We summarize the results from analysis presented in the first technical appendix. But we do not make the result a rich vs poor issue, or even an income redistribution one. The lower income households—below an ever growing poverty standard or minimum income level (exemptions, etc., figure 1b)—must be provided for and hopefully should not be a pool made up of the same households. Social mobility should be possible and encouraged.

First, in summarizing earlier analysis, the simple choice between consumption (C) and saving (S) out of income (Y) may be seen as being depicted by the utility-maximizing analysis presented above. Defining the saving to income ratio over time, $S(t)/Y(t) = k$, *noting the equality of*

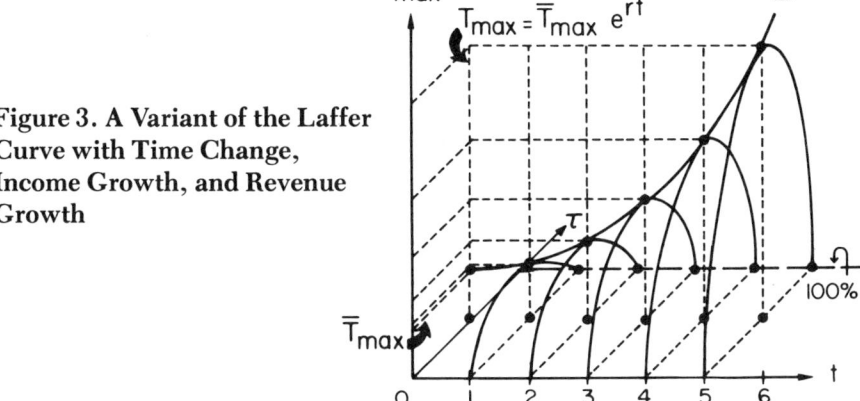

Figure 3. A Variant of the Laffer Curve with Time Change, Income Growth, and Revenue Growth

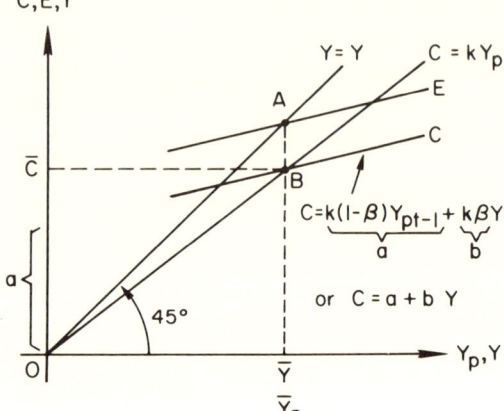

Figure 4. The Keynesian Plane: Long- and Short-Run Functions

saving and investment, $S(t) = I(t)$, stating the ratio of capital to income, $K(t)/Y(t) = g$, and noting that investment is simply an increment in capital, $I(t) = dK(t)/dt$, we have a system of equations which may be reduced to the solution equation,

$$Y_{max} = \bar{Y}_{max} e^{(k/g)t} \quad (1)$$

It is dealt with in the first technical appendix and as a matter of fact it simply depicts a growth curve for income with the growth rate, $a (a = k/g)$, where the notation (subscript max) signifies the underlying consumption-saving/utility-max orientation.

Second, recalling the Laffer-curve discussion, $T = f(\tau, Y_{const.})$ and $dT/d\tau = 0$, a growth equation for total revenue (T) may be written,

$$T_{max} = T e^{rt} \quad (2)$$

where r is the growth rate for tax revenue. Combining the variant of the Laffer curve in figure 2 with the revenue growth features leads to the three-dimensional sketch shown as figure 3. The exponential curve denoted I in figure 3 is also analogous to the growth path denoted I in figure 1 of technical appendix one (p. 807).

Increasing the saving to income ratio, S/Y or k in equation (1), rotates the growth curve for Y_{max} upward with the intercept $\bar{Y}_{max}$ being the fixed point about which the rotation occurs. In figure 3, the revenue-growth curve also rotates upward with its intercept $\bar{T}_{max}$ at time zero fixed.

Appendix Two: A Variant of the Laffer Curve

There is still further meaning in terms of Friedman's consumption function (text, p. 83, 441-443), $C = k(i,...)Y_P$, shown in figure 4. It is shown there as it gets imposed on the common Keynesian income (Y), expenditure (E) plane with consumption (C). Raising the real rate of return (i) will rotate downward the line depicting consumption as a proportion of permanent income, $C = kY_P$. Friedman defined his function with the following equation:

$$C(T) = k\beta \int_{-\infty}^{T} e^{(\beta-a)(t-T)} Y(t) \, dt \qquad (3)$$

where T denotes a future time horizon, the households' expectations are being formed by looking back into the past $(-\infty)$ and into the future (T), e is the growth constant, and a is the growth rate $(= k/g)$. The growth rate may be obtained from independent estimates, as Friedman said, but the parameter β is obtained from a distributed lag estimation technique.

Substituting from equation (1) for Y(t) in equation (3),

$$Y_P(T) = \beta \int_{-\infty}^{T} \exp \beta(t-T) \exp at \, dt \qquad (4)$$

From operations performed on this (p. 807) there is the simple restriction, $(\beta+a)T > 1$. Given this, however, an increase in a increases permanent income. Returning to equation (3), and keeping in mind equation (4), consumption will vary directly with the growth rate $a(a = k/g)$. Tax cuts that raise the saving to income ratio (i.e., k) will also increase consumption, $C(T) = k(\ )Y_P$, where k is distinct from k (p. 808).

Decreasing the saving to income ratio reverses all the above changes—the growth curve for income rotates downward, the growth in tax revenue to the government declines, and the real rate of interest declines.

As long as the ceiling on marginal tax rates is lowered to bring the marginal rate curve into line with the average rate curve, there is no further restriction on the immediately foregoing analysis, $T_{max} = f(\tau \text{ and } Y_{max})$. Tax cuts that raise the saving to income ratio also increase consumption, C(T), and tax revenue. The Laffer curve, maximizing condition imposed by the equality of the ceiling (floor) on the marginal tax rate and the average tax rate $(\tau' = \tau)$, places a limit on the tax cuts as far as revenue maximization goes. The limit does not apply, if we ignore the more static analysis concerning the variant of the Laffer analysis, and the dynamic analysis could still be invoked without reference to even the modified Laffer curve.

V. Income Redistribution and Monetary Effects

The "linchpin hypothesis" of the Keynesian system, as already noted, was associated in the 1930s and 1940s and beyond with notions of demand management which, as we now point out, also concerned attempts to moderate the inequality of income. The simple consumption function posited, as we recall, a tendency for high income households to save a disproportionately large part of income. Further, this relatively static analysis of consumption was virtually identical to much earlier analysis where utility was treated as a function of income, such that a dollar yielded more additional utility to a low income household than to a high income household. And, although these respective and virtually identical analyses were static, they nevertheless were considered as holding over time, and they appeared to justify a redistribution of income to favor the lower income households and hence increase total spending.

To be sure, it seemed plausible in the presence of what appeared as excess saving and inadequate demand to achieve full employment, that government tax and transfer payments could be used to transfer income from high to low income households—all with the view to achieving social justice as well as greater spending. Indeed, the simple utility function—which has been referred to as the Lerner justification for income distribution (Lerner 1944, chap. 3)—influenced academic writers who justified the progressive income tax.

Whatever the merits of the foregoing arguments, in the light of changing circumstances, they still appear and find support from studies of household budgets as far as short-term analysis goes. The static consumption function one did so as late as the 1981 debates over President Reagan's tax cut bill.

The problem with the use of the simple consumption function as an argument for income redistribution is that the argument is reversible when the economic problem it addresses is reversed (i.e., when the economic problem changes from oversupply to undersupply and excessive spending for consumption purposes). Thus, we have tax actions and transfer payments that may serve to decrease the saving to income ratio, on the one hand, and that may serve to increase saving, on the other. In the light of the analysis of the last sub-section, moreover, the foregoing arguments play quite dynamic roles.

Increasing k (the growth rate a, $a = k/g$, $k = S/Y$) increases income growth, tax-revenue growth, and rotates upward the respective growth curves (including curve I, in figure 3). A tax cut and related policy behind this we call "trickle down" policy. From discussion surrounding equation (3), however, it should be clear that consumption, $C(T)$, is also made greater by these developments than would be the case with the reverse policy.

The reverse policy we call "trickle up" (i.e., the policy of decreasing k), because of the argument that it increases consumption (actually C/Y ratio), which increases sales, and hence some capital spending—all with some benefits flowing to those who provide capital. Decreasing k rotates

Appendix Two: A Variant of the Laffer Curve 831

the growth curves for income and taxes downward (including curve I, in figure 3).

A neutral tax cut occurs (neither "trickle down" nor "trickle up") where the relative positions of the "agents," the households and the firm, are left unchanged. An across-the-board tax cut of a given percentage of tax liability of households illustrates this neutral cut. Further, the present analysis of tax cuts proceeds from whatever tax and government-transfer-payment (tax/income redistribution) system exists at the time, and monetary policy plays a role in assuring non-inflationary economic growth.

Setting aside the matter of the productivity of resources in the private vis-à-vis the goverment sector (pp. 219-220, 222), the neutral cut is complicated by the role for monetary policy. There are two parts to the reasoning, starting with no change in monetary policy (i.e., the monetary reserves, or base money, grow at a constant rate). First, the tax cuts with equal cuts in government spending simply transfer activity from the government to the private sector. The monetary policy (constant money growth) reassures income growth and the path I for revenue growth in figure 2, as activity is transferred from the government to the private sector. Second, the tax cuts with deficits to be financed at a given time (i.e., with "crowding out" of private financing and spending, as introduced in section I) call forth offsetting results. The positive effects of the tax cuts on spending in this case are offset by the negative effects from crowding out of spending.

The Tax Reduction Act of 1981 and the 1982 Tax Equity and Fiscal Responsibility Act had mixed effects in the foregoing terms, as no doubt expected. There were features that contributed to saving and capital accumulation (tax credits, expanded IRA, and the reduction in the limit on the marginal tax rate) and hence some "trickle down" effect. Most of the tax changes (reduced marriage penalty, the across-the-board part of the cuts), however, fall into the neutral class of changes. Most of the cuts of 5, 10, and 10 percent of tax liability over a three year period probably did no more than to partially neutralize bracket creep. However, the failure of Congress to reduce spending to match the cuts in revenue, and the resulting deficits ($195.4 billion for fiscal year ended Sept. 30, 1983) combined with monetary policy probably would have contributed to some crowding out of the private sector except that an unanticipated result came about, namely: as the U.S. economy and government appeared increasingly stable in relation to the rest of the world, large amounts of capital funds flowed into the U.S. from abroad to support the public and private financing efforts in the U.S. (pp. 683-685).

Notes to Appendix Two

1. This argument on Evans's part is in fact a counterpart to the assumption underlying the Laffer curve analysis set forth by Wanniski (1978, 97-103), namely:

> "The goal of the politician in setting the tax rate in general is (should be) that of maximizing the revenue to the government."

2. Where we have switched here from consumption to saving to consumption and investment, the reader may wish to recall the discussion of the flow of saving into investment (sect. I).

References to Appendix Two

Canto, Victor A.; Joines, Douglas H.; and Laffer, Arthur B., eds. 1983. *Foundations of Supply-Side Economics*. New York: Academic Press.

Evans, Michael K. 1969. *Macroeconomic Activity: Theory, Forecasting, and Control—An Econometric Approach*. New York: Harper & Row, Publishers.

Frazer, William. 1980. *Expectations, Forecasting and Control: A Provisional Textbook of Macroeconomics*, vols. I & II. Lanham, Md.: University Press of America, Inc.

Kelcher, Robert E. and Orzechowski, William. 1980. "Supply-Side Effects of Fiscal Policy: Some Historical Perspective." Working Paper Series, Federal Reserve Bank of Atlanta, August.

Kelcher, Robert E. 1982. "Historical Origins of Supply-Side Economics." *Economic Review*. Federal Reserve Bank of Atlanta (January): 12-19.

Keynes, John Maynard. 1936. *The General Theory of Employment, Interest, and Money*. New York: Harcourt, Brace, and Company.

Laffer, Arthur. 1981. "Supply-Side Economics." *MacNeil-Lehrer Report*, transcript (February 19).

Lerner, Abba P. 1944. *The Economics of Control*. New York: The Macmillian Company.

Wanniski, Jude. 1978. *The Way the World Works*. New York: Simon and Schuster.

Index

Index

A

advocacy,
  role of, 482-483
  should not be costless, 483, 491
agenda, hidden,
  (see "hidden agenda")
Alchian, Armen, 301-305
Allais, Maurice, 173, 731
Allende, Salvador,
  death, 330
  Marxist, 327-328
  methods, 329
Angell, James,
  course in monetary economics, 138, 376 n49
antitrust,
  paradox of, 320-321
  start of, 308
antitrust law,
  economic argument controls, 318
  empirical considerations, 318-321
antitrust policy,
  central goal of, 308, 314
  (see "second best" condition)
aristocracy,
  member by birth, 204
  paternalistic, 204
Arrow, Kenneth,
  on mathematical statistics, 160
  welfare economics, 308, 378 n51
"as if" principle,
  effect of behavior is "as if," 125-127, 131, 319
  (see famous 1953 essay)
"assumer" science,
  theory of price, 294
  (see axioms)
assumptions,
  descriptive accuracy of, 195-196, 208, 307
  significance of role, 127
  truth of, 86, 229
  vs predictions, 195-196
  (see axioms, homogeneous product; truth in economics)
Austrian School, 281
axioms,
  antitrust and, 309
  as conclusions or theorems, 127
  converse to truth of, 113
  Friedman's reaction, 229
  Friedman's view, 319-320
  in Ricardo's work, 49
  key passage on, 113
  modus ponens, 34, 41
  monopolistic competition and, 311
  theory of firm, 34
  truth and, 34, 62, 312
  vs prediction, 122-123, 126, 128
  (see assumer science; assumptions; "as if" principle; conventionalists; famous 1953 essay; homogeneous product axiom; truth)
axioms controversy, 108
  problem of reversing mode, 128
  (see *modus ponens*; *modus tollens*)
axioms, role of,
  perfect market, 194-195, 202

B

Baker, James, 634
balanced budget, constitutional
  requirement, 515, 535, 690
  Burns and Friedman, 243, 261
  Burns's support of, 243
  Friedman's effort, 535
  Reagan's call for, 680
  Samuelson on, 773 n75
Bank of England,
  control difficulties, 552-558, 594
Banking Acts of 1933 and 1935,
  open market operations, 258
banking view of interest rates,
  envisioned i-control, 211-212, 259
  (see liquidity preference; i-regime)
Bayesian learning,
  learning from mistakes, 124
  personalistic probability, 120-122
  (see economic Bayesian)
Becker, Gary, 772 n50, 818 n11
Bentham, Jeremy, 457
"biased double standard," 332-333, 337, 502
  Kissinger and Friedman, 346-347, 348-349, 363-364
big government,
  (see government, big)
Big U-Turn, defined, 692
Bloomsbury group,
  composition of, 762 n11
Boland, Lawrence,
  "hidden agenda," 703, 714-715
  logical defense of Friedman's essay, 114, 125, 128-132
  on appropriate treatment of time, 726-727
  on equilibrium, 722-723

Index 835

on forms of logical
  argument, 725
on Keynes, 716
on neoclassical economics, 717-723
Bork, Robert, 631, 677, 698
  antitrust, 309, 316-323
  oligopoly and, 315-316
  "second best" condition and, 314-315
Borts, George, 410
"bracket creep," also "tax trap," 225
  definition, 803
British case,
  unique features, 26-27
British coal miners,
  (see coal miners, British)
British economic system,
  success and decline of, 37, 57
British government,
  budgeting procedures, 781 n64
  elections, 525, 596
  overseer role for Cabinet, 590-591, 612-613
  political parties before Thatcher, 762 n39
  structure of, 575, 623, 779 n12, 781 n58
  (see coal miners, British)
British socialism, 23-24
British tradition,
  economics in, 4, 31-32, 37-39
  economic system and, 37
  Keynes as a departure from, 38
  summary of, 30-36
Brittan, Samuel, 432, 449-452
Britton, John, 511-512
Bronfenbrenner, Martin, 283
Brunner, Karl, 361, 598, 708
  at UCLA, 304
  in U.S., 109
Buchanan, James,
  new area of economics, 277
  on "economic man," 766 n35
  on Knight, 306
  on Marshall and Friedman, 119
  prospect of prediction, 300
  "public choice" economics, 297-301
  welfare economics, 153
  Wicksell's influence, 297
bureaucratic inertia,
  law of, 505
Burns, Arthur,
  as inflation fighter, 221
  as insider, 164, 221
  as Keynesian, 230
  at age 70, 256
  at the Fed, 648
  characterization of, 255
  data on, 144-146
  economic laws not working, 234-235
  flaws in position, 263
  Friedman's eulogy of, 257
  Friedman tie, 138, 140, 144-145
  independence of Fed and, 217-218
  independence of White House, 237
  micromanagement of policy, 216, 221, 235, 263-264
  Mitchell protégé, 138, 144, 153
  Nixon White House, 232, 233
  on independence of Fed, 250, 259
  on Marxian perception, 467
  on Schumpeter, 467-468
  replacement of, 216
business cycle, political,
  definition of, 213
  Kennedy election, 231
  timing of business conditions, 242
  (see government budget constraint; Fed, political role of)
business cycle,
  Burns's view endogenous, 241, 258
  elimination of, 35
  Mitchell, Wesley, 138, 148
  (see "endogenous"/"exogenous"; time series)
business organization,
  (see corporate form)

C

Caldwell, Bruce, 711-712
Cambridge style,
  complexities of life, 56
  schedules, method of, 56
  [see realitic (sic) theory]
capital flows, international,
  interest rates vs sound economy, 535
capital, human,
  (see Becker, Gary)
capital spending,
  i-regime, 59
  in Ricardo's work, 49
"capital," "capitalism,"
  terms, 466
capital-led recovery, 1981-1982,
  (see recovery from 1981-82 recession)
Capitalism and Freedom, 530-531
  as a popular work, 152
  Chile and, 343, 346, 363
  vis-à-vis *Free to Choose*, 178
capitalism

    as being materialistic, 485, 495
    bourgeoisie disciplines, 532
    "economic apologist," 503
    freedom for non-materialist, 492
    Friedman's essential notion of, 476-477
    "grave diggers," 503
    high capitalism, xi
    Jewish involvement, 704
    Jews and, 386-387 n13 and n18
    Manchester as model, 53
    Marxist view of history, 502-503
    Marx's revolution, 38
    Marx's view, 54, 467, 497
    mode of organization, end of, 489
    moral beliefs and, 495, 509
    necessary condition for freedom, 490
    overthrow of capitalist, 467, 497, 503
    religion and, 647
    Schumpeter's view 467-468
    (see communism; free enterprise; social market economy)
capitalist and socialist ethics,
    choice between, 6
    Ruskin and Marx, 22
    (see capitalist ethic; socialist ethic)
capitalist economy,
    (see free enterprise)
capitalist ethic,
    absence in Mill, 52
    bourgeois distribution of income, 493
    corollary to another principle, 509
    freedom as goal, 140-141, 151-152
    Friedman's controversies, 140
    Friedman's vacillation, 494-495, 504-505, 509
    not ethical principle, 509
    payment according to, 22
    Ricardo's work, 49
    statement of, 494, 504, 509
    (see marginal product)
Carter Administration,
    failure of, 23, 60
    Miller at Fed, 261-262
    Volcker appointment, 262
Carter, Jimmy,
    "a national malaise," 632
    unemployment and, 433
Castro, Fidel, 329-330
causation,
    common stimuli, 309
causation, money to income,
    leading time rate of change, 539, 544-545
    Walters's test, 603
    (see Kaldor, Nicolas)
central bank,

    independence of, 217, 235, 260-261, 264, 273, 568
    (see Federal Reserve, political role of)
ceteris paribus,
    Hayek and, 175
    impounding change, 294
    use in economics, 109, 119
    (see Hayek, Friedrich von)
Chamberlin, Edward,
    Young, Allan, 311
change, normal and revolutionary, 711-715
change, social and convention,
    complexity of, 702
    Plato's and Aristotle's views, 703
    three views of, 701
    '20s and '30s as time of, 703
    (see change, normal and revolutionary; convention)
Chicago school(s),
    anti-monopolistic competition, 307
    egalitarian sentiments, 287, 290
    Hayek and, 175
    income tax, 289-290
    labor unions, 290
    overview, 305-306
    three schools, 276-277, 281-306
    UCLA, 301-304
    (see Hayek, Friedrich von)
Chicago type,
    characteristics, 301, 305
    not majority, 305
Chicago, University of,
    "Chicago boys," 343, 338, 327, 352, 362
    involvement with Chile, 327, 333, 362
    [see Chicago School(s); Harberger, Arnold]
Chile, 327-364
    China and double standard, 347
    economic miracle, 338, 350
    economic performance, 348-350
    Friedman's involvement, 327
    "lab test for a theorist," 351
    military coup, 330
    upheavals, 328-330
    U.S. involvement, 330-333
    (see Allende, Salvador; Chile, Junta government; Pinochet, Augusto)
Chile, Junta government,
    declaration of principles, 341-442
    economic policies, 343-344
    payment on foreign debt, 352-353
Chou En-lai, 331
Churchill, Winston,

Index 837

Keynes and, 1920s, 419, 422-423
Clark, Lindley, H.,
  on Friedman, 710
closed economy,
  idea of, 426
coal miners,
  Britain's, bellweather of union strength, 625
  Churchill and Keynes, 423
  "Miner's Rule O.K.?", 628
  role in 1920s, 423, 625
  Thatcher government and, 606-607, 625
Coase theorem, 378 n51
communism,
  double standard for judgement, 502
  ideal, 502
comparisons, 285
  anti-monopolistic
    competition, 308-312
  axioms controversy and, 125-128
  British/U.S. economies, 530-571
  British/U.S. euphemisms and rhetoric, 631
  countervailing ideas, 701-702
  econometrics and Friedman's statistics, 68-87, 735-760, 740-741
  economic theories, 70, 455
  Friedman/the Cowles
    Commission, 84-87, 706-707
  Friedman/Galbraith, 201-202, 208, 229-230, 274
  Friedman/Hayek, 173, 176-179
  Friedman/Keynes, 25, 178-179, 408, 527, 762 n11
    style, 25-26
    dynamic analysis, 32
  Friedman/Samuelson
    methodologies, 90-92, 107, 718-719
  Friedman/Simons, 288-291
  Reagan/Roosevelt, 631, 789 n2
  Thatcher/Reagan, 538, 626, 632-633
  Thatcher/Reagan tasks, 626
  U.K. Radcliffe Report/U.S. monetary matters, 600, 757-758
  (see capitalist and socialist ethics; Hotelling's line; power theories vs monetary theories)
competition,
  in Marx's model, 54
competition, imperfect, works on, 197
competition, perfect, equilibrium and individualism, 721-723
  imperfect competition problem, 722
competitive model, as ideological abstraction, 318-319

"conditioning,"
  of agents, 461-464, 486
Congdon, Tim, 545-546, 569
Congressional Budget Committee,
  Act of 1974, 242, 634
  Stockman's use of, 634
Connally, John, 233
conservatism,
  conventional meaning, 232-233
  Heflin, Howard, 309
  "old time religion," 238
conspiracy theory of history,
  (see history, conspiracy theory of)
Constitution, U.S.,
  First Amendment, 204, 391 n34
constitutional amendment to balance the budget,
  (see balanced budget)
constitutional amendments,
  balanced budget and flat rate tax, 514-518, 523-524
  (see special interests; voting)
consumption,
  capital as sacrifice of, 54
consumption function,
  income redistribution and, 826-830
  Keynes's, 440
  "Lerner justification," 813
  out-reaching effects, 440
  social mobility, 20-21
  tax cuts and, 440-441
  (see Friedman's consumption function) *contraction*
controversy,
  Friedman's work, 7
  in proportion to merit of contribution, 105
  special reasons for contribution, 111
  (see differences of opinion, reconciliation of)
convention,
  change and, 701
  defined, 701
  "hidden agenda" case, 701
  role of, 703
  (see change, social; "hidden agenda")
conventionalism,
  monopolistic competition, 312-313
  the two Cambridges, 306
conventionalist,
  assumptions, truth of, 34, 129
  (see "economic man" concepts)
conventionalist's view,
  assume truth of assumptions, 129

the two Cambridges, 306
corporate form of business,
   gain in prominence, 308
   rise of, 12-13
Council of Economic Advisors,
   during Nixon years, 233-237
   during Reagan Presidency, 634
Cournot, Augustin,
   French mathematician, 370, n67
Cowles Commission, 705-706
   at Chicago, 161, 162
   struggle at Chicago, 289
creative work,
   source of insights, 107
   (see demarcation problem; peer review process)
Crusoe, Robinson,
   economics, 306
culture,
   autonomous units, 11, 23
currency, key,
   definition, 412

D

Dallek, Robert, 632, 676-677
Darman, Richard, 634
Das Kapital, 367 n21
   and cotton, 12, 367 n21
   writing of, 53-54
Davenport, John, 281, 287, 290
deceleration of inflation,
   shock or gradual, 585
   (see government, unwinding of)
deficits (trade and domestic),
   and the dollar, 669, 677, 689
   central bank and deficits, 567
   defense vs social spending, 238, 731 n7
   future agenda, 686
   government, reducing size of, 675, 677
   means of adjustment, 677
   monetary discipline, 649-653, 669
   reflows argument, 643, 674
   sources, summary of, 688-689
   (see tax cuts)
deficits and the Crash of 1987, 534-535
   computer trading, 686
   financing, three needs, 683
   inflow of foreign funds, 683, 689
   vanishing levitation, 685
   [see capital-led recovery, 1983-1984; deficits (trade and domestic) and the dollar]
deficits, federal budget,
   as owed to ourselves, 59
   conventions of Marshall's era, 701
   financing of, 534, 804
   importance of, 534
   rationalized role, 435
   relation to money and credit, 441
   understanding Keynes provided, 435
   (see government budget constraint)
demand curve,
   downward sloping, 307-308, 310
   identification of, 319
   relation to law, 319
demand for money,
   (see money demand)
Dewey, John, 133-135, 737
differences of opinion,
   purpose of statistical analysis, 135, 744
   reconciled by evidence, 123
   resolution of, 744, 758
   reconciliation, Klein and Friedman, 75-77, 103, 772, n48
   Samuelson and Friedman, 87-88, 90, 103-104
   Simon and Friedman, 87-88, 105
   (see consensus in economics; controversy)
Director, Aaron, 287, 291-292
   Knight group in mid-1930s, 161
   law and economics, 316-323, 324
Director, Rose,
   data on, 151, 183
   libertarian leanings, 162
   political views of economists, 288
Disraeli, Benjamin,
   assimilated Jew, 168, 171
   Victoria and, 13
distribution/redistribution of income,
   class struggle, 487, 489
   Friedman on government, 470
   Friedman on proximity fuses, 156, 157
   Friedman's background in probability, 512-513
   Friedman's egalitarian sentiment, 140
   Friedman's resolution of sentiments, 151-153, 162
   inequality, causes of, 510
   inequality in inheritance, 510
   Marx on, 493
   permanent income hypothesis, 510
   practical technological rule, 12
   rules governing, 337
   saga of, 496-503
   Samuelson as egalitarian, 487
   Savage connection, 160
   (see consumption function; freedom; minimum wages; utility of income)

Domar model, 808
double standard,
  (see biased double standard)
Douglas, Paul H., 283-284
  income distribution, market demand and Ruskin, 283-284
dynamics,
  entropy time, 120
  Friedman's reorientation of theory, 108, 117
  monetary analysis, 31-32, 111
  sidereal time, 120
  time rates of change vs levels, 126, 121
  (see episodic change; Bayesian learning)

E

econometric forecasts,
  CEA 1970-1971, 235-236
  forecasting models, 643, 645-646
econometrics,
  conflict with indirect method, 558-559
  control (?) of key variables, 550, 552, 559-560
  definition of, 33
  effects, separation of, 552, 559
  fashionable, 542, 552, 559-560
  forecasting models, 643, 645-646
  Friedman's critics, 84-87, 699, chap. 18
  identification problem, money demand, 743
  Keynesian model, 646
  Klein's approach, 74-84, 735, 749
  model building and use of force, 545
economic analysis,
  alternative systems of, 70, 455, 698
economic Bayesian,
  effects, separation of, 552, 559
  fashionable, 542, 552, 559-560
  forecasting models, 643, 645-646
  Friedman's critics, 84-87, 699, chap. 18
  identification problem, money demand, 743
  Keynesian model, 646
  Klein's approach, 84-84, 735, 749
  "modern econometricians," 553
  "prevailing fashion," 597
  prior belief, 122
  separation of effects error, 804
  Walter's textbook, 597
  (see Bayesian learning; Henry, David and Ericsson, Neil; personalistic probability; statistical methods)
economic development,
  dependence on, 339
economic ideas, reasons for,
  visibility in 1980s, 39
economic instability,
  source of, 529
economic man controversy,
  Buchanan on, 766 n35
economic man concepts, 30, 34, 277
  avoided by Friedman, 118-122
  Galbraith and Friedman, 203
  retreat from, 462, 476
  utility maximization, etc. 118, 125
  (see utility maximization)
economic man assumptions (axioms),
  calculus and, 293
economic man,
  materialism, 342
economic policies, the future agenda, 686
  open economy competition, 688-689
economic policy, goals and instruments,
  mathematical idea of, 566
economic policy,
  as physical science, 457-458, 463-464
  as solution to problems, 123
  assumer science, 459, 490
  background in pre-WW I, 435
  definition (allocation of scarce means), 458, 464, 490
  mathematical ideal of goals and instruments, 566
  political dimension, 449-452
  positive and normative, 459-460
  Public Choice, 449
  "Robinson Crusoe," 457-458, 462, 464, 476, 490
  two-track system, 418, 454
  (see fiscal policy; monetary policy; Public Choice; society, problems of; welfare economics; values, social)
economic science,
  a priori speculation, 57
  (see statistical methods, uses of)
economic theory, 123, 135
  abstraction vs detail, 126
  arguments for social reform, 123-124
  as different from physical sciences, 119-120
  crisis in, 574
  engine of analysis, 117, 119
  Friedman as NBER theorist, 153-155
  Friedman's complex framework, 117, 119, 139
  Friedman's purpose, 309-310, 313
  Galbraith's purpose, 203-204
  General Theory, roots of, 425
  general vs description, 311-312

Manchester as model, 508
"no theory without facts," 153
policy orientation, 132
policy purpose, 114-115
position and motion, 744-748
prediction as purpose, 112, 122-133, 135
purpose of, 33, 108, 307, 309, 319-320, 324
refutation of, 124
relation to policy and hypothesis, 123-124
standards for testing, 125, 157
sticky prices, Friedman and indexation, 223
test of one against another, 115-116, 126
theories as instruments, 115
(see demarcation problem; hypothesis testing; instrumentalism; Marshallian demand curve; mechanical apparatus; monetarism; perfect market; prediction; price theory; simplicity; society, problems of; testing)

economics, non political,
groundwork for, 457, 463
Hotelling's line, 410
Keynes's anti-scientism, 463-464, 465
value free, 457
(see Hotelling's line; political economy)

economics,
as martial art, 201, 580, 709
as useful subject, 193
British socialism, 23-24
coherent whole, 35
divergence of views in, 35
founding of, 23
high on Thatcher and Reagan agendas, 635
inconsistent views, 720
institutional factors and, 553-554
methodology of, 21-22
move in empirical direction, 295
no political neutrality, 141
political neutrality, 397 n22
purpose, policy orientation, 40
real world and, 637
science view of, 30, 35
simplicity, 22
"superstars in," 580
Swedish use of term, 372 n3
two-track, micro-macro system, 716, 727-728
whole view of, 35
(see economic science; economic theory; ideology; political economy)

economics, and physical science methods,
Knight vs Friedman, 68-87, 463-464, 466, 491

economics, normative and positive distinction,
Friedman's policy orientation, 132
J.N. Keynes's book, 112
prediction for policy purpose, 112
(see Mitchell, Wesley)

economics,
Robinson Crusoe, 457-458, 476
separated economics from polity, 490

"economics" and "political economy," usages, 276

economists, academic,
circumvented by Friedman, 541
Thatcher's opposition to, 541
(see peer review system)

"economists of the city," City of London, 779 n4
definition, 575
early response of, 779 n4

"efficiency,"
allocative efficiency, 313
antitrust law and, 318
productive efficiency, 313-314

elections, government support of,
(see advocacy)

elitist view,
Galbraith, 204
Plato, 336
"wisest and best," 336

empirical economics,
Hume and, 37
modern computer and, 37

empirical hypothesis, fruitful,
definition of, 57
search for, 57

"empirical scientist,"
ambitious dreams, 56
reference to Friedman, 153, 180
reference to Mitchell, 153, 180

empiricism,
belief and, 129

empiricists,
ambitious dreams, 56

Employment Act of 1946, 254, 427-428, 434

"endogenous"/"exogenous," terms, 241, 258

ends and means, 464, 484-486

"engine of analysis", 324
emphasis on, 277, 284

episodic change,
as isolated events, 120-121
(see evolutionary change and nonrepetitive events; Friedman's adjustments for episodes)

Index

equation systems,
  recognized by Marshall, 55
equilibrium,
  Friedman on, 563-564, 696-697
  in economics, 459
  in Friedman's economics, 742
  laureates' attention, 33
  Marshall's, 56-57
  unemployment, 58
  (see general equilibrium analysis; Walrasian model)
ethic, socialist,
  (see socialist ethic)
ethical beliefs, shared, need for support and understanding, 463, 489-490, 495
  (see capitalist ethic; social values)
Evans, Michael, 818 n4, 821
  analysis of tax cuts, 671-675
  criticisms of book, 789-790 n9
  on supply-side economics, 638, 641
evidence,
  independent, 121-122
  scientific, 121-122
evolution,
  antitrust and, 321-322
  principles of, 278
  Spencer, Veblen, et al., 321-322, 324-325
evolutionary change and nonrepetitive events, 120-121
exchange economy,
  features of, 478
  monopoly as problem, 478, 480-499
  (see freedom; voluntary association)
exchange rates,
  "dirty float," 416
  fixed, 415
  floating, 415-416
exogenous variable,
  control variable, 59
  (see "endogenous"/"exogenous")
expectations, inflationary,
  main features, 747
  structure underlying shift in, 562, 564-565, 595-596, 652, 668-669
  (see liquidity preference; New York's revenge; stock market)
expectations of the future,
  Keynes's emphasis, 58
externalities,
  defined, 461

F

Fabian Society,
  British socialism, 23-24
  founding of, 23
"facts without theory," 38, 53, 153, 732,
  in relation to econometrics, 741
  NBER's pre-Friedman research, 153
  (see Koopmans, Tjalling)
famous 1953 essay, 695, 724, 731
  avoidance of methodological error, 129, 134
  Burns's comments on, 164
  controversial, 107-108, 111-112
  key passages, 113
  Koopmans as critic, 129-131
  laureates' attention, 33
  marketing masterpiece, 108
  prepublication title, 36, 112, 139
  reflects breadth of monetarism, 139
  Samuelson as critic, 131-132
  title of, 36
  Walter's econometrics, 597
  (see "as if" principle; Boland, Lawrence; logical defense)
fascism,
  Pareto as ideologue, 489
"Fed bashing,"
  definition of, 651
Federal Reserve, independence of,
  Burns on, 250, 259, 260
  Carter White House and, 262
  compensating for errors, 259
  myth, widely held, 635, 680
  only justification for, 252
  Reagan turn in policy, 648-670
  two sorts of independence, 260
Federal Reserve, monetary policy,
  muted tones vis-à-vis Thatcher, 621
  (see monetary policy)
Federal Reserve, monetary accommodation, 545, 574, 644, 648, 651, 687, 751
  energy crisis, 243, 252, 271
  Friedman analysis, 243-246
Federal Reserve,
  and discretionary judgement, 257-258,
  as "deep dark hole," 635
  assumption of independence of, 217
  chasing interest rates, 237-238
  Constitution and, 235
  crash of 1929, 424-425, 431
  exhortation and open mouth policy, 221
  Galbraith on appointments, 265-266
  government budget constraint, 217
  independence, political neutrality, 235
  interest rate control, 535, 556-557, 561-562
  monetary rule, the, 215
  more sophisticated in '87 than '29, 686

pegged interest rates, 217
transition to M-regime, 447-448
Treasury-Fed accord, 428 3/1951
turning point in inflation policy, 243
under Treasury, 215, 218

Federal Reserve, political role of, 218
Congress's wishes, 235
elections of 1960, 233, 254
elections of 1972, 254, 255, 257, 263
elections of 1980, 273
independence, etc., 260-261, 264, 273
make subordinate to Treasury, 257, 273
Nixon's view, 236, 253-254
(see government budget constraint;
Federal Reserve, monetary
accommodation; Friedman's rule)

Federal Reserve, October 6, 1979
announcement,
(see October 6 announcement)

Federal Reserve, control difficulties,
"base drift," and M1 control, 656-659, 664
deregulation of interest rates, 656-657
practice of LLR, 657-658
(see October 6 announcement)

finance,
integration in economics, 308

"fine tuning," 207, 433
Carter administration, 269, 433, 439
expansion in 1960s, 218
Nixon CEA, 232-238
Nixon White House, 232-240
old-time religion, 238
(see quick fix)

fiscal policy,
defined as deficit, 234
definition of, 286
government budget
constraint, etc., 271-272
introduced by Keynes, 59
OFP balance rule, 237, 250
related to flawed view of monetary policy,
258-259

Fisher, Irving,
interest rate equation, 212
pre-Keynes quantity theory, 414
price adjustments, 447
rate of interest (i), 448
rate of return vs i, 448-449

Fisher, Ronald A., 70, 148, 697

flat-rate tax,
analysis, 822-824
emergence of, 503-507
first statement of, 495-496
legislation on, 488
moving toward, 640

perspective on, 772 n10
tax loopholes, 671
value judgement, relation to, 508-509
(see tax reform)

flexible wages,
indexation, 585-586
(see rigid wages)

forecasting,
by Marx and Engels, 55

forecasts,
Friedman cases, 224
Friedman, M., 251, 263
Stein and Heller, 224
(see historical prophecies)

free enterprise economy,
fresher view of, 637
maturity of, 526
redirection of, 529
(see exchange economy)

"free market,"
characteristics, social, 337
(see freedom, economic/political)

free market, advocacy of,
a growth industry, 780 n51

free market,
bulwark of liberty, 281

free society,
dispersing power, 141
minority rights, 141
need for understanding, 489-490
(see ethical beliefs, shared; freedom; social
values)

Free to Choose, 707
"Economic Bill of Rights," 677
"nuts and bolts" book, 301
popularity of, 264-265
relation to Galbraith, 264

Free to Choose, television series,
BBC screening, 588, 780 n51
Galbraith series, 264-265

free trade,
Friedman's support of, 535-536
Reagan, 535-536
Reagan and Thatcher, 536, 626
Thatcher commitment, 591, 626

freedom, 460-464, 482-486
and Jewish values, 170
as highest goal, 62, 485, 492, 509
believers in, 473
businessmen and professors, 472
conflict unavoidable, 482
distribution of income and, 408

Index

enabling role of the market, 476
ends and means, 484-485
for non-materialistic, 492
Friedman on Smith, 45
Friedman's highest goal, 494-495
Goldwater, 473, 484
market economy, 533
need for by minority, 532
"political freedom," meaning of, 479
preeminence of, 204
role of the market, 532
source of, 481
the exchange economy, 478
vs coercion, 478-479, 491
(see advocacy; capitalist ethic; free market; minority freedom; monopoly; voluntary association)

freedom, economic/political, 337
freedom, individual,
Jew and capitalism, 386-387 n18
Friedman and Keynes,
comparison, 178-179
Friedman and Dicey, 475
Reagan on "quick fix," 651-652
"stay the course," 642, 675, 788
Friedman, David,
as economist, 184
on father, 183
Friedman, early views of,
Goldwater campaign, 631
"Satan and the imps," 588
"Friedmanesque,"
definition of term, 236
Nixon's CEA, 235, 270-271
relation to Friedman, 394 n18
Friedman juggernaut,
canons of revolutionary change, 713-714
Friedman, Milton,
acquired diverse knowledge, 146-151, 155-160, 741
a paradox, 171
as economic Bayesian, 122, 740
as heretic, 266
a summary, 687-688
at Hoover Institution, 188-189
backed away from *modus ponens*, 719-720
background of, 116-119, 148-151, 159, 160
banking, 182
birth of, 18
British tradition, 31-32,
Chilean involvement, 327, 325-333
Chilean/Nobel period, 344-362, 35-37
Chile lecture topics, 340
coauthored dissertation, 382 n26

combined strands of thought, 139, 159, 160,
comparison with Disraeli, 171-172
conflicting influences, 460
conflicts with Harvard, 282
controversies, list of, 140, 149, 161
counter to convention, 702
cultural influence, 18-21
differences vis-à-vis others, 278
diverse education, xii, 20, 160
dominance at Chicago, 706-707
effective onslaught, 600
events of 1974, 191-192, 205-206
explicit reference to, 562, 577, 599, 600, 602, 604-605
facts and theory, 735
features of writings, 339
first open lecture, 779 n4
formative years, 5, 139
going public, 5, 26-27
Goldwater campaign, 473, 530, 569
hallmark of Chicago, 282
hallmark of, 758-759
Hotelling, SRG, NBER, 155-159
influences, 71, 77, 148-149
indirect approach, 110, 112, 134
influence on Reagan presidency, 687-688
influence on antitrust, 278, 309
intellectual minority, 172
interest in exercise, 143
interrelated accomplishments, 748-749
juxtaposed with others, 60-62
Kemp, A., on strands of influence, 178, 710
language style vs Keynes, 762 n11
Marshall, view of, 56-57, 61
masterful peddler, 25
mathematical statistician, 148-149, 155-159
mid-1970s period, 191, 350-362
migration of parents, 16-17
moral courage, 19
NBER theorist, 153-154, 155
on imperfect competition, 307
on fundamental value, 476
open economy, 322-323
optimistic outlook, 496-497, 514
outsider, 164, 698, 702, 731-732
overview of policy, theory, methods, 758-760
public visibility of, 710-711
putting act together, 724-725
qualities of, 203
radical right, 171
read Marshall differently, 202, 208, 229
receipt of Nobel prize, 184-186
recognition, 180-189

844

reliance on, good thing, 301
Rosten's portrait of, 771-772 n9 and n16
Rudgers days, 143-144
saw big picture, 710
sequential analysis, 382 n53
shifts attention to money, 209-210
simplicity of argument, 476
simplicity of statements, 22
spokesman for freedom, 171
style, personal, 707-711, 771-772 n9 and n16
summary of impact, 687-688
system of thought, 708
teaching, research and recognition, 180-189
"The Ghost of Montague Norman," 588
thrived on personal contact, 178
views in antitrust writings, 318-32 178, 182
Wallis and, 184-189
workshop in money and banking, 182
years of going public, 141
(see comparisons; controversy; dynamics; economic Bayesian; "empirical scientist;" famous 1953 essay; freedom; free enterprise; Friedman, David; Friedman's ideas; Friedman's ideas in London; Friedman's uses of statistical methods; indirect approach; indirect method; individualism, institutional, instrumentalism; "laissez faire;" long run; Mitchell, Wesley Clair; monetarism; monetary economics; Popper, Karl; primal equation; simplicity; Walrasian approach)

Friedman quotations,
  absolute truth, 135, 744
  advancing scientific understanding, 121
  bureaucratic inertia, 505
  "mistakes of good men," 344
  on fundamental value, 476
  on people who have freedom, 471
  on scientific understanding, 109
  other people's money, 344
  "political crystal ball," 438-439
  purpose of statistical analysis, 135

Friedman, Rose
  (see Director, Rose)

Friedman, Stigler and Wallis,
  as a group, 161, 162
  (see SRG; Stigler, George; Wallis, Allen)

Friedman's adjustments for episodes, 655, 658, 791 n65, 751-752
  data adjustments, 750-751
  Huhne on H/E, 738-740

statistical errors and episodic change, 751
  (see episodic change)
Friedman's advocacy of ideas,
  contrast with Adam Smith, 474
  masterful peddler, 474
Friedman's career,
  early hints of interest, 724, 731
  outcome of bold moves, 731
Friedman's Chicago, 291-293
  success of, 283
Friedman's consumption function, 61, 441-443, 825-829
  welfare economics, etc. 459
  (see great ratios of economics)
Friedman's controversies—mid-1970s, tied to, 209
Friedman's economics,
  aggregation and time, 728-731
  anticipation of, 295
  antidote and new direction, 574
  arrival in London, 528
  as broad view, 276
  as dynamic, 442-443
  as empirically oriented science, 491
  "as if" methodology, 131, 719
  as policy oriented science, 132
  as political/empirical oriented, 276
  as system of analysis, 698-699
  attributes of, 133, 278, 728-731
  awareness of problems (as listed), 132
  background of, 116-119, 148-151, 159, 160
  Chile lecture topics, 340
  combined strands of thought, 139, 159, 160
  comprehensive, most, 639-640
  consumption function, 61, 441-443
  cycles, trends and episodes, 443
  early hints about, 724-725
  essay on Mitchell, 180-181
  evolutionary change, 278, 321-322
  facts and theory, 735
  features of, 491, 495, 496, 497, 502, 508, 512-514
  features of writings, 339
  formative years, 139
  Friedman's law, 567, 650-651, 731
  hallmark of, 758-759
  holistic system, 119, 139, 160
  "holistic" view, 295
  impact, a summary of, 687-688
  indirect approach, 110, 112, 134
  interrelated parts, 636-637, 737, 748-749
  interrelated systems, 110, 121, 132
  isolated events, 120-121
  juxtaposed with others, 60-62

Kuznets and GNP data, 210 49, 155-159
liquidity preference, 61, 443-448, 744-748
meets Boland's criteria, 727-731
methodological underpinnings, 133
misinterpretation of, 35-36
modus tollens, 725-726
monetary part, 636-637
monopoly and evolution, 321-322
open economy, 322-323
own underpinnings, 735
package, whole, 636-637
parts, interrelated, 636-638
permanent income and competition, 637-638
philosophical roots, 107, 116-119
policy orientation, 112, 115-116
policy, theory, methods—an overview, 758-760
price and monetary theory, 294
probability and, 68-71
production and distribution, 637
Reagan, Regan and Sprinkel, 759
theory of price, 294
three interrelated parts, 737, 748-749
total system of thought, 178, 182
unconditional predictions, 123
views in antitrust writings, 318-321, 324
years of going public, 141

Friedman's education,
extraordinary, 159, 160
intellectual life, 162

Friedman's essay on Mitchell, anticipates dissertations, 181

Friedman's formative years, aspects of background converge, 210

Friedman's ideas in London,
effective onslaught, 600
explicit reference to, 562, 577, 599, 600, 602
first open lecture, 779 n4
first Wincott lecture, 574, 779 n4
inflation as a tax, 584
intrusion of, 541, 573, 575, 628
Johnson, Harry, 598
Kaldor on, 527, 541, 562-563, 599
monetarist at Treasury post, 624
Radcliffe Report vs, 600
Times coverage, 573
TV series, 588, 780, n51
unwinding government, 579-580, 584-589
Walters connection, 575, 597, 600, 624
(see monetarist ties in U.S.; Thatcher government)

Friedman's Jewish connection,
cultural influences, 18-21
paradoxes, two, 162, 166-172
(see Jew; Judaism)

Friedman's law,
statement of, 567, 650-651, 731

Friedman's monetarism,
Reagan, Regan and Sprinkel, 759
(see monetarism, Friedman's)

Friedman's Nobel prize,
announcement of, 354
controversy over, 356-362
"Down with Capitalism," 344, 364
first word of, 354-355

Friedman's revolution, 418, 731-733
consumption function, 441-443
liquidity preference, 443-448
(see freedom; monetary revolution)

Friedman's rule,
as monetary standard, 412, 535, 548-549
Burns's discussion of, 241
institutions vs men, 124
monetary discipline, 649-653
monetary rule, 234, 260
placing Fed under Treasury, 791 n112
restatement, 649-650, 688
statement of, 412
time frame of, 549
variations of, 549

Friedman's style,
"blind leading the blind," 165
Daniel in the lion's den, 164
language style, 762 n11
personal style, 707-711

Friedman's theory,
no centerpiece, 41
(see monetarism, Friedman's)

Friedman's uses of statistical methods,
data adjustments, 750
distinguishable features, 741-744
evolution of, 748-755
identifying a demand curve, 743
indirect method, 741
late attention to, 736
"phase averaging," "triplet," 741, 750, 756
purpose of statistical analysis, 288, 397 n22, 507, 693-695, 744
statistical tests, 744
vs Knight's "honor among scientists," 464
(see Friedman's adjustment for episodes; Friedman's economics; *Guardian* articles; monetarism, Friedman's; Leamer problem; statistical methods, uses of)

Friedman/Burns, 1974 episode, outline of, 239-240

full employment,

846   U-Turn

deficits rationalized, 545
  in expansion of 1906s, 217, 219
  Keynesian = 4 percent unemployment, 237
  maintenance of, 526
  resolute position by government, 530
future research,
  interest rate, real, 535, 809-812, 815-817
  the great constants, 727-731
  topics for, 300, 530, 760
  sources of growth(?), 553-554, 562, 588-589, 596, 608, 614

G

Galbraith, John Kenneth,
  and Friedman's popular writings, 264-265
  BBC's TV series, 264
  data on, 194-204
  defrocking of Friedman, 240, 264-269
  entry in prominent ways, 140
  Great Crash, 201
  influence on K-J, 231
  influential phrase, 264
  Joan Robinson and, 196, 229
  M-regime, monetarism, 140
  New Industrial State, 435
  "of the chosen," 197
  on First Amendment, 391 n34
  on Friedman, 201
  on power, ix, 363
  practicing martial art, 264-269
  price controls, 140
  price czar, 197-199, 233
  purpose, 203
  qualities shared with Friedman, 203
  sketch of, 200
  social values, 463, 507
  subject of money, 265-266
  symbol of transition, 140
  Warburg chair, 201
  (see Robinson, Joan)
Galbraith quotations,
  a job and no visible work, 200
  claim to worldly position, 196
  economist without a price system, 199
  history of money, 266, 274
  Japanese attack, 197
  salvation in witchcraft, 240, 265
  sudden loss of power, 199
  "well modulated voice"/"polished table," 267
  wisdom by appointment, 206
general equilibrium analysis,
  story of, 706
  (see equilibrium; individualism, atomistic; Walrasian equations)

General Theory, Keynes's, as specific theory, 58, 59
  backdrop of, 526
  roots to, 58-60
  (see "rigid wages")
German reparations payments,
  problem of in 1920s, 424
  (see Schacht, Hjalmar)
GNP potential,
  natural rate of unemployment and, 214
gold,
  artificiality of, 417
  "barbarous relic," 417
  Commission, 642
  Commission report, 548-549, 791 n112
  Keynes on gold issue, 420
  post WW II, U.S., 427-428
  price and hedge against dollar, 648
  (see Friedman's rule; gold-flows mechanism)
gold-flows mechanism,
  discipline of, 413
  dispersement of power, 62
  financial unification, 549-550
  substance of, 413
gold, ownership of,
  by U.S. citizens, 416
gold standard,
  regulation of trade, 11-12
  pre-WW I stability, 412-417, 434
  Waterloo to WW I, 11-12
Goldwater, Barry,
  "extremism in defense of liberty," 473, 484
  intellectual homogeneity, 26
  nomination speech, 530
  presidential campaign, 5, 26, 149
Goldwater campaign, 149,
  antecedents to Reagan presidency, 473
  Friedman and Reagan, 631, 676, 789 n3
  Friedman on '64 election, 766 n66, 767 n74
Goodhart, Charles, 540, 544, 552, 553, 736-737, 748
government,
  accommodation of wage and price changes, 176
  as employer of last resort, 214, 216
  as the problem, 633
  defense as percent of GNP, 234, 238
  defense spending, 238, 731 n7
  evolutionary change and, 322-323
  goal of restricting growth, 534, 675, 677, 679, 690
  "government planning," 172

individual and, 304
Keynes's belief in, 438-439
market and, 479-484
nonproductive jobs and, 219, 221
political cures and, 301
rigidity vs flexibility, 628
senior civil servants, 592, 615, 634, 781 n61
state financed campaign funds, 483
"Vietnam dividend," 238
Walter's appointment, 598-599
(see advocacy; British government; long run/short run political view; political business cycle; voting)
government budget constraint,
central bank and deficits, 567
crowding in and out, 271-272
definition of, 217
fiscal policy and, 259
Friedman's arguments, 674
Friedman's law and, 567
independence of Fed and 217-218
Lord Kaldor and, 218
nullifying fiscal policy, 218
perspective on, 689
government, democratic,
belief in civil servants, 438
Carter administration, 433, 439
"educated Bourgeoisie," 434
"fine tuning," 433
overextended, 434-435, 438
political market place, 449-452
(see political business cycle)
government, growth of, 219, 221
aggregate of special interest, 221
deficits and monetary policy, 568
government, reducing size of as goal,
Friedman and Reagan, 675, 677, 679
goal/policy, 675, 677
government, role of,
changes concerning it, 514-515
"regulated economic malfunctioning," 473
government, unwinding of, 191, 221-228, 579-580, 596, 604
announcement in advance, 226
British case, 226-228
Friedman and Thatcher, 614
"hard slog," 587
Galbraith to economic freedom, 225
gradualism vs shock, 225-227
"Light Brigade," poem, 607, 783 n95
shock treatment or gradual, 585
steps in, 225
transition imperfect, 688
turn in monetary policy, 648-670

Gramm, W. Phil, 675, 790 n14
"Boll Weevils," 638
Gramm-Rudman bill, 514, 682
kicked in, 679
Great Depression, 426-427, 431-432
as failure of capitalism, 286
failure of policy, 286
influence of, 702
role of monetary policy downplayed, 217
turning points, 285
views on cause, 23
great ratios of economics, 524
attention to, 409
Greenspan, Alan,
Crash of 1987, 686
on Burns, 256-257
on controlling money stock, 263
Reagan supporter, 790 n13
sketch of, 200
growth, economic,
recognized by Marshall, 55
without recession, 206-207
growth, real, sources of,
long-run/institutional factors, 553-554, 562, 588-589, 596, 608, 614
saving-to-income ratio, 805-808, 826-830
"Victorian values," 615
Guardian articles, 738-741
"Emperor of International Monetarism," 739

H
Hadjimichalahis, Michael, 664
Hansen, Alvin, 427, 436
at Harvard, 198-199
stagnation thesis, 762 n58
Harberger, Arnold, 333, 362
Nobel letter on Friedman, 358
on Chilean economy, 348-349
"hard slog," 587
(see government, unwinding of)
Harrod, Sir Roy, 448-449
on Friedman, 25
Hayek, Friedrich von, 585, 780 n51
basic propositions to work, 176-177
comparison with Friedman, 176
data on, 175-180
liberty, Thatcher government, 140
money area work, 175
organized Mont Pelerin Society, 162
rivalry with Keynes, 175
(see Mont Pelerin Society)

"helicopter money," 446
Heller, Walter,
  as a Keynesian, 140
  data on, 205-208
  events of 1974, 191-192, 205, 206
  full employment surplus, 237
  on Phillips curve, 214
  sketch of, 200
  Wisconsin and, 165, 205
  Wisconsin/Friedman incident, 165
Hendry, David and Ericsson, Neil,
  charges against F/S, 736-737
  econometric approach vs Friedman, 755-758
  Guardian articles, 737-741
Hicks, Sir John,
  events of 1974, 205
  (see Hicks's drama)
Hicks's drama, 412-413
"hidden agenda" in economics,
  definition of, 703
  methodologist and, 703
  neoclassical economics and, 714-715
Hildebrand, George,
  stereotyped, 303
historical determinism,
  denied in Chile, 330
  Moynihan on, 332-333, 364
  (see historicism)
historical prophecies,
  as found in Marx and Mill, 122
historicism (also historical or sociological determinism), 333, 573, 779 n2
  Burns on Marx, 467
  capitalist mode of
    organization, 489
  Friedman reference to, 779 n2
  Marx, Hegel, Mill, Compte, Plato, 779 n2
  Marxist-Leninist state, 333
  prophecy, dream of, 779 n2
  questioned by Friedman, 467-468, 472
history, aberration in, 411, 452-453
  pre-WW I stability, 435
history, conspiracy theory of, 124
  Friedman, 170
  Popper, 124
  (see historical prophecies)
Hobson, John A., 284, 493
homogeneous product axiom,
  concerning the perfect market, 125
  imperfect competition, 127-128
  (see axioms)
homogeneous product,
  key axiom, 194, 202, 208, 229, 307

notion of an industry, 307
  (see product differentiation)
Hotelling, Harold, 731-732
  at Columbia, 69, 77, 138, 148, 159
  SRG, 157
Hotelling's line, 409-410, 614
  capitalist ethic, 504
  code words of the left, 172
  East European type economy, 606, 613
  economic ideas and, 627
  Friedman vs Samuelson, 486-490
  ideological shifts, 514
  "muddle of the middle," 627
  muddle of the synthesis, 274
  parlor socialist, 171
  polarization of parties, 604, 616
  political left and right, 409-410
  SDP centrist movement, 603, 616-617
  Thatcher's need for "centrist," 577
  Thatcher's 1983 elections and, 622-623
  Thatcher's Tories to right, 617
  (see capitalist ethic; freedom; middle road; political left, right; socialist ethic)
Hume, David,
  British tradition and, 38
  empirical method, 37
  gold flows, 413-416
  Smith and, 37, 41-45
  quantity theory of money, 139, 413-416
hypothesis,
  definition, 21
  purpose of theory, 108
  relation to policy, 123-124
  speculative method, 110
  (see regularities; stable relationship)
hypothesis, fruitful,
  empirical, 33, 41
  essentially an abstraction, 202
  (see regularities; stable relationship)
hypothesis testing,
  persuasion and debate, 486
  (see persuasion)

I

i-regime, 452-453
  and fiscal policy, 258
  conditions of '30s and fiscal policy, 258
  control via bank rate, 24
  independence of Fed, 217
  in Keynes's work, 59
  interest rate fungible, 218
  Keynes's legacy, 217
  Lord Croham on i control, 562
  pegged-rate effort, 217
  pro-cyclical policy, 212, 215, 220

tight money, 258
Treas./Fed accord, 260
(compare with monetarism)

i-regime to M-regime, 61
Bank of England, 552-558, 626-627
central bank independence,
 issue of, 568, 648
differences of opinion,
 reconciliation of, 744, 758
Fed's movement, 230
government budget constraint, 567-568
"hard slog," 613-616
ideal not reality, 615
ideas in summary, 688
lags in adjustment, 558
power theories vs money, 197-230
source of shift, 686
transition, 220-222, 230, 447-448, 570-571, 602-613, 626-627
transition imperfect, 688
velocity/interest-rate association, 655
(see monetarism; M-regime)

ideal as enemy of the good,
 antitrust law and, 319

ideas,
 in political process, 528
 power of in Mill, 368 n55
 pre-WW I and 1980s, 411-412, 452-453
 (see British tradition; Friedman, M;
  Friedman's economics; Friedman's
  ideas in London; Keynes, J.M.)

ideas, acceptance of,
 as viewed by Mill, 51
 crisis, ix
 resistance to, 33
 vacuum of power needed for, ix

ideas, Friedman's,
 Reagan and Thatcher, 604
 ten in relation to political action, 532-536
 Walters's emphasis, 600
 (see Friedman's economics; Friedman's
  ideas in London)

identification problem, money demand, 210

ideology,
 antitrust and, 319
 in differences of opinion, 396 n22

imperfect competition,
 testing of, 127-128
 theory of, 127-128
 the two Cambridges, 306-307
 (see homogeneous product; monopolistic
  competition)

income, distribution of,
 market demand and, 283-284, 815-817
 (see distribution of income)

income, real,
 GNP (constant dollars), 676
 (see growth, real)

income, redistribution,
 monetary effects and, 831-832
 (see trickle-up and trickle-down theory)

income tax, negative, 409, 518-522
 initial advancement, 500-502
 role of, 495

income tax, progressive,
 loopholes and all, 511
 Samuelson and Friedman, 488
 social mobility, 512
 tax on becoming wealthy, 510, 515
 thinking behind, 408, 459, 493-495
 (see special interests)

income tax,
 Chicago egalitarian, 287, 289-290
 Friedman's flat tax, 290
 withholding of income at source, 504-505
 (see flat-rate tax; income tax, negative;
  income tax, progressive)

indexation,
 comprehensive use of escalator clause, 223
 of income tax, 230
 overall, 222-225
 wage contracts, 191

indirect approach,
 Friedman's, 110, 112, 134-135

indirect method,
 central features, 542
 contrast with Laidler, 560-561, 776 n69

individual, the,
 demands on, 336-337
 (see open society)

individualism,
 cultural conditioning and, 465
 cultural heterogeneity and, 476
 false individualism, 477
 Junta government's principles, 342
 "revival of," 592
 Robinson Crusoe economics, 457-458, 476, 490
 stress/future, 336-337
 (see "free market"; individual)

individualism, atomistic,
 equilibrium and, 721-723
 methodological, 721
 neoclassical economics, 701
 (see individualism, institutional)

individualism, institutional, 537, 647
 choice and societal influence, 701
 Friedman and, 701, 730, 732
 (see individualism, atomistic)

induction,
belief in empiricism, 378 n67
problem of, 34, 125, 378 n16
induction, problem of, 715-716, 720
accepting hypothesis a matter of
judgement, 129
avoided by Friedman, 129, 134-135
conventionalism and, 720
Friedman and, 720
Friedman's awareness, 132
inductive logic,
unsatisfactory theory, 126
(see induction, problem of)
industrial revolution,
financial markets and, 308
inflation,
as a tax, 584
Chile, 329
Friedman's theory as antidote, 229
monetary accommodation, 530
money and features of, 339
power theory of, 208, 209, 229, 545-546
shift from production, 565
shock treatment for, 339-340, 346, 348-349, 353-354, 363
"suitcase money," 610
wage induced, 429
(see wages)
inflation, causes of,
price indexes vs monetary
accommodation, 790-791 n52
inflation, power theories vs monetary,
accommodation, 790-791 n52
price indexes and monetary discipline,
652, 790-791 n52
(see Friedman's law; monetary policy;
monetary discipline)
inflation rate,
controlled by monetary authority, 743
inflationary expectations,
structural shift, 446-447
(see "New York's revenge")
inflationary recession,
Keynesian policy and, 192
Institute of Economic Affairs (IEA),
contact with Friedman, 573
role of, 528
institutional economics,
Commons and Mitchell, 163-164
(see Veblen, Thorstein)
instrumentalism,
Friedman's variant, 34, 114-115, 133-134

theories, instruments of prediction, 130-131, 133
instrumentalist school,
Dewey and Friedman, 134-135
tie to Dewey, 134
intellectuals, bias of,
double standard, 347
socialist trend, 332-333
(see double standard; historical
determinism)
interest rate, real, 809-812
definition of, 32
Reagan/Mondale debate, 809
tax and monetary powers of the state, 212-213, 815-817
tax cuts and, 815-816
(see liquidity preference with
overshooting)
interest rate and expected inflation,
Fisher equation, 652-655
interest rate analysis,
control mechanism, in relation to, 655
Fisher equation, 652-653
Thatcher/Reagan positions, 535
interest rate(s),
chasing of, 567
control of, 535, 536-537, 561-562
controlled by central bank, 535, 561-562
Fed's chasing of, 297-298
Fisher equation, 212
inelasticity of, 526
inflation-rate component, 616
observed without error, 261
pegged, 217
price of credit (not money), 557, 783 n79
Thatcher on inflation-rate component,
610
tied to expected inflation, 212-213
Treasury/Fed accord, 217
(see banking view of; interest rates and
expected inflation; interest rates; i-regime to M-regime; liquidity
preference with overshooting; "New
York's revenge")
International Monetary Fund, 427
interwatershed period,
aberration in history, 411, 452-453
(see Hicks's drama)
investment demand,
inelasticity of (def), 526
Iran/Contra episode, 632-633, 635, 677

J

Jew,

anti-market, 170
as merchants, 366 n19
banking tradition, 12-13, 166,
Bonaparte, Napoleon, 10-11
capitalism and, 386-387 n13 and n18, 704
Friedman on, 166-172
in economics, 19, 704
in finance, 366 n19, 367 n27
in trade, 366 n15
left wing causes, 167
liberalism, 10
market and freedom, the, 166
migration to U.S., 13-18, 705
nationhood, separate, 10-11
political equality, 167-168
settlement in U.S., 17-18
social consciousness of, 702
stereotype, 167, 171
success in finance, 12-13
(see usury)

Jew, paradox of,
free society, 166
20th century, 11

Jewish culture,
entry into economics, 19

Jewish history,
Americana, 9-27
Friedman's lecture and great migration, 16-17
Pale of Settlements, 14-16
relevance of, 4
tradition of scholarship, 144
(see Friedman's Jewish connections)

Johnson, Harry, 291
Friedman's Chicago, 291-292
U.K. and Friedman connection, 598-599

Johnson, Lyndon,
social programs, 234, 238

Jones, Homer, 138, 144

Joseph, Sir Keith (later Lord),
appointment by Thatcher, 577
at Friedman's '76 lecture, 580, 709
godfather to Thatcher, 575
industry department, 612
Walters's appointment, 598

Judaism,
hero type in, 19

K

Kaldor, Lord Nicolas,
causation, 730
causation controversy, 545
control of key variables, 550
monetary accommodation, 740
on Friedman's monetarism, 521, 541, 562-563
on Keynes and money, 445
on monetarism, long run, 562-565
on monetary revolution, 418
on Phillips Curve trade off, 563
on *The General Theory*, 429
on Walrasian model, 563-564
"The New Monetarism," 527, 599

Kane, Edward, 239, 255, 260, 261

Kaufman, Henry, 206

Kennedy-Johnson movement,
four fronts, 231

Keynes, John Neville, 116, 460

Keynes, John Maynard,
atmosphere of '20s, 419-425
Bloomsbury credentials, 417, 453
born a Roman, 26
Churchill and, 419, 422-423
compromise with Marx, 58
data on, 57-62
"Economic Consequences of Mr. Churchill," 419, 625
"educated Bourgeoisie," 434
faith in civil servants, 420-421
father, 57
features of his theory, 408
Friedman on, 551
i-regime, 420-421
managed currency, 417
monetary economist, 58
monetary revolution, 31
political and social atmosphere, 590, 780 n55
reactions in 1920s, 414-415, 417-423
Tract on Monetary Reform, 417-418, 551
unemployment, interest in, 58
(see *General Theory*, Keynes's; Keynesian revolution; Paris Peace Conference; socialism, British; *Treatise on Probability*)

Keynes's consumption function,
utility of income and, 408, 459, 493-495

Keynes's economics,
extended by Friedman, 456
output vs price adjustments, 447
(see labor)

Keynesian economics,
analysis of deterioration, 580-584
center of, 565
Chile lecture and, 341
crisis in, 205-206
events of 1974, 191-192, 205-206
expansion of the 1960s, 206-207, 217
Fed in 1920s, OMO, 286

market power theory of prices, 208, 209, 229, 545-546
  Reagan on, 678
  short run benefits, 215
  (see inflation; labor standard; Radcliffe Report)

Keynesian era, transition from,
  analysis of, 533-534
  Bank of England, difficulties, 552-558, 594
  "economics of joy," 533, 536, 638, 687
  Fed's control difficulties, 656-658
  Friedman's influence, summary of, 688
  "hard slog," 533, 536-537
  monetarist/supply-side recession, 659-664
  personalities, 537
  (see government, unwinding of)

Keynesian era, 23
  "consensus government," 578-579, 613
  dominance of Keynesian economics, 436-437
  Friedman's research and, 569
  government intrusion, 434
  in U.K., 611, 613
  Nixon devaluation of dollar, 231-232
  overview, 269-274
  rationalized deficits, 435
  shift in structure underlying inflationary expectations, 562, 564-565
  (see "New York's revenge")

Keynesian fiscal policy,
  Wallis on war effort, 383 n61

Keynesian pillows,
  (see consumption function; liquidity preference)

Keynesian revolution, 430-437
  failure of, 437-452, 454
  (see monetary revolution)

Keynesian thinking, 24
  (see i-regime)

Keynesian unemployment, rate of 4 percent, 232, 237
  as low rate, 234
  (see GNP potential)

Keynesians,
  aspects of deficits avoided, 441

Kissinger, Henry,
  Chilean upheavals, 328-330
  on "biased double standard," 346

Klamer, Arjo, 693-694, 715, 723

Knight, Frank,
  and Friedman, 147, 148, 152, 153, 161, 162
  anti-scientism, 463-464
  as leader at Chicago, 161, 162
  Ayers, Clarence and, 786 n35
  Buchanan's tie, 297
  Friedman's departure, 116, 118, 306
  Mont Pelerin Society, 173
  reaction to economics, 306, 459, 463
  risk and uncertainty, 722-723
  "Robinson Crusoe" economics, 457-458, 476
  persuasion as false argument, 486
  view of economics, 311
  Young Allan, 311
  (see "assumer science;" Buchanan, James)

Koopmans, Tjalling, 703, 706, 717
  Friedman and NBER critic, 129-130

Kuhn, Thomas,
  scientific revolution, nature of, 711-715

Kuznets, Simon, 361
  associate of Friedman, 98, 149
  role of, 99

Kuznets's findings, relation to consumption function, 441-442

L

labor,
  mobility of, 43, 49
  (see mobility, social)

Labour party in Britain, outgrowth of, 24
  rise in 1920s, 416, 419

labor standard,
  Hicks's Act III, 427-429

labor theory of value,
  as flaw in Marx's theory, 54, 507-508
  in *Das Kapital*, 54
  one hundred percent, 32
  Ricardo and Marx, 30, 37-38
  Stigler on Ricardo, 370 n8
  (see time preference for income)

labor unions,
  Chicago view, 290
  (see sticky prices)

Laffer, Arthur,
  data on, 641
  "economics of joy," 533, 536, 638, 687
  (see Laffer curve)

Laffer curve,
  analytical problems, 671
  elements of, 824-825
  "Friedmanesque" variant of, 821-833
  myth of reflows, 641
  myths of, 821
  1980 elections and, 670
  pre-1981 form, 670

reflows agrement, 638, 640, 721
Laidler, David,
   money analysis, not Friedman, 560-561, 776 n34
"laissez faire,"
   meaning of, 286, 460, 466-467
   vs free enterprise, 467
Langer, Oscar, 706
   at Chicago, 178, 289
Laughlin, J. Lawrence, 282
   on Mill, 52
Law of bureaucratic inertia,
   Friedman's statement of, 505
Law of one price,
   (see price, law of one)
leading time rate of change in the money stock,
   causation controversy, 736
   early controversy, 735-736
Leamer problem,
   Friedman and, 742, 750
   statement of, 741
left wing,
   attention to Chile, 346-348
   Chile, 327-330
   frustration over Chile, 332
   (see intellectuals, bias of; historical determinism; Marxist socialism)
Lehman Brothers, 12-13, 366-367 n20
   cotton/textile business, 12
   post-WW II relief, 200
Lerner, Abba, 151, 379 n19, 483, 795 n19, 813, 831
liberal,
   economic liberalism, 366, n6
   socialist liberalism, 367 n47
"liberalism,"
   Friedman on term, 470-471
Liberty, Statue of,
   Lazarus's poem, 18
Liebhofsky, H. H., 399 n104
Lilley, Peter, 437
   and Friedman's consumption function, 442
liquidity preference with overshooting, 745-748
   effects, order listed, 567
   Friedman and Reagan, 652-653
   idea, action on, 535
liquidity preference,
   idea in U.K., 600
   i-regime to M-regime, 208-221
   liquidity effect, 211
   overshooting, 212
   post-WW II thinking, 428
   shift in liquidity on world scale, 689
   Thatcher on interest rate, 610-611
   (see banking view of interest rates; inflationary expectations; velocity/interest rate association)
LMWK group,
   members of, 638
   Mundell, data on, 641-642
   return to goal, 642
   ties to Kemp-Roth, 640
logic,
   independent of interpretation, 130
   limits of, 129
   logical validity, not truth, 129
   purpose of, 128
   reversing mode of argument, 128-129
   (see conventionalists)
Logical Positivism, 107
   misidentified with Friedman, 109-111, 178
long run, trends of opinion,
   Friedman's interest, 475, 510
long run, political,
   Friedman and, 430, 449, 536
   "political crystal ball," 438-439
   political/economic summary, 688
   trends of opinion, 475, 438-439, 510
   (see "quick fix")
long run,
   Friedman and, 536
   Keynes vs Friedman, 475
"long run" as guide to affairs,
   "we are all dead," 417
   quantity theory equation, 417
long-run/short-run, equilibrium, etc., 563-564
   income, real, 553-554, 562
   (see equilibrium)
Lucas, Robert, 694, 716, 722
Lucas-Sargent RE, 716
   equilibrium and, 722
   Friedman/Schwartz on, 723
   Knight and, 722-723

M

M-regime,
   not rigid Friedman rule, 680
   Reagan orientation, 635, 687-689
   Washington and London, 61

854   U-Turn

(see Friedman's ideas in London;
    Friedman's monetarism; Friedman's
    rule)
macroeconomics,
    counterrevolution to, 573-574
Mao Tse-tung,
    China objective, 328-329
marginal analysis,
    rediscovery of calculus, 293-294
marginal product, payment according to,
    "pocket money society," 573
    (see capitalist ethic)
market,
    government and, 479-484
    morals and, 482, 495
    role of, 532
market behavior,
    roots in Jewish trade, 11
market power theory of prices,
    contrast to Friedman, 211
    Friedman's theory as antidote, 229
    inflation and the Keynesian economy, 208,
        209, 229
    Keynesian, 199, 208, 229
    no attention to money stock, 209
    (see Keynesian era; Phillips curve)
market structure(s),
    Bork on, 318
    competition, etc., 295-296
    definition of, 307
    detailed description, 310
    extremes and other cases, 309
Marshall, Alfred,
    conventions of his era, 701
    data on, 55-57
    different readings of, 56-57, 61, 202, 208,
        209
    drew on Mill, 31
    concept of a market, 34
    "engine of analysis," 229
    Friedman's interest, 56-57
    Friedman's reading, 118-119, 229
    Friedman's view, 56-57, 61
    mathematics background, 55
    orthodoxy which followed, 701
    perfect competition and, 308-309
    Principles of Economics, 56
    (see Cambridge style; Marshall's
        economics; neoclassical economics)
market system,
    evolutionary change and, 321-322
Marshall, Alfred, Friedman's reading, 118-
    119
    price theoretic tie to M, 211, 229

Marshall's economics,
    price adjustments in, 58
    price adjustments vs output, 447
Marshall's technique,
    appropriate to problem, 313
Marshallian demand curve,
    Friedman's tie between statics and
        dynamics, 118
    Friedman's treatment, 209, 289
Marshallian industries,
    vs product differentiation, 312-313
Marx and Engels,
    cotton in Alabama, 12
    cotton/textile business, 12
Marx, Karl,
    British tradition and, 38
    Das Kapital, writing of, 53-54
    data on, 52-53
    distribution of income, 493, 503
    Highgate cemetery, 573
    history, theory of, 30, 32, 54, 55
    labor theory of value, 493, 496-497, 507
        (compare pp. 507-508)
    Manchester as model, 508
    reasons for inclusion, 39
    revolution against
        capitalism, 38
    revolution in Russia, 55
    (see historicism; labor theory of value;
        Marxist socialism; socialist ethic)
Marxist and socialist movement,
    Jews in, 168-169
Marxist socialism,
    Chile, 327-331
    Cuba, 329
    objective, 329
    (see historical determinism)
mathematical elegance,
    Mill on, 51
mathematics in economics,
    equation systems, 55-57
    growth, 55
    Marshall, 55-57
Mayer, Thomas, 540, 544
McKinney, John, 460-461, 482, 486
mechanical apparatus,
    Keynesian, 82-84, 194-195, 141-448, 637-
        638, 649-652, 745-747
    Marshallian tie to velocity equation, 650,
        747-748, 759
    (see Slutsky equation)
Meese, Edwin, 634
meritocracy,
    based on merit, 204

(compare aristocracy)
method, indirect, 541-544
  approach, 77-82
  contrast with Laidler, 560-561
  examples, 82-84
methodology in economics,
  unpopular, gains visibility, 703
micro management of macro policy, 264
  no scope for, 562-563
  (see Burns, Arthur)
middle road,
  Keynes as compromise, 58
  socialist liberalism, 367, n47
  (see Hotelling's line; big government, growth of)
Mill, John Stuart,
  data on, 50-52
  distribution, theory of, 496
  on impact of ideas, 368 n55
  science in economics, 30
  style of writing, 31, 52
  working-class movements, 56
Miller, James C.,
  physician's code, 686
minimum wage,
  Friedman on, 498-500, 519, 771 n16
  means of subsistence and, 503
minority freedom, 474, 481-482
  majority action and, 484
  (see power, dispersion of; freedom)
Mitchell, Wesley Clair,
  early days at Chicago, 133-134, 181
  Friedman's essay on, 152, 154, 180-181
  Friedman tie, whole view, 277-278, 282
  grand design for research, 153-155
  relevance of position to normative economics, 112, 123, 132, 153
  Veblen/Dewey connection, 181
  Veblen, Dewey, Friedman, 282
  Veblen's intellectual heir, 181, 196
  (see Burns, Arthur; "empirical scientist")
Mitchell's NBER research,
  end of, 539
mobility, social/economic,
  "fair social progress," 342
  mobility of labor, 43, 49
  social change, 337
  teaching slave to reason, 337
  (see consumption function, Friedman's; income distribution)
models, big,
  adding detail, 114, 121, 132
  choosing between, 115-116
modus ponens (axioms),
  Friedman's shift of emphasis, 278
  Friedman's view, 130
  Koopman's interpretation, 130
  truth of assumptions, 128
modus tollens
  falsity of conclusion, 128
  reverse logic, 34
monetarism,
  catalytic event, 139, 146
  dissertations under Friedman, 155
  encompassing nature of, 139
  Kaldor on, 527, 541
  major works at NBER, 140
  not politically neutral, 566, 569
  opposition to, 541
  swings long vs long run, 547, 562-563
  use of term, 139
  word as a label, 529, 762 n3
  (see money, quantity theory of)
monetarism, Friedman's,
  attributes of, 60-62
  defined, 229
  emergence of, 209-211
  features embraced by, 211, 229
  (see M-regime)
monetarist economics,
  leader of, 527
  (see Friedman's economics)
monetarist ties in U.S.,
  Sprinkel, 634
  (see Greenspan, Allan; Friedman's ideas in London)
monetary accommodation,
  as "quick fix," 608, 616
  further statement of, 651
  public sector borrowing requirement, 593, 608
  (compare with Friedman's rule)
  (see political business cycle)
monetary analysis,
  integration of, 30-32
  revolution of 20th century, 60
  Ricardo's work, 48-49
  separate from production, 30, 48, 119
  (see dynamics; Keynes, J.M., and Friedman, M.)
monetary economics,
  Hayek on Keynes, 178-179
  Hayek's work, 175-176
  Keynes's interest, 57-58
  money and production, separate, 30, 48, 179

(see Friedman, M.; Keynes, J.M.;
    monetary theory; production and
    money)
monetary economy,
    relation to underground economy, 533
    (compare underground economy)
Monetary History,
    controversy over, 539
    Crash of 1929, 424-425, 539
monetary policy in the U.K.,
    British connection, 539-571
    "corset," 593-594, 615
    Friedman and, 562, 577, 599, 600, 602,
        604-605, 779 n4
    "Ghost of Montague Norman," 588
    money growth in 1980, 782 n76
    PSBR, 593, 608
    (see monetary accommodation)
monetary policy,
    accommodation and episodes, 751
    accommodative, 545, 574, 644, 648, 651,
        687
    deficit and tax matters interrelated, 635
    destabilizing force, 529-530
    discretionary control, 550-551
    i-regime to M-regime, 145
    micro management, 216
    "monetary discipline," 669
    1981-1982 recession, 669-670
    powerful in effects, 629
    power of, 653
    power of U.S. disinflation, 644
    price index vs monetary discipline, 790-
        791 n52
    reasons for inattention to, 635
    topics bearing on '81 turn, 648, 790 n47
    (see Friedman's rule; inflation; interest
        rates, control of; monetary policy in the
        U.K.; money and credit aggregates; M-
        regime)
monetary revolution,
    British connection, 539-571
    financial trappings, 35
    Friedman and, 562, 577, 599, 600, 602,
        604-605, 779 n4
    "Ghost of Montague Norman," 588
    in economics, 418
    in Kuhn sense, 711-714, 732
    Keynes and Friedman, 31, 408-409, 732
    Keynes's link to, 418, 445-446, 456
    two main crises, 408,
    (see Friedman Juggernaut; monetary
        theory)
monetary standard(s),
    gold, etc., 412-416
    inconsistent course for U.S., 427

key currency, 412
    (see gold-flows mechanism; labor
        standard)
monetary system,
    market's need for, 532, 569
monetary theory,
    price index and demand curve, 209
    price theoretic tie to M, 211, 229
    statement of motion, 409, 418
    theory of price and, 294-295
    (see Friedman, M.; Marshallian demand
        curve; monetary economics)
Monetary Trends,
    attention shifts to statistical methods, 540
    British connection, 539-571
    new contributions, 546-554
    past themes, 544-546
    (see primal equation; statistical methods)
monetary/fiscal policy mix,
    muddle of, 235-236
money,
    assets serving as, 569-570
    bonds and, 418
    credit distinct from, 557
    definition of, 526
    definition of, Keynes and Friedman, 654
    motives for holding, 418, 729, 776 n69
    motives, Keynes and
        Friedman, 729, 748
    satisfaction of wants, indirect, 478, 529,
        532
    transactions demand, 659
    (see monetary aggregates; money and
        credit aggregates; money demand;
        money stock; quantity theory
        equation(s); velocity of money)
money and credit aggregates,
    control of, 554-558
    estimating one aggregate from another,
        658, 673, 791 n65, 750-751
    money base, 556
    nominal stock, as controlled, 743
    stable relation adjustment for episodes,
        655, 658, 791 n65
    (see i-regime to M-regime)
money balances,
    measurement of turnover, 209-210
    (see money demand)
money demand,
    agents determine real stock, 743
    approach to identification problem, 543
    early post-WW II thinking, 428
    elasticity, old measure, 548
    income elasticity for, 548-549
    liquidity preference, overshooting, 567

Index   857

long swings vs long run, 547, 562-563
transactions, speculations, precautionary,
  58, 59, 418, 478, 529, 532, 748
(see liquidity preference; money; velocity
  of money)
money, finance and real-goods, interaction
  of, 417
money, price of,
  reciprocal of price level, 557
money, quantity theory of,
  Keynes in 1920s, 414-415, 417-423
(see "helicopter money"; quantity theory
  equation(s); money, velocity of)
money, study of,
  complexity of, 635
  not politically neutral, 569
money, velocity of,
  volatile variable, 417
(see money balances; money, motives for
  holding)
monopolistic competition, 311-313
(see imperfect competition)
monopoly,
  as one firm, 310
  problem of, 479-480
  technical, 479-480
  unlawful, 308
(see market structure)
Mont Pelerin Society,
  data on, 172-174
  first meeting, Popper et al., 117, 140, 162
Moynihan, Daniel
  Nixon White House, 232
  on socialist trend, 332-333
  welfare reform, 520-522
muddle of the middle,
  Nixon policy mix, 235-239, 272, 274
Muth, John, 716

N
nationalized industries,
  Thatcher government and, 586, 783 n100
(see "privatization")
natural order philosophy,
  Locke, John, 457
natural rate of unemployment,
  controversy, 215
  definition, 214
  Nixon CEA and Burns, 234
  rose in early '70s, 216
  variable rate, 263-264
  vs target rate, 433
(see GNP potential; unemployment)
"natural,"

use of term, 809
neighborhood effects, 402, n1
(see third party effects)
neoclassical economics,
  definition of, 293
  high value on agreement, 720
  omission of monetary disturbances, 526
  Patinkin, 715
  pre-WW I stability, 434
  Samuelson, 715
(see Marshall, Alfred; science, normal
  view of)
New Classical School's RE, not Friedman's,
  562
"New York's revenge," 447, 545, 653, 668
  change in structure, inflationary
    expectations, 562, 564, 565, 567
  combination of developments, 447
  stock market variant of, 685
Niehans, Jurg, 594
Niskanen, William, 439
Nixon administration,
  Friedman's ideas at the CEA, 234
  policy mix, 235-239, 272
  policy orientation, 232
  price controls, 236-237
Nixon White House,
  Friedman's welfare reform, 520
  "Now I am a Keynesian," 237
Nixon years,
  unprepared, 270
Nobel prize,
  criteria for award, 372 n1
  economics, 35
noblesse oblige, 204
normative economics,
  Mitchell, Wesley, 507
  relevance to positive economics, 507

O   1979
October 6 announcement, 555, 648-649,
  642, 669-670
  change in technique (not policy), 656, 658
  Friedman on, 262-263
  Greenspan on, 262-263
"oligopoly,"
  meaning of, 315
(see market structure)
open economy,
(see free trade)
open market operations,
  emergence of, 418
open society, the,

abstract, 336
   Socratic/Popperian/Friedmanian, 335-336
output and price adjustments, 530
   (see "rigid wages")

P

Pareto's criterion, 434
Pareto, Vilfredo,
   ideologue of fascism, 489
Paris Peace Conference,
   Jewish nationhood, 10-11
   Keynes, J.M., 57
"peer review,"
   Friedman on, 707-708
   Galbraith and, 193-194
   value placed on agreement, 720
perfect competition, theory of,
   Ricardo's work, 49
   (see perfect market)
perfect market, 194-197, 308-309
   (compare imperfect competition)
   (see homogeneous product axiom)
persuasion,
   clientele classes, 25
   Friedman's advocacy, 474
   Friedman's overpowering argument, 146
   Knight's conditioning, 461-464, 486
   open to religious groups, 502
   social values and, 204
   special role for, 482, 486
   Stigler on, 24-25
   (see advocacy; "conditioning"; power, conditioned)
persuasion, ideas and,
   Reagan presidency, 631
   Thatcher and Reagan, 604
   (see ideas, Friedman's)
Phillips curve,
   appendage to Keynesian economics, 195, 209
   counter argument, 547
   Friedman's depiction, 213-214
   initial depiction, 213-214
   Keynesian economics, 565
   Phillips, A.W., 213
   Thatcher on, 610-611
   Times paraphrase, 581-582
   trade off, 208
   trade off only temporary, 214
Pinochet, Augusto,
   Chilean Junta, 335
   economic performance, 348-350
   free-market policies, 337-338
   Friedman meeting, 346

planning,
   grand scheme of state, 415
planning, government,
   vs free society, 172
policy, ideal,
   enemy of the good, 35
political business cycle, 432, 438
   Gallop's rolodex, 616
   U.S. portrayal of, 616
   (see business cycle, political; government, democratic)
"political crystal ball," 438-439
   Friedman and the long run, 440
political economy,
   "capitalist apologetics," 457
   doubt about political cures, 301
   fading away of political concerns, 462-463
   Marshall's shift, 56
   the term, 276, 281, 434
   (see economics, non-political)
political left, right, 537-538
   "the enemy within," 538
   (see Hotelling's line)
political left,
   parlor socialist, 171
   (see Hotelling's line)
political views of economist,
   Friedman, Rose, 288
   normative economics, 288
Popper, Karl,
   Friedman tie, 107, 115, 117, 119-124, 173
positive economics,
   relation to normative, 378 n51
Posner, Richard, 293
poverty,
   Marshall's emphasis, 55-56
   war on, 219
power,
   coercion, 478-479, 491
   dispersion of, 415, 434, 477, 491
   the state and, 435
Power and Ideas,
   concept of persuasion, ix
   five extended themes, 704
   Friedman as instrument for the study, 698
   goals of, xii
   Jewish connection, 704-707
   non-political neutrality of economics, 410, 693, 698
   perspectives of, 892
   themes of, 692-698
   thesis, 279
   three perspectives, 701

(see monetary revolution; power, conditioned; uses of statistical methods to resolve differences of opinion)
power, conditioned,
  definition, ix
  Friedman, 21-26
  Galbraith, ix
  Keynes, ix, 25
  "power in the name of ideas," 627
  Stigler, 24-25
power, dispersion of, 415, 434, 491
  admits freedom, 477
  (see gold flows mechanism)
power of ideas,
  persuasion, 21-26
power, persuasive,
  Ricardo, 32, 40, 48
  (see ideas)
prediction,
  conditional and unconditional, 117, 119-120
  conditional, example of, 196
  (compare with assumptions)
  essay title, 36
  Friedman contrast to Knight, 118
  only useful function of statistician, 157
  testing for truth, 126, 135
  theory purpose, 34
  (see instrumentalism; unqualified predictions)
prediction, unconditional, example of, 215
price adjustments,
  Marshall's economics, 58
  (see Say's law of markets)
price controls,
  Baruch plan, 199
  Burns's flirtation, 263
  complex system of, 197-199, 208
  euphoric state, 197, 237
  Kaldor's position, 566
  Nixon White House, 221, 230
  (see Galbraith, J.K.)
price, law of one,
  statement of, 421-422
price theory,
  detailed description and, 310
  Friedman's Chicago teaching, 180, 182
  Friedman's economics and, 294-295
  law and economics, 316-323
  market structure and, 310-316
  monetary disturbances and relative prices, 563-564
  price system, markets, government, 177
  relation to price index, 118, 209
  statement of position, 119

(see market structure; Stigler, G.)
prices,
  consumer price index, 684
  U.S. in late 1920s, 424
primal equation, 79, 539, 541
  contrast with Laidler, 560-561
  Friedman's, 79, 541, 743, 744, 747, 753
  velocity of money and, 747, 753
  (see indirect method; money demand)
"privatization,"
  Britain British merchant banks, 624
  Friedman's answer, 781 n63
  nationalized industries, 613, 615, 624, 625
probability,
  analogy to random walk, 739-740
  delineation of schools via probability, 277
  distribution of income, relation to, 512-513
  evolutionary change, 321-322
  Friedman, "economic Bayesian," 740, 744
  random walk, 756-757
  Savage, Leonard, 68-70, 277
  testing one theory against another, 744
  "will o' the wisp," 754
  (see Bayesian learning; Knight, risk and uncertainty)
probability, personalistic, difference of opinion, 135
probability, theory of,
  Friedman and Savage, 32, 68-70, 507
product differentiation, as control over price, 310-312
production and money,
  Keynes's integration, 58, 59-60
  Ricardo's separation, 30, 48, 59
production, theory of,
  Mill and Marx, 30, 51
  separate from distribution, 30, 52
Proxmire, William,
  Friedman/Burns episode, 240-255
"public choice" economics, 490
  Buchanan et al., 297-301
  Knight's influence, 460
public finance,
  as science, 287
  Wicksell and Buchanan, 297
purchasing-power parity/exchange rate,
  exchange ratio and price level, 550-551
  law of one price, 421-423, 549-550

Q

quantity theory equation(s)
  before Keynes, 414
  Cambridge form, 417

implicit in *General Theory*, 418, 445
(see primal equation)
purchasing-power parity, 421
(see price, law of one)
quantity theory of money,
Friedman's preference, 139
Hume and, 38
(see Friedman's monetarism; monetarism; primal equation)
"quick fix,"
approach to the economy, 213
Carter and, 221, 632, 659-660
disregard of long run, 616
expedient to expedient, 606
Gallop's rolodex, 616
Keynesian policy, 213
Reagan's discussion of, 651-652
short-run Keynesian measures, 432
Thatcher on, 536
vs long run, 536
(see long-run/short run political view; Thatcher's resolute approach)
quotations,
(see Friedman quotations; Galbraith quotations; Thatcher quotations)

R

Radcliffe Committee,
thinking on money, 445, 447
Radcliffe Report, 565
contrast with Friedman, 600
radical left,
(see Hotelling's line; left wing)
radical right, 104,
(see Hotelling's line; right wing)
Rand Corporation, 303
Reagan and Roosevelt, 631, 789 n2
Reagan presidency,
achievements on economic front, 687-688
as symbol of strong economy, 683
Bork nomination, 309
distinct but partially over-lapping groups, 636-638
foreign funds inflow, 683-685
Friedman/Reagan, shared stances, 680-681
Friedman's influence, on deficits, 675, 677
Friedman's influence, summary, 687-688
Friedman's monetary influence, 670
future agenda, 687
ideological, 631, 633, 634, 696
"lame duck," period, 677-678
legal trends before, 320
monetary disinflation, 644, 648-670

organization, 633-634
record victory in '84, 675-676
revolutionary, 632-633, 687
revolutionary pattern of changes, 635-636
stock market boom, 683-686
(see Greenspan, Alan; Reagan's political umbrella; recovery from '81-'82 recession; Sprinkel, Beryl; "symbolic presidency")
Reagan, Ronald,
as redefining popularism, 633
beginnings and beyond, 646-648
dollar exchange rate, 626
Friedman analysis of interest rates, 653, 791 n56
Friedmanite, 639
Friedman/Reagan goal of freedom, 679
Gipper speech, 531
Goldwater campaign, 530-531, 631, 647, 791 n109
ideology, 537
individual freedom, 647
1964 television
presentation, 530-531
on exchange and stock markets, 535
on Keynesian theory, 678
personal charm, 648, 678
success, two sources for, 633
Thatcher and, 538, 626, 632-633
U.K. context, 604, 626
Reagan's political umbrella,
diverse groups under, 638
pragmatic tradition, 790 n13
tax and public choice
specialist, 790 n12
(see Gramm, Phil; LMWK; Stockman, David)
real rate of interest,
(see interest rate, real; time preference for income)
realitic (sic) theory, 696, 714
approach, 31-32, 696
theory, Cambridge style, 60, 696, 714
vs mathematical elegance, 31
vs pure theory, 418
(see Cambridge style)
recovery from 1981-1982 recession, 664-666
deficits, but not Keynesian, 665-666
GNP growth, 675-676
record performance, 675-676
Reder, Melvin, 282
Regan, Donald T.,
at Treasury and Chiefs of Staff, 634, 639
on econometric models, 645-646
regression analysis,

Index

regression equation, 41, 110, 121, 272
separation of effects error, 82, 751
simple method, 742, 752
(see econometrics; Leamer problem)

regularities, 35
(see stable relation)

research, future, 530
(see future research)

revolutionaries,
criteria for inclusion, 39-40

Ricardo, David,
bare-bone method, 496
corn laws, 497
data on, 45-49
labor theory of value, 496-497
margin of subsistence, 496
persuasion and corn laws, 32, 40, 48-49
style of writing, 47
writings of, 47

right wing,
Chile, 327
Heflin quote, 309
(see "biased double standard")

"rigid wages,"
government position, 530, 628
Keynes's wage units, 546
labor standard, 527, 529-530
rigidity in government vs private sector, 628
Thatcher and, 536
under Thatcher, 628-629
(see sticky prices; wage adjustments)

Robinson, Joan,
Galbraith and, 197, 229
price theory and, 197
the two Cambridges, 306-307

Roosevelt, Franklin D.,
Alvin Hansen's students, 436
New Deal, 426, 434

Rosten, Leo, vi, 771-772 n9 and n16
reference to Friedman, 495
quotes Oscar Wilde, 495

rules vs authority,
monetary rule, 215

Ruskin, John, 22, 284, 493
distribution of income, 284
socialist ethic, 78, 204

S

Samuelson, Paul,
as Friedman critic, 87-88, 90, 103, 131-132
as leading Keynesian, 84-87, 102-103
as neoclassicist, 91-92
as political advisor, 92
avoidance of empirical work, 93
blood in the streets, 773 n74
data on, 84-87
on discussion of methodology, 379 n72
on Jew as intellectual, 705
on Keynesian revolution, 92-93
roles of, 103-104
sources on ideological position, 91-92
tautological avoidance, 718-719
textbook, 92
the mixed economy, 487, 488, 522-523
vs Friedman, 486-490

Savage, Leonard ("Jimmy"), 486
association with Friedman, 160
as recalled by Friedman, 135
on Friedman's grand design, 160
SRG and background, 383 n60
SRG, influence on, 383 n60

saving to income ratio (s/y),
also consumption to income, 123
(see consumption function; great ratios)

Say's law of markets, 58, 195, 417, 637, 790 n10
Friedman vs Keynes's attack, 529, 805
price adjustments, 58
statement of, 195

Schacht, Hjalmar, 432-433
(see German reparations)

Schultz, George, 233

Schumpeter, Joseph,
Brittan on, 449
Burns on, 467-468
Samuelson on, 489

Schwartz, Anna,
Commission on gold, 548-549
Friedman's association with, 382 n48, 775 n1
Friedman-focus note, 737

science,
(see economics; science, social)

science in economics,
meaning of term, 32, 51
Mill's view of, 30, 51
natural order, 30, 51

science, normal view of,
"mopping up activity," 712
"puzzle-solving activity," 712, 732

science, social,
boundary between science/pseudo science, 720-721
enterprise built upon criticism, 721

(see neoclassical economics)
"second-best" condition,
  description of, 314
  set aside by Bork, 314-315
Selden, Richard, 301, 305
Shoup, Carl, 150-151
  Friedman's tie, 165
Silk, Leonard, 487, 506
  New York Times writer, 150-153
  "Old Time Religion," 470
  on Friedman, 382 n29
  on tax reform, 679
Simons, Henry, 286-288
  influence of, 152, 277
  Mont Pelerin Society, 173
  100 percent reserve proposal, 289
simplicity,
  analogy to Euclidian geometry, 502
  homogeneous workers, 493
    (compare human capital, p. 508)
  relevance of, 126
  Ricardo's method, 496
  (see axioms, homogeneous product; modus ponens; realitic (sic) approach)
simplification,
  Ricardo's simplification, 49
  versus detail in theory, 40, 49
  (see theory, purpose of)
Skidelsky, Robert, 434-439
Slutsky equation,
  Friedman and Marshallian demand curve, 118, 209, 377 n34
Smith, Adam,
  competition in, 308
  data on, 41-45
  invisible hand, 43
  Wealth of Nations, 10, 37, 42-43, 45, 46, 490, 526
social change,
  Plato's problem, 336
  (see open society)
Social Democratic Party,
  centrist movement, 603, 616-617
  gains from "hard slog," 616-617
  "patch of middle ground," 621
  Thatcher's '83 campaign and, 622
socialism, British,
  theoretical basis of, 780-781 n57
"social market economy,"
  use of term, 402
social mobility,
  Friedman and, 495
  Friedman's function, 409, 489
  Jewish history and, 20, 138, 171

Jews and, 171
live-to-work behavior, 502
vs equality, 512
(see mobility, social/economic)
social organization,
  culture, 11
  market behavior, 11
social values,
  competitive capitalism and, 170
  economic man and, 203
  economists and, 397-398 n22
  emphasis on 203,
  fundamental value, the, 280
  government as instrument, 229
  "In my father's house are many mansions," 170
  use of power and, 203-204
socialist ethic, 493-494, 504
  found in Ruskin, 55
  Ruskin and, 204
  stated in Marx, 55
society,
  open vs closed, 279
society, problems of,
  caused by good people, 124
Sombart, Warner, 704
  Friedman on, 386-387 n18
special interest,
  bundling together, 640, 687
  cost of, 515
  packaging of, 452-454, 473-474, 488, 515, 517
  pooling of, 452
  six-month window and, 631
  tax cuts and, 452
special interests, problem of, 593
Spencer, Herbert, 278
Sprinkel, Beryl,
  data on, 639
  monetarist tie, 634-635
  on Fed policy, 660-664
stable relation,
  and scientific understanding, 121
  focus on, 105, 108-109
  Friedman and, 35
stable relationship, search for,
  great ratios of economics, 743
  (see Friedman's adjustments for episodes; primal equation)
statistical methods,
  adding detail, 114, 132
  F/S use of, 540
  prevailing fashion, 121-122
  purpose of, 135, 744, 758

Index 863

relation to philosophy, 134-135
shift in controversy, 7
(see indirect method; regression analysis)
Statistical Research Group (SRG),
  data on, 155-159
  Wald's work with, 383 n60
statistical methods, uses of, 121-122
  effects, separation of, 82, 552, 561
  Friedman as mathematical statistician, 148-149, 155-159
  Friedman's practical relation to philosophy, 134
  reconciling differences of opinion, 288, 397 n22, 507, 693-695
  separation of effects, 82, 552, 561
  (see econometrics; indirect method; primal equation)
statistical tests,
  economic hypotheses and, 173
  Granger causality tests, 756
  Granger-Sims test, 736
  "true" test of a theory, 112-113
statistics,
  as reconciling differences, 288, 397 n22, 507, 693-695
  role of, 357
Stein, Herbert, 603-604
sticky prices (wages),
  downward adjustments and indexation, 223, 230
  Friedman tied to indexation, 230
  indexation of contracts, 191
  Keynesian theory and, 223
sticky wages,
  origin of notion, 191
  prices and, 195
  (compare with perfect market)
Stigler, George, 397 n13, 398 n44
  Friedman and, 293-297
  Friedman and price theory, 293-294, 312-313, 323-324
  Mont Pelerin Society, 173
  photo, 296
  role of axioms, 398 n69
stock market crash(es),
  liquidity crisis, 286
stock market, New York,
  crash of 1929, 424-425
  crash of 1987, 683-686
  differences between '29/'87, 686
  great booms, 683-684
  inflationary expectations reduced, 668-669
  (see deficits and the '87 crash)
Stockman, David,

data on, 642-646
ideologue, in-house, 639
initially pro "economics of joy" (reflected reflows argument), 687
initially separated money analysis from tax cut, 687
packaging special interest, 687
"pointman" on the budget, 634, 638, 687
"random elements," of history, 643-644
reflows argument, 643, 674, 687
sources of his dejection, 687
"trickle down" theory, 643, 818 n2
(see government, regulating size of; special interest, bundling together)
supply-side economics,
  anticipation of, 268-269, 274
  distinction to "demand management," 636
  enduring truth of, 638
  Evans on, 641
  fundamental underpinning, 533, 635
  ideas under label, 528, 533
  monetarist label in London only, 527, 541, 562, 781 n61
  policy mix, 236, 259
  policy timing and '81-'82 recession, 669-670
  steps in U.K. transition, 586-587
  truths of, 821
  (see Friedman's ideas in London; Reagan's political umbrella)
"symbolic presidency,"
  symbolism and meaning, 632

T

tax cut(s),
  analysis of, 802-819
  a reflows argument, 207
  effects dependent on monetary policy, 802
  expansion of the 1960s, 207
  Friedman's analysis of, 804-805
  Friedman's arguments, 673-674
  goals of, 533
  Heller and, 207, 208
  income, growth and consumption, 808
  in U.K. vs U.S., 596, 608
  Kemp-Roth, 670-675
  Kennedy, 218
  main ones, U.S., 671
  monetary analysis of, 804
  reflows concept, 674
  tax ratio, 1962-1964, 218
  "trickle-up," "trickle-down," 638
  (see flat-rate tax; tax reform; special interests trickle-up and trickle-down theory)
tax cuts, ceiling on marginal rates,

in U.K., 608
"tax expenditures,"
 Friedman on, 471
tax rates,
 marginal ceiling on, 671, 690
 (see flat-rate tax)
tax reform,
 flat-rate tax as, 680
 Reagan's, 675, 677, 679-683
 summary of, 690
taxes,
 bracket creep, 221
 constitutional amendment and, 475, 515-518
 income tax as drag, 208
 indexation of, 191, 221-225
 inflation's trap, 221, 225
 tax trap, 224-225
 (see income tax)
testing,
 competing statements, 132
 Galbraith and, 196
 Mitchell and NBER, 196
 one theory against another, 125
 prediction, 127-128, 132
 standards for, 125
 (see prediction)
Thatcher, Margaret,
 and "rigid wages," 536
 as "authoritarian schoolmaster," 620
 background, 576-578
 "centrist henchmen," 577
 Churchill and 1920s, 420-423, 430
 "conviction politician," 579
 early '60s, 530
 "enemy within," 538
 Friedman as "intellectual begetter," 588
 "Friedmanite believer," 590, 602
 Goldwater lines, 531
 monetarist economic policies, 602
 on economic/institutional factors, 553-554
 "pocket money society," 573
 polarization of left and right, 604, 617
 Reagan comparison, 538, 626, 632-633
 Samuelson on class struggle, 489
 Tobin on, 420
 unions and, 602-603, 625
 (see coalminers, Britain's; Thatcher's resolute approach)
Thatcher quotations,
 "conviction politician," 579
 on bad schools, 576
 "progressive consensus," 578
 "propagandist for a socialist society," 578
 on the quick fix, 606

truth as same old story, 606
Thatcher's 1983 elections,
 decline in "misery index," 622
 Falkland's episode, 619-621
 French experience, 617-619
 Friedman on Thatcher vs Mitterrand, 618
 ideological choice, 621-622
 people vs the government, 621
 returns for '79, '83, '87, 622
 song, "Maggie may," 621
 two key developments, 617
Thatcher's government,
 Walters's assessment, 628-629
Thatcher's resolute approach, 537, 622, 627
 conviction politician, 579
 "kamikaze trip," 607
 "Light Brigade," 607
 "power in the name of ideas," 627
 SDP and, 616
 "short-term trouble," 615
 vis-à-vis "muted threat," 621
 (see long-run/short-run, political view)
"Thatcherism," 538
the two Cambridges, 306-307
 (see monopolistic competition)
theorems and proofs, 98, 717-718
theory, meaning of term, 35
 revolutions in, 39-41
 Ricardo's simplification, 49, 797 n75
 simplification vs detail, 40, 78, 742
 (see hypothesis)
third party effects, 410, 467
 also neighborhood effects, 478-480
 externalities defined, 461
 (see neighborhood effects)
time,
 Boland on treatment of, 726-727
 Friedman's theory and, 726-727
 position and motion, 744-748
 primal equation and, 731
 psychological, 731, 742
 time rate of change, 79, 82-84, 146, 149, 210, 214-215, 443, 446, 542, 741
time preference for income,
 flaw in Marx's theory, 507-508
 (see interest rate, real)
time series, permanent and transitory components, 117
 Hotelling and, 155
 seeds of consumption function, 149
 (see business cycle; consumption function; liquidity preference)
Tobin, James,
 on Friedman at Yale, 709-710

Index 865

on indexation, 224
on Thatcher, 620-621
Tool, Mark, 511-512
trade unions,
  coal miners, 423
  incomes policies, 430
  Labor party, 416, 419
  (see coal miners, British; sticky wages)
Treatise on Probability,
  Keynes's early work, 57
  personalistic probability, 57
"trickle-up" and "trickle-down" theory, 812-816
  consumption function and, 813-817
  income distribution and, 813-817
  "Lerner justification," 813
  original usage, 818
  (see income redistribution)
trust, the,
  as financial arrangement, 308
  restraint of trade, 308
truth,
  as an empirical matter, 128
  as convention, 129
  axioms and, 312
  conventionalist search, 307
  Friedman on, 134-135
  meaning of, 135
  progress of knowledge, 124
  relation to scientific progress, 134
  search for, 133
  search for one true theory, 115
  testing for, 126
  (see testing)
truth in economics,
  detailed description vs abstraction, 202
  modus ponens, 82, 209
  problem of, 202
  (see statistical tests)
Tullock, Gordon,
  public choice economics, 298-301

U

U-Turn, 692
  Big, ix, 6
  concept of, 276
  in thinking and in policy, 276
  (see Hotelling's line)
UCLA, 301-305
uncertainty,
  money and, 418
  (see probability)
unconditional prediction,
  monetary example, 215

underground economy, 825-827
  "black economy," 629
  in U.K., 594
unemployment,
  Britain in 1920s, 416
  dependance on, 179
  futile effort at control, 24
  Hayek on Keynes, 178-179
  Keynes's equilibrium, 58
  Keynes's solution, temporary, 432
unemployment, natural rate,
  as variable rate, 582-583
  mobility of labor, 591-592
  (see natural rate of unemployment)
unqualified predictions,
  list of Friedman's work, 123
  (see predictions)
use of statistical methods,
  (see statistical methods, uses of)
"usury," 366 n19
  church's view, 166
utility analysis,
  Mill and Bentham, 50
  pleasure-pain calculus, 30, 50
utility maximization
  antecedents, 457
  utilitarians, 461
utility of income,
  declining marginal, 408, 459, 494-495, 507, (compare pp. 510-514)
  Hobson on, 493
  Keynes's consumption function, 408, 459, 493-494, 507

V

valid orthodoxy, 119
value added tax (VAT),
  Friedman's early role, 504
  Friedman and Reagan, 681
"value" as price, 458
value judgment,
  widely accepted, 463, 489-490
  (see capitalist ethic; conditioning)
values,
  morals and the market, 482, 491, 495
values, social, 463
  better ends, striving for, 464
  capitalist ethic, relation to, 509
  economic science and, 287
  Friedman on Galbraith, 288
  ends and means, 484-486
  imposing on others, 494, 502
  other people's money, 409
  (see individualism)

866 U-TURN

Veblen, Thorstein, 282, 704-705
  as institutionalist, 134
  at Chicago, 181
  Galbraith and, 196
  Mitchell and NBER, 196
  (see institutionalist school)
velocity of money,
  art work, 663
  as money demand, 543
  as random walk, 756-757
  as stable phenomenon, 753-754, 756-757
  great ratio of economics, 743
  inverse of income elasticity, 747-748
  post-WW II rise, 428
  Radcliffe Commission, 754
  two-country comparison, 256
  "will 'o the wisp," 754
  (see money demand)
velocity/interest-rate association,
  as stable relation, 655
  Fed's control mechanism, 655-656
Victoria, Queen,
  (see Disraeli, Benjamin)
Victorian values,
  pre-WW I stability, 435
  Thatcher and, 419
  (see Bloomsbury)
Vietnam dividend, defined, 238
Volcker, Paul
  appointment of, 648-649, 669
  as Under Secretary, 225
  early 1980 actions, 262
  Fed appointment, 262
  Reagan developments and, 670, 687
voluntary association,
  "agents" in a market, 533
  and freedom, 43, 476-477, 509-510
  market arrangements, 11
  monetary economy, 825
  (see exchange economy; wants, indirect satisfaction of)
von Neumann and Morgenstern, 705
voting,
  bare majority, 481
  essential consensus (super majority), 481, 482, 518
  market and, 481
  minority, 481
  self-denying ordinance, 481

W

wage adjustments,
  full employment and, 530, 533
  (see "rigid wages")

wages,
  component of prices, 413
  downward adjustments, 415
  labor standard, 425-426
  "sticky" vs Thatcher, 420
  Tobin on Thatcher, 420
  "wage units" in *General Theory*, 429
  (see sticky prices; trade unions)
Wald, Abraham, 705
Wallis, W. Allen, 184-189, 609
  data on, 302-303
Walrasian approach,
  identified, 39
  vis-à-vis Marshall, 117-118
Walrasian equations,
  Friedman on Marshall and Walras, 724
  mathematical elegance and, 696
  (see general equilibrium analysis)
Walrasian model,
  Friedman's position, 564
  long run vs long swings, 547, 562-563, 688
Walters, Alan W.,
  connection with Friedman, 575, 597, 628
  data on, 597-602
  economics background, 783 n79
  on Thatcher government's record, 628-629
  Thatcher advisor, 575
  title, 624
Wanninski, Jude, 638, 641, 825
wants, satisfaction of,
  indirect, 529, 532
  money system involved, 569
  (see money)
Weintraub, Roy, 706
welfare (also normative) economics,
  as normative economics, 152
  Friedman on, 378 n51, 382 n42, 766-767 n68
  Lerner's work, 152-153, 117
  Pigou, A.C., 459
  problems of, 378 n51
  social control, 460
  (see Buchanan, J.; normative economics; public finance; utility of income)
welfare optimum, 308
  allocative efficiency and, 313-314
  basis for antitrust, 309, 317
  consumer welfare, 308
  goal with dynamic element, 320
  maximum C.S., 314
  problem with antitrust goal, 319
  (see antitrust policy; "second-best" condition; welfare economics)
White, Harry, 772 n40

Wicksell, Knut, 100-102
　influence on Buchanan, 297
work,
　living to work, 19
　WW II, U.S. recovery following, 23
　WW II, work effort, 383 n61
　(see social mobility)

This volume is printed on archival **quality "acid free"** paper.

424 Eng problem